Seven
Plays
of
the
Modern
Theater

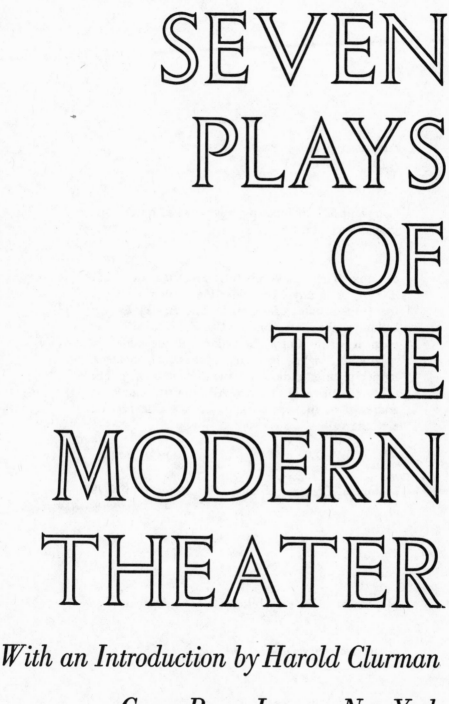

SEVEN PLAYS OF THE MODERN THEATER

With an Introduction by Harold Clurman

Grove Press, Inc.   *New York*

Contents

INTRODUCTION

by

Harold Clurman

"I hate love!," Jo, the seventeen-year-old girl of Shelagh Delaney's *A Taste of Honey*, exclaims at one point of the play. But the play as well as the person are notably tender.

I begin my remarks on the plays collected here with this observation because many critics have held most of them to be conspicuously lacking in love. I myself have occasionally dubbed the trend which these plays represent as the "theater of negation." I do not retract this earlier designation, but I now find that like most labels it indicates only a partial truth and thus misleads.

As Albert Camus once made clear, there really is no such thing as nihilistic literature. The act of writing is in itself an affirmation, and when one affirms one does so in behalf of something. It is also worth remembering, as John Berger the English art critic has wittily observed, "The despair of the artist is often misunderstood. It is never total. It excepts his own work . . . there is hope of reprieve."

The seven plays in this volume—American, French, Irish, and English, produced between 1952 and 1960—though diverse in style, quality, and stress, have one thing in common: they are all products of the age of nuclear fission; they bear witness to the atomization of the human personality. They may even be construed as protests against the dehumanization of man, which, historically speaking, culminated but did not begin with the bomb.

Unity of character seems to have dissolved with the attrition, decay, and dissolution of fixed moral standards. Lacking these, men lose a sense of continuity, direction, and finally a sense of their own identity. They must therefore fail not only as "protagonists" of dramas they esteem important, they can hardly recognize themselves—except through anguish and pain—as men. They are reduced to a series of nervous impulses.

The sentiment they are left with is a kind of disgust—with the world and with themselves. "When disgust leads a man to stop singing," notes Werner Haftmann in *Painting in the Twentieth Century*, "he begins to curse." The plays in this volume are replete with

vii

curses. Hence the earlier cliché designation "theater of negation." But on rereading the plays—and with repeated views of them on the stage—I have come to see them in a different light.

There are more than curses in these plays: there is a kind of song. And because one world—our world—has made these plays, they have a curious kinship. Out of the disarray and disharmony of our present situation a new sort of music is being wrought—cacophonous and repellent at first hearing—but in the end inescapable and haunting.

A catchall title for this book might be: *At the End of Our Ropes!* (I do not refer to the hanging in Brendan Behan's *The Quare Fellow!*) The plays all concern creatures (they are rarely characters) *in extremis.* Here is a passage from Harold Pinter's *The Birthday Party:*

STANLEY: How would you like to go away with me?
LULU: Where?
STANLEY: Nowhere. Still we could go.
LULU: But where would we go?
STANLEY: Nowhere. There's nowhere to go. So we could just go. It wouldn't matter.
LULU: We might as well stay here.
STANLEY: No. It's no good here.
LULU: Well, where else is there?
STANLEY: Nowhere.

Does this not parallel the first lines of Samuel Beckett's *Waiting for Godot*—the key play of the European postwar generation? "Nothing to be done," says Estragon; then, soon after: "Don't let's do anything. It's safer." The world is at an impasse and nothing's to be done in any of these plays except—short of self-annihilation—to go on living "a minute at a time" as the fellow says in *The Quare Fellow* when he is asked how one lives through eleven years in prison.

The jacket of the Grove Press paperback edition of *The Birthday Party* reads: "With superb dramatic tact, the tragedy is concealed beneath layer and layer of rough comedy." It is not tact which causes this dramatic effect but an attitude, an esthetic, or, more properly, the play's essential nature.

All these despairing dramas are comedies! Ionesco has spoken of the Marx brothers in connection with *Rhinoceros;* the first person who ever mentioned *Godot* to me intimated that it might be played by Chaplin. There is a burlesque aspect to all these plays. They often verge on nonsense, even idiocy. For where there is no spiritual geography, no wrong or right, no intellectual or moral guiding lines, there can hardly be tragedy: there can only be absurdity or nightmare.

The playwrights do not commit themselves. The world appears to have deprived them of a meaningful vocabulary of firm values. Thus we get only a remnant of age-old sentience and sensibility. That is why one of the things the plays share in common (particularly in those of Beckett, Pinter, and Ionesco) is a parody of the banality, repetitiousness, and emptiness of ordinary conversation. To generalize convincingly is impossible in an environment where inherited dogmas no longer jibe with existing conditions. Hence the bareness of speech where the crudest facts are dealt with and abracadabra where ideas demand utterance.

For a man to undertake determined action he must believe in his aims; he must have purpose. Where everything is doubted and where problems find no acceptable or accepted answers, action becomes erratic, ridiculous, or destructive. Most of these plays have no action in the traditional sense. What action there is tends toward the semi-suicidal (as in *The Connection*) or what may be called passive action—as in most of the others. In *Rhinoceros* there is the half promise of an action: to resist the drive toward mindlessness toward which all but one of the play's people are rushing.

With purpose gone and action chiefly reflexive, little remains of character except contour. No wonder then that most of the figures in these plays are virtually anonymous. Pozzo, Lucky, Estragon, Vladimir are tags, not names. In *The Quare Fellow,* the main figures are Prisoners A , B , etc. McCann and Goldberg in *The Birthday Party* are symbolic gags; Leach, Ernie, and the others in *The Connection* are cases. The Logician and the Old Gentleman as names are more emblematic of *Rhinoceros* than the cognomen Berenger, which is hardly more specific than "Smith" or Mr. Ordinary Man. In *The Balcony,* the nomenclature is designedly fraudulent, certainly abstract. We hardly remember any of the people in these plays by their names (except possibly Jo and Helen in *A Taste of Honey*) as we do Hamlet, Candida, Trigorin.

"Atmosphere," in the sense in which it pervades a specific place, is vague and general (less so in the English, Irish, and American plays, which tend toward greater "realism," than in the French). There is no horizon, almost no décor. Where there is, the stage director does well to simplify it to the barest signs. "A country road. A tree." is sufficient indication of locale in *Godot*. We are repeatedly confronted by a sort of compressed vacuum—a no man's land. Even the more full-bodied Jo and Helen in their "comfortless flat in Manchester" seem at the last curtain to fade from sight and remain in our memories as figments of our imagination.

Still—in apparent paradox—at least two figures always fix themselves and stand out in the featureless surroundings as if they were the last living beings in the cosmos. They usually treat each other with deliberate cruelty or aggressive indifference—even while they cling to one another. The pattern is constant even where the number exceeds two as in *The Connection*, where extremes of individual isolation do not altogether separate the men caught in an identical narcotic maze.

Yet all this subtraction of sustaining elements finally adds up to a definite mood and a positive significance. There is terror here, the terror of "absence." Everything is absent which goes into the making of a complete world, a world in which, as the French say, one can make a reason for oneself. But it is this very absence which foreshadows its opposite.

The plays are barely disguised outcries for the presence of meaning: we want to know, they say, what it is of which we are bereaved; we want to recover some principle or magnetic and cohesive force which might bind us and make the world whole or real to us again. The exploration of nothingness which constitutes the "argument" of most of these plays is an oblique quest for something approximating a lost or abandoned truth. Even the most anarchic of these playwrights—Jean Genet—speaks of creating an image of truth to be born out of a false show.

When Huysmans, the typical decadent of late nineteenth-century French literature, wrote *Against the Grain*, a critic remarked that after such a book the author would have to choose between suicide and the cross. The writers of the present tragi-comedies abjure the cross and do not choose to die. Even the sorriest prisoner in *The Quare Fellow* finds life "a bloody sight better than death any day of the world."

"I'm frightened," says the little man of *Rhinoceros*, and when asked what he is frightened of answers: "I don't know exactly . . . . I feel out of place in life . . . . I don't even know I'm me." He has no explanation for anything. When explanations are offered they usually amount to nothing better than chop logic or to such hysterical regurgitations of highfalutin or low-breed slogans as those spewed by Lucky in *Godot*.

Yet when pressed to the limit the little man does speak out despite himself. His girl says in the brazen voice of our delinquent generation: "Don't speak to me about mankind. . . . Humanism is all washed up . . . . What's wrong with being a rhinoceros? . . . I feel a bit ashamed of what you call love . . . . It just doesn't compare with the ardour and tremendous energy emanating from all these creatures around us." In torment because he has lost a sense of his own justification, the little man shouts out: "I'm staying as I am, I'm a human being. . . . I'm not capitulating."

Though all the definitions seem to break down, a basic humanism reasserts itself against the "progress" which manifests itself in change or novelty without content ("progress" which is nothing but arbitrary movement), "progress" which prides itself in sheer energy and power as ends in themselves. There is latent within poor Berenger an echo of ancient verities seeking to find a new articulation. The negative clamors for the positive from which it has been wrested. Naked man cries for fresh clothes.

The special tone of these plays arises from an avoidance, an almost morbid rejection of the metaphysical. It is this tearing off of the false face of ancient rituals and outworn interpretations—this dread of being hoodwinked by faiths that did not keep the faith—which so often causes these plays to appear bloodless and fleshless. No crocodile tears for these dramatic rebels! It is not a lack of humanity that is at the root of their disturbance but a too fierce and absolute hunger for it.

The Connection, perhaps the most "naturalistic" of these plays, is not so much about addiction to drugs as it is about this desperate attempt to fill the void resulting from default and treachery of a society given over almost entirely to Production, Energy, Power, and Success as ultimate values. Gelber will abide "no doctors, no heroes, no martyrs, no Christs." The men "hooked" by heroin in *The Connection* are "hungry for a little hope, a fix to forget. A fix to remember, to be sad, to be happy, to be, to be."

No "heroes"? Of course not. The very notion of heroism smacks of artifice and display, of the world of *The Balcony* in which revolutionaries castrate themselves so that they may be aligned in the illusionists' gallery where everyone merely counterfeits somebody real and important. What is one to do in such a world? It is obscene to be either master or slave—Pozzo or Lucky. There is no ready answer to anything. One must wait. Waiting bespeaks an agonized tension, keeping oneself prepared for the signal, the redeeming act, the road to grace.

That is *Godot's* "message." Many of us who have written about *Godot* previously have overlooked the burst of eloquence which in its final moments interrupts the staccato of the first part of the play. "Let us do something, while we have a chance! . . . To all mankind they were addressed, those cries for help still ringing in our ears! But at this place, at this moment of time, all mankind is us, whether we like it or not. Let us make the most of it, before it is too late! Let us represent worthily for once the foul brood to which a cruel fate consigned us! . . . It is true that when with folded arms we weigh the pros and cons we are no less a credit to our species. . . . What are we doing here, *that* is the question. And we are blessed in this, that we happen to know the answer. Yes, in this immense confusion one thing alone is clear. We are waiting for Godot . . . . "

Beckett would deny that Godot might be equated with God. In his view the term has become hopelessly compromised if not tainted. But just the same we know what he means. "We have kept our appointment. . . . We are not saints, but we have kept our appointment. How many people can boast as much?"

Godot is an ascetic's play and, if you will, a religious one. It marks a pilgrimage to the edge of the abyss and a summons to have the essential question of our life and times answered. What we do with ourselves if the Bomb should fall is of far less moment than what we do with ourselves here and now before its possible fall. Nothing less than the answer will do. Beckett and his coevals demand everything of us. That is why their plays are among the truly significant expressions of our day. Without being what we used to call "social" plays they voice the deepest dilemma of our civilization. And if they do not suggest or contain the answer except through the urgency of their questions—as some hold that Bertolt Brecht's work does—they issue from a source that is at bottom related to the problems posed in another way by the German master dramatist. All together these plays constitute (along with Brecht's) the most valuable because the most provocative testimony that the contemporary theater now has to offer.

Waiting for Godot

Tragicomedy
by
Samuel Beckett

Translated from his original French text
by the author

WAITING FOR GODOT was first presented (as *En Attendant Godot*) at the Théâtre de Babylone, 38 Boulevard Raspail, Paris, during the season of 1952-53. The play was directed by Roger Blin, with décor by Sergio Gerstein, and with the following cast:

ESTRAGON . . . . Pierre Latour

VLADIMIR . . . . Lucien Raimbourg

POZZO . . . . Roger Blin

LUCKY . . . . Jean Martin

A BOY . . . . Serge Lecointe

The play is in two acts

ACT ONE

A country road. A tree.

Evening.

ESTRAGON, *sitting on a low mound, is trying to take off his boot. He pulls at it with both hands, panting. He gives up, exhausted, rests, tries again. As before.*

Enter VLADIMIR.

ESTRAGON (*giving up again*): Nothing to be done.

VLADIMIR (*advancing with short, stiff strides, legs wide apart*): I'm beginning to come round to that opinion. All my life I've tried to put it from me, saying, Vladimir, be reasonable, you haven't yet tried everything. And I resumed the struggle. (*He broods, musing on the struggle. Turning to* ESTRAGON.) So there you are again.

ESTRAGON: Am I?

VLADIMIR: I'm glad to see you back. I thought you were gone for ever.

ESTRAGON: Me too.

VLADIMIR: Together again at last! We'll have to celebrate this. But how? (*He reflects.*) Get up till I embrace you.

ESTRAGON (*irritably*): Not now, not now.

VLADIMIR (*hurt, coldly*): May one inquire where His Highness spent the night?

ESTRAGON: In a ditch.

VLADIMIR (*admiringly*): A ditch! Where?

ESTRAGON (*without gesture*): Over there.

VLADIMIR: And they didn't beat you?

ESTRAGON: Beat me? Certainly they beat me.

VLADIMIR: The same lot as usual?

ESTRAGON: The same? I don't know.

VLADIMIR: When I think of it . . . all these years . . . but for me . . . where would you be . . . (*Decisively.*) You'd be nothing more than a little heap of bones at the present minute, no doubt about it.

3

ESTRAGON: And what of it?

VLADIMIR (*gloomily*): It's too much for one man. (*Pause. Cheerfully.*) On the other hand what's the good of losing heart now, that's what I say We should have thought of it a million years ago, in the nineties.

ESTRAGON: Ah stop blathering and help me off with this bloody thing.

VLADIMIR: Hand in hand from the top of the Eiffel Tower, among the first. We were respectable in those days. Now it's too late. They wouldn't even let us up. (ESTRAGON *tears at his boot.*) What are you doing?

ESTRAGON: Taking off my boot. Did that never happen to you?

VLADIMIR: Boots must be taken off every day, I'm tired telling you that. Why don't you listen to me?

ESTRAGON (*feebly*): Help me!

VLADIMIR: It hurts?

ESTRAGON (*angrily*): Hurts! He wants to know if it hurts!

VLADIMIR (*angrily*): No one ever suffers but you. I don't count. I'd like to hear what you'd say if you had what I have.

ESTRAGON: It hurts?

VLADIMIR (*angrily*): Hurts! He wants to know if it hurts!

ESTRAGON (*pointing*): You might button it all the same.

VLADIMIR (*stooping*): True. (*He buttons his fly.*) Never neglect the little things of life.

ESTRAGON: What do you expect, you always wait till the last moment.

VLADIMIR (*musingly*): The last moment . . . (*He meditates.*) Hope deferred maketh the something sick, who said that?

ESTRAGON: Why don't you help me?

VLADIMIR: Sometimes I feel it coming all the same. Then I go all queer. (*He takes off his hat, peers inside it, feels about inside it shakes it, puts it on again.*) How shall I say? Relieved and at the same time . . . (*He searches for the word.*) . . . appalled. (*With emphasis.*) AP-PALLED. (*He takes off his hat again, peers inside it.*) Funny. (*He knocks on the crown as though to dislodge a foreign body, peers into it again, puts it on again.*) Nothing to be done. (ESTRAGON *with a supreme effort succeeds in pulling off his boot. He peers inside it, feels about inside it, turns it upside down, shakes it, looks on the ground to see if anything has fallen out, finds nothing, feels inside it again, staring sightlessly before him.*) Well?

ESTRAGON: Nothing.

VLADIMIR: Show.

ESTRAGON: There's nothing to show.

VLADIMIR: Try and put it on again.

ESTRAGON (*examining his foot*): I'll air it for a bit.

VLADIMIR: There's man all over for you, blaming on his boots the faults of his feet. (*He takes off his hat again, peers inside it, feels about inside it, knocks on the crown, blows into it, puts it on again.*) This is getting alarming. (*Silence.* VLADIMIR *deep in thought,* ESTRAGON *pulling at his toes.*) One of the thieves was saved. (*Pause.*) It's a reasonable percentage. (*Pause.*) Gogo .

ESTRAGON: What?

VLADIMIR: Suppose we repented.

ESTRAGON: Repented what?

VLADIMIR: Oh . . . (*He reflects.*) We wouldn't have to go into the details.

ESTRAGON: Our being born?

VLADIMIR *breaks into a hearty laugh which he immediately stifles, his hand pressed to his pubis, his face contorted.*

VLADIMIR: One daren't even laugh any more.

ESTRAGON: Dreadful privation.

VLADIMIR: Merely smile. (*He smiles suddenly from ear to ear, keeps smiling, ceases as suddenly.*) It's not the same thing. Nothing to be done. (*Pause.*) Gogo.

ESTRAGON (*irritably*): What is it?

VLADIMIR: Did you ever read the Bible?

ESTRAGON: The Bible . . . (*He reflects.*) I must have taken a look at it.

VLADIMIR: Do you remember the Gospels?

ESTRAGON: I remember the maps of the Holy Land. Coloured they were. Very pretty. The Dead Sea was pale blue. The very look of it made me thirsty. That's where we'll go, I used to say, that's where we'll go for our honeymoon. We'll swim. We'll be happy.

VLADIMIR: You should have been a poet.

ESTRAGON: I was. (*Gesture towards his rags.*) Isn't that obvious?

Silence.

VLADIMIR: Where was I . . . How's your foot?

ESTRAGON: Swelling visibly.

VLADIMIR: Ah yes, the two thieves. Do you remember the story?

ESTRAGON: No.

VLADIMIR: Shall I tell it to you?

ESTRAGON: No.

VLADIMIR: It'll pass the time. *(Pause.)* Two thieves, crucified at the same time as our Saviour. One—

ESTRAGON: Our what?

VLADIMIR: Our Saviour. Two thieves. One is supposed to have been saved and the other . . . *(He searches for the contrary of saved.)* . . . damned.

ESTRAGON: Saved from what?

VLADIMIR: Hell.

ESTRAGON: I'm going.

He does not move.

VLADIMIR: And yet . . . *(Pause)* . . . how is it—this is not boring you I hope—how is it that of the four Evangelists only one speaks of a thief being saved. The four of them were there—or thereabouts—and only one speaks of a thief being saved. *(Pause.)* Come on, Gogo, return the ball, can't you, once in a way?

ESTRAGON *(with exaggerated enthusiasm)*: I find this really most extraordinarily interesting.

VLADIMIR: One out of four. Of the other three two don't mention any thieves at all and the third says that both of them abused him.

ESTRAGON: Who?

VLADIMIR: What?

ESTRAGON: What's this all about? Abused who?

VLADIMIR: The Saviour.

ESTRAGON: Why?

VLADIMIR: Because he wouldn't save them.

ESTRAGON: From hell?

VLADIMIR: Imbecile! From death.

ESTRAGON: I thought you said hell.

VLADIMIR: From death, from death.

ESTRAGON: Well what of it?

VLADIMIR: Then the two of them must have been damned.

ESTRAGON: And why not?

VLADIMIR: But one of the four says that one of the two was saved.

ESTRAGON: Well? They don't agree and that's all there is to it.

VLADIMIR: But all four were there. And only one speaks of a thief being saved. Why believe him rather than the others?

ESTRAGON: Who believes him?

VLADIMIR: Everybody. It's the only version they know.

ESTRAGON: People are bloody ignorant apes.

He rises painfully, goes limping to extreme left, halts, gazes into distance off with his hand screening his eyes, turns, goes to extreme right, gazes into distance. VLADIMIR *watches him, then goes and picks up the boot, peers into it, drops it hastily.*

VLADIMIR: Pah!

He spits. ESTRAGON *moves to center, halts with his back to auditorium.*

ESTRAGON: Charming spot. (*He turns, advances to front, halts facing auditorium.*) Inspiring prospects. (*He turns to* VLADIMIR.) Let's go.

VLADIMIR: We can't.

ESTRAGON: Why not?

VLADIMIR: We're waiting for Godot.

ESTRAGON (*despairingly*): Ah! (*Pause.*) You're sure it was here?

VLADIMIR: What?

ESTRAGON: That we were to wait.

VLADIMIR: He said by the tree. (*They look at the tree.*) Do you see any others.

ESTRAGON: What is it?

VLADIMIR: I don't know. A willow.

ESTRAGON: Where are the leaves?

VLADIMIR: It must be dead.

ESTRAGON: No more weeping.

VLADIMIR: Or perhaps it's not the season.

ESTRAGON: Looks to me more like a bush.

VLADIMIR: A shrub.

ESTRAGON: A bush.

VLADIMIR: A—. What are you insinuating? That we've come to the wrong place?

ESTRAGON: He should be here.

VLADIMIR: He didn't say for sure he'd come.

ESTRAGON: And if he doesn't come?

VLADIMIR: We'll come back to-morrow.

ESTRAGON: And then the day after to-morrow.

VLADIMIR: Possibly.

ESTRAGON: And so on.

VLADIMIR: The point is—

ESTRAGON: Until he comes.

VLADIMIR: You're merciless.

ESTRAGON: We came here yesterday.

VLADIMIR: Ah no, there you're mistaken.

ESTRAGON: What did we do yesterday?

VLADIMIR: What did we do yesterday?

ESTRAGON: Yes.

VLADIMIR: Why . . . (*Angrily.*) Nothing is certain when you're about.

ESTRAGON: In my opinion we were here.

VLADIMIR (*looking round*): You recognize the place?

ESTRAGON: I didn't say that.

VLADIMIR: Well?

ESTRAGON: That makes no difference.

VLADIMIR: All the same . . . that tree . . . (*Turning towards auditorium.*) that bog . . .

ESTRAGON: You're sure it was this evening?

VLADIMIR: What?

ESTRAGON: That we were to wait.

VLADIMIR: He said Saturday. (*Pause.*) I think.

ESTRAGON: You think.

VLADIMIR: I must have made a note of it. (*He fumbles in his pockets, bursting with miscellaneous rubbish.*)

ESTRAGON (*very insidious*): But what Saturday? And is it Saturday? Is it not rather Sunday? (*Pause.*) Or Monday? (*Pause.*) Or Friday?

VLADIMIR (*looking wildly about him, as though the date was inscribed in the landscape*): It's not possible!

ESTRAGON: Or Thursday?

VLADIMIR: What'll we do?

ESTRAGON: If he came yesterday and we weren't here you may be sure he won't come again to-day.

VLADIMIR: But you say we were here yesterday.

ESTRAGON: I may be mistaken. (*Pause.*) Let's stop talking for a minute, do you mind?

VLADIMIR (*feebly*): All right. (ESTRAGON *sits down on the mound.*

VLADIMIR *paces agitatedly to and fro, halting from time to time to gaze into distance off.* ESTRAGON *falls asleep.* VLADIMIR *halts finally before* ESTRAGON.) Gogo! ... Gogo! ... GOGO!

ESTRAGON *wakes with a start.*

ESTRAGON (*restored to the horror of his situation*): I was asleep! (*De spairingly.*) Why will you never let me sleep?
VLADIMIR: I felt lonely.
ESTRAGON: I had a dream.
VLADIMIR: Don't tell me!
ESTRAGON: I dreamt that—
VLADIMIR: DON'T TELL ME!
ESTRAGON (*gesture towards the universe*): This one is enough for you? (*Silence.*) It's not nice of you, Didi. Who am I to tell my private nightmares to if I can't tell them to you?
VLADIMIR: Let them remain private. You know I can't bear that.
ESTRAGON (*coldly*): There are times when I wonder if it wouldn't be better for us to part.
VLADIMIR: You wouldn't go far.
ESTRAGON: That would be too bad, really too bad. (*Pause.*) Wouldn't it, Didi, be really too bad? (*Pause.*) When you think of the beauty of the way. (*Pause.*) And the goodness of the wayfarers. (*Pause. Wheedling.*) Wouldn't it, Didi?
VLADIMIR: Calm yourself.
ESTRAGON (*voluptuously*): Calm ... calm ... The English say cawm. (*Pause.*) You know the story of the Englishman in the brothel?
VLADIMIR: Yes.
ESTRAGON: Tell it to me.
VLADIMIR: Ah stop it!
ESTRAGON: An Englishman having drunk a little more than usual proceeds to a brothel. The bawd asks him if he wants a fair one, a dark one or a red-haired one. Go on.
VLADIMIR: STOP IT!

Exit VLADIMIR *hurriedly.* ESTRAGON *gets up and follows him as far as the limit of the stage. Gestures of* ESTRAGON *like those of a spectator encouraging a pugilist. Enter* VLADIMIR. *He brushes past* ESTRAGON, *crosses the stage with bowed head.* ESTRAGON *takes a step towards him, halts.*

ESTRAGON (*gently*): You wanted to speak to me? (*Silence.* ESTRAGON *takes a step forward.*) You had something to say to me? (*Silence. Another step forward.*) Didi ...

VLADIMIR (*without turning*): I've nothing to say to you.

ESTRAGON (*step forward*): You're angry? (*Silence. Step forward.*) Forgive me. (*Silence. Step forward.* ESTRAGON *lays his hand on* VLADIMIR's *shoulder.*) Come, Didi. (*Silence.*) Give me your hand. (VLADIMIR *half turns.*) Embrace me! (VLADIMIR *stiffens.*) Don't be stubborn! (VLADIMIR *softens. They embrace.* ESTRAGON *recoils.*) You stink of garlic!

VLADIMIR: It's for the kidneys. (*Silence.* ESTRAGON *looks attentively at the tree.*) What do we do now?

ESTRAGON: Wait.

VLADIMIR: Yes, but while waiting.

ESTRAGON: What about hanging ourselves?

VLADIMIR: Hmm. It'd give us an erection.

ESTRAGON (*highly excited*): An erection!

VLADIMIR: With all that follows. Where it falls mandrakes grow. That's why they shriek when you pull them up. Did you not know that?

ESTRAGON: Let's hang ourselves immediately!

VLADIMIR: From a bough? (*They go towards the tree.*) I wouldn't trust it.

ESTRAGON: We can always try.

VLADIMIR: Go ahead.

ESTRAGON: After you.

VLADIMIR: No no, you first.

ESTRAGON: Why me?

VLADIMIR: You're lighter than I am.

ESTRAGON: Just so!

VLADIMIR: I don't understand.

ESTRAGON: Use your intelligence, can't you?

VLADIMIR *uses his intelligence.*

VLADIMIR (*finally*): I remain in the dark.

ESTRAGON: This is how it is. (*He reflects.*) The bough ... the bough ... (*Angrily.*) Use your head, can't you?

VLADIMIR: You're my only hope.

ESTRAGON (*with effort*): Gogo light—bough not break—Gogo dead.
Didi heavy—bough break—Didi alone. Whereas—

VLADIMIR: I hadn't thought of that.

ESTRAGON: If it hangs you it'll hang anything.

VLADIMIR: But am I heavier than you?

ESTRAGON: So you tell me. I don't know. There's an even chance. Or
nearly.

VLADIMIR: Well? What do we do?

ESTRAGON: Don't let's do anything. It's safer.

VLADIMIR: Let's wait and see what he says.

ESTRAGON: Who?

VLADIMIR: Godot.

ESTRAGON: Good idea.

VLADIMIR: Let's wait till we know exactly how we stand.

ESTRAGON: On the other hand it might be better to strike the iron
before it freezes.

VLADIMIR: I'm curious to hear what he has to offer. Then we'll take
it or leave it.

ESTRAGON: What exactly did we ask him for?

VLADIMIR: Were you not there?

ESTRAGON: I can't have been listening.

VLADIMIR: Oh . . . Nothing very definite.

ESTRAGON: A kind of prayer.

VLADIMIR: Precisely.

ESTRAGON: A vague supplication.

VLADIMIR: Exactly.

ESTRAGON: And what did he reply?

VLADIMIR: That he'd see.

ESTRAGON: That he couldn't promise anything.

VLADIMIR: That he'd have to think it over.

ESTRAGON: In the quiet of his home.

VLADIMIR: Consult his family.

ESTRAGON: His friends.

VLADIMIR: His agents.

ESTRAGON: His correspondents.

VLADIMIR: His books.

ESTRAGON: His bank account.

VLADIMIR: Before taking a decision.

ESTRAGON: It's the normal thing.

VLADIMIR: Is it not?

ESTRAGON: I think it is.
VLADIMIR: I think so too

Silence.

ESTRAGON (*anxious*): And we?
VLADIMIR: I beg your pardon?
ESTRAGON: I said, And we?
VLADIMIR: I don't understand.
ESTRAGON: Where do we come in?
VLADIMIR: Come in?
ESTRAGON: Take your time.
VLADIMIR: Come in? On our hands and knees.
ESTRAGON: As bad as that?
VLADIMIR: Your Worship wishes to assert his prerogatives?
ESTRAGON: We've no rights any more?

Laugh of VLADIMIR, *stifled as before, less the smile.*

VLADIMIR: You'd make me laugh if it wasn't prohibited.
ESTRAGON: We've lost our rights?
VLADIMIR (*distinctly*): We got rid of them.

Silence. They remain motionless, arms dangling, heads sunk, sagging at the knees.

ESTRAGON (*feebly*): We're not tied? (*Pause.*) We're not—
VLADIMIR: Listen!

They listen, grotesquely rigid.

ESTRAGON: I hear nothing.
VLADIMIR: Hsst! (*They listen.* ESTRAGON *loses his balance, almost falls. He clutches the arm of* VLADIMIR *who totters. They listen, huddled together.*) Nor I.

Sighs of relief. They relax and separate.

ESTRAGON: You gave me a fright.
VLADIMIR: I thought it was he.

ESTRAGON: Who?

VLADIMIR: Godot.

ESTRAGON: Pah! The wind in the reeds.

VLADIMIR: I could have sworn I heard shouts.

ESTRAGON: And why would he shout?

VLADIMIR: At his horse.

Silence.

ESTRAGON (*violently*): I'm hungry!

VLADIMIR: Do you want a carrot?

ESTRAGON: It that all there is?

VLADIMIR: I might have some turnips.

ESTRAGON: Give me a carrot. (VLADIMIR *rummages in his pockets, takes out a turnip and gives it to* ESTRAGON *who takes a bite out of it. Angrily.*) It's a turnip!

VLADIMIR: Oh pardon! I could have sworn it was a carrot. (*He rummages again in his pockets, finds nothing but turnips.*) All that's turnips. (*He rummages.*) You must have eaten the last. (*He rummages.*) Wait, I have it. (*He brings out a carrot and gives it to* ESTRAGON.) There, dear fellow. (ESTRAGON *wipes the carrot on his sleeve and begins to eat it.*) Make it last, that's the end of them.

ESTRAGON (*chewing*): I asked you a question.

VLADIMIR: Ah.

ESTRAGON: Did you reply?

VLADIMIR: How's the carrot?

ESTRAGON: It's a carrot.

VLADIMIR: So much the better, so much the better. (*Pause.*) What was it you wanted to know?

ESTRAGON: I've forgotten. (*Chews.*) That's what annoys me. (*He looks at the carrot appreciatively, dangles it between finger and thumb.*) I'll never forget this carrot. (*He sucks the end of it meditatively.*) Ah yes, now I remember

VLADIMIR: Well?

ESTRAGON (*his mouth full, vacuously*). We're not tied?

VLADIMIR: I don't hear a word you're saying.

ESTRAGON (*chews, swallows*): I'm asking you if we're tied

VLADIMIR: Tied?

ESTRAGON: Ti-ed.

VLADIMIR: How do you mean tied?

ESTRAGON: Down.

VLADIMIR: But to whom? By whom?

ESTRAGON: To your man.

VLADIMIR: To Godot? Tied to Godot! What an idea! No question of it. (*Pause.*) For the moment.

ESTRAGON: His name is Godot?

VLADIMIR: I think so.

ESTRAGON: Fancy that. (*He raises what remains of the carrot by the stub of leaf, twirls it before his eyes.*) Funny, the more you eat the worse it gets.

VLADIMIR: With me it's just the opposite.

ESTRAGON: In other words?

VLADIMIR: I get used to the muck as I go along.

ESTRAGON (*after prolonged reflection*): Is that the opposite?

VLADIMIR: Question of temperament.

ESTRAGON: Of character.

VLADIMIR: Nothing you can do about it.

ESTRAGON: No use struggling.

VLADIMIR: One is what one is.

ESTRAGON: No use wriggling.

VLADIMIR: The essential doesn't change.

ESTRAGON: Nothing to be done. (*He proffers the remains of the carrot to* VLADIMIR.) Like to finish it?

A terrible cry close at hand. ESTRAGON *drops the carrot. They remain motionless, then together make a sudden rush towards the wings.* ESTRAGON *stops halfway, runs back, picks up the carrot, stuffs it in his pocket, runs to rejoin* VLADIMIR *who is waiting for him, stops again, runs back, picks up his boot, runs to rejoin* VLADIMIR. *Huddled together, shoulders hunched, cringing away from the menace, they wait.*

Enter POZZO *and* LUCKY. POZZO *drives* LUCKY *by means of a rope passed round his neck, so that* LUCKY *is the first to enter, followed by the rope which is long enough to let him reach the middle of the stage before* POZZO *appears.* LUCKY *carries a heavy bag, a folding stool, a picnic basket and a greatcoat,* POZZO *a whip.*

POZZO (*off*): On! (*Crack of whip.* POZZO *appears. They cross the stage.*

LUCKY *passes before* VLADIMIR *and* ESTRAGON *and exit.* POZZO *at the sight of* VLADIMIR *and* ESTRAGON *stops short. The rope tautens.* POZZO *jerks at it violently.*) Back!

Noise of LUCKY *falling with all his baggage.* VLADIMIR *and* ESTRAGON *turn towards him, half wishing half fearing to go to his assistance.* VLADIMIR *takes a step towards* LUCKY, ESTRAGON *holds him back by the sleeve.*

VLADIMIR: Let me go!

ESTRAGON: Stay where you are!

POZZO: Be careful! He's wicked. (VLADIMIR *and* ESTRAGON *turn towards* POZZO.) With strangers.

ESTRAGON (*undertone*): Is that him?

VLADIMIR: Who?

ESTRAGON (*trying to remember the name*): Er ..

VLADIMIR: Godot?

ESTRAGON: Yes.

POZZO: I present myself: Pozzo.

VLADIMIR (*to* ESTRAGON): Not at all!

ESTRAGON: He said Godot.

VLADIMIR: Not at all!

ESTRAGON (*timidly, to* POZZO): You're not Mr. Godot, Sir?

POZZO (*terrifying voice*): I am Pozzo! (*Silence.*) Pozzo! (*Silence.*) Does that name mean nothing to you? (*Silence.*) I say does that name mean nothing to you?

VLADIMIR *and* ESTRAGON *look at each other questioningly.*

ESTRAGON (*pretending to search*): Bozzo ... Bozzo ...

VLADIMIR (*ditto*): Pozzo ... Pozzo ...

POZZO: PPPOZZZO!

ESTRAGON: Ah! Pozzo ... let me see ... Pozzo ...

VLADIMIR: Is it Pozzo or Bozzo?

ESTRAGON: Pozzo ... no ... I'm afraid I ... no ... I don't seem to ...

VLADIMIR (*conciliating*): I once knew a family called Gozzo. The mother had the clap.

ESTRAGON (*hastily*): We're not from these parts, Sir.

POZZO (*halting*): You are human beings none the less. (*He puts on his glasses.*) As far as one can see. (*He takes off his glasses.*) Of the same species as myself. (*He bursts into an enormous laugh.*) Of the same species as Pozzo! Made in God's image!

VLADIMIR: Well you see—

POZZO (*peremptory*): Who is Godot?

ESTRAGON: Godot?

POZZO: You took me for Godot.

VLADIMIR: Oh no, Sir, not for an instant, Sir.

POZZO: Who is he?

VLADIMIR: Oh he's a . . . he's a kind of acquaintance.

ESTRAGON: Nothing of the kind, we hardly know him.

VLADIMIR: True . . . we don't know him very well . . . but all the same . . .

ESTRAGON: Personally I wouldn't even know him if I saw him.

POZZO: You took me for him.

ESTRAGON (*recoiling before* POZZO): That's to say . . . you understand . . . the dusk . . . the strain . . . waiting . . . I confess . . . I imagined . . . for a second . . .

POZZO: Waiting? So you were waiting for him?

VLADIMIR: Well you see—

POZZO: Here? On my land?

VLADIMIR: We didn't intend any harm.

ESTRAGON: We meant well.

POZZO: The road is free to all.

VLADIMIR: That's how we looked at it.

POZZO: It's a disgrace. But there you are.

ESTRAGON: Nothing we can do about it.

POZZO (*with magnanimous gesture*): Let's say no more about it. (*He jerks the rope.*) Up pig! (*Pause.*) Every time he drops he falls asleep. (*Jerks the rope.*) Up hog! (*Noise of* LUCKY *getting up and picking up his baggage.* POZZO *jerks the rope.*) Back! (*Enter* LUCKY *backwards.*) Stop! (*LUCKY stops.*) Turn! (*LUCKY turns. To* VLADIMIR *and* ESTRAGON, *affably.*) Gentlemen, I am happy to have met you. (*Before their incredulous expression.*) Yes yes, sincerely happy. (*He jerks the rope.*) Closer! (*LUCKY advances.*) Stop! (*LUCKY stops.*) Yes, the road seems long when one journeys all alone for . . . (*He consults his watch.*) . . . yes . . . (*He calculates.*) . . . yes, six hours, that's right, six hours on end, and never a soul in sight. (*To* LUCKY.) Coat! (LUCKY *puts down the bag, advances, gives the coat, goes back to his place, takes up the bag.*) Hold that! (POZZO *holds out the whip.* LUCKY *advances and, both his hands being occupied, takes the whip in his mouth, then goes back to his place.* POZZO *begins to put on his coat, stops.*) Coat! (LUCKY *puts down bag, basket and stool, advances, helps* POZZO *on with his coat, goes back to his place and takes up bag, basket and stool.*) Touch of autumn in the air this evening. (POZZO *finishes buttoning his coat, stoops, inspects himself, straightens up.*) Whip! (LUCKY *advances, stoops,* POZZO *snatches the whip from his mouth,* LUCKY *goes back to his place.*) Yes, gentlemen, I cannot go for long without the society of my likes (*He puts on his glasses and looks at the two likes.*) even when the likeness is an imperfect one. (*He takes off his glasses.*) Stool! (LUCKY *puts down bag and basket, advances, opens stool, puts it down, goes back to his place, takes up bag and basket.*) Closer! (LUCKY *puts down bag and basket, advances, moves stool, goes back to his place, takes up bag and basket.* POZZO *sits down, places the butt of his whip against* LUCKY'S *chest and pushes.*) Back! (LUCKY *takes a step back.*) Further! (LUCKY *takes another step back.*) Stop! (LUCKY *stops. To* VLADIMIR *and* ESTRAGON.) That is why, with your permission, I propose to dally with you a moment, before I venture any further. Basket! (LUCKY *advances, gives the basket, goes back to his place.*) The fresh air stimulates the jaded appetite. (*He opens the basket, takes out a piece of chicken and a bottle of wine.*) Basket! (LUCKY *advances, picks up the basket and goes back to his place.*) Further! (LUCKY *takes a step back.*) He stinks. Happy days!

> *He drinks from the bottle, puts it down and begins to eat. Silence.* VLADIMIR *and* ESTRAGON, *cautiously at first, then more boldly, begin to circle about* LUCKY, *inspecting him up and down.* POZZO *eats his chicken voraciously, throwing away the bones after having sucked them.* LUCKY *sags slowly, until bag and basket touch the ground, then straightens up with a start and begins to sag again. Rhythm of one sleeping on his feet.*

ESTRAGON: What ails him?

VLADIMIR: He looks tired.

ESTRAGON: Why doesn't he put down his bags?

VLADIMIR: How do I know? (*They close in on him.*) Careful!

ESTRAGON: Say something to him.

VLADIMIR: Look!

ESTRAGON: What?

VLADIMIR (*pointing*): His neck!

ESTRAGON (*looking at the neck*): I see nothing.

VLADIMIR: Here.

ESTRAGON *goes over beside* VLADIMIR.

ESTRAGON: Oh I say!

VLADIMIR: A running sore!

ESTRAGON: It's the rope.

VLADIMIR: It's the rubbing.

ESTRAGON: It's inevitable.

VLADIMIR: It's the knot.

ESTRAGON: It's the chafing.

They resume their inspection, dwell on the face.

VLADIMIR (*grudgingly*): He's not bad looking.

ESTRAGON (*shrugging his shoulders, wry face*): Would you say so?

VLADIMIR: A trifle effeminate.

ESTRAGON: Look at the slobber.

VLADIMIR: It's inevitable.

ESTRAGON: Look at the slaver.

VLADIMIR: Perhaps he's a halfwit.

ESTRAGON: A cretin.

VLADIMIR (*looking closer*): Looks like a goiter.

ESTRAGON (*ditto*): It's not certain.

VLADIMIR: He's panting.

ESTRAGON: It's inevitable.

VLADIMIR: And his eyes!

ESTRAGON: What about them?

VLADIMIR: Goggling out of his head.

ESTRAGON: Looks at his last gasp to me.

VLADIMIR: It's not certain. (*Pause.*) Ask him a question.

ESTRAGON: Would that be a good thing?

VLADIMIR: What do we risk?

ESTRAGON (*timidly*): Mister . . .

VLADIMIR: Louder.

ESTRAGON (*louder*): Mister . . .

POZZO: Leave him in peace! (*They turn towards* POZZO *who, having finished eating, wipes his mouth with the back of his hand.*) Can't you see he wants to rest? Basket! (*He strikes a match and begins to light his pipe.* ESTRAGON *sees the chicken bones on the ground and stares at them greedily. As* LUCKY *does not move* POZZO *throws the match angrily away and jerks the rope.*) Basket! (LUCKY *starts, almost falls, recovers his senses, advances, puts the bottle in the basket and goes back to his place.* ESTRAGON *stares at the bones.* POZZO *strikes another match and lights his pipe.*) What can you expect, it's not his job. (*He pulls at his pipe, stretches out his legs.*) Ah! That's better.

ESTRAGON (*timidly*): Please Sir . . .

POZZO: What is it, my good man?

ESTRAGON: Er . . . you've finished with the . . . er . . . you don't need the . . . er . . . bones, Sir?

VLADIMIR (*scandalized*): You couldn't have waited?

POZZO: No no, he does well to ask. Do I need the bones? (*He turns them over with the end of his whip.*) No, personally I do not need them any more. (ESTRAGON *takes a step towards the bones.*) But . . . (ESTRAGON *stops short.*) . . . but in theory the bones go to the carrier. He is therefore the one to ask. (ESTRAGON *turns towards* LUCKY, *hesitates.*) Go on, go on, don't be afraid, ask him, he'll tell you.

ESTRAGON *goes towards* LUCKY, *stops before him.*

ESTRAGON: Mister . . . excuse me, Mister . . .

POZZO: You're being spoken to, pig! Reply! (*To* ESTRAGON.) Try him again.

ESTRAGON: Excuse me, Mister, the bones, you won't be wanting the bones?

LUCKY *looks long at* ESTRAGON.

POZZO (*in raptures*): Mister! (LUCKY *bows his head.*) Reply! Do you want them or don't you? (*Silence of* LUCKY. *To* ESTRAGON.)

They're yours. (ESTRAGON *makes a dart at the bones, picks them up and begins to gnaw them.*) I don't like it. I've never known him refuse a bone before. (*He looks anxiously at* LUCKY.) Nice business it'd be if he fell sick on me!

He puffs at his pipe.

VLADIMIR (*exploding*): It's a scandal!

Silence. Flabbergasted, ESTRAGON *stops gnawing, looks at* POZZO *and* VLADIMIR *in turn.* POZZO *outwardly calm.* VLADIMIR *embarrassed.*

POZZO (*to* VLADIMIR): Are you alluding to anything in particular?
VLADIMIR (*stutteringly resolute*): To treat a man . . . (*Gesture towards* LUCKY.) . . . like that . . . I think that . . . no . . . a human being . . . no . . . it's a scandal!
ESTRAGON (*not to be outdone*): A disgrace! (*He resumes his gnawing.*)
POZZO: You are severe. (*To* VLADIMIR.) What age are you, if it's not a rude question? (*Silence.*) Sixty? Seventy? (*To* ESTRAGON.) What age would you say he was?
ESTRAGON: Eleven.
POZZO: I am impertinent. (*He knocks out his pipe against the whip, gets up.*) I must be getting on. Thank you for your society. (*He reflects.*) Unless I smoke another pipe before I go. What do you say? (*They say nothing.*) Oh I'm only a small smoker, a very small smoker, I'm not in the habit of smoking two pipes one on top of the other, it makes (*Hand to heart, sighing.*) my heart go pit-a-pat. (*Silence.*) It's the nicotine, one absorbs it in spite of one's precautions. (*Sighs.*) You know how it is. (*Silence.*) But perhaps you don't smoke? Yes? No? It's of no importance. (*Silence.*) But how am I to sit down now, without affectation, now that I have risen? Without appearing to—how shall I say—without appearing to falter. (*To* VLADIMIR.) I beg your pardon? (*Silence.*) Perhaps you didn't speak? (*Silence.*) It's of no importance. Let me see . . . (*He reflects.*)
ESTRAGON: Ah! That's better. (*He puts the bones in his pocket.*)
VLADIMIR: Let's go.
ESTRAGON: So soon?
POZZO: One moment! (*He jerks the rope.*) Stool! (*He points with his*

whip. LUCKY *moves the stool.*) More! There! (*He sits down.* LUCKY *goes back to his place.*) Done it! (*He fills his pipe.*)

VLADIMIR (*vehemently*): Let's go!

POZZO: I hope I'm not driving you away. Wait a little longer, you'll never regret it.

ESTRAGON (*scenting charity*): We're in no hurry.

POZZO (*having lit his pipe*): The second is never so sweet . . . (*He takes the pipe out of his mouth, contemplates it.*) . . . as the first I mean. (*He puts the pipe back in his mouth.*) But it's sweet just the same.

VLADIMIR: I'm going.

POZZO: He can no longer endure my presence. I am perhaps not particularly human, but who cares? (*To* VLADIMIR.) Think twice before you do anything rash. Suppose you go now while it is still day, for there is no denying it is still day. (*They all look up at the sky.*) Good. (*They stop looking at the sky.*) What happens in that case— (*He takes the pipe out of his mouth, examines it.*)—I'm out— (*He relights his pipe.*)—in that case— (*Puff.*)—in that case— (*Puff.*)—what happens in that case to your appointment with this . . . Godet . . . Godot . . . Godin . . . anyhow you see who I mean, who has your future in his hands . . . (*Pause.*) . . . at least your immediate future?

VLADIMIR: Who told you?

POZZO: He speaks to me again! If this goes on much longer we'll soon be old friends.

ESTRAGON: Why doesn't he put down his bags?

POZZO: I too would be happy to meet him. The more people I meet the happier I become. From the meanest creature one departs wiser, richer, more conscious of one's blessings. Even you . . . (*He looks at them ostentatiously in turn to make it clear they are both meant.*) . . . even you, who knows, will have added to my store.

ESTRAGON: Why doesn't he put down his bags?

POZZO: But that would surprise me.

VLADIMIR: You're being asked a question.

POZZO (*delighted*): A question! Who? What? A moment ago you were calling me Sir, in fear and trembling. Now you're asking me questions. No good will come of this!

VLADIMIR (*to* ESTRAGON): I think he's listening.

ESTRAGON (*circling about* LUCKY): What?

VLADIMIR: You can ask him now. He's on the alert.

ESTRAGON: Ask him what?

VLADIMIR: Why he doesn't put down his bags.

ESTRAGON: I wonder.

VLADIMIR: Ask him, can't you?

POZZO (*who has followed these exchanges with anxious attention, fearing lest the question get lost*): You want to know why he doesn't put down his bags, as you call them.

VLADIMIR: That's it.

POZZO (*to* ESTRAGON): You are sure you agree with that?

ESTRAGON: He's puffing like a grampus.

POZZO: The answer is this. (*To* ESTRAGON.) But stay still, I beg of you, you're making me nervous!

VLADIMIR: Here.

ESTRAGON: What is it?

VLADIMIR: He's about to speak.

> ESTRAGON *goes over beside* VLADIMIR. *Motionless, side by side, they wait.*

POZZO: Good. Is everybody ready? Is everybody looking at me? (*He looks at* LUCKY, *jerks the rope.* LUCKY *raises his head.*) Will you look at me, pig! (LUCKY *looks at him.*) Good. (*He puts the pipe in his pocket, takes out a little vaporizer and sprays his throat, puts back the vaporizer in his pocket, clears his throat, spits, takes out the vaporizer again, sprays his throat again, puts back the vaporizer in his pocket.*) I am ready. Is everybody listening? Is everybody ready? (*He looks at them all in turn, jerks the rope.*) Hog! (LUCKY *raises his head.*) I don't like talking in a vacuum. Good. Let me see. (*He reflects.*)

ESTRAGON: I'm going.

POZZO: What was it exactly you wanted to know?

VLADIMIR: Why he—

POZZO (*angrily*): Don't interrupt me! (*Pause. Calmer.*) If we all speak at once we'll never get anywhere. (*Pause.*) What was I saying? (*Pause. Louder.*) What was I saying?

> VLADIMIR *mimics one carrying a heavy burden.* POZZO *looks at him, puzzled.*

ESTRAGON (*forcibly*): Bags. (*He points at* LUCKY.) Why? Always hold. (*He sags, panting.*) Never put down. (*He opens his hands, straightens up with relief.*) Why?

POZZO: Ah! Why couldn't you say so before? Why he doesn't make himself comfortable? Let's try and get this clear. Has he not the right to? Certainly he has. It follows that he doesn't want to. There's reasoning for you. And why doesn't he want to? (*Pause.*) Gentlemen, the reason is this.

VLADIMIR (*to* ESTRAGON): Make a note of this.

POZZO: He wants to impress me, so that I'll keep him.

ESTRAGON: What?

POZZO: Perhaps I haven't got it quite right. He wants to mollify me, so that I'll give up the idea of parting with him. No, that's not exactly it either.

VLADIMIR: You want to get rid of him?

POZZO: He wants to cod me, but he won't.

VLADIMIR: You want to get rid of him?

POZZO: He imagines that when I see how well he carries I'll be tempted to keep him on in that capacity.

ESTRAGON: You've had enough of him?

POZZO: In reality he carries like a pig. It's not his job.

VLADIMIR: You want to get rid of him?

POZZO: He imagines that when I see him indefatigable I'll regret my decision. Such is his miserable scheme. As though I were short of slaves! (*All three look at* LUCKY.) Atlas, son of Jupiter! (*Silence.*) Well, that's that I think. Anything else?

Vaporizer.

VLADIMIR: You want to get rid of him?

POZZO: Remark that I might just as well have been in his shoes and he in mine. If chance had not willed otherwise. To each one his due.

VLADIMIR: You waagerrim?

POZZO: I beg your pardon?

VLADIMIR: You want to get rid of him?

POZZO: I do. But instead of driving him away as I might have done, I mean instead of simply kicking him out on his arse, in the goodness of my heart I am bringing him to the fair, where I hope to get a good price for him. The truth is you can't drive such creatures away. The best thing would be to kill them.

LUCKY *weeps.*

ESTRAGON: He's crying!

POZZO: Old dogs have more dignity. (*He proffers his handkerchief to* ESTRAGON.) Comfort him, since you pity him. (ESTRAGON *hesitates.*) Come on. (ESTRAGON *takes the handkerchief.*) Wipe away his tears, he'll feel less forsaken.

ESTRAGON *hesitates.*

VLADIMIR: Here, give it to me, I'll do it.

ESTRAGON *refuses to give the handkerchief. Childish gestures.*

POZZO: Make haste, before he stops. (ESTRAGON *approaches* LUCKY *and makes to wipe his eyes.* LUCKY *kicks him violently in the shins.* ESTRAGON *drops the handkerchief, recoils, staggers about the stage howling with pain.*) Hanky!

LUCKY *puts down bag and basket, picks up handkerchief and gives it to* POZZO, *goes back to his place, picks up bag and basket.*

ESTRAGON: Oh the swine! (*He pulls up the leg of his trousers.*) He's crippled me!

POZZO: I told you he didn't like strangers.

VLADIMIR (*to* ESTRAGON): Show. (ESTRAGON *shows his leg. To* POZZO, *angrily.*) He's bleeding!

POZZO: It's a good sign.

ESTRAGON (*on one leg*): I'll never walk again!

VLADIMIR (*tenderly*): I'll carry you. (*Pause.*) If necessary.

POZZO: He's stopped crying. (*To* ESTRAGON.) You have replaced him as it were. (*Lyrically.*) The tears of the world are a constant quantity. For each one who begins to weep somewhere else another stops. The same is true of the laugh. (*He laughs.*) Let us not then speak ill of our generation, it is not any unhappier than its predecessors. (*Pause.*) Let us not speak well of it either. (*Pause.*) Let us not speak of it at all. (*Pause. Judiciously.*) It is true the population has increased.

VLADIMIR: Try and walk.

ESTRAGON *takes a few limping steps, stops before* LUCKY *and spits on him, then goes and sits down on the mound.*

POZZO: Guess who taught me all these beautiful things. (*Pause. Pointing to* LUCKY.) My Lucky!

VLADIMIR (*looking at the sky*): Will night never come?

POZZO: But for him all my thoughts, all my feelings, would have been of common things. (*Pause. With extraordinary vehemence.*) Professional worries! (*Calmer.*) Beauty, grace, truth of the first water, I knew they were all beyond me. So I took a knook.

VLADIMIR (*startled from his inspection of the sky*): A knook?

POZZO: That was nearly sixty years ago . . . (*He consults his watch.*) . . . yes, nearly sixty. (*Drawing himself up proudly.*) You wouldn't think it to look at me, would you? Compared to him I look like a young man, no? (*Pause.*) Hat! (LUCKY *puts down the basket and takes off his hat. His long white hair falls about his face. He puts his hat under his arm and picks up the basket.*) Now look. (POZZO *takes off his hat.*[1] *He is completely bald. He puts on his hat again.*) Did you see?

VLADIMIR: And now you turn him away? Such an old and faithful servant!

ESTRAGON: Swine!

POZZO *more and more agitated.*

VLADIMIR: After having sucked all the good out of him you chuck him away like a . . . like a banana skin. Really . . .

POZZO (*groaning, clutching his head*): I can't bear it . . . any longer . . . the way he goes on . . . you've no idea . . . it's terrible . . . he must go . . . (*He waves his arms.*) . . . I'm going mad . . . (*He collapses, his head in his hands.*) . . . I can't bear it . . . any longer . . .

[1] *All four wear bowlers.*

Silence All look at POZZO.

VLADIMIR: He can't bear it.

ESTRAGON: Any longer.

VLADIMIR: He's going mad.

ESTRAGON: It's terrible.

VLADIMIR (*to* LUCKY): How dare you! It's abominable! Such a good master! Crucify him like that! After so many years! Really!

POZZO (*sobbing*). He used to be so kind . . . so helpful . . . and entertaining . . . my good angel . . . and now . . . he's killing me.

ESTRAGON (*to* VLADIMIR): Does he want to replace him?

VLADIMIR: What?

ESTRAGON: Does he want someone to take his place or not?

VLADIMIR: I don't think so.

ESTRAGON: What?

VLADIMIR: I don't know.

ESTRAGON: Ask him.

POZZO (*calmer*): Gentlemen, I don't know what came over me. Forgive me. Forget all I said. (*More and more his old self.*) I don't remember exactly what it was, but you may be sure there wasn't a word of truth in it. (*Drawing himself up, striking his chest.*) Do I look like a man that can be made to suffer? Frankly? (*He rummages in his pockets.*) What have I done with my pipe?

VLADIMIR: Charming evening we're having.

ESTRAGON: Unforgettable.

VLADIMIR: And it's not over.

ESTRAGON: Apparently not.

VLADIMIR: It s only beginning.

ESTRAGON: It's awful.

VLADIMIR: Worse than the pantomime.

ESTRAGON: The circus.

VLADIMIR: The music-hall.

ESTRAGON: The circus.

POZZO: What can I have done with that briar?

ESTRAGON: He's a scream. He's lost his dudeen. (*Laughs noisily.*)

VLADIMIR: I'll be back. (*He hastens towards the wings.*)

ESTRAGON: End of the corridor, on the left.

VLADIMIR: Keep my seat.

Exit VLADIMIR.

POZZO (*on the point of tears*): I've lost my Kapp and Peterson!

ESTRAGON (*convulsed with merriment*): He'll be the death of me!

POZZO: You didn't see by any chance—. (*He misses* VLADIMIR.) Oh! He's gone! Without saying goodbye! How could he! He might have waited!

ESTRAGON: He would have burst.

POZZO: Oh! (*Pause.*) Oh well then of course in that case . . .

ESTRAGON: Come here.

POZZO: What for?

ESTRAGON: You'll see.

POZZO: You want me to get up?

ESTRAGON: Quick! (POZZO *gets up and goes over beside* ESTRAGON. ESTRAGON *points off.*) Look!

POZZO (*having put on his glasses*): Oh I say!

ESTRAGON: It's all over.

> Enter VLADIMIR, *somber. He shoulders* LUCKY *out of his way, kicks over the stool, comes and goes agitatedly.*

POZZO: He's not pleased.

ESTRAGON (*to* VLADIMIR): You missed a treat. Pity.

> VLADIMIR *halts, straightens the stool, comes and goes, calmer.*

POZZO: He subsides. (*Looking round.*) Indeed all subsides. A great calm descends. (*Raising his hand.*) Listen! Pan sleeps.

VLADIMIR: Will night never come?

> *All three look at the sky.*

POZZO: You don't feel like going until it does?

ESTRAGON: Well you see—

POZZO: Why it's very natural, very natural. I myself in your situation, if I had an appointment with a Godin . . . Godet . . . Godot . . . anyhow you see who I mean, I'd wait till it was black night before I gave up. (*He looks at the stool.*) I'd very much like to sit down, but I don't quite know how to go about it.

ESTRAGON: Could I be of any help?

POZZO: If you asked me perhaps.

ESTRAGON: What?

POZZO: If you asked me to sit down.

ESTRAGON: Would that be a help?

POZZO: I fancy so.

ESTRAGON: Here we go. Be seated, Sir, I beg of you.

POZZO: No no, I wouldn't think of it! (*Pause. Aside.*) Ask me again.

ESTRAGON: Come come, take a seat I beseech you, you'll get pneumonia.

POZZO: You really think so?

ESTRAGON: Why it's absolutely certain.

POZZO: No doubt you are right. (*He sits down.*) Done it again! (*Pause.*) Thank you, dear fellow. (*He consults his watch.*) But I must really be getting along, if I am to observe my schedule.

VLADIMIR: Time has stopped.

POZZO (*cuddling his watch to his ear*): Don't you believe it, Sir, don't you believe it. (*He puts his watch back in his pocket.*) Whatever you like, but not that.

ESTRAGON (*to* POZZO): Everything seems black to him to-day.

POZZO: Except the firmament. (*He laughs, pleased with this witticism.*) But I see what it is, you are not from these parts, you don't know what our twilights can do. Shall I tell you? (*Silence.* ESTRAGON *is fiddling with his boot again,* VLADIMIR *with his hat.*) I can't refuse you. (*Vaporizer.*) A little attention, if you please. (VLADIMIR *and* ESTRAGON *continue their fiddling,* LUCKY *is half asleep.* POZZO *cracks his whip feebly.*) What's the matter with this whip? (*He gets up and cracks it more vigorously, finally with success.* LUCKY *jumps.* VLADIMIR's *hat,* ESTRAGON's *boot,* LUCKY's *hat, fall to the ground.* POZZO *throws down the whip.*) Worn out, this whip. (*He looks at* VLADIMIR *and* ESTRAGON.*) What was I saying?

VLADIMIR: Let's go.

ESTRAGON: But take the weight off your feet, I implore you, you'll catch your death.

POZZO: True. (*He sits down. To* ESTRAGON.*) What is your name?

ESTRAGON: Adam.

POZZO (*who hasn't listened*): Ah yes! The night. (*He raises his head.*) But be a little more attentive, for pity's sake, otherwise we'll never get anywhere. (*He looks at the sky.*) Look! (*All look at the sky except* LUCKY *who is dozing off again.* POZZO *jerks the rope.*) Will you look at the sky, pig! (LUCKY *looks at the sky.*) Good, that's enough. (*They stop looking at the sky.*) What is there so extraordinary about it? Qua sky. It is pale and luminous like any sky at this hour of the day. (*Pause.*) In these latitudes.

(*Pause.*) When the weather is fine. (*Lyrical.*) An hour ago (*He looks at his watch, prosaic.*) roughly (*Lyrical.*) after having poured forth even since (*He hesitates, prosaic.*) say ten o'clock in the morning (*Lyrical.*) tirelessly torrents of red and white light it begins to lose its effulgence, to grow pale (*Gesture of the two hands lapsing by stages.*) pale, ever a little paler, a little paler until (*Dramatic pause, ample gesture of the two hands flung wide apart.*) pppfff! finished! it comes to rest. But— (*Hand raised in admonition.*)—but behind this veil of gentleness and peace night is charging (*Vibrantly.*) and will burst upon us (*Snaps his fingers.*) pop! like that! (*His inspiration leaves him.*) just when we least expect it. (*Silence. Gloomily.*) That's how it is on this bitch of an earth.

Long silence.

ESTRAGON: So long as one knows.

VLADIMIR: One can bide one's time.

ESTRAGON: One knows what to expect.

VLADIMIR: No further need to worry.

ESTRAGON: Simply wait.

VLADIMIR: We're used to it. (*He picks up his hat, peers inside it, shakes it, puts it on.*)

POZZO: How did you find me? (VLADIMIR *and* ESTRAGON *look at him blankly.*) Good? Fair? Middling? Poor? Positively bad?

VLADIMIR (*first to understand*): Oh very good, very very good.

POZZO (*to* ESTRAGON): And you, Sir?

ESTRAGON: Oh tray bong, tray tray tray bong.

POZZO (*fervently*): Bless you, gentlemen, bless you! (*Pause.*) I have such need of encouragement! (*Pause.*) I weakened a little towards the end, you didn't notice?

VLADIMIR: Oh perhaps just a teeny weeny little bit.

ESTRAGON: I thought it was intentional.

POZZO: You see my memory is defective.

Silence.

ESTRAGON: In the meantime nothing happens.

POZZO: You find it tedious?

ESTRAGON: Somewhat.

POZZO (*to* VLADIMIR): And you, Sir?

VLADIMIR: I've been better entertained.

> *Silence.* POZZO *struggles inwardly.*

POZZO: Gentlemen, you have been .. civil to me.

ESTRAGON: Not at all!

VLADIMIR: What an idea!

POZZO: Yes yes, you have been correct. So that I ask myself is there anything I can do in my turn for these honest fellows who are having such a dull, dull time.

ESTRAGON: Even ten francs would be a help.

VLADIMIR: We are not beggars!

POZZO: Is there anything I can do, that's what I ask myself, to cheer them up? I have given them bones, I have talked to them about this and that, I have explained the twilight, admittedly. But is it enough, that's what tortures me, is it enough?

ESTRAGON: Even five.

VLADIMIR (*to* ESTRAGON, *indignantly*): That's enough!

ESTRAGON: I couldn't accept less.

POZZO: Is it enough? No doubt. But I am liberal. It's my nature. This evening. So much the worse for me. (*He jerks the rope.* LUCKY *looks at him.*) For I shall suffer, no doubt about that. (*He picks up the whip.*) What do you prefer? Shall we have him dance, or sing, or recite, or think, or—

ESTRAGON: Who?

POZZO: Who! You know how to think, you two?

VLADIMIR: He thinks?

POZZO: Certainly. Aloud. He even used to think very prettily once, I could listen to him for hours. Now . . . (*He shudders.*) So much the worse for me. Well, would you like him to think something for us?

ESTRAGON: I'd rather he'd dance, it'd be more fun.

POZZO: Not necessarily.

ESTRAGON: Wouldn't it, Didi, be more fun?

VLADIMIR: I'd like well to hear him think.

ESTRAGON: Perhaps he could dance first and think afterwards, if it isn't too much to ask him.

VLADIMIR (*to* POZZO): Would that be possible?

POZZO: By all means, nothing simpler. It's the natural order. (*He laughs briefly.*)

VLADIMIR: Then let him dance.

Silence.

POZZO: Do you hear, hog?

ESTRAGON: He never refuses?

POZZO: He refused once. (*Silence.*) Dance, misery!

> LUCKY *puts down bag and basket, advances towards front, turns to* POZZO. LUCKY *dances. He stops.*

ESTRAGON: Is that all?

POZZO: Encore!

> LUCKY *executes the same movements, stops.*

ESTRAGON: Pooh! I'd do as well myself. (*He imitates* LUCKY, *almost falls.*) With a little practice.

POZZO: He used to dance the farandole, the fling, the brawl, the jig, the fandango and even the hornpipe. He capered. For joy. Now that's the best he can do. Do you know what he calls it?

ESTRAGON: The Scapegoat's Agony.

VLADIMIR: The Hard Stool.

POZZO: The Net. He thinks he's entangled in a net.

VLADIMIR (*squirming like an aesthete*): There's something about it . . .

> LUCKY *makes to return to his burdens.*

POZZO: Woaa!

> LUCKY *stiffens.*

ESTRAGON: Tell us about the time he refused.

POZZO: With pleasure, with pleasure. (*He fumbles in his pockets.*) Wait. (*He fumbles.*) What have I done with my spray? (*He fumbles.*) Well now isn't that . . . (*He looks up, consternation on his features. Faintly.*) I can't find my pulverizer!

ESTRAGON (*faintly*): My left lung is very weak! (*He coughs feebly. In ringing tones.*) But my right lung is as sound as a bell!

POZZO (*normal voice*): No matter! What was I saying. (*He ponders.*) Wait. (*Ponders.*) Well now isn't that . . . (*He raises his head.*) Help me!

ESTRAGON: Wait!

VLADIMIR: Wait!

POZZO: Wait!

> *All three take off their hats simultaneously, press their hands to their foreheads, concentrate.*

ESTRAGON (*triumphantly*): Ah!

VLADIMIR: He has it.

POZZO (*impatient*): Well?

ESTRAGON: Why doesn't he put down his bags?

VLADIMIR: Rubbish!

POZZO: Are you sure?

VLADIMIR: Damn it haven't you already told us?

POZZO: I've already told you?

ESTRAGON: He's already told us?

VLADIMIR: Anyway he has put them down.

ESTRAGON (*glance at* LUCKY): So he has. And what of it?

VLADIMIR: Since he has put down his bags it is impossible we should have asked why he does not do so.

POZZO: Stoutly reasoned!

ESTRAGON: And why has he put them down?

POZZO: Answer us that.

VLADIMIR: In order to dance.

ESTRAGON: True!

POZZO: True!

> *Silence. They put on their hats.*

ESTRAGON: Nothing happens, nobody comes, nobody goes, it's awful!

VLADIMIR (*to* POZZO): Tell him to think.

POZZO: Give him his hat.

VLADIMIR: His hat?

POZZO: He can't think without his hat.

VLADIMIR (*to* ESTRAGON): Give him his hat.

ESTRAGON: Me! After what he did to me! Never!
VLADIMIR: I'll give it to him. (*He does not move.*)
ESTRAGON (*to* POZZO): Tell him to go and fetch it.
POZZO: It's better to give it to him.
VLADIMIR: I'll give it to him.

> *He picks up the hat and tenders it at arm's length to* LUCKY,
> *who does not move.*

POZZO: You must put it on his head.
ESTRAGON (*to* POZZO): Tell him to take it.
POZZO: It's better to put it on his head.
VLADIMIR: I'll put it on his head.

> *He goes round behind* LUCKY, *approaches him cautiously, puts*
> *the hat on his head and recoils smartly.* LUCKY *does not move.*
> *Silence.*

ESTRAGON: What's he waiting for?
POZZO: Stand back! (VLADIMIR *and* ESTRAGON *move away from* LUCKY.
POZZO *jerks the rope.* LUCKY *looks at* POZZO.) Think, pig! (*Pause.*
LUCKY *begins to dance.*) Stop! (LUCKY *stops.*) Forward! (LUCKY
advances.) Stop! (LUCKY *stops.*) Think!

> *Silence.*

LUCKY: On the other hand with regard to—
POZZO: Stop! (LUCKY *stops.*) Back! (LUCKY *moves back.*) Stop! (LUCKY
stops.) Turn! (LUCKY *turns towards auditorium.*) Think!

> *During* LUCKY's *tirade the others react as follows.*
> 1) VLADIMIR *and* ESTRAGON *all attention,* POZZO *dejected and*
>   *disgusted.*
> 2) VLADIMIR *and* ESTRAGON *begin to protest,* POZZO's *sufferings*
>   *increase.*
> 3) VLADIMIR *and* ESTRAGON *attentive again,* POZZO *more and*
>   *more agitated and groaning.*
> 4) VLADIMIR *and* ESTRAGON *protest violently.* POZZO *jumps up,*
>   *pulls on the rope. General outcry.* LUCKY *pulls on the rope,*

staggers, shouts his text. All three throw themselves on LUCKY *who struggles and shouts his text.*

LUCKY: Given the existence as uttered forth in the public works of Puncher and Wattmann of a personal God quaquaquaqua with white beard quaquaquaqua outside time without extension who from the heights of divine apathia divine athambia divine aphasia loves us dearly with some exceptions for reasons unknown but time will tell and suffers like the divine Miranda with those who for reasons unknown but time will tell are plunged in torment plunged in fire whose fire flames if that continues and who can doubt it will fire the firmament that is to say blast hell to heaven so blue still and calm so calm with a calm which even though intermittent is better than nothing but not so fast and considering what is more that as a result of the labors left unfinished crowned by the Acacacacademy of Anthropopopometry of Essy-in-Possy of Testew and Cunard it is established beyond all doubt all other doubt than that which clings to the labors of men that as a result of the labors unfinished of Testew and Cunard it is established as hereinafter but not so fast for reasons unknown that as a result of the public works of Puncher and Wattmann it is established beyond all doubt that in view of the labors of Fartov and Belcher left unfinished for reasons unknown of Testew and Cunard left unfinished it is established what many deny that man in Possy of Testew and Cunard that man in Essy that man in short that man in brief in spite of the strides of alimentation and defecation wastes and pines wastes and pines and concurrently simultaneously what is more for reasons unknown in spite of the strides of physical culture the practice of sports such as tennis football running cycling swimming flying floating riding gliding conating camogie skating tennis of all kinds dying flying sports of all sorts autumn summer winter winter tennis of all kinds hockey of all sorts penicilline and succedanea in a word I resume flying gliding golf over nine and eighteen holes tennis of all sorts in a word for reasons unknown in Feckham Peckham Fulham Clapham namely concurrently simultaneously what is more for reasons unknown but time will tell fades away I resume Fulham Clapham in a word the dead loss per head since the death of Bishop Berkeley being to the tune of one inch four ounce per head approximately by and large more or less to the nearest decimal good measure round figures stark naked in the stockinged feet in Connemara in a word for reasons unknown no matter what matter the facts are there and considering what is more much more grave that in the light of the labors lost of Steinweg and Peterman it appears what is more much more grave that in the light the light the light of the labors lost of Steinweg and Peterman that in the plains in the mountains by the seas by the rivers running water running fire the air is the same and then the earth namely the air and then the earth in the great cold the great dark the air and the earth abode of stones in the great cold alas alas in the year of their Lord six hundred and something the air the earth the sea the earth abode of stones in the great deeps the great cold on sea on land and in the air I resume for reasons unknown in spite of the tennis the facts are there but time will tell I resume alas alas on on in short in fine on on abode of stones who can doubt it I resume but not so fast I resume the skull fading fading fading and concurrently simultaneously what is more for reasons unknown in spite of the tennis on on the beard the flames the tears the stones so blue so calm alas alas on on the skull the skull the skull the skull in Connemara in spite of the tennis the labors abandoned left unfinished graver still abode of stones in a word I resume alas alas abandoned unfinished the skull the skull in Connemara in spite of the tennis the skull alas the stones Cunard (*Mêlée, final vociferations.*) tennis . . . the stones . . . so calm . . . Cunard . . . unfinished . . .

POZZO: His hat!

> VLADIMIR *seizes* LUCKY's *hat. Silence of* LUCKY. *He falls. Silence. Panting of the victors.*

ESTRAGON: Avenged!

> VLADIMIR *examines the hat, peers inside it.*

POZZO: Give me that! (*He snatches the hat from* VLADIMIR, *throws it on the ground, tramples on it.*) There's an end to his thinking!
VLADIMIR: But will he be able to walk?
POZZO: Walk or crawl! (*He kicks* LUCKY.) Up pig!
ESTRAGON: Perhaps he's dead.

VLADIMIR: You'll kill him.

POZZO: Up scum! (*He jerks the rope.*) Help me!

VLADIMIR: How?

POZZO: Raise him up!

> VLADIMIR *and* ESTRAGON *hoist* LUCKY *to his feet, support him an instant, then let him go. He falls.*

ESTRAGON: He's doing it on purpose!

POZZO: You must hold him. (*Pause.*) Come on, come on, raise him up.

ESTRAGON: To hell with him!

VLADIMIR: Come on, once more.

ESTRAGON: What does he take us for?

> *They raise* LUCKY, *hold him up.*

POZZO: Don't let him go! (VLADIMIR *and* ESTRAGON *totter.*) Don't move! (POZZO *fetches bag and basket and brings them towards* LUCKY.) Hold him tight! (*He puts the bag in* LUCKY's *hand.* LUCKY *drops it immediately.*) Don't let him go! (*He puts back the bag in* LUCKY's *hand. Gradually, at the feel of the bag,* LUCKY *recovers his senses and his fingers finally close round the handle.*) Hold him tight! (*As before with basket.*) Now! You can let him go. (VLADIMIR *and* ESTRAGON *move away from* LUCKY *who totters, reels, sags, but succeeds in remaining on his feet, bag and basket in his hands.* POZZO *steps back, cracks his whip.*) Forward! (LUCKY *totters forward.*) Back! (LUCKY *totters back.*) Turn! (LUCKY *turns.*) Done it! He can walk. (*Turning to* VLADIMIR *and* ESTRAGON.) Thank you, gentlemen, and let me . . . (*He fumbles in his pockets.*) . . . let me wish you . . . (*Fumbles.*) . . . wish you . . . (*Fumbles.*) . . . what have I done with my watch? (*Fumbles.*) A genuine half-hunter, gentlemen, with deadbeat escapement! (*Sobbing.*) Twas my granpa gave it to me! (*He searches on the ground,* VLADIMIR *and* ESTRAGON *likewise.* POZZO *turns over with his foot the remains of* LUCKY's *hat.*) Well now isn't that just—

VLADIMIR: Perhaps it's in your fob.

POZZO: Wait! (*He doubles up in an attempt to apply his ear to his stomach, listens. Silence.*) I hear nothing. (*He beckons them to approach.* VLADIMIR *and* ESTRAGON *go over to him, bend over his stomach.*) Surely one should hear the tick-tick.

VLADIMIR: Silence!

All listen, bent double.

ESTRAGON: I hear something.
POZZO: Where?
VLADIMIR: It's the heart.
POZZO (*disappointed*): Damnation!
VLADIMIR: Silence!
ESTRAGON: Perhaps it has stopped.

They straighten up.

POZZO: Which of you smells so bad?
ESTRAGON: He has stinking breath and I have stinking feet.
POZZO: I must go.
ESTRAGON: And your half-hunter?
POZZO: I must have left it at the manor.

Silence.

ESTRAGON: Then adieu.
POZZO: Adieu.
VLADIMIR: Adieu.
POZZO: Adieu.

Silence. No one moves.

VLADIMIR: Adieu.
POZZO: Adieu.
ESTRAGON: Adieu.

Silence.

POZZO: And thank you.
VLADIMIR: Thank *you*.
POZZO: Not at all.
ESTRAGON: Yes yes.
POZZO: No no.
VLADIMIR: Yes yes.

ESTRAGON: No no.

Silence.

POZZO: I don't seem to be able . . . (*Long hesitation.*) . . . to depart.
ESTRAGON: Such is life.

POZZO *turns, moves away from* LUCKY *towards the wings, paying out the rope as he goes.*

VLADIMIR: You're going the wrong way.
POZZO: I need a running start. (*Having come to the end of the rope, i.e. off stage, he stops, turns and cries.*) Stand back! (VLADIMIR *and* ESTRAGON *stand back, look towards* POZZO. *Crack of whip.*) On! On!
ESTRAGON: On!
VLADIMIR: On!

LUCKY *moves off.*

POZZO: Faster! (*He appears, crosses the stage preceded by* LUCKY. VLADIMIR *and* ESTRAGON *wave their hats. Exit* LUCKY.) On! On! (*On the point of disappearing in his turn he stops and turns. The rope tautens. Noise of* LUCKY *falling off.*) Stool! (VLADIMIR *fetches stool and gives it to* POZZO *who throws it to* LUCKY.) Adieu!

VLADIMIR ⎫
ESTRAGON ⎭ (*waving*): Adieu! Adieu!
POZZO: Up! Pig! (*Noise of* LUCKY *getting up.*) On! (*Exit* POZZO.) Faster! On! Adieu! Pig! Yip! Adieu!

Long silence.

VLADIMIR: That passed the time.
ESTRAGON: It would have passed in any case.
VLADIMIR: Yes, but not so rapidly.

Pause.

ESTRAGON: What do we do now?

VLADIMIR: I don't know.
ESTRAGON: Let's go.
VLADIMIR: We can't.
ESTRAGON: Why not?
VLADIMIR: We're waiting for Godot.
ESTRAGON (*despairingly*): Ah!

Pause.

VLADIMIR: How they've changed!
ESTRAGON: Who?
VLADIMIR: Those two.
ESTRAGON: That's the idea, let's make a little conversation.
VLADIMIR: Haven't they?
ESTRAGON: What?
VLADIMIR: Changed.
ESTRAGON: Very likely. They all change. Only we can't.
VLADIMIR: Likely! It's certain. Didn't you see them?
ESTRAGON: I suppose I did. But I don't know them.
VLADIMIR: Yes you do know them.
ESTRAGON: No I don't know them.
VLADIMIR: We know them, I tell you. You forget everything. (*Pause. To himself.*) Unless they're not the same . . .
ESTRAGON: Why didn't they recognize us then?
VLADIMIR: That means nothing. I too pretended not to recognize them. And then nobody ever recognizes us.
ESTRAGON: Forget it. What we need—ow! (VLADIMIR *does not react.*) Ow!
VLADIMIR (*to himself*): Unless they're not the same . . .
ESTRAGON: Didi! It's the other foot! (*He goes hobbling towards the mound.*)
VLADIMIR: Unless they're not the same . . .
BOY (*off*): Mister!

ESTRAGON *halts. Both look towards the voice.*

ESTRAGON: Off we go again.
VLADIMIR: Approach, my child.

Enter BOY, *timidly. He halts.*

BOY: Mister Albert . . . ?
VLADIMIR: Yes.
ESTRAGON: What do you want?
VLADIMIR: Approach!

The BOY *does not move.*

ESTRAGON (*forcibly*): Approach when you're told, can't you?

The BOY *advances timidly, halts.*

VLADIMIR: What is it?
BOY: Mr. Godot . . .
VLADIMIR: Obviously . . . (*Pause.*) Approach.
ESTRAGON (*violently*): Will you approach! (*The* BOY *advances timidly.*)
    What kept you so late?
VLADIMIR: You have a message from Mr. Godot?
BOY: Yes Sir.
VLADIMIR: Well, what is it?
ESTRAGON: What kept you so late?

The BOY *looks at them in turn, not knowing to which he
should reply.*

VLADIMIR (*to* ESTRAGON): Let him alone.
ESTRAGON (*violently*): You let me alone. (*Advancing, to the* BOY.)
    Do you know what time it is?
BOY (*recoiling*): It's not my fault, Sir.
ESTRAGON: And whose is it? Mine?
BOY: I was afraid, Sir.
ESTRAGON: Afraid of what? Of us? (*Pause.*) Answer me!
VLADIMIR: I know what it is, he was afraid of the others.
ESTRAGON: How long have you been here?
BOY: A good while, Sir.
VLADIMIR: You were afraid of the whip?
BOY: Yes Sir.
VLADIMIR: The roars?
BOY: Yes Sir.
VLADIMIR: The two big men.
BOY: Yes Sir.

VLADIMIR: Do you know them?

BOY: No Sir.

VLADIMIR: Are you a native of these parts? (*Silence.*) Do you belong
to these parts?

BOY: Yes Sir.

ESTRAGON: That's all a pack of lies. (*Shaking the* BOY *by the arm.*)
Tell us the truth!

BOY (*trembling*): But it is the truth, Sir!

VLADIMIR: Will you let him alone! What's the matter with you?
(ESTRAGON *releases the* BOY, *moves away, covering his face with
his hands.* VLADIMIR *and the* BOY *observe him.* ESTRAGON *drops
his hands. His face is convulsed.*) What's the matter with you?

ESTRAGON: I'm unhappy.

VLADIMIR: Not really! Since when?

ESTRAGON: I'd forgotten.

VLADIMIR: Extraordinary the tricks that memory plays!

> ESTRAGON *tries to speak, renounces, limps to his place, sits down
> and begins to take off his boots.*

(*To* BOY.) Well?

BOY: Mr. Godot—

VLADIMIR: I've seen you before, haven't I?

BOY: I don't know, Sir.

VLADIMIR: You don't know me?

BOY: No Sir.

VLADIMIR: It wasn't you came yesterday?

BOY: No Sir.

VLADIMIR: This is your first time?

BOY: Yes Sir.

> *Silence.*

VLADIMIR: Word words. (*Pause.*) Speak.

BOY (*in a rush*): Mr. Godot told me to tell you he won't come this
evening but surely to-morrow.

> *Silence.*

VLADIMIR: Is that all?

BOY: Yes Sir.

Silence.

VLADIMIR: You work for Mr. Godot?
BOY: Yes Sir.
VLADIMIR: What do you do?
BOY: I mind the goats, Sir.
VLADIMIR: Is he good to you?
BOY: Yes Sir.
VLADIMIR: He doesn't beat you?
BOY: No Sir, not me.
VLADIMIR: Whom does he beat?
BOY: He beats my brother, Sir.
VLADIMIR: Ah, you have a brother?
BOY: Yes Sir.
VLADIMIR: What does he do?
BOY: He minds the sheep, Sir.
VLADIMIR: And why doesn't he beat you?
BOY: I don't know, Sir.
VLADIMIR: He must be fond of you.
BOY: I don't know, Sir.

Silence.

VLADIMIR: Does he give you enough to eat? (*The* BOY *hesitates.*) Does he feed you well?
BOY: Fairly well, Sir.
VLADIMIR: You're not unhappy? (*The* BOY *hesitates.*) Do you hear me?
BOY: Yes Sir.
VLADIMIR: Well?
BOY: I don't know, Sir.
VLADIMIR: You don't know if you're unhappy or not?
BOY: No Sir.
VLADIMIR: You're as bad as myself. (*Silence.*) Where do you sleep?
BOY: In the loft, Sir.
VLADIMIR: With your brother?
BOY: Yes Sir.
VLADIMIR: In the hay?
BOY: Yes Sir.

Silence.

VLADIMIR: All right, you may go.

BOY: What am I to tell Mr. Godot, Sir?

VLADIMIR: Tell him . . . (*He hesitates.*) . . . tell him you saw us. (*Pause.*) You did see us, didn't you?

BOY: Yes Sir. (*He steps back, hesitates, turns and exit running.*)

> *The light suddenly fails. In a moment it is night. The moon rises at back, mounts in the sky, stands still, shedding a pale light on the scene.*

VLADIMIR: At last!

> ESTRAGON *gets up and goes towards* VLADIMIR, *a boot in each hand. He puts them down at edge of stage, straightens and contemplates the moon.*

What are you doing?

ESTRAGON: Pale for weariness.

VLADIMIR: Eh?

ESTRAGON: Of climbing heaven and gazing on the likes of us.

VLADIMIR: Your boots, what are you doing with your boots?

ESTRAGON (*turning to look at the boots*): I'm leaving them there. (*Pause.*) Another will come, just as . . . as . . . as me, but with smaller feet, and they'll make him happy.

VLADIMIR: But you can't go barefoot!

ESTRAGON: Christ did.

VLADIMIR: Christ! What has Christ got to do with it? You're not going to compare yourself to Christ!

ESTRAGON: All my life I've compared myself to him.

VLADIMIR: But where he lived it was warm, it was dry!

ESTRAGON: Yes. And they crucified quick.

Silence.

VLADIMIR: We've nothing more to do here.

ESTRAGON: Nor anywhere else.

VLADIMIR: Ah Gogo, don't go on like that. To-morrow everything will be better.

ESTRAGON: How do you make that out?

VLADIMIR: Did you not hear what the child said?

ESTRAGON: No.

VLADIMIR: He said that Godot was sure to come to-morrow. (*Pause.*) What do you say to that?

ESTRAGON: Then all we have to do is to wait on here.

VLADIMIR: Are you mad? We must take cover. (*He takes* ESTRAGON *by the arm.*) Come on. (*He draws* ESTRAGON *after him.* ESTRAGON *yields, then resists. They halt.*)

ESTRAGON (*looking at the tree*): Pity we haven't got a bit of rope.

VLADIMIR: Come on. It's cold. (*He draws* ESTRAGON *after him. As before.*)

ESTRAGON: Remind me to bring a bit of rope to-morrow.

VLADIMIR: Yes. Come on. (*He draws him after him. As before.*)

ESTRAGON: How long have we been together all the time now?

VLADIMIR: I don't know. Fifty years maybe.

ESTRAGON: Do you remember the day I threw myself into the Rhone?

VLADIMIR: We were grape harvesting.

ESTRAGON: You fished me out.

VLADIMIR: That's all dead and buried.

ESTRAGON: My clothes dried in the sun.

VLADIMIR: There's no good harking back on that. Come on. (*He draws him after him. As before.*)

ESTRAGON: Wait!

VLADIMIR: I'm cold!

ESTRAGON: Wait! (*He moves away from* VLADIMIR.) I sometimes wonder if we wouldn't have been better off alone, each one for himself. (*He crosses the stage and sits down on the mound.*) We weren't made for the same road.

VLADIMIR (*without anger*): It's not certain.

ESTRAGON: No, nothing is certain.

VLADIMIR *slowly crosses the stage and sits down beside* ESTRAGON.

VLADIMIR: We can still part, if you think it would be better.

ESTRAGON: It's not worth while now.

Silence.

VLADIMIR: No, it's not worth while now.

Silence.

ESTRAGON: Well, shall we go?
VLADIMIR: Yes, let's go.

They do not move.

Curtain.

ACT TWO

Next day. Same time.

Same place.

ESTRAGON'S *boots front center, heels together, toes splayed.* LUCKY'S *hat at same place. The tree has four or five leaves. Enter* VLADIMIR *agitatedly. He halts and looks long at the tree, then suddenly begins to move feverishly about the stage. He halts before the boots, picks one up, examines it, sniffs it, manifests disgust, puts it back carefully Comes and goes. Halts extreme right and gazes into distance off, shading his eyes with his hand. Comes and goes. Halts extreme left, as before. Comes and goes. Halts suddenly and begins to sing loudly*

VLADIMIR:

A dog came in—

(*Having begun too high he stops, clears his throat, resumes.*)

A dog came in the kitchen
And stole a crust of bread.
Then cook up with a ladle
And beat him till he was dead.

Then all the dogs came running
And dug the dog a tomb—

(*He stops, broods, resumes.*)

Then all the dogs came running
And dug the dog a tomb
And wrote upon the tombstone
For the eyes of dogs to come:

A dog came in the kitchen

And stole a crust of bread.
Then cook up with a ladle
And beat him till he was dead.

Then all the dogs came running
And dug the dog a tomb—

(*He stops, broods, resumes.*)

Then all the dogs came running
And dug the dog a tomb—

(*He stops, broods. Softly.*)

And dug the dog a tomb . . .

He remains a moment silent and motionless, then begins to move feverishly about the stage. He halts before the tree, comes and goes, before the boots, comes and goes, halts extreme right, gazes into distance, extreme left, gazes into distance. Enter ESTRAGON *right, barefoot, head bowed. He slowly crosses the stage.* VLADIMIR *turns and sees him.*

VLADIMIR: You again! (ESTRAGON *halts but does not raise his head.* VLADIMIR *goes towards him.*) Come here till I embrace you
ESTRAGON: Don't touch me!

VLADIMIR *holds back, pained.*

VLADIMIR: Do you want me to go away? (*Pause.*) Gogo! (*Pause.* VLADIMIR *observes him attentively.*) Did they beat you? (*Pause.*) Gogo! (ESTRAGON *remains silent, head bowed.*) Where did you spend the night?
ESTRAGON: Don't touch me! Don't question me! Don't speak to me! Stay with me!
VLADIMIR: Did I ever leave you?
ESTRAGON: You let me go.
VLADIMIR: Look at me. (ESTRAGON *does not raise his head. Violently.*) Will you look at me!

ESTRAGON *raises his head. They look long at each other, then suddenly embrace, clapping each other on the back. End of the embrace.* ESTRAGON, *no longer supported, almost falls.*

ESTRAGON: What a day!

VLADIMIR: Who beat you? Tell me.

ESTRAGON: Another day done with.

VLADIMIR: Not yet.

ESTRAGON: For me it's over and done with, no matter what happens. (*Silence.*) I heard you singing.

VLADIMIR: That's right, I remember.

ESTRAGON: That finished me. I said to myself, He's all alone, he thinks I'm gone for ever, and he sings.

VLADIMIR: One is not master of one's moods. All day I've felt in great form. (*Pause.*) I didn't get up in the night, not once!

ESTRAGON (*sadly*): You see, you piss better when I'm not there.

VLADIMIR: I missed you . . . and at the same time I was happy. Isn't that a queer thing?

ESTRAGON (*shocked*): Happy?

VLADIMIR: Perhaps it's not quite the right word.

ESTRAGON: And now?

VLADIMIR: Now? . . . (*Joyous.*) There you are again . . . (*Indifferent.*) There we are again . . . (*Gloomy.*) There I am again.

ESTRAGON: You see, you feel worse when I'm with you. I feel better alone too.

VLADIMIR (*vexed*): Then why do you always come crawling back?

ESTRAGON: I don't know.

VLADIMIR: No, but I do. It's because you don't know how to defend yourself. I wouldn't have let them beat you.

ESTRAGON: You couldn't have stopped them.

VLADIMIR: Why not?

ESTRAGON: There was ten of them.

VLADIMIR: No, I mean before they beat you. I would have stopped you from doing whatever it was you were doing.

ESTRAGON: I wasn't doing anything.

VLADIMIR: Then why did they beat you?

ESTRAGON: I don't know.

VLADIMIR: Ah no, Gogo, the truth is there are things escape you that don't escape me, you must feel it yourself.

ESTRAGON: I tell you I wasn't doing anything.

VLADIMIR: Perhaps you weren't. But it's the way of doing it that counts, the way of doing it, if you want to go on living.

ESTRAGON: I wasn't doing anything.

VLADIMIR: You must be happy too, deep down, if you only knew it.

ESTRAGON: Happy about what?

VLADIMIR: To be back with me again.

ESTRAGON: Would you say so?

VLADIMIR: Say you are, even if it's not true.

ESTRAGON: What am I to say?

VLADIMIR: Say, I am happy.

ESTRAGON: I am happy.

VLADIMIR: So am I.

ESTRAGON: So am I.

VLADIMIR: We are happy.

ESTRAGON: We are happy. (*Silence.*) What do we do now, now that we are happy?

VLADIMIR: Wait for Godot. (ESTRAGON *groans. Silence.*) Things have changed here since yesterday.

ESTRAGON: And if he doesn't come.

VLADIMIR (*after a moment of bewilderment*): We'll see when the time comes. (*Pause.*) I was saying that things have changed here since yesterday.

ESTRAGON: Everything oozes.

VLADIMIR: Look at the tree.

ESTRAGON: It's never the same pus from one second to the next.

VLADIMIR: The tree, look at the tree.

ESTRAGON *looks at the tree.*

ESTRAGON: Was it not there yesterday?

VLADIMIR: Yes of course it was there. Do you not remember? We nearly hanged ourselves from it. But you wouldn't. Do you not remember?

ESTRAGON: You dreamt it.

VLADIMIR: Is it possible you've forgotten already?

ESTRAGON: That's the way I am. Either I forget immediately or I never forget.

VLADIMIR: And Pozzo and Lucky, have you forgotten them too?

ESTRAGON: Pozzo and Lucky?

VLADIMIR: He's forgotten everything!

ESTRAGON: I remember a lunatic who kicked the shins off me. Then he played the fool.

VLADIMIR: That was Lucky.

ESTRAGON: I remember that. But when was it?

VLADIMIR: And his keeper, do you not remember him?

ESTRAGON: He gave me a bone.

VLADIMIR: That was Pozzo.

ESTRAGON: And all that was yesterday, you say?

VLADIMIR: Yes of course it was yesterday.

ESTRAGON: And here where we are now?

VLADIMIR: Where else do you think? Do you not recognize the place?

ESTRAGON (*suddenly furious*): Recognize! What is there to recognize? All my lousy life I've crawled about in the mud! And you talk to me about scenery! (*Looking wildly about him.*) Look at this muckheap! I've never stirred from it!

VLADIMIR: Calm yourself, calm yourself.

ESTRAGON: You and your landscapes! Tell me about the worms!

VLADIMIR: All the same, you can't tell me that this (*Gesture.*) bears any resemblance to .. (*He hesitates.*) . . . to the Macon country for example. You can't deny there's a big difference.

ESTRAGON: The Macon country! Who's talking to you about the Macon country?

VLADIMIR: But you were there yourself, in the Macon country.

ESTRAGON: No I was never in the Macon country! I've puked my puke of a life away here, I tell you! Here! In the Cackon country!

VLADIMIR: But we were there together, I could swear to it! Picking grapes for a man called . . . (*He snaps his fingers.*) . . . can't think of the name of the man, at a place called . . . (*Snaps his fingers.*) . . . can't think of the name of the place, do you not remember?

ESTRAGON (*a little calmer*): It's possible. I didn't notice anything.

VLADIMIR: But down there everything is red!

ESTRAGON (*exasperated*): ı didn't notice anything, I tell you!

Silence. VLADIMIR *sighs deeply.*

VLADIMIR: You're a hard man to get on with, Gogo.

ESTRAGON: It'd be better if we parted.

VLADIMIR: You always say that and you always come crawling back.

ESTRAGON: The best thing would be to kill me, like the other.

VLADIMIR: What other? (*Pause.*) What other?

ESTRAGON: Like billions of others.

VLADIMIR (*sententious*): To every man his little cross. (*He sighs.*) Till he dies. (*Afterthought.*) And is forgotten.

ESTRAGON: In the meantime let us try and converse calmly, since we are incapable of keeping silent.

VLADIMIR: You're right, we're inexhaustible.

ESTRAGON: It's so we won't think.

VLADIMIR: We have that excuse.

ESTRAGON: It's so we won't hear.

VLADIMIR: We have our reasons.

ESTRAGON: All the dead voices.

VLADIMIR: They make a noise like wings.

ESTRAGON: Like leaves.

VLADIMIR: Like sand.

ESTRAGON: Like leaves.

Silence.

VLADIMIR: They all speak at once.

ESTRAGON: Each one to itself.

Silence.

VLADIMIR: Rather they whisper.

ESTRAGON: They rustle.

VLADIMIR: They murmur.

ESTRAGON: They rustle.

Silence.

VLADIMIR: What do they say?

ESTRAGON: They talk about their lives.

VLADIMIR: To have lived is not enough for them.

ESTRAGON: They have to talk about it.

VLADIMIR: To be dead is not enough for them.

ESTRAGON: It is not sufficient.

Silence.

VLADIMIR: They make a noise like feathers.

ESTRAGON: Like leaves.
VLADIMIR: Like ashes.
ESTRAGON: Like leaves.

Long silence.

VLADIMIR: Say something!
ESTRAGON: I'm trying.

Long silence.

VLADIMIR (*in anguish*): Say anything at all!
ESTRAGON: What do we do now?
VLADIMIR: Wait for Godot.
ESTRAGON: Ah!

Silence.

VLADIMIR: This is awful!
ESTRAGON: Sing something.
VLADIMIR: No no! (*He reflects.*) We could start all over again perhaps.
ESTRAGON: That should be easy.
VLADIMIR: It's the start that's difficult.
ESTRAGON: You can start from anything.
VLADIMIR: Yes, but you have to decide.
ESTRAGON: True.

Silence.

VLADIMIR: Help me!
ESTRAGON: I'm trying.

Silence.

VLADIMIR: When you seek you hear.
ESTRAGON: You do.
VLADIMIR: That prevents you from finding.
ESTRAGON: It does.
VLADIMIR: That prevents you from thinking.
ESTRAGON: You think all the same.

VLADIMIR: No no, impossible.

ESTRAGON: That's the idea, let's contradict each other.

VLADIMIR: Impossible.

ESTRAGON: You think so?

VLADIMIR: We're in no danger of ever thinking any more.

ESTRAGON: Then what are we complaining about?

VLADIMIR: Thinking is not the worst.

ESTRAGON: Perhaps not. But at least there's that.

VLADIMIR: That what?

ESTRAGON: That's the idea, let's ask each other questions.

VLADIMIR: What do you mean, at least there's that?

ESTRAGON: That much less misery.

VLADIMIR: True.

ESTRAGON: Well? If we gave thanks for our mercies?

VLADIMIR: What is terrible is to *have* thought.

ESTRAGON: But did that ever happen to us?

VLADIMIR: Where are all these corpses from?

ESTRAGON: These skeletons.

VLADIMIR: Tell me that.

ESTRAGON: True.

VLADIMIR: We must have thought a little.

ESTRAGON: At the very beginning.

VLADIMIR: A charnel-house! A charnel-house!

ESTRAGON: You don't have to look.

VLADIMIR: You can't help looking.

ESTRAGON: True.

VLADIMIR: Try as one may.

ESTRAGON: I beg your pardon?

VLADIMIR: Try as one may.

ESTRAGON: We should turn resolutely towards Nature.

VLADIMIR: We've tried that.

ESTRAGON: True.

VLADIMIR: Oh it's not the worst, I know.

ESTRAGON: What?

VLADIMIR: To have thought.

ESTRAGON: Obviously.

VLADIMIR: But we could have done without it.

ESTRAGON: Que voulez-vous?

VLADIMIR: I beg your pardon?

ESTRAGON: Que voulez-vous.

VLADIMIR: Ah! que voulez-vous. Exactly.

Silence.

ESTRAGON: That wasn't such a bad little canter.
VLADIMIR: Yes, but now we'll have to find something else.
ESTRAGON: Let me see. (*He takes off his hat, concentrates.*)
VLADIMIR: Let me see. (*He takes off his hat, concentrates. Long silence.*) Ah!

They put on their hats, relax.

ESTRAGON: Well?
VLADIMIR: What was I saying, we could go on from there.
ESTRAGON: What were you saying when?
VLADIMIR: At the very beginning.
ESTRAGON: The very beginning of WHAT?
VLADIMIR: This evening . . . I was saying . . . I was saying . . .
ESTRAGON: I'm not a historian.
VLADIMIR: Wait . . . we embraced . . . we were happy . . . happy . . what do we do now that we're happy . . . go on waiting . . . waiting . . . let me think . . . it's coming . . . go on waiting . . . now that we're happy . . . let me see . ah! The tree!
ESTRAGON: The tree?
VLADIMIR: Do you not remember?
ESTRAGON: I'm tired.
VLADIMIR: Look at it.

They look at the tree.

ESTRAGON: I see nothing.
VLADIMIR: But yesterday evening it was all black and bare. And now it's covered with leaves.
ESTRAGON: Leaves?
VLADIMIR: In a single night.
ESTRAGON: It must be the Spring.
VLADIMIR: But in a single night!
ESTRAGON: I tell you we weren't here yesterday. Another of your nightmares.
VLADIMIR: And where were we yesterday evening according to you?

ESTRAGON: How would I know? In another compartment. There's no lack of void.

VLADIMIR *(sure of himself)*: Good. We weren't here yesterday evening. Now what did we do yesterday evening?

ESTRAGON: Do?

VLADIMIR: Try and remember.

ESTRAGON: Do . . . I suppose we blathered.

VLADIMIR *(controlling himself)*: About what?

ESTRAGON: Oh . . . this and that I suppose, nothing in particular. *(With assurance.)* Yes, now I remember, yesterday evening we spent blathering about nothing in particular. That's been going on now for half a century.

VLADIMIR: You don't remember any fact, any circumstance?

ESTRAGON *(weary)*: Don't torment me, Didi.

VLADIMIR: The sun. The moon. Do you not remember?

ESTRAGON: They must have been there, as usual.

VLADIMIR: You didn't notice anything out of the ordinary?

ESTRAGON: Alas!

VLADIMIR: And Pozzo? And Lucky?

ESTRAGON: Pozzo?

VLADIMIR: The bones.

ESTRAGON: They were like fishbones.

VLADIMIR: It was Pozzo gave them to you.

ESTRAGON: I don't know.

VLADIMIR: And the kick.

ESTRAGON: That's right, someone gave me a kick.

VLADIMIR: It was Lucky gave it to you.

ESTRAGON: And all that was yesterday?

VLADIMIR: Show your leg.

ESTRAGON: Which?

VLADIMIR: Both. Pull up your trousers. (ESTRAGON *gives a leg to* VLADIMIR, *staggers.* VLADIMIR *takes the leg. They stagger.*) Pull up your trousers.

ESTRAGON: I can't.

VLADIMIR *pulls up the trousers, looks at the leg, lets it go.* ESTRAGON *almost falls.*

VLADIMIR: The other. (ESTRAGON *gives the same leg.*) The other, pig!

(ESTRAGON *gives the other leg. Triumphantly.*) There's the wound! Beginning to fester!

ESTRAGON: And what about it?

VLADIMIR (*letting go the leg*): Where are your boots?

ESTRAGON: I must have thrown them away.

VLADIMIR: When?

ESTRAGON: I don't know.

VLADIMIR: Why?

ESTRAGON (*exasperated*): I don't know why I don't know!

VLADIMIR: No, I mean why did you throw them away?

ESTRAGON (*exasperated*): Because they were hurting me!

VLADIMIR (*triumphantly, pointing to the boots*): There they are! (ESTRAGON *looks at the boots.*) At the very spot where you left them yesterday!

ESTRAGON *goes towards the boots, inspects them closely.*

ESTRAGON: They're not mine.

VLADIMIR (*stupefied*): Not yours!

ESTRAGON: Mine were black. These are brown.

VLADIMIR: You're sure yours were black?

ESTRAGON: Well they were a kind of gray.

VLADIMIR: And these are brown. Show.

ESTRAGON (*picking up a boot*): Well they're a kind of green.

VLADIMIR: Show. (ESTRAGON *hands him the boot.* VLADIMIR *inspects it, throws it down angrily.*) Well of all the—

ESTRAGON: You see, all that's a lot of bloody—

VLADIMIR: Ah! I see what it is. Yes, I see what's happened.

ESTRAGON: All that's a lot of bloody—

VLADIMIR: It's elementary. Someone came and took yours and left you his.

ESTRAGON: Why?

VLADIMIR: His were too tight for him, so he took yours.

ESTRAGON: But mine were too tight.

VLADIMIR: For you. Not for him.

ESTRAGON (*having tried in vain to work it out*): I'm tired! (*Pause.*) Let's go.

VLADIMIR: We can't.

ESTRAGON: Why not?

VLADIMIR: We're waiting for Godot.

ESTRAGON: Ah! (*Pause. Despairing.*) What'll we do, what'll we do!

VLADIMIR: There's nothing we can do.

ESTRAGON: But I can't go on like this!

VLADIMIR: Would you like a radish?

ESTRAGON: Is that all there is?

VLADIMIR: There are radishes and turnips.

ESTRAGON: Are there no carrots?

VLADIMIR: No. Anyway you overdo it with your carrots.

ESTRAGON: Then give me a radish. (VLADIMIR *fumbles in his pockets, finds nothing but turnips, finally brings out a radish and hands it to* ESTRAGON *who examines it, sniffs it.*) It's black!

VLADIMIR: It's a radish.

ESTRAGON: I only like the pink ones, you know that!

VLADIMIR: Then you don't want it?

ESTRAGON: I only like the pink ones!

VLADIMIR: Then give it back to me.

ESTRAGON *gives it back.*

ESTRAGON: I'll go and get a carrot.

He does not move.

VLADIMIR: This is becoming really insignificant.

ESTRAGON: Not enough.

Silence.

VLADIMIR: What about trying them.

ESTRAGON: I've tried everything.

VLADIMIR: No, I mean the boots.

ESTRAGON: Would that be a good thing?

VLADIMIR: It'd pass the time. (ESTRAGON *hesitates.*) I assure you, it'd be an occupation.

ESTRAGON: A relaxation.

VLADIMIR: A recreation.

ESTRAGON: A relaxation.

VLADIMIR: Try.

ESTRAGON: You'll help me?

VLADIMIR: I will of course.

ESTRAGON: We don't manage too badly, eh Didi, between the two of us?

VLADIMIR: Yes yes. Come on, we'll try the left first.

ESTRAGON: We always find something, eh Didi, to give us the impression we exist?

VLADIMIR (*impatiently*): Yes yes, we're magicians. But let us persevere in what we have resolved, before we forget. (*He picks up a boot.*) Come on, give me your foot. (ESTRAGON *raises his foot.*) The other, hog! (ESTRAGON *raises the other foot.*) Higher! (*Wreathed together they stagger about the stage.* VLADIMIR *succeeds finally in getting on the boot.*) Try and walk. (ESTRAGON *walks.*) Well?

ESTRAGON: It fits.

VLADIMIR (*taking string from his pocket*): We'll try and lace it.

ESTRAGON (*vehemently*): No no, no laces, no laces!

VLADIMIR: You'll be sorry. Let's try the other. (*As before.*) Well?

ESTRAGON (*grudgingly*): It fits too.

VLADIMIR: They don't hurt you?

ESTRAGON: Not yet.

VLADIMIR: Then you can keep them.

ESTRAGON: They're too big.

VLADIMIR: Perhaps you'll have socks some day.

ESTRAGON: True.

VLADIMIR: Then you'll keep them?

ESTRAGON: That's enough about these boots.

VLADIMIR: Yes, but—

ESTRAGON (*violently*): Enough! (*Silence.*) I suppose I might as well sit down.

He looks for a place to sit down, then goes and sits down on the mound.

VLADIMIR: That's where you were sitting yesterday evening.

ESTRAGON: If I could only sleep.

VLADIMIR: Yesterday you slept.

ESTRAGON: I'll try.

He resumes his foetal posture, his head between his knees.

VLADIMIR: Wait. (*He goes over and sits down beside* ESTRAGON *and begins to sing in a loud voice.*)

> Bye bye bye bye
> Bye bye—

ESTRAGON (*looking up angrily*): Not so loud!

VLADIMIR (*softly*):

> Bye bye bye bye
> Bye bye bye bye
> Bye bye bye bye
> Bye bye . . .

ESTRAGON *sleeps.* VLADIMIR *gets up softly, takes off his coat and lays it across* ESTRAGON'S *shoulders, then starts walking up and down, swinging his arms to keep himself warm.* ESTRAGON *wakes with a start, jumps up, casts about wildly.* VLADIMIR *runs to him, puts his arms round him.*

There . . . there . . . Didi is there . . . don't be afraid . . .

ESTRAGON: Ah!

VLADIMIR: There . . . there . . . it's all over.

ESTRAGON: I was falling—

VLADIMIR: It's all over, it's all over.

ESTRAGON: I was on top of a—

VLADIMIR: Don't tell me! Come, we'll walk it off.

He takes ESTRAGON *by the arm and walks him up and down until* ESTRAGON *refuses to go any further.*

ESTRAGON: That's enough. I'm tired.

VLADIMIR: You'd rather be stuck there doing nothing?

ESTRAGON: Yes.

VLADIMIR: Please yourself.

He releases ESTRAGON, *picks up his coat and puts it on.*

ESTRAGON: Let's go.

VLADIMIR: We can't.

ESTRAGON: Why not?

VLADIMIR: We're waiting for Godot.

ESTRAGON: Ah!

VLADIMIR *walks up and down*

Can you not stay still?

VLADIMIR: I'm cold.

ESTRAGON: We came too soon.

VLADIMIR: It's always at nightfall.

ESTRAGON: But night doesn't fall.

VLADIMIR: It'll fall all of a sudden, like yesterday.

ESTRAGON: Then it'll be night.

VLADIMIR: And we can go.

ESTRAGON: Then it'll be day again. (*Pause. Despairing.*) What'll we do, what'll we do!

VLADIMIR (*halting, violently*): Will you stop whining! I've had about my bellyful of your lamentations!

ESTRAGON: I'm going.

VLADIMIR (*seeing* LUCKY's *hat*): Well!

ESTRAGON: Farewell.

VLADIMIR: Lucky's hat. (*He goes towards it.*) I've been here an hour and never saw it. (*Very pleased.*) Fine!

ESTRAGON: You'll never see me again.

VLADIMIR: I knew it was the right place. Now our troubles are over. (*He picks up the hat, contemplates it, straightens it.*) Must have been a very fine hat. (*He puts it on in place of his own which he hands to* ESTRAGON.) Here.

ESTRAGON: What?

VLADIMIR: Hold that.

ESTRAGON *takes* VLADIMIR's *hat.* VLADIMIR *adjusts* LUCKY's *hat on his head.* ESTRAGON *puts on* VLADIMIR's *hat in place of his own which he hands to* VLADIMIR. VLADIMIR *takes* ESTRAGON's *hat.* ESTRAGON *adjusts* VLADIMIR's *hat on his head.* VLADIMIR *puts on* ESTRAGON's *hat in place of* LUCKY's *which he hands to* ESTRAGON. ESTRAGON *takes* LUCKY's *hat.* VLADIMIR *adjusts* ETRAGON's *hat on his head.* ESTRAGON *puts on* LUCKY's *hat in place of* VLADIMIR's *which he hands to* VLADIMIR. VLADIMIR *takes his hat.* ESTRAGON *adjusts* LUCKY's *hat on his head.* VLADIMIR *puts on his hat in place of* ESTRAGON's *which he hands to* ESTRAGON. ESTRAGON *takes his hat.* VLADIMIR *adjusts his hat on his head.* ESTRAGON *puts on his hat in place of* LUCKY's *which he hands to* VLADIMIR. VLADIMIR *takes* LUCKY's *hat.* ESTRAGON *adjusts his hat on his head.* VLADIMIR *puts on* LUCKY's *hat in place of his own which he hands to* ESTRAGON. ESTRAGON *takes* VLADIMIR's *hat.* VLADIMIR *adjusts* LUCKY's *hat on his head.* ESTRAGON *hands* VLADIMIR's *hat back to* VLADIMIR *who takes it and hands it back to* ESTRAGON *who takes it and hands it back to* VLADIMIR *who takes it and throws it down.*

How does it fit me?

ESTRAGON: How would I know?

VLADIMIR: No, but how do I look in it?

He turns his head coquettishly to and fro, minces like a mannequin.

ESTRAGON: Hideous.

VLADIMIR: Yes, but not more so than usual?

ESTRAGON: Neither more nor less.

VLADIMIR: Then I can keep it. Mine irked me   (*Pause.*) How shall I say? (*Pause.*) It itched me.

He takes off LUCKY's *hat, peers into it, shakes it, knocks on the crown, puts it on again.*

ESTRAGON: I'm going.

Silence.

VLADIMIR: Will you not play?

ESTRAGON: Play at what?

VLADIMIR: We could play at Pozzo and Lucky.

ESTRAGON: Never heard of it.

VLADIMIR: I'll do Lucky, you do Pozzo. (*He imitates* LUCKY *sagging under the weight of his baggage.* ESTRAGON *looks at him with stupefaction.*) Go on.

ESTRAGON: What am I to do?

VLADIMIR: Curse me!

ESTRAGON (*after reflection*): Naughty!

VLADIMIR: Stronger!

ESTRAGON: Gonococcus! Spirochete!

VLADIMIR *sways back and forth, doubled in two.*

VLADIMIR: Tell me to think.
ESTRAGON: What?
VLADIMIR: Say, Think, pig!
ESTRAGON: Think, pig!

Silence.

VLADIMIR: I can't!
ESTRAGON: That's enough of that.
VLADIMIR: Tell me to dance.
ESTRAGON: I'm going.
VLADIMIR: Dance, hog! (*He writhes. Exit* ESTRAGON *left, precipitately.*) I can't! (*He looks up, misses* ESTRAGON.) Gogo! (*He moves wildly about the stage. Enter* ESTRAGON *left, panting. He hastens towards* VLADIMIR, *falls into his arms.*) There you are again at last!
ESTRAGON: I'm accursed!
VLADIMIR: Where were you? I thought you were gone for ever.
ESTRAGON: They're coming!
VLADIMIR: Who?
ESTRAGON: I don't know.
VLADIMIR: How many?
ESTRAGON: I don't know.
VLADIMIR (*triumphantly*): It's Godot! At last! Gogo! It's Godot! We're saved! Let's go and meet him! (*He drags* ESTRAGON *towards the wings.* ESTRAGON *resists, pulls himself free, exit right.*) Gogo! Come back! (VLADIMIR *runs to extreme left, scans the horizon. Enter* ESTRAGON *right, he hastens towards* VLADIMIR, *falls into his arms.*) There you are again again!
ESTRAGON: I'm in hell!
VLADIMIR: Where were you?
ESTRAGON: They're coming there too!
VLADIMIR: We're surrounded! (ESTRAGON *makes a rush towards back.*) Imbecile! There's no way out there. (*He takes* ESTRAGON *by the arm and drags him towards front. Gesture towards front.*) There! Not a soul in sight! Off you go! Quick! (*He pushes* ESTRAGON *towards auditorium.* ESTRAGON *recoils in horror.*) You won't? (*He contemplates auditorium.*) Well I can understand that. Wait till I see. (*He reflects.*) Your only hope left is to disappear.

ESTRAGON: Where?

VLADIMIR: Behind the tree. (ESTRAGON *hesitates.*) Quick! Behind the tree. (ESTRAGON *goes and crouches behind the tree, realizes he is not hidden, comes out from behind the tree.*) Decidedly this tree will not have been the slightest use to us.

ESTRAGON (*calmer*): I lost my head. Forgive me. It won't happen again. Tell me what to do.

VLADIMIR: There's nothing to do.

ESTRAGON: You go and stand there. (*He draws* VLADIMIR *to extreme right and places him with his back to the stage.*) There, don't move, and watch out. (VLADIMIR *scans horizon, screening his eyes with his hand.* ESTRAGON *runs and takes up same position extreme left. They turn their heads and look at each other.*) Back to back like in the good old days. (*They continue to look at each other for a moment, then resume their watch. Long silence.*) Do you see anything coming?

VLADIMIR (*turning his head*): What?

ESTRAGON (*louder*): Do you see anything coming?

VLADIMIR: No.

ESTRAGON: Nor I.

They resume their watch. Silence.

VLADIMIR: You must have had a vision.

ESTRAGON (*turning his head*): What?

VLADIMIR (*louder*): You must have had a vision.

ESTRAGON: No need to shout!

They resume their watch. Silence.

VLADIMIR ⎱
ESTRAGON ⎰ (*turning simultaneously*): Do you—

VLADIMIR: Oh pardon!

ESTRAGON: Carry on.

VLADIMIR: No no, after you.

ESTRAGON: No no, you first.

VLADIMIR: I interrupted you.

ESTRAGON: On the contrary.

They glare at each other angrily.

VLADIMIR: Ceremonious ape!

ESTRAGON: Punctilious pig!

VLADIMIR: Finish your phrase, I tell you!

ESTRAGON: Finish your own!

Silence. They draw closer, halt.

VLADIMIR: Moron!

ESTRAGON: That's the idea, let's abuse each other.

They turn, move apart, turn again and face each other.

VLADIMIR: Moron!

ESTRAGON: Vermin!

VLADIMIR: Abortion!

ESTRAGON: Morpion!

VLADIMIR: Sewer-rat!

ESTRAGON: Curate!

VLADIMIR: Cretin!

ESTRAGON (*with finality*): Crritic!

VLADIMIR: Oh!

He wilts, vanquished, and turns away.

ESTRAGON: Now let's make it up.

VLADIMIR: Gogo!

ESTRAGON: Didi!

VLADIMIR: Your hand!

ESTRAGON: Take it!

VLADIMIR: Come to my arms!

ESTRAGON: Your arms?

VLADIMIR: My breast!

ESTRAGON: Off we go!

They embrace. They separate. Silence.

VLADIMIR: How time flies when one has fun!

Silence.

ESTRAGON: What do we do now?
VLADIMIR: While waiting.
ESTRAGON: While waiting.

Silence.

VLADIMIR: We could do our exercises.
ESTRAGON: Our movements.
VLADIMIR: Our elevations.
ESTRAGON: Our relaxations.
VLADIMIR: Our elongations.
ESTRAGON: Our relaxations.
VLADIMIR: To warm us up.
ESTRAGON: To calm us down.
VLADIMIR: Off we go.

VLADIMIR *hops from one foot to the other.* ESTRAGON *imitates him.*

ESTRAGON (*stopping*): That enough. I'm tired.
VLADIMIR (*stopping*): We're not in form. What about a little deep breathing?
ESTRAGON: I'm tired breathing.
VLADIMIR: You're right. (*Pause.*) Let's just do the tree, for the balance.
ESTRAGON: The tree?

VLADIMIR *does the tree, staggering about on one leg.*

VLADIMIR (*stopping*): Your turn.

ESTRAGON *does the tree, staggers.*

ESTRAGON: Do you think God sees me?
VLADIMIR: You must close your eyes.

ESTRAGON *closes his eyes, staggers worse.*

ESTRAGON (*stopping, brandishing his fists, at the top of his voice*): God have pity on me!
VLADIMIR (*vexed*): And me?

ESTRAGON: On me! On me! Pity! On me!

> *Enter* POZZO *and* LUCKY. POZZO *is blind.* LUCKY *burdened as before. Rope as before, but much shorter, so that* POZZO *may follow more easily.* LUCKY *wearing a different hat. At the sight of* VLADIMIR *and* ESTRAGON *he stops short.* POZZO, *continuing on his way, bumps into him.*

VLADIMIR: Gogo!

POZZO (*clutching on to* LUCKY *who staggers*): What is it? Who is it?

> LUCKY *falls, drops everything and brings down* POZZO *with him They lie helpless among the scattered baggage.*

ESTRAGON: It is Godot?

VLADIMIR: At last! (*He goes towards the heap.*) Reinforcements at last!

POZZO: Help!

ESTRAGON: Is it Godot?

VLADIMIR: We were beginning to weaken. Now we're sure to see the evening out.

POZZO: Help!

ESTRAGON: Do you hear him?

VLADIMIR: We are no longer alone, waiting for the night, waiting for Godot, waiting for . . . waiting. All evening we have struggled, unassisted. Now it's over. It's already to-morrow.

POZZO: Help!

VLADIMIR: Time flows again already. The sun will set, the moon rise and we away . . . from here.

POZZO: Pity!

VLADIMIR: Poor Pozzo!

ESTRAGON: I knew it was him.

VLADIMIR: Who?

ESTRAGON: Godot.

VLADIMIR: But it's not Godot.

ESTRAGON: It's not Godot?

VLADIMIR: It's not Godot.

ESTRAGON: Then who is it?

VLADIMIR: It's Pozzo.

POZZO: Here! Here! Help me up!

VLADIMIR: He can't get up.

ESTRAGON: Let's go.

VLADIMIR: We can't.

ESTRAGON: Why not?

VLADIMIR: We're waiting for Godot.

ESTRAGON: Ah!

VLADIMIR: Perhaps he has another bone for you.

ESTRAGON: Bone?

VLADIMIR: Chicken. Do you not remember?

ESTRAGON: It was him?

VLADIMIR: Yes.

ESTRAGON: Ask him.

VLADIMIR: Perhaps we should help him first.

ESTRAGON: To do what?

VLADIMIR: To get up.

ESTRAGON: He can't get up?

VLADIMIR: He wants to get up.

ESTRAGON: Then let him get up.

VLADIMIR: He can't.

ESTRAGON: Why not?

VLADIMIR: I don't know.

POZZO *writhes, groans, beats the ground with his fists.*

ESTRAGON: We should ask him for the bone first. Then if he refuses we'll leave him there.

VLADIMIR: You mean we have him at our mercy?

ESTRAGON: Yes.

VLADIMIR: And that we should subordinate our good offices to certain conditions?

ESTRAGON: What?

VLADIMIR: That seems intelligent all right. But there's one thing I'm afraid of.

POZZO: Help!

ESTRAGON: What?

VLADIMIR: That Lucky might get going all of a sudden. Then we'd be ballocksed.

ESTRAGON: Lucky?

VLADIMIR: The one that went for you yesterday.

ESTRAGON: I tell you there was ten of them.

VLADIMIR: No, before that, the one that kicked you.

ESTRAGON: Is he there?

VLADIMIR: As large as life. (*Gesture towards* LUCKY.) For the moment he is inert. But he might run amuck any minute.

POZZO: Help!

ESTRAGON: And suppose we gave him a good beating the two of us?

VLADIMIR: You mean if we fell on him in his sleep?

ESTRAGON: Yes.

VLADIMIR: That seems a good idea all right. But could we do it? Is he really asleep? (*Pause.*) No, the best would be to take advantage of Pozzo's calling for help—

POZZO: Help!

VLADIMIR: To help him—

ESTRAGON: *We* help *him*?

VLADIMIR: In anticipation of some tangible return.

ESTRAGON: And suppose he—

VLADIMIR: Let us not waste our time in idle discourse! (*Pause. Vehemently.*) Let us do something, while we have the chance! It is not every day that we are needed. Not indeed that we personally are needed. Others would meet the case equally well, if not better. To all mankind they were addressed, those cries for help still ringing in our ears! But at this place, at this moment of time, all mankind is us, whether we like it or not. Let us make the most of it, before it is too late! Let us represent worthily for once the foul brood to which a cruel fate consigned us! What do you say? (ESTRAGON *says nothing.*) It is true that when with folded arms we weigh the pros and cons we are no less a credit to our species. The tiger bounds to the help of his congeners without the least reflexion, or else he slinks away into the depths of the thickets. But that is not the question. What are we doing here, *that* is the question. And we are blessed in this, that we happen to know the answer. Yes, in this immense confusion one thing alone is clear. We are waiting for Godot to come—

ESTRAGON: Ah!

POZZO: Help!

VLADIMIR: Or for night to fall. (*Pause.*) We have kept our appointment and that's an end to that. We are not saints, but we have kept our appointment. How many people can boast as much?

ESTRAGON: Billions.

VLADIMIR: You think so?

ESTRAGON: I don't know.

VLADIMIR: You may be right.

POZZO: Help!

VLADIMIR: All I know is that the hours are long, under these conditions, and constrain us to beguile them with proceedings which— how shall I say—which may at first sight seem reasonable, until they become a habit. You may say it is to prevent our reason from foundering. No doubt. But has it not long been straying in the night without end of the abyssal depths? That's what I sometimes wonder. You follow my reasoning?

ESTRAGON (*aphoristic for once*): We are all born mad. Some remain so.

POZZO: Help! I'll pay you!

ESTRAGON: How much?

POZZO: One hundred francs!

ESTRAGON: It's not enough.

VLADIMIR: I wouldn't go so far as that.

ESTRAGON: You think it's enough?

VLADIMIR: No, I mean so far as to assert that I was weak in the head when I came into the world. But that is not the question.

POZZO: Two hundred!

VLADIMIR: We wait. We are bored. (*He throws up his hand.*) No, don't protest, we are bored to death, there's no denying it. Good. A diversion comes along and what do we do? We let it go to waste. Come, let's get to work! (*He advances towards the heap, stops in his stride.*) In an instant all will vanish and we'll be alone once more, in the midst of nothingness! (*He broods.*)

POZZO: Two hundred!

VLADIMIR: We're coming!

He tries to pull POZZO *to his feet, fails, tries again, stumbles, falls, tries to get up, fails.*

ESTRAGON: What's the matter with you all?

VLADIMIR: Help!

ESTRAGON: I'm going.

VLADIMIR: Don't leave me! They'll kill me!

POZZO: Where am I?

VLADIMIR: Gogo!

POZZO: Help!

VLADIMIR: Help!

ESTRAGON: I'm going.

VLADIMIR: Help me up first, then we'll go together.

ESTRAGON: You promise?

VLADIMIR: I swear it!

ESTRAGON: And we'll never come back?

VLADIMIR: Never!

ESTRAGON: We'll go to the Pyrenees.

VLADIMIR: Wherever you like.

ESTRAGON: I've always wanted to wander in the Pyrenees.

VLADIMIR: You'll wander in them.

ESTRAGON (*recoiling*): Who farted?

VLADIMIR: Pozzo.

POZZO: Here! Here! Pity!

ESTRAGON: It's revolting!

VLADIMIR: Quick! Give me your hand!

ESTRAGON: I'm going. (*Pause. Louder.*) I'm going.

VLADIMIR: Well I suppose in the end I'll get up by myself. (*He tries, fails.*) In the fullness of time.

ESTRAGON: What's the matter with you?

VLADIMIR: Go to hell.

ESTRAGON: Are you staying there?

VLADIMIR: For the time being.

ESTRAGON: Come on, get up, you'll catch a chill.

VLADIMIR: Don't worry about me.

ESTRAGON: Come on, Didi, don't be pig-headed!

He stretches out his hand which VLADIMIR *makes haste to seize.*

VLADIMIR: Pull!

ESTRAGON *pulls, stumbles, falls. Long silence.*

POZZO: Help!

VLADIMIR: We've arrived.

POZZO: Who are you?

VLADIMIR: We are men.

Silence.

ESTRAGON: Sweet mother earth!

VLADIMIR: Can you get up?

ESTRAGON: I don't know.

VLADIMIR: Try.

ESTRAGON: Not now, not now.

Silence.

POZZO: What happened?

VLADIMIR (*violently*): Will you stop it, you! Pest! He can think of nothing but himself!

ESTRAGON: What about a little snooze?

VLADIMIR: Did you hear him? He wants to know what happened!

ESTRAGON: Don't mind him. Sleep.

Silence.

POZZO: Pity! Pity!

ESTRAGON (*with a start*): What is it?

VLADIMIR: Were you asleep?

ESTRAGON: I must have been.

VLADIMIR: It's this bastard Pozzo at it again.

ESTRAGON: Make him stop it. Kick him in the crotch.

VLADIMIR (*striking* POZZO): Will you stop it! Crablouse! (POZZO *extricates himself with cries of pain and crawls away. He stops, saws the air blindly, calling for help.* VLADIMIR, *propped on his elbow, observes his retreat.*) He's off! (POZZO *collapses.*) He's down!

ESTRAGON: What do we do now?

VLADIMIR: Perhaps I could crawl to him.

ESTRAGON: Don't leave me!

VLADIMIR: Or I could call to him.

ESTRAGON: Yes, call to him.

VLADIMIR: Pozzo! (*Silence.*) Pozzo! (*Silence.*) No reply.

ESTRAGON: Together.

VLADIMIR: } Pozzo! Pozzo!
ESTRAGON: }

VLADIMIR: He moved.

ESTRAGON: Are you sure his name is Pozzo?

VLADIMIR (*alarmed*): Mr. Pozzo! Come back! We won't hurt you!

Silence.

ESTRAGON: We might try him with other names.

VLADIMIR: I'm afraid he's dying.

ESTRAGON: It'd be amusing.

VLADIMIR: What'd be amusing?

ESTRAGON: To try him with other names, one after the other. It'd pass the time. And we'd be bound to hit on the right one sooner or later.

VLADIMIR: I tell you his name is Pozzo.

ESTRAGON: We'll soon see. (*He reflects.*) Abel! Abel!

POZZO: Help!

ESTRAGON: Got it in one!

VLADIMIR: I begin to weary of this motif.

ESTRAGON: Perhaps the other is called Cain. Cain! Cain!

POZZO: Help!

ESTRAGON: He's all humanity. (*Silence.*) Look at the little cloud.

VLADIMIR (*raising his eyes*): Where?

ESTRAGON: There. In the zenith.

VLADIMIR: Well? (*Pause.*) What is there so wonderful about it?

Silence.

ESTRAGON: Let's pass on now to something else, do you mind?

VLADIMIR: I was just going to suggest it.

ESTRAGON: But to what?

VLADIMIR: Ah!

Silence.

ESTRAGON: Suppose we got up to begin with?

VLADIMIR: No harm trying.

They get up.

ESTRAGON: Child's play.

VLADIMIR: Simple question of will-power.

ESTRAGON: And now?

POZZO: Help!

ESTRAGON: Let's go.

VLADIMIR: We can't.

ESTRAGON: Why not?

VLADIMIR: We're waiting for Godot.

ESTRAGON: Ah! (*Despairing.*) What'll we do, what'll we do!

POZZO: Help!

VLADIMIR: What about helping him?

ESTRAGON: What does he want?

VLADIMIR: He wants to get up.

ESTRAGON: Then why doesn't he?

VLADIMIR: He wants us to help him to get up.

ESTRAGON: Then why don't we? What are we waiting for?

They help POZZO *to his feet, let him go. He falls.*

VLADIMIR: We must hold him. (*They get him up again.* POZZO *sags between them, his arms round their necks.*) Feeling better?

POZZO: Who are you?

VLADIMIR: Do you not recognize us?

POZZO: I am blind.

Silence.

ESTRAGON: Perhaps he can see into the future.

VLADIMIR: Since when?

POZZO: I used to have wonderful sight—but are you friends?

ESTRAGON (*laughing noisily*): He wants to know if we are friends!

VLADIMIR: No, he means friends of his.

ESTRAGON: Well?

VLADIMIR: We've proved we are, by helping him.

ESTRAGON: Exactly. Would we have helped him if we weren't his friends?

VLADIMIR: Possibly.

ESTRAGON: True.

VLADIMIR: Don't let's quibble about that now.

POZZO: You are not highwaymen?

ESTRAGON: Highwaymen! Do we look like highwaymen?

VLADIMIR: Damn it can't you see the man is blind!

ESTRAGON: Damn it so he is. (*Pause.*) So he says.

POZZO: Don't leave me!

VLADIMIR: No question of it.

ESTRAGON: For the moment.

POZZO: What time is it?

VLADIMIR (*inspecting the sky*): Seven o'clock . . . eight o'clock . . .

ESTRAGON: That depends what time of year it is.

POZZO: Is it evening?

Silence. VLADIMIR *and* ESTRAGON *scrutinize the sunset.*

ESTRAGON: It's rising.

VLADIMIR: Impossible.

ESTRAGON: Perhaps it's the dawn.

VLADIMIR: Don't be a fool. It's the west over there.

ESTRAGON: How do you know?

POZZO (*anguished*): Is it evening?

VLADIMIR: Anyway it hasn't moved.

ESTRAGON: I tell you it's rising.

POZZO: Why don't you answer me?

ESTRAGON: Give us a chance.

VLADIMIR (*reassuring*): It's evening, Sir, it's evening, night is drawing nigh. My friend here would have me doubt it and I must confess he shook me for a moment. But it is not for nothing I have lived through this long day and I can assure you it is very near the end of its repertory. (*Pause.*) How do you feel now?

ESTRAGON: How much longer are we to cart him around. (*They half release him, catch him again as he falls.*) We are not caryatids!

VLADIMIR: You were saying your sight used to be good, if I heard you right.

POZZO: Wonderful! Wonderful, wonderful sight!

Silence.

ESTRAGON (*irritably*): Expand! Expand!

VLADIMIR: Let him alone. Can't you see he's thinking of the days when he was happy. (*Pause.*) *Memoria praeteritorum bonorum*—that must be unpleasant.

ESTRAGON: We wouldn't know.

VLADIMIR: And it came on you all of a sudden?

POZZO: Quite wonderful!

VLADIMIR: I'm asking you if it came on you all of a sudden.

POZZO: I woke up one fine day as blind as Fortune. (*Pause.*) Sometimes I wonder if I'm not still asleep.

VLADIMIR: And when was that?

POZZO: I don't know.

VLADIMIR: But no later than yesterday—

POZZO (*violently*): Don't question me! The blind have no notion of time. The things of time are hidden from them too.

VLADIMIR: Well just fancy that! I could have sworn it was just the opposite.

ESTRAGON: I'm going.

POZZO: Where are we?

VLADIMIR: I couldn't tell you.

POZZO: It isn't by any chance the place known as the Board?

VLADIMIR: Never heard of it.

POZZO: What is it like?

VLADIMIR (*looking round*): It's indescribable. It's like nothing. There's nothing. There's a tree.

POZZO: Then it's not the Board.

ESTRAGON (*sagging*): Some diversion!

POZZO: Where is my menial?

VLADIMIR: He's about somewhere.

POZZO: Why doesn't he answer when I call?

VLADIMIR: I don't know. He seems to be sleeping. Perhaps he's dead.

POZZO: What happened exactly?

ESTRAGON: Exactly!

VLADIMIR: The two of you slipped. (*Pause.*) And fell.

POZZO: Go and see is he hurt.

VLADIMIR: We can't leave you.

POZZO: You needn't both go.

VLADIMIR (*to* ESTRAGON): You go.

ESTRAGON: After what he did to me? Never!

POZZO: Yes yes, let your friend go, he stinks so. (*Silence.*) What is he waiting for?

VLADIMIR: What you waiting for?

ESTRAGON: I'm waiting for Godot.

Silence.

VLADIMIR: What exactly should he do?

POZZO: Well to begin with he should pull on the rope, as hard as he likes so long as he doesn't strangle him. He usually responds to that. If not he should give him a taste of his boot, in the face and the privates as far as possible.

VLADIMIR (*to* ESTRAGON): You see, you've nothing to be afraid of. It's even an opportunity to revenge yourself.

ESTRAGON: And if he defends himself?

POZZO: No no, he never defends himself.

VLADIMIR: I'll come flying to the rescue.

ESTRAGON: Don't take your eyes off me.

He goes towards LUCKY.

VLADIMIR: Make sure he's alive before you start. No point in exerting yourself if he's dead.

ESTRAGON (*bending over* LUCKY): He's breathing.

VLADIMIR: Then let him have it.

With sudden fury ESTRAGON *starts kicking* LUCKY, *hurling abuse at him as he does so. But he hurts his foot and moves away, limping and groaning.* LUCKY *stirs.*

ESTRAGON: Oh the brute!

He sits down on the mound and tries to take off his boot. But he soon desists and disposes himself for sleep, his arms on his knees and his head on his arms.

POZZO: What's gone wrong now?

VLADIMIR: My friend has hurt himself.

POZZO: And Lucky?

VLADIMIR: So it is he?

POZZO: What?

VLADIMIR: It is Lucky?

POZZO: I don't understand.

VLADIMIR: And you are Pozzo?

POZZO: Certainly I am Pozzo.

VLADIMIR: The same as yesterday?

POZZO: Yesterday?

VLADIMIR: We met yesterday. (*Silence.*) Do you not remember?

POZZO: I don't remember having met anyone yesterday. But to-morrow

I won't remember having met anyone to-day. So don't count on me to enlighten you.

VLADIMIR: But—

POZZO: Enough! Up pig!

VLADIMIR: You were bringing him to the fair to sell him. You spoke to us. He danced. He thought. You had your sight.

POZZO: As you please. Let me go! (VLADIMIR *moves away.*) Up!

LUCKY *gets up, gathers up his burdens.*

VLADIMIR: Where do you go from here.

POZZO: On. (LUCKY, *laden down, takes his place before* POZZO.) Whip! (LUCKY *puts everything down, looks for whip, finds it, puts it into* POZZO's *hand, takes up everything again.*) Rope!

LUCKY *puts everything down, puts end of rope into* POZZO's *hand, takes up everything again.*

VLADIMIR: What is there in the bag?

POZZO: Sand. (*He jerks the rope.*) On!

VLADIMIR: Don't go yet.

POZZO: I'm going.

VLADIMIR: What do you do when you fall far from help?

POZZO: We wait till we can get up. Then we go on. On!

VLADIMIR: Before you go tell him to sing.

POZZO: Who?

VLADIMIR: Lucky.

POZZO: To sing?

VLADIMIR: Yes. Or to think. Or to recite.

POZZO: But he is dumb.

VLADIMIR: Dumb!

POZZO: Dumb. He can't even groan.

VLADIMIR: Dumb! Since when?

POZZO (*suddenly furious*): Have you not done tormenting me with your accursed time! It's abominable! When! When! One day, is that not enough for you, one day he went dumb, one day I went blind, one day we'll go deaf, one day we were born, one day we shall die, the same day, the same second, is that not enough for you? (*Calmer.*) They give birth astride of a grave, the light

gleams an instant, then it's night once more. (*He jerks the rope.*)
On!

> *Exeunt* POZZO *and* LUCKY. VLADIMIR *follows them to the edge
> of the stage, looks after them. The noise of falling, reinforced
> by mimic of* VLADIMIR, *announces that they are down again.
> Silence.* VLADIMIR *goes towards* ESTRAGON, *contemplates him a
> moment, then shakes him awake.*

ESTRAGON (*wild gestures, incoherent words. Finally*): Why will you
never let me sleep?

VLADIMIR: I felt lonely.

ESTRAGON: I was dreaming I was happy.

VLADIMIR: That passed the time.

ESTRAGON: I was dreaming that—

VLADIMIR (*violently*): Don't tell me! (*Silence.*) I wonder is he really
blind.

ESTRAGON: Blind? Who?

VLADIMIR: Pozzo.

ESTRAGON: Blind?

VLADIMIR: He told us he was blind.

ESTRAGON: Well what about it?

VLADIMIR: It seemed to me he saw us.

ESTRAGON: You dreamt it. (*Pause.*) Let's go. We can't. Ah! (*Pause.*)
Are you sure it wasn't him?

VLADIMIR: Who?

ESTRAGON: Godot.

VLADIMIR: But who?

ESTRAGON: Pozzo.

VLADIMIR: Not at all! (*Less sure.*) Not at all! (*Still less sure.*) Not
at all!

ESTRAGON: I suppose I might as well get up. (*He gets up painfully.*)
Ow! Didi!

VLADIMIR: I don't know what to think any more.

ESTRAGON: My feet! (*He sits down again and tries to take off his
boots.*) Help me!

VLADIMIR: Was I sleeping, while the others suffered? Am I sleeping
now? To-morrow, when I wake, or think I do, what shall I say
of to-day? That with Estragon my friend, at this place, until the
fall of night, I waited for Godot? That Pozzo passed, with his

carrier, and that he spoke to us? Probably. But in all that what truth will there be? (ESTRAGON, *having struggled with his boots in vain, is dozing off again.* VLADIMIR *looks at him.*) He'll know nothing. He'll tell me about the blows he received and I'll give him a carrot. (*Pause.*) Astride of a grave and a difficult birth. Down in the hole, lingeringly, the grave-digger puts on the forceps. We have time to grow old. The air is full of our cries. (*He listens.*) But habit is a great deadener. (*He looks again at* ESTRAGON.) At me too someone is looking, of me too someone is saying, He is sleeping, he knows nothing, let him sleep on. (*Pause.*) I can't go on! (*Pause.*) What have I said?

He goes feverishly to and fro, halts finally at extreme left, broods. Enter BOY *right. He halts. Silence.*

BOY: Mister ... (VLADIMIR *turns.*) Mister Albert ...
VLADIMIR: Off we go again. (*Pause.*) Do you not recognize me?
BOY: No Sir.
VLADIMIR: It wasn't you came yesterday.
BOY: No Sir.
VLADIMIR: This is your first time.
BOY: Yes Sir.

Silence.

VLADIMIR: You have a message from Mr. Godot.
BOY: Yes Sir.
VLADIMIR: He won't come this evening.
BOY: No Sir.
VLADIMIR: But he'll come to-morrow.
BOY: Yes Sir.
VLADIMIR: Without fail.
BOY: Yes Sir.

Silence.

VLADIMIR: Did you meet anyone?
BOY: No Sir.
VLADIMIR: Two other ... (*He hesitates.*) ... men?
BOY: I didn't see anyone, Sir.

Silence.

VLADIMIR: What does he do, Mr. Godot? (*Silence.*) Do you hear me?
BOY: Yes Sir.
VLADIMIR: Well?
BOY: He does nothing, Sir.

Silence.

VLADIMIR: How is your brother?
BOY: He's sick, Sir.
VLADIMIR: Perhaps it was he came yesterday.
BOY: I don't know, Sir.

Silence.

VLADIMIR (*softly*): Has he a beard, Mr. Godot?
BOY: Yes Sir.
VLADIMIR: Fair or . . . (*He hesitates.*) . . . or black?
BOY: I think it's white, Sir.

Silence.

VLADIMIR: Christ have mercy on us!

Silence.

BOY: What am I to tell Mr. Godot, Sir?
VLADIMIR: Tell him . . . (*He hesitates.*) . . . tell him you saw me and
that . . .(*He hesitates.*) . . , that you saw me. (*Pause.* VLADIMIR
advances, the BOY *recoils.* VLADIMIR *halts, the* BOY *halts. With
sudden violence.*) You're sure you saw me, you won't come and
tell me to-morrow that you never saw me!

Silence. VLADIMIR *makes a sudden spring forward, the* BOY
*avoids him and exit running. Silence. The sun sets, the moon
rises. As in Act One.* VLADIMIR *stands motionless and bowed.*
ESTRAGON *wakes, takes off his boots, gets up with one in each
hand and goes and puts them down center front, then goes
towards* VLADIMIR.

ESTRAGON: What's wrong with you?
VLADIMIR: Nothing.
ESTRAGON: I'm going.
VLADIMIR: So am I.
ESTRAGON: Was I long asleep?
VLADIMIR: I don't know.

Silence.

ESTRAGON: Where shall we go?
VLADIMIR: Not far.
ESTRAGON: Oh yes, let's go far away from here.
VLADIMIR: We can't.
ESTRAGON: Why not?
VLADIMIR: We have to come back to-morrow.
ESTRAGON: What for?
VLADIMIR: To wait for Godot.
ESTRAGON: Ah! (*Silence.*) He didn't come?
VLADIMIR: No.
ESTRAGON: And now it's too late.
VLADIMIR: Yes, now it's night.
ESTRAGON: And if we dropped him? (*Pause.*) If we dropped him?
VLADIMIR: He'd punish us. (*Silence. He looks at the tree.*) Everything's
    dead but the tree.
ESTRAGON (*looking at the tree*): What is it?
VLADIMIR: It's the tree.
ESTRAGON: Yes, but what kind?
VLADIMIR: I don't know. A willow.

ESTRAGON *draws* VLADIMIR *towards the tree. They stand motionless before it. Silence.*

ESTRAGON: Why don't we hang ourselves?
VLADIMIR: With what?
ESTRAGON: You haven't got a bit of rope?
VLADIMIR: No.
ESTRAGON: Then we can't.

Silence.

VLADIMIR: Let's go.

ESTRAGON: Wait, there's my belt.

VLADIMIR: It's too short.

ESTRAGON: You could hang on to my legs.

VLADIMIR: And who'd hang on to mine?

ESTRAGON: True.

VLADIMIR: Show all the same. (ESTRAGON *loosens the cord that holds up his trousers which, much too big for him, fall about his ankles. They look at the cord.*) It might do at a pinch. But is it strong enough?

ESTRAGON: We'll soon see. Here.

> *They each take an end of the cord and pull. It breaks. They almost fall.*

VLADIMIR: Not worth a curse.

> *Silence.*

ESTRAGON: You say we have to come back to-morrow?

VLADIMIR: Yes.

ESTRAGON: Then we can bring a good bit of rope.

VLADIMIR: Yes.

> *Silence.*

ESTRAGON: Didi.

VLADIMIR: Yes.

ESTRAGON: I can't go on like this.

VLADIMIR: That's what you think.

ESTRAGON: If we parted? That might be better for us.

VLADIMIR: We'll hang ourselves to-morrow. (*Pause.*) Unless Godot comes.

ESTRAGON: And if he comes?

VLADIMIR: We'll be saved.

> VLADIMIR *takes off his hat* (LUCKY'S), *peers inside it, feels about inside it, shakes it, knocks on the crown, puts it on again.*

ESTRAGON: Well? Shall we go?

VLADIMIR: Pull on your trousers.

ESTRAGON: What?

VLADIMIR: Pull on your trousers.

ESTRAGON: You want me to pull off my trousers?

VLADIMIR: Pull ON your trousers.

ESTRAGON (*realizing his trousers are down*): True. (*He pulls up his trousers.*)

VLADIMIR: Well? Shall we go?

ESTRAGON: Yes, let's go.

They do not move.

Curtain.

The Quare Fellow

A Comedy-Drama
by
Brendan Behan

THE QUARE FELLOW was first presented in this version by Theatre Workshop at the Theatre Royal, Stratford, London, May 24, 1956; directed by Joan Littlewood and with the following cast:

Prisoners

DUNLAVIN . . . . Maxwell Shaw
NEIGHBOUR . . . . Gerard Dynevor
PRISONER A, *hard case* . . . . Glynn Edwards
PRISONER B, *the man of thirty* . . . . Brian Murphy
LIFER . . . . Bill Grover
THE OTHER FELLOW . . . . Ron Brooker
MICKSER . . . . Eric Ogle
ENGLISH VOICE . . . . John Rutley
YOUNG PRISONER 1, SCHOLARA . . . . Timothy Harley
YOUNG PRISONER 2, SHAYBO . . . . George Eugeniou
PRISONER C, *the boy from the island* . . . . . Henry Livings
PRISONER D, *the embezzler* . . . . Barry Clayton
PRISONER E, *the bookie* . . . . Brian Murphy

Warders

CHIEF WARDER . . . . Maxwell Shaw
REGAN . . . . Dudley Foster
CRIMMIN . . . . Brian Nunn
DONELLY, *Warder 1* . . . . Clive Goodwin
THE NEW ONE, *Warder 2* . . . . Fred Cooper
THE PRISON GOVERNOR . . . . Robert Henderson
HOLY HEALEY . . . . Barry Clayton
THE HANGMAN . . . . Gerry Raffles
JENKINSON . . . . Brian Murphy

The play is in three acts

ACT ONE

A prisoner sings: he is in one of the punishment cells.

> A hungry feeling came o'er me stealing
> And the mice were squealing in my prison cell,
> And that old triangle
> Went jingle jangle,
> Along the banks of the Royal Canal.

The curtain rises.

The scene is the bottom floor or landing of a wing in a city prison, 'B.1." The cell doors are of metal with a card giving the name, age and religion of the occupant. Two of the cells have no cards. The left of the stage leads to the circle, the administrative heart of the prison, and on the right, in the wall and at right angles to the audience, is a window, from which a view may be had of the laundry yard of the women's prison. On the wall and facing the audience is printed in large block shaded Victorian lettering the word "SILENCE."

PRISONER:

> To begin the morning
> The warder bawling
> Get out of bed and clean up your cell,
> And that old triangle
> Went jingle jangle,
> Along the banks of the Royal Canal.

A triangle is beaten, loudly and raucously. A WARDER *comes briskly and, swinging a bunch of keys, goes to the vacant cells, looks in the spyholes, takes two white cards from his pocket, and puts one on each door. Then he goes to the other doors, looks in the spyholes and unlocks them.*

Meanwhile the singer in the base punishment cells is on his third verse:

87

> The screw was peeping
> And the lag was weeping . . .

But this only gets as far as the second line, for the WARDER *leans over the stairs and shouts down . . .*

WARDER: The screw is listening as well as peeping, and you'll be bloody well weeping if you don't give over your moaning. We might go down there and give you something to moan about. (*The singing stops and he turns and shouts up and down the landing.*) B. Wings: two, three and one. Stand to your doors. Come on, clean up your cells there. (*He goes off* R.)

> PRISONERS A *and* B *come out of their cells, collect buckets and brushes, and start the morning's chores.* A *is a man of 40, he has done two "laggings," a sentence of five years or more, and some preventive detention.* B *is a gentle-looking man and easygoing.*

PRISONER A: Nice day for the races.

PRISONER B: Don't think I can make it today. Too much to do in the office. Did you hear the commotion last night round in D. Wing? A reprieve must have come through.

PRISONER A: Aye, but there's two for a haircut and shave, I wonder which one's been chucked?

PRISONER B: Dunlavin might know; give him a call there.

PRISONER A: Dunlavin!

VOICE (*from cell*):

> There are hands that will welcome you in
> There are lips that I am burning to kiss
> There are two eyes that shine . . .

PRISONER A: Hey, Dunlavin, are you going to scrub that place of yours away?

VOICE:

> Far away where the blue shadows fall
> I will come to contentment and rest,
> And the toils of the day
> Will be all charmed away . . .

PRISONER A: Hey, Dunlavin.

DUNLAVIN *appears in the door of the cell polishing a large enamel chamber pot with a cloth. An old man, he has spent most of his life in jail. Unlike most old lags he has not become absolutely dulled from imprisonment.*

DUNLAVIN: . . . In my little grey home in the West.

PRISONER A: What do you think that is you're polishing—the Railway Cup?

DUNLAVIN: I'm shining this up for a special visitor. Healey of the Department of Justice is coming up today to inspect the cells.

PRISONER A: Will he be round again so soon?

DUNLAVIN: He's always round the day before an execution. I think he must be in the hanging and flogging section.

PRISONER B: Dunlavin, there you are, at the corner of the wing, with the joints in the hot-water pipes bringing you news from every art and part, any time you put your ear to it.

DUNLAVIN: Well? Well?

PRISONER B: Well, what was the commotion last night round in D. Wing? Did the quare fellow get a reprieve?

DUNLAVIN: Just a minute till I put back me little bit of china, and I'll return and tell all. Now which quare fellow do you mean? The fellow beat his wife to death with the silver-topped cane, that was a presentation to him from the Combined Staffs, Excess and Refunds branch of the late Great Southern Railways, was reprieved, though why him any more than the other fellow is more nor I can tell.

PRISONER A: Well, I suppose they looked at it, he only killed her and left it at that. He didn't cut the corpse up afterwards with a butcher's knife.

DUNLAVIN: Yes, and then of course the other fellow used a meat-chopper. Real bog-man act. Nearly as bad as a shotgun, or getting the weed-killer mixed up in the stir-about. But a man with a silver-topped cane, that's a man that's a cut above meat-choppers whichever way you look at it.

PRISONER A: Well, I suppose we can expect Silver-top round soon to start his life.

PRISONER B: Aye, we've a couple of vacancies.

PRISONER A: There's a new card up here already.

DUNLAVIN: I declare to God you're right. (*Goes to read one of the cards.*) It's not him at all, it's another fellow, doing two year, for . . . oh, the dirty beast, look what the dirty man-beast is in for. 'Clare to God, putting the likes of that beside me. They must think this is the bloody sloblands.

PRISONER B: There's another fellow here.

DUNLAVIN: I hope it's not another of that persuasion. (*Reads the card.*) Ah, no, it's only the murderer, thanks be to God.

The others have a read of the card and skip back to their own cells.

DUNLAVIN: You wouldn't mind old Silver-top. Killing your wife is a natural class of a thing could happen to the best of us. But this other dirty animal on me left . . .

PRISONER B: Ah well, now he's here he'll just have to do his birdlime like anyone else.

DUNLAVIN: That doesn't say that he should do it in the next flowery dell to me. Robbers, thieves and murderers I can abide, but when it comes to that class of carry-on—Good night, Joe Doyle.

PRISONER A (*indicates 22*): This fellow was dead lucky.

PRISONER B: Live lucky.

PRISONER A: Two fellows waiting to be topped and he's the one that gets away. As a general rule they don't like reprieving one and topping the other.

DUNLAVIN: So as to be on the safe side, and not to be making fish of one and flesh of the other, they usually top both. Then, of course, the Minister might have said, enough is as good as a feast.

They rest on their brooms.

PRISONER B: It must be a great thing to be told at the last minute that you're not going to be topped after all. To be lying there sweating and watching. The two screws for the death watch coming on at twelve o'clock and the two going off shaking hands with you, and you go to bed, and stare up at the ceiling.

DUNLAVIN: And the two screws nod to each other across the fire to make a sup of tea, but to do it easy in case they wake you, and you turn round in the bed towards the fire and you say "I'll take a sup as you're at it" and one of the screws says "Ah, so you're awake, Mick. We were just wetting it; isn't it a good job you spoke up in time."

PRISONER A: And after that, the tea is drunk and they offer you cigarettes, though the mouth is burned off you from smoking and anyway you've more than they have, you've got that many you'll be leaving them after you, and you lie down and get up, and get up and lie down, and the two screws not letting on to be minding you and not taking their eyes off you for one half-minute, and you walk up and down a little bit more . . .

PRISONER B: And they ask you would you like another game of draughts or would you sooner write a letter, and getting on to morning you hear a bell out in the city, and you ask them the time, but they won't tell you.

DUNLAVIN: But they put a good face on it, and one says "There's that old watch stopped again" and he says to the other screw "Have you your watch, Jack?" and the other fellow makes a great joke of it "I'll have to take a run up as far as the North City Pawn shop and ask them to let me have a look at it." And then the door is unlocked and everyone sweats blood, and they come in and ask your man to stand up a minute, that's if he's able, while they read him something: "I am instructed to inform you that the Minister has, he hasn't, he has, he hasn't recommended to the President, that . . ."

PRISONER A: And the quare fellow says "Did you say 'has recommended or has not recommended . . . ?' I didn't quite catch that."

DUNLAVIN: My bloody oath but he catches it. Although I remember once in a case like now when there were two fellows to be topped over two different jobs, didn't the bloody fellow from the Prison Board, as it was then, in old Max Greeb's time, didn't he tell the wrong man he was reprieved? Your man was delighted for a few hours and then they had to go back and tell him "Sorry, my mistake, but you're to be topped after all"?

PRISONER B: And the fellow that was reprieved, I bet he was glad.

DUNLAVIN: Of course he was glad, anyone that says that a condemned man would be better off hung than doing life, let them leave it to his own discretion Do you know who feels it worse going out to be topped?

PRISONER A: Corkmen and Northerners . . . they've such bloody hard necks.

DUNLAVIN: I have to do me funny half-hour for Holy Healey. I'm talking serious now.

PRISONER A: All right, come on, let's have it—

DUNLAVIN: The man that feels it worst, going into that little house with the red door and the silver painted gates at the bottom of D. Wing, is a man that has been in the nick before, when some other merchant was topped; or he's heard screws or old lags in the bag shop or at exercise talking about it. A new chap that's never done anything but murder, and that only once, is usually a respectable man, such as this Silver-top here. He knows nothing about it, except the few lines that he'd see in the papers. "Condemned man entered the hang-house at seven fifty-nine. At eight three the doctor pronounced life extinct."

PRISONER B: That's a lot of mullarkey. In the first place the doctor has his back turned after the trap goes down, and doesn't turn and face it until a screw has caught the rope and stopped it wriggling. Then they go out and lock up the shop and have their breakfast and don't come back for an hour. Then they cut your man down and the doctor slits the back of his neck to see if the bones are broken. Who's to know what happens in the hour your man is swinging there, maybe wriggling to himself in the pit.

PRISONER A: You're right there. When I was in the nick in England, there was a screw doing time, he'd been smuggling out medical reports on hangings and selling them to the Sunday papers, and he told me that one bloke had lived seventeen minutes at the end of a rope.

DUNLAVIN: I don't believe that! Seventeen minutes is a bloody long time to be hanging on the end of a rope.

PRISONER A: It was their own medical report.

PRISONER B: I'll lay odds to a make that Silver-top isn't half charmed with himself he's not going with the meat-chopper in the morning.

DUNLAVIN: You could sing that if you had an air to it.

PRISONER A: They'll have him down to reception, changed into Fry's and over here any time now.

DUNLAVIN: Him and this other jewel here. Bad an' all as Silver-top was to beat his wife's brains out, I'd as lief have him near to me as this article. Dirty beast! I won't have an hour's luck for the rest of me six months, and me hoping to touch Uncle Healey today for a letter to the Room-Keepers for when I'd go out.

PRISONER B: Eh, Dunlavin, is the Department trying to reform, reconstruct and rehabilitate you in your old age?

DUNLAVIN: Ah no, it's nothing to do with the Department. Outside his job in the Department, Uncle Healey's in some holy crowd, that does good be stealth. They never let the right hand know what the left hand doeth, as the man said. Of course they never put either hand in their pocket, so you'd never get money off them, but they can give letters to the Prisoners' Aid and the Room-Keepers. Mind you. Healey's not here today as a holy man. He'll just be fixing up the man that's getting hung in the morning, but if I can get on the right side of him, he might mix business with pleasure and give me a letter for when I get out.

PRISONER B: Now we know the cause of all the spring-cleaning.

DUNLAVIN: And a fellow in the kitchen told us they're doing a special dinner for us on account of Uncle Healey's visit.

PRISONER A: Do you mean we're getting food with our meals today?

DUNLAVIN: That's right, and I can't be standing yapping to youse. I've to hang up my holy pictures and think up a few funny remarks for him. God, what Jimmie O'Dea is getting thousands for I've to do for a pair of old socks and a ticket for the Prisoners' Aid.

DUNLAVIN *goes into his cell. Two* YOUNG PRISONERS *aged about seventeen go past with sweeping brushes in front of them, singing softly and in unison.*

YOUNG PRISONERS:
> Only one more cell inspection
> We go out next Saturday,
> Only one more cell inspection
> And we go far, far away.

PRISONER A: What brings you fellows round here this morning?

YOUNG PRISONER 1: Our screw told us to sweep all round the Juvenile Wing and then to come round here and give it a bit of a going over.

PRISONER B: And have you your own wing done?

YOUNG PRISONER 2: No, but if we did our wing first, we'd miss the mots hanging out the laundry. You can't see them from our wing.

PRISONER A: Just as well, maybe; you're bad enough as it is.

YOUNG PRISONER 1: But I tell you what you will see from our wing this morning. It's the carpenter bringing up the coffin for the quare fellow and leaving it over in the mortuary to have it handy for the morning. There's two orderlies besides us over in the Juveniles, and we were going to toss up who'd come over here, but they're country fellows and they'd said they'd sooner see the coffin. I'd sooner a pike at a good-looking mot than the best coffin in Ireland, wouldn't you, Shaybo?

YOUNG PRISONER 2: Certainly I would, and outside that, when you're over here, there's always a chance of getting a bit of education about screwing jobs, and suchlike, from experienced men. Do you think Triplex or celluloid is the best for Yale locks, sir?

YOUNG PRISONER 1: Do you carry the stick all the time, sir?

PRISONER A: If I had a stick I'd know where to put it, across your bloody . . .

YOUNG PRISONER 2: Scholara, get sweeping, here's the screw.

They drift off sweeping and singing softly.

PRISONER B: He's bringing one of 'em. Is it Silver-top or the other fellow?

PRISONER A: Silver-top. I remember him being half carried into the circle the night he was sentenced to death.

PRISONER B: He has a right spring in his step this morning then.

PRISONER A: He's not looking all that happy. Still, I suppose he hasn't got over the shock yet.

> WARDER *and a* PRISONER *come on* L. *The* PRISONER *is in early middle age; when he speaks he has a "good accent." He is carrying a pillow slip which contains his sheets and other kit. The* WARDER *halts him.*

WARDER REGAN: Stand by the door with your name on it. Later on when you've seen the doctor these fellows will show you how to lay your kit. Stand there now, till the doctor is ready to see you. (*He goes. There is a pause, while the* PRISONERS *survey the new-comer.*)

PRISONER B: He'll bloody well cheer the place up, won't he?

LIFER: Have any of you got a cigarette?

PRISONER A: That's a good one. You're not in the condemned cell now, you know. No snout allowed here.

PRISONER B: Unless you manage to scrounge a dog-end off the remands.

PRISONER A: Or pick one up in the exercise yard after a man the like of yourself that's allowed them as a special concession. Not, by

God, that we picked up much after you. What did you do with your dog-ends?

LIFER: Threw them in the fire.

PRISONER B: You what!

PRISONER A: How was it the other poor bastard, that's got no reprieve and is to be topped in the morning—how was it he was always able to leave a trail of butts behind him when he went off exercise?

LIFER: I've never been in prison before; how was I to know?

PRISONER A: You're a curse of God liar, my friend, you did know; for it was whispered to him by the fellows from the hospital bringing over the grub to the condemned cell. He never gave them as much as a match! And he couldn't even bring his dog-ends to the exercise yard and drop them behind for us to pick up when we came out later.

PRISONER B: I bet you're charmed with yourself that you're not going through the iron door tomorrow morning.

The LIFER doesn't speak, but looks down at his suit.

PRISONER A: Aye, you're better off in that old suit, bad as it is, than the wooden overcoat the quare fellow is going to get tomorrow morning.

PRISONER B: The longest you could do would be twenty years. More than likely you'll get out in half of that. Last man to finish up in the Bog, he done eleven.

LIFER: Eleven. How do you live through it?

PRISONER A: A minute at a time.

PRISONER B: You haven't got a bit of snout for him, have you? (PRISONER A *shakes his head.*) Maybe Dunlavin has. Hey, Dunlavin, have you e'er a smoke you'd give this chap? Hey, Dunlavin.

DUNLAVIN (*coming from his cell*): Yes, what is it? Anyone there the name of headache?

PRISONER B: Could you manage to give this chap something to smoke? E'er a bit of snout at all.

DUNLAVIN: There's only one brand of tobacco allowed here—"Three Nuns." None today, none tomorrow, and none the days after. (*He goes back into his cell.*)

PRISONER B: Eh, Dunlavin, come back to hell out of that.

DUNLAVIN: Well, what?

PRISONER B: This poor chap after being smoking about sixty a day . .

DUNLAVIN: Where?

PRISONER B: In the condemned cell—where else?

DUNLAVIN: Now I have you. Sure I thought you were the other fellow, and you're not, you're only the murderer. God comfort you. (*Shakes hands.*) Certainly so. (*Takes off his jacket, looks up and down the wing, undoes his trousers and from the depths of his combinations he produces a cigarette end, and a match, and presents them to the* LIFER.) Reprieved in the small hours of this morning. Certainly so. The dead arose and appeared to many, as the man said, but you'll be getting yourself a bad name standing near that other fellow's door. This is your flowery dell, see? It has your name there on that little card. And all your particulars. Age forty-three. Religion R.C.

LIFER (*reads*): Life.

DUNLAVIN: And a bloody sight better than death any day of the week.

PRISONER B: It always says that. The Governor will explain it all to you later this morning.

DUNLAVIN: Or maybe they'll get holy Uncle Healey to do it.

PRISONER B: Go into your cell and have a smoke for yourself. Bring in your kit bag. (*Passes in kit to* LIFER.) Have a quiet burn there before the screw comes round; we'll keep nick. (LIFER *closes the door of his cell.*)

DUNLAVIN: God knows I got the pick of good neighbours. Lovely people. Give me a decent murderer though, rather than the likes of this other fellow. Well, I'll go into me little place and get on with me bit of dobying so as to have it all nice for Healey when he comes round. (*He goes back to his cell.*)

PRISONER B (*to* LIFER): Don't light up yet! Here's the screw coming.

PRISONER A: With the other fellow.

WARDER REGAN *and another prisoner, "the* OTHER FELLOW," *an anxious-faced man, wearing prison clothes and carrying a kit bag come on* L.

WARDER REGAN: Yes, this is your flowery dell. Leave in your kitbag and stand at your door and wait for the doctor. These other fellows will show you where to go when he comes.

OTHER FELLOW: Right, sir. Very good, sir.

WARDER REGAN *goes, the* OTHER FELLOW *has a look round.*

PRISONER B: There's a bloke in the end cell getting himself a quiet burn. Why don't you join him before the screws get back?

The OTHER FELLOW *notices the card on* LIFER's *cell.*

OTHER FELLOW: My God! Is this what I've come to, mixing with murderers! I'd rather not, thank you, though I could do with a smoke. I'll have to spend long months here, even if I get my remission, with murderers and thieves and God knows what! You're not all murderers are you? You haven't killed anyone, have you?

PRISONER B: Not for a while, I haven't.

OTHER FELLOW: I cannot imagine any worse crime than taking a life, can you?

PRISONER B: It'd depend whose life.

OTHER FELLOW: Of course. I mean, a murderer would be justified in taking his own life, wouldn't he? "We send him forth" says Carlisle—you've heard of Carlisle haven't you?—"We send him forth, back to the void, back to the darkness, far out beyond the stars. Let him go from us."

DUNLAVIN (*head out of door of cell*): Oh. (*Looks at* OTHER FELLOW.) I thought it was Healey from the Department or someone giving it out of them.

PRISONER A: Looks like this man is a bit of an intellectual.

DUNLAVIN: Is that what they call it now?

LIFER: Thanks for the smoke, Mr. Dunlavin.

DUNLAVIN: Not at all, sure, you're welcome, call again when you're passing. But remember the next wife you kill and you getting forty fags a day in the condemned cell, think of them as is not so fortunate as yourself and leave a few dog-ends around the exercise yard after you. Here's these noisy little gets again.

The two YOUNG PRISONERS *come round from the left; their sweeping brushes in front of them and singing their song. The* OTHER FELLOW *stands quite still at his door.*

YOUNG PRISONERS:
> Only one more cell inspection
> We go out next Saturday

Only one more cell inspection
Then we go far far away.

(*They are sweeping near the* LIFER.)

Only one more cell inspection
We go out next Saturday
Only one more cell . . .

LIFER: For God's sake shut up that squeaking . . .

YOUNG PRISONER 1: We've as much right to open our mouth as what you have, and you only a wet day in the place.

PRISONER B: Leave the kids alone. You don't own the place, you know. They're doing no harm. (*To the* YOUNG PRISONERS.) You want to sweep this bit of floor away?

DUNLAVIN: What brings you round here so often? If you went over to the remand wings you might pick up a bit of snout or a look at the paper.

YOUNG PRISONER 1: We get a smoke and the *Mail* every day off a limey on our road that's on remand. He's in over the car smuggling. But round here this morning you can see the mots from the laundry over on the female side hanging out the washing in the exercise yard. Do youse look at them? I suppose when you get old, though, you don't much bother about women.

PRISONER B: I'm thirty-six, mac.

YOUNG PRISONER 1: Ah, I thought that. Don't suppose you care if you never see a mot. There's Shaybo there and he never thinks of anything else. Do you think of anything else but women, Shaybo?

YOUNG PRISONER 2: Yes. Robbing and stealing, Scholara. You go to the window and keep an eye out for them and I'll sweep on round here till you give us a call.

YOUNG PRISONER 1: Right, Shaybo, they should be nearly out now. (*Goes up and stands by window.*)

PRISONER B: I forgot about the women.

DUNLAVIN: I didn't. It's a great bit of a treat today—that and having me leg rubbed. Neighbour and I wait in for it.

YOUNG PRISONER 1 (*from the window, in a coarse whisper*): Shaybo, you can see them now.

YOUNG PRISONER 2: The blondy one from North Crumlin?

YOUNG PRISONER 1: Yes, and there's another one with her. I don't know her.

YOUNG PRISONER 2: Must be a country mot. Scholara doesn't know her. Women.

DUNLAVIN: Women.

PRISONER A: I see the blondy one waving.

YOUNG PRISONER 1: If it's all the one to you, I'd like you to know that's my mot and it's me she's waving at.

PRISONER A: I'll wave you a thick ear.

DUNLAVIN: Hey, Neighbour! Where the hell is he this morning? Neighbour!

AN OLD MAN'S CREAKING VOICE: Here I am, Neighbour, here I am.

NEIGHBOUR, *a bent old man, comes from* L., *hobbling as quickly as he can on a stick.*

DUNLAVIN: Ah, you lost mass.

NEIGHBOUR: What, are they gone in already?

DUNLAVIN: No, but they're finished hanging up the top row of clothes. There'll be no stretching or reaching off chairs.

NEIGHBOUR: Still, thanks be to God for small mercies. They'll be out again this day week.

PRISONER A: If you lives to see it.

NEIGHBOUR: Why wouldn't I live to see it as well as what you would? This is not the nearest I was to fine women, nor are they the first good-looking ones I saw.

PRISONER A: With that old cough of yours they could easy be the last.

NEIGHBOUR: God, you're a desperate old gas bag. We remember better-looking women than ever they were, don't we, Dunlavin? Meena La Bloom, do you remember her?

DUNLAVIN: Indeed and I do; many's the seaman myself and Meena gave the hey and a do, and Mickey Finn to.

NEIGHBOUR: And poor May Oblong.

DUNLAVIN: Ah, where do you leave poor May? The Lord have mercy on her, wasn't I with her one night in the digs, and there was a Member of Parliament there, and May after locking him in the back room and taking away his trousers, with him going over the north wall that morning to vote for Home Rule. "For the love of your country and mine," he shouts under the door to May, "give me back me trousers." "So I will," says May, "if you shove a fiver out under the door."

NEIGHBOUR: He had the wad hid? Dirty suspicious old beast.

DUNLAVIN: That's right. He was cute enough to hide his wad some-where, drunk and all as he was the previous night. All we got in his trousers was a locket of hair of the patriotic plumber of Dol-phin's barn that swore to let his hair grow till Ireland was free.

NEIGHBOUR: Ah, poor May, God help her, she was the heart of the roll.

DUNLAVIN: And when she was arrested for carrying on after the cur-few, the time of the trouble, she was fined for having concealed about her person two Thompson submachine guns, 1921 pattern three Mills bombs, and a stick of dynamite.

NEIGHBOUR: And will you ever forget poor Lottie L'Estrange, that got had up for pushing the soldier into Spencer Dock?

DUNLAVIN: Ah, God be with the youth of us.

NEIGHBOUR: And Cork Annie, and Lady Limerick.

DUNLAVIN: And Julia Rice and the Goofy One.

NEIGHBOUR (*turns towards window*): Hey, you, move out of the way there and give us a look. Dunlavin, come up here before they go, and have a look at the blondy one.

YOUNG PRISONER 1: Go 'long, you dirty old dog. That's my mot you're speaking about. (*Shoves* NEIGHBOUR.) You old heap of dirt, to wave at a decent girl.

PRISONER A: Hey, snots, d'you think you own the bloody place?

YOUNG PRISONER 1: Would you like it, to have that dirty old eyebox looking at your mot?

PRISONER B: He's not going to eat her.

DUNLAVIN (*from behind*): No, but he'd like to.

YOUNG PRISONER 2: That's right, and Scholara is nearly married to her. At least she had a squealer for him and he has to pay her money every week. Any week he's outside like, to give it, or her to get it.

YOUNG PRISONER 1 (*blows a kiss*): That's right, and I have him putting his rotten old eye on her.

OTHER FELLOW (*at his doorway*) : God preserve us.

PRISONER A: Well, you don't own the bloody window. (*Shoves* YOUNG PRISONER 1 *out of way and brings over* NEIGHBOUR.) Come on, you, if you want to see the May procession.

NEIGHBOUR: Ah, thanks, butty, your blood's worth bottling.

PRISONER A: I didn't do it on account of you, but if you let them young pups get away with too much they'd be running the place.

YOUNG PRISONER 2: Come on, Scholara, we'll mosey back. The screw will think we're lost.

They go back down the stairs, pick up their brushes, and start sweeping again and singing.

YOUNG PRISONER 1:

> Only one more cell inspection
> We go out next Saturday

YOUNG PRISONER 2:

> Only one more cell inspection . . .

LIFER: Shut your bloody row, can't you?

DUNLAVIN: Shut up yourself; you're making more noise than any of them.

YOUNG PRISONER 1: Don't tell us to shut up, you bastard.

PRISONER B: Ah leave him alone; he started life this morning.

YOUNG PRISONER 1: Ah we're sorry, mister, ain't we, Shaybo?

YOUNG PRISONER 2: God, we are. Go over and take a pike at the female yard. They hang up the clothes now and Scholara's mot is over there. You can have a look at her. Scholara won't mind, will you, Schol?

YOUNG PRISONER 1: Certainly and I won't. Not with you going to the Bog to start life in a couple of days, where you won't see a woman.

YOUNG PRISONER 2: A child.

YOUNG PRISONER 1: A dog.

YOUNG PRISONER 2: A fire.

PRISONER A: Get to hell out of that round to your own wing. Wouldn't you think a man would know all that forbye you telling it to him?

YOUNG PRISONER 2: We were going anyway. We've seen all we wanted to see. It wasn't to look at a lot of old men we came here, but to see mots hanging out the washing.

YOUNG PRISONER 1: And eitherways, we'll be a lot nearer the women than you'll be next Saturday night. Think of us when you're sitting locked up in the old flowery, studying the Bible, Chapter 1, verse 2, and we trucking round in chase of charver.

They samba out with their brushes for partners, humming the Wedding Samba.

PRISONER A: Them young gets have too much old gab out of them altogether. I was a Y.P. in Walton before the war and I can tell you they'd be quiet boys if they got the larrying we used to get.

OTHER FELLOW: And talking so disrespectfully about the Bible.

NEIGHBOUR: Belied and they needn't; many's the time the Bible was a consolation to a fellow all alone in the old cell. The lovely thin paper with a bit of mattress coir in it, if you could get a match or a bit of tinder or any class of light, was as good a smoke as ever I tasted. Am I right, Dunlavin?

DUNLAVIN: Damn the lie, Neighbour. The first twelve months I done, I smoked my way half-way through the book of Genesis and three inches of my mattress. When the Free State came in we were afraid of our life they were going to change the mattresses for feather beds. And you couldn't smoke feathers, not, be God, if they were rolled in the Song of Solomon itself. But sure, thanks to God, the Free State didn't change anything more than the badge on the warders' caps.

OTHER FELLOW: Can I be into my cell for a while?

PRISONER B: Until the doctor calls you. (*Goes into his cell.*)

PRISONER A: Well, I'm going to have a rest. It's hard work doing a lagging.

LIFER: A lagging? That's penal servitude, isn't it?

DUNLAVIN: Three years or anything over.

LIFER: Three years is a long time.

DUNLAVIN: I wouldn't like to be that long hanging.

NEIGHBOUR: Is he the . .

DUNLAVIN (*sotto voce*): Silver-top! (*Aloud.*) Started life this morning.

NEIGHBOUR: So they're not going to top you after all? Well, you're a lucky man. I worked one time in the hospital, helping the screw there, and the morning of the execution he gave me two bottles of stout to take the hood off the fellow was after being topped. I wouldn't have done it a second time for two glasses of malt, no, nor a bottle of it. I cut the hood away; his head was all twisted and his face black, but the two eyes were the worst; like a rabbit's; it was fear that had done it.

LIFER: Perhaps he didn't feel anything. How do you know?

NEIGHBOUR: I only seen him. I never had a chance of asking him. (NEIGHBOUR *goes to the murderer's door.*) Date of expiration of sentence, life. In some ways I wouldn't mind if that was my lot. What do you say?

DUNLAVIN: I don't know; it's true we're too old and bet for lobby-watching and shaking down anywhere, so that you'd fall down and sleep on the pavement of a winter's night and not know but you were lying snug and comfortable in the Shelbourne.

NEIGHBOUR: Only then to wake up on some lobby and the hard floor-boards under you, and a lump of hard filth for your pillow, and the cold and the drink shaking you, wishing it was morning for the market pubs to open, where if you had the price of a drink you could sit in the warm anyway. Except, God look down on you, if it was Sunday.

DUNLAVIN: Ah, there's the agony. No pub open, but the bells battering your bared nerves and all you could do with the cold and the sickness was to lean over on your side and wish that God would call you.

LIFER: If I was outside my life wouldn't be like that.

NEIGHBOUR: No, but ours would.

DUNLAVIN (*quietly*): See, we're selfish, mister, like everyone else.

WARDER (*shouts off*): Medical applications and receptions. Fall in for the doctor.

LIFER *looks lost.*

DUNLAVIN: Yes, that's you. Go up there to the top of the wing and wait there till the screw tells you to go in. Neighbour, call them other fellows.

Exit LIFER.

NEIGHBOUR: Come on—the vet's here.

DUNLAVIN (*calling in to the* OTHER FELLOW): Hey, come out and get gelded.

OTHER FELLOW *and* PRISONERS A *and* B *come out of cells.*

NELGHBOUR: You're for the doctor. Go on up there with the rest of them. Me and Dunlavin don't go up. We only wait to be rubbed.

DUNLAVIN: Don't have any chat at all with that fellow. D'you see what he's in for?

NEIGHBOUR *goes and looks. Exit* OTHER FELLOW *and* PRISONERS A *and* B.

NEIGHBOUR: What the hell does that mean?

DUNLAVIN: A bloody sex mechanic.

NEIGHBOUR: I didn't know.

DUNLAVIN: Well, you know now. I'll go in and get me chair. You can sit on it after me. It'll save you bringing yours out.

NEIGHBOUR: Well, if you go first and you have a chance of a go at the spirit bottle, don't swig the bloody lot. Remember I'm for treatment too.

DUNLAVIN: Don't be such an old begrudger. He'll bring a quart bottle of it, and who could swallow that much methylated spirit in the few drops you'd get at it?

NEIGHBOUR: You could, or a bucket of it, if it was lying anywhere handy. I seen you do it, bluestone and all, only buns to a bear as far as you were concerned.

DUNLAVIN: Do you remember the old doctor they had here years ago?

NEIGHBOUR: The one they used to call Crippen.

DUNLAVIN: The very man. There was one day I was brought in for drinking the chat and I went to court that morning and was here in the afternoon still as drunk as Pontius Pilate. Crippen was examining me. "When I put me hand there you cough," and all to that effect. "Did you ever have V.D.?" says he. "I haven't got your habits," says I to him. These fellows weren't long.

Re-enter PRISONERS A *and* B.

NEIGHBOUR: What did he give youse?

PRISONER B (*passing into cell*): Extra six ounces of bread. Says we're undernourished.

PRISONER A: Is the bar open yet?

NEIGHBOUR: Never you mind the bar. I've cruel pains in my leg that I want rubbed to take out the rheumatics, not to be jeered at, and I've had them genuine since the war.

PRISONER A: What war? The economic war?

NEIGHBOUR: Ah, you maggot. It's all your fault, Dunlavin, telling them fellows we do get an odd sup out of the spirit bottle. Letting everyone know our business.

PRISONERS A *and* B *go into cells and shut the doors.*

DUNLAVIN: No sign of Holy Healey yet.

NEIGHBOUR: You're wasting your time chasing after old Healey. He told me here one day, and I trying to get myself an old overcoat out of him, that he was here only as a head man of the Department of Justice, and he couldn't do other business of any other sort or size whatever, good, bad or indifferent. It's my opinion that old Healey does be half-jarred a deal of the time anyway.

DUNLAVIN: The likes of Healey would take a sup all right, but being a high-up civil servant, he wouldn't drink under his own name. You'd see the likes of Healey nourishing themselves with balls of malt, at eleven in the morning, in little back snugs round Merrion Row. The barman would lose his job if he so much as breathed their name. It'd be "Mr. H. wants a drop of water but not too much." "Yes, Mr. O." "No, sir, Mr. Mac wasn't in this morning." "Yes, Mr. D. Fine morning; it will be a lovely day if it doesn't snow." Educated drinking, you know. Even a bit of chat about God at an odd time, so as you'd think God was in another department, but not long off the Bog, and they was doing Him a good turn to be talking well about Him.

NEIGHBOUR: Here's the other two back. The M.O. will be down to us soon.

LIFER *and* OTHER FELLOW *go into cells and shut the doors.*

DUNLAVIN: That other fellow's not looking as if this place is agreeing with him.

NEIGHBOUR: You told me a minute ago that I wasn't even to speak to him.

DUNLAVIN: Ah, when all is said and done, he's someone's rearing after all, he could be worse, he could be a screw or an official from the Department.

WARDER REGAN *comes on with a bottle marked "methylated spirit."*

WARDER REGAN: You're the two for rubs, for your rheumatism.'

DUNLAVIN: That's right, Mr. Regan sir, old and bet, sir, that's us. And the old pains is very bad with us these times, sir.

WARDER REGAN: Not so much lip, and sit down whoever is first for treatment.

DUNLAVIN: That's me, sir. Age before ignorance, as the man said. (*Sits in the chair.*)

WARDER REGAN: Rise the leg of your trousers. Which leg is it?

DUNLAVIN: The left, sir.

WARDER REGAN: That's the right leg you're showing me.

DUNLAVIN: That's what I was saying, sir. The left is worst one day and the right is bad the next. To be on the safe side, you'd have to do two of them. It's only the mercy of God I'm not a centipede, sir, with the weather that's in it.

WARDER REGAN: Is that where the pain is?

DUNLAVIN (*bending down slowly towards the bottle*): A little lower down, sir, if you please. (*Grabs the bottle and raises it to his mouth.*) Just a little lower down, sir, if it's all equal to you.

> REGAN *rubs, head well bent, and* DUNLAVIN *drinks long and deeply and as quickly lowers the bottle on to the floor again, wiping his mouth and making the most frightful grimaces, for the stuff doesn't go down easy at first. He goes through the pantomime of being burnt inside for* NEIGHBOUR'*s benefit and rubs his mouth with the back of his hand.*

DUNLAVIN: Ah, that's massive, sir. 'Tis you that has the healing hand. You must have desperate luck at the horses; I'd only love to be with you copying your dockets. (REGAN *turns and pours more spirit on his hands.*) Ah, that's it, sir, well into me I can feel it going. (*Reaches forward towards the bottle again, drinks.*) Ah, that's it, I can feel it going right into me. And doing me all the good in the world. (REGAN *reaches and puts more spirit on his hand and sets to rubbing again.*) That's it, sir, thorough does it; if you're going to do a thing at all you might as well do it well. (*Reaches forward for the bottle again and raises it.* NEIGH-BOUR *looks across in piteous appeal to him not to drink so much, but he merely waves the bottle in elegant salute, as if to wish him good health, and takes another drink.*) May God reward you, sir, you must be the seventh son of the seventh son or one of the Lees from Limerick on your mother's side maybe. (*Drinks again.*) Ah, that's the cure for the cold of the wind and the world's neglectment.

WARDER REGAN: Right, now you.

> NEIGHBOUR *comes forward.*

WARDER DONELLY (*offstage*): All present and correct, Mr. Healey, sir.
DUNLAVIN: Holy Healey!

Enter WARDER DONELLY.

WARDER DONELLY: This way, Mr. Healey.
WARDER REGAN: Attention! Stand by your doors.
DUNLAVIN: By the left, laugh.
WARDER DONELLY: This way.

Enter MR. HEALEY, *an elegantly dressed gentleman.*

HEALEY: Good morning.
WARDER DONELLY: Any complaints?
PRISONER A: No, sir.
HEALEY: Good morning!
WARDER DONELLY: Any complaints?
OTHER FELLOW: ⎫
PRISONER B: ⎭ No, sir.
HEALEY: Good morning all! Well, now, I'm here representing the Department of Justice, if there are any complaints now is the time to make them.
SEVERAL PRISONERS: No complaints, sir.
WARDER REGAN: All correct, sir. Two receiving medical treatment here, sir.
DUNLAVIN: Just getting the old leg rubbed, sir, Mr. Healey.
HEALEY: Well, well, it almost smells like a bar.
DUNLAVIN: I'm near drunk myself on the smell of it, sir.
HEALEY: Don't let me interrupt the good work.
DUNLAVIN: Ah, the old legs. It's being out in all weathers that does it, sir. Of course we don't have that to contend with while we're here, sir.
HEALEY: Out in all weathers, I should think not indeed. Well, my man, I will be inspecting your cell amongst others in due course.
DUNLAVIN: Yes, sir.
HEALEY: It's always a credit to you, I must say that. (*He turns to* REGAN.) Incorrigible, some of these old fellows, but rather amusing.
WARDER REGAN: Yes, sir.
HEALEY: It's Regan, isn't it?

WARDER REGAN: Yes, sir.

HEALEY: Ah yes, you're helping the Canon at the execution tomorrow morning, I understand.

WARDER REGAN: Well, I shall be with the condemned man sir, seeing that he doesn't do away with himself during the night and that he goes down the hole with his neck properly broken in the morning, without making too much fuss about it.

HEALEY: A sad duty.

WARDER REGAN: Neck breaking and throttling, sir? (HEALEY *gives him a sharp look.*) You must excuse me, sir. I've seen rather a lot of it. They say familiarity breeds contempt.

HEALEY: Well, we have one consolation, Regan, the condemned man gets the priest and the sacraments, more than his victim got maybe. I venture to suggest that some of them die holier deaths than if they had finished their natural span.

WARDER REGAN: We can't advertise "Commit a murder and die a happy death," sir. We'd have them all at it. They take religion very seriously in this country.

HEALEY: Quite, quite so! Now, I understand you have the reprieved man over here, Regan.

WARDER REGAN: No. Twenty-six sir.

DUNLAVIN: Just beside me, sir.

HEALEY: Ah, yes! So here we are! Here's the lucky man, eh? Well, now, the Governor will explain your position to you later in the day. Your case will be examined every five years. Meanwhile I thought you might like a holy picture to hang up in your cell. Keep a cheerful countenance, my friend. God gave you back your life and the least you can do is to thank him with every breath you draw! Right? Well, be of good heart. I will call in and see you again, that is, if duty permits. (*He moves to* DUN-LAVIN's *cell.*)

HEALEY (*at* DUNLAVIN's *cell*): Very creditable. Hm.

DUNLAVIN: Well, to tell you the truth, sir, it's a bit extra special to-day. You see, we heard you was here.

HEALEY: Very nice.

DUNLAVIN: Of course I do like to keep my little place as homely as I can with the little holy pictures you gave me of Blessed Martin, sir.

HEALEY: I see you don't recognize the colour bar.

DUNLAVIN: The only bar I recognize, sir, is the Bridge Bar or the Beamish House the corner of Thomas Street.

HEALEY: Well, I must be off now, and I'm glad to see you're being well looked after.

DUNLAVIN: It's neither this nor that, but if you could spare a minute, sir?

HEALEY: Yes, what is it? But hurry; remember I've a lot to do today.

DUNLAVIN: It's like this, sir. I won't always be here, sir, having me leg rubbed and me bit of grub brought to me. As it says in the Bible, sir, have it yourself or be without it and put ye by for the rainy day, for thou knowest not the night thou mayest be sleeping in a lobby.

HEALEY: Yes, yes, but what is it you want?

DUNLAVIN: I've the chance of a little room up round Buckingham Street, sir, if you could only give me a letter to the Room-Keepers after I go out, for a bit of help with the rent.

HEALEY: Well, you know, when I visit the prison, I'm not here as a member of any outside organization of which I may be a member but simply as an official of the Department of Justice.

DUNLAVIN: Yes, but where else would I be likely to meet you, sir? I'd hardly bump into you in the Bridge Bar when I'd be out side, would I, sir?

HEALEY: No, no, certainly not. But you know the Society offices in the Square. See me there any Friday night, between eight and nine.

DUNLAVIN: Thank you, sir, and a bed in heaven to you, sir.

HEALEY: And the same to you. (*Goes to next cell.*)

DUNLAVIN: And many of them, and I hope we're all here this time next year (*Venomously after* MR. HEALEY.) that it may choke you.

WARDER DONELLY *bangs on* LIFER's *closed door, then looks in.*

WARDER DONELLY: Jesus Christ, sir. He's put the sheet up! Quick.

REGAN *and* DONELLY *go into* LIFER's *cell. He is hanging. They cut him down.*

WARDER REGAN: Gently does it.

They lay him down in the passage and try to restore him.

HEALEY: What a dreadful business, and with this other coming off tomorrow.

THE PRISONERS *crowd out of line.*

WARDER DONELLY: Get back to your cells!

HEALEY: Is he still with us?

WARDER REGAN: He'll be all right in an hour or two. Better get the M.O., Mr. Donelly.

The triangle sounds.

WARDER DONELLY: B. Wing, two, three and one. Stand by your doors. Right, lead on. Now come on, come on, this is no holiday. Right sir, over to you. Lead on, B.1.

WARDER REGAN *and* HEALEY *are left with the unconscious* LIFER.

HEALEY: Dear, dear. The Canon will be very upset about this.

WARDER REGAN: There's not much harm done, thank God. They don't have to put a death certificate against the receipt for his live body.

HEALEY: That doesn't seem a very nice way of looking at it, Regan.

WARDER REGAN: A lot of people mightn't consider ours a very nice job, sir.

HEALEY: Ours?

WARDER REGAN: Yes, ours, sir. Mine, the Canon's, the hangman's, and if you don't mind my saying so, yours, sir.

HEALEY: Society cannot exist without prisons, Regan. My job is to bring what help and comfort I can to these unfortunates. Really, a man with your outlook, I cannot see why you stay in the service.

WARDER REGAN: It's a soft job, sir, between hangings.

The triangle is heard. The M.O. *comes on with two stretcher-bearers.*

The curtain falls.

ACT TWO

The curtain rises.

The prison yard, a fine evening.

VOICE OF PRISONER (*off-stage, singing*):

> A hungry feeling came o'er me stealing
> And the mice were squealing in my prison cell
> And the old triangle
> Went jingle jangle
> Along the banks of the Royal Canal.

WARDER DONELLY: B.1. B.2. B.3. Head on for exercise, right! Lead on, B.1. All one, away to exercise.

> *The prisoners file out,* WARDER DONELLY *with them.*

> On a fine spring evening,
> The lag lay dreaming
> The seagulls wheeling high above the wall,
> And the old triangle
> Went jingle jangle
> Along the banks of the Royal Canal.
> The screw was peeping
> The lag was sleeping,

> *The prisoners wander where they will; most go and take a glance at the half-dug grave.*

> While he lay weeping for the girl Sal,

WARDER DONELLY: Who's the bloody baritone? Shut up that noise, you. Where do you think you are?

NEIGHBOUR: It's not up here, sir; it's one of the fellows in the basement, sir, in the solitary.

WARDER DONELLY: He must be getting birdseed with his bread and water. I'll bloody well show him he's not in a singing house. (*Song is still going on.*) Hey, shut up that noise! Shut up there or I'll leave you weeping. Where do you think you are? (*Song stops.*) You can get sitting down any of you that wants it. (DUN-LAVIN *sits.*)

NEIGHBOUR (*at the grave*): They'll have to bottom out another couple of feet before morning.

PRISONER B: They! Us you mean; they've got four of us in a working party after tea.

NEIGHBOUR: You want to get that clay nice and neat for filling in. (*He spits and wanders away.*)

PRISONER B: We'll get a couple of smokes for the job at least.

They wander.

NEIGHBOUR: How are you, Neighbour?

DUNLAVIN: Dying.

NEIGHBOUR: If you are itself, it's greed that's killing you. I only got a sup of what was left.

DUNLAVIN: I saved your life then; it was very bad meths.

PRISONER B: What did Regan say when he caught youse lying in the cell?

NEIGHBOUR: He wanted to take us up for drinking it on him, but Dunlavin said we were distracted with the events of the morning and didn't know what we were doing. So he just told us to get to hell out of it and he hoped it would destroy us for life.

DUNLAVIN: May God forgive him.

NEIGHBOUR: I thought it was as good a drop of meths as ever I tasted. It would never come up to the pre-war article, but between the spring-time and the warmth of it, it would put new life into you. Oh, it's a grand evening and another day's work behind us.

PRISONER B: With the winter over, Neighbour, I suppose you don't feel a day over ninety.

NEIGHBOUR: If you'd have done all the time I have you wouldn't look so young.

PRISONER A: What time? Sure, you never done a lagging in your life. A month here and a week there for lifting the collection box out of a chapel or running out of a chemist's with a bottle of cheap wine. Anything over six months would be the death of you.

NEIGHBOUR: Oh, you're the hard chaw.

PRISONER A: Two laggings, I've done. Five year and |seven, and a bit of Preventive Detention, on the Moor and at Parkhurst.

NEIGHBOUR: What for? Ferocious begging?

PRISONER A: I've never been a grasshopper or a nark for the screws anyway, wherever I was; and if you were in a lagging station I know what they'd give you, shopping the poor bastard that was singing in the chokey. He was only trying to be company for himself down there all alone and not knowing whether it was day or night.

NEIGHBOUR: I only did it for his own good. If the screw hadn't checked him the Principal might have been coming out and giving him an extra few days down there.

DUNLAVIN: Will youse give over the pair of youse for God's sake. The noise of youse battering me bared nerves is unhuman. Begod, an Englishman would have more nature to a fellow lying with a sick head. A methylated martyr, that's what I am.

NEIGHBOUR (*to* PRISONER A): Meself and that man sitting there, we done time before you came up. In Kilmainham, and that's where you never were. First fourteen days without a mattress, skilly three times a day. None of your sitting out in the yard like now-adays. I got my toe amputated by one of the old lags so I could get into hospital for a feed.

DUNLAVIN (*looks up and feebly moans*): A pity you didn't get your head amputated as you were at it. It would have kept you quiet for a bit.

NEIGHBOUR: I got me mouth to talk, the same as the next man. Maybe we're not all that well up, that we get up at the Christmas con- cert and do the electrocutionist performance, like some I could mention.

DUNLAVIN: It's neither this nor that, Neighbour, but if you would only give over arguing the toss about nothing and change over to a friendly subject of mutual interest—like the quare fellow that's to be topped in the morning.

NEIGHBOUR: True, true, Dunlavin, and a comfortable old flowery dell he'll have down there. (*He prods the grave with his stick.*) We'll be eating the cabbages off that one in a month or two.

PRISONER A: You're in a terrible hurry to get the poor scut under the cabbages. How do you know he won't get a reprieve, like old Silver-top?

LIFER: Jesus, Mary and Joseph, you'd like to see me in there, wouldn't you! (*He moves violently away from them.*)

NEIGHBOUR: Your man doesn't like any talk about hanging.

PRISONER A: No more would you, if you'd tried to top yourself this morning.

NEIGHBOUR: Anyway he's gone now and we can have a chat about it in peace. Sure we must be saying something and it's better than scandalizing our neighbours.

PRISONER B: You never know what might happen to the quare fellow. God is good.

PRISONER C: And has a good mother.

They look in surprise at the young person who has quietly joined them.

DUNLAVIN: No, no, it's too late now for him to be chucked.

PRISONER A: It has been known, a last-minute reprieve, you know.

NEIGHBOUR: He bled his brother into a crock, didn't he, that had been set aside for the pig-slaughtering and mangled the remains beyond all hope of identification.

PRISONER C: Go bfoiridh Dia reinn.

NEIGHBOUR: He hasn't got a chance, never in a race of cats. He'll be hung as high as Guilderoy.

PRISONER A: You're the life of the party, aren't you? You put me in mind of the little girl who was sent in to cheer her father up. She was so good at it that he cut his throat.

PRISONER E: Ah, sure he was only computing the odds to it. He'll be topped.

NEIGHBOUR: I'd lay me Sunday bacon on it if anyone would be idiot enough to take me up.

PRISONER E, *a bookie, has been listening.*

PRISONER E: I wouldn't take your bacon, but I'll lay it off for you if you like.

Another prisoner watches for the screws. PRISONER E *acts as if he were a tick-tack man at the races.*

PRISONER E: The old firm. Here we are again. Neighbour lays his

Sunday bacon the quare fellow will be topped tomorrow morning. Any takers?

PRISONER D: Five snout.

PRISONER E: Away home to your mother.

MICKSER: Half a bacon.

PRISONER E: Half a . . .

NEIGHBOUR: Even bacons.

PRISONER E: Even bacons. Even bacons any takers? Yourself, sir, come on now, you look like a sportsman.

PRISONER A: I wouldn't eat anything after he'd touched it, not if I were starving.

NEIGHBOUR: Is that so . . .

PRISONER E: Now, now, now, don't interrupt the betting. Any takers?

DUNLAVIN: I'll take him up if only to shut his greedy gob.

NEIGHBOUR: You won't! You're having me on!

DUNLAVIN: No, I'll bet you my Sunday bacon that a reprieve will come through before morning. I feel it in my bones.

NEIGHBOUR: That's the rheumatics.

PRISONER E: Is he on, Neighbour?

NEIGHBOUR: He is.

PRISONER E: Shake on it, the two of youse!

DUNLAVIN: How d'ye do, Lord Lonsdale!

NEIGHBOUR: Never mind all that. The minute the trap goes down tomorrow morning your Sunday bacon is mine.

PRISONER A: God leave you health to enjoy it.

NEIGHBOUR: He'll be topped all right.

PRISONER A: And if he isn't, I'm the very man will tell him you bet your bacon on his life.

NEIGHBOUR: You never would.

PRISONER A: Wouldn't I?

NEIGHBOUR: You'd never be bad enough.

PRISONER A: And what would be bad about it?

NEIGHBOUR: Causing a dissension and a disturbance.

The two YOUNG PRISONERS *enter.*

PRISONER A: You mean he mightn't take it for a joke.

PRISONER B: Here's them two young prisoners; they've the life of Reilly, rambling round the place. Where youse wandering off to now?

YOUNG PRISONER 1: We came over here to see a chiner of ours. He turned twenty the day before yesterday, so they shifted him away from the Juveniles to here. (*He sees* PRISONER C.) Ah, there you are. We were over in the hospital being examined for going out on Saturday and we had a bit of snout to give you. (*Takes out a Woodbine package, extracts a cigarette from it and gives it to* PRISONER C, *who shyly stands and takes it.*)

PRISONER C (*quietly*): Thanks.

YOUNG PRISONER 1: Gurra morra gut, you mean.

PRISONER C (*smiles faintly*): Go raibh maith agat.

YOUNG PRISONER 1 (*grandly*): Na bac leis. (*To the other prisoners.*) Talks Irish to beat the band. Comes from an island between here and America. And Shaybo will give you a couple of strikers.

YOUNG PRISONER 2 (*reaches in the seams of his coat and takes out a match which he presents to* PRISONER C): Here you are. It's a bloody shame to shove you over here among all these old men even if you are twenty itself, but maybe you won't be long after us, and you going home.

PRISONER C (*Kerry accent*): I will, please God. It will be summer-time and where I come from is lovely when the sun is shining.

They stand there, looking embarrassed for a moment.

DUNLAVIN: Go on, why don't you kiss him good-bye.

YOUNG PRISONER 2: Eh, Schol, let's have a pike at the grave before the screw comes out.

YOUNG PRISONER 1: Ah, yes, we must have a look at the grave.

They dive into the grave, the old men shout at them, but WARDER DONELLY *comes to the door of the hospital.*

WARDER DONELLY: Get up to hell out of that and back to your own wing, youse two. (*Shouts to the warders in the prison wing.*) Two on you there, pass them fellows into the Juveniles. Get to hell out of that!

The YOUNG PRISONERS *samba off, give the so-called V-sign, slap the right biceps with the left palm, and turning lightly, run in through the door.*

NEIGHBOUR: Aren't they the impudent pups? Too easy a time they have of it. I'd tan their pink backsides for them. That'd leave them fresh and easy. Impudent young curs is going these days. No respect for God nor man, pinch anything that wasn't nailed down.

PRISONER B: Neighbour, the meths is rising in you.

DUNLAVIN: He might as well rave there as in bed.

ENGLISH VOICE (*from one of the cell windows*): I say, I say, down there in the yard.

DUNLAVIN: The voice of the Lord!

PRISONER A: That's the geezer from London that's in over the car smuggling.

ENGLISH VOICE: I say, down there.

PRISONER B: Hello, up there.

NEIGHBOUR: How are you fixed for fillet?

PRISONER B: Shut up a minute. Wait till we hear what is it he wants.

ENGLISH VOICE: Is there any bloke down there going out this week?

PRISONER B: Mickser is going out tomorrow. He's on this exercise. (*Shouts.*) Hold on a minute. (*Looks round.*) Hey, Mickser.

MICKSER: What's up?

PRISONER B: That English fellow that's on remand over the cars, he wants to know if there's anyone going out this week? You're going out tomorrow, ain't you?

MICKSER: Yes, I am. I'm going out in the morning. (*To* ENGLISH PRISONER.) What do you want?

ENGLISH VOICE: I want you to go up and contact my mate. He's in Dublin. It's about bail for me. I can write his name and address here and let it down to you on my string. I didn't want the law to get his address in Dublin, so I can't write to him. I got a quid in with me, without the screw finding it, and I'll let it down with the address if you'll do it.

MICKSER: Good enough. Let down the address and the quid.

ENGLISH VOICE: My mate will give you some more when you see him.

MICKSER: That's all right. Let the quid down now and the address before the screw comes out of the hospital. I'm going out tomorrow and I'll see him for you, soon as we get out of the market pubs at half two.

PRISONER B: He's letting it down now.

MICKSER: There's the quid anyway. (*Reading the note.* NEIGHBOUR

gets to his feet and goes behind and peers over his shoulder.
MICKSER *sees him.*) Get to hell out of it, you.

NEIGHBOUR: I only just wanted to have a look at what he wrote.

MICKSER: And have his mate in the Bridewell, before the day was out.
I know you, you bloody old stag.

NEIGHBOUR: I saw the day you wouldn't say the like of that.

MICKSER (*proffering him the pound*): Here, get a mass said for
yourself.

NEIGHBOUR: It wouldn't do you much harm to put yourself under the
hand of a priest either.

MICKSER (*laughs at him*): That's for sinners. Only dirty people has to
wash.

NEIGHBOUR: A man of your talent and wasting your time here.

MICKSER (*going back to walk with the prisoners behind*): Good luck
now, Neighbour. I'll call up and see you in the hospice for the
dying.

NEIGHBOUR (*stands and calls loudly after him*): You watch yourself.
I saw the quare fellow in here a couple of years ago. He was a
young hard chaw like you in all the pride of his strength and
impudence. He was kicking a ball about over in A yard and I
was walking around with poor old Mockridge, neither of us
minding no one. All of a sudden I gets such a wallop on the
head it knocks the legs from under me and very nigh cuts off my
ear. "You headed that well," says he, and I deaf for three days
after it! Who's got the best of it now, young as he is and strong
as he is? How will his own ear feel tomorrow morning, with the
washer under it, and whose legs will be the weakest when the
trap goes down and he's slung into the pit? And what use is the
young heart?

*Some of the prisoners walking round stop and listen to him,
but* MICKSER *gives him a contemptuous look and walks on,
shouting at him in passing.*

MICKSER: Get along with you, you dirty half animal.

A WARDER *passes, sounds of the town heard, factory sirens,
distant ships. Some of the prisoners pace up and down like
caged animals.*

NEIGHBOUR: Dunlavin, have you the loan of a pencil for a minute?

DUNLAVIN: What do you want it for?

NEIGHBOUR: I just want to write something to that English fellow about his bail.

DUNLAVIN: You'd better hurry, before the screw comes back out.

NEIGHBOUR *writes.*

NEIGHBOUR: Hey, you up there that's looking for the bail.

ENGLISH VOICE: Hello, you got the quid and the address?

PRISONER A: What's the old dog up to?

DUNLAVIN: Ah, leave him alone. He's a bit hasty, but poor old Neighbour has good turns in him.

PRISONER A: So has a corkscrew.

NEIGHBOUR: Let down your string and I'll send you up this bit of a message.

ENGLISH VOICE (*his hands can be seen at the window holding the note*): "Get a bucket and bail yourself out." (*Shouts in rage.*) You dirty bastard bleeder to take my quid and I'll tell the bloody screw I will; I'll shop you, you bleeding . . .

MICKSER: What's up with you?

NEIGHBOUR: Get a bucket and bail yourself out. (*Laughing an old man's cackle.*)

ENGLISH VOICE: You told me to get a bucket and bail my bleeding self out, but I'll tell the screw; I'll shop you about that quid.

MICKSER (*shouts up to the window*): Shut your bloody big mouth for a minute. I told you nothing.

PRISONER A: It was this old get here.

MICKSER: I sent you no message; it was this old pox bottle.

NEIGHBOUR (*ceases to laugh, is alarmed at the approach of* MICKSER): Now, now, Mickser, take a joke, can't you, it was only a bit of gas.

MICKSER (*advancing*): I'll give you gas.

MICKSER *advances on* NEIGHBOUR. *The lags stop and look—suddenly* MICKSER *seizes the old man and, yelling with delight, carries* NEIGHBOUR *over to the grave and thrusts him into it. The prisoners all crowd around kicking dirt on to the old man and shouting "Get a bucket and bail yourself out."*

PRISONER B: Nick, Mickser, nick, nick, here's the screw.

PRISONER A: It's only the cook with the quare fellow's tea.

> *A* PRISONER *comes through the hospital gate and down the steps. He wears a white apron, carries a tray and is surrounded by an interested band, except for the* LIFER, *who stands apart, and* DUNLAVIN, *who lies prone on the front asleep. From the prisoners around the food rises an excited chorus.*

PRISONER A: Rashers and eggs.

PRISONER B: He got that last night.

MICKSER: Chicken.

NEIGHBOUR: He had that for dinner.

PRISONER B: Sweet cake.

PRISONER A: It's getting hung he is, not married.

NEIGHBOUR: Steak and onions.

MICKSER: Sausages and bacon.

PRISONER B: And liver.

PRISONER A: Pork chops.

PRISONER B: Pig's feet.

PRISONER A: Salmon.

NEIGHBOUR: Fish and chips.

MICKSER: Jelly and custard.

NEIGHBOUR: Roast lamb.

PRISONER A: Plum pudding.

PRISONER B: Turkey.

NEIGHBOUR: Goose.

PRISONERS A, B, AND NEIGHBOUR: Rashers and eggs.

ALL: Rashers and eggs, rashers and eggs, and eggs and rashers and eggs and rashers it is.

COOK (*desperate*): Ah, here, lads.

PRISONERS: Here, give us a look, lift up the lid, eh, here, I never seen it.

> *The* COOK *struggles to protect his cargo, the* PRISONERS *mill round in a loose scrum of excitement and greed, their nostrils mad almost to the point of snatching a bit. There is a roar from the gate.*

WARDER DONELLY (*from inside the hospital gate*): Get to hell out of that. What do youse think you are on?

The PRISONERS *scatter in a rush.*

The COOK *with great dignity carries on.*

NEIGHBOUR (*sitting down*): Oh, the two eggs, the yolk in the middle like . . . a bride's eye under a pink veil, and the grease of the rashers . . . pale and pure like melted gold.

DUNLAVIN: Oh, may God forgive you, as if a body wasn't sick enough as it is.

NEIGHBOUR: And the two big back rashers.

PRISONER A: Go along, you begrudging old dog. Maybe when you go back the standard of living in your town residence, No. 1 St. James Street, might be gone up. And they'll be serving rashers and eggs. You'd do a lot for them, when you'd begrudge them to a man for his last meal on this earth.

NEIGHBOUR: Well, it's not his last meal if you want to know. He'll get a supper tonight and a breakfast in the morning, and I don't begrudge him the little he'll eat of that, seeing the rope stew to follow, and lever pudding and trap door doddle for desert. And anyway didn't you run over the same as the rest of us to see what he was getting?

PRISONER A: And if I did, it wasn't to begrudge it to the man.

PRISONER B: Sure we all ran over, anything to break the monotony in a kip like this.

The triangle is heard.

PRISONER A (*gloomily*): I suppose you're right. In Strangeways, Manchester, and I in it during the war, we used to wish for an airraid. We had one and we were left locked up in our cells. We stood up on our tables and took the blackouts off the windows and had a grand-stand view of the whole city burning away under us. The screws were running round shouting in the spyholes at us to get down from the windows, but they soon ran off down the shelters. We had a great view of the whole thing till a bomb landed on the Assize Court next door, and the blast killed twenty of the lags. They were left standing on their tables without a mark on them, stone dead. Sure anyway, we all agreed it broke the monotony.

Enter WARDER DONELLY.

WARDER DONELLY: Right, fall in there!

PRISONER B: Don't forget the bet, Neighbour.

WARDER DONELLY: Come on, get in line there.

PRISONER A: And don't forget what I'm going to tell the quare fellow.

WARDER DONELLY: Silence there. (*Search begins.*) What's this you've got in your pocket? A file? Scissors out of the bag shop? No? A bit of rope? Oh, your handkerchief, so it is. (*Searching next* PRISONER). You here, what's this? A bit of wax end, you forgot to leave in the bag shop? Well, don't forget the next time. What's this? (*Man takes out two inches of rope.*) What's this for? You were roping mail bags today, and after all they don't rope themselves. Ah, you forgot to leave it behind? Well, go easy, save as much as that each time and in five years' time you'd have enough to make a rope ladder. Oh, you're only doing six months? Well maybe you want to save the taxpayers a few quid and hang yourself. Sorrow the loss if you did, but they'd want to know where you got the rope from. (PRISONERS *laugh as they are expected to do.*) Come on, next man. (*He hurries along now.*) Come along now, no mailbags, scissors, needles, knives, razor blades, guns, hatchets or empty porter bottles. No? (*To the last* PRISONER.) Well, will you buy a ticket to the Police Ball?

PRISONERS *laugh dutifully.*

WARDER REGAN (*voice from prison wing*): All done, sir?

PRISONER A: Don't forget, Neighbour.

WARDER DONELLY: Right, sir, on to you, sir. (*Gate swings open.*) Right, lead on, B.1.

NEIGHBOUR: Anyway, his grave's dug and the hangman's on his way.

PRISONER A: That doesn't mean a thing, they always dig the grave; just to put the wind up them—

WARDER DONELLY: Silence!

The prisoners march, the gate clangs behind them; the tramp of their feet is heard as they mark time inside.

WARDER REGAN (*voice from the prison wing*): Right, B. Wing, bang out your doors. B.1, get in off your steps and bang out your

doors, into your cells and bang out your doors. Get locked up.
BANG THEM DOORS! GET INSIDE AND BANG OUT
THEM DOORS!

*The last door bangs lonely on its own and then there is
silence.*

VOICE FROM BELOW (*singing*):

> The wind was rising,
> And the day declining
> As I lay pining in my prison cell
> And that old triangle
> Went jingle jangle

*The triangle is beaten, the gate of the prison wing opens and
the* CHIEF *and* WARDER DONELLY *come down the steps and
approach the grave.*

Along the banks of the Royal Canal.

CHIEF (*resplendent in silver braid*): Who's that singing?
WARDER DONELLY: I think it's one of the prisoners in the chokey, sir.
CHIEF: Where?
WARDER DONELLY: In the punishment cells, sir.
CHIEF: That's more like it. Well, tell him to cut it out.

SONG:

> In the female prison
> There are seventy women . . .

WARDER DONELLY (*goes down to the area and leans and shouts*): Hey,
you down there, cut it out, or I'll give you jingle jangle.

The song stops. WARDER DONELLY *walks back.*

CHIEF: Is the quare fellow finished his tea?
WARDER DONELLY: He is. He is just ready to come out for exercise,
now. The wings are all clear. They're locked up having their
tea. He'll be along any minute.

CHIEF: He's coming out here?

WARDER DONELLY: Yes, sir.

CHIEF (*exasperated*): Do you want him to see his grave, bloody well half dug? Run in quick and tell those bloody idiots to take him out the side door, and exercise him over the far side of the stokehold, and tell them to keep him well into the wall where he'll be out of sight of the cell windows. Hurry and don't let him hear you. Let on it's something about another duty. Warders! You'd get better in Woolworths.

He goes to the area and shouts down.

Hey, you down there. You in the cell under the steps. You do be singing there to keep yourself company? You needn't be afraid, it's only the Chief. How long you doing down there? Seven days No. 1 and twenty-one days No. 2. God bless us and love us, you must have done something desperate. I may be able to do something for you, though God knows you needn't count on it, I don't own the place. You what? With who? Ah sure, I often have a bit of a tiff with the same man myself. We'll see what we can do for you. It's a long time to be stuck down there, no matter who you had the tiff with.

Enter WARDER DONELLY.

CHIEF: Well?

WARDER DONELLY: It's all right, they've brought him out the other way.

They look out beyond the stage.

CHIEF: Looks as if they're arguing the toss about something.

WARDER DONELLY: Football.

CHIEF: Begod, look at them stopping while the quare fellow hammers his point home.

WARDER DONELLY: I was down in the condemned cell while he was getting his tea. I asked him if it was all right. He said it was, and "Aren't the evenings getting a grand stretch?" he says.

CHIEF: Look at him now, putting his nose to the air.

WARDER DONELLY: He's a grand evening for his last.

CHIEF: I took the name of the fellow giving the concert in the punishment cells. In the morning when we get this over, see he's shifted to Hell's gates over the far side. He can serenade the stokehold wall for a change if he's light enough to make out his music.

WARDER DONELLY *copies the name and number.*

CHIEF: I have to attend to every mortal thing in this place. None of youse seem to want to do a hand's turn, bar draw your money—you're quick enough at that. Well, come on, let's get down to business.

WARDER DONELLY *goes and uncovers the grave.*

CHIEF (*looking off*): Just a minute. It's all right. They've taken him round the back of the stokehold. (*Looking at the grave.*) Not so bad, another couple of feet out of the bottom and we're elected. Regan should be down with the working party any minute, as soon as the quare fellow's finished his exercise.

WARDER DONELLY: There, he's away in now, sir. See him looking at the sky?

CHIEF: You'd think he was trying to kiss it good-bye. Well, that's the last he'll see of it.

WARDER DONELLY: No chance of a reprieve, sir?

CHIEF: Not a chance. Healey never even mentioned fixing up a line with the Post Office. If there'd been any chance of developments he'd have asked us to put a man on all night. All he said was "The Governor will get the last word before the night's out.' That means only one thing. Go ahead.

WARDERS REGAN *and* CRIMMIN *come out with* PRISONERS A, B, C, *and* D.

WARDER REGAN: Working party all correct, sir. Come on, get those boards off. Bottom out a couple more feet and leave the clay at the top, nice and neat.

CHIEF: Oh, Mr. Regan.

WARDER REGAN: Take over, Mr. Crimmin.

CHIEF: Mr. Regan. All I was going to say was—why don't you take yourself a bit of a rest while these fellows are at work on the grave. It's a long old pull till eight tomorrow morning.

WARDER REGAN: Thank you, sir.

CHIEF: Don't mention it. I'll see you before you go down to the cell. Get yourself a bit of a smoke, in the hospital. Don't forget now.

He and WARDER DONELLY *go back in.*

WARDER REGAN: Mr. Crimmin. The Chief, a decent man, he's after giving us his kind permission to go into hospital and have a sit down and a smoke for ourselves when these fellows have the work started. He knew we'd go in anyway, so he saw the chance of being floochalach, at no expense to the management. Here (*Takes out a packet of cigarettes, and takes some from it.*), here's a few fags for the lads.

CRIMMIN: I'll give them some of mine too.

WARDER REGAN: Don't do anything of the sort. One each is enough, you can slip them a couple when they're going to be locked up, if you like, but if these fellows had two fags each, they'd not work at all but spend the time out here blowing smoke rings in the evening air like lords. I'll slip in now, you come in after me. Tell them not to have them in their mouths if the Chief or the Governor comes out.

He goes up the steps to the hospital.

CRIMMIN (*calls* PRISONER C): Hey!

PRISONER C (*comes to him*): Seadh a Thomais?

CRIMMIN (*gives him cigarettes and matches*): Seo, cupla toitin. Taim f hein is an screw eile ag did isteach chiung an oispeasdal, noimest Roinn amach no toitini siud, is glacfaidh sibh gal, M. thagann an Governor nor Chief, no an Principal, no blodh in bhur mbeil agaib iad. A' tuigeann tu?

PRISONER C: Tuigim, a Thomais, go raidh maith agat.

CRIMMIN (*officially*): Right, now get back to your work.

PRISONER C: Yes, sir.

CRIMMIN *goes up the hospital steps.*

PRISONER C: He gave me some cigarettes.

PRISONER D *has gone straight to the grave,* PRISONER B *is near it.*

PRISONER A: May I never dig a grave for less! You two get on and do a bit of digging while we have a quiet burn, then we'll take over.

PRISONER C: He said to watch out for the Chief and them.

PRISONER B: Pass down a light to your man. He says he'd enjoy it better down there, where he can't be seen! Decent of him and Regan wasn't it?

PRISONER A: They'd have you dead from decency. That same Regan was like a savage in the bag shop today, you couldn't get a word to the fellow next to you.

PRISONER C: I never saw him like that before.

PRISONER B: He's always the same at a time like this, hanging seems to get on his nerves.

PRISONER A: Why should he worry, he won't feel it.

PRISONER B: He's on the last watch. Twelve till eight.

PRISONER A: Till death do us part.

PRISONER C: The quare fellow asked for him, didn't he?

PRISONER A: They all do.

PRISONER C: He asked to have Mr. Crimmin too.

PRISONER A: It'll break that young screw up, and him only a wet day in the place.

PRISONER B: Funny the way they all ask for Regan. Perhaps they think he'll bring them good luck, him being good living.

PRISONER A: Good living! Whoever heard of a good living screw? Did you never hear of the screw, married the prostitute?

PRISONER B: No, what happened to him?

PRISONER A: He dragged her down to his own level.

PRISONER B: He told me once that if I kept off the beer I need never come back here. I asked him what about himself, and he told me he was terrible hardened to it and would I pray for him.

PRISONER C: When I was over in the Juveniles he used to talk like that to us. He said that the Blessed Virgin knew us better than the police or the judges—or ourselves even. We might think we were terrible sinners but she knew we were good boys only a bit wild . . .

PRISONER A: Bloody mad he is.

PRISONER C: And that we were doing penance here for the men who took us up, especially the judges, they being mostly rich old men with great opportunity for vice.

PRISONER D *appears from the grave.*

PRISONER A: The dead arose and appeared to many.

PRISONER A *goes and rearranges the work which* PRISONER D *has upset.*

PRISONER B: What's brought you out of your fox hole?

PRISONER D: I thought it more discreet to remain in concealment while I smoked but I could not stop down there listening to talk like that, as a ratepayer, I couldn't stand for it, especially those libellous remarks about the judiciary.

He looks accusingly at the boy.

PRISONER C: I was only repeating what Mr. Regan said, sir.

PRISONER D: He could be taken up for it. According to that man, there should be no such thing as law and order. We could all be murdered in our beds, the innocent prey of every ruffian that took it into his head to appropriate our goods, our lives even. Property must have security! What do you think society would come to without police and judges and suitable punishments? Chaos! In my opinion hanging's too good for 'em.

PRISONER C: Oh, Mr. Regan doesn't believe in capital punishment, sir.

PRISONER D: My God, the man's an atheist! He should be dismissed from the public service. I shall take it up with the Minister when I get out of here. I went to school with his cousin.

PRISONER A: Who the hell does he think he is, a bloody high court judge?

PRISONER D: Chaos!

PRISONER B: He's in for embezzlement, there were two suicides and a bye-election over him.

PRISONER D: There are still a few of us who care about the state of the country, you know. My family's national tradition goes back to the Land War. Grandfather did four weeks for incitement to mutiny—and we've never looked back since. One of my young nephews, as a matter of fact, has just gone over to Sandhurst.

PRISONER B: Isn't that where you done your four years?

PRISONER A: No, that was Parkhurst.

PRISONER C (*to others*): A college educated man in here, funny, isn't it?

PRISONER D: I shall certainly bring all my influence to bear to settle this Regan fellow.

PRISONER C: You must be a very important man, sir.

PRISONER D: I am one of the Cashel Carrolls, my boy, related on my mother's side to the Killens of Killcock.

PRISONER B: Used to wash for our family.

PRISONER C: Go bfoiridh. Dia rainn.

PRISONER D: Irish speaking?

PRISONER C: Yes, sir.

PRISONER D: Then it might interest you to know that I took my gold medal in Irish.

PRISONER C: Does that mean he speaks Irish?

PRISONER D: Of course.

PRISONER C: Oh sir. Ta Caoliumn go leor agamsa. O'n gobliabh an amach, sir.

PRISONER B: That's fixed you.

PRISONER D: Quite. Tuighin thu.

PRISONER B: The young lad's from Kerry, from an island where they don't speak much else.

PRISONER D: Kerry? Well of course you speak with a different dialect to the one I was taught.

PRISONER B: The young screw Crimmin's from the same place. He sneaks up to the landing sometimes when the other screws aren't watching and there they are for hours talking through the spy-hole, all in Irish.

PRISONER D: Most irregular.

PRISONER B: There's not much harm in it.

PRISONER D: How can there be proper discipline between warder and prisoner with that kind of familiarity?

PRISONER C: He does only be giving me the news from home and who's gone to America or England; he's not long up here and neither am I . . . the two of us do each be as lonely as the other.

PRISONER B: The lad here sings an old song betimes. It's very nice. It makes the night less lonely, each man alone and sad maybe in the old cell. The quare fellow heard him singing and after he was sentenced to death he sent over word he'd be listening every night around midnight for him.

PRISONER A: You'd better make a big effort tonight, kid, for his last concert.

PRISONER C: Ah, God help him! Sure, you'd pity him all the same. It must be awful to die at the end of a swinging rope and a black hood over his poor face.

PRISONER A: Begod, he's not being topped for nothing—to cut his own brother up and butcher him like a pig.

PRISONER D: I must heartily agree with you sir, a barbarian if ever there was one.

PRISONER C: Maybe he did those things, but God help him this minute and he knowing this night his last on earth. Waiting over there he is, to be shaken out of his sleep and rushed to the rope.

PRISONER A: What sleep will he take? They won't have to set the alarm clock for a quarter to eight, you can bet your life on that.

PRISONER C: May he find peace on the other side.

PRISONER A: Or his brother waiting to have a word with him about being quartered in such an unmannerly fashion.

PRISONER C: None of us can know for certain.

PRISONER D: It was proved in a court of law that this man had experience as a pork butcher and put his expert knowledge to use by killing his brother with an axe and dismembering the body, the better to dispose of it.

PRISONER C: Go bfoiridh. Dia rainn.

PRISONER A: I wouldn't put much to the court of law part of it, but I heard about it myself from a fellow in from his part of the country. He said he had the brother strung up in an outhouse like a pig.

PRISONER D: Actually he was bleeding him into a farmhouse vessel according to the evidence. He should be hung three or four times over.

PRISONER A: Seeing your uncle was at school with the President's granny, perhaps he could fix it up for you.

PRISONER C: I don't believe he is a bad man. When I was on remand he used to walk around with me at exercise every day and he was sad when I told him about my brother, who died in the Yank's army, and my father, who was buried alive at the demolition of Manchester . . . He was great company for me who knew no one, only jackeens would be making game of me, and I'm sorry for him.

PRISONER A: Sure, it's a terrible pity about you and him. Maybe the jackeens should spread out the red carpet for you and every other Bog barbarian that comes into the place.

He moves away irritably.

Let's get a bit more off this bloody hole.

PRISONER B: Nick. Nick.

WARDER REGAN (*entering with* CRIMMIN): I've been watching you for the last ten minutes and damn the thing you've done except yap, yap, yap the whole time. The Chief or the Governor or any of them could have been watching you. They'd have thought it was a bloody mothers' meeting. What with you and my other bald mahogany gas pipe here.

PRISONER D: We were merely exchanging a few comments, sir.

WARDER REGAN: That's a lie and it's not worth a lie.

PRISONER A: All right! So we were caught talking at labour. I didn't ask to be an undertaker's assistant. Go on, bang me inside and case me in the morning! Let the Governor give me three days of No. 1.

WARDER REGAN: Much that'd worry you.

PRISONER A: You're dead right.

WARDER REGAN: Don't be such a bloody big baby. We all know you're a hard case. Where did you do your lagging? On the Bog?

PRISONER A: I did not. Two laggings I done! At Parkhurst and on the Moor.

WARDER REGAN: There's the national inferiority complex for you. Our own Irish cat-o'-nine-tails and the batons of the warders loaded with lead from Carrick mines aren't good enough for him. He has to go Dartmooring and Parkhursting it. It's a wonder you didn't go further while you were at it, to Sing Sing or Devil's Island.

PRISONER A (*stung*): I'm not here to be made a mock of, whether I done a lagging in England or not.

WARDER REGAN: Who said a word about it, only yourself—doing the returned Yank in front of these other fellows? Look, the quare fellow's got to be buried in the morning, whether we like it or not, so cut the mullarkey and get back to work.

PRISONER A: I don't let anyone make game of me!

WARDER REGAN: Well, what are you going to do about it? Complain to Holy Healey's department? He's a fine bloody imposter, isn't he? Like an old I.R.A. man with a good agency in the Sweep now.

Recommend me to the respectable people! Drop it for Christ's sake, man. It's a bad night for all of us. Fine job, isn't it, for a young fellow like him, fresh from his mother's apron strings. You haven't forgotten what it's like to come from a decent home, have you, with the family rosary said every night?

PRISONER A: I haven't any time for that kind of gab. I never saw religion do anything but back up the screws. I was in Walton last Christmas Eve, when the clergyman came to visit a young lad that had been given eighteen strokes of the cat that morning. When the kid stopped moaning long enough to hear what he had to say, he was told to think on the Lord's sufferings, then the cell door closed with a bang, leaving a smell of booze that would have tripped you up.

He takes a look at the quare fellow's side of the stage and, muttering to himself, goes back to work.

WARDER REGAN: You should pray for a man hardened in drink. Get back to it, all of you, and get that work a bit more advanced. Myself and Crimmin here have a long night ahead of us; we don't want to be finishing off your jobs for you.

They get into the grave.

PRISONER A: I never seen a screw like that before.
PRISONER B: Neither did anyone else.

They work.

CRIMMIN: What time is it, sir?
WARDER REGAN: Ten to seven.
CRIMMIN: Is himself here yet?
WARDER REGAN: Yes, he came by last night's boat. He's nervous of the 'plane, says it isn't natural. He'll be about soon. He's been having a sleep after the trip. We'll have to wait till he's measured the quare fellow for the drop, then we can go off till twelve.
CRIMMIN: Good.
WARDER REGAN: And for Christ's sake try to look a bit more cheerful when you come back on.
CRIMMIN: I've never seen anyone die, Mr. Regan.

WARDER REGAN: Of course, I'm a callous savage that's used to it.

CRIMMIN: I didn't mean that.

WARDER REGAN: I don't like it now any more than I did the first time.

CRIMMIN: No sir.

WARDER REGAN: It was a little Protestant lad, the first time; he asked if he could be walked backwards into the hanghouse so as he wouldn't see the rope.

CRIMMIN: God forgive them.

WARDER REGAN: May He forgive us all. The young clergyman that was on asked if the prison chaplain could accompany him; it was his first hanging too. I went to the Canon to ask him, a fine big man he was. "Regan," he says, "I thought I was going to escape it this time, but you never escape. I don't suppose neither of us ever will. Ah well," he says, "maybe being hung twenty times will get me out of purgatory a minute or two sooner."

CRIMMIN: Amen, a Thighearna Dhia.

WARDER REGAN: The young clergyman was great; he read a bit of the Bible to the little Protestant lad while they waited and he came in with him, holding his hand and telling him, in their way, to lean on God's mercy that was stronger than the power of men. I walked beside them and guided the boy on to the trap and under the beam. The rope was put round him and the washer under his ear and the hood pulled over his face. And still the young clergyman called out to him, in a grand steady voice, in through the hood: "I declare to you, my living Christ this night . . ." and he stroked his head till he went down. Then he fainted; the Canon and myself had to carry him out to the Governor's office.

A pause. We are aware of the men working at the grave.

WARDER REGAN: The quare fellow asked for you especially, Crimmin; he wanted you because you're a young lad, not yet practised in badness. You'll be a consolation to him in the morning when he's surrounded by a crowd of bigger bloody ruffians than himself, if the truth were but told. He's depending on you, and you're going to do your best for him.

CRIMMIN: Yes, Mr Regan.

REGAN *walks to the grave.*

WARDER REGAN: How's it going?

PRISONER A: Just about done, sir.

WARDER REGAN: All right, you can leave it.

They get up.

WARDER REGAN: Leave your shovels; you'll be wanting them in the morning. Go and tell the warder they've finished, Mr. Crimmin. I'll turn them over.

He searches the PRISONERS, *finds a cigarette end on* A *and sniffs it.*

Coffin nail. Most appropriate. (*He goes towards exit and calls.*) You needn't bother searching them, sir. I've turned them over.

PRISONER A (*aside*): He's as mad as a coot.

PRISONER C: But charitable.

WARDER REGAN: Right, lead on there!

PRISONER D: This is no place for charity, on the taxpayers' money.

PRISONER A: Take it up with your uncle when you get back into your stockbroker's trousers.

WARDER REGAN: Silence. Right, sir, working party off.

As the PRISONERS *march off, the* HANGMAN *comes slowly down the steps.*

CRIMMIN: Is this . . .

WARDER REGAN: Himself.

HANGMAN: It's Mr. Regan, isn't it? Well, as the girl said to the soldier "Here we are again."

WARDER REGAN: Nice evening. I hope you had a good crossing.

HANGMAN: Not bad. It's nice to get over to old Ireland you know, a nice bit of steak and a couple of pints as soon as you get off the boat. Well, you'll be wanting to knock off, won't you? I'll just pop down and have a look, then you can knock off.

WARDER REGAN: We were just waiting for you.

HANGMAN: This young man coming with us in the morning?

CRIMMIN: Yes, sir.

HANGMAN: Lend us your cap a minute, lad.

CRIMMIN: I don't think it would fit you, sir.

HANGMAN: We don't have to be so particular. Mr. Regan's will do. It ought to fit me by this time, and he won't catch cold the time I'll be away.

He goes out.

CRIMMIN: What does he want the cap for?

WARDER REGAN: He gets the quare fellow's weight from the doctor so as he'll know what drop to give him, but he likes to have a look at him as well, to see what build he is, how thick his neck is, and so on. He says he can judge better with the eye. If he gave him too much one way he'd strangle him instead of breaking his neck, and too much the other way he'd pull the head clean off his shoulders.

CRIMMIN: Go bhoiridh Dia orainm.

WARDER REGAN: You should have lent him your cap. When he lifts the corner of the spy-hole all the quare fellow can see is the peak of a warder's cap. It could be you or me or anyone looking at him. Himself has no more to do with it than you or I or the people that pay us, and that's every man or woman that pays taxes or votes in elections. If they don't like it, they needn't have it.

The HANGMAN *comes back.*

HANGMAN: Well set up lad. Twelve stone, fine pair of shoulders on him. Well, I expect you'll give us a call this evening over at the hospital. I'm in my usual apartments. This young man is very welcome, too, if he wants to join the company.

WARDER REGAN: Right, sir.

HANGMAN: See you later.

He goes out.

WARDER REGAN: Right, Crimmin. Twelve o'clock and look lively. The quare fellow's got enough on his plate without putting him in the blue jigs altogether. As the old Home Office memorandum says "An air of cheerful decorum is indicated, as a readiness to play such games as draughts, ludo, or snakes and ladders; a readiness to enter into conversations on sporting topics will also be appreciated."

CRIMMIN: Yes, sir.

WARDER REGAN (*as they go*): And, Crimmin . . .

CRIMMIN: Yes, sir?

WARDER REGAN: Take off your watch.

They go out.

NEIGHBOUR (*from his cell*): Hey, Dunlavin. Don't forget that Sunday bacon. The bet stands. They're after being at the grave. I just heard them. Dunlavin, do you hear me?

PRISONER A: Get down on your bed, you old Anti-Christ. You sound like something in a week-end pass out of Hell.

ENGLISH PRISONER: Hey, you bloke that's going out in the morning. Don't forget to see my chiner and get him to bail me out.

NEIGHBOUR: Get a bucket and bail yourself out.

SONG:
> The day was dying and the wind was sighing,
> As I lay crying in my prison cell,
> And the old triangle
> Went jingle jangle
> Along the banks of the Royal Canal.

The curtain falls.

ACT THREE

SCENE ONE

Later the same night. Cell windows lit. A blue lamp in the courtyard
A faint tapping is heard intermittently.

As the curtain rises, two WARDERS *are seen. One is* DONELLY, *the other*
a fellow new to the job.

WARDER 1: Watch the match.

WARDER 2: Sorry.

WARDER 1: We're all right for a couple of minutes, the Chief'll have
plenty to worry him tonight; he's not likely to be prowling about.

WARDER 2: Hell of a job, night patrol, at any time.

WARDER 1: We're supposed to pass each cell every half-hour tonight,
but what's the use? Listen to 'em.

The tapping can be distinctly heard.

WARDER 2: Yap, yap, yap. It's a wonder the bloody old hot-water pipes
aren't worn through.

Tapping.

WARDER 1: Damn it all, they've been yapping in association since seven
o'clock.

Tapping.

WARDER 2: Will I go round the landings and see who it is?

WARDER 1: See who it is? Listen!

WARDER 2: Do you think I should go?

WARDER 1: Stay where you are and get youself a bit of a burn. Devil
a bit of use it'd be anyway. As soon as you lifted the first spy-hole,
the next fellow would have heard you and passed it on to the
whole landing. Mind the cigarette, keep it covered. Have you
ever been in one of these before?

137

WARDER 2: No.

WARDER 1: They'll be at it from six o'clock tomorrow morning, and when it comes a quarter to eight it'll be like a running commentary in the Grand National.

Tapping.

WARDER 1 (*quietly*): Shut your bloody row! And then the screeches and roars of them when his time comes. They say it's the last thing the fellow hears.

Tapping dies down.

WARDER 2: Talk about something else.

Tapping.

WARDER 1: They're quietening down a bit. You'd think they'd be in the humour for a read or a sleep, wouldn't you?

WARDER 2: It's a hell of a job.

WARDER 1: We're in it for the three P's, boy, pay, promotion and pension, that's all that should bother civil servants like us.

WARDER 2: You're quite right.

WARDER 1: And without doing the sergeant major on you, I'm senior man of us two, isn't that right, now?

WARDER 2: I know what you mean.

WARDER 1: Well, neither bragging nor boasting—God gives us the brains and no credit to ourselves—I think I might speak to you as a senior man, if you didn't mind.

WARDER 2: Not at all. Any tip you could give me I'd be only too grateful for it. Sure it'd only be a thick wouldn't improve his knowledge when an older man would be willing to tell him something that would be of benefit to him in his career.

WARDER 1: Well now, would I be right in saying that you've no landing of your own?

WARDER 2: Quite right, quite right. I'm only on here, there or any old where when you or any other senior man is wanting me.

WARDER 1: Well, facts is facts and must be faced. We must all creep before we can walk, as the man said; but I may as well tell you straight, what I told the Principal about you.

WARDER 2: Tell me face to face. If it's fault you found in me I'd as lief hear it from me friend as from me enemy.

WARDER 1: It was no fault I found in you. If I couldn't do a man a good turn—I'd be sorry to do him a bad one.

WARDER 2: Ah, sure I know that.

WARDER 1: What I said to the Principal about you was: that you could easily handle a landing of your own. If it happened that one was left vacant. And I don't think I'm giving official information away, when I say that such a vacancy may occur in the near future. Before the month is out. Have you me?

WARDER 2: I have you, and I'm more than grateful to you. But sure I'd expect no less from you. You're all nature.

WARDER 1: It might happen that our Principal was going to the Bog on promotion, and it might happen that a certain senior officer would be promoted in his place.

WARDER 2: Ah, no.

WARDER 1: But ah, yes.

WARDER 2: But there's no one in the prison but'd be delighted to serve under you. You've such a way with you. Even with the prisoners.

WARDER 1: Well, I hope I can do my best by me fellow men, and that's the most any can hope to do, barring a double-dyed bloody hypocrite like a certain party we needn't mention. Well, him and me have equal service and it's only the one of us can be made Principal, and I'm damn sure they're not going to appoint a half-lunatic that goes round asking murderers to pray for him.

WARDER 2: Certainly they're not, unless they're bloody-well half-mad themselves.

WARDER 1: And I think they know him as well as we do.

WARDER 2: Except the Canon, poor man; he has him well recommended.

WARDER 1: You can leave out the "poor man" part of it. God forgive me and I renounce the sin of it, the Lord says "touch not my anointed," but the Canon is a bloody sight worse than himself, if you knew only the half of it.

WARDER 2: Go to God.

WARDER 1: Right, I'll tell you now. He was silenced for something before he came here and this is the *only* job he can get. Something terrible he did, though God forgive us, maybe it's not right to talk of it.

WARDER 2: You might sing it.

WARDER 1: I hear it was the way that he made the housekeeper take a girl into the house, the priest's house, to have a baby, an illegitimate!

WARDER 2: And could a man like that be fit to be a priest!

WARDER 1: He'd hardly be fit to be a prison chaplain, even. Here's the Chief or one of them coming. Get inside quick and let on you're looking for them fellows talking on the hot-water pipes, and not a word about what I said. That's between ourselves.

WARDER 2: Ah sure I know that's under foot. Thanks anyway.

WARDER 1: You're more than welcome. Don't be surprised if you get your landing sooner than you expected. Thirty cells all to yourself before you're fifty.

WARDER 2: I'll have the sister's children pray for you.

Enter CHIEF WARDER.

WARDER 1: All correct, sir.

CHIEF: What the hell do you mean, "All correct, sir"? I've been watching you this half-hour yapping away to that other fellow.

WARDER 1: There were men communicating on the hot-water pipes, sir, and I told him ten times if I told him once to go inside the landing and see who it was; it's my opinion, sir, the man is a bit thick.

CHIEF: It's your opinion. Well, you're that thick yourself you ought to be a fair judge. And who the bloody hell are you to tell anyone to do anything? You're on night patrol the same as what he is.

WARDER 1: I thought, sir, on account of the night that's in it.

CHIEF: Why, is it Christmas? Listen here, that there is an execution in the morning is nothing to do with you. It's not your job to care, and a good job too, or you'd probably trip over the rope and fall through the bloody trap. What business have you out here, anyway?

WARDER 1: I thought I had to patrol by the grave, sir.

CHIEF: Afraid somebody might pinch it? True enough, this place is that full of thieves, you can leave nothing out of your hand. Get inside and resume your patrol. If you weren't one of the old hands I'd report you to the Governor. Get along with you and we'll forget about it.

WARDER 1: Very good, sir, and thank you, sir.

Tapping.

CHIEF: And stop that tapping on the pipes.

WARDER 1: I will, sir, and thanks again, sir.

> FIRST WARDER *salutes, goes up the steps to the prison gates, which open. The* GOVERNOR *comes in in evening dress. The* FIRST WARDER *comes sharply to attention, salutes and goes off. The* GOVERNOR *continues down the steps and over to the* CHIEF WARDER.

CHIEF: All correct, sir.

GOVERNOR: Good. We had final word about the reprieve this afternoon. But you know how these things are, Chief, hoping for last-minute developments. I must say I should have been more than surprised had the Minister made a recommendation. I'll go down and see him before the Canon comes in. It makes them more settled for confession when they know there is absolutely no hope. How is he?

CHIEF: Very well, sir. Sitting by the fire and chatting to the warders. He says he might go to bed after he sees the priest.

GOVERNOR: You'll see that there's a good breakfast for himself and the two assistants?

CHIEF: Oh, yes, sir, he's very particular about having two rashers and eggs. Last time they were here, some hungry pig ate half his breakfast and he kicked up murder.

GOVERNOR: See it doesn't happen this time.

CHIEF: No indeed. There's a fellow under sentence of death next week in the Crumlin; we don't want him going up to Belfast and saying we starved him.

GOVERNOR: Have they come back from town yet?

CHIEF (*looks at his watch*): It's after closing time. I don't expect they'll be long now. I put Clancy on the side gate to let them in. After he took the quare fellow's measurements he went over to the place he drinks in. Some pub at the top of Grafton Street. I believe he's the life of the bar there, sir; the customers think he's an English traveller. The publican knows who he is, but then they're both in the pub business, and sure that's as tight a trade as hanging.

GOVERNOR: I suppose his work here makes him philosophical, and they say that drink is the comfort of the philosophers.

CHIEF: I wouldn't doubt but you'd be right there, sir. But he told me himself he only takes a drink when he's on a job. The rest of the time he's serving behind his own bar.

GOVERNOR: Is Jenkinson with him?

CHIEF: Yes, sir. He likes to have him with him, in case he gets a bit jarred. Once he went straight from the boat to the pubs and spent the day in them, and when he got here wasn't he after leaving the black box with his rope and his washers and his other little odds and ends behind him in a pub and forgot which one it was he left them in.

GOVERNOR: Really.

CHIEF: You could sing it. You were in Limerick at the time, sir, but here we were, in a desperate state. An execution coming off in the morning and we without the black box that had all his tools in it. The Governor we had then, he promised a novena to St. Anthony and two insertions in the *Messenger* if they were found in time. And sure enough after squad cars were all over in the city, the box was got in a pub down the North Wall, the first one he went into. It shows you the power of prayer, sir.

GOVERNOR: Yes, I see what you mean.

CHIEF: So now he always brings Jenkinson with him. You see, Jenkinson takes nothing, being very good living. A street preacher he is, for the Methodists or something. Himself prefers T.T.s. He had an Irishman from Clare helping one time, but he sacked him over the drink. In this Circus, he said, there's only one allowed to drink and that's the Ringmaster.

GOVERNOR: We advertised for a native hangman during the Economic War. Must be fluent Irish speaker. Cauliochtai do rior Meamram V.7. There were no suitable applicants.

CHIEF: By the way, sir, I must tell you that the warders on night patrol were out here conversing, instead of going round the landings.

GOVERNOR: Remind me to make a note of it tomorrow.

CHIEF: I will, sir, and I think I ought to tell you that I heard the principal warder make a joke about the execution.

GOVERNOR: Good God, this sort of thing is getting out of hand. I was at my School Union this evening. I had to leave in sheer embarrassment; supposedly witty remarks made to me at my own table. My eldest son was furious with me for going at all. He was at a table with a crowd from the University. They were even worse.

One young pup went so far as to ask him if he thought I would oblige with a rendering of "The night before Larry was stretched." I shall certainly tell the Principal that there's at least one place in this city where an execution is taken very seriously indeed. Good night to you.

CHIEF: Good night, sir.

Tapping. The CHIEF WARDER *walks up and down.* REGAN *enters.*

Ah, Mr. Regan, the other man coming along?

WARDER REGAN: He'll be along in a minute.

CHIEF: I don't know what we'd do without you, Regan, on these jobs. Is there anything the Governor or I could do to make things easier?

WARDER REGAN: You could say a decade of the rosary.

CHIEF: I could hardly ask the Governor to do that.

WARDER REGAN: His prayers would be as good as anyone else's.

CHIEF: Is there anything on the practical side we could send down?

WARDER REGAN: A bottle of malt.

CHIEF: Do you think he'd drink it?

WARDER REGAN: No, but I would.

CHIEF: Regan, I'm surprised at you.

WARDER REGAN: I was reared among people that drank at a death or prayed. Some did both. You think the law makes this man's death someway different, not like anyone else's. Your own, for instance.

CHIEF: I wasn't found guilty of murder.

WARDER REGAN: No, nor no one is going to jump on you in the morning and throttle the life out of you, but it's not him I'm thinking of. It's myself. And you're not going to give me that stuff about just shoving over the lever and bob's your uncle. You forget the times the fellow gets caught and has to be kicked off the edge of the trap hole. You never heard of the warders down below swinging on his legs the better to break his neck, or jumping on his back when the drop was too short.

CHIEF: Mr. Regan, I'm surprised at you.

WARDER REGAN: That's the second time tonight.

Tapping. Enter CRIMMIN.

CRIMMIN: All correct, sir.

CHIEF: Regan, I hope you'll forget those things you mentioned just now. If talk the like of that got outside the prison . . .

WARDER REGAN (*almost shouts*): I think the whole show should be put on in Croke Park; after all, it's at the public expense and they let it go on. They should have something more for their money than a bit of paper stuck up on the gate.

CHIEF: Good night, Regan. If I didn't know you, I'd report what you said to the Governor.

WARDER REGAN: You will anyway.

CHIEF: Good night, Regan.

WARDER REGAN (*to* CRIMMIN): Crimmin, there you are. I'm going into the hospital to fix up some supper for us. An empty sack won't stand, as the man said, nor a full one won't bend.

He goes. CRIMMIN *strolls. Traffic is heard in the distance, drowning the tapping. A drunken crowd are heard singing.* DONELLY *and the* NEW WARDER *appear in the darkness.*

WARDER 1: Is that young Mr. Crimmin?

CRIMMIN: Yes, it's me.

WARDER 1: You've a desperate job for a young warder this night. But I'll tell you one thing, you've a great man with you. Myself and this other man here are only after being talking about him.

WARDER 2: That's right, so we were. A grand man and very good living.

WARDER 1: There's someone coming. Too fine a night to be indoors. Good night, Mr. Crimmin.

CRIMMIN: Good night, sir.

WARDER 1 (*as they go off*): Come on, let's get a sup of tea.

CRIMMIN waits. Tapping heard. WARDER REGAN *re-enters.*

WARDER REGAN: Supper's fixed. It's a fine clear night. Do you hear the buses? Fellows leaving their mot's home, after the pictures or coming from dances, and a few old fellows well jarred but half sober for fear of what herself will say when they get in the door. Only a hundred yards up there on the bridge, and it might as well be a hundred miles away. Here they are back from the pub.

Voices are heard in the dark approaching. Enter HANGMAN *and* JENKINSON.

HANGMAN (*sings*):
> She was lovely and fair like the rose of the summer,
> Though 'twas not her beauty alone that won me,
> Oh, no, 'twas the truth in her eyes ever shining,
> That made me love Mary the Rose of Tralee.

Don't see any signs of Regan.

JENKINSON: He's probably had to go on duty. You've left it too late.

HANGMAN: Well, if the mountain won't come to M'ammed then the M'ammed must go to the mountain.

WARDER REGAN (*from the darkness*): As the girl said to the soldier.

HANGMAN: As the girl said to the soldier. Oh, it's you, Regan. Will you have a drink?

WARDER REGAN: I'm afraid we've got to be off now.

HANGMAN: Never mind off now. Have one with me. It's a pleasure to see you again. We meet all too seldom. You have one with me. Adam, give him a bottle of stout.

He sings again.

> Oh, no, 'twas the truth in her eyes ever shining,
> That made me love Mary the Rose of Tralee.

Not bad for an old 'un. Lovely song, in't it? Very religious though. "The Poor Christian Fountain." I'm very fond of the old Irish songs; we get a lot of Irish in our place on a Saturday night, you know.

WARDER REGAN: Is it what they call a sporting pub?

HANGMAN: That's just what it is, and an old sport behind the bar counter an' all. All the Irish come in, don't they, Adam?

JENKINSON (*gloomily*): Reckon they do. Perhaps because no one else would go in it.

HANGMAN: What do you mean? It's best beer in the district. Not that you could tell the difference.

WARDER REGAN: Good health.

HANGMAN: May we never do worse. (*To* JENKINSON.) You're in a right cut, aren't you, making out there's nobody but Irish coming into my pub? I've never wanted for friends. Do you know why? Be-

cause I'd go a 'undred mile to do a man a good turn. I've always
tried to do my duty.

JENKINSON: And so have I.

HANGMAN: Do you remember the time I got out from a sickbed
'ang a soldier at Strangeways, when I thought you and Christmas
'adn't had enough experience?

JENKINSON: Aye, that's right enough.

HANGMAN: I'm not going to quarrel with you. Here, go and fetch your
concertina and sing 'em that hymn you composed.

JENKINSON *hesitates.*

HANGMAN: Go on. It's a grand tune, a real credit to you. Go on, lad.

JENKINSON: Well, only for the hymn, mind.

He goes off to fetch it.

WARDER REGAN: Sure, that's right.

HANGMAN: 'E's a good lad is our Adam, but 'e's down in the dumps
at the moment. 'Im and Christmas, they used to sing on street
corners with the Band of Holy Joy, every Saturday night, concertina and all. But some of the lads found out who they were and
started putting bits of rope in collection boxes; it's put them off
outdoor testimony. But this 'ymn's very moving about hanging
and mercy and so forth. Brings tears to your eyes to 'ear Adam
and Christmas singing it.

JENKINSON *returns.*

JENKINSON: Right?

HANGMAN: Right!

JENKINSON (*sings*):

> My brother, sit and think.
> While yet some time is left to thee
> Kneel to thy God who from thee does not shrink
> And lay thy sins on Him who died for thee.

HANGMAN: Take a fourteen-stone man as a basis and giving him a drop
of eight foot . . .

JENKINSON:

> Men shrink from thee but not I,
> Come close to me I love my erring sheep.
> My blood can cleanse thy sins of blackest dye,
> I understand if thou canst only weep.

HANGMAN: Every half-stone lighter would require a two-inch longer drop, so for weight thirteen and a half stone—drop eight feet two inches, and for weight thirteen stone—drop eight feet four inches.

JENKINSON:

> Though thou hast grieved me sore,
> My arms of mercy still are open wide,
> I still hold open Heaven's shining door
> Come then, take refuge in my wounded side.

HANGMAN: Now he's only twelve stone so he should have eight foot eight, but he's got a thick neck on him so I'd better give him another couple of inches. Yes, eight foot ten.

JENKINSON:

> Come now, the time is short.
> Longing to pardon and bless I wait.
> Look up to me, my sheep so dearly bought
> And say, forgive me, ere it is too late.

HANGMAN: Divide 412 by the weight of the body in stones, multiply by two gives the length of the drop in inches. (*He looks up and seems sobered.*) 'E's an R.C., I suppose, Mr. Regan? (*Puts book in his pocket.*)

WARDER REGAN: That's right.

HANGMAN: That's all, then. Good night.

JENKINSON: Good night.

WARDER REGAN: Good night. (*The* HANGMAN *and* JENKINSON *go off.*) Thanks for the hymn. Great night for stars. If there's life on any of them, I wonder do the same things happen up there? Maybe some warders on a planet are walking across a prison yard this minute and some fellow up there waiting on the rope in the morning, and looking out through the bars, for a last look at our earth and the moon for the last time. Though I never saw them to bother much about things like that. It's nearly always letters to their wives or mothers, and then we don't send them— only throw them into the grave after them. What'd be the sense of broadcasting such distressful rubbish?

PRISONER C (*sings from his cell window*): Is e fath mo bhuadhartha na bhaghaim cead curts.

WARDER REGAN: Regular choir practice going on round here tonight.

CRIMMIN: He's singing for . . . for . . .

WARDER REGAN: For the quare fellow.

CRIMMIN: Yes. Why did the Englishman ask if he was a Catholic?

WARDER REGAN: So as they'd know to have the hood slit to anoint him on the rope, and so as the fellows below would know to take off his boots and socks for the holy oil on his feet when he goes down.

PRISONER C (*sings*):

> N'il gaoth adtuaidh ann,
> N'il sneachta cruaidh ann . . .

WARDER REGAN: We'd better be getting in. The other screws will be hopping mad to get out; they've been there since four o'clock today.

PRISONER C (*sings*): Mo whuirnin bhan . . .

His song dies away and the empty stage is gradually lightened for

SCENE TWO

The prison yard. It is morning.

WARDER 1: How's the time?

WARDER 2: Seven minutes.

WARDER 1: As soon as it goes five to eight they'll start. You'd think they were working with stop watches. I wish I was at home having my breakfast. How's the time?

WARDER 2: Just past six minutes.

MICKSER'S VOICE: Bail o dhis orribh go leir a chairdre.

WARDER 1: I knew it. That's that bloody Mickser. I'll fix him this time.

MICKSER'S VOICE: And we take you to the bottom of D. Wing.

WARDER 1: You bastard, I'll give you D. Wing.

MICKSER'S VOICE: We're ready for the start, and in good time, and who do I see lined up for the off but the High Sheriff of this ancient city of ours, famous in song and story as the place where the pig ate the whitewash brushes and—(*The* WARDERS *remove their caps.*) We're off, in this order: the Governor, the Chief, two screws Regan and Crimmin, the quare fellow between them, two more screws and three runners from across the Channel, getting well in front, now the Canon. He's making a big effort for the last two furlongs. He's got the white pudding bag on his head, just a short distance to go. He's in.

A clock begins to chime the hour. Each quarter sounds louder.

His feet to the chalk line. He'll be pinioned, his feet together. The bag will be pulled down over his face. The screws come off the trap and steady him. Himself goes to the lever and . . .

The hour strikes. The WARDERS *cross themselves and put on their caps. From the* PRISONERS *comes a ferocious howling.*

PRISONERS: One off, one away, one off, one away.

WARDER 1: Shut up there.

WARDER 2: Shut up, shut up.

WARDER 1: I know your windows, I'll get you. Shut up.

The noise dies down and at last ceases altogether.

Now we'll go in and get that Mickser. (*Grimly.*) *I'll* soften his cough. Come on . . .

WARDER REGAN *comes out.*

WARDER REGAN: Give us a hand with this fellow.

WARDER 1: We're going after that Mickser.

WARDER REGAN: Never mind that now, give us a hand. He fainted when the trap was sprung.

WARDER 1: These young screws, not worth a light.

They carry CRIMMIN *across the yard.*

NEIGHBOUR'S VOICE: Dunlavin, that's a Sunday bacon you owe me. Your man was topped, wasn't he?

PRISONER A.'s VOICE: You won't be long after him.

DUNLAVIN'S VOICE: Don't mind him, Neighbour.

NEIGHBOUR'S VOICE: Don't you forget that bacon, Dunlavin.

DUNLAVIN'S VOICE: I forgot to tell you, Neighbour.

NEIGHBOUR'S VOICE: What did you forget to tell me?

ENGLISH VOICE: Where's the bloke what's going out this morning?

NEIGHBOUR'S VOICE: He's up in Nelly's room behind the clock. What about that bacon, Dunlavin?

ENGLISH VOICE: You bloke that's going out this morning, remember to see my chiner and tell him to 'ave me bailed out.

NEIGHBOUR'S VOICE: Get a bucket and bail yourself out. What about me bacon, Dunlavin?

ENGLISH VOICE: Sod you and your bleeding bacon.

DUNLAVIN'S VOICE: Shut up a minute about your bail, till I tell Neighbour about his bet.

NEIGHBOUR'S VOICE: You lost it, that's all I know.

DUNLAVIN'S VOICE: Yes, but the doctor told me that me stomach was out of order; he's put me on a milk diet.

CHIEF (*comes through prison gates and looks up*): Get down from those windows. Get down at once. (*He beckons inside and* PRISONERS A, B, C, *and* D *file past him and go down on the steps.* PRISONER B *is carrying a cold hammer and chisel.*) Hey, you there in front, have you the cold chisel and hammer?

PRISONER B: Yes, sir.

CHIEF: You other three, the shovels are where you left them; get to work there and clear the top and have it ready for filling in.

They go on to the canvas, take up the shovels from behind and begin work. PRISONER B *stands on the foot of the steps with his cold chisel while the* CHIEF *studies his paper to give final instructions.*

CHIEF: Yes, that's it. You're to carve E. 777. Got that?

PRISONER B: Yes, sir. E. 777.

CHIEF: That's it. It should be E.779 according to the book, but a "7" is easier for you to do than a "9." Right, the stone in the wall that's nearest to the spot. Go ahead now. (*Raising his voice.*) There's the usual two bottles of stout a man, but only if you work fast.

WARDER 1: I know the worst fellow was making this noise, sir. It was Mickser, sir. I'm going in to case him now. I'll take an hour's overtime to do it, sir.

CHIEF: You're a bit late. He was going out this morning and had his civilian clothing on in the cell. We were only waiting for this to be over to let him out.

WARDER 1: But . . . Sir, he was the whole cause.

CHIEF: Well, what do you want me to do, run down the Circular Road after him? He went out on remission. We could have stopped him. But you were too bloody slow for that.

WARDER 1: I was helping to carry . . .

CHIEF: You were helping to carry . . . Warders! I'd get better in Woolworths.

WARDER 2: To think of that dirty savage getting away like that. Shouting and a man going to his God.

WARDER 1: Never mind that part of it. He gave me lip in the woodyard in '42, and I couldn't do anything because he was only on remand. I've been waiting years to get that fellow.

WARDER 2: Ah, well, you've one consolation. He'll be back.

At the grave PRISONER A *is the only one visible over the canvas.*

PRISONER B: Would you say that this was the stone in the wall nearest to it?

PRISONER A: It'll do well enough. It's only for the records. They're not likely to be digging him up to canonize him.

PRISONER B: Fair enough. E.777.

REGAN *drops the letters into the grave, and goes.*

PRISONER A: Give us them bloody letters. They're worth money to one of the Sunday papers.

PRISONER B: So I understood you to say yesterday.

PRISONER A: Well, give us them.

PRISONER D: They're not exclusively your property any more than anyone else's.

PRISONER B: There's no need to have a battle over them. Divide them. Anyone that likes can have my share and I suppose the same goes for the kid.

PRISONER D: Yes, we can act like businessmen. There are three. One each and toss for the third. I'm a businessman.

PRISONER A: Fair enough. Amn't I a businessman myself? For what's a crook, only a businessman without a shop.

PRISONER D: What side are you on? The blank side or the side with the address?

VOICE OF PRISONER BELOW (*singing*):
> In the female prison
> There are seventy women
> I wish it was with them that I did dwell,
> Then that old triangle
> Could jingle jangle
> Along the banks of the Royal Canal.

The curtain falls.

A
Taste
of
Honey

by
Shelagh Delaney

A TASTE OF HONEY was first presented by Theatre Workshop at the Theatre Royal, Stratford, London, May 27, 1958. On February 10, 1959, it was presented by Donald Albery and Oscar Lewenstein Ltd., at Wyndham's Theatre, London; directed by Joan Littlewood with sets by John Bury, costumes by Una Collins, and with the following cast:

HELEN . . . . Avis Bunnage

JOSEPHINE, *her daughter* . . . . Frances Cuka

PETER, *her friend* . . . . Nigel Davenport

THE BOY . . . . Clifton Jones

GEOFFREY . . . . Murray Melvin

THE APEX JAZZ TRIO . . . . Johnny Wallbank, *cornet*
Barry Wright, *guitar*
Christopher Capon, *double bass*

The play is in two acts and is
set in Salford, Lancashire, today

ACT ONE

SCENE ONE

The stage represents a comfortless flat in Manchester and the street outside. Jazz music. Enter HELEN, *a semi-whore, and her daughter,* JO. *They are loaded with baggage.*

HELEN: Well! This is the place.

JO: And I don't like it.

HELEN: When I find somewhere for us to live I have to consider something far more important than your feelings . . . the rent. It's all I can afford.

JO: You can afford something better than this old ruin.

HELEN: When you start earning you can start moaning.

JO: Can't be soon enough for me. I'm cold and my shoes let water . . . what a place . . . and we're supposed to be living off her immoral earnings.

HELEN: I'm careful. Anyway, what's wrong with this place? Everything in it's falling apart, it's true, and we've no heating—but there's a lovely view of the gasworks, we share a bathroom with the community and this wallpaper's contemporary. What more do you want? Anyway it'll do for us. Pass me a glass, Jo.

JO: Where are they?

HELEN: I don't know.

JO: You packed 'em. She'd lose her head if it was loose.

HELEN: Here they are. I put 'em in my bag for safety. Pass me that bottle—it's in the carrier.

JO: Why should I run round after you? (*Takes whisky bottle from bag.*)

HELEN: Children owe their parents these little attentions.

JO: I don't owe you a thing.

HELEN: Except respect, and I don't seem to get any of that.

JO: Drink, drink, drink, that's all you're fit for. You make me sick.

HELEN: Others may pray for their daily bread, I pray for . . .

JO: Is that the bedroom?

HELEN: It is. Your health, Jo.

155

JO: We're sharing a bed again, I see.

HELEN: Of course, you know I can't bear to be parted from you.

JO: What I wouldn't give for a room of my own! God! It's freezing! Isn't there any sort of fire anywhere, Helen?

HELEN: Yes, there's a gas-propelled thing somewhere.

JO: Where?

HELEN: Where? What were you given eyes for? Do you want me to carry you about? Don't stand there shivering; have some of this if you're so cold.

JO: You know I don't like it.

HELEN: Have you tried it?

JO: No.

HELEN: Then get it down you! (*She wanders around the room searching for fire.*) "Where!" she says. She can never see anything till she falls over it. Now, where's it got to? I know I saw it here somewhere . . . one of those shilling in the slot affairs; the landlady pointed it out to me as part of the furniture and fittings. I don't know. Oh! It'll turn up. What's up with you now?

JO: I don't like the smell of it.

HELEN: You don't smell it, you drink it! It consoles you.

JO: What do you need consoling about?

HELEN: Life! Come on, give it to me if you've done with it. I'll soon put it in a safe place. (*Drinks.*)

JO: You're knocking it back worse than ever.

HELEN: Oh! Well, it's one way of passing time while I'm waiting for something to turn up. And it usually does if I drink hard enough. Oh my God! I've caught a shocking cold from somebody. Have you got a clean hanky, Jo? Mine's wringing wet with dabbing at my nose all day.

JO: Have this, it's nearly clean. Isn't that light awful? I do hate to see an unshaded electric light bulb dangling from the ceiling like that.

HELEN: Well, don't look at it then.

JO: Can I have that chair, Helen? I'll put my scarf round it.

JO *takes chair from* HELEN, *stands on it and wraps her scarf round light bulb—burning herself in the process.*

HELEN: Wouldn't she get on your nerves? Just when I was going to

take the weight off my feet for five minutes. Oh! my poor old
nose.

JO: Christ! It's hot.

HELEN: Why can't you leave things alone? Oh! she gets me down. I'll
buy a proper shade tomorrow. It's running like a tap. This is the
third hanky today.

JO: Tomorrow? What makes you think we're going to live that long?
The roof's leaking!

HELEN: Is it? No, it's not, it's just condensation.

JO: Was it raining when you took the place?

HELEN: It is a bit of a mess, isn't it.

JO: You always have to rush off into things. You never think.

HELEN: Oh well, we can always find something else.

JO: But what are you looking for? Every place we find is the same.

HELEN: Oh! Every time I turn my head my eyeballs hurt. Can't we
have a bit of peace for five minutes?

JO: I'll make some coffee.

HELEN: Do what you like. I feel rotten. I've no business being out of
bed.

JO: Where's the kitchen?

HELEN: Where's the—through there. I have to be really bad before I
can go to bed, though. It's the only redeeming feature in this
entire lodging house. I've got it in my throat now too. I hope
you're going to make full use of it.

JO: There's a gas stove in here.

HELEN: It hurts when I swallow. Of course there is!

JO: It looks a bit ancient. How do I light it?

HELEN: How do I—with a match. Wouldn't she drive you mad?

JO: I know that, but which knob do I turn?

HELEN: Turn 'em all, you're bound to find the right one in the end.
She can't do a thing for herself, that girl. Mind you don't gas
yourself. Every time I comb my hair it goes right through me I
think it's more than a cold, you know—more likely it's 'flu! Did
you find it?

Loud bang.

JO: Yes.

HELEN: The way she bangs about! I tell you, my head's coming off.

JO: Won't be long now. Who lives here besides us, Helen? Any young people?

HELEN: Eh? Oh! Yes, I did see a lad hanging around here when I called last week. Handsome, long-legged creature—just the way I like 'em. Perhaps he's one of the fixtures. He'd just do for you, Jo; you've never had a boy friend, have you?

JO: No. I used to like one of your fancy men though.

HELEN: Oh! Which one?

JO: I thought I was in love with him.

HELEN: Which one does she mean?

JO: I thought he was the only man I'd ever love in my life and then he ran off with that landlady's daughter.

HELEN: Oh! Him.

JO: And I cried myself to sleep for weeks.

HELEN: She was a silly cat if ever there was one. You should have seen her. Honest to God! She was a sight for sore eyes. I'll have to tell you about her too sometime.

JO: I saw him again one day, on the street.

HELEN: Did you?

JO: I couldn't believe my eyes. He was thin, weak-chinned, with a funny turned-up nose.

HELEN: It wasn't his nose I was interested in.

Tugboat heard.

JO: Can you smell that river?

HELEN: I can't smell a thing! I've got such a cold.

JO: What's that big place over there?

HELEN: The slaughterhouse. Where all the cows, sheep and pigs go in and all the beef, pork and mutton comes out.

JO: I wonder what it'll be like here in the summer. I bet it'll smell.

HELEN: This whole city smells. Eee, there's a terrible draught in here. Where's it coming from? Look at that! What a damn silly place to put a window. This place is cold enough, isn't it, without giving shelter to the four winds.

JO: Helen, stop sniffing. It sounds awful.

HELEN: I can't help it. You'd sniff if you had a cold like this. She's not got a bit of consideration in her. It's self all the time.

JO: I'm going to unpack my bulbs. I wonder where I can put them.

HELEN: I could tell you.

JO: They're supposed to be left in a cool, dark place.

HELEN: That's where we all end up sooner or later. Still, it's no use worrying, is it?

JO: I hope they bloom. Always before when I've tried to fix up a window box nothin's ever grown in it.

HELEN: Why do you bother?

JO: It's nice to see a few flowers, isn't it?

HELEN: Where did you get those bulbs?

JO: The Park. The gardener had just planted about two hundred. I didn't think he'd miss half a dozen.

HELEN: That's the way to do things. If you see something you want, take it. That's my daughter for you. If you spent half as much time on me as you do on them fiddling bits of greenery I'd be a damn sight better off. Go and see if that kettle's boiling.

JO: See yourself. I've got to find somewhere for my bulbs.

HELEN: See yourself! Do everything yourself. That's what happens. You bring 'em up and they turn round and talk to you like that. I would never have dared talk to my mother like that when I was her age. She'd have knocked me into the middle of next week. Oh! my head. Whenever I walk, you know how it is! What a journey! I never realized this city was so big. Have we got any aspirins left, Jo?

JO: No. I dreamt about you last night, Helen.

HELEN: You're going to have a shocking journey to school each day, aren't you? It must be miles and miles.

JO: Not for much longer.

HELEN: Why, are you still set on leaving school at Christmas?

JO: Yes.

HELEN: What are you going to do?

JO: Get out of your sight as soon as I can get a bit of money in my pocket.

HELEN: Very wise too. But how are you going to get your money in the first place? After all, you're not very fond of work, are you?

JO: No. I take after you.

HELEN (*looking at the aspidistra*): That's nice, isn't it? Puts me in mind of my first job, in a tatty little pub down Whit Lane. I thought it was wonderful . . . You know, playing the piano and all that; a real get-together at weekends. Everybody standing up and giving a song. I used to bring the house down with this one. (*Sings.*)

I'd give the song birds to the wild wood
I'd give the sunset to the blind
And to the old folks I'd give the memory
of the baby upon their knee.

(*To orchestra.*) Come on, vamp it in with me.

JO: You can't play to that. It's got no rhythm.

HELEN: Oh! They'd tear it up, wouldn't they? (*She sings another verse.*) It's nice though, isn't it?

JO: What would you say if I did something like that?

HELEN: I should have taken up singing—everybody used to tell me. What did you say?

JO: I said what would you say if I got a job in a pub?

HELEN: You can't sing, can you? Anyway, it's your life, ruin it your own way. It's a waste of time interfering with other people, don't you think so? It takes me all my time to look after myself, I know that.

JO: That's what you said, but really you think you could make a better job of it, don't you?

HELEN: What?

JO: Ruining my life. After all, you've had plenty of practice.

HELEN: Yes, give praise where praise is due, I always say. I certainly supervised my own downfall. Oh! This chair's a bit low, isn't it? Could do with a cushion.

JO: Anyway I'm not getting married like you did.

HELEN: Oh!

JO: I'm too young and beautiful for that.

HELEN: Listen to it! Still, we all have funny ideas at that age, don't we—makes no difference though, we all end up same way sooner or later. Anyway, tell me about this dream you had.

JO: What dream?

HELEN: You said you had a dream about me.

JO: Oh that! It was nothing much. I was standing in a garden and there were some policemen digging and guess what they found planted under a rosebush?

HELEN: You.

JO: No—you.

HELEN: Why, had we run short of cemetery space? Well, I've always said we should be used for manure when we're gone. Go and see to that coffee. I'm dying for a hot drink. This bloody cold!

It's all over me. I'm sure it's 'flu—I suppose I'd better clear some of this stuff away. She wouldn't think. Well, they don't at that age, do they? Oh! It gets me right here when I try to do anything when I bend, you know. Have you ever had it? I was thinking of washing my hair tonight, but I don't think it's wise to . . . Christ! what the hell's she got in here . . . sooner her than me . . . what's this? (*Seeing drawings.*) Hey Jo, Jo, what's this?

JO: What's what?

HELEN: Did you do this?

JO: Put it down.

HELEN: I thought you said you weren't good at anything.

JO: It's only a drawing.

HELEN: It's very good. Did you show them this at school?

JO: I'm never at one school long enough to show them anything.

HELEN: That's my fault, I suppose.

JO: You will wander about the country.

HELEN: It's the gipsy in me. I didn't realize I had such a talented daughter. Look at that. It's good, isn't it?

JO: I'm not just talented, I'm geniused.

HELEN: I think I'll hang this on the wall somewhere. Now, where will it be least noticeable? Don't snatch. Have you no manners? What's these?

JO: Self-portraits. Give 'em here.

HELEN: Self-portraits? Oh! Well, I suppose you've got to draw pictures of yourself, nobody else would. Hey! Is that supposed to be me?

JO: Yes.

HELEN: Don't I look a misery? They're very artistic though, I must say. Have you ever thought of going to a proper art school and getting a proper training?

JO: It's too late.

HELEN: I'll pay. You're not stupid. You'll soon learn.

JO· I've had enough of school. Too many different schools and too many different places.

HELEN: You're wasting yourself.

JO: So long as I don't waste anybody else. Why are you so suddenly interested in me, anyway? You've never cared much before about what I was doing or what I was trying to do or the difference between them.

HELEN: I know, I'm a cruel, wicked woman.

JO: Why did we have to come here anyway? We were all right at the other place.

HELEN: I was fed up with the other place.

JO: You mean you're running away from somebody.

HELEN: You're asking for a bloody good hiding, lady. Just be careful. Oh! She'd drive you out of your mind. And my head's splitting. Splitting in two.

JO: What about me? Don't you think I get fed up with all this flitting about? Where's the bathroom? I'm going to have a bath.

HELEN: You're always bathing.

JO: I'm not like you. I don't wait until it becomes necessary before I have a good wash.

HELEN: You'll find the communal latrine and wash-house at the end of the passage. And don't throw your things about, this place is untidy enough as it is.

JO: That's all we do, live out of a travelling-bag.

HELEN: Don't worry, you'll soon be an independent working woman and free to go where you please.

JO: The sooner the better. I'm sick of you. You've made my life a misery. And stop sneezing your 'flu bugs all over me. I don't want to catch your cold.

HELEN: Oh! Get out of my sight. Go and have your bath. .

JO: You can get your own coffee too. Why should I do anything for you? You never do anything for me.

Music. Enter PETER, *a brash car salesman, cigar in mouth.*

HELEN: Oh! My God! Look what the wind's blown in. What do you want?

PETER: Just passing by, you know. Thought I'd take a look at your new headquarters.

HELEN: Just passing . . . How did you find my address?

PETER: I found it. Did you think you could escape me, dear?

JO: So that's what she was running away from.

PETER: Who's this?

HELEN: My daughter.

PETER: Oh! Hello there. That puts another ten years on her.

JO: What's this one called?

HELEN: Smith.

JO: You told me not to trust men calling themselves Smith.

HELEN: Oh go and have your bath.

JO: I don't know where the bathroom is.

HELEN: It's in a little hole in the corridor.

JO: Is he staying?

PETER: Yes, I'm staying.

JO: Then I'll go for my bath later.

HELEN: What did you want to follow me here for?

PETER (*fumbling*): You know what I want.

HELEN: Give over! Jo, go and see to that coffee! He would show up just when I've got her hanging round my neck.

PETER: Do what your mother tells you.

JO: Ordering me about like a servant! (*She goes.* PETER *makes another pass at* HELEN.) The kettle's not boiling. I suppose she hasn't told you about me.

PETER: Christ!

HELEN: Go and lay the table.

JO: No.

HELEN: Well, do something. Turn yourself into a bloody termite and crawl into the wall or something, but make yourself scarce.

PETER: Get rid of her.

HELEN: I can't. Anyway, nobody asked you to come here.

PETER: Why did you come here? I had to chase all over town looking for you, only to finish up in this dump.

HELEN: Oh shut up! I've got a cold.

PETER: What on earth made you choose such a ghastly district?

HELEN: I can't afford to be so classy.

PETER: Tenements, cemetery, slaughterhouse.

HELEN: Oh we've got the lot here.

PETER: Nobody could live in a place like this.

JO: Only about fifty thousand people.

PETER: And a snotty-nosed daughter.

HELEN: I said nobody asked you to come. Oh my God! I'll have to have a dose of something. My head's swimming. Why did you?

PETER: Why did I what?

HELEN: Follow me here?

PETER: Now you know you're glad to see me, kid.

HELEN: No I'm not. The only consolation I can find in your immediate presence is your ultimate absence.

PETER: In that case, I'll stay.

HELEN: I warned you. I told you I was throwing my hand in. Now didn't I?

PETER: You did.

HELEN: Oh! Throw that cigar away. It looks bloody ridiculous stuck in your mouth like a horizontal chimney.

PETER: Your nose is damp. Here, have this.

HELEN: Oh go away!

PETER: Give it a good blow.

HELEN: Leave it alone.

PETER: Blow your nose, woman. (*She does.*) And while you're at it blow a few of those cobwebs out of your head. You can't afford to lose a man like me.

HELEN: Can't I?

PETER: This is the old firm. You can't renege on the old firm.

HELEN: I'm a free lance. Besides, I'm thinking of giving it up.

PETER: What?

HELEN: Sex! Men!

PETER: What have we done to deserve this?

HELEN: It's not what you've done. It's what I've done.

PETER: But (*Approaching her.*), darling, you do it so well.

HELEN: Now give over, Peter. I've got all these things to unpack.

PETER: Send her to the pictures.

HELEN: I don't feel like it.

PETER: What's wrong?

HELEN: I'm tired. It's terrible when you've got a cold, isn't it? You don't fancy anything.

PETER: Well, put your hat on, let's go for a drink. Come on down to the church and I'll make an honest woman of you.

HELEN (*she goes to put her coat on, then changes her mind*): No, I don't fancy it.

PETER: I'm offering to marry you, dear.

HELEN: You what?

PETER: Come on, let's go for a drink.

HELEN: I told you I don't fancy it.

PETER: You won't find anything better.

HELEN: Listen, love, I'm old enough to be your mother.

PETER (*petting her*): Now you know I like this mother and son relationship.

HELEN: Stop it!

PETER: Aren't you wearing your girdle?

HELEN: Now, Peter.

PETER: Whoops!

HELEN: Well, you certainly liberate something in me. And I don't think it's maternal instincts either.

PETER (*sings*) : "Walter, Walter, lead me to the altar!"

HELEN: Some hopes.

PETER: Helen, you don't seem to realize what an opportunity I'm giving you. The world is littered with women I've rejected, women still anxious to indulge my little vices and excuse my less seemly virtues. Marry me, Helen. I'm young, good-looking and well set up. I may never ask you again.

HELEN: You're drunk.

PETER: I'm as sober as a judge.

HELEN: If you ask me again I might accept.

PETER (*sings*): "I see a quiet place, a fireplace, a cosy room."

HELEN: Yes, the tap room at the Red Lion. What are you after?

PETER: You know what I like.

JO (*coughs, enters*): Here's your coffee. Excuse me if I interrupted something. I'm sorry the crockery isn't very elegant, but it's all we've got.

PETER: Don't run away.

JO: I'm not running. (*Sits.*)

PETER: Is she always like this?

HELEN: She's jealous . . .

PETER: That's something I didn't bargain for.

HELEN: Can't bear to see me being affectionate with anybody.

JO: You've certainly never been affectionate with me.

PETER: Still, she's old enough to take care of herself. What sort of coffee is this anyway? It can hardly squeeze itself through the spout.

HELEN: She always does that. Makes it as weak as she can because she knows I like it strong. Don't drink that, it isn't worth drinking. Leave it.

JO: She should be in bed.

PETER: I know she should.

JO: You look very pale and sickly, Helen.

HELEN: Thank you.

JO: Is he going?

HELEN: Yes, come on, you'd better go before you catch my cold.

He pulls her to him as she passes.

PETER: Come outside then.

HELEN: No.

PETER: What does the little lady want? An engagement ring?

JO: I should have thought their courtship had passed the stage of symbolism.

HELEN: I always accept the odd diamond ring with pleasure.

PETER: I know it's my money you're after.

HELEN: Are you kidding?

JO: Hey!

> *He embraces* HELEN *at the door and begins to tell her a dirty story.*

PETER: Did I ever tell you about the bookie who married the prostitute?

HELEN: No. Go on.

JO: Hey! What sort of a cigar is that?

PETER: Why don't you go home to your father?

JO: He's dead.

PETER: Too bad. Anyway, this bookie . . .

JO: Is it a Havana?

HELEN: Yes.

PETER: A rich, dark Havana, rolled on the thigh of a coal black mammy.

JO: You want to be careful. You never know where a coal black mammy's thigh's been.

HELEN: Take no notice of her. She think's she's funny.

JO: So does he! I bet he's married.

> HELEN *bursts out laughing at his joke.*

You're not really going to marry her, are you? She's a devil with the men.

PETER: Are you, Helen?

HELEN: Well, I don't consider myself a slouch. Now come on then, if you've finished what you came for you'd better get going. We've all this to clear away before we go to bed.

PETER: Well, I won't be round tomorrow; the cat's been on the straw-
berries.

HELEN: Get going.

PETER: Don't forget me.

JO: Shall I withdraw while you kiss her good night?

HELEN: I'll kiss you good night in a minute, lady, and it really will be
good night.

PETER: Well, take care of your mother while she's ailing, Jo. You
know how fragile these old ladies are.

HELEN: Go on, get! (*Exit* PETER.) Well, I'm going to bed. We'll shift
this lot tomorrow. There's always another day.

JO: It's dark out there now. I think I'll have my bath in the morning.

HELEN: Are you afraid of the dark?

JO: You know I am.

HELEN: You should try not to be.

JO: I do.

HELEN: And you're still afraid?

JO: Yes.

HELEN: Then you'll have to try a bit harder, won't you?

JO: Thanks. I'll do that. What's the bed like?

HELEN: Like a coffin only not half as comfortable.

JO: Have you ever tried a coffin?

HELEN: I dare say I will one day. I do wish we had a hot water bottle.

JO: You should have asked him to stay. It wouldn't be the first time
I've been thrown out of my bed to make room for one of your . . .

HELEN: For God's sake shut up! Close your mouth for five minutes.
And you can turn the light off and come to bed.

JO: Aren't we going to clear this lot up?

HELEN: No, it'll look all right in the dark.

JO: Yes, it's seen at its best, this room, in the dark.

HELEN: Everything is seen at its best in the dark—including me. I love
it. Can't understand why you're so scared of it.

JO: I'm not frightened of the darkness outside. It's the darkness inside houses I don't like.

HELEN: Come on! Hey, Jo, what would you do if I told you I was
thinking of getting married again?

JO: I'd have you locked up in an institution right away!

HELEN: Come on.

Music. Fade out.

SCENE TWO

JO *and her* BOY FRIEND, *a coloured naval rating, walking on the street. They stop by the door.*

JO: I'd better go in now. Thanks for carrying my books.

BOY: Were you surprised to see me waiting outside school?

JO: Not really.

BOY: Glad I came?

JO: You know I am.

BOY: So am I.

JO: Well, I'd better go in.

BOY: Not yet! Stay a bit longer.

JO: All right! Doesn't it go dark early? I like winter. I like it better than all the other seasons.

BOY: I like it too. When it goes dark early it gives me more time for— (*He kisses her.*)

JO: Don't do that. You're always doing it.

BOY: You like it.

JO: I know, but I don't want to do it all the time.

BOY: Afraid someone'll see us?

JO: I don't care.

BOY: Say that again.

JO: I don't care.

BOY: You mean it too. You re the first girl I've met who really didn't care. Listen, I'm going to ask you something. I'm a man of few words. Will you marry me?

JO: Well, I'm a girl of few words. I won't marry you but you've talked me into it.

BOY: How old are you?

JO: Nearly eighteen.

BOY: And you really will marry me?

JO: I said so, didn't I? You shouldn't have asked me if you were only kidding me up. (*She starts to go.*)

BOY: Hey! I wasn't kidding. I thought you were. Do you really mean it? You will marry me?

JO: I love you.

BOY: How do you know?

JO: I don't know why I love you but I do.

BOY: I adore you. (*Swinging her through the air.*)

JO: So do I. I can't resist myself.

BOY: I've got something for you.

JO: What is it? A ring!

BOY: This morning in the shop I couldn't remember what sort of hands you had, long hands, small hands or what. I stood there like a damn fool trying to remember what they felt like. (*He puts the ring on and kisses her hand.*) What will your mother say?

JO: She'll probably laugh.

BOY: Doesn't she care who her daughter marries?

JO: She's not marrying you, I am. It's got nothing to do with her.

BOY: She hasn't seen me.

JO: And when she does?

BOY: She'll see a coloured boy.

JO: No, whatever else she might be, she isn't prejudiced against colour. You're not worried about it, are you?

BOY: So long as you like it.

JO: You know I do.

BOY: Well, that's all that matters.

JO: When shall we get married?

BOY: My next leave? It's a long time, six months.

JO: It'll give us a chance to save a bit of money. Here, see . . . this ring . . . it's too big; look, it slides about . . . And I couldn't wear it for school anyway. I might lose it. Let's go all romantic. Have you got a bit of string?

BOY: What for?

JO: I'm going to tie it round my neck. Come on, turn your pockets out. Three handkerchiefs, a safety pin, a screw! Did that drop out of your head? Elastic bands! Don't little boys carry some trash. And what's this?

BOY: Nothing.

JO: A toy car! Does it go?

BOY: Hm hm!

JO: Can I try it? (*She does.*)

BOY: She doesn't even know how it works. Look, not like that.

He makes it go fast.

JO: I like that. Can I keep it?

BOY: Yes, take it, my soul and all, everything.

JO: Thanks. I know, I can use my hair ribbon for my ring. Do it up for me.

BOY: Pretty neck you've got.

JO: Glad you like it. It's my schoolgirl complexion. I'd better tuck this out of sight. I don't want my mother to see it. She'd only laugh. Did I tell you, when I leave school this week I start a part-time job in a bar? Then as soon as I get a full-time job, I'm leaving Helen and starting up in a room somewhere.

BOY: I wish I wasn't in the Navy.

JO: Why?

BOY: We won't have much time together.

JO: Well, we can't be together all the time and all the time there is wouldn't be enough.

BOY: It's a sad story, Jo. Once, I was a happy young man, not a care in the world. Now! I'm trapped into a barbaric cult . . .

JO: What's that? Mau-Mau?

BOY: Matrimony.

JO: Trapped! I like that! You almost begged me to marry you.

BOY: You led me on. I'm a trusting soul. Who took me down to that deserted football pitch?

JO: Who found the football pitch? I didn't even know it existed. And it just shows how often you must have been there, too . . . you certainly know where all the best spots are. I'm not going there again . . . It's too quiet. Anything might happen to a girl.

BOY: It almost did. You shameless woman!

JO: That's you taking advantage of my innocence.

BOY: I didn't take advantage. I had scruples.

JO: You would have done. You'd have gone as far as I would have let you and no scruples would have stood in your way.

BOY: You enjoyed it as much as I did.

JO: Shut up! This is the sort of conversation that can colour a young girl's mind.

BOY: Women never have young minds. They are born three thousand years old.

JO: Sometimes you look three thousand years old. Did your ancestors come from Africa?

BOY: No. Cardiff. Disappointed? Were you hoping to marry a man whose father beat the tom-tom all night?

JO: I don't care where you were born. There's still a bit of jungle in

you somewhere. (*A siren is heard.*) I'm going in now, I'm hungry.
A young girl's got to eat, you know.

BOY: Honey, you've got to stop eating. No more food, no more make-up, no more fancy clothes; we're saving up to get married.

JO: I just need some new clothes too. I've only got this one coat. I have to use it for school and when I go out with you. I do feel a mess.

BOY: You look all right to me.

JO: Shall I see you tonight?

BOY: No, I got work to do.

JO: What sort of work?

BOY: Hard work, it involves a lot of walking.

JO: And a lot of walking makes you thirsty. I know, you're going drinking.

BOY: That's right. It's one of the lads' birthdays. I'll see you tomorrow.

JO: All right. I'll tell you what, I won't bother going to school and we can spend the whole day together. I'll meet you down by that ladies' hairdressing place.

BOY: The place that smells of cooking hair?

JO: Yes, about ten o'clock.

BOY: Okay, you're the boss.

JO: Good night.

BOY: Aren't you going to kiss me good night?

JO: You know I am. (*Kisses him.*) I like kissing you. Good night.

BOY: Good night.

JO: Dream of me.

BOY: I dreamt about you last night. Fell out of bed twice.

JO: You're in a bad way.

BOY: You bet I am. Be seeing you!

JO (*as she goes*): I love you.

BOY: Why?

JO: Because you're daft.

He waves good-bye, turns and sings to the audience, and goes.
HELEN *dances on to the music, lies down and reads an evening
paper.* JO *dances on dreamily.*

HELEN: You're a bit late coming home from school, aren't you?

JO: I met a friend.

HELEN: Well, he certainly knows how to put stars in your eyes.

JO: What makes you think it's a he?

HELEN: Well, I certainly hope it isn't a she who makes you walk round in this state.

JO: He's a sailor.

HELEN: I hope you exercised proper control over his nautical ardour. I've met a few sailors myself.

JO: He's lovely.

HELEN: Is he?

JO: He's got beautiful brown eyes and gorgeous curly hair.

HELEN: Has he got long legs?

JO: They're all right.

HELEN: How old is he?

JO: Twenty-two. He's doing his national service, but before that he was a male nurse.

HELEN: A male nurse, eh? That's interesting. Where did he do his nursing?

JO: In a hospital, of course! Where else do they have nurses?

HELEN: Does he ever get any free samples? We could do with a few contacts for things like that.

JO: Oh shut up, Helen. Have a look in that paper and see what's on at the pictures tomorrow night.

HELEN: Where is it? Oh yes . . . *I was a Teenage* . . . what? You can't go there anyway, it's a proper little flea pit. *The Ten Commandments,* here, that'd do you good. *Desire Under the* . . . oh! What a funny place to have desire! You might as well have it at home as anywhere else, mightn't you? No, there's nothing here that I fancy.

JO: You never go to the pictures.

HELEN: I used to but the cinema has become more and more like the theatre, it's all mauling and muttering, can't hear what they're saying half the time and when you do it's not worth listening to. Look at that advertisement. It's pornographic. In my opinion such a frank and open display of the female form can only induce little boys of all ages to add vulgar comments in pencil. I ask you, what sort of an inflated woman is that? She's got bosom, bosom and still more bosom. I bet every inch of her chest is worth it's weight in gold. Let's have a look at you. I wonder if I could turn you into a mountain of voluptuous temptation?

JO: Why?

HELEN: I'd put you on films.

JO: I'd sooner be put on't streets. It's more honest.

HELEN: You might have to do that yet.

JO: Where did this magazine come from?

HELEN: Woman downstairs give it me.

JO: I didn't think you'd buy it.

HELEN: Why buy when it's cheaper to borrow?

JO: What day was I born on?

HELEN: I don't know.

JO: You should remember such an important event.

HELEN: I've always done my best to forget that.

JO: How old was I when your husband threw you out?

HELEN: Change the subject. When I think of her father and my husband it makes me wonder why I ever bothered, it does really.

JO: He was rich, wasn't he . . .

HELEN: He was a rat!

JO: He was your husband. Why did you marry him?

HELEN: At the time I had nothing better to do. Then he divorced me; that was your fault.

JO: I agree with him. If I was a man and my wife had a baby that wasn't mine I'd sling her out.

HELEN: Would you? It's a funny thing but I don't think I would. Still, why worry?

JO (*reading from magazine*): It says here that Sheik Ahmed—an Arabian mystic—will, free of all charge, draw up for you a complete analysis of your character and destiny.

HELEN: Let's have a look.

JO: There's his photograph.

HELEN: Oh! He looks like a dirty little spiv. Listen Jo, don't bother your head about Arabian mystics. There's two w's in your future. Work or want, and no Arabian Knight can tell you different. We're all at the steering wheel of our own destiny. Careering along like drunken drivers. I'm going to get married. (*The news is received in silence.*) I said, I'm going to get married.

JO: Yes, I heard you the first time. What do you want me to do, laugh and throw pennies? Is it that Peter Smith?

HELEN: He's the unlucky man.

JO: You're centuries older than him.

HELEN: Only ten years.

JO: What use can a woman of that age be to anybody?

HELEN: I wish you wouldn't talk about me as if I'm an impotent, shriv-
elled old woman without a clue left in her head.

JO: You're not exactly a child bride.

HELEN: I have been one once, or near enough.

JO: Just imagine it, you're forty years old. I hope to be dead and
buried before I reach that age. You've been living for forty years.

HELEN: Yes, it must be a biological phenomena.

JO: You don't look forty. You look a sort of well-preserved sixty.

Music. Enter PETER *carrying a large bouquet and a box of
chocolates and looking uncomfortable.*

HELEN: Oh look, and it's all mine!

JO: Hello, Daddy.

PETER: Oh! So you told her.

HELEN: Of course. Come in and sit down. On second thoughts lie
down, you look marvellous.

He gives her the bouquet.

Oh! really, you shouldn't have bothered yourself. I know the
thought was there, but . . . here, Jo, have we got a vase, put
these in some water.

JO: How did she talk you into it? You must be out of your mind.

PETER: That's possible, I suppose.

JO: Flowers and all the trimmings. Helen can't eat anything sweet
and delicious. She's got to watch her figure.

HELEN: Nonsense! My figure hasn't altered since I was eighteen.

JO: Really?

HELEN: Not an inch.

JO: I hope I'm luckier with mine.

HELEN: Do you see anything objectionable about my figure, Peter?

PETER: I find the whole thing most agreeable.

JO: You've got to say that, you're marrying it!

PETER: The chocolates are for you, Jo.

JO: Buying my silence, hey? It's a good idea. I like chocolates.

HELEN: Help yourself to a drink, Peter, and I'll go and put my glad
rags on. (*Exit.*)

PETER: Don't let's be long, huh? I've booked a table. Dammit, I
thought you'd be ready.

JO: She's got no sense of time.

PETER: Don't sit there guzzling all those chocolates at once.

She throws the lid at him.

What the hell are you playing at . . . sit down and behave yourself, you little snip.

JO: Hey! Don't start bossing me about. You're not my father.

PETER: Christ Almighty! Will you sit down and eat your chocolates.
Do what you like but leave me alone.

Suddenly she attacks him, half-laughing, half-crying.

JO: You leave me alone. And leave my mother alone too.

HELEN *enters.*

PETER: Get away! For God's sake go and . . .

HELEN: Leave him alone, Jo. He doesn't want to be bothered with you.
Got a cigarette, Peter? Did you get yourself a drink?

PETER: No, I . . .

JO: Do I bother you, Mister Smith, or must I wait till we're alone for
an answer?

PETER: Can't you keep her under control?

HELEN: I'll knock her head round if she isn't careful. Be quiet, Jo.
And don't tease him.

PETER: Tonight's supposed to be a celebration.

JO: What of?

HELEN: He's found a house. Isn't he marvellous? Show her the photo
of it, Peter. I shan't be a tick!

JO: You've certainly fixed everything up behind my back.

HELEN: Don't you think it's nice? One of his pals had to sell, moving
into something smaller. (*Goes.*)

PETER *throws snap on to the table.*

JO: It's not bad. White walls, tennis courts. Has it got a swimming
pool?

PETER: It has twelve swimming pools.

JO: Can I see the other photos?

PETER: Which photos?

JO: In your wallet. I suppose you thought I didn't notice.

PETER: Oh! These. Yes, well, that's a photograph of my family, my mother, my father, my sister, my brother and . . . (*To himself.*) all the rest of the little bastards.

JO: Is this a wedding group?

PETER: My brother's wedding.

JO: They only just made it, too, from the look of his wife. You can tell she's going to have a baby.

PETER: Oh? Thank you.

JO: You can have it back if I can see the others.

PETER: Which others? What are you talking about?

JO: Do you want me to tell my mother?

PETER: I don't give a damn what you tell your mother.

JO: They're all women, aren't they? I bet you've had thousands of girl friends. What was this one with the long legs called?

PETER: Ah! Yes, number thirty-eight. A charming little thing.

JO: Why do you wear that black patch?

PETER: I lost an eye.

JO: Where?

PETER: During the war.

JO: Were you in the Navy?

PETER: Army.

JO: Officer?

PETER: Private.

JO: I thought you would have been somebody very important.

PETER: A private is far more important than you think. After all, who does all the dirty work?

JO: Yes, a general without any army wouldn't be much use, would he? Can I see your eye? I mean can I see the hole?

PETER: There's nothing to see.

JO: Do you wear that patch when you go to bed?

PETER: That's something about which I don't care to make a public statement.

JO: Tell me.

PETER: Well, there is one highly recommended way for a young girl to find out.

JO (*glancing through photos in wallet*): I don't like this one. She's got too much stuff on her eyes.

PETER: That's the sort of thing your sex goes in for.

JO: I don't. I let my natural beauty shine through.

PETER: Is there no alternative?

JO: Don't you like shiny faces?

PETER: I suppose they're all right on sweet young things but I just don't go for sweet young things—

JO: Do you fancy me?

PETER: Not yet.

JO: You prefer old women.

PETER: She isn't old.

JO: She soon will be.

PETER: Ah well, that's love. (*Sings.*) "That wild, destructive thing called love."

JO: Why are you marrying Helen?

PETER: Why shouldn't I marry Helen?

JO: Your generation has some very peculiar ideas, that's all I can say.

PETER: Could I have my photographs back, please?

JO: There . . .

PETER: You don't like your mother much do you?

JO: She doesn't much care for me either.

PETER: I can understand that.

JO (*looking over his shoulder at photographs*): I like that one with the shaggy hair cut. She's got nice legs too. Nearly as nice as mine.

PETER: Would you care for a smoke?

JO: Thanks.

> HELEN *is heard singing off stage.*

HELEN: Jo! Where's my hat?

JO: I don't know. Where you left it. It's no use getting impatient, Peter. The art work takes a long time. Are you sure you lost your eye during the war? What happened?

PETER: Go and tell your mother I'll wait for her in the pub.

JO: Are you married?

PETER (*going*): No, I'm still available.

HELEN (*entering*): But only just.

PETER: Helen, you look utterly fantastic.

HELEN: Thanks. Put that cigarette out, Jo, you've got enough bad habits without adding to your repertoire. Do you like my hat, Peter?

PETER: Bang-on, darling!

HELEN: What are all these books doing all over the place? Are you planning a moonlight flit, Jo? Stop it, Peter.

PETER: Got your blue garters on?

HELEN: Now, Peter. Come on, Jo, shift these books.

JO: I'm sorting them.

PETER (*taking* HELEN's *hat*): How do I look?

HELEN: Peter!

JO: Have you forgotten I'm leaving school this week?

HELEN: Peter, give it here. Stop fooling about. It took me ages to get this hat on right. Jo, do as you're told.

JO: All right.

HELEN: Peter! Don't do that. Give it to me. It's my best one. Put it down.

PETER (*to himself*): No bloody sense of humour.

HELEN: What has she got here? Look at 'em. *Selected Nursery Rhymes*, Hans Andersen's *Fairy Tales, Pinocchio*. Well, you certainly go in for the more advanced types of literature. And what's this? The Holy Bible!

JO: You ought to read it. I think it's good.

HELEN: The extent of my credulity always depends on the extent of my alcoholic intake. Eat, drink and be merry—

JO: And live to regret it.

PETER: God! We've got a founder member of the Lord's Day Observance Society here.

JO: What are you marrying him for?

HELEN: He's got a wallet full of reasons.

JO: Yes. I've just seen 'em too.

HELEN: Can you give us a quid, Peter? I'd better leave her some money. We might decide to have a weekend at Blackpool and she can't live on grass and fresh air.

JO: I won't set eyes on her for a week now. I know her when she's in the mood. What are you going to do about me, Peter? The snotty-nosed daughter? Don't you think I'm a bit young to be left like this on my own while you flit off with my old woman?

PETER: She'll be all right, won't she? At her age.

HELEN: We can't take her with us. We will be, if you'll not take exception to the phrase, on our honeymoon. Unless we change our minds.

PETER: I'm not having her with us.

HELEN: She can stay here then. Come on. I'm hungry.

JO: So am I.

HELEN: There's plenty of food in the kitchen.

JO: You should prepare my meals like a proper mother.

HELEN: Have I ever laid claim to being a proper mother? If you're too idle to cook your own meals you'll just have to cut food out of your diet altogether. That should help you lose a bit of weight, if nothing else.

PETER: She already looks like a bad case of malnutrition.

JO: Have you got your key, Helen? I might not be here when you decide to come back. I'm starting work on Saturday.

HELEN: Oh yes, she's been called to the bar.

PETER: What sort of a bar?

JO: The sort you're always propping up. I'm carrying on the family traditions. Will you give me some money for a new dress, Helen?

HELEN: If you really want to make a good investment, you'll buy a needle and some cotton. Every article of clothing on her back is held together by a safety pin or a knot. If she had an accident in the street I'd be ashamed to claim her.

PETER: Are we going?

JO: Can't I come with you?

HELEN: Shut up! You're going to have him upset. You jealous little cat! Come on, Peter.

PETER: All right, all right, don't pull. Don't get excited. And don't get impatient. Those bloody little street kids have probably pulled the car to pieces by now but we needn't worry about that, need we . . .

HELEN: I told you you'd upset him.

PETER: Upset? I'm not upset. I just want to get to hell out of this black hole of Calcutta.

They leave flat. JO *looks after them for a moment then turns to bed—she lies across it, crying. Music.* BLACK BOY *enters.*

BOY (*calling*): Jo!

She doesn't move.

BOY: Joe!

JO: Coming.

They move towards each other as if dancing to the music. The music goes, the lights change.

JO: Oh! It's you! Come in. Just when I'm feeling and looking a mess.

BOY: What's wrong? You been crying?

JO: No.

BOY: You have. Your eyes are red.

JO: I don't cry. I've got a cold.

BOY: I think you have, too. Yes, you've got a bit of a temperature. Have you been eating?

JO: No.

BOY: You're a fine sight. Where's the kitchen?

JO: Through there. What are you going to do?

BOY: Fix you a cold cure. Where do you keep the milk?

JO: Under the sink. I hate milk.

BOY: I hate dirt. And this is just the dirtiest place I've ever seen. The children round here are filthy.

JO: It's their parents' fault. What are you putting in that milk?

BOY: A pill.

JO: I bet it's an opium pellet. I've heard about men like you.

BOY: There isn't another man like me anywhere. I'm one on his own.

JO: So am I.

BOY: Who was that fancy bit I saw stepping out of here a few minutes ago?

JO: If she was dressed up like Hope Gardens it was my mother.

BOY: And who is the Pirate King?

JO: She's marrying him. Poor devil!

BOY: You'll make a pretty bridesmaid.

JO: Bridesmaid! I'd sooner go to my own funeral.

BOY: You'd better drink this first.

JO: I don't like it.

BOY: Get it down you.

JO: But look, it's got skin on the top.

BOY: Don't whine. I'm not spending the evening with a running-nosed wreck. Finish your milk.

JO: Did you treat your patients in hospital like this?

BOY: Not unless they were difficult. Your mother looks very young, Jo, to have a daughter as old as you.

JO: She can still have children.

BOY: Well, that's an interesting bit of news. Why should I worry if she can have children or not?

JO: Do you fancy her?

BOY: That isn't the sort of question you ask your fiancé.

JO: It doesn't really matter if you do fancy her, anyway, because she's gone. You're too late. You've had your chips.

BOY: I'll be gone soon, too. What then?

JO: My heart's broke.

BOY: You can lie in bed at night and hear my ship passing down the old canal. It's cold in here. No fire?

JO: It doesn't work.

BOY: Come and sit down here. You can keep me warm.

JO: Is it warm where you're going?

BOY: I guess so.

JO: We could do with a bit of sunshine. In this country there are only two seasons, winter and winter. Do you think Helen's beautiful?

BOY: Who's Helen?

JO: My mother. Honestly, you are slow sometimes. Well, do you think she's beautiful?

BOY: Yes.

JO: Am I like her?

BOY: No, you're not at all like her.

JO: Good. I'm glad nobody can see a resemblance between us.

BOY: My ring's still round your neck. Wear it. Your mother isn't here to laugh.

JO: Unfasten it, then.

BOY: Pretty neck you've got.

JO: Glad you like it.

BOY: No! Let me put it on.

JO: Did it cost very much?

BOY: You shouldn't ask questions like that. I got it from Woolworths!

JO: Woolworth's best! I don't care. I'm not proud. It's the thought that counts and I wonder what thought it was in your wicked mind that made you buy it.

BOY: I've got dishonourable intentions.

JO: I'm so glad.

BOY: Are you? (*He embraces her.*)

JO: Stop it.

BOY: Why? Do you object to the "gross clasps of the lascivious Moor"?

JO: Who said that?

BOY: Shakespeare in *Othello*.

JO: Oh! Him. He said everything, didn't he?

BOY: Let me be your Othello and you my Desdemona.

JO: All right.

BOY: "Oh ill-starred wench."

JO: Will you stay here for Christmas?

BOY: If that's what you want.

JO: It's what you want.

BOY: That's right.

JO: Then stay.

BOY: You naughty girl!

JO: I may as well be naughty while I've got the chance. I'll probably never see you again. I know it.

BOY: What makes you say that?

JO: I just know it. That's all. But I don't care. Stay with me now, it's enough, it's all I want, and if you do come back I'll still be here.

BOY: You think I'm only after one thing, don't you?

JO: I know you're only after one thing.

BOY: You're so right. (*He kisses her.*) But I will come back. I love you.

JO: How can you say that?

BOY: Why or how I say these things I don't know, but whatever it means it's true.

JO: Anyway, after this you might not want to come back. After all, I'm not very experienced in these little matters.

BOY: I am.

JO: Anyway, it's a bit daft for us to be talking about you coming back before you've gone. Can I leave that hot milk?

BOY: It would have done you good. Never mind. (*Embraces her.*)

JO: Don't do that.

BOY: Why not?

JO: I like it.

> *Fade out. Music. Wedding bells.* HELEN's *music. She dances on with an assortment of fancy boxes, containing her wedding clothes.*

HELEN: Jo! Jo! Come on. Be sharp now.

> JO *comes on in her pyjamas. She has a heavy cold.*

For God's sake give me a hand. I'll never be ready. What time is
it? Have a look at the church clock.

JO: A quarter past eleven, and the sun's coming out.

HELEN: Oh! Well, happy the bride the sun shines on.

JO: Yeah, and happy the corpse the rain rains on. You're not getting
married in a church, are you?

HELEN: Why, are you coming to throw bricks at us? Of course not. Do
I look all right? Pass me my fur. Oh! My fur! Do you like it?

JO: I bet somebody's missing their cat.

HELEN: It's a wedding present from that young man of mine. He
spends his money like water, you know, penny wise, pound foolish. Oh! I am excited. I feel twenty-one all over again. Oh! You
would have to catch a cold on my wedding day. I was going to
ask you to be my bridesmaid too.

JO: Don't talk daft.

HELEN: Where did you put my shoes? Did you clean 'em? Oh! They're
on my feet. Don't stand there sniffing, Jo. Use a handkerchief.

JO: I haven't got one.

HELEN: Use this, then. What's the matter with you? What are you trying to hide?

JO: Nothing.

HELEN: Don't try to kid me. What is it? Come on, let's see.

JO: It's nothing. Let go of me. You're hurting.

HELEN: What's this?

JO: A ring.

HELEN: I can see it's a ring. Who give it to you?

JO: A friend of mine.

HELEN: Who? Come on. Tell me.

JO: You're hurting me.

HELEN *breaks the cord and gets the ring.*

HELEN: You should have sewn some buttons on your pyjamas if you
didn't want me to see. Who give it you?

JO: My boy friend. He asked me to marry him.

HELEN: Well, you silly little bitch. You mean that lad you've been
knocking about with while we've been away?

JO: Yes.

HELEN: I could choke you.

JO: You've already had a damn good try.

HELEN: You haven't known him five minutes. Has he really asked you to marry him?

JO: Yes.

HELEN: Well, thank God for the divorce courts! I suppose just because I'm getting married you think you should.

JO: Have you got the monopoly?

HELEN: You stupid little devil! What sort of a wife do you think you'd make? You're useless. It takes you all your time to look after yourself. I suppose you think you're in love. Anybody can fall in love, do you know that? But what do you know about the rest of it?

JO: Ask yourself.

HELEN: You know where that ring should be? In the ashcan with everything else. Oh! I could kill her, I could really.

JO: You don't half knock me about. I hope you suffer for it.

HELEN: I've done my share of suffering if I never do any more. Oh Jo, you're only a kid. Why don't you learn from my mistakes? It takes half your life to learn from your own.

JO: You leave me alone. Can I have my ring back, please?

HELEN: What a thing to happen just when I'm going to enjoy myself for a change.

JO: Nobody's stopping you.

HELEN: Yes, and as soon as my back's turned you'll be off with this sailor boy and ruin yourself for good.

JO: I'm already ruined.

HELEN: Yes, it's just the sort of thing you'd do. You make me sick.

JO: You've no need to worry, Helen. He's gone away. He may be back in six months, but there again, he may . . .

HELEN: Look, you're only young. Enjoy your life. Don't get trapped. Marriage can be hell for a kid.

JO: Can I have your hanky back?

HELEN: Where did you put it?

JO: This is your fault too.

HELEN: Everything's my fault. Show me your tongue.

JO: Breathing your 'flu bugs all over me.

HELEN: Yes, and your neck's red where I pulled that string.

JO: Will you get me a drink of water, Helen?

HELEN: No, have a dose of this. (*Offering whisky.*) It'll do you more good. I might as well have one myself while I'm at it, mightn't I?

JO: You've emptied more bottles down your throat in the last few weeks than I would have thought possible. If you don't watch it, you'll end up an old down-and-out boozer knocking back the meths.

HELEN: It'll never come to that. The devil looks after his own, they say.

JO: He certainly takes good care of you. You look marvellous, considering.

HELEN: Considering what?

JO: The wear and tear on your soul.

HELEN: Oh well, that'll have increased its market value, won't it?

JO: Old Nick'll get you in the end.

HELEN: Thank God for that! Heaven must be the hell of a place. Nothing but repentant sinners up there, isn't it? All the pimps, prostitutes and politicians in creation trying to cash in on eternity and their little tin god. Where's my hat?

JO: Where's your husband?

HELEN: Probably drunk with his pals somewhere. He was going down to the house this morning to let some air in. Have you seen a picture of the house? Yes, you have. Do you like it? (*She peers and primps into mirror.*)

JO: It's all right if you like that sort of thing, and I don't.

HELEN: I'll like it in a few years, when it isn't so new and clean. At the moment it's like my face, unblemished! Oh look at that, every line tells a dirty story, hey?

JO: Will you tell me something before you go?

HELEN: Oh! You can read all about that in books.

JO: What was my father like?

HELEN *turns away.*

HELEN: Who?

JO: You heard! My father! What was he like?

HELEN: Oh! Him.

JO: Well, was he so horrible that you can't even tell me about him?

HELEN: He wasn't horrible. He was just a bit stupid, you know. Not very bright.

JO: Be serious, Helen.

HELEN: I am serious.

JO: Are you trying to tell me he was an idiot?

HELEN: He wasn't an idiot, he was just a bit—retarded.

JO: You liar!

HELEN: All right, I'm a liar.

JO: Look at me.

HELEN: Well, am I?

JO: No.

HELEN: Well, now you know.

JO: How could you give me a father like that?

HELEN: I didn't do it on purpose. How was I to know you'd materialize out of a little love affair that lasted five minutes?

JO: You never think. That's your trouble.

HELEN: I know.

JO: Was he like a . . . a real idiot?

HELEN: I've told you once. He was nice though, you know, a nice little feller!

JO: Where is he now, locked up?

HELEN: No, he's dead.

JO: Why?

HELEN: Why? Well, I mean, death's something that comes to us all, and when it does come you haven't usually got time to ask why.

JO: It's hereditary, isn't it?

HELEN: What?

JO: Madness.

HELEN: Sometimes.

JO: Am I mad?

HELEN: Decide for yourself. Oh, Jo, don't be silly. Of course you're not daft. Not more so than anybody else.

JO: Why did you have to tell me that story? Couldn't you have made something up?

HELEN: You asked for the truth and you got it for once. Now be satisfied.

JO: How could you go with a half-wit?

HELEN: He had strange eyes. You've got 'em. Everybody used to laugh at him. Go on, I'll tell you some other time.

JO: Tell me now!

HELEN: Mind my scent!

JO: Please tell me. I want to understand.

HELEN: Do you think I understand? For one night, actually it was the afternoon, I loved him. It was the first time I'd ever really been with a man . . .

JO: You were married.

HELEN: I was married to a Puritan—do you know what I mean?

JO: I think so.

HELEN: And when I met your father I was as pure and unsullied as I fondly, and perhaps mistakenly, imagine you to be. It was the first time and though you can enjoy the second, the third, even the fourth time, there's no time like the first, it's always there. I'm off now. I've got to go and find my husband. Now don't sit here sulking all day.

JO: I was thinking.

HELEN: Well, don't think. It doesn't do you any good. I'll see you when the honeymoon's over. Come on, give us a kiss. You may as well. It's a long time since you kissed me.

JO: Keep it for him.

HELEN: I don't suppose you're sorry to see me go.

JO: I'm not sorry and I'm not glad.

HELEN: You don't know what you do want.

JO: Yes, I do. I've always known what I want.

HELEN: And when it comes your way will you recognize it?

JO: Good luck, Helen.

HELEN: I'll be seeing you. Hey! If he doesn't show up I'll be back.

JO: Good luck, Helen.

Exit HELEN. *"Here comes the Bride" on the cornet.*

Curtain.

ACT TWO

SCENE ONE

As the curtain goes up fairground music can be heard in the distance.
JO and a boy can be heard playing together. When they enter the fla .
they have been playing about with a bunch of brightly coloured
balloons. It is summer now and JO's pregnancy is quite obvious.

JO (*as she falls on a couch in the darkened room*): Let me lie here and
    don't wake me up for a month.

GEOF: Shall I put the light on?

JO: No. Don't you dare put that light on.

GEOF: Did you enjoy the fair?

JO: Loved it. I haven't been to a fair since Christmas.

GEOF: Those roundabouts are still going. Can you hear 'em?

JO: I should be up at half past seven tomorrow morning. I'll never
    make it. I'll just have to be late. Anyway, why should I slave away
    for anybody but me? Haven't you got a home to go to, Geof?

GEOF: Of course.

JO: Well, why are you lurking about? Come in if you want to.

GEOF: Thanks.

JO: There's some biscuits and a flask of coffee in the kitchen only I'm
    too tired to get 'em. Aren't you hungry?

GEOF: No, but you are.

JO: That's right. Go and get 'em for me, Geof.

GEOF: Where's the kitchen?

JO: Straight on.

GEOF: I'll put the light on.

JO: No, you won't! I like this romantic half-light, it just goes with
    this Manchester maisonette!

GEOF: Take four paces forward, turn right, turn left, once round the
    gasworks and straight on up the creek. (*He bangs into a chair or*
    table and cries or swears.)

JO: Put a match on, you daft thing.

GEOF *strikes a match.*

188

GEOF: Ee, this place is enormous, isn't it?

JO: I know. I've got to work all day in a shoe shop and all night in a bar to pay for it. But it's mine. All mine.

GEOF: I can tell it's yours from the state it's in. No wonder you won't put the light on. Where do you keep the cups?

JO: In the sink.

GEOF: Isn't this place a bit big for one, Jo?

JO: Why? Are you thinking of moving in?

GEOF: Not likely.

JO: You are, you know. Put 'em down here. Don't you want any?

GEOF: No.

JO: Well, hand 'em over to me because I'm starved. Has your landlady thrown you out?

GEOF: Don't be silly.

JO: I've been wondering why you were so anxious to see me home. You didn't fancy sleeping under the arches, did you? Why did your landlady throw you out, Geoffrey? I'll let you stay here if you tell me.

GEOF: I was behind with the rent.

JO: That's a lie for a start.

GEOF: I don't tell lies.

JO: Come on, let's have some truth. Why did she throw you out?

GEOF: I've told you why.

JO (*switches on light*): Come on, the truth. Who did she find you with? Your girl friend? It wasn't a man, was it?

GEOF: Don't be daft.

JO: Look, I've got a nice comfortable couch, I've even got some sheets. You can stay here if you'll tell me what you do. Go on, I've always wanted to know about people like you.

GEOF: Go to hell.

JO: I won't snigger, honest I won't. Tell me some of it, go on. I bet you never told a woman before.

GEOF: I don't go in for sensational confessions.

JO: I want to know what you do. I want to know why you do it. Tell me or get out.

GEOF: Right! (*He goes to the door.*)

JO: Geof, don't go. Don't go, Geof! I'm sorry. Please stay.

GEOF: Don't touch me.

JO: I didn't mean to hurt your feelings.

GEOF: I can't stand women at times. Let go of me.

JO: Come on, Geof. I don't care what you do.

GEOF: Thank you. May I go now, please?

JO: Please stay here Geof. I'll get those sheets and blankets.

GEOF: I can't stand people who laugh at other people. They'd get a bigger laugh if they laughed at themselves.

JO: Please stay, Geof. (*She goes off for the sheets and blankets. He finds her book of drawings on the table and glances through them.*)

GEOF: Are these yours?

JO: No, why? Put them down, Geof.

GEOF: Obviously they are. They're exactly like you.

JO: How do you mean?

GEOF: Well, there's no design, rhythm or purpose.

JO: Hey?

GEOF: Where's the design in that? It's all messy, isn't it? Charcoal. I don't like it.

JO: I do.

GEOF: What made you choose that for a subject?

JO: I like . . .

GEOF: They're all sentimental.

JO: Me? Sentimental?

GEOF: No. No. I don't like 'em.

JO: Do you really think they're sentimental?

GEOF: Well, look. I mean . . .

JO: I'm sorry you don't like them.

GEOF: Why don't you go to a decent school?

JO: I've never been to any school.

GEOF: You want taking in hand.

JO: No, thanks.

GEOF: Has anybody ever tried?

JO: What?

GEOF: Taking you in hand.

JO: Yes.

GEOF: What happened to him?

JO: He came in with Christmas and went out with the New Year.

GEOF: Did you like him?

JO: He was all right . . .

GEOF: Did you love him?

JO: I don't know much about love. I've never been too familiar with it. I suppose I must have loved him. They say love creates. And

I'm certainly creating at the moment. I'm going to have a baby.

GEOF: I thought so. You're in a bit of a mess, aren't you?

JO: I don't care.

GEOF: You can get rid of babies before they're born, you know.

JO: I know, but I think that's terrible.

GEOF: When's it due?

JO: Reckon it up from Christmas.

GEOF: About September.

JO: Yes.

GEOF: What are you going to do? You can't be on your own.

JO: There's plenty of time.

GEOF: Got any money?

JO: Only my wages and they don't last long. By the time I've bought all I need, stockings and make-up and things, I've got nothing left.

GEOF: You can do without make-up.

JO: I can't. I look like a ghost without it.

GEOF: At your age?

JO: What's age got to do with it? Anyway, I'm not working for much longer. I'm not having everybody staring at me.

GEOF: How are you going to manage then?

JO: There's no need for you to worry about it.

GEOF: Somebody's got to. Anyway, I like you.

JO: I like you too.

GEOF: Your mother should know.

JO: Why?

GEOF: Well, she's your mother. Do you know her address?

JO: No. She was supposed to be marrying some man. They live in a big, white house somewhere.

GEOF: What sort of a woman is she?

JO: She's all sorts of woman. But she's got plenty of money.

GEOF: That's all you need to be interested in. You've got to buy all sorts of things for the baby. Clothes, a cot and a pram. Here, that teddy bear we won tonight'll come in handy, won't it? I can make things too. I'll help . . .

JO: Shut up! I'm not planning big plans for this baby, or dreaming big dreams. You know what happens when you do things like that. The baby'll be born dead or daft!

GEOF: You're feeling a bit depressed, Jo.

JO: I'm feeling nothing.

GEOF: You'll be your usual self soon.

JO: And what is my usual self? My usual self is a very unusual self, Geoffrey Ingram, and don't forget it. I'm an extraordinary person. There's only one of me like there's only one of you.

GEOF: We're unique!

JO: Young.

GEOF: Unrivalled!

JO: Smashing!

GEOF: We're bloody marvellous!

JO: Hey! Do you like beer?

GEOF: Yes.

JO: Whisky.

GEOF: Yes.

JO: Gin?

GEOF: Yes. Have you got some?

JO: No, but if I had I'd give it all to you. I'd give everything I had to you. Here, have a biscuit. You'll like these. They taste like dog food.

GEOF: Spratts!

JO: You look like a spratt. Jack Spratt, who'd eat no fat, his wife would eat no lean and so between them both, you see, they licked the platter clean. Did you enjoy that dramatic recitation?

GEOF: Very moving.

JO: You say one.

GEOF:
> There was a young man of Thessaly,
> And he was wondrous wise.
> He jumped into a quickset hedge
> And scratched out both his eyes.
> And when he saw his eyes were out,
> With all his might and main
> He jumped into another hedge
> And scratched them in again.

JO: I like that. Do you know any more?

GEOF:
> As I was going up Pippin Hill,
> Pippin Hill was dirty.
> And there I met a pretty miss
> And she dropped me a curtsy.
> Little miss, pretty miss,
> Blessings light upon you.

> If I had half a crown a day
> I'd gladly spend it on you.

JO: Would you?

GEOF: I would.

JO: Silly things nursery rhymes when you weigh them up.

GEOF: I like them. Do you want a cigarette?

JO: How many have you got left?

GEOF: I've got enough for one each.

JO: No, you keep 'em. They don't bother me really. I used to smoke just to annoy my mother. What's that?

GEOF: A free gift coupon.

JO: Everything you buy lately has a free gift coupon in it. It's coming to something when they have to bribe the public to buy their stuff. What's this one for?

GEOF: There's a whole list of things to send for if you have enough coupons. Hee, there's even a car, smoke forty thousand cigarettes a day for the next ten thousand years and you'll get a Lagonda

JO: What's that?

GEOF: A car.

JO: A nice car?

GEOF: A wonderful car.

JO: I'll buy you one for Christmas. If you ask me nice I'll buy you two.

GEOF: Thanks.

JO: Oh! I'm tired. This couch isn't going to be very comfortable, is it?

GEOF: It'll do.

JO: What are you going to sleep in?

GEOF: My shirt!

JO: I'm that tired! I haven't the energy to get myself to bed. You won't sleep very well on this couch, Geof.

GEOF: It's all right. Beggars can't be choosers.

JO: We're both beggars. A couple of degenerates.

GEOF: The devil's own!

JO (*she goes to bed.* GEOF *starts to undress*): Hey! You'd better turn that light out, or I might be after you. (*He turns the light out and then gets into bed. She begins to sing the song "Black Boy" as she lies on her bed.*)

> Black boy, black boy, don't you lie to me.
> Where did you stay last night?
> In the pines, in the pines where the sun never shines,
> I shivered the whole night through.

GEOF: Jo!

JO: Yes.

GEOF: What was that boy like?

JO: Which boy?

GEOF: You know.

JO: Oh! Him. He wasn't a bit like you. He could sing and dance and he was as black as coal.

GEOF: A black boy?

JO: From darkest Africa! A Prince.

GEOF: A what?

JO: A Prince, son of a chieftain.

GEOF: I'll bet he was too.

JO: Prince Ossini!

GEOF: What was he doing here?

JO: He was a male nurse in the Navy.

GEOF: Do you wish he was still here?

JO: Not really. I think I've had enough. I'm sick of love. That's why I'm letting you stay here. You won't start anything.

GEOF: No, I don't suppose I will.

JO: You'd better not. I hate love.

GEOF: Do you, Jo?

JO: Yes, I do.

GEOF: Good night.

JO: Good night.

GEOF: You needn't lock the bedroom door.

JO: I'm in bed. Geoffrey! Geoffrey!

GEOF: What do you want?

JO: What time have you got to be up in the morning?

GEOF: I don't go to school tomorrow. I'll stay here and clear this place up a bit. And make you a proper meal. Now go to sleep, hey?

JO: Geoffrey!

GEOF: What's wrong now?

JO (*laughing*): You're just like a big sister to me.

> *Music to black out. Then quick as lights go up. Waking, GEOF dances and goes off with bedclothes. JO dances off. GEOF dances in with props for the next scene, which in reality would be a month or two later. GEOF is cutting out a baby's gown. JO wanders about the room.*

JO: God! It's hot.

GEOF: I know it's hot.

JO: I'm so restless.

GEOF: Oh, stop prowling about.

JO: This place stinks. (*Goes over to the door. Children are heard singing in the street.*) That river, it's the colour of lead. Look at that washing, it's dirty, and look at those filthy children.

GEOF: It's not their fault.

JO: It's their parents' fault. There's a little boy over there and his hair, honestly, it's walking away. And his ears. Oh! He's a real mess! He never goes to school. He just sits on that front doorstep all day. I think he's a bit deficient.

The children's voices die away. A tugboat hoots.

His mother ought not to be allowed.

GEOF: Who?

JO: His mother. Think of all the harm she does, having children.

GEOF: Sit down and read a book, Jo.

JO: I can't.

GEOF: Be quiet then. You're getting on my nerves.

Suddenly she yells and whirls across the room.

JO: Wheee! Come on rain. Come on storm. It kicked me, Geof. It kicked me!

GEOF: What?

JO: It kicked me.

GEOF *runs to her and puts his head on her belly.*

GEOF: Will it do it again?

JO: It shows it's alive anyway. Come on, baby, let's see what big sister's making for us.

GEOF: Put it down.

JO: What a pretty little dress.

GEOF: It's got to wear something. You can't just wrap it up in a bundle of newspaper.

JO: And dump it on a doorstep. How did Geoffrey find out the measurements?

GEOF: Babies are born to the same size more or less.

JO: Oh, no, they're not. Some are thin scrappy things and others are huge and covered in rolls of fat.

GEOF: Shut up, Jo, it sounds revolting.

JO: They are revolting. I hate babies.

GEOF: I thought you'd change. Motherhood is supposed to come natural to women.

JO: It comes natural to you, Geoffrey Ingram. You'd make somebody a wonderful wife. What were you talking about to that old mare downstairs?

GEOF: I was giving her the rent. I got my grant yesterday.

JO: You're as thick as thieves, you two.

GEOF: She's going to make the baby a cradle.

JO: What?

GEOF: You know, she makes wicker baskets.

JO: A wicker basket!

GEOF: It's the best we can do, unless you want to go down to the river plaiting reeds.

JO: I don't want her poking her nose into my affairs.

GEOF: You're glad enough to have me dancing attendance on you.

JO: Only because I thought you'd leave me alone. Why don't you leave me alone? (*She cries and flings herself down on the couch.*) I feel like throwing myself in the river.

GEOF: I wouldn't do that. It's full of rubbish.

JO: Well that's all I am, isn't it?

GEOF: Stop pitying yourself.

JO: Don't jump down my throat.

GEOF: How much longer is this going on?

JO: What?

GEOF: Your present performance.

JO: Nobody asked you to stay here. You moved in on me, remember, remember? If you don't like it you can get out, can't you? But you wouldn't do that, would you, Geoffrey? You've no confidence in yourself, have you? You're afraid the girls might laugh . . .

GEOF: Read that book and shut up. When the baby comes, if it ever does, you won't know one end of it from the other.

JO: *Looking After Baby.* Isn't that nice? Three months, exercises, constipation. Four months, relaxation. It even tells you how to wash nappies. How lovely. There's a little job for you, Geoffrey.

GEOF: Drink that. (*He hands her a glass of milk.*)

JO (*flirting with him*): Does it tell you how to feed babies, Geoffrey?

GEOF: Even you know that.

JO: I know about that way, breast feeding, but I'm not having a little animal nibbling away at me, it's cannibalistic. Like being eaten alive.

GEOF: Stop trying to be inhuman. It doesn't suit you.

JO: I mean it. I hate motherhood.

GEOF: Well, whether you hate it or not you've got it coming to you so you might as well make a good job of it.

JO: I've got toothache.

GEOF: I've got bloody heartache!

JO: I think you'd like everybody to think this baby's yours, wouldn't you, Geoffrey?

GEOF: Not likely.

JO: After all, you don't show much sign of coming fatherhood, do you? You like babies, don't you, Geof?

GEOF: Yes, I do.

JO (*coquettes with him*): Geoffrey, have you got any of that toothache cure?

He moves away.

Geoffrey, have you got any of that toothache cure?

GEOF: The only cure for the toothache is a visit to the dentist. Drink your milk.

JO: I hate milk. (*She looks out of the window.*) I never thought I'd still be here in the summer. (*She puts her arms round* GEOF *playfully.*) Would you like to be the father of my baby, Geoffrey?

GEOF: Yes, I would.

JO *stands in the doorway. The children can be heard singing again.*

What time is it?

JO: Half-past four by the church clock. Why do you stay here, Geof?

GEOF: Someone's got to look after you. You can't look after yourself.

JO: I think there's going to be a storm. Look at that sky. It's nearly black. And you can hear the kids playing, right over there on the croft.

A silence in the room: we hear the children singing.

GEOF: What would you say if I started something?

JO: Eh!

GEOF: I said what would you say if I started something?

JO: In my condition, I'd probably faint.

GEOF: No, I mean after.

JO: I don't want you.

GEOF: Am I repulsive to you?

JO: You're nothing to me. I'm everything to myself.

GEOF: No, you're not. You're going to need me after.

JO: I won't be here after.

GEOF: Do you still think he might come back?

JO: I've forgotten him.

She turns towards him, he to her.

GEOF: You do need me, Jo, don't you?

JO: Let go of me. You're squeezing my arm.

GEOF: I've never kissed a girl.

JO: That's your fault.

GEOF: Let me kiss you.

JO: Let go of me. Leave me alone.

She struggles but he kisses her.

GEOF: How was that for first time?

JO: Practise on somebody else.

GEOF: I didn't mean to hurt you.

JO: Look Geof, I like you, I like you very much, but I don't enjoy all this panting and grunting . . .

GEOF: Marry me, Jo.

JO: Don't breathe all over me like that, you sound like a horse. I'm not marrying anybody.

GEOF: I wouldn't ask you to do anything you didn't want to do.

JO: Yes, you would.

GEOF: Jo, I don't mind that you're having somebody else's baby. What you've done, you've done. What I've done, I've done.

JO: I like you, Geof, but I don't want to marry you.

GEOF: Oh, all right. Anyway, I don't suppose I could live up to that black beast of a prince of yours. I bet you didn't struggle when he made love to you.

JO: It might have been better if I had.

GEOF (*he gives her a bar of chocolate*): Have some chocolate.

JO: Thanks. Do you want some?

GEOF: No.

JO: Go on.

GEOF: I said no.

JO: You like strawberry cream.

GEOF: I don't want any, Jo. I've made my mind up.

JO: Don't be daft, have some chocolate.

GEOF: No ∴.

She gives a piece of chocolate to him just the same.

JO: I think it would be best if you left this place, Geof. I don't think it's doing you any good being here with me all the time.

GEOF: I know that, but I couldn't go away now.

JO: You'll have to go some time. We can't stay together like this for ever.

GEOF: I'd sooner be dead than away from you.

JO: You say that as if you mean it.

GEOF: I do mean it.

JO: Why?

GEOF: Before I met you I didn't care one way or the other—I didn't care whether I lived or died. But now . . .

JO: I think I'll go and lie down. (*She goes to bed and lies across it.*)

GEOF: There's no need for me to go, Jo. You said yourself you didn't want anybody else here and I'm only interested in you. We needn't split up need we, Jo?

JO: I don't suppose so.

Music. Enter HELEN.

HELEN: Jo! Your beloved old lady's arrived. Well, where is she, Romeo?

GEOF: Don't tell her I came for you.

HELEN: What? Don't mumble.

GEOF: I said don't tell her I came for you.

HELEN: All right, all right. This place hasn't changed much, has it?

Still the same old miserable hole. Well, where's the lady in question?

GEOF: In there.

HELEN: What, lazing in bed, as usual? Come on, get up; plenty of girls in your condition have to go out to work and take care of a family. Come on, get up.

JO: What blew you in?

HELEN: Let's have a look at you.

JO: Who told you about me?

HELEN: Nobody.

JO: How did you get to know then?

HELEN: Come on, aren't you going to introduce me to your boy friend? Who is he?

JO: My boy friend. Oh, it's all right, we're so decent we're almost dead I said who told you about me?

HELEN: Does it matter?

JO: I told you to keep out of my affairs, Geoffrey. I'm not having anybody running my life for me. What do you think you're running? A "Back to Mother" movement?

GEOF: Your mother has a right to know.

JO: She's got no rights where I'm concerned.

HELEN: Oh, leave him alone. You're living off him, by all accounts.

JO: Who've you been talking to? That old hag downstairs?

HELEN: I didn't need to talk to her. The whole district knows what's been going on here.

JO: And what has been going on?

HELEN: I suppose you think you can hide yourself away in this chicken run, don't you? Well, you can't. Everybody knows.

GEOF: She won't go out anywhere, not even for a walk and a bit or fresh air. That's why I came to you.

HELEN: And what do you think I can do about it? In any case, bearing a child doesn't place one under an obligation to it.

GEOF: I should have thought it did.

HELEN: Well, you've got another think coming. If she won't take care of herself that's her lookout. And don't stand there looking as if it's my fault.

GEOF: It's your grandchild.

HELEN: Oh, shut up, you put years on me. Anyway, I'm having nothing to do with it. She's more than I can cope with, always has been.

GEOF: That's obvious.

HELEN: And what's your part in this little Victorian melodrama? Nursemaid?

JO: Serves you right for bringing her here, Geof.

HELEN: It's a funny-looking set-up to me.

JO: It's our business.

HELEN: Then don't bring me into it. Where's the loving father? Distinguished by his absence, I suppose.

JO: That's right.

HELEN (*to* GEOF): Did she hear any more of him?

JO: No, she didn't.

HELEN: When I'm talking to the organ grinder I don't expect the monkey to answer.

JO: I could get him back tomorrow if I wanted to.

HELEN: Well, that's nice to know. He certainly left you a nice Christmas box. It did happen at Christmas, I suppose? When the cat's away.

GEOF: You've been away a long time.

HELEN: Oh, you shut up. Sling your hook!

JO: Will you keep out of this, Geoffrey?

HELEN: Well, come on, let's have a look at you.

JO *turns away.*

What's up? We're all made the same, aren't we?

JO: Yes we are.

HELEN: Well then. Can you cut the bread on it yet?

JO *turns.*

Yes, you're carrying it a bit high, aren't you? Are you going to the clinic regularly? Is she working?

GEOF: No, I told you, she doesn't like people looking at her.

HELEN: Do you think people have got nothing better to do than look at you?

JO: Leave me alone.

HELEN: She'd be better off working than living off you like a little bloodsucker.

GEOF: She doesn't live off me.

JO: No, we share everything, see! We're communists too.

HELEN: That's his influence I suppose.

JO: Get out of here. I won't go out if I don't want to. It's nothing to do with you. Get back to your fancy man or your husband, or whatever you like to call him.

HELEN *begins to chase her.*

Aren't you afraid he'll run off and leave you if you let him out of your sight?

HELEN: I'll give you such a bloody good hiding in a minute, if you're not careful. That's what you've gone short of!

JO: Don't show yourself up for what you are!

HELEN: You couldn't wait, could you? Now look at the mess you've landed yourself in.

JO: I'll get out of it, without your help.

HELEN: You had to throw yourself at the first man you met, didn't you?

JO: Yes, I did, that's right.

HELEN: You're man mad.

JO: I'm like you.

HELEN: You know what they're calling you round here? A silly little whore!

JO: Well, they all know where I get it from too.

HELEN: Let me get hold of her! I'll knock her bloody head round!

JO: You should have been locked up years ago, with my father.

HELEN: Let me get hold of her!

GEOF: Please, Jo, Helen, Jo, please!

HELEN: I should have got rid of you before you were born.

JO: I wish you had done. You did with plenty of others, I know.

HELEN: I'll kill her. I'll knock the living daylights out of her.

GEOF: Helen, stop it, you will kill her!

JO: If you don't get out of here I'll . . . jump out of the window.

There is a sudden lull.

GEOF (*yelling*): Will you stop shouting, you two?

HELEN: We enjoy it.

GEOF: Helen!

HELEN: Now you're going to listen to a few home truths, my girl.

JO: We've had enough home truths!

HELEN: All right, you thought you knew it all before, didn't you? But

you came a cropper. Now it's "poor little Josephine, the tragedy
queen, hasn't life been hard on her." Well, you fell down, you get
up . . . nobody else is going to carry you about. Oh, I know
you've got this pansified little freak to lean on, but what good
will that do you?

JO: Leave Geof out of it!

HELEN: Have you got your breath back? Because there's some more
I've got to get off my chest first.

JO: You don't half like the sound of your own voice.

GEOF: If I'd known you were going to bully her like this I'd never
have asked you to come here.

HELEN: You can clear off! Take your simpering little face out of it!

JO: Yes, buzz off, Geof! Well, who brought her here? I told you what
sort of a woman she was. Go and . . . go and make a cup of tea.

He goes.

HELEN: Look at your arms. They're like a couple of stalks! You look
like a ghost warmed up. And who gave you that haircut, him?
Don't sit there sulking.

JO: I thought it was the tea break.

HELEN: I didn't come here to quarrel.

JO: No?

HELEN: I brought you some money.

JO: You know what you can do with that.

HELEN: All right! You've said your piece. Money doesn't grow on
trees. I'll leave it on the table. Have you been collecting your
maternity benefit or . . .

JO: Or are you too idle to walk down to the post office? Don't be daft!
I'm not entitled to it. I haven't been earning long enough.

HELEN: You've no need to go short of anything.

JO: It's taken you a long time to come round to this, hasn't it?

HELEN: What?

JO: The famous mother-love act.

HELEN: I haven't been able to sleep for thinking about you since he
came round to our house.

JO: And your sleep mustn't be disturbed at any cost.

HELEN: There'll be money in the post for you every week from now
on.

JO: Until you forget.

HELEN: I don't forget things; it's just that I can't remember anything. I'm going to see you through this whether you like it or not. After all I am . . .

JO: After all you are my mother! You're a bit late remembering that, aren't you? You walked through that door with that man and didn't give me a second thought.

HELEN: Why didn't you tell me?

JO: You should have known. You're nothing to me.

PETER *appears.*

PETER: What the hell's going on? Do you expect me to wait in the filthy street all night?

HELEN: I told you to stay outside.

PETER: Don't point your bloody finger at me.

HELEN: I said I'd only be a few minutes and I've only been a few minutes. Now come on, outside!

PETER: Ah! The erring daughter. There she is. (*Sings.*) "Little Josephine, you're a big girl now." Where d'you keep the whisky?

HELEN: They haven't got any. Now, come on.

PETER (*seeing* GEOF): What's this, the father? Oh Christ, no!

GEOF: Who's he?

HELEN: President of the local Temperance Society!

PETER (*singing*): "Who's got a bun in the oven? Who's got a cake in the stove?"

HELEN: Leave her alone.

PETER: Oh, go to hell!

JO: I've got nothing to say . . .

PETER: Go on, have your blasted family reunion, don't mind me! (*Notices* GEOF *again.*) Who's this? Oh, of course! Where are the drinks, Lana? (*He falls into the kitchen, singing.*) "Getting to know you, getting to know all about you . . ."

HELEN: Jo, come on . . .

There is a loud crash in the kitchen.

And the light of the world shone upon him.

PETER *enters.*

PETER: Cheer up, everybody. I am back. Who's the lily? Look at Helen, well, if she doesn't look like a bloody unrestored oil painting. What's the matter everybody? Look at the sour-faced old bitch! Well, are you coming for a few drinks or aren't you?

HELEN: The pubs aren't open yet.

JO: Do you mind getting out of here?

PETER: Shut your mouth, bubble belly! Before I shut it for you. Hey! (*To* GEOF.), Mary, come here. Did I ever tell you about the chappie who married his mother by mistake?

JO: I said get him out of here, Helen. His breath smells.

HELEN: I can't carry him out, can I?

PETER: His name was Oedipus, he was a Greek I think. Well, the old bag turned out to be his mother . . .

HELEN: Shut up, Peter, for God's sake!

PETER: So he scratched out both his eyes.

HELEN: Cut the dirty stories!

PETER: But I only scratched out one of mine. Well, are you coming or not?

HELEN: I'm not.

PETER: Well, is anybody coming for a few drinks? You staying with the ladies, Jezebel?

GEOF: Listen, mister, this is my friend's flat . . .

PETER: And what do you do, Cuddles? Don't worry, I know this district. Look at Helen, isn't she a game old bird? Worn out on the beat but she's still got a few good strokes left.

HELEN: Get out of here, you drunken sot.

PETER: Now I told you to moderate your language. What's this? Giving my money away again?

HELEN: Take your bloody money and get out!

PETER: Thank you.

HELEN: You dirty bastard!

PETER: You should have heard her the other night. You know what happened? Her wandering boy returned. He hadn't been home for two weeks and do you know why? He picked up a couple of grapefruit on a thirty-two bust, rich, young and juicy . . . hey! Where's the smallest room?

GEOF: This way.

PETER: And she went off the deep end. (*Sings as he goes. Another crash offstage.*)

HELEN (*to* GEOF): You'd better go with him or Lord knows where he'll end up.

GEOF: I hope the landlady hasn't heard him.

HELEN: Cigarette?

JO: No. Yes, I will. I'll keep it for Geof.

HELEN: You'd better have the whole bloody packet if you're in such a state.

JO: Well, he couldn't hold it any more, could he?

HELEN: No one could hold that much.

JO: How long has he been like this?

HELEN: What does that boy friend of yours do for a living?

JO: He's an art student. I suppose that's what's been keeping you occupied?

HELEN: An art student. I might have known. Does he live here?

JO: Why should I answer your questions? You never answer any of mine.

HELEN: Look at you! Why don't you take a bit of pride in yourself? Grow your hair properly?

JO: Look at you. Look what your pride in yourself has done for you.

HELEN: Come and stay with me, Jo; there's a nice room and plenty of food.

JO: No, thanks.

HELEN: You prefer to stay in this hole with that pansified little freak?

GEOF: Shall I go?

HELEN: I didn't know you'd come.

JO: Would you go and live with her if you were me, Geof?

GEOF: No, I don't think I would.

JO: Neither would anybody in their right mind.

GEOF: She always said you were a pretty rotten sort of woman. I thought she was exaggerating.

HELEN: Look, can't you get it into your stupid head that I'm offering you a decent home?

PETER *enters, more sober, more unpleasant.*

PETER: Bloody cockroaches are playing leapfrog in there.

HELEN: Look, I'll tell you again, in front of him, my home is yours.

PETER: Ah! Shut up!

HELEN: I'll take care of you and see you through it.

JO: The time to have taken care of me was years ago, when I couldn't take care of myself.

HELEN: All right, but we're talking about here and now. When I really set out to take care of somebody I usually do the job properly.

JO: So I see.

PETER: I'm not having that bloody slut at our place. I'll tell you that for nothing.

HELEN: Take no notice. The house is half mine.

PETER: Like hell it is. I could throw you out tomorrow.

JO: I don't think . . .

PETER: And don't bring that little fruitcake parcel either! (*Mumbles.*) I can't stand the sight of him. Can't stand 'em at any price.

HELEN: Oh, keep out of it. Jo, I can't bear to think of you sitting here in this dump!

PETER: Neither can I. Now let's get going.

HELEN: The whole district's rotten, it's not fit to live in.

PETER: Let's go before we grow old sitting here.

HELEN: Shut up, the pubs will be open in ten minutes.

PETER: You're wrong there. (*Looking at his watch.*) They're open now. What time do you make it?

GEOF: There's one thing about this district, the people in it aren't rotten. Anyway, I think she's happier here with me than in that dazzling white house you're supposed to be so'. . .

PETER: Dazzling bunch of bul . . . lot of bloody outsiders, no class at all. What's the time anyway?

HELEN (*to* GEOF): You shut up! I know what she needs if she's not going to finish up in a box.

PETER: What's the time by your watch, sonny?

GEOF: It's never been right since it last went wrong.

PETER: Neither have I. How long are we going to sit around in this room? I don't like the smell of unwashed bodies, woman. I dragged you out of the gutter once. If you want to go back there it's all the same to me. I'm not having this shower at any price. I'm telling you for the last time because I'm getting out of it. Stay if you want, it's all the same to me; it's your own bloody level. Well, are you coming or not?

HELEN: I'm not.

PETER: I said are you coming?

HELEN: And I said I'm not.

PETER: Well, you can just go and take a flying flip out of the window. (*He goes.*)

HELEN: I'll . . . I'll . . . would you sooner I stayed here with you?

JO: No, thanks.

PETER: Helen . . . (*Calling.*) . . . come on!

HELEN: I'll send you some money.

JO: Keep it. You might need it.

PETER: Helen!

HELEN: Go to . . .

PETER: Are you coming?

HELEN (*yelling*): Yes. (*To* GEOF.) See that she goes to the clinic regularly and be sure she gets enough to eat.

GEOF: She has been doing that.

HELEN: I'll see you around. (*She goes.*)

JO: Well, here endeth the third lesson.

GEOF: At least she left you some money. We can get some . . .

JO: He took it back. I got you a cigarette though, love.

GEOF: Oh, smashing! I was out.

Music. They dance together. Fade out.

SCENE TWO

GEOFFREY *dances in with a mop and bucket and begins to clean the place.* JO *dances back and sits on the table reading. She is wearing a long white housecoat and again, in reality, months have passed between this and the previous scene. Music out.*

JO: "Ninth month, everything should now be in readiness for the little stranger." Where did you find this book, Geoffrey? It reads like *Little Women*.

GEOF: I got it for fourpence off a book barrow.

JO: You've got terrible tendencies, haven't you?

GEOF: How do you mean?

JO: You like everything to be just that little bit out of date, don't you? Clothes, books, women.

GEOF: You've got no choice, have you? I mean you all start by living in the past. Well look, it's all around you, isn't it?

JO: I wonder if we ever catch up with ourselves?

GEOF: I don't know.

JO: Now you're a real Edwardian, aren't you?

GEOF: What's that?

JO: A proper Ted! And me, I'm contemporary.

GEOF: God help us!

JO: I really am, aren't I? I really do live at the same time as myself, don't I?

GEOF: Do you mind? I've just done all that. Oh come on! Get off!

He pushes her with the mop.

JO: Hey, hey!

GEOF: Women!

JO: You haven't noticed my home dressmaking.

GEOF: No. I've been trying to ignore it. What is it?

JO: A housecoat.

GEOF: It looks more like a badly tailored shroud.

JO: What the well-dressed expectant mother is wearing this year. I feel wonderful. Aren't I enormous?

GEOF: You're clever, aren't you?

JO: What's in the oven, Geoffrey?

GEOF: You what?

JO: What's cooking?

GEOF: A cake.

JO: Mm, you're wonderful, aren't you?

GEOF: Pretty good.

JO: I know, you make everything work. The stove goes, now we eat. You've reformed me, some of the time at any rate.

GEOFFREY *shifts the sofa. There is old rubbish and dirt under it.*

GEOF: Oh, Jo!

JO: I wondered where that had got to.

GEOF: Now you know. It's disgusting, it really is.

JO: Oh Geof, the bulbs I brought with me!

GEOF: Haven't you shifted the sofa since then?

JO: They never grew.

GEOF: No, I'm not surprised.

JO: They're dead. It makes you think, doesn't it?

GEOF: What does?

JO: You know, some people like to take out an insurance policy, don't they?

GEOF: I'm a bit young for you to take out one on me.

JO: No. You know, they like to pray to the Almighty just in case he turns out to exist when they snuff it.

GEOF (*brushing under the sofa*): Well, I never think about it. You come, you go. It's simple.

JO: It's not, it's chaotic—a bit of love, a bit of lust and there you are. We don't ask for life, we have it thrust upon us.

GEOF: What's frightened you? Have you been reading the newspapers?

JO: No, I never do. Hold my hand, Geof.

GEOF: Do you mind? Halfway through this?

JO: Hold my hand.

> *He does.*

GEOF: Hey, Jo. Come on, silly thing, it's all right. Come on there.

JO: You've got nice hands, hard. You know I used to try and hold my mother's hands, but she always used to pull them away from me. So silly really. She had so much love for everyone else, but none for me.

GEOF: If you don't watch it, you'll turn out exactly like her.

JO: I'm not like her at all.

GEOF: In some ways you are already, you know.

> *She pushes his hand away.*

Can I go now?

JO: Yes.

GEOF: Thank you very much! (*He is pushing the couch back into position.*)

JO: "And he took up his bed and walked." You can stay here if you tell me what you do. Do you remember, Geoffrey? I used to think you were such an interesting, immoral character before I knew you. I thought you were like that . . . for one thing.

> GEOFFREY *chases her with the mop all through this speech.*

You're just like an old woman really. You just unfold your bed, kiss me good night and sing me to sleep. Hey, what's the matter? Don't you like living here with me?

GEOF: It has its lighter moments, but on the whole it's a pretty trying prospect.

JO: Why do you wear black shirts? They make you look like a spiv.

GEOF: They do, Jo, but I can't be too particular. Good clothes cost money.

JO: Well, I weigh in with my share, don't I? That's a nice little job you got me, retouching those bloody photographs. What was it supposed to do, prove I was the artistic type? Of course we can't all be art students, going to our expensive art schools, nursing our little creative genius.

GEOF: Must you shout?

JO: I'm Irish.

GEOF: Never mind, it's not your fault.

JO (*laughing*): I like you.

GEOF: Do you like me more than you don't like me or don't you like me more than you do?

JO: Now you're being Irish.

GEOF: Fine Irishwoman you are. Where did your ancestors fall, in the Battle of Salford Town Hall?

JO: My mother's father was Irish.

GEOF: You'll find any excuse.

JO: And she had me by an Irishman—the village idiot, from what I can make out.

GEOF: What do you mean?

JO: A frolic in a hay loft one afternoon. You see her husband thought sex was dirty, and only used the bed for sleeping in. So she took to herself an idiot. She said he'd got eyes like me.

GEOF: Are you making it up?

JO: He lived in a twilight land, my daddy. The land of the daft.

GEOF: Did she tell you all this?

JO: Yes.

GEOF: I'm not surprised. It sounds like Ibsen's *Ghosts*. I don't know where Helen gets them from, I don't really.

JO: I had to drag it out of her. She didn't want to tell me.

GEOF: That doesn't mean to say it's the truth. Do people ever tell the truth about themselves?

JO: Why should she want to spin me a yarn like that?

GEOF: She likes to make an effect.

JO: Like me?

GEOF: You said it. You only have to let your hair grow for a week for Helen to think you're a cretin.

JO: What?

GEOF: I said you've only got to let your hair grow for a week for Helen to think you're a cretin. She always looks at me as though I should be put away for treatment, doesn't she?

JO: Yes.

GEOF: I know, you don't have to tell me! Have you been worrying about that all these months?

JO: No.

GEOF: You have.

JO: I haven't.

GEOF: Well, I didn't think you could be so daft. Can you see Helen going out with a real loony!

JO: Well, now you put it like that, no, I can't!

GEOF: No, neither can—I don't know. Anyway, who knows who are the fools and the wise men in this world?

JO: I wouldn't be surprised if all the sane ones weren't in the bin.

GEOF: You're probably right. Anyway everyone knows you're as cracked as an old bedbug.

JO (*laughing*): Thanks, Geof. You know, you're a cure.

GEOF: I used to be a patrol leader in the Boy Scouts.

JO: So long as you weren't Scoutmaster! You know, I wish she was here all the same.

GEOF: Why? You'd only quarrel. You know you always say you hate the sight of her.

JO: I do.

GEOF: Well then.

JO: She must know my time has almost come. When do your exams finish?

GEOF: On Thursday.

JO: I wonder which day it'll be? Put your arms round me, Geof. I don't want you to be worried while your exams are on.

GEOF: Then you shouldn't have asked me to put my arms round you, should you?

JO: Ah well, it doesn't matter if you fail. In this country the more you know the less you earn.

GEOF: Yes, you're probably right. I've got something for you. Oh Jo, I'm daft at times.

JO: I know that. I was wondering what it was.

GEOF (*from his pack he takes a life-sized doll*): There—isn't it nice? I thought you could practise a few holds on it over the weekend. You've got to be able to establish your superiority over the little devils. I don't know where that goes. There, look, isn't it good?

JO (*seeing the doll*): The colour's wrong.

GEOF: Jo.

JO: The colour's wrong. (*Suddenly and violently flinging the doll to the ground.*) I'll bash its brains out. I'll kill it. I don't want his baby, Geof. I don't want to be a mother. I don't want to be a woman.

GEOF: Don't say that, Jo.

JO: I'll kill it when it comes, Geof, I'll kill it.

GEOF: Do you want me to go out and find that chap and bring him back? Is that what you want?

JO: I don't want that. I don't want any man.

GEOF: Well, if you're going to feel like that about it you might as well have it adopted. I thought you'd feel differently as time went on.

JO: I won't.

GEOF: Perhaps you will when you see the baby.

JO: No, I won't.

GEOF: Do you still love him?

JO: I don't know. He was only a dream I had. You know, he could sing and he was so tender. Every Christmas Helen used to go off with some boy friend or other and leave me all on my own in some sordid digs, but last Christmas I had him.

GEOF: Your black prince.

JO: What was his name?

GEOF: Prince Ossini.

JO: No, it was Jimmie!

GEOF: Oh well, the dream's gone, but the baby's real enough.

JO: My mother always used to say you remember the first time all your life, but until this moment I'd forgotten it.

GEOF: Do you remember when I asked you to marry me?

JO: Yes.

GEOF: Do you?

JO: No. What did I say?

GEOF: You just went and lay on the bed.

JO: And you didn't go and follow me, did you?

GEOF: No.

JO: You see, it's not marrying love between us, thank God.

GEOF: You mean you just like having me around till your next prince comes along?

JO: No.

GEOF: Oh well, you need somebody to love you while you're looking for someone to love.

JO: Oh Geof, you'd make a funny father. You are a funny little man. I mean that. You're unique.

GEOF: Am I?

JO: I always want to have you with me because I know you'll never ask anything from me. Where are you going?

GEOFFREY *goes to the kitchen.*

GEOF: To see the cake.

JO *follows him.*

JO: I'll set the cups and we'll have a celebration, then you'll have to study for your exams. It's a bit daft talking about getting married, isn't it? We're already married. We've been married for a thousand years.

They march in together from the kitchen, he with the cake, she with the tea things.

GEOF (*putting it down*): Here, look at that. What are you going to call it?

JO: What, the cake?

GEOF (*laughing*): No, Jo, the baby.

JO: I think I'll give it to you, Geof. You like babies, don't you? I might call it Number One. It'll always be number one to itself.

HELEN *enters, loaded with baggage as in Act One, Scene One.*

HELEN: Anybody at home? Well, I'm back. You see, I couldn't stay away, could I? There's some flowers for you, Jo. The barrows are smothered in them. Oh! How I carried that lot from the bus stop I'll never know. The old place looks a bit more cheerful, doesn't it? I say, there's a nice homely smell. Have you been doing a bit of baking? I'll tell you one thing, it's a lovely day for flitting.

JO: Would you like a cup of tea, Helen?

HELEN: Have you got anything stronger? Oh no, course you haven't! Go on, I'll have a cup with you. Let's have a look at you, love. I arrived just in time, by the look of things, didn't I? How are you, love? Everything straightforward? Been having your regular check-up and doing all them exercises and all the things they go in for nowadays? That's a good girl. Have you got everything packed?

JO: Packed?

HELEN: Yes.

JO: But I'm not going into hospital.

HELEN: You're not having it here, are you?

GEOF: Yes, she didn't want to go away.

HELEN: Oh my God, is he still here? I thought he would be.

GEOF: Do you want a piece of cake, Jo?

JO: Yes, please.

HELEN: You can't have a baby in this dump. Why don't you use a bit of sense for once and go into hospital? They've got everything to hand there. I mean, sometimes the first one can be a bit tricky.

GEOF: There's going to be nothing tricky about it; it's going to be perfectly all right, isn't it, Jo?

HELEN: Who do you think you are, the Flying Doctor?

JO: Look, I've made up my mind I want to have it here. I don't like hospitals.

HELEN: Have you ever been in a hospital?

JO: No.

HELEN: Well, how do you know what it's like? Oo! Give me a cup of tea quick.

GEOF: Oh well, we've got a district nurse coming in.

HELEN: Oh my God, my feet are killing me. How I got that lot from the bus stop I'll never know.

JO: Well what are you lugging all the cases about for?

HELEN: I've come to look after you. It's just as well, by the look of things. (*Whispers to* JO.)

JO: Well, it's going to be a bit crowded, you know. Is your husband coming and all? Is he moving in too?

HELEN: There wouldn't be much room for two of us on that couch, would there?

JO: That's Geoffrey's bed.

GEOF: It's all right, Jo, I don't mind moving out.

JO: For Heaven's sake, you don't have to start wilting away as soon as she barges in.

GEOF: I don't.

HELEN: I could do with a drink.

JO: Start barging around just like a bull in a china shop.

HELEN: I've got some lovely things for the baby, Jo. Where did I put them? Where's that other case, Jo? Oh!

GEOF: Jo, will you sit down. I'll get it.

HELEN: Look, love. I've come here to talk to my daughter. Can you make yourself scarce for a bit?

GEOF: I've got to go, we need some things for the weekend.

JO: You don't have to let her push you around.

GEOF: I don't.

HELEN. Oh I do wish he wouldn't mumble. It does get on my nerves. What's he saying?

GEOF: Where's my pack?

JO: What a couple of old women.

GEOF: Look here, Jo!

JO: Look, just a minute will you. I . . . look I . . . there's nothing . . .

GEOF: How can I stay . . .

HELEN: Come here. How long is he going to stick around here. Bloody little pansy . . .

JO: Look, if you're going to insult Geof . . .

HELEN: I'm not insulting him.

JO: Yes you are.

HELEN: I'm not. I just don't like his style, that's all.

GEOF: It's all right, Mrs. Smith . . .

HELEN: Look, love, I just want five minutes alone with her. Do you mind? Is it too much to ask?

GEOF: Do you want any cotton wool?

HELEN: Good God, does he knit an' all?

JO: You don't have to go.

GEOF: Jo, I've got to go, I'll only be a couple of minutes.

JO: There's plenty of stuff in the kitchen. Now look . . .

GEOFFREY *goes.*

HELEN: You don't mean to tell me he's really gone?

JO: Now that you've been rude to my friend ...

HELEN: What an arty little freak! I wasn't rude to him. I never said a word. I never opened my mouth.

JO: Look, he's the only friend I've got, as a matter of fact.

HELEN: Jo! I thought you could find yourself something more like a man.

JO: Why were you so nasty to him?

HELEN: I wasn't nasty to him. Besides, I couldn't talk to you in front of him, could I? Hey, wait till you see these things for the baby.

JO: You hurt people's feelings and you don't even notice.

HELEN: Jo, I just wanted to get rid of him, that's all. Look at those, Jo. Look, isn't that pretty, eh? The baby's going to be dressed like a prince, isn't he?

JO: We're all princes in our own little kingdom. You're not to insult Geoffrey. Will you leave him alone?

HELEN: Hey, look at this Jo, isn't it pretty? Oh, I love babies—aren't they lovely?

JO: Has your husband thrown you out?

HELEN: Oh come off it, Jo. I had to be with you at a time like this, hadn't I? And what about this sailor lad of yours, have you made any attempt to trace him? He's entitled to keep his child, you know.

JO: I wouldn't do that, it's degrading.

HELEN: What do you call this set-up?

JO: It's all right. There's no need for you to worry about me. I can work for the baby myself.

HELEN: Who's going to look after it when you're out at work? Have you thought about that?

JO: Yes, I have.

HELEN: Well, you can't do two jobs at once, you know. Who's going to nurse it? Him?

JO: That's my business. I can do anything when I set my mind to it.

HELEN: Very clever, aren't you?

JO: There's no need to be so superior. Look where all your swanking's landed you. What does the little lady want—an engagement ring? And now he's thrown you out, hasn't he, and you have to come crawling back here.

HELEN: Well, it was good while it lasted.

JO: Making a fool of yourself over that throw-back.

HELEN: He threw his money about like a man with no arms.

JO: This is my flat now, Helen.

HELEN: It's all right, love, I've got a bit of money put by.

JO: You're a real fool, aren't you?

HELEN: Oh, Jo, look. I'm back aren't I? Forget it. Don't keep on about it.

JO: Do you know what I think?

HELEN: What?

JO: I think you're still in love with him.

HELEN: In love? Me?

JO: Yes.

HELEN: You must be mad.

JO: What happened?

HELEN: He's gone off with his bit of crumpet. Still, it was good while it lasted. Anyway. I'll shift some of this, Jo.

JO: So we're back where we started. And all those months you stayed away from me because of him! Just like when I was small.

HELEN: I never thought about you! It's a funny thing, I never have done when I've been happy. But these last few weeks I've known I should be with you.

JO: So you stayed away—

HELEN: Yes. I can't stand trouble.

JO: Oh, there's no trouble. I've been performing a perfectly normal, healthy function. We're wonderful! Do you know, for the first time in my life I feel really important. I feel as though I could take care of the whole world. I even feel as though I could take care of you, too!

HELEN: Here, I forgot to tell you, I've ordered a lovely cot for you.

JO: We've got one.

HELEN: It's lovely. It's got pink curtains, you know, and frills.

JO *gets wicker basket from under bed.*

Oh, I don't like that. What is it?

JO: It's wicker work. Geof got it.

HELEN: It's a bit old-fashioned, isn't it?

JO: We like it.

HELEN: Look love, why don't you go and lie down? You look as though you've got a bit of a headache.

JO: Do you wonder?

HELEN: Well, go and have a rest, there's a good girl. I'm going to tidy this place up for you. I'm going to make it just the way you like it. Go on.

JO: Oh no!

HELEN: Go on, Jo. Go on. It looks more like a laundry basket, doesn't it! Oh! The state of this place! We'll never have it right. Living like pigs in a pigsty—

GEOFFREY *enters.*

Oh, you're back are you? Well, come in if you're coming.

GEOF: Where's Jo?

HELEN: She's in bed. Where do you think she is? She's having a little sleep, so don't you dare wake her up.

GEOF: I wouldn't do that. (*He places pack filled with food on the table.*)

HELEN: Don't put that bag on there, I'm cleaning this place up.

GEOF: You know I just did it before you came.

HELEN: It doesn't look like it. Look, son, we're going to have the midwife running in and out of here before long. We want this place all clean and tidy, all hygienic-looking, if that's possible.

GEOF: Well, it's clean.

JO: Is that Geof?

HELEN: Now look what you've done!

GEOF: Yes, Jo.

JO: Have you got any of those headache pills, love?

GEOF: Yes, I'll get you some.

HELEN: If you're going in there take these flowers with you and put them in water. You might as well make yourself useful. They look as though they're withering away. (*She peers into the pack.*) What the devil's he got here? What's that? Spaghetti! I don't know how people can eat it. And that's a funny looking lettuce. What the hell's that? Hey, what's this here?

GEOF: What?

HELEN: All this muck in here?

GEOF: Well, Jo likes that type of food.

HELEN: Since when? She needs proper food down her at a time like this.

GEOF: Oh!

HELEN *points to wicker basket.*

HELEN: Hey, you can throw that bloody thing out for a start.

GEOF: What thing?

HELEN: That thing there. You're not putting my grandchild in a thing like that. Oh, this place! It's filthy! I don't know what you've been doing between the two of you. You might have kept it a bit cleaner than this. Just look at it! Don't stand there looking silly holding that thing, throw it away, or do something with it! I've ordered a proper cot of the latest design, it's got all the etceteras and everything. This place! You're living like pigs in a pigsty. Oh, for God's sake give it here, I'll do something with it.

GEOF: Yes, but Jo likes it.

HELEN: Well, I suppose it will come in handy for something. (*She enters the kitchen.*) Oh my God, it's the same in here! Nowhere to put anything . . . Are you off now?

GEOF: Yes.

HELEN: Well, take that muck with you as you're going.

GEOF: I don't want it.

HELEN: I'm sure I don't.

GEOF: Mrs. Smith, I . . . I . . .

HELEN: Are you talking to me?

GEOF: Yes, I wanted to ask you something.

HELEN: Well, get it said. Don't mumble.

GEOF: I don't want you to take offence.

HELEN: Do I look the type that takes offence?

GEOF: Would you not frighten Jo?

HELEN: I thought you said you were going.

GEOF: I said would you not frighten Jo.

HELEN: What are you talking about, frightening her?

GEOF: You know, telling her that it might be tricky or that she might have trouble, because she's going to be all right.

HELEN: Are you trying to tell me what to do with my own daughter?

GEOF: Oh no.

HELEN: Well, are you going?

GEOF: Yes, although she said she didn't want a woman with her when she had it.

HELEN: She said what?

GEOF: She said she wanted me with her when she had it because she said she wouldn't be frightened if I was with her.

HELEN: How disgusting!

GEOF: There's nothing disgusting about it.

HELEN: A man in the room at a time like this!

GEOF: Husbands stay with their wives.

HELEN: Are you her husband?

GEOF: No.

HELEN: Well, get.

GEOF: I'm going. She can't cope with the two of us. Only just don't frighten her, that's all.

HELEN: I've told you we don't want that.

GEOF: Yes I know, but she likes it.

HELEN: You can bloody well take it with you, we don't want it.

GEOFFREY *empties food from his pack on to the table while* HELEN *thrusts it back.* HELEN *finally throws the whole thing, pack and all, on to the floor.*

GEOF: Yes, the one thing civilization couldn't do anything about— women. Good-bye Jo, and good luck. (*He goes.*)

JO *stirs on the bed.*

HELEN: It's all right, love, I'm here and everything's all right. Are you awake now?

JO: Hello. Yes . . . What's it like?

HELEN: What?

JO: Is there much pain?

HELEN: No! It's not so much pain as hard work, love. I was putting my Christmas pudding up on a shelf when you started on me. There I was standing on a chair singing away merry as the day is long . . .

JO: Did you yell?

HELEN: No, I ran.

JO: Do you know, I had such a funny dream just now.

HELEN: Oh Jo, you're always dreaming, aren't you. Well, don't let's talk about your dreams or we'll get morbid.

JO: Where would you like those flowers putting?

HELEN: Over . . . over there . . . Come on, you come and do it, love.

JO: Hasn't Geof come back yet?

HELEN: No, he hasn't.

JO: Well, where are you going to sleep, Helen?

HELEN: It's all right, love. Don't fall over, now.

JO: You know, I've got so used to old Geof lying there on that couch like—like an old watchdog. You aren't . . .

HELEN: It's all right, love, don't you worry about me, I'll find somewhere.

JO: I wonder where he is . . . Oh!

HELEN: Oh Jo, careful . . . Hold on, love, hold on! It'll be all right. The first one doesn't last long. Oh my God, I could do with a drink now. Hold on.

JO *kneels on bed.* HELEN *strokes her hair.*

JO: That's better.

HELEN: Are you all right now? There we are.

Children sing outside.

Can you hear those children singing over there on the croft, Jo?

JO: Yes, you can always hear them on still days.

HELEN: You know when I was young we used to play all day long at this time of the year; in the summer we had singing games and in the spring we played with tops and hoops, and then in the autumn there was the Fifth of November, then we used to have bonfires in the street, and gingerbread and all that. Have I ever told you about the time when we went to a place called Shining Clough? Oh, I must have done. I used to climb up there every day and sit on the top of the hill, and you could see the mills in the distance, but the clough itself was covered in moss. Isn't it funny how you remember these things? Do you know, I'd sit there all day long and nobody ever knew where I was. Shall I go and make us a cup of tea?

HELEN *enters kitchen and fiddles with stove.*

Oh Jo, I've forgotten how we used to light this thing.

JO: Turn on all the knobs. Mind you don't gas yourself.

HELEN: I still can't do it.

JO: Geof'll fix it.

HELEN: No, it's all right.

JO: Helen.

HELEN: Yes.

JO: My baby may be black.

HELEN: You what, love?

JO: My baby will be black.

HELEN: Oh, don't be silly, Jo. You'll be giving yourself nightmares.

JO: But it's true. He was black.

HELEN: Who?

JO: Jimmie.

HELEN: You mean to say that . . . that sailor was a black man? . . . Oh my God! Nothing else can happen to me now. Can you see me wheeling a pram with a . . . Oh my God, I'll have to have a drink.

JO: What are you going to do?

HELEN: I don't know. Drown it. Who knows about it?

JO: Geoffrey.

HELEN: And what about the nurse? She's going to get a bit of a shock, isn't she?

JO: Well, she's black too.

HELEN: Good, perhaps she'll adopt it. Dear God in heaven!

JO: If you don't like it you can get out. I didn't ask you to come here.

HELEN: Where's my hat?

JO: On your head.

HELEN: Oh yes . . . I don't know what's to be done with you, I don't really. (*To the audience.*) I ask you, what would you do?

JO: Are you going?

HELEN: Yes.

JO: Are you just going for a drink?

HELEN: Yes.

JO: Are you coming back?

HELEN: Yes.

JO: Well, what are you going to do?

HELEN: Put it on the stage and call it Blackbird. (*She rushes out.*)

> JO *watches her go, leaning against the doorpost. Then she looks round the room, smiling a little to herself—she remembers* GEOF.

JO.   As I was going up Pippin Hill,
        Pippin Hill was dirty.

And there I met a pretty miss,
And she dropped me a curtsy.
Little miss, pretty miss,
Blessings light upon you.
If I had half a crown a day,
I'd gladly spend it on you.

Curtain.

The Connection

by
Jack Gelber

CAROLE

THE CONNECTION was first produced at The Living Theatre, New York, July 15, 1959; directed by Judith Malina, designed by Julian Beck, original tunes by Freddie Redd, and with the following cast:

JIM DUNN	Leonard Hicks
JAYBIRD	Ira Lewis
LEACH	Warren Finnerty
SOLLY	Jerome Raphel
SAM	John McCurry
ERNIE	Garry Goodrow
FIRST MUSICIAN	Freddie Redd
FOURTH MUSICIAN	Michael Mattos
FIRST PHOTOGRAPHER	Louis McKenzie
SECOND PHOTOGRAPHER	Jamil Zakkai
SECOND MUSICIAN	Jackie McLean
THIRD MUSICIAN	Larry Ritchie
HARRY	Henry Proach
SISTER SALVATION	Barbara Winchester
COWBOY	Carl Lee

The play is in two acts

NOTE: The jazz played is in the tradition of Charlie Parker. There are approximately thirty minutes of jazz in each act. Its division within the act is a matter of pacing which can only be worked out on stage. The musicians use their own names throughout the play. In casting I think of JIM DUNN, JACK, LEACH, SOLLY, ERNIE, and SECOND PHOTOGRAPHER as Caucasians; SAM, COWBOY, SISTER SALVATION, HARRY, and FIRST PHOTOGRAPHER as Negroes. However, there need not be any rigidity in casting. In the original production SAM and COWBOY were Negroes.

ACT ONE

The players arrange themselves on stage a few minutes before the play begins. SOLLY *is looking out of a window with binoculars. Behind him is a room full of homemade furniture. In center stage* SAM *is stretched out sleeping on a bed. Downstage left* LEACH *and* ERNIE *are slumped over a table. The* FIRST *and* FOURTH MUSICIANS *are at extreme right dozing at a piano. A small green light bulb hangs in the center of the room. A door to the toilet is rear left. There is, perhaps, a sign on the wall, "Heaven or Hell: which road are you on?" Perhaps there is a painting or an orange crate bookcase in the room. The house lights dim.* JIM DUNN *and* JAYBIRD *stroll up the aisle. They are wearing suits. Perhaps* JAYBIRD *has a darker shirt. They jump or hop on stage.*

JIM: Hello there! I'm Jim Dunn and I'm producing *The Connection*. This is Jaybird, the author. Hardly a day goes by without the daily papers having some item involving narcotics. Any number of recent movies, plays and books have been concerned with the peculiar problems of this anti-social habit. Unfortunately few of these have anything to do with narcotics. Sometimes it is treated as exotica and often as erotica. Jaybird has spent some months living among drug addicts. With the help of [name of director] we have selected a few addicts to improvise on Jaybird's themes. I can assure you that this play does not have a housewife who will call the police and say, "Would you please come quickly to the [name of theatre]. My husband is a junkie."

   House lights up.

   Please turn the house lights down.
FOURTH MUSICIAN: Hey, Jim, is Cowboy back?
JIM: No, man, Cowboy is not back.

   FIRST MUSICIAN *plays his instrument hurriedly.*

JIM: Stop it kids. We haven't begun yet. I'm not finished. Turn those lights down.

228

Lights down.

Yes. We shall hear more from the musicians. A little better than
that. That's what hooked me into this thing: jazz. I mean the
music they try to stuff into movies and plays can't be called jazz.
Not really. Tonight will be different. (*Loses his place.*) When
you're dealing with a taboo such as narcotics and trying to use
the theatre in a way that it hasn't quite been tried before, you—
I am taking a big gamble. Of course we are starting small. The
[name of theatre] is small. I think playgoers should have some
place to . . . you know what I mean.

JAYBIRD: Jimmie, you're goofing. You've got your speeches mixed.
What Jim is trying to say is that I am interested in an improvised
theatre. It isn't a new idea. It just isn't being done. Remember:
for one night this scene swings. But as a life it's a damn bore.
When all the changes have been played, we'll all be back where
we started. We end in a vacuum. I am not a moralist. However,
some of you will leave this theatre with the notion that jazz and
narcotics are inextricably connected. That is your connection,
not—

JIM: This word magician here has invented me for the sole purpose
of explaining that I and this entire evening on stage are merely
a fiction. And don't be fooled by anything anyone else tells you.
Except the jazz. As I've said, we do stand by the authenticity of
that improvised art. But as for the rest it has no basis in naturalism. None. Not a bit. Absol—

JAYBIRD: This is getting embarrassing. We've gone through this. The
improvising comes later.

JIM: What I mean to say is that we are not actually using real heroin.
You don't think we'd use the real stuff? After all, narcotics are
illegal.

A knock. Everyone stiffens. LEACH *opens the door. Enter* SECOND
and THIRD MUSICIANS.

SECOND MUSICIAN: Have we started yet?

JIM: Emphatically not! Not until I'm finished. Dig?

SECOND MUSICIAN: What are you selling this time, Jim? Aren't you the
cat that was trying to sell me valve oil last week?

JIM: I only asked you—oh, what's the use? Can't you do something?

JAYBIRD: Why should I? Pay no attention to them. My primitive tribe is getting restless.

SECOND MUSICIAN: I have a gig for us. They're even going to pay us money.

JIM: You see, I am taking a gamble. But why are salesmen put down? I'm selling an idea. What's so immoral about that?

SECOND MUSICIAN: Swing Baby. [FIRST MUSICIAN's name], we have to get some tunes prepared.

JIM: Anyway, I was talking about the problem of naturalism. Did I say anything about that? Well, it's out of the question. Where could it lead? A sociologist's report on the pecking order of Bowery bums. No, out of the question. Right, Jaybird? Right.

JAYBIRD: No!

House lights on.

JIM: Again? What's happening backstage? Is everyone high before we start? Turn those damn lights off!

JAYBIRD: I have had enough for now. Isn't it time to leave?

Exits into the audience. House lights down.

SECOND MUSICIAN: Please don't leave us! Please don't leave us!

JIM: Why don't we do the whole play in the dark? There's an idea for you, Jaybird.

JAYBIRD: I've had enough of your ideas.

JIM: Well, Jaybird did have some prepared things about unions that I thought were pretty funny, but—I shall return.

Exit JIM. LEACH *stands up and unfolds a tablecloth. He snaps it and lays it out. With a large knife he starts cutting a pineapple. He has a handkerchief around a boil on his neck.*

LEACH: I'm hungry. This is my place, why shouldn't I eat? These people never eat. Don't they know it's nutritious? Oh, this boil. Damn this boil. Dream world. Narcotics. I live comfortable. I'm not a Bowery bum. Look at my room. It's clean. Except for the people who come here and call themselves my friends. My friends? Huh! They come here with a little money and they expect me to use my hard earned connections to supply them with heroin. And when I take a little for myself they cry, they scream. The bastards. They wait here and make me nervous. Sleeping. That's all they can do. Sleep. Last night I dreamt I was on a ladder. I wish Solly were awake. You know what I mean? He'd know. There were a hundred clowns dangling on this rope ladder, laughing to someone. You know what I mean? Then it was all a painting and the name psychology was written on the bottom.

> *Rapid entrance of* JIM *with* FIRST *and* SECOND PHOTOGRAPHERS. FIRST PHOTOGRAPHER *is a Negro in a white suit, the* SECOND PHOTOGRAPHER *white in a black suit. The* FIRST *is swift and agile, the* SECOND *slow and clodlike. As the play unfolds they exchange, piece-by-piece, their clothing and personalities.*

JIM: I hope I haven't interrupted anything, Leach? I couldn't have. In keeping with our improvisation theme, I have an announcement. Have you been introduced to the cast?
LEACH: Aw, Jimmie, I didn't want to wake anybody up.
JIM: How kind of you. First things first. This is Leach.
LEACH (*staring ahead and saluting*): Yessir!
JIM: This is Ernie. He's our dope-addict psychopath.

> ERNIE *blows his mouthpiece.*

JIM: Solly? Wake up, Solly.
SOLLY (*raises his hand and waves*): Ad sum!
JIM: Sam is our expert in folk lore.
SAM: Don't fire until you see the whites of their eyes.
JIM: These are the musicians. I'm sure they need no introduction. This is (names all the musicians.)

> FIRST, SECOND *and* THIRD MUSICIAN *stand, bow their heads, and sit. The* FOURTH MUSICIAN *is asleep.* JIM *tugs at him.*

FOURTH MUSICIAN (*reaching for his sleeve*): Cowboy here?
JIM: No, he is not. Now, friends—
FIRST MUSICIAN: I can't tell the performance from the rehearsal.
JIM: Steady, boys, we have a long trip. Our other actors are off in the real world procuring heroin.
LEACH: Actors?

JIM: All right, junkies. During our trip we will incorporate an allied art—the motion picture.

JAYBIRD (*from the audience*): What?

JIM: This is the ad lib part. Don't worry. Money! And, if everything goes right, you will be able to see the film version of this play. It was the only hip thing to do.

SECOND MUSICIAN: You're hip, my ass!

LEACH (*to* JIM): Will you stop this cornball stuff.

ERNIE: I knew they would pull something like this. I told you I didn't trust this cat!

JIM: Come on, Jaybird. This can't go on like this.

JAYBIRD: So far so good. Don't worry. Conflict!

JIM: It just means more money. For you and for me. Besides, we aren't going Hollywood. They're making an avant-garde movie. The photographers know something about Griffith and Eisenstein.

LEACH: You sure have to mention the right names.

SOLLY: Leave him be.

JIM: Okay, you cats ought to smoke pot instead of using junk. It would make you more agreeable. (*Exit.*)

ERNIE (*to* FIRST PHOTOGRAPHER): How much they paying you, man?

FIRST PHOTOGRAPHER *ignores him and moves in and about the stage with a light meter, framing with his fingers different parts of the set.*

What are you getting out of this, man?

SECOND PHOTOGRAPHER: Oh, it'll pay the rent. Oh. Ah. Er. I'm visual, you see. I'm not able to express, ah, myself. Let's get the rest of the equipment. Ah.

FIRST PHOTOGRAPHER *mentally adds up on his fingers, and they exit into the audience.*

LEACH: Do you see that lightbulb? Do you realize that light travels at 186,000 miles per second per second? Solly, wake up. I want you to hear this.

SOLLY (*apparently asleep*): I haven't slept since the night I met you. Two years ago. But, for once, pretend that I am asleep.

LEACH: So, I was saying that light travels at 186,000 miles per second per second. You know what I mean? We, the human race, are being bombarded constantly with the light particles. And now the question is: why aren't we dead? At 186,000 miles per second per second we should be annihilated. But we aren't. Why? I'll tell you. Man is transparent. You know what I mean? Man is transparent. Yes, transparent. That's why the light goes through him and doesn't hurt me or you. Now this is the interesting part. Are you listening, Solly? (*Pause.*) If man is transparent, how do you account for his shadow? You know? To tell you the truth, I don't know the whole answer. You know what I mean? But I think that it has something to do with the alchemical nature of man. Got it? Some weird alchemical changes make the light's color different shades of black. Not too sure of that. Solly, what do you think of it? Does it have something to do with Indian philosophy?

SOLLY: I'm hungry. What are you cutting to death today?

LEACH (*places fruit on a dish*): Hey, Sam, you want some pineapple? (*Pushes* SAM.) Don't you want to eat?

SAM: Now, man, you know I hate to be pushed. I have but one life. I'm waiting on Cowboy. What happened to Cowboy? And Leonard the Locomotive?

LEACH: They ran off and got married! How do I know? Go on, eat something.

SAM: No, I's sick. Honest, I couldn't eat a thing.

LEACH: Hey, Ernie! Wake up, boy! Time to eat. Huh? Here's some nourishment.

ERNIE: Don't be a drag, man. Where's Cowboy and Leonard the Locomotive?

LEACH: Cowboy, Cowboy. You rotten junkies. Is that all you can think about is dope? Dope? Dope?

SECOND MUSICIAN: Somebody call me?

THIRD MUSICIAN (*to himself*): My wife thinks I'm insane for doing this.

LEACH: I'm offering you the fruit of the land. Cowboy is just going to kill you. I want to save you.

ERNIE: Come off it, man. You steal so much shit from us that there are rumors of you opening a drug store.

SOLLY: Sure, Leach is trying to turn on the whole world.

LEACH: That's right. I'm saving all the heroin I can so that I can put it in vitamin pills. Can't you see everyone in the whole world being hooked without them knowing it? (*Totters and laughs.*)

Besides, I only take what's coming to me, and you don't have to come up here. (*Crosses to* FIRST MUSICIAN.) How about you, man? Pineapple?

> FIRST MUSICIAN'S *head slowly falls and his body lapses into a deep sleep.*

Hey, man. Pineapple?

FIRST MUSICIAN (*just before falling off his chair he straightens up*): What's happening? What tune are we blowing? Cowboy back?

THIRD MUSICIAN: My wife thinks I'm insane.

LEACH: No, Cowboy is not back.

SECOND MUSICIAN: Cowboy went to cop and got copped.

FIRST MUSICIAN: Oh. (*Starts falling asleep again.*)

FIRST PHOTOGRAPHER (*in audience. Enthusiastically*): That's the way it really is. That's the way it is.

SOLLY: I'm hungry, Leach.

LEACH: Okay. (*Hands him the plate.*) Take the whole thing.

SOLLY: Ernie, do you see where you make your mistake? Ask and you shall receive.

ERNIE: I'm not much for tact. I guess I'll never be.

SOLLY: Well, man, it is a very rotting black shadow that seeps through your body.

LEACH: So you were listening? Maybe you know that you're not the only one who thinks about these things. (*Holds his neck.*) My lousy boil!

SOLLY: Put some hot water on it.

LEACH: I think I will. Maybe I'll shave.

ERNIE (*to the audience*): Cut your throat.

LEACH: I've invited some chicks over. Jimmie thought it was a good idea to put in a little battle of the sexes. Where does he get his ideas? If anybody knocks you take care of it, Solly. I don't feel like being arrested today. I haven't had dinner yet. Or my fix. (*Exits to toilet.*)

ERNIE: Hey, Solly, what were you talking about morals?

SOLLY: Nothing much. I thought it would be easier if you pretended that Leach was a very good friend of yours. Let him think he's helping you.

ERNIE: Oh. I thought you wanted me to follow the ten commandments or something.

SAM (*reclining*): Not a bad idea. I'm sick. Oh, powerful sick and hungry. I hope Cowboy gets back soon. I didn't like the idea of Leonard the Locomotive going with him. He's a practical joker. Every day he goes out. Or I go out. Or we're both way out. Every day. (*Sings.*) Sko-bah-dee. Skee-boh-dah. Same old stuff. (*Laughs.*) Yeah. Where is the old Cowboy? I remember when I got out of Quentin with the Cowboy a few years ago. We were walking down Broadway. (*Gets up and walks in place.*) We swore off of swearing anything off. That's the way it is—you know something in your mind for so long and you know that talking nonsense is just that and nothing more. Yeah, man, we were going to stay clean. Clean, man, clean. We collared the first connection we could find. I said, "What am I doing?" Just one fix won't hurt anything. (*Starts jogging in place.*) What is this thing I'm fighting? That taste come back to your mouth. And that's what you want. That taste, that little taste. If you don't find it there you look some place else. And you're running, man. Running. It doesn't matter how or why it started. You don't think about anything and you start going back, running back. I used to think that the people who walk the streets, the people who work every day, the people who worry so much about the next dollar, the next new coat, the chlorophyll addicts, the aspirin addicts, the vitamin addicts, those people are hooked worse than me. Worse than me. Hooked. (*Stops jogging and falls on the bed.*)

SOLLY: They are. Man, they sure are. You happen to have a vice that is illegal.

FIRST PHOTOGRAPHER (*in audience*): That's the way it is. That's the way it really is.

SAM: I guess so. What am I talking about?

SOLLY: You are fed up with everything for the moment. And like the rest of us you are a little hungry for a little hope. So you wait and worry. A fix of hope. A fix to forget. A fix to remember, to be sad, to be happy, to be, to be. So we wait for the trustworthy Cowboy to gallop in upon a white horse. Gallant white powder.

SAM: There ain't nothing gallant about heroin, baby.

ERNIE: Will you stop talking about it? You cats are a drag. It's getting on my nerves. I've got a job tonight and I've got to get straight. (*Blows his mouthpiece.*) Why doesn't that bastard get here? He probably took all our money and burned us.

Knock.

LEACH (*off stage*): See who it is, Solly.

SOLLY (*at the window*): It's Harry. He's got his suitcase.

LEACH (*off stage*): Let him in. I hope he doesn't want to stay here.

> SOLLY *opens the door and* HARRY *walks in and looks around. Then he goes to the light socket in center stage and plugs in the cord of the portable phonograph. He opens the phonograph and puts on a Charlie Parker record—all in silence. The record plays for two minutes. Everyone assumes an intense pose of listening. Afterwards there is a silence and* HARRY *carefully picks up the record, closes the phonograph, unplugs the cord, and leaves. There is a long pause. One of the musicians starts playing and the others join him in cementing their feelings. They play for about one minute.*

JAYBIRD (*enters from the audience*): Cut it! Cut it! You are murdering the play. What are you doing? Let's go over it again. You're to give the whole plot in the first act. So far not one of you has carried out his dramatic assignment.

> *Calms himself.* LEACH *enters.*

I had characters, with biographies for each of them. I thought that was clear. This is improvised theatre! And what have you provided? Do you think you are doing a slice of life?

SOLLY (*shouting*): Stop! Stop the action! Why did you seek out dope addicts? We didn't have to go through with this. Now quit complaining. Besides you've changed into a monster. Why don't you stay on stage with us?

JAYBIRD: Never mind that now. There are to be no realistic body movements as we rehearsed. No longer is your hand your own hand. You are part of something infinitely larger. Solly, where is the philosophy I put into your mouth?

SOLLY: It went up in smoke before the show.

JAYBIRD: A monster? I'm a monster? What do you know about the theatre? (*Pause. Softly.*) Leach, where is the plot? Give it away, expose it, say it three times. Don't be anal.

LEACH: I flushed it down the toilet.

JAYBIRD: Sam, Ernie, is this a conspiracy? Where are your confessions? Your capsule comments?

ERNIE: Where are my capsules?

SAM: Man, you've been telling us to act natural. Now we don't own our own hands.

JAYBIRD: You may know more about junk, but let me swing with this production. Okay, let's get on with it.

SOLLY: Go ahead [name of FIRST MUSICIAN], it's our stage now.

JAYBIRD *exits into the audience to the jeers of those on stage. The musicians play for five minutes while the photographers move about the stage with their camera and glaring lights.*

FIRST PHOTOGRAPHER: Take 27-A.

SECOND PHOTOGRAPHER: This is terrific stuff! I wonder how much will have to be cut out of it? Terrific! Do you think we'll get a shot of the connection?

FIRST PHOTOGRAPHER: You mean Cowboy or Leonard the Locomotive?

SECOND PHOTOGRAPHER: No, no. I mean the man behind them. I mean the big connection.

FIRST PHOTOGRAPHER: If I were him I wouldn't want to show my face.

LEACH: So you fellows want to see the man, the man behind the man.

SECOND PHOTOGRAPHER: Will he be here?

LEACH: No, kiddies, he will not. I have been on this scene for a long, long time and I have never seen him. Sit down. Sit down. I have never seen the man because there is no man.

SECOND PHOTOGRAPHER: You mean there isn't any organized international setup?

LEACH: No.

ERNIE: Sure there is.

SECOND PHOTOGRAPHER: Then somebody must be the head of it.

ERNIE: No, I don't think there's any head.

SECOND PHOTOGRAPHER: If you have an organization, somebody must be in charge. Hey, Sam, who's in charge?

SAM: I am.

SECOND PHOTOGRAPHER: You are?

SAM: Sure. I am the man as much as anyone. Listen, I am your man if you come to me. You are my man if I go to you.

SECOND PHOTOGRAPHER: Well, where does it start?

SOLLY: Right here!

SAM: Or over there.

SECOND PHOTOGRAPHER: I don't understand.

SOLLY (*at the window with binoculars*): Nobody here understands that. They wouldn't be here if they were that interested. To us here it is a mystery where Cowboy goes. Anyone coming to Leach feels that he is the central actor in his own drama. An artificial and melodramatic organization. But that is the setup. Surely it starts in the ground and grows up as a poppy. After that it is a mundane game for me, that is, for me.

FIRST PHOTOGRAPHER: That's the way it is. Really, that's the way it is.

SOLLY: The man is you. You are the man. You are your own connection. It starts and stops here. You come here to take pictures. And now you're getting involved at your own risk.

LEACH: You think we ought to turn them on, Solly?

SAM: I'm not donating anything.

LEACH: I'm not asking you.

SOLLY: Don't look at me. Ask them.

LEACH: Well?

SECOND PHOTOGRAPHER: They say one shot and you can never stop. You're hooked.

LEACH *laughs.*

FIRST PHOTOGRAPHER: You got any pot?

LEACH (*laughs*): Oh, this is the end. They send two square photographers. And one of them turns out to be a pot-head.

FIRST PHOTOGRAPHER (*to* SECOND PHOTOGRAPHER): Marijuana.

LEACH: Mari-juana. No, I don't have any pot. But how quaint of you to ask.

SECOND PHOTOGRAPHER: They say marijuana leads to the stronger stuff.

FIRST PHOTOGRAPHER: Shut up.

LEACH (*pointing to the* FIRST PHOTOGRAPHER): I'd like to turn that one on. He'd be crazy. I'd like to see that.

ERNIE: No, I'd like to turn the other one on, and knock him out. Oh, he'd be helpless. At first, that is.

SAM: You are certainly a mean bunch of boys.

LEACH: Mind your own business.

SOLLY (*looking out of the window*): I can't see you. Yes, now you are in focus.

LEACH: Is that Cowboy and Leonard the Locomotive?

SOLLY: No, man, I'm looking for a woman.

Exit photographers into the audience.

Goodbye.

ERNIE: I'm tired of waiting. Let's do something.

SOLLY: Hello there! I'm the nineteenth century and I'm producing the twentieth. Unfortunately, the twentieth century has developed anti-social habits. There isn't a day that goes by without some item in the daily papers involving insanity. We've gone out and bribed a few natives. Actually, I'm the only white man the natives trust. If we can start a small opium war—I always wanted to start a war.

LEACH: Cool it, Solly. Those cats make our living. Oh, my neck. My boil!

SOLLY: You're right. I've always wanted an audience, but now I've got one. Imagine someone wanting to have real junkies on stage. Wow! Believe me, we're not here for the money.

ERNIE: Speak for yourself.

SOLLY: It's not that much. As you have gathered, we are, as they say in the tabloids, dope fiends. We are waiting. We have waited before. The connection is coming. He is always coming. But so is education, for example. The man who will whisper the truth in your ear. Or the one who will shout it out among the people. I can't generalize and believe it. I'm not made that way. Perhaps Jaybird has chosen this petty and miserable microcosm because of its self-annihilating aspects. This tells us something about Jaybird, but nothing about me. Hurry, hurry, hurry. The circus is here. Suicide is not uncommon among us. The seeking of death is at once fascinating and repellent. The overdose of heroin is where that frail line of life and death swings in a silent breeze of ecstatic summer. The concept of this limbo you can hold in your palsied hand. Who else can make so much out of passing out? But existence on another plane is sought, whether to alleviate the suffering from this one, or to wish for death, it doesn't matter. I hate over-simplification. Sam! Sam is simple. Sam, someone, say something. Say something to the customers.

FIRST PHOTOGRAPHER (*in audience*): Man, that's the way it really is.

SAM: Oh, man. I'm not much for this sort of thing.

SOLLY: Pay your dues. Pay your dues.

SAM: Okay. If that's the way it is. But who's to say? Who's there to squeeze the ball into his own shape and tell me this is right. You know that. What does Jaybird want? A soft shoe dance? I don't need any burnt cork, you know. Now, Solly, you know Leach. When you met him he came on with how easy it would be to exist if you two shared expenses. I remember you slept there. It was cheap. Little rent, some food here and there whenever the bastard felt like sharing what he had. Or Cowboy cooking up a storm of food that he swiped in the supermarket. But Leach, man, Leach is a queer without being queer. He thinks like a chick. You wouldn't live with that. I certainly wouldn't. Sometimes I wish he would stop fighting it and make the homosexual scene. It would be easier on all of us. Besides, he would swing more himself. Now he's undependable, like a womans. He's like everybody's mother. Cowboy treats him like a womans and everything is fine. I can't do it. I just look at him, and I can't do it. And there's Solly. Man, he's hard to figure. Educated, shit, he knows an awful lot. But then he's here waiting on the same stuff I am. And he ain't rich. He don't get high unless he's happy. I can never figure that out. Most cats get high when they're down. Not him. Mostly I sees him in my mind with dancing on the street. Yeah, dancing down through the people. Sometimes yelling, sometimes whispering to people. Always with a book. I don't remember ever seeing him on the street without a book. He watches everything. I was playing with this hoop (*Picks up hoop.*) and he tells me about the Roman's symbols of death or some shit like that. He's always telling me what I do is got to do with the Africans or the Navahos. He breaks me up. A stand up cat. I like him. (*Pause.*) Ernie? (*Pause.*)

ERNIE: What do you want? Get us all busted?

SAM: You don't want much. A little dope and your horn. I don't trust you.

ERNIE: The same. (*Blows his mouthpiece.*)

LEACH: Your confession is next, son. Shut up. You think it's easy?

SAM: As long as Ernie is straight with me, I am with him. But I don't like him. I hold back, you know? He has no will power when it comes to not having anything to get high with. Hey, is there any beer left?

SECOND MUSICIAN: No.

LEACH: My neck hurts. I'm going to put more hot water on it. (*Exits to toilet.*)

SAM: They have a saying in this world: It isn't the shit that will do you in, it's the lack of it. I can't put Ernie down too hard. I steal. But I steal from people I don't like, and I wouldn't touch a match stick of a friend of mine. Listen! I like telling stories best. I have quite a rep . . . repi . . . quite a lot of stories that would tickle the hairs on your ass. But I'm kinda sick right now. You can imagine. I mean, you've seen pictures of guys like me. It's torturous. Well, I'm coming off this here stage in a minute or so and I'll be in the lobby. I could use a little money.

Music begins softly.

Only till I get myself straightened out. I'm supposed to see this guy next week about working in a book store. Solly introduced me. Didn't you, Solly? Well, I'll be making a lot of bread then. I's sick, good people. I'll talk to you when I come offen this silly stage. I got some powerful stories in me when that shit flows in my veins. Right now I'm going to lay down for a minute. Maybe the music will help.

Musicians play for about five minutes.

ERNIE: Trust me? Man, I don't care one way or the other. Sam's right about me in his own way—I only care to play. And . . . (*Smile.*) . . . a little dope makes life enjoyable. I play the same—with or without it. (*Blows his mouthpiece here, and throughout the speech.*) That's the truth. No square bullshitter is going to change me. That's for sure. I've had to hock my horn. Do you know what that feels like? I take the few measly pennies to some connection and get high. That's where my horn is now—the hock shop. I got a job tonight and no horn. Maybe someone will borrow me theirs. I don't know. I'm lonely! Not for you or anybody on this stage. I know these people. I've known them a long time. Too long. (*Walks over to* SECOND MUSICIAN.) Can I use your horn tonight, man? (*No answer.*) Did you see? Do you? Sam isn't too bad. He could of told some really rotten bits that people tell about me. Thanks, Sam. (*No answer.*) They say I threw a kid out the window, after he took an overdose. Don't believe it.

Photographers enter and circle around ERNIE.

Well, there's Leach. An orphan. Not too many people know that. Yeah, his old man was a musician. Died when he was eight. County authorities took him to a farm until he was seventeen. Poor kid. Bah! Leach went to work in a book store and one day he left with everything in the till and went to New York. He became a cheap businessman. He's always trying to be so hip. He still is just a petty conniving businessman. Leach has run away with the till from more cities and people than I'll ever know. Of course, Leach tells another story: he was cheated, he was insulted, he was dealing with squares, he was . . . you know the story. (*Smiles.*) So do I, for that matter. Get this straight. I admit when I've sinned. That's more than you will get from most.

VOICE: Come off it.

ERNIE: Who said that? (*No answer.*) Money and sex. That's all I hear from you. So here it is right back. Leach, sexually speaking, can't be with a girl for more than one night. He likes the courtship. The playing up. The making out. Not it itself. You don't like hearing the truth, do you, Leach? (*No answer.*) Leach uses junk that way. He doesn't enjoy junk, ever. I'm suspicious of people who never enjoy getting high. Oh, but he loves the excitement of getting it.

VOICE: Come off it.

ERNIE: Leonard the Locomotive? Cowboy? Hey, Solly, didn't that sound like Leonard the Locomotive? (*No answer.*) He's crazy, that Leonard is. He must have been crazy about trains when he was a kid. He really thinks he's a locomotive at times. You photographers stop taking my picture! Where's Jim? We aren't being paid for being film actors. (*Pause.*) Solly and Sam are very much alike. Surprise you? It's funny, in a way. They are of course very different people. Solly can read Greek and Hebrew. (*Speaking progressively faster.*) I don't think Sam can read English. But they are the same. In this way. They swing with being high. Sam has been around junk and junkies all his life and no one is more familiar with that peculiar code that goes with it, you dig? He learned the hard way. Solly knows instinctively. I mean he was born hip. God knows why he's here. I tell everyone that he is just like that damned author who wrote this damned play. He just came around and acted like he was a junkie so that he could go home to his wife and kids and get us on paper. No, that was a bad act and everyone knew it. Not Solly. If he's acting then I'm fooled. And yet—well. (*Toots mouthpiece. Starts again, slowly.*) Well, Sam is going to be around junk and junkies the rest of his life. He has no choice. Really. I don't feel that way about Solly. Both of them dig music. I mean they dig it. I mean they have an emotional digging. Which brings us to Cowboy. He's a good businessman. Some cats think he is a sweetheart. I mean he's noted for his honesty. I mean I hope he gets here soon, but he is the guy who will not run out. I think it's good business. Not a kind heart. After all, cross country gossip travels at high speed in my world. And nobody cheats him. And he used to blow [name of horn] like myself. I mean I still blow [name of horn] but he used to.

VOICE: Come off it.

ERNIE: Magic. That's what Cowboy does. I mean he makes something out of nothing. I've got the horrors. Where is Cowboy? Oh, he's fast with a knife. I saw him in action. I never believed it but there it was: knowing the danger before it happened. And then the quick move.

VOICE: Come off it.

ERNIE: Stop it. Shit! Shit! I don't trust any of you. Yes, I've tied everything into nice small packages for you. You can go home and say that Ernie really knows. Boy, he really can rip things apart. Shit. Do you hear? I don't trust one son of a bitch here or in the audience. Why? Because I really don't believe any of you understand what this is about. You're stupid. Why are you here? Because you want to see someone suffer. You want to laugh at me? You don't want to know me. And these people? Sam doesn't care about me or my music when it comes right down to it. He's for number one—himself. Solly's young. Besides, he won't be a junkie all his life. He will be so far out of it he won't have to hear the rotten stories about his life being vomited up by thieves and misfits. It's Cowboy's business to screw me. And Leach? He wants to have me begging. He wants my guts out. I knew this would happen when I started talking. I knew it. I've tried. I just can't make it. I can't explain any more to you. I tried. A little anyway. I tried. My old man made me work on his farm every day until I was seventeen and never paid me a dime. All I got was a slap across the face for thanks. Where's Cowboy? Where is he? That bastard better come back. It's no use. No use. I want my money. Where is my pay? We're supposed to be paid. Jaybird, where's my pay? I'll kill you. Do you hear?

> *Starts off stage.* SOLLY *restrains him. Photographers exit.* JAYBIRD *leaves the theatre.*

He's leaving, Solly. That's what the confession was for, wasn't it? Solly, he's leaving. We'll never get paid. I won't sign the confession. I won't sign! We'll never get paid. They made movies and it's no use. No use. (*Sits down. Mumbles.*) No use. No use.

> *Silence.* SECOND MUSICIAN *falls off his seat. He gets up and starts playing. The others join him for about five minutes of music.*

ERNIE: Give me a cigarette.
SECOND MUSICIAN: Let's split. No sense getting hung on a hanger. Cowboy got himself busted.
FIRST MUSICIAN: He'll be here. Let's stick.
THIRD MUSICIAN: My wife thinks I'm insane.

> SAM *gives him a cigarette.* ERNIE *lights it and throws the match on the floor.*

LEACH (*enters and looks around. His boil still hurts*): Who threw the match on the floor? What do you think I'm running here? A hotel for slobs? I feed you and even give you my clothes. And what do you do? Look at this place! Look at it! It's a pigsty. A pigsty. I just mopped the floor, too. Oh, what else could I expect? (*Pause.*) Where's Cowboy? (*No answer.*) Oh, my neck! Solly, what do you think I ought to do? Solly, Sam? Ernie, take a look at this. Will you?

> ERNIE *examines* LEACH's *neck*

ERNIE: Looks bad, Leach. I'd see a doctor. I hope you might die. And listen: I threw the match on the floor. I want my money. I want out. Now.

LEACH: What do you mean? (*Turns suddenly and* ERNIE *accidentally breaks the boil.*) Aaaaah!

Everyone except SOLLY *runs to him.* LEACH *is on the verge of tears.* SAM *takes control of the situation and puts* LEACH *on the bed.* ERNIE, *in disgust, stands next to* SOLLY *at the window. Everyone calms down.* SAM *gets a clean cloth and wraps it around* LEACH'S *neck.* LEACH *brushes everyone aside, picks up a mirror, examines his boil, and then turns to* ERNIE.

Ernie, I'm a man of principle. I want you to pick up that match and whatever else you've thrown on the floor. Or get out.

ERNIE (*pause*): Man, I'm a musician. I blow my horn. I'm no goddamn housekeeper. Not for you or anyone else.

LEACH: I think you better leave.

ERNIE: I'm waiting on the Cowboy. I got my bread in his pocket. And I'm not leaving until I get my fix.

LEACH: How many times have I turned you on? For nothing! How many times did you flop here? Have I ever turned you out into the cold? Man, you're ungrateful. You're selfish. And don't forget it.

ERNIE: I'm going to vomit. Man, I can't take this. Give me back my bread and I'll get out of here.

LEACH: You didn't give me any money. Besides, I haven't got any money.

FIRST PHOTOGRAPHER (*in audience*): That's the way it is. Man, that's the way it really is.

ERNIE: You've got enough on you. You always have enough on you. Miserly bastard. Like what happened to the dollar cap, to the three dollar bag? And that was some good shit, too.

LEACH: Man, you are living in another time. That was years ago. Don't blame me for what it costs.

ERNIE: Who else is there to blame? As far as I know you're just a screwball who is playing the small businessman.

LEACH: Get out! Get out! Why don't you stop pretending that you're a musician? Why do you carry that silly mouthpiece? Why?

You're never going to use it. You can't play any more. You've got to practice, you dig?

ERNIE: What do I do now? Drop my pants and bend over? I'm waiting for Cowboy. And I'm not leaving until he gets back.

SOLLY *picks up a chair and smashes it on the floor. Silence*

LEACH: What did you do that for?

SOLLY: I hate petty arguments. Besides, Cowboy's coming.

LEACH: What do you mean?

SOLLY: Cowboy's coming.

LEACH: Let me have the binoculars. (*Pause.*) Who is that with him? It doesn't look like Leonard the Locomotive. Man, it's someone in uniform. It's the cops.

SOLLY: No. No. It isn't any cop. Take another look. (*Laughs.*)

LEACH: It's some kind of uniform. I don't like it. Who is it?

SOLLY: It's some kind of salvation sister.

LEACH: Are you sure?

SOLLY: I'm not sure of anything. I think it's beautiful. Whatever Cowboy's up to certainly is good for a laugh.

LEACH: What in the world is he doing with a salvation sister? Do you think he's going to bring her in here? He's crazy. Crazy! And what happened to Leonard the Locomotive?

JIM (*quick entrance with a cigarette with holder in one hand*): Hello again. Did you miss me, my charming audience? Ah, how sweet. Things are getting exciting around here. Don't you think so?

Photographers enter and move around him while he is thinking of what to say. He dismisses them with a movement.

I am told that Leach has invited some lovely ladies to our little party. We shall see what we shall see. I may even convince Jaybird to come back.

ERNIE: Where's our money?

SOLLY: Cool it. (*To* JIM.) You'd better come through. I'm not responsible for what Ernie will do.

JIM: Huh? Good people, do not be intimidated by any of these boys during the intermission. No matter what they tell you they will be turned on a scientifically accurate amount of heroin in the next act. And that is their payment for the performance, excluding the money made on the movie. Also, we are selling some Turkish delight [and whatever else that is sold] in the lobby. Now . . . anyone in the audience for a smoke?

Lights slowly fade.

ACT TWO

Music, then lights slowly up. As the music continues for about five minutes, the musicians take turns going into the toilet. As the las musician exits, ERNIE *enters the toilet.* SOLLY *is sleeping at the window.* SISTER SALVATION *is looking around the room on tiptoe.* SAM, *on the center couch, begins to stir and the* SISTER *"shshes" him. The music ends.* ERNIE *enters, high, spots a chair and goes to it.* COWBOY *enters: he has a red bandana around his neck.*

COWBOY: Sam?

SAM: Coming, right now.

SISTER: Shsh. You heard Brother Cowboy. There's a nice young woman next door that is very sick. Now please don't make any noise. One can say things in a tiny voice as well as a big one.

COWBOY: Thank you, Sister Salvation. You are a great help to all of us.

SISTER: Is there a bathroom, Brother Cowboy?

COWBOY: Yes, mam. But Sam here hasn't had a bath in a long time. I thought I'd help him wash away those sins of his. Understand?

SISTER: Surely, Brother Cowboy.

SAM *and* COWBOY *exit.*

(*To* ERNIE.) You look very pale, son. Is something the matter? Hungry, son?

ERNIE: Leave me alone. I'm in no mood for conversation.

SISTER: Soul. Yes, my dear child, the soul. I'm sure of it.

ERNIE: You have invited yourself to a den of vipers, Sister Salvation. I'm sure you will find enough sins crossing your path today. So leave me alone.

COWBOY *enters.*

COWBOY: Understand this, Brother Rat, Brother Sun and Brother Eel! Leonard the Locomotive and I met this fine woman just one mile from our home. You know where the central police station is? Not far from there, under a flag symbolizing American freedom of speech and religion, I stopped to hear the words of the Lord.

SISTER: Amen.

COWBOY: Amen. A few gentlemen we know began a conversation with me. They asked the all important questions. Where were you? What have you been doing? How was the rodeo and horse tricks? Leonard the Locomotive succeeded in attracting some attention with his famous locomotive yell, and this worker of the Lord . . .

SISTER: Amen.

COWBOY: . . . this worker and I engaged in a most enlightening discussion. We took a quiet walk home and I invited her up for a little tea.

LEACH: Orange Pekoe.

COWBOY: Possibly she, Leonard the Locomotive, and the power of the Lord saved us all. For the moment, that is.

SISTER: Amen to that, Brother Cowboy.

COWBOY: Amen, Sister Salvation. Now excuse me please. (*Exit.*)

SOLLY: Sister Salvation, Sister Salvation, when did your record of saving souls start?

LEACH: Cool, cool water, Solly.

SOLLY: Have a little trust in the Lord, friend.

SISTER: Brother, I began in the service of the Lord fourteen years ago. But I have only been active these past seven. If you could see the hundreds of faces smile and light up when someone holds out a helping hand to show the path of salvation, it would warm your heart. You haven't known joy until you have seen the way to God. (*Pause.*) Do you know Harry McNulty?

LEACH: We don't know anyone.

COWBOY *enters.*

COWBOY: Excuse me, Sister Salvation. Solly, you're next.

SISTER: There's something crazy going on.

SAM (*following* COWBOY): Save yourself, you sinners! Brother Cowboy has some potent medicine made from the rarest, finest witch doctor white flower that ever grew. (*Laughs.*) Shiiiit. Oh, excuse me, Sister Salvation.

COWBOY: Leach, how about making Sister Salvation a nice cup of tea while you're waiting.

LEACH: I'm waiting to get on. Man, I'm sick.

SOLLY (*at the toilet door*): I don't take long. Start the tea, I'll finish it. (*Exits with* COWBOY.)

> ERNIE *starts playing "There is a Fountain Filled with Blood" on his mouthpiece. Then he starts singing it. After a few lines the words disappear and he is scat singing.* SISTER SALVATION *claps her hands in time and everyone joins her. The photographers enter from the audience.*

SISTER: Oh, it is good, good, good to hear such young men appreciate songs like that. (*Notices the photographers.*) Who are they? Where did they come from?

LEACH: They're all right. Friends of the family. Did Jaybird come back?

FIRST PHOTOGRAPHER: Not yet.

SISTER: What's a nice Negro boy like you doing here?

SAM: I've seen the light! (*Melodramatically.*) Yes, I've seen the light! Brethren, I used to be a sinner! A sinner!

> LEACH *and* ERNIE *laugh. Photographers exit.*

A sinner that done bad to his fellow man. But now! Praise the Lord!

SISTER: Amen.

SAM: I am redeemed! From my eternal suffering I am redeemed! Like a pawn ticket.

> *Laughter.*

I want to take the opportunity to thank each and every kind, gentle and good contributor in the audience. You have helped a most noble cause, and a cause that is dear to our hearts. That goodness, that goodness that flows in our veins is the evidence —is the evidence of our gratitude toward you and every one of our fellow men.

SISTER: Amen.

LEACH: I'm not on yet.

SAM: You, too, Brother Eel, will be saved by Brother Cow in just . . .

> SOLLY *enters with* COWBOY.

Ah, you see before you with your very own eyes Brother Sol. Hello, Brother.

SOLLY: You weren't kidding, Sambo. This is powerful medicine. I'm going around and will become butter any minute.

SAM: I should wash your mouth out with soap.

SISTER: Amen. Amen. Are you through in the bathroom, Brother Cowboy?

Exit LEACH.

COWBOY: There is just Brother Leach, mam. And then our baptism will be all over.

Exit COWBOY.

SISTER: That's all right, Brother Cowboy. You just keep working.

SECOND MUSICIAN *falls to the floor and* FIRST MUSICIAN *helps him up.* SISTER SALVATION *starts over to him, but* SOLLY *interrupts her.*

SOLLY: Praise the Lord!

SISTER: Amen.

SOLLY: Sister Salvation, I want you to see the light. I mean, man, light travels at 186,000 miles per second per second. I'd like to see that, too. Watch it closely. Faster and faster around your head. Now let your eyes cross. The light is forming an enormous circle around you. You're not helping me, baby. Help me. (*Starts to fall.* SAM *catches him and carries him to his seat.*) Mercy on me. I falleth before the Lord. Oh, man, it is too tiring. Man, whew! Where do all those sinners get the energy to be saved? Fantastic. I couldn't make it. You have to hand it to them. Day after day, trudging and pulling, they seek out energetic sinners. Each of them is saved ten or twenty times. It's just too much.

SAM: You got to let yourself go. When you feel it inside, just let yourself go and wail.

SOLLY: Man, I feel it inside, but I can't move. I'm stoned. (*Sits at window.*)

SISTER (*to* ERNIE): Where do you come from, son?

ERNIE (*almost asleep*): What?

SISTER: Are you all right, son?

ERNIE: Yeah. Sure. Of course, baby, I'm all right. Where do I come from? See, I can remember.

SISTER: Yes. Where do you come from?

ERNIE: California.

SISTER: That's marvelous.

ERNIE: What's so marvelous about it?

SISTER: It's so clean and healthy there. The trees, and everything is so green. (*Pause.*) I thought perhaps—perhaps you know Harry McNulty. He's Irish.

ERNIE: Yes. (*Falling asleep.*) It is. Green.

Falls out of the chair. SISTER SALVATION *helps him up and* COWBOY *comes over and slaps him gently.*

I'm all right. Man. Leave me alone. It's green. I want to sleep.

COWBOY: The poor boy hasn't slept in days.

SISTER: Oh, we better leave him alone. He looks like a good prospect to save.

COWBOY: Why don't you make yourself a nice cup of tea.

SISTER SALVATION *exits.*

LEACH: I'm not even high. I don't feel a thing. I don't feel a thing.

SAM: If you don't feel a thing, man, then you're higher than any of us.

LEACH: You gave them more. How much did you give Ernie, Cowboy? He's knocked out. And I don't feel a thing.

COWBOY: Cool it. You know Ernie has been chipping. I gave him the same as you, but you got a higher tolerance. Dig?

Photographers enter from the audience.

SECOND PHOTOGRAPHER: I . . . I don't know how to say this.

COWBOY: I don't know you, man. Who are you?

SECOND PHOTOGRAPHER: I'm here to do the film.

LEACH: Jim sent him. But weren't you the one that was so afraid? Yeah. What about the other photographer?

FIRST PHOTOGRAPHER: Count me out. I don't want nothing to do with this.

LEACH (*laughs*): This is going to be fun. Cowboy, give him a taste.

COWBOY: Not out of mine.

LEACH: Out of mine. Go ahead, give him a little taste.

COWBOY: Are you sure you want to go through with this?

SECOND PHOTOGRAPHER (*mumbles*): Yes.

JAYBIRD (*enters from the audience*): Okay. Okay. Aren't you carrying this too far? What is happening here? You aren't here to do this sort of thing. Destroy yourself, but this wasn't in our deal.

COWBOY: Jaybird, I don't want to initiate anyone into the club. This boy is asking for it. You stop him. I'm too tired to talk.

JAYBIRD: I don't like it. It's not supposed to work this way. I've given you latitude. But this is too much.

LEACH: Hey, Jaybird, you've never made it. Why don't you find out what it's all about before you put it down.

JAYBIRD: Me? No. Not me. Never. Me?

LEACH: You're supposed to know all about it. I mean this all is a play, man. It's not really real. (*Snicker.*) Hey, I want to watch.

COWBOY: Let's not talk here. (*Smiling.*) You stay, Leach. Come on back.

Exit COWBOY, FIRST PHOTOGRAPHER *and* JAYBIRD.

LEACH: So Jaybird will take a little taste for himself.

SISTER (*enters. Walks to the window*): Where are all those people coming from? Who are they? I don't see anybody out there. (*Uses binoculars.*) I don't see anyone out there at all. This is very confusing. (*To Solly.*) Do you know Harry McNulty?

SOLLY: No. There are some questions I can't answer. That's one of them.

SISTER: [Gives a short description of actor who plays Harry.]

SOLLY: What makes you think I would know him?

SISTER: Oh, he loves jazz music. I thought perhaps . . . never mind, I'm probably wrong anyway. The Lord willing, that is.

SECOND MUSICIAN *falls off his seat.* FIRST MUSICIAN *mechanically picks him up.*

FIRST PHOTOGRAPHER: That is the way it is. Really, it is that way.

SAM: Yes, it is. As long as we are talking religion, I got one that happened not too long ago. (*To the musicians.*) You know Abdul the drummer? Well, Abdul is from Harlem and he has

taken up the Moslem faith. A religious man if I ever saw one. Is
there any beer?

SECOND MUSICIAN: No.

SAM: One night Abdul and Cowboy and me were looking for some
small connection. No luck anywhere. Everybody is tearing their
hair out. Cowboy and I decide to try to score outside the city.
Abdul gave us some money and told us to meet him at his pad. We
go outside the city and score and everything is crazy. It is getting
light out by now and we hurry back to town and go to Abdul's
pad. We knock. No answer. Knock again. No answer. Cowboy
tries the door and it's open. We go in and there is Abdul in his
underwear kneeling on this rug and he got his hands clasped
together and eyes is tight shut. I say, "Abdul, we're back." No
answer. "Abdul, baby, everything's cool. We made it." Still no
answer. Cowboy tries to stop me from talking to him because
Cow figures it must be important if Abdul won't even turn
around. We sit down. I can't stand the silence any more. So I
say, "Abdul, what the hell you doing, man? Do you know who
I am? What are you doing on your knees, baby?" He turns around
and stares at me. Finally, he says, "Man, I was praying that you
would come back and turn me on!"

SISTER (*pause*): That's a wicked story! Such language!

LEACH (*enters*): Here's your cup of tea, Sister Salvation.

SISTER: Thank you, brother.

COWBOY *enters with* SECOND PHOTOGRAPHER *and* JAYBIRD. JAY-
BIRD *has* COWBOY's *red bandana around his neck,* FIRST PHOTOG-
RAPHER *exits to the audience.* SECOND PHOTOGRAPHER *takes*
SISTER SALVATION's *cup and sits.*

COWBOY: Well, what's been happening? Sister Salvation, the bathroom is yours. (SISTER *exits.*) What have you been doing to that
chick? I don't want her to leave with a suspicious thought in her
head.

LEACH: You shouldn't have brought her here. I think she knows
what's happening. Or she doesn't know and wants to.

COWBOY: There were two narcotic bulls on my back. Leonard the
Locomotive went one way, and they followed him. I left with her.
Man, it was close. I was about to throw the shit away.

SAM: What happened in there?

COWBOY: What a miserable sight it was. A night for comedy. I think Jaybird is pretty sick. (*Pointing to the* SECOND PHOTOGRAPHER.) He is.

LEACH: He's out of his skull. Look at him. Hey, man, how do you feel?

SECOND PHOTOGRAPHER: Don't be a drag, man.

They all laugh.

JAYBIRD: I've got to lie down.

LEACH: Go ahead! There's a bed.

JAYBIRD: No, not here. (*Whispers.*) There are too many people around. Wait a minute. I'm sick. (*Exits to toilet.*)

SISTER (*entering*): Drink! (*Backs up* JAYBIRD. JAYBIRD *runs into toilet, holding his mouth.*) That's what you've been doing in there!

COWBOY: What do you mean, Sister Salvation?

SISTER: What do you mean, Brother Cowboy? There are at least ten bottles of wine in the bathroom. All empty. Oh, Lord, before my very own eyes I have been deceived. Wine is a mocker, strong drink is raging: and whosoever is deceived thereby is not wise.

The following dialogue is underscored with the bass playing with SOLLY, *and the horn with* SISTER SALVATION.

SOLLY: A false balance is an abomination to the Lord; but a just weight is his delight.

SAM: Swing!

SISTER: Be not among winebibbers, among riotous eaters of flesh. For the drunkard and glutton shall come to poverty. Who hath woe? Who hath sorrow? Who hath babbling? Who hath wounds without cause? Who hath redness of eyes? They that tarry long at the wine. They that go to seek mixed wine. At last it biteth like a serpent and stingeth like an adder.

SOLLY: Who invented that uniform?

SISTER: What?

SOLLY: Who invented the uniform you are wearing?

SISTER: I don't know. What has that got to do with it? It isn't what I was talking about. You can't get out of this that easily. You will pay . . .

SOLLY: Foggy day in London, London, London town. It's the War

Congress. 1878. Winter. The flock is assembling. Coming back to you now, Sister Salvation? Elijah Cadmen stood up and said, (*Sotto voce.*) "We need a military type uniform. War to the teeth and salvation to the world."

SISTER: I thought that General Booth invented . . . I could look it up in the library. Where did you learn these things? You would like our library. It's open to the public.

SOLLY: Your bonnet was invented by the General's wife. There will be equality of the sexes, they scream. Dress shall be according to climate. 1880. International meeting. Fur caps in the Arctic. Veils in India. All embracing salvation.

SISTER: I give up. I give up. Stop.

SOLLY: Don't surrender now. Or do. It was just, just, just, just one of those things.

SISTER: What's a nice young man like you doing here?

Laughter by all.

I don't understand. Why do you . . . ?

Laughter by all.

SOLLY: No more war. You had better leave while the spirit of brotherhood prevails.

SISTER: I don't want to leave. I know I'm a burden. I went to see about my funeral. The man at Morgen's funeral parlor said it would cost three hundred dollars for opening and closing the grave. Eighty-five dollars for the head stone. I'm growing old and my eyes are going. I don't want to leave. I've been in the hospital. They put the needle in my arm, too.

SOLLY: Cowboy? (*Nods to him.*) Go ahead, Sister Salvation, before we tell you who Harry McNulty is.

SISTER (COWBOY *takes her to the door*): You are not alone. You are not alone. (*Exit.*) You are not alone.

JAYBIRD (*enters from toilet*): Glad to have met you? (*Laughs and sits down to sleep.*)

The musicians play for about ten minutes. When finished there is a pause. JIM *enters, taking notes.*

JIM: Leach? Leach? Where are the chicks? Where are the chicks?

LEACH: Oh, man, my job was to invite them. I didn't guarantee anything. They'll probably show up. Hold your pants.

COWBOY: Hey, man, are we getting any extra money for being in this movie scheme?

JIM: You would have. (*Pointing to* SECOND PHOTOGRAPHER.) He isn't going to make any movies so far as I can see.

COWBOY: Do I detect a note of hostility?

JIM: No. No, but it wasn't right for you to give these people dope. Look at Jaybird. Oh, Jaybird!

COWBOY: I didn't want to give either of them anything. It's their own responsibility. Man, they're old enough to know what they're doing.

JIM: Okay. All right. I'm not a moralist. But we should get the chicks here. Oh, it didn't have to be chicks. Homosexuals would do. Some kind of chorus. I should have seen to it myself. You people are so unreliable.

JAYBIRD (*mumbles*): It's out of my hands! It's out of my hands! There is this wall between you and me, Jim. So that's what it does!

JIM: I want a good show too. Is that too much? You know it's every penny I've got. You can't go on amusing yourself! Get girls or something. I'm telling you that'll do it, man.

LEACH: Maybe you would like to turn on, too. Since you're not a moralist.

JIM: No. (*Points to his head.*) I've got a brain. Why are you cats really here?

LEACH: It's fun.

SOLLY: The money.

ERNIE: It's something to do.

COWBOY: Because we all love you.

JIM *exits.*

LEACH: I'm not high, Cowboy.

COWBOY: Wait awhile, man. Don't hurry it. Enjoy it, baby.

LEACH: I didn't get a flash, Cowboy, I didn't get a flash.

COWBOY (*laughs*): It's been ten years since I've had a flash. Just sit down and look at a picture book.

ERNIE *blows his mouthpiece.*

Not while I'm around. No, no. Practice in your bathroom. Hey, Solly, what did your White Sox [or any current sports reference] do today?

SOLLY: The Yankees [or any appropriate sports reference] beat them. Again. There's the worst habit I know—the congenital losers.

COWBOY: It's only a game. How did that new shortstop do?

LEACH: You square bastards! Square daytime bastards. Baseball ain't hip.

SAM: I ain't hip. Do you call it hip spending half the time in jail? (*Nods.*)

LEACH: They haven't got me yet.

COWBOY: You better expect it. Besides, what's wrong with day jobs? Or being square? Man, I haven't anything against them. There are lousy hipsters and lousy squares. Personally I couldn't make the daily work scene. I like my work hours as they are. But it doesn't make me any better. No, man, no.

LEACH: You know what I'd do if I had a day job? Man, I'd work about six months and then establish credit. You know what I mean? Then I'd get every charge card there is. Food, liquor and travel. Man, I'd go all over the world. What could they do? Throw me in debtor's prison? Not in America. No sir, we're free here. You know what I mean? Man . . .

COWBOY: What movies you been watching?

LEACH: Others have done it.

COWBOY: Seems like a lot of work. An awful lot of work. Could you work six months? At what? (*Sings.*) I'm dreaming of a white Christmas, just like the ones I used to know. (*Says.*) You know we live in a white society. Did you ever see black snow?

SAM (*wakes up*): Who said snow?

SOLLY: I've seen brown heroin from Mexico.

COWBOY: But that's Mexico.

LEACH: I'm not high, Cowboy, I'm not high.

COWBOY: Give it time. Go eat something. Read a picture book. Man, walk outside and let life—

MAN (*in audience*): I gave Sam five bucks and I want a story. I want a story from Sam.

COWBOY: Who said that? Stand up.

MAN (*stands*): I want a story.

COWBOY: Insistent bastard. (*Takes hoop and wakes* SAM.) Here, man, roll out some kind of jive. It's that cat there. Did he give you five?

SAM: Yeah. Can't you see that someone gave me five?

COWBOY: Then tell him a story.

SAM (*intermittently scratching his face and body*): Three, four years ago: let's see, there was me and the Cowboy and Leach. Yeah. Leach was selling books downtown. He always walked out of that store with one under his coat. Cowboy and he had a pad down near the waterfront. Me? I was scuffling. As usual. The point is we were very hot. I don't know whose fault that was. Leach can be loud. Scream like a bitch in heat. Of course, Cowboy's and my record speak for itself. Anyway, what I last remember how it first began. Shiiit. Is that what I wanted to say? Man, this is very nice stuff. Anyway, there was a party. Leach was bribing this hustler with good old heroin. Funny thing, Leach always seems to have a place. If he and I have the same amount of money, I wind up on the street and he always got a weird kind of joint with foolish signs all around. This party. Did I tell you about the party? Kelly was there. He had his harem, too. That was when we called Kelly "Upsidedownface!" He didn't like it. He did have that kind of head. But, he always had three or four chicks with him. And did he like them go-go pills! Man, he took thirty or forty benzedrine a day. And believe me, I was brought up to believe that it was best to have just one man and one bitch in bed at the same time. But Upsidedownface wouldn't be satisfied with less than two and usually more. Maybe that's got something to do with him hanging himself. I don't know. That night one of his chicks was taking the trouble to bring me beer and to rub up against me. Man, she was a beautiful animal. Oh! Well, she was hung up in her head like everyone else I know. She kept talking about how she always wanted to marry a Negro. She came from the South or something. She kept calling me her Black Prince. Well, I don't care what a bitch say with her mouth. It's what she say with her body that has got my eye. Upsidedownface is a generous person. If you let him announce to everyone what you can take away from him. You dig? While he was announcing the departure of the chick from his harem, the phonograph was playing and Leach was arguing with this bitch he invited. I think he was kissing her breasts or something. What made it an argument was that there were so many people around. Prostitutes sure can have prissy morals. The woman next door started complaining, knocking on the walls. Finally she came over. Leach told her off. About ten minutes later the cops knock politely on the door. They come in. What's going on here? Who rents this apartment? What's your name? and yours? Those sort of questions. We all played it cool. No searching. Nothing like that. The party went on. Not the same. The cops shake everyone. But, in a curious way, most cops and junkies are alike. Sado . . . Solly, sado what?

SOLLY: Masochist.

SAM: Anyway, we wondered if they would come back. People left, the music stopped. Leach started bitching. He felt insulted that everyone was going. The cops didn't come back. About a week later to the day we three were in the pad again. Cowboy cooked dinner that night. Ham. And peas. Yeah. We were finished eating and Leach was teaching me how to play chess. Which meant that he was playing with himself. He moved all the pieces and I would sit back and stroke my chin and say, "Yeah. Yeah." Cowboy was reading some kind of hot book. The phone rings and it is some chick that doesn't particularly knock Leach out. But he gives a story and makes a date. I suppose this was to make Cowboy and me jealous. Leach has a funny mind. He tell us that he will be back at eleven o'clock. Sure. After he leaves, Cowboy pulls out some marijuana and we get high and have a few laughs about Leach. I was going to sleep.

Footsteps offstage, coming and going.

On the wall that I was looking at was a painting in orange and red, circles and lines. They began moving out of the painting and in my head, you know what I mean? Next thing I know the door is knocked down and these two guys with guns are over Cowboy and me. Wham! We're thrown against the wall. Well, this is old stuff in a way. If that sort of thing can ever be old stuff. First there is the scare. A few wacks and threats and we are supposed to tell all. All? Actually, Cowboy and I didn't know Leach had hidden about a quarter of an ounce in the couch. The greedy bastard! Then something funny happened. It seemed that they were after Leach. They looked at our arms. They could have thrown us in jail for those long snakes of old needle marks. Or they could have claimed that it was our stuff that they had found. But no. For some reason they know that Leach rented the apartment and they wanted him. Perhaps they thought he was the King of the Junkie World. That's what the papers call every squirt that is caught. Cowboy tells them that we are supposed to meet Leach in a certain bar not too far. Meanwhile, it is getting very close to eleven o'clock. They fall for it and we leave and start walking up the block. Arm in arm, of course. Leach is walking straight towards us. He's got this chick with him. Cowboy drops his cigarette and bends down to get it. While the cops are watching him, I raised my hand to my mouth. Leach got the idea, and kicks the chick who is about to scream hello to us. They walked right by. We didn't see Leach for two years. Heard he went to Texas, or some place unfit for humans. Anyway, we go into this candle-lighted bar and the Cowboy looks very carefully at everyone. The cops hurry him up. So Cowboy gets mad and picks out a rather well-tailored looking kid. Bing! They collar him, and take him along with us to the station. That poor kid screamed all the way down to the station and they put him in the observation room. They let us go. I don't know if they ever let that kid go. Man, that was a long one. I'm tired. (*Mumbles and stretches, then sits.*)

JAYBIRD (*stands. Scratches face and body*): You cats are actors?

COWBOY: I'm not acting. You should have thought about that when you hired us.

JAYBIRD: I'm not angry. Just amused. All you do is talk, talk, talk. Is there no end to this babbling? (*Calms himself.*) This part was to be blood and guts drama. It's not for me that I plead with you. Think of the audience. Jimmie thinks of the audiences. I dream about them. So far one would think this was a drawing room comedy. If you were in the audience you'd know what I'm talking about. Listen, I researched everything carefully. I lived among you. Now what are you doing? You've all changed. Man, you aren't supposed to change. Just act naturally. Is that all you know—destruction? I know better. Maybe it's the audience. It's that? They're making you nervous. They're making me nervous Maybe we should have tried it without an audience the first few nights. (*Starts to fall asleep.*)

COWBOY: It's not the audience, Jaybird.

JAYBIRD: Don't feel inadequate. After all, I have a prison record too.

We've all been in the army. We're veterans, you and I. We're veterans. (*Laughs.*)

ERNIE *blows his mouthpiece.*

COWBOY: I feel great, don't you, man?

JAYBIRD: I don't know . . . I don't know what's happening to me. (*Wearily.*) I do know that there isn't any hero in this play. I wrote a play with four heroes. Didn't I explain that part? You are all heroes. I mean in the theatrical sense. Cowboy, can't you act like a hero? It's the basis of Western drama, you know. Can't you make an heroic speech? You have not been upstaging it, at all. Look what you've done to the cameraman. Where's the other photographer?

FIRST PHOTOGRAPHER *enters from audience.*

We want some angle shots of Cowboy. Our hero.

SECOND PHOTOGRAPHER *wakes up and wobbles around* COWBOY *with* FIRST PHOTOGRAPHER.

Cowboy, you can do for the show, Cowboy. We're all together. Say something.

COWBOY: It's too much risk going out and scoring every night. I mean I'm followed every night and I have to scheme a way of getting back here. I'm tired. Man, I've been moving my whole life. You think I enjoy leaving love behind? I haven't anything to say. Is that what you wanted, Author? (*To the photographers.*) I'm sick of the sight of you fake beboppers. (*He takes hold of the* FIRST PHOTOGRAPHER *and pushes him to the end of the stage.*) Get out of here! I'm sick of the sight of you. (*To the author.*) Sit down and quit worrying about your precious play. Sit down, Mother. Damn it! You can't find anything out about anything by flirting with people. What do you think we live in, a freak show? You be the hero. Relax, we won't run out on you. You're just high.

LEACH (*softly at first*): I'm not high. I'm not high at all. You know what I mean? I want more. Cowboy? Cowboy? You have some left. I'm not high. It's mine, Cowboy. Strictly speaking, it's mine and I want some more. Everybody's high and I'm not. You didn't give me as much as you gave them.

COWBOY: Now, baby, why should I want to cheat you?

LEACH: I want more.

COWBOY: Man, you are high. That shit is in your system.

LEACH: I want more.

COWBOY: Okay, it's your life.

Exit COWBOY. *Musicians play.* COWBOY *enters and gives* LEACH *a small package.* LEACH *performs the ritual of fixing and taking the heroin. No one pays any attention to him. He falls, dropping the "works."*

COWBOY: There goes my last spike! (*Goes to* LEACH. *He realizes* LEACH *has taken an overdose.*) Sam!

SAM *slowly goes to him. One by one the musicians stop playing.* COWBOY *and* SAM *bring* LEACH *to the couch.* COWBOY *starts artificial respiration.*

SECOND MUSICIAN: Give him a salt shot.

COWBOY: That was my last spike.

THIRD MUSICIAN: Let's pack up.

FOURTH MUSICIAN: Let's get to that gig.

COWBOY *and* SAM *walk* LEACH *back and forth. He doesn't respond. They lay him on the couch.* JAYBIRD *starts to* LEACH *but stops and sits again.*

ERNIE: I'm leaving. I don't like it. You know what I mean? I've got a gig tonight. I've got to find a horn to use. You dig?

SECOND MUSICIAN: Can we help?

SAM: No, you might as well make that gig.

ERNIE *exits.*

Chicken shit!

Musicians exit, each saying: "*We'll see you tomorrow,* COWBOY."

Later on, gentlemen, later on. (*Looks at* SOLLY.) Why don't you go, too?

SOLLY: I'm not in a hurry.

SAM (*picks up and plays with the hoop*): I'm sorry, Solly. But that bastard Ernie just upsets me. He always runs out. He hasn't played that rotten horn for five years now. And him coming on like he was the great artist of something or other. Bullshitter.

JAYBIRD *again starts to* LEACH *but stops and sits.*

SOLLY: How is he?

COWBOY: Not good.

SOLLY: Shall I get a doctor?

COWBOY: No, not yet. No use of all of us getting in trouble.

SAM: I remember when that bastard Ernie threw a kid who took an overdose out the window. Didn't even know whether he was dead or not.

SOLLY: We never found out for sure.

SAM: I always believed it. (*Rolls hoop to the other side of the stage.*)

LEACH (*mumbles*): Three eighty four. Three eighty four. My number's up. I can see it. (*Laughs crazily.*)

JAYBIRD: Is he dying? (*Mumbles.*) Why did I start this? (*Sits next to* SOLLY.)

SOLLY: I don't blame Ernie for leaving. Listen to that madman.

SAM: Well, he's alive.

SOLLY: Which one? (*Pause.*) I ever tell you the Chinese laundry story? It was in Chicago. I was living above this Chinese laundry and one day the owner knocked on my door and told me that my bathroom was leaking into his store. I told him he could fix it if he wanted to. And he did! Which flipped me because he was a notorious cheap skate. At that time shit was relatively scarce and I had to go out of the city to score. One afternoon I happened to be sitting on the front fire escape and I noticed some photographers taking pictures of the building. I couldn't figure it out. Besides, I was very high and got paranoid and went inside. That afternoon the headlines were screaming about the biggest narcotics ring in America being rounded up. Where? Downstairs. Two million dollars worth of opium right under my leaking bathroom and I had to go miles to get a pittance. At least I made the front page.

SAM: That's a good five dollar story.

LEACH (*still in a coma*): They're coming! Hide! Hide. You can't have me!

SOLLY: Is he all right?

COWBOY: The more he talks the better I'll feel.

SOLLY: Yes, he'll probably live. Whatever that means. I don't think there is such a thing as learning a lesson. At least not with him. Somehow you get the feeling Leach will try again and again until he kills himself. Or the cops get him and he spends a few years in jail. Talking calms me. There is something perverse in me looking for meaning all the time.

LEACH: Who killed Cock Robin? (*Insistent.*) Who killed Cock Robin?

COWBOY: I don't know what he's talking about and I don't know what you're talking about. And once more, babies, I don't care. But, both of you keep blowing. Just blow.

SOLLY: I can remember that when I was a kid the word marijuana was in the dictionary between marigold and marimba.

SAM: It probably still is. (*Lights a book of matches, then stamps them out.*) Hey, man, how long has heroin been illegal?

SOLLY: In this country since 1928, I think.

SAM: Why? I mean, man, why did they make it illegal?

SOLLY: I really don't know. To protect people from themselves. Maybe popular opinion. Maybe the liquor lobby. I once heard it was a plot of the rich. Beats me.

SAM: I wish I knew.

COWBOY: Who cares? Man, they got a bomb, haven't they? Protect us from ourselves. Man, the Japanese cats don't feel that way. That's your theory, Solly. Just a theory. Doesn't have anything to do with us.

SOLLY: Well, Leach doesn't need any theories, if that's what you mean.

COWBOY: Everything that's illegal is illegal because it makes more money for more people that way.

SOLLY: That may be right. But, junk does take its effect.

COWBOY: We all pay our dues whatever we do.

JAYBIRD (*mumbles incoherently. Wakes up*): So they all left. What happened to the ending? We've lost the end. Well, well. All's well. Is he dead?

COWBOY: No.

SOLLY: You look like the Jaybird I first met.

JAYBIRD: Mmph. I'm here and you're here. Just like a couple of months ago. Something happened in between. Maybe the idea of an audience. But . . . (*He touches* SOLLY's *shoulder.*) I'm still alone and naïve. And hooked on people. All sentiment aside, why don't you cats kick junk?

SOLLY: How many times have we heard someone swearing he was going to kick? (*No answer.*) I look out this window and watch the crowds looking into store windows. I try to remember that they are human beings. Most of the time, it doesn't make sense. When I talk, I'm a pessimist. Yet, I want to live. I don't jump into the street against the lights and just miss killing myself a hundred times a day. That's what happens out there. And in here, too. Why are some hunted and others hunt? The tyranny of the majority. I remember once I moved out of a hotel without paying the old Italian who ran it. Two months later I was walking by the hotel and he ran out after me. He wanted to grab me by the collar and start a fight. Instead he looked at me and said, "You aren't one of the people." Now what in God's creation did he mean?

Pause on stage.

JIM (*enters from audience*): I'm getting panicked. I'm getting panicked. There's a rumor the fuzz are coming. The fuzz are coming. We're going to get busted. Busted. Oh, the publicity! What's wrong with you?

JAYBIRD: I'm sick. We've lost it. We've lost it. (*Stands.*)

JIM: What have we lost?

JAYBIRD: The end, you fool. The end.

JIM (*thinks*): We'll all die. That's a great idea for you. We just die.

SOLLY: Don't be silly. I can't. I'm out of it.

JIM: That's not the point. How do you propose to get off stage logically? Ah, you see. Shakespeare, tragedy, that sort of thing has been making it for a long time. This is a time-tested formula. What more can you ask? I'll die too. Don't think I'm not willing to die. If it will bring in the revenue. I'll die of exhaustion of carrying you off. (*Laughs.*) You see? Perfect plot, eh, Jaybird.

JAYBIRD: You stink!

JIM: All right so I hired photographers. One of them had to take a shot.

JAYBIRD: I'm not blaming you. How did I ever get into this? Oh, yes

... (*Pacing the stage.*) ... I wanted to do something far out. Yes, I'm guilty of trying to have a little shock value. Is there a politician in the house? Then I've failed.

JIM: It wasn't your fault. We should have had chicks. You planned it with chicks and it was my fault they didn't show up. Maybe we'll get them for the movie version. Besides I thought you'd be delighted with my photographer idea. I thought you liked Dada.

JAYBIRD: Shut up! (*Long pause.*) It was my fault. I thought perhaps the doctors would take over. That's the message for tonight from me. Maybe I'm supposed to be the hero. But I'm not a martyr. We don't need women. We need a martyr. Let Dada doctors take control of narcotics.

COWBOY: Man, doctors wouldn't help me. I'd be out of a job. Hell, the doctors would be the big connection.

SOLLY: I don't trust them. Those are the people who mildly electrocute thousands of people every year. And how many prefrontal lobotomies are performed? Oh, no. I don't trust them as a group any more than I trust the police as a group. Or Junkies, especially the likes of Ernie and Leach.

JAYBIRD: Yes.

SAM: Why didn't you get on the H-bomb riff? If you needed a riff. I've always liked mushrooms.

JIM: I've had a run for my money.

JAYBIRD: All right. All right. So that isn't the answer. I've lost it. But one thing I've learned about the theatre. I believe it all fits together.

SOLLY: It doesn't have to fit.

JAYBIRD: Yes. Yes, it does. We wouldn't all be on stage if it didn't fit. That's what I had in mind in the first place. I didn't learn anything. I knew it. Find a horror. Then you try to tell people it isn't a horror. And then I have the gall to be horrified. Well, if it wasn't junk, I would have been involved with something else. (*Takes off* COWBOY's *red bandana.*)

COWBOY: Well, doctor, that's very heroic.

Loud knocking on the door.

JAYBIRD: No doctors, no heroes, no martyrs, no Christs. That's a very good score. I didn't get burned. Maybe short counted, but not burned. (*Pacing.*) It's all yours now.

Pause on stage. JIM *opens the door. It is* HARRY. *He performs his record ritual. Lights slowly fade. Music ends in the dark.*

END

The Balcony

by
Jean Genet

Translated by Bernard Frechtman

The first American performance of THE BALCONY was presented at Circle In The Square, New York City, March, 3, 1960. It was directed by José Quintero, scenery and lights by David Hays, costumes by Patricia Zipprodt, and with the following cast:

THE BISHOP . . . . F. M. Kimball

IRMA . . . . Nancy Marchand

THE WOMAN PENITENT . . . . Grayson Hall

THE THIEF . . . . Sylvia Miles

THE JUDGE . . . . Arthur Malet

THE EXECUTIONER . . . . John Perkins

THE GENERAL . . . . John S. Dodson

THE GIRL . . . . Salome Jens

CARMEN . . . . Betty Miller

THE CHIEF OF POLICE . . . . Roy Poole

THE ENVOY . . . . Jock Livingston

ROGER . . . . Joseph Daubenas

THE SLAVE . . , ... William Goodwin

THE MAN, ARTHUR, GEORGETTE, CHANTAL, THE WOUNDED MAN, ARMAND, LUKE, LOUIS, MARK, ROSINE, THE BEGGAR, FIRST PHOTOGRAPHER, SECOND PHOTOGRAPHER, THIRD PHOTOGRAPHER, THE QUEEN

The play is in nine scenes

SCENE ONE

On the ceiling, a chandelier, which will remain the same in each scene. The set represents a sacristy, formed by three blood-red, cloth folding-screens. The one at the rear has a built-in door. Above, a huge Spanish crucifix. On the right wall, a mirror, with a carved gilt frame, reflects an unmade bed which, if the room were arranged logically, would be in the first rows of the orchestra. A table with a large jug. A yellow arm-chair. On the chair, a pair of black trousers, a shirt and a jacket. THE BISHOP, *in miter and gilded cope, is sitting in the chair. He is obviously larger than life. The role is played by an actor wearing tragedian's cothurni about twenty inches high. His shoulders, on which the cope lies, are inordinately broadened so that when the curtain rises he looks huge. He wears garish make-up. At the side, a* WOMAN, *rather young, highly made up and wearing a lace dressing-gown, is drying her hands with a towel. Standing by is another woman,* IRMA. *She is about forty, dark, severe-looking, and is wearing a black tailored suit.*

THE BISHOP (*sitting in the chair, middle of the stage; in a low but fervent voice*): In truth, the mark of a prelate is not mildness or unction, but rather the most rigorous intelligence. Our heart is our undoing. We think we are master of our kindness; we are the slave of a serene laxity. In fact, it is something quite other than intelligence that is involved . . . (*He hesitates.*) It may be cruelty. And beyond that cruelty—and through it—a skilful, vigorous heading towards Absence. Towards Death. God? (*Smiling.*) I can read your mind! (*To his miter.*) Miter, bishop's bonnet, when my eyes close for the last time, it is you that I shall see behind my eyelids, you, my beautiful gilded hat . . . you, my handsome ornaments, copes, laces. . . .

IRMA (*bluntly; throughout the scene she will hardly move. She is standing very near the door*): An agreement's an agreement. When a deal's been made. . . .

THE BISHOP (*very gently, waving her aside with a gesture*): And when the die is cast. . . .

IRMA: No. Twenty. Twenty, and no nonsense. Or I'll lose my temper. And that's not like me. . . . Now, if you have any difficulties. . . .

271

THE BISHOP (*curtly, and tossing away the miter*): Thank you.

IRMA: And don't break anything. We need that. (*To* THE WOMAN.) Put it away. (*She lays the miter on the table, near the jug.*)

THE BISHOP (*after a deep sigh*): I've been told that this house is going to be besieged? The rebels have already crossed the river.

IRMA: You can slip around behind the Archbishop's Palace. Then, down Fishmarket Street. . . .

Suddenly a scream of pain, uttered by a woman off-stage.

IRMA (*annoyed*): But I instructed them to be quiet. Good thing I took care to cover the windows with padded curtains. (*Suddenly amiable, insidious.*) Well, and what was it this evening? A blessing? A prayer? A mass? A perpetual adoration?

THE BISHOP (*gravely*): Let's not talk about that now. It's over. I'm concerned only about getting home. . . .

THE WOMAN: There was a blessing, Madame. Then, my confession. . . .

IRMA: And after that?

THE BISHOP: That'll do!

THE WOMAN: That was all. At the end, my absolution.

IRMA: Won't anyone be able to witness it? Just once?

THE BISHOP (*frightened*): No, no. Those things must remain secret, and they shall. It's indecent enough to talk about them while I'm being undressed. Nobody. And all the doors must be closed. Oh, firmly closed, shut, buttoned, laced, hooked, sewn. . . .

IRMA: I merely asked. . . .

THE BISHOP: Sewn, Madame.

IRMA (*annoyed*): You'll allow me at least, won't you, to feel a little uneasy . . . professionally? I said twenty.

THE BISHOP (*his voice suddenly grows clear and sharp, as if he were awakening; he displays a little annoyance*): We didn't tire ourselves. Barely six sins, and far from my favorite ones.

THE WOMAN: Six, but deadly ones! And it was a job finding *those*.

THE BISHOP (*uneasy*): What? You mean they were false?

THE WOMAN: They were real, all right! I mean it was a job committing them. If only you realized what it takes, what a person has to go through, in order to reach the point of disobedience.

THE BISHOP: I can imagine, my child. The order of the world is so lax that you can do as you please there—or almost. But if your sins were false, you may say so now.

IRMA: Oh no! I can already hear you complaining the next time you come. No. They were real. (*To* THE WOMAN.) Untie his laces. Take off his shoes. And when you dress him, be careful he doesn't catch cold. (*To* THE BISHOP.) Would you like a toddy, a hot drink?

THE BISHOP: Thank you. I haven't time. I must be going. (*Dreamily.*) Yes, six, but deadly ones!

IRMA: Come here, we'll undress you!

THE BISHOP (*pleading, almost on his knees*): No, no, not yet.

IRMA: It's time. Come on! Quick! Make it snappy!

> *While they talk, the women undress him. Or rather they merely remove pins and untie cords that seem to secure the cope, stole and surplice.*

THE BISHOP (*to* THE WOMAN): About the sins, you really did commit them?

THE WOMAN: I did.

THE BISHOP: You really made the gestures? All the gestures?

THE WOMAN: I did.

THE BISHOP: When you moved towards me with your face forward, was it really aglow with the light of the flames?

THE WOMAN: It was.

THE BISHOP: And when my ringed hand came down on your fore-head, forgiving it. . . .

THE WOMAN: It was.

THE BISHOP: And when my gaze pierced your lovely eyes?

THE WOMAN: It was.

IRMA: Was there at least a glimmer of repentance in her lovely eyes, your Lordship?

THE BISHOP (*standing up*): A fleeting glimmer. But was I seeking re-pentance in them? I saw there the greedy longing for trans-gression. In flooding it, evil all at once baptized it. Her 'big eyes opened on the abyss . . . a deathly pallor lit up—yes, Madame —lit up her face. But our holiness lies only in our being able to forgive you your sins. Even if they're only make-believe.

THE WOMAN (*suddenly coy*): And what if my sins were real?

THE BISHOP (*in a different, less theatrical tone*): You're mad! I hope you really didn't do all that!

IRMA (*to* THE BISHOP): Don't listen to her. As for her sins, don't worry. Here there's no. . .

THE BISHOP (*interrupting her*): I'm quite aware of that. Here there's no possibility of doing evil. You live in evil. In the absence of remorse. How could you do evil? The Devil makes believe. That's how one recognizes him. He's the great Actor. And that's why the Church has anathematized actors.

THE WOMAN: Reality frightens you, doesn't it?

THE BISHOP: If your sins were real, they would be crimes, and I'd be in a fine mess.

THE WOMAN: Would you go to the police?

> IRMA *continues to undress him. However, he still has the cope on his shoulders.*

IRMA: Stop plaguing her with all those questions.

> *The same terrible scream is heard again.*

IRMA: They're at it again! I'll go shut them up.

THE BISHOP: That wasn't a make-believe scream.

IRMA: How do we know? And what does it matter?

THE BISHOP (*going slowly to the mirror. He stands in front of it*): Now answer, mirror, answer me. Do I come here to discover evil and innocence? (*To* IRMA, *very gently.*) Leave the room! I want to be by myself.

IRMA: It's late. And the later it gets, the more dangerous it'll be. . . .

THE BISHOP (*pleading*): Just one more minute.

IRMA: You've been here two hours and twenty minutes. In other words, twenty minutes too long. . . .

THE BISHOP (*suddenly incensed*): I want to be by myself. Eavesdrop, if you want to—I know you do, anyway—and don't come back till I've finished.

> *The two women leave with a sigh, looking as if they were out of patience.* THE BISHOP *remains alone.*

THE BISHOP (*after making a visible effort to calm himself, in front of the mirror and holding his surplice*): Now answer, mirror, answer me. Do I come here to discover evil and innocence? And

in your gilt-edged glass, what was I? Never—I affirm it before
God Who sees me—I never desired the episcopal throne. To become bishop, to work my way up—by means of virtues or vices
—would have been to turn away from the ultimate dignity of
bishop. I shall explain: (THE BISHOP *speaks in a tone of great
precision, as if pursuing a line of logical reasoning.*) in order to
become a bishop, I would have had to make a zealous effort not
to be one, but to do what would have resulted in my being one.
Having become a bishop, in order to be one I would have had—
in order to be one for myself, of course!—I would have had to be
constantly aware of being one so as to perform my function. (*He
seizes the flap of his surplice and kisses it.*) Oh laces, laces, fash-
ioned by a thousand little hands to veil ever so many panting
bosoms, buxom bosoms, and faces, and hair, you illustrate me
with branches and flowers! Let us continue. But—there's the
crux! (*He laughs.*) So I speak Latin!—a function is a function.
It's not a mode of being. But a bishop—that's a mode of being.
It's a trust. A burden. Miters, lace, gold-cloth and glass trinkets,
genuflexions. . . . F . . k the function!

Crackling of machine-gun fire.

IRMA (*putting her head through the door*): Have you finished?
THE BISHOP: For Christ's sake, leave me alone. Get the hell out! I'm
questioning myself.

IRMA *shuts the door.*

THE BISHOP (*to the mirror*): The majesty, the dignity, that light up
my person, do not emanate from the attributions of my function.
—No more, good heavens! than from my personal merits.—The
majesty, the dignity that light me up come from a more mysterious brilliance: the fact that the bishop precedes me. Do I
make myself clear, mirror, gilded image, ornate as a box of
Mexican cigars? And I wish to be bishop in solitude, for appearance alone. . . . And in order to destroy all function, I want to
cause a scandal and feel you up, you slut, you bitch, you trollop,
you tramp. . . .
IRMA (*entering*): That'll do now. You've got to leave.
THE BISHOP: You're crazy! I haven't finished.

Both women have entered.

IRMA: I'm not trying to pick an argument, and you know it, but you've no time to waste. . . .

THE BISHOP (*ironically*): What you mean is that you need the room for someone else and you've got to arrange the mirrors and jugs.

IRMA (*very irritated*): That's no business of yours. I've given you every attention while you've been here. And I repeat that it's dangerous for anyone to loiter in the streets.

Sound of gunfire, in the distance.

THE BISHOP (*bitterly*): That's not true! You don't give a damn about my safety. When the job's finished, you don't give a damn about anyone!

IRMA (*to* THE GIRL): Stop listening to him and undress him.

IRMA (*to* THE BISHOP, *who has stepped down from his cothurni and has now assumed the normal size of an actor, of the most ordinary of actors*): Lend a hand. You're stiff.

THE BISHOP (*with a foolish look*): Stiff? I'm stiff? A solemn stiffness! Final immobility. . . .

IRMA (*to* THE GIRL): Hand him his jacket. . . .

THE BISHOP (*looking at his clothes, which are heaped on the floor*): Ornaments, laces, through you I re-enter myself. I reconquer a domain. I beleaguer a very ancient place from which I was driven. I install myself in a clearing where suicide at last becomes possible. The judgment depends on me, and here I stand, face to face with my death.

IRMA: That's all very fine, but you've got to go. You left your car at the front door, near the power-station.

THE BISHOP (*to* IRMA): Because our Chief of Police, that wretched incompetent, is letting us be slaughtered by the rabble! (*Turning to the mirror and declaiming.*) Ornaments! Miters! Laces! You, above all, oh gilded cope, you protect me from the world. Where are my legs, where are my arms? Under your wavy, lustrous flaps, what have my hands been doing? Fit only for fluttering gestures, they've become mere stumps of wings—not of angels, but of partridges!—rigid cope, you make it possible for the most tender and luminous sweetness to ripen in warmth and darkness. My charity, a charity that will flood the world—it

was under this carapace that I distilled it. . . . Would my hand
emerge at times, knifelike, to bless? Or cut, mow down? My
hand, the head of a turtle, would push aside the flaps. A turtle
or a cautious snake? And go back into the rock. Underneath, my
hand would dream. . . . Ornaments, gilded copes. . . .

*The stage moves from left to right, as if it were plunging into
the wings. The following set then appears.*

Same chandelier. <u>*Three brown folding-screens.*</u> *Bare walls. At right, same mirror, in which is reflected the same unmade bed as in the first scene. A woman, young and beautiful, seems to be chained, with her wrists bound. Her muslin dress is torn. Her breasts are visible. Standing in front of her is* THE EXECUTIONER. *He is a giant, stripped to the waist. Very muscular. His whip has been slipped through the loop of his belt, in back, so that he seems to have a tail. A* JUDGE, *who, when he stands up, will seem larger than life (he, too, is mounted on cothurni, which are invisible beneath his robe, and his face is made up), is crawling towards the woman, who shrinks as he approaches.*

THE THIEF (*holding out her foot*): Not yet! Lick it! Lick it first. . . .

> THE JUDGE *makes an effort to continue crawling. Then he stands up and, slowly and painfully, though apparently happy, goes and sits down on a stool.* THE THIEF (*the woman described above*) *drops her domineering attitude and becomes humble.*

THE JUDGE (*severely*): For you're a thief! You were caught. . . . Who? The police. . . . Have you forgotten that your movements are constricted by a strong and subtle network, my brawny cops? They're watchful, swivel-eyed insects that lie in wait for you. All of you! And they bring you captive, all of you, to the Bench. . . . What have you to say for yourself? You were caught. . . . Under your skirt . . . (*To* THE EXECUTIONER.) Put your hand under her skirt. You'll find the pocket, the notorious Kangaroo Pocket . . . (*To* THE THIEF.) that you fill with any old junk you pick up. Because you're an idiot to boot. . . . (*To* THE EXECUTIONER.) What was there in that notorious Kangaroo Pocket? In that enormous paunch?

THE EXECUTIONER: Perfumes, Your Honor, a flashlight, a bottle of Fly-tox, some oranges, several pairs of socks, bear-skins, a Turkish towel, a scarf. (*To* THE JUDGE.) Do you hear me? I said: a scarf.

THE JUDGE (*with a start*): A scarf? Ah ha, so that's it? Why the scarf? Eh? What were you going to do with it? Whom were you planning to strangle? Answer. Who? . . . Are you a thief or a strangler?

(*Very gently, imploringly.*) Tell me, my child, I beg of you, tell me you're a thief.

THE THIEF: Yes, your Honor.

THE EXECUTIONER: No!

THE THIEF (*looking at him in surprise*): No?

THE EXECUTIONER: That's for later.

THE THIEF: Eh?

THE EXECUTIONER: I mean the confession is supposed to come later. Plead not guilty.

THE THIEF: What, and get beaten again!

THE JUDGE (*mealy-mouthed*): Exactly, my child: and get beaten. You must first deny, then admit and repent. I want to see hot tears gush from your lovely eyes. Oh! I want you to be drenched in them. The power of tears! Where's my statute-book? (*He fishes under his robe and pulls out a book.*)

THE THIEF: I've already cried. . . .

THE JUDGE (*he seems to be reading*): Under the blows. I want tears of repentance. When I see you wet as a meadow I'll be utterly satisfied!

THE THIEF: It's not easy. I tried to cry before. . . .

THE JUDGE (*no longer reading; in a half-theatrical, almost familiar tone*): You're quite young. Are you new here? At least you're not a minor?

THE THIEF: Oh no, sir.

THE JUDGE: Call me Your Honor. How long have you been here?

THE EXECUTIONER: Since the day before yesterday, Your Honor.

THE JUDGE (*reassuming the theatrical tone and resuming the reading*): Let her speak. I like that puling voice of hers, that voice without resonance. . . . Look here: you've got to be a model thief if I'm to be a model judge. If you're a fake thief, I become a fake judge. Is that clear?

THE THIEF: Oh yes, Your Honor.

THE JUDGE (*he continues reading*): Good. Thus far everything has gone off well. My executioner has hit hard . . . for he too has his function. We are bound together, you, he and I. For example, if he didn't hit, how could I stop him from hitting? Therefore, he must strike so that I can intervene and demonstrate my authority. And you must deny your guilt so that he can beat you. (*A noise is heard, as of something having fallen in the next room. In a natural tone*.) What's that? Are all the doors firmly shut? Can anyone see us, or hear us?

THE EXECUTIONER: No, no, you needn't worry. I bolted the door. (*He goes to examine a huge bolt on the rear door.*) And the corridor's out of bounds.

THE JUDGE (*in a natural tone*): Are you sure?

THE EXECUTIONER: You can take my word for it. (*He puts his hand into his pocket.*) Can I have a smoke?

THE JUDGE (*in a natural tone*): The smell of tobacco inspires me. Smoke away. (*Same noise as before.*) Oh, what *is* that? What *is* it? Can't they leave me in peace? (*He gets up.*) What's going on?

THE EXECUTIONER (*curtly*): Nothing at all. Someone must have dropped something. You're getting nervous.

THE JUDGE (*in a natural tone*): That may be, but my nervousness makes me aware of things. It keeps me on my toes. (*He gets up and moves towards the wall.*) May I have a look?

THE EXECUTIONER: Just a quick one, because it's getting late. (THE EXECUTIONER *shrugs his shoulders and exchanges a wink with* THE THIEF.)

THE JUDGE (*after looking*): It's lit up. Brightly lit, but empty.

THE EXECUTIONER (*shrugging his shoulders*): Empty!

THE JUDGE (*in an even more familiar tone*): You seem anxious. Has anything new happened?

THE EXECUTIONER: This afternoon, just before you arrived, the rebels took three key-positions. They set fire to several places. Not a single fireman came out. Everything went up in flames. The Palace. . . .

THE JUDGE: What about the Chief of Police? Twiddling his thumbs, as usual?

THE THIEF: There's been no news of him for four hours. If he can get away, he's sure to come here. He's expected at any moment.

THE JUDGE (*to* THE THIEF, *and sitting down*): In any case, he'd better not plan to come by way of Queen's Bridge. It was blown up last night.

THE THIEF: We know that. We heard the explosion from here.

THE JUDGE (*resuming his theatrical tone; he reads the statute-book*): All right. Let's get on with it. Thus, taking advantage of the sleep of the just, taking advantage of a moment's inattention, you rob them, you ransack, you pilfer and purloin. . . .

THE THIEF: No, Your Honor, never. . . .

THE EXECUTIONER: Shall I tan her hide?

THE THIEF (*crying out*): Arthur!

THE EXECUTIONER: What's eating you? Don't address me. Answer His Honor. And call me Mr. Executioner.

THE THIEF: Yes, Mr. Executioner.

THE JUDGE (*reading*): I continue: did you steal?

THE THIEF: I did. I did, Your Honor.

THE JUDGE (*reading*): Good. Now answer quickly, and to the point: what else did you steal?

THE THIEF: Bread, because I was hungry.

THE JUDGE (*he draws himself up and lays down the book*): Sublime! Sublime function! I'll have all that to judge. Oh, child, you reconcile me with the world. A judge! I'm going to be judge of your acts! On me depends the weighing, the balance. The world is an apple. I cut it in two: the good, the bad. And you agree, thank you, you agree to be the bad! (*Facing the audience.*) Right before your eyes: nothing in my hands, nothing up my sleeve, remove the rot and cast it off. But it's a painful occupation. If every judgment were delivered seriously, each one would cost me my life. That's why I'm dead. I inhabit that region of exact freedom. I, King of Hell, weigh those who are dead, like me. She's a dead person, like myself.

THE THIEF: You frighten me, sir.

THE JUDGE (*very bombastically*): Be still. In the depths of Hell I sort out the humans who venture there. Some to the flames, the others to the boredom of the fields of asphodel. You, thief, spy, she-dog, Minos is speaking to you, Minos weighs you. (*To* THE EXECUTIONER.) Cerberus?

THE EXECUTIONER (*imitating the dog*): Bow-wow, bow-wow!

THE JUDGE: You're handsome! And the sight of a fresh victim makes you even handsomer. (*He curls up* THE EXECUTIONER's *lips.*) Show your fangs. Dreadful. White. (*Suddenly he seems anxious. To* THE THIEF.) But at least you're not lying about those thefts— you did commit them, didn't you?

THE EXECUTIONER: Don't worry. She committed them, all right. She wouldn't have dared not to. I'd have made her.

THE JUDGE: I'm almost happy. Continue. What did you steal? (*Suddenly, machine-gun fire.*)

THE JUDGE: There's simply no end to it. Not a moment's rest.

THE THIEF: I told you: the rebellion has spread all over the north of the city. . . .

THE EXECUTIONER: Shut up!

THE JUDGE (*irritated*): Are you going to answer, yes or no? What else have you stolen? Where? When? How? How much? Why? For whom?

THE THIEF: I very often entered houses when the maids were off. I used the service entrance. . . . I stole from drawers, I broke into children's piggy-banks. (*She is visibly trying to find words.*) Once I dressed up as a lady. I put on a dark brown suit, a black straw hat with cherries, a veil and a pair of black shoes—with Cuban heels—then I went in. . . .

THE JUDGE (*in a rush*): Where? Where? Where? Where—where—where? Where did you go in?

THE THIEF: I can't remember. Forgive me.

THE EXECUTIONER: Shall I let her have it?

THE JUDGE: Not yet. (*To* THE THIEF.) Where did you go in? Tell me where?

THE THIEF (*in a panic*): But I swear to you, I don't remember.

THE EXECUTIONER: Shall I let her have it? Shall I, Your Honor?

THE JUDGE (*to* THE EXECUTIONER, *and going up to him*): Ah! ah! your pleasure depends on me. You like to thrash, eh? I'm pleased with you, Executioner! Masterly mountain of meat, hunk of beef that's set in motion at a word from me! (*He pretends to look at himself in* THE EXECUTIONER.) Mirror that glorifies me! Image that I can touch, I love you. Never would I have the strength or skill to leave streaks of fire on her back. Besides, what could I do with such strength and skill? (*He touches him.*) Are you there? You're all there, my huge arm, too heavy for me, too big, too fat for my shoulder, walking at my side all by itself! Arm, hundred-weight of meat, without you I'd be nothing. . . . (*To* THE THIEF.) And without you too, my child. You're my two perfect complements. . . . Ah, what a fine trio we make! (*To* THE THIEF.) But you, you have a privilege that he hasn't, nor I either, that of priority. My being a judge is an emanation of your being a thief. You need only refuse—but you'd better not!—need only refuse to be who you are—what you are, therefore who you are—for me to cease to be . . . to vanish, evaporated. Burst. Volatized. Denied. Hence: good born of . . . What then? What then? But you won't refuse, will you? You won't refuse to be a thief? That would be wicked.

It would be criminal. You'd deprive me of being! (*Imploringly.*) Say it, my child, my love, you won't refuse?

THE THIEF (*coyly*): I might.

THE JUDGE: What's that? What's that you say? You'd refuse? Tell me where. And tell me again what you've stolen.

THE THIEF (*curtly, and getting up*): I won't.

THE JUDGE: Tell me where. Don't be cruel. . . .

THE THIEF: Your tone is getting too familiar. I won't have it!

THE JUDGE: Miss. . . . Madame. I beg of you. (*He falls to his knees.*) Look, I beseech you. Don't leave me in this position, waiting to be a judge. If there were no judges, what would become of us, but what if there were no thieves?

THE THIEF (*ironically*): And what if there weren't?

THE JUDGE: It would be awful. But you won't do that to me, will you? Please understand me: I don't mind your hiding, for as long as you can and as long as my nerves can bear it, behind the refusal to confess—it's all right to be mean and make me yearn, even prance, make me dance, drool, sweat, whinny with impatience, crawl . . . do you want me to crawl?

THE EXECUTIONER (*to* THE JUDGE): Crawl.

THE JUDGE: I'm proud!

THE EXECUTIONER (*threateningly*): Crawl! (THE JUDGE, *who was on his knees, lies flat on his stomach and crawls slowly towards* THE THIEF. *As he crawls forward,* THE THIEF *moves back.*)

THE EXECUTIONER: Good. Continue.

THE JUDGE (*to* THE THIEF): You're quite right, you rascal, to make me crawl after my judgeship, but if you were to refuse for good, you hussy, it would be criminal. . . .

THE THIEF: Call me Madame, and ask politely.

THE JUDGE: Will I get what I want?

THE THIEF (*coyly*): It costs a lot—stealing does.

THE JUDGE: I'll pay! I'll pay whatever I have to, Madame. But if I no longer had to divide the Good from the Evil, of what use would I be? I ask you?

THE THIEF: I ask myself.

THE JUDGE (*infinitely sad*): A while ago I was going to be Minos. My Cerberus was barking. (*To* THE EXECUTIONER.) Do you remember? (THE EXECUTIONER *interrupts* THE JUDGE *by cracking his whip.*) You were so cruel, so mean! So good! And me, I was pitiless. I was going to fill Hell with the souls of the damned, to fill prisons.

Prisons! Prisons! Prisons, dungeons, blessed place where evil is impossible since they are the crossroads of all the malediction in the world. One cannot commit evil in evil. Now, what I desire above all is not to condemn, but to judge. . . . (*He tries to get up.*)

THE EXECUTIONER: Crawl! And hurry up, I've got to go and get dressed.

THE JUDGE (*to* THE THIEF): Madame! Madame, please, I beg of you. I'm willing to lick your shoes, but tell me you're a thief. . . .

THE THIEF (*in a cry*): Not yet! Lick! Lick! Lick first!

The stage moves from left to right, as at the end of the preceding scene, and plunges into the right wing. In the distance, machine-gun fire.

SCENE THREE

*Three dark green folding-screens, arranged as in the preceding
scenes. The same chandelier. The same mirror reflecting the unmade
bed. On an armchair, a horse of the kind used by folk-dancers, with
a little kilted skirt. In the room, a timid-looking gentleman:* THE
GENERAL. *He removes his jacket, then his bowler hat and his gloves.*
IRMA *is near him.*

THE GENERAL (*pointing to the hat, jacket and gloves*): Have that
    cleared out.
IRMA: It'll be folded and wrapped.
THE GENERAL: Have it removed from sight.
IRMA: It'll be put away. Even burned.
THE GENERAL: Yes, yes, of course, I'd like it to burn! Like cities at
    twilight.
IRMA: Did you notice anything on the way?
THE GENERAL: I ran very serious risks. The populace has blown up
    dams. Whole areas are flooded. The arsenal in particular. So
    that all the powder kegs are wet. And the weapons rusty. I had
    to make some rather wide detours—though I didn't trip over a
    single drowned body.
IRMA: I wouldn't take the liberty of asking you your opinions. Every-
    one is free, and I'm not concerned with politics.
THE GENERAL: Then let's talk of something else. The important thing
    is how I'm going to get out of this place. It'll be late by the time
    I leave. . . .
IRMA: About it's being late. . . .
THE GENERAL: That does it. (*He reaches into his pocket, takes out
    some banknotes, counts them and gives some to* IRMA. *She keeps
    them in her hand.*)
THE GENERAL: I'm not keen about being shot down in the dark when
    I leave. For, of course, there won't be anyone to escort me?
IRMA: I'm afraid not, unfortunately. Arthur's not free. (*A long
    pause.*)
THE GENERAL (*suddenly impatient*): But . . . isn't she coming?
IRMA: I can't imagine what she's doing. I gave instructions that every-
    thing was to be ready by the time you arrived. The horse is
    already here. . . . I'll ring.

THE GENERAL: Don't, I'll attend to that. (*He rings.*) I like to ring! Ringing's authoritative. Ah, to ring out commands.

IRMA: In a little while, General. Oh, I'm so sorry, here am I giving you your rank. . . . In a little while you'll. . . .

THE GENERAL: Sh! Don't say it.

IRMA: You have such force, such youth! such dash!

THE GENERAL: And spurs. Will I have spurs? I said they were to be fixed to my boots. Oxblood boots, right?

IRMA: Yes, General. Oxblood. And patent-leather.

THE GENERAL: Patent-leather very well, but with mud?

IRMA: With mud and perhaps a little blood. I've had the decorations prepared.

THE GENERAL: Authentic ones?

IRMA. Authentic ones.

Suddenly a woman's long scream.

THE GENERAL: What's that? (*He starts going to the right wall and is already bending down to look, as if there were a small crack, but* IRMA *steps in front of him.*)

IRMA: Nothing. There's always some carelessness, on both sides.

THE GENERAL: But that cry? A woman's cry. A call for help perhaps? My pounding heart skips a beat. . . . I spring forward. . . .

IRMA: What on earth can she be doing?

She goes to ring, but by the rear door enters a very beautiful young woman, red-headed, hair undone, disheveled. Her bosom is almost bare. She is wearing a black corset, black stockings and very high-heeled shoes. She is holding a general's uniform, complete with sword, cocked hat and boots.

THE GENERAL (*severely*): So you finally got here? Half an hour late. That's more than's needed to lose a battle.

IRMA: She'll redeem herself, General, I know her.

THE GENERAL (*looking at the boots*): What about the blood? I don't see any blood.

IRMA: It dried. Don't forget that it's the blood of your past battles. Well, then, I'll leave you. Do you have everything you need?

THE GENERAL (*looking to the right and left*): You're forgetting. . . .

IRMA: Good God! Yes, I was forgetting.

She lays on the chair the towels she has been carrying on her arm. Then she leaves by the rear. THE GENERAL *goes to the door, then locks it. But no sooner is the door closed than someone knocks.* THE GIRL *goes to open it. Behind, and standing slightly back,* THE EXECUTIONER, *sweating, wiping himself with a towel.*

THE EXECUTIONER: Is Mme. Irma here?

THE GIRL (*curtly*): In the Rose-garden. (*Correcting herself.*) I'm sorry, in the Funeral Chapel. (*She closes the door.*)

THE GENERAL (*irritated*): I'll be left in peace, I hope. And you're late. Where the hell were you? Didn't they give you your feed-bag? You're smiling, are you? Smiling at your rider? You recognize his hand, gentle but firm? (*He strokes her.*) My proud steed! My handsome mare, we've had many a spirited gallop together!

THE GIRL: And that's not all! I want to trip through the world with my nervous legs and well-shod hooves. Take off your pants and shoes so I can dress you.

THE GENERAL (*he has taken the cane*): All right, but first down on your knees! Come on, come on, bend your knees, bend them. . . .

The girl rears, utters a whinny of pleasure and kneels like a circus horse before THE GENERAL.

THE GENERAL: Bravo! Bravo, Dove! You haven't forgotten a thing. And now, you're going to help me and answer my questions. It's fitting and proper for a nice filly to help her master unbutton himself and take off his gloves, and to be at his beck and call. Now start by untying my laces.

During the entire scene that follows, THE GIRL *helps* THE GENERAL *remove his clothes and then dress up as a general. When he is completely dressed, he will be seen to have taken on gigantic proportions, by means of trick effects: invisible foot-gear, broadened shoulders, excessive make-up.*

THE GIRL: Left foot still swollen?

THE GENERAL: Yes. It's my leading-foot. The one that prances. Like your hoof when you toss your head.

THE GIRL: What am I doing? Unbutton yourself.

THE GENERAL: Are you a horse or an illiterate? If you're a horse, you toss your head. Help me. Pull. Don't pull so hard. See here, you're not a plough-horse.

THE GIRL: I do what I have to do.

THE GENERAL: Are you rebelling? Already? Wait till I'm ready. When I put the bit into your mouth. . . .

THE GIRL: Oh no, not that.

THE GENERAL: A general reprimanded by his horse! You'll have the bit, the bridle, the harness, the saddlegirth, and I, in boots and helmet, will whip and plunge!

THE GIRL: The bit is awful. It makes the gums and the corners of the lips bleed. I'll drool blood.

THE GENERAL: Foam pink and spit fire! But what a gallop! Along the ryefields, through the alfalfa, over the meadows and dusty roads, over hill and dale, awake or asleep, from dawn to twilight and from twilight. . . .

THE GIRL: Tuck in your shirt. Pull up your suspenders. It's quite a job dressing a victorious general who's to be buried. Do you want the sabre?

THE GENERAL: Let it lie on the table, like Lafayette's. Conspicuously, but hide the clothes. Where? How should *I* know? Surely there's a hiding-place somewhere. (THE GIRL *bundles up his clothes and hides them behind the armchair.*)

THE GENERAL: The tunic? Good. Got all the medals? Count 'em.

THE GIRL (*after counting them, very quickly*): They're all here, sir.

THE GENERAL: What about the war? Where's the war?

THE GIRL (*very softly*): It's approaching, sir. It's evening in an apple-orchard. The sky is calm and pink. The earth is bathed in a sudden peace—the moan of doves—the peace that precedes battles. The air is very still. An apple has fallen to the grass. A yellow apple. Things are holding their breath. War is declared. The evening is very mild. . . .

THE GENERAL: But suddenly?

THE GIRL: We're at the edge of the meadow. I keep myself from flinging out, from whinnying. Your thighs are warm and you're pressing my flanks. Death. . . .

THE GENERAL: But suddenly?

THE GIRL: Death has pricked up her ears. She puts a finger to her lips, asking for silence. Things are lit up with an ultimate goodness. You yourself no longer heed my presence. . . .

THE GENERAL: But suddenly?

THE GIRL: Button up by yourself, sir. The water lay motionless in the pools. The wind itself was awaiting an order to unfurl the flags. . . .

THE GENERAL: But suddenly?

THE GIRL: Suddenly? Eh? Suddenly? (*She seems to be trying to find the right words.*) Ah, yes, suddenly all was fire and sword! Widows! Miles of crape had to be woven to put on the standards. The mothers and wives remained dry-eyed behind their veils. The bells came clattering down the bombed towers. As I rounded a corner I was frightened by a blue cloth. I reared, but, steadied by your gentle and masterful hand, I ceased to quiver. I started forward again. How I loved you, my hero!

THE GENERAL: But . . . the dead? Weren't there any dead?

THE GIRL: The soldiers died kissing the standard. You were all victory and kindness. One evening, remember. . . .

THE GENERAL: I was so mild that I began to snow. To snow on my men, to shroud them in the softest of winding-sheets. To snow. Moskova!

THE GIRL: Splinters of shell had gashed the lemons. Now death was in action. She moved nimbly from one to the other, deepening a wound, dimming an eye, tearing off an arm, opening an artery, discoloring a face, cutting short a cry, a song. Death was ready to drop. Finally, exhausted, herself dead with fatigue, she grew drowsy and rested lightly on your shoulder, where she fell asleep.

THE GENERAL (*drunk with joy*): Stop, stop, it's not time for that yet, but I feel it'll be magnificent. The cross-belt? Good. (*He looks at himself in the mirror.*) Austerlitz! General! Man of war and in full regalia, behold me in my pure appearance. Nothing, no contingent trails behind me. I appear, purely and simply. If I went through wars without dying, went through sufferings, without dying, it was for this minute close to death. (*Suddenly he stops; he seems troubled by an idea.*) Tell me, Dove?

THE GIRL: What is it, sir?

THE GENERAL: What's the Chief of Police been doing? (THE GIRL *shakes her head.*) Nothing? Still nothing? In short, everything slips through his fingers. And what about us, are we wasting our time?

THE GIRL (*imperiously*): Not at all. And, in any case, it's no business of ours. Continue. You were saying: for this minute close to death ... and then?

THE GENERAL (*hesitating*): ... close to death ... where I shall be nothing, though reflected *ad infinitum* in these mirrors, nothing but my image. ... Quite right, comb your mane. Curry yourself. I require a well-groomed filly. So, in a little while, to the blare of trumpets, we shall descend—I on your back—to death and glory, for I am about to die. It is indeed a descent to the grave. ...

THE GIRL: But, sir, you've been dead since yesterday.

THE GENERAL: I know ... but a formal and picturesque descent, by unexpected stairways. ...

THE GIRL: You are a dead general, but an eloquent one.

THE GENERAL: Because I'm dead, prating horse. What is now speaking, and so beautifully, is Example. I am now only the image of my former self. Your turn, now. Lower your head and hide your eyes, for I want to be a general in solitude. Not even for myself, but for my image, and my image for its image, and so on. In short, we'll be among equals. Dove, are you ready? (THE GIRL *nods*.) Come now. Put on your bay dress, horse, my fine Arab steed. (THE GENERAL *slips the mock-horse over her head. Then he cracks his whip*.) We're off! (*He bows to his image in the mirror*.) Farewell, general! (*Then he stretches out in the armchair with his feet on another chair and bows to the audience, holding himself rigid as a corpse*. THE GIRL *places herself in front of the chair and, on the spot, makes the movements of a horse in motion*.)

THE GIRL: The procession has begun. ... We're passing through the City. ... We're going along the river. I'm sad. ... The sky is overcast. The nation weeps for that splendid hero who died in battle. ...

THE GENERAL (*starting*): Dove!

THE GIRL (*turning around, in tears*): Sir?

THE GENERAL: Add that I died with my boots on! (*He then resumes his pose*.)

THE GIRL: My hero died with his boots on! The procession continues. Your aides-de-camp precede me. ... Then come I, Dove, your war-horse. ... The military band plays a funeral march. ... (*Marching in place*, THE GIRL *sings Chopin's* Funeral March, *which is continued by an invisible orchestra* [*with brasses*]. *Far off, machine-gun fire*.)

SCENE FOUR

A room, the three visible panels of which are three mirrors in which is reflected a little old MAN, *dressed as a tramp though neatly combed. He is standing motionless in the middle of the room. Near him, looking very indifferent, a very beautiful red-haired* GIRL. *Leather corselet, leather boots. Naked and beautiful thighs. Fur jacket. She is waiting. So is the man. He is impatient, nervous. The girl is motionless.*

The man removes his torn gloves tremblingly. He takes from his pocket a handkerchief and mops his face. He takes off his glasses, folds them and puts them into a case, which he slips into his pocket. He wipes his hands with his handkerchief.

All the gestures of the little old man are reflected in the three mirrors. (Three actors are needed to play the roles of the reflections.)

At length, there are three raps at the rear door. The red-haired girl goes to the door. She says: "Yes." The door opens a little, and through the opening appear IRMA'S *hand and arm holding a whip and a very dirty and shaggy wig. The girl takes them. The door closes.*

The man's face lights up. The red-haired girl has an exaggeratedly lofty and cruel air. She puts the wig on his head roughly.

The man takes a bouquet of artificial flowers from his pocket. He holds it as if he were going to offer it to the girl, who whips him and lashes it from his hand. The man's face is lit up with tenderness.

Very nearby, machine-gun fire.

The man touches his wig.

THE MAN: What about the lice?
THE GIRL (*very coarsely*): They're there.

IRMA's *room. Very elegant. It is the same room that was reflected in the mirrors in the first three scenes. The same chandelier. Large lace hangings suspended from the flies. Three arm-chairs. Large window at left; door at right.* IRMA *is sitting at her dressing-table, going over her accounts. Near her, a girl:* CARMEN. *Machine-gun fire.*

CARMEN (*counting*): The bishop, twenty . . . the judge, twenty. . . . (*She raises her head.*) No, Madame, nothing yet. No Chief of Police.

IRMA (*irritated*): And yet!

CARMEN: Yes, I know: it takes all kinds to make a world. But no Chief of Police. (*She counts again.*) The general, twenty . . . the sailor, thirty . . . the baby . . .

IRMA: I've told you, Carmen, I don't like that.

CARMEN (*sharply*): A person can make a mistake.

IRMA: And no back-talk either. And I demand respect for the visitors. Vi-si-tors! I don't allow myself—my own self (*she stresses the word "own"*)—even to refer to them as clients. And yet! . . . (*She flashily snaps the sheaf of fresh banknotes that she has in her hand.*)

CARMEN (*severely; she has turned around and is glaring at* IRMA): For you, yes: cash and refinement.

IRMA (*trying to be conciliatory*): Those eyes! Don't be unjust. You've been irritable for some time now. I know that everyone's upset by what's going on, but things will quiet down. The sun will come out again. George. . . .

CARMEN: Ah, him!

IRMA: Don't sneer at the Chief of Police. If not for him we'd be in a fine mess. Yes, we, because you're tied up with me. And with him. (*A long pause.*) What disturbs me most is your sadness. (*Wisely.*) You've changed, Carmen.

CARMEN: There's nothing much left for me to do at your place, Mme. Irma.

IRMA (*disconcerted*): But . . . I've put you in charge of my bookkeeping. You sit down at my desk, and all at once my entire life opens out before you. I haven't a secret left, and you're not happy?

292

CARMEN: Of course, I'm grateful to you for your confidence, but . . . it's not the same thing.

IRMA: Do you miss "that," Carmen? (CARMEN *is silent.*) Come, come, Carmen, when you mounted the snow-covered rock with the yellow paper rosebush—by the way, I'm going to have to store that in the cellar—and when the miraculously-healed leper swooned at the sight of you, you didn't take yourself seriously, did you, Carmen? (*Brief silence.*)

CARMEN: When our sessions are over, Madame, you never allow anyone to talk about them. So you have no idea of how we really feel. You observe it all from a distance. But if ever you once put on the dress and the blue veil, or if you were the unbuttoned penitent, or the general's mare, or the country girl tumbled in the hay. . . .

IRMA (*shocked*): Me!

CARMEN: Yes, you, Mme. Irma. Or the maid in a pink apron, or the archduchess deflowered by the policeman, or . . . but I'm not going to run through the whole list . . . you'd know what that does to a girl's soul, and that she's got to use a little irony in self-defense. But no, you don't even want us to talk about it among ourselves. You're afraid of a smile, of a joke.

IRMA (*very severely*): True, I don't allow any joking. A giggle, or even a smile, spoils everything. A smile means doubt. The clients want sober ceremonies. My house is a severe place. You're allowed to play cards.

CARMEN: Then don't be surprised that we're sad. But I'm thinking of my daughter.

IRMA (*she stands—for a bell has buzzed—and goes to a curious piece of furniture at the left, a kind of switchboard with a view-finder and earphone. While talking, she looks into the view-finder, after pushing down a switch*): Every time I ask you a slightly intimate question, you shut up like a clam, and you throw your daughter up to me. Are you still set on going to see her? Don't be a fool. Between this place and the nursery in the country there's fire and water, rebellion and bullets. I even wonder whether . . . (*The bell buzzes again.* MME. IRMA *pulls up the switch and pushes down another.*) . . . whether they didn't get George on the way. Though a Chief of Police knows how to take care of himself. (*She looks at a watch that she takes from her bosom.*) He's late.

CARMEN: In order to get to your studios, those gentlemen of yours go

through gunfire without fear, whereas I, in order to see my
daughter. . . .

IRMA: Without fear? In a state of jitters that excites them. Their
gaping nostrils can sniff the orgy behind the wall of flame and
steel. As for you, the orgies of your heart. . . .

CARMEN: . . . they don't help matters, Madame. My daughter loves me.

IRMA: You're the fairy godmother who comes to see her with toys and
perfumes. She pictures you in Heaven. (*Bursting out laughing.*)
Ah, that's the limit—to think there's someone for whom my
brothel—which is Hell—is Heaven! It's Heaven for your brat!
(*She laughs.*) Are you going to make a whore of her later on?

CARMEN: Mme. Irma!

IRMA: That's right! I ought to leave you to your secret brothel, your
precious pink cat-house, your soulful whorehouse. . . . You think
I'm cruel? This rebellion is getting me down, too. Yet I've tried
everything, even prayer. (*She smiles.*) Like your miraculously-
healed leper. Have I wounded you?

CARMEN (*with decision*): Twice a week, on Tuesdays and Fridays, I
had to be the Immaculate Conception of Lourdes and appear to
a bankclerk of the National City. For you it meant money in the
bank and justified your brothel, whereas for me, a believer, it
was. . . .

IRMA (*astonished*): You agreed to it. You didn't seem to mind it.

CARMEN: Mind it! I was happy.

IRMA: Well? Where's the harm?

CARMEN: I saw the effect I had on him. I saw his state of terror, how
he'd break out in a sweat, I heard the rattle in his throat. . . .

IRMA: That'll do. He doesn't come any more. I wonder why. Maybe
his wife found out.

CARMEN: Who cares! But you can understand, Madame, that this
world of illusion oppresses me and that everything inside me
yearns for my daughter. She's in a real garden. . . .

IRMA: You'll have a hard time getting to her, and before long the
garden will be in your heart.

CARMEN: Be still!

IRMA (*inexorably*): The city is full of corpses. All the roads are cut
off. The peasants are also going over to the rebels. I wonder why?
Contagion? The rebellion is an epidemic. It has the same fatal
and sacred character. In any case, we're going to find ourselves
more and more isolated. The rebels have it in for the Clergy, for

the Army, for the Magistracy, for me, Irma, a bawd and madame of a whorehouse. As for you, you'll be killed, disemboweled, and your daughter will be adopted by some virtuous rebel.

Suddenly a buzz. IRMA *runs to the apparatus and looks and listens as before.*

IRMA: Studio 24, Chamber of the Sands. What's going on?

She watches very attentively. A long pause.

CARMEN (*she has sat down at* IRMA's *table and gone back to the accounts. Without raising her head*): The Foreign Legion?

IRMA (*with her eye still glued to the apparatus*): Yes. It's the heroic Legionnaire falling to the sand. And that idiot Rachel has thrown a dart at his ear. He might have been disfigured. What an idea, having himself shot at as if by an Arab, and dying—if you want to call it that!—at attention, on a sand pile! (*A silence. She watches attentively.*) Ah, Rachel's doctoring him. She's preparing a dressing for him, and he has a happy look. (*Very much interested.*) My, my, he seems to like it. I have a feeling he wants to alter his scenario and that starting today he's going to die in the military hospital, tucked in by his nurse. . . . Another uniform to buy. Always expenses. (*Suddenly anxious.*) Say, I don't like that. Not one bit. I'm getting more and more worried about Rachel. She'd better not double-cross me the way Chantal did. (*Turning around, to* CARMEN:) By the way, no news of Chantal?

CARMEN: No, none.

IRMA (*picks up the apparatus again*): And the machine's not working right! What's he saying to her? He's explaining . . . she's listening . . . she understands. I'm afraid he understands too. (*Buzzing again. She pushes down another switch and looks.*) False alarm. It's the plumber leaving.

CARMEN: Which one?

IRMA: The real one.

CARMEN: Which is the real one?

IRMA: The one who repairs the taps.

CARMEN: Is the other one fake?

IRMA (*shrugs her shoulders and pushes down the first switch*): Ah, I told you so: the three or four drops of blood from his ear have inspired him. Now he's having her pamper him. Tomorrow morning he'll be in fine fettle for going to his Embassy.

CARMEN: He's married, isn't he?

IRMA: As a rule, I don't like to talk about the private life of my visitors. The Grand Balcony has a world-wide reputation. It's the most artful, yet the most decent house of illusions. . . .

CARMEN: Decent?

IRMA: Discreet. But I might as well be frank with you, you inquisitive girl. Most of them are married.

CARMEN: When they're with their wives, whom they love, do they keep a tiny, small-scale version of their revels in a brothel. . . .

IRMA: Bitch!

CARMEN: Excuse me, Madame . . . in a house of illusions. I was saying: do they keep their revels in a house of illusions tucked away in the back of their heads in miniature form, far off? But present?

IRMA: It's possible, child. No doubt they do. Like a Chinese lantern left over from a carnival, and waiting for the next one, or, if you prefer, like an imperceptible light in the imperceptible window of an imperceptible castle that they can enlarge instantly whenever they feel like going there to relax.

CARMEN: All the same, it must be nice in a real house.

IRMA: Who knows! But Carmen, if my girls start bothering their heads about such things, it'll be the ruin of the brothel. I really think you miss your apparition. Look, I can do something for you. I did promise it to Regina, but I promise it to you. If you want to, of course. Someone rang me up yesterday and asked for a Saint Theresa. . . . (*A pause.*) Ah, obviously, it's a come-down from the Immaculate Conception to Saint Theresa, but it's not bad either. . . . (*A pause.*) Well, what do you say? It's for a banker. Very clean, you know. Not demanding.

CARMEN: I liked my dress and veil and rosebush.

IRMA: There's a rosebush in the "Saint Theresa" too. Think it over.

A pause.

CARMEN: And what'll the authentic detail be?

IRMA: The ring. He's got it all worked out. The wedding ring. You know that every nun wears a wedding ring, as a bride of God. (CARMEN *makes a gesture of astonishment.*) That's so. That's how he'll know he's dealing with a real nun.

CARMEN: What about the fake detail?

IRMA: It's almost always the same: black lace under the homespun skirt. Well, how about it? You have the kind of gentleness he likes. He'll be pleased.

CARMEN: It's really very kind of you, to think of him.

IRMA: I'm thinking of you.

CARMEN: You're so kind, Madame—I wasn't being ironic. The thing to be said for your house is that it brings consolation. You set up and prepare their secret theatres. . . . You've got your feet on the ground. The proof is that you rake in money. Whereas they . . . their awakening must be brutal. No sooner is it finished than it starts all over again.

IRMA: Luckily for me.

CARMEN: . . . starts all over again, and always the same adventure. They'd like it never to end.

IRMA: You miss the entire point. When it's over, their minds are clear. I can tell from their eyes. Suddenly they understand mathematics. They love their children and their country. Like you.

CARMEN (*puffing herself up*): I'm the daughter of a high-ranking officer. . . .

IRMA: I know. There always has to be one in a brothel. But bear in mind that General, Bishop and Judge are, in real life. . . .

CARMEN: Which are you talking about?

IRMA: Real ones.

CARMEN: Which are real? The ones here?

IRMA: The others. In real life they're the props of a display that they have to drag in the mud of the real and commonplace. Here, Comedy and Appearance remain pure, and the Revels intact.

CARMEN: The revels that I indulge in. . . .

IRMA (*interrupting her*): I know what they are: to forget theirs.

CARMEN: Do you blame me for that?

IRMA: And theirs are to forget yours. They, too, love their children. Afterwards.

Buzzing again, as before. IRMA, who has been sitting all the while near the apparatus, turns about, looks into the view-finder and puts the receiver to her ear. CARMEN goes back to her accounts.

CARMEN (*without raising her head*): The Chief of Police?

IRMA: No. The waiter who just arrived. He's going to start complaining again . . . there he goes, he's flaring up because Elyane is handing him a white apron.

CARMEN: I warned you. He wants a pink one.

IRMA: Go to the Five-and-Ten tomorrow, if it's open. And buy a duster for the railwayman. A green one.

CARMEN: If only Elyane doesn't forget to drop the tip on the floor. He demands a true revolt. And dirty glasses.

IRMA: They all want everything to be as true as possible. . . . Minus something indefinable, so that it won't be true. (*Changing her tone.*) Carmen, it was I who decided to call my establishment a house of illusions, but I'm only the manager. Each individual, when he rings the bell and enters, brings his own scenario, perfectly thought out. My job is merely to rent the hall and furnish the props, actors and actresses. My dear, I've succeeded in lifting it from the ground—do you see what I mean? I unloosed it long ago and it's flying. I cut the moorings. It's flying. Or, if you like, it's sailing in the sky, and I with it. Well, my darling . . . may I say something tender—every madame always, traditionally, has a slight partiality for one of her young ladies. . . .

CARMEN: I had noticed it, Madame, and I too, at times. . . . (*She looks at* IRMA *languidly.*)

IRMA (*standing up and looking at her*): I have a strange feeling, Carmen. (*A long pause.*) But let's continue. Darling, the house really does take off, leaves the earth, sails in the sky when, in the secrecy of my heart, I call myself, but with great precision, a keeper of a bawdy-house. Darling, when secretly, in silence, I repeat to myself silently, "You're a bawd, boss of a whorehouse," darling, everything (*Suddenly lyrical.*), everything flies off—chandeliers, mirrors, carpets, pianos, caryatids and my studios, my famous studios: the studio known as the Hay Studio, hung with rustic scenes, the Studio of the Hangings, spattered with blood and tears, the Throne Room Studio, draped in velvet with a fleur-de-lys pattern, the Studio of Mirrors, the Studio of State, the Studio of the Perfumed Fountains, the Urinal Studio, the Amphitrite Studio, the Funeral Studio, adorned with marble urns, the Moonlight Studio, everything flies off: studios—Oh! I was forgetting the studio of the beggars, of the tramps, where filth and poverty are magnified. To continue: studios, girls, crystals, laces, balconies, everything takes it on the lam, rises up and carries me off!

A long pause. The two women are standing motionless, facing each other.

CARMEN: How well you speak.

IRMA (*modestly*): I went through elementary school.

CARMEN: So I assumed. My father, the artillery colonel. . . .

IRMA (*correcting her sharply*): You mean cavalry, my dear.

CARMEN: Excuse me. That's right. The cavalry colonel wanted me to have an education. Alas. . . . As for you, you've been successful. You've been able to surround your loveliness with a sumptuous theatre, a gala, the splendors of which envelop you and hide you from the world. Your whoredom required such pomp. But what about me, am I to have only myself and be only myself? No, Madame. {Thanks to vice and men's heartache, I too have had my moment of glory!} With the receiver at your ear, you could see me through the view-finder, standing erect, sovereign and kind, maternal yet feminine, with my heel on the cardboard snake and the pink paper-roses. You could also see the bankclerk from the National City kneeling before me and swooning when I appeared to him. Unfortunately he had his back to you and so you weren't aware of the ecstasy on his face and the wild pounding of my heart. My blue veil, my blue robe, my blue apron, my blue eyes. . . .

IRMA: They're hazel.

CARMEN: They were blue that day. For him I was Heaven in person descending on his brow. I was a Madonna to whom a Spaniard might have prayed and sworn an oath. He hymned me, fusing me with his beloved color, and when he carried me to bed, it was into the blue that he penetrated. Unhappily, I won't ever appear to him again.

IRMA: I've offered you Saint Theresa.

CARMEN: I'm not prepared, Mme. Irma. One has to know what the client's going to require. Has everything been worked out?

IRMA: Every whore should be able—I hope you'll excuse me, but since we've gone so far, let's talk man to man—should be able to handle any situation.

CARMEN: I'm one of your whores, Mme. Irma, and one of your best. I boast of it. In the course of an evening, I can . . .

IRMA: I'm aware of your feats. But when you start glorifying yourself as soon as you hear the word whore, which you keep repeating to yourself and which you flaunt as if it were a title, it's not quite the same as when I use the word to designate a function. But you're right, darling, to extol your profession and to glory in it. Make it shine. Let it illuminate you, if that's the only thing you have. (*Tenderly.*) I'll do all I can to help you. . . . You're not only the purest jewel of all my girls, you're the one on whom I bestow all my tenderness. You realize I can do that only in secret, because of Arthur. . . .

A knock at the door. IRMA *starts.*

IRMA (*lowering her voice*): Speak of the devil. . . . (*To* CARMEN.) Quick, make up your mind. Are you staying? (CARMEN *is silent.*) Say yes. A grey homespun dress, Carmen, a bouquet of roses. . .

Knocking at the door again.

CARMEN: But, Madame, I believe in her. . . .

Knocking again, more imperious.

IRMA: You're a fool! . . . Come in!

The door opens. Enter THE EXECUTIONER, *whom hereafter we shall call* ARTHUR. *Classical pimp's outfit: light grey suit, white felt hat, etc. He finishes knotting his tie.*)

IRMA: Is the session over? He went through it fast.

ARTHUR: Yes, the little geezer's buttoning up. He's pooped. Two sessions in half an hour.

IRMA: You went easy, I hope? Last time, the poor girl was laid up for two days.

ARTHUR: Don't pull that kind-hearted-whore stuff on me. Both last time and tonight she got what was coming to her: in dough and in wallops. Right on the line. The banker wants to see stripes on her back. So I stripe it.

IRMA: At least you don't get any pleasure out of it?

ARTHUR: Not with her. You're my only love. And a job's a job. I'm conscientious about my work.

IRMA (*sternly*): I'm not jealous of the girl, but I wouldn't want you to disable the personnel. It's getting harder and harder to replace.

ARTHUR: I tried a couple of times to draw marks on her back with purple paint, but it didn't work. The old guy inspects her when he arrives and insists I deliver her in good shape.

IRMA: Paint? Who gave you permission?

ARTHUR (*shrugging his shoulders*): What's one illusion more or less! I thought I was doing the right thing. But don't worry. Now I whip, I flagellate, she screams, and he crawls.

IRMA: In any case, be careful. The house is being watched.

ARTHUR: I know. All the north part of town was taken last night. Too bad the Judge wants screaming.

IRMA: The Bishop's less dangerous. He's satisfied with pardoning sins.

CARMEN: Though he gets pleasure out of pardoning, he expects you to commit them. No, the best of the lot is the one you tie up, spank, whip and soothe, and then he snores.

ARTHUR: Who cuddles him? (*To* CARMEN.) You? Do you give him your breast?

CARMEN (*curtly*): I do my job right, too.

ARTHUR: Would the young lady like to give me a lesson?

IRMA: Let Carmen alone. She's suffering. (*To* CARMEN.) Well, what about Saint Theresa? Will you?

CARMEN (*plaintively*): Let me think it over a little longer.

ARTHUR (*bowing to* CARMEN *ironically*): Her cashier? No, I beg your pardon, her bookkeeper? (*To* IRMA.) How much did you take in today?

IRMA (*on the defensive*): Carmen and I haven't finished the accounts.

ARTHUR: But I have. According to my calculations, it runs to a good two hundred.

IRMA: That's possible. In any case, don't worry. I don't cheat.

ARTHUR: I believe you, my love, but I can't help it: the figures arrange themselves in my head. Two hundred! War, rebellion, shooting, frost, hail, rain, showers of shit, nothing stops them! On the contrary. People are killing each other in the streets, the joint's being watched, but all the same, they come charging in. As for me, I've got you right at home, sweetie-pie, otherwise. . . .

IRMA (*bluntly*): You'd be cowering in a cellar, paralyzed with fear.

ARTHUR (*ambiguously*): I'd do as the others do, my love. You're not forgetting my little percentage?

IRMA: I give you what you need.

ARTHUR: My love! I've ordered the silk shirts. And do you know what kind of silk? And what color?

IRMA (*tenderly*): All right, cut it. Not in front of Carmen.

ARTHUR: On the contrary. Do you know what kind of silk?

IRMA: Darling! The thought that Carmen will know that your chest—in the silk of my blouses. . . . Oh, darling . . . be still. . . .

ARTHUR: Then it's O.K.?

IRMA: Our accounts aren't done.

ARTHUR: And do you know what else? You should have seen the shirt-maker's face. I insisted that they button on the left. As if they were for you!

IRMA: My love!

ARTHUR: Then it's O.K.?

IRMA: Yes.

ARTHUR: How much?

IRMA (*regaining her self-possession*): We'll see. I have to go over the accounts with Carmen.

ARTHUR: You'll tell me when I get back. I trust you. I've got to deliver the rest of the stuff—I've got my orders. You might have asked the Bishop to remember me in his prayers. . . . It's true I don't interest him. I wonder whether I'll bring your Arthur back all in one piece. No, I'm not keen about it. If I could. . . .

IRMA (*severely*): You've no right. You've no right to hesitate. You were entrusted with a mission, and you accepted it. You'll carry it out. And me ready to tremble for your life.

ARTHUR: Don't work yourself up. I'm going. But at the risk of my life, whereas you're under cover in a nice warm place, waiting for George to arrive.

IRMA: If I belonged entirely to you and only you, we'd be in clover. Get going. And be back fairly soon. You have a session this evening. Did you know?

ARTHUR (*on his way to the door*): This evening? Another one? What is it?

IRMA: I thought I told you: a corpse.

ARTHUR: How delightful! And what am I supposed to do?

IRMA: Nothing. You're to remain motionless, and you'll be buried. You'll be able to rest.

ARTHUR: Ah, because I'm the one who . . . ? All right. Who's the client? Someone new?

IRMA (*mysteriously*): A very important person, and stop asking questions.

ARTHUR (*starting to leave, then hesitating*): You bitch! (*He turns round and smiles.*) You adorable bitch! (*He exits.*)

IRMA (*to* CARMEN, *after a pause*): Let's get back to the accounts, shall we?

CARMEN: In all, counting the sailor and the simple jobs, it comes to three hundred twenty.

IRMA: Splendid. The more killing there is in the working-class districts, the more the men roll into my studios.

CARMEN: The men?

IRMA (*after a pause*): Some men. Drawn by my mirrors and chandeliers, always the same ones. As for the others, heroism takes the place of women.

CARMEN (*bitterly*): Women?

IRMA: What shall I call you, my big, long, sterile girls? Their seed never ripens in you, and yet . . . if you weren't there?

CARMEN: You have your revels, Mme. Irma.

IRMA: Be still. It's this chilling game that makes me sad and melancholy. Fortunately I have my jewels. Which, as it happens, are in great danger. I may lose them at any moment.

Machine-gun fire.

You hear?

CARMEN: The Army is fighting bravely.

IRMA: And the Rebels even more bravely. And we're in the shadow of the cathedral, a few feet from the Archbishop's Palace. There's no price on my head. No, that would be too much to expect, but it's known that I serve supper to prominent people. So they're out to get me. And there are no men in the house.

CARMEN: Arthur will be back.

IRMA: Are you trying to be funny? He's no man, he's my stage-prop.

CARMEN: Assuming the worst. . . .

IRMA: If the Rebels win? I'm a goner. They're workers. Without imagination. Prudish and maybe chaste.

CARMEN: It won't take them long to get used to debauchery. Just wait till they get a little bored. . . .

IRMA: You're wrong. Or else they won't let themselves get bored. But I'm the one who's most exposed. For you it's different. In every revolution there's the glorified whore who sings an anthem and is virginified. That'll be you. The others'll piously bring water for the dying to drink. Afterwards . . . they'll marry you off. Would you like to get married?

CARMEN: Orange blossoms, tulle. . . .

IRMA: Wonderful! To you, getting married means masquerading. Darling, you certainly are one of us. No, I can't imagine you married either. Besides, what they're really dreaming of doing is murdering us. We'll have a lovely death, Carmen. It will be terrible and sumptuous. They may break into my studios, shatter the crystals, tear the brocades and slit our throats. . . .

CARMEN: They'll take pity. . . .

IRMA: They won't. They'll thrill at the thought that their fury is sacrilegious. All bedraggled, with caps on their heads, or in helmets and boots, they'll destroy us by fire and sword. It'll be very beautiful. We oughtn't to wish for any other kind of end, and you, you're thinking of leaving. . . .

CARMEN: But Mme. Irma. . . .

IRMA: Yes, yes. When the house is about to go up in flames, when the rose is about to be stabbed, all you think of, Carmen, is fleeing.

CARMEN: If I wanted to be elsewhere, you know very well why.

IRMA: Your daughter? But your daughter is dead. . . .

CARMEN: Madame!

IRMA: Whether dead or alive, your daughter is dead. Think of the charming grave, adorned with daisies and artificial wreaths, at the far end of the garden . . . and that garden in your heart, where you'll be able to look after it. . . .

CARMEN: I'd have loved to see her again. . . .

IRMA: You'll keep her image in the image of the garden and the garden in your heart under the flaming robe of Saint Theresa. And you hesitate? I offer you the very finest of deaths, and you hesitate? Are you a coward?

CARMEN: You know very well I'm devoted to you.

IRMA: Well? Will you stay? I'll teach you figures! The wonderful figures that we'll spend nights together calligraphing.

CARMEN (*softly*): The war is raging. As you said, it's the horde.

IRMA (*triumphantly*): The horde, but we have our cohorts, our armies, our hosts, legions, batallions, vessels, heralds, clarions, trumpets, our colors, streamers, standards, banners. . . . And yet you tremble? But darling, all's not lost. They'll be crushed. George is still all-powerful. In any case, I hope he'll get through. A Chief of Police always finds a way. Now come and dress me. But first I want to see how Rachel's getting on.

> *Same buzzing as before.* IRMA *glues her eyes to the view-finder. A pause. She peers.*

Christ is leaving with his paraphernalia. I've never been able to understand why he has himself tied to the cross with ropes that he brings in a valise. Maybe they're ropes that have been blessed. Where does he put them when he gets home? Who the hell cares! Let's take a look at Rachel. (*She pushes down another switch.*) Ah, they've finished. They're talking. They're putting away the little arrows, the bow, the gauze bandages, the white officer's cap. . . . No, I don't at all like the way they're looking at each other: it's too candid and straightforward. (*She turns to* CARMEN.) There you have the dangers of regularity. It would be a catastrophe if my clients and girls smiled at each other affectionately. It would be an even greater catastrophe than if it were a question of love. (*She presses the switch mechanically and lays down the receiver. Pensively.*) Dress me.

CARMEN: What are you wearing?
IRMA: The cream-colored negligee.

> CARMEN *opens the door of a closet and takes out the negligee, while* IRMA *unhooks her suit.*

Tell me, Carmen, what about Chantal? . . .
CARMEN: Madame?

> *A pause.*

IRMA: Yes. About Chantal, tell me, what do you know about her?
CARMEN: I've questioned all the girls: Rosine, Elyane, Florence, Marlyse. They've each prepared a little report. I'll let you have them. But I didn't get much out of them. It's possible to spy beforehand. During the fighting, it's harder. For one thing, the camps are more sharply defined. You can choose. When there's

peace, it's too vague. You don't quite know whom you're betraying. Nor even whether you're betraying. There's no news
about Chantal. They don't even know whether she's still alive.

IRMA: But, tell me, wouldn't you have any scruples about it?

CARMEN: No. Entering a brothel means rejecting the world. Here I
am and here I stay. Your laws and orders and the passions are
my reality. What jewels are you wearing?

IRMA: The pearls. My jewels. They're the only things I have that are
real. I feel everything else is sham. I have my jewels as others
have little girls in gardens.—Who's double-crossing? You're hesitating.

CARMEN: The girls all mistrust me. I collect their little report. I pass
it on to you. You pass it on to the police. The police check on
it. . . . Me, I know nothing.

IRMA: You're cautious. Give me a handkerchief.

CARMEN: No. Viewed from here, where, in any case, men show their
naked selves, life seems to me so remote, so profound, that it has
all the unreality of a film or of the birth of Christ in the manger.
When I'm in a room with a man and he forgets himself so far
as to say to me: "The arsenal will be taken tomorrow night," I
feel as if I were reading an obscene scrawl. His act becomes as
mad, as . . . voluminous as those described in a certain way on
certain walls. . . .

A knocking. IRMA *rushes to her apparatus and, by means of a
mechanism, conceals it in the wall. Then she cries out.*

IRMA: Yes. Come in. (*To* CARMEN.) You, leave the room.

CARMEN *starts leaving, but, from the rear, enters* THE CHIEF OF
POLICE. *Heavy fur-lined coat, hat, cigar.*

THE CHIEF OF POLICE: No, no, stay, Carmen. I like having you around.

*He keeps his hat and coat on. Does not remove his cigar from
his mouth, but bows to* IRMA.

Pleasant warmth, light fragrance. . . . (*Kissing* IRMA'S *hand.*)
Beautiful lady!

IRMA (*breathlessly*): Put your hand here. (*On her breast.*) I'm all tense. I'm still wrought up. I knew you were on your way, which meant you were in danger. I waited for you all a-tremble.

THE CHIEF OF POLICE: Easy, easy, let me take it all in. You were saying?

IRMA: You rat.

THE CHIEF OF POLICE: All right, that'll do. Let's cut the comedy. The situation's getting more and more serious—it's not desperate, but it will be before long—hap-pi-ly! The Royal Palace is surrounded. The Queen's in hiding. The city—it's a miracle that I got through —the city's being ravaged by fire and sword. Out there the rebellion is tragic and joyous, whereas in this house everything's dying a slow death. So, today's my day. By tonight I'll be in the grave or on a pedestal. So whether I love you or desire you is unimportant. How are things going at the moment?

IRMA: Marvelously. I had some great performances.

THE CHIEF OF POLICE (*impatiently*): What kind?

IRMA: Carmen has a talent for description. Ask her.

THE CHIEF OF POLICE (*to* CARMEN): Tell me, still. . . ?

CARMEN: Yes, sir, still. Still the pillars of the Empire: the Judge . . .

THE CHIEF OF POLICE (*ironically*): Our allegories, our talking weapons. And is there also. . . ?

CARMEN: As every week, a new theme.

THE CHIEF OF POLICE *makes a gesture of curiosity.*

This time it's the baby who gets slapped, spanked, tucked in, then cries and is cuddled.

THE CHIEF OF POLICE (*impatiently*): Fine. But. . . .

CARMEN: He's charming, Sir. And so sad!

THE CHIEF OF POLICE (*exploding*): Well, yes or no, is there a simulation. . . .

CARMEN (*bewildered*): Simulation?

THE CHIEF OF POLICE: You idiot! Yes! An impersonation of the Chief of Police?

Very heavy silence.

IRMA: The time's not ripe. My dear, your function isn't noble enough to offer dreamers an image that would enshrine them. Perhaps because it lacks illustrious ancestors? No, my dear fellow. . . .

You have to resign yourself to the fact that your image does not yet conform to the liturgies of the brothel.

THE CHIEF OF POLICE: Who's represented in them?

IRMA: You know who. You have your index-cards. (*She enumerates on her fingers.*) There are two kings of France with coronation ceremonies and different rituals, an admiral at the stern of his sinking destroyer, a bishop during the perpetual adoration, a judge performing his functions, a general on horseback, a dey of Algiers surrendering, a fireman putting out a fire, a goat attached to a stake, a housewife returning from market, a pickpocket, a robbed man who's bound and beaten up, a Saint Sebastian, a farmer in his barn . . . but no chief of police . . . nor colonial administrator, though there *is* a missionary dying on the cross, and Christ in person.

THE CHIEF OF POLICE (*after a pause*): You're forgetting the mechanic.

IRMA: He doesn't come any more. What with tightening screws, he'd have ended by constructing a machine. And it might have worked. Back to the factory!

THE CHIEF OF POLICE: So not a single one of your clients has had the idea . . . the remotest idea, the barest suggestion. . . .

IRMA: No. I know you do what you can. You try hatred and love. But glory gives you the cold shoulder.

THE CHIEF OF POLICE (*forcefully*): My image is growing bigger and bigger. It's becoming colossal. Everything around me repeats and reflects it. And you've never seen it represented in this place?

IRMA: In any case, even if it were celebrated here, I wouldn't see anything. The ceremonies are secret.

THE CHIEF OF POLICE: You liar. You've got secret peep-holes in every wall. Every partition, every mirror, is rigged. In one place, you can hear the sighs, in another the echo of the moans. You don't need me to tell you that brothel tricks are mainly mirror tricks. . . . (*Very sadly.*) Nobody yet! But I'll make my image detach itself from me. I'll make it penetrate into your studios, force its way in, reflect and multiply itself. Irma, my function weighs me down. Here, it will appear to me in the blazing light of pleasure and death.

IRMA: You must keep killing, my dear George.

THE CHIEF OF POLICE: I do what I can, I assure you. People fear me more and more.

IRMA: Not enough. You must plunge into darkness, into shit and blood.

THE CHIEF OF POLICE (*very irritated*): I repeat: I do what I can to prove to the nation that I'm a leader, a lawgiver, a builder. . . .

IRMA (*uneasily*): You're raving. Or else you really do expect to build an empire. In which case you're raving.

THE CHIEF OF POLICE (*with conviction*): When the rebellion's been put down, and put down by me, when I've been appealed to by the Queen and have the nation behind me, nothing can stop me. Then, and only then, will you see who I now am! (*Musingly.*) Yes, my dear, I want to build an empire . . . so that the empire will, in exchange, build *me*. . . .

IRMA: . . . a tomb.

THE CHIEF OF POLICE (*somewhat taken aback*): But, after all, why not? Doesn't every conqueror have one? So? (*Exalted.*) Alexandria! I'll have my tomb, Irma. And when the cornerstone is laid, you'll be guest of honor.

IRMA: Thank you. (*To* CARMEN.) Carmen, my dress.

THE CHIEF OF POLICE (*to* CARMEN, *who is about to leave*): Just a minute, Carmen. What do you think of the idea?

CARMEN: That you want to merge your life with one long funeral, Sir.

THE CHIEF OF POLICE (*aggressively*): Is life anything else? You seem to know everything—so tell me: in this sumptuous theatre where every moment a drama is performed—in the sense that the outside world says a mass is celebrated—what have you observed?

CARMEN (*after a hesitation*): As for anything serious, anything worth reporting, only one thing: that without the thighs it contained, a pair of pants on a chair is beautiful, Sir. Emptied of our little old men, our ornaments are deathly sad. They're the ones that are placed on the catafalques of high dignitaries. They cover only corpses that never stop dying. And yet, . . .

IRMA (*to* CARMEN): That's not what the Chief of Police is asking.

THE CHIEF OF POLICE: Let her alone, my dear. I'm used to Carmen's speeches. (*To* CARMEN.) You were saying: and yet . . . ?

CARMEN: And yet, I'm sure that the sudden joy in their eyes when they see the cheap finery is really the gleam of innocence. . . .

THE CHIEF OF POLICE: People claim that our house sends them to Death.

Suddenly a ringing. IRMA *starts. A pause.*

IRMA: Someone's opened the door. Who can it be at this hour? (*To* CARMEN.) Carmen, go down and shut the door.

> CARMEN *exits. A rather long silence between* IRMA *and* THE CHIEF OF POLICE, *who remain alone.*

IRMA: It was I who rang. I wanted to be alone with you for a moment. (*A pause, during which they look into each other's eyes seriously.*) Tell me, George.... (*She hesitates.*)

THE CHIEF OF POLICE (*a little annoyed*): Say it.

IRMA: Do you still insist on keeping up the game? No, no, don't be impatient. Aren't you tired of it?

THE CHIEF OF POLICE: But. . . . What do you mean? In a little while I'll be going home.

IRMA: If you can. If the rebellion leaves you free to go.

THE CHIEF OF POLICE: Irma, you're mad. Or you're acting as if you were. The rebellion itself is a game. From here you can't see anything of the outside, but every rebel is playing a game. And he loves his game.

IRMA: But supposing they let themselves be carried beyond the game? I mean if they get so involved in it that they destroy and replace everything. Yes, yes, I know, there's always the false detail that reminds them that at a certain moment, at a certain point in the drama, they have to stop, and even withdraw. . . . But what if they're so carried away by passion that they no longer recognize anything and leap, without realizing it, into . . .

THE CHIEF OF POLICE: You mean into reality? What of it? Let them try. I do as they do, I penetrate right into the reality that the game offers us, and since I have the upper hand, it's I who score.

IRMA: They'll be stronger than you.

THE CHIEF OF POLICE: Why do you say "they'll be"? Don't I have treasures invested, a thousand resources? All right, enough of that. Are you or aren't you the mistress of a house of illusions? You are. Good. If I come to your place, it's to find satisfaction in your mirrors and their trickery. (*Tenderly.*) Don't worry. Everything will be just as it's always been.

IRMA: I don't know why, but today I feel uneasy. Carmen seems strange to me. The rebels—how shall I put it?—have a kind of gravity. . . .

THE CHIEF OF POLICE: Their role requires it.

IRMA: No, no, a kind of determination. They walk by the windows threateningly, but they don't sing. The threat is in their eyes.

THE CHIEF OF POLICE: What of it? Supposing it is, do you take me for a coward? Do you think I should give up and go home?

IRMA (*pensively*): No. Besides, I think it's too late.

THE CHIEF OF POLICE: Do you have any news?

IRMA: From Chantal, before she lit out. The power-house will be occupied around 3 A.M.

THE CHIEF OF POLICE: Are you sure? Who told her?

IRMA: The partisans of the Fourth Sector. The "Andromeda Sector."

THE CHIEF OF POLICE: That's plausible. How did she find out?

IRMA: It's through her that there were leaks, and through her alone. So don't belittle my house. . . .

THE CHIEF OF POLICE: Your cat-house, my love.

IRMA: Cat-house, whorehouse, bawdyhouse. Brothel. F . . kery. Call it anything you like. So Chantal's the only one who's on the other side. . . . She lit out. But before she did, she confided in Carmen, and Carmen's no fool.

THE CHIEF OF POLICE: Who tipped her off?

IRMA: Roger. The plumber. An idiotic affair. It's not easy for men to get into this place: it's a convent. By "men" you know whom I mean . . . ?

THE CHIEF OF POLICE: The ones with cool heads.

IRMA: Very neatly put. Well, I allowed him to come to repair the plumbing. Wear and tear's pretty heavy here: piping costs me a hundred a month. . . . Does that interest you?

THE CHIEF OF POLICE: Your plumbing? I'll send around the head of my works department.

IRMA: To continue: I let the plumber come. How do you imagine him? Young and handsome? No. He's forty. Thick-set. Serious, with ironic eyes. Chantal spoke to him. I put him out: too late. He belongs to the Andromeda network.

THE CHIEF OF POLICE: Andromeda? Splendid. The rebellion's riding high, it's moving out of this world. If it gives its sectors the names of constellations, it'll evaporate in no time and be metamorphosed into song. Let's hope the songs are beautiful.

IRMA: And what if their songs give the rebels courage? What if they're willing to die for them?

THE CHIEF OF POLICE: The beauty of their songs will make them soft. Unfortunately, they haven't yet reached the point of either beauty or softness. In any case, Chantal's tender passions were providential.

IRMA: Don't bring God into. . . .

THE CHIEF OF POLICE: I'm a freemason. Therefore. . . .

IRMA: You? You never told me.

THE CHIEF OF POLICE (*solemnly*): Sublime Prince of the Royal Secret.

IRMA (*ironically*): You, a brother in a little apron! With a hood and taper and a little mallet! That's odd. (*A pause.*) You too?

THE CHIEF OF POLICE: Why? You too?

IRMA (*with mock solemnity*): I'm a guardian of far more solemn rites. (*Suddenly sad.*) Since that's all I am now.

THE CHIEF OF POLICE: As usual, you're going to bring up our grand passion.

IRMA (*gently*): Not our passion, but the time when we loved each other.

THE CHIEF OF POLICE (*ironically*): Well, would you like to give a historical account of it and deliver a eulogy? You think my visits would have less zest if you didn't flavor them with the memory of a pretended innocence?

IRMA: It's a question of tenderness. Neither the wildest concoctions of my clients nor my own fancies nor my constant endeavor to enrich my studios with new themes nor the passing of time nor the gilding and crystals nor bitter cold can dispel the moments when you cuddled in my arms or keep me from remembering them.

THE CHIEF OF POLICE: Do you really miss them?

IRMA (*tenderly*): I'd give my kingdom to relive a single one of them! And you know which one. I need just one word of truth—as when one looks at one's wrinkles at night, or rinses one's mouth. . . .

THE CHIEF OF POLICE: It's too late. (*A pause.*) Besides, we couldn't cuddle each other eternally. You don't know what I was already secretly moving towards when I was in your arms.

IRMA: I know that I loved you. . . .

THE CHIEF OF POLICE: Could you give up Arthur?

IRMA: It was you who forced him on me. You insisted on there being a man here—against my better judgment—in a domain that should have remained virgin. . . . You fool, don't laugh. Virgin, that is, sterile. But you wanted a pillar, a shaft, a phallus present —an upright bulk. Well, it's here. You saddled me with that hunk of congested meat, that milksop with wrestler's arms. He may look like a strong man at a fair, but you don't realize how fragile he is. You stupidly forced him on me because you felt yourself aging.

THE CHIEF OF POLICE: Be still.

IRMA (*with rising vehemence*): No. I feel like talking. Catastrophe is at my door. . . .

THE CHIEF OF POLICE: You've nothing to fear. The house is guarded by the police.

IRMA (*shrugging her shoulders*): Who's guarding the police? But I feel like talking because in this tense situation it's the only thing I can do to share your emotion. I repeat, you felt yourself aging. You were concerned with power, but without fulfilling yourself. And you relaxed here through Arthur.

THE CHIEF OF POLICE: The danger of the situation has banished boredom and the taste for pleasure by proxy. In acting I've become active again and I want to have you. Kick Arthur out.

IRMA: I need him. I have no illusions. I'm his man and he relies on me, but I need that rugged storewindow dummy hanging onto my skirts. He's my body, as it were, but set beside me.

THE CHIEF OF POLICE: I'm jealous!

IRMA: Of that big doll made up as an executioner in order to satisfy a phony judge? Look, darling, the spectacle of me under the spectacle of that magnificent body never used to bother you. . . . Let me repeat. . . .

THE CHIEF OF POLICE (*he slaps* IRMA, *who falls on the sofa*): And don't blubber or I'll break your jaw. If ever I hear that you've told anyone what happened, I'll send your joint up in smoke. I'll set fire to your hair and bush and I'll turn you loose. I'll light up the town with blazing whores. (*Very gently.*) Do you think I'm capable of it?

IRMA (*in a panting whisper*): Yes, darling.

THE CHIEF OF POLICE: All right, add up the accounts for me. If you like, you can deduct Apollo's crepe de Chine. And hurry up. I've got to get back to my post. For the time being, I have to act.

Afterwards. . . . Afterwards, things'll run themselves. My name will act in my place. Well, what about Arthur?

IRMA: He'll be dead this evening.

THE CHIEF OF POLICE: Dead? You mean . . . really . . . really dead?

IRMA (*with resignation*): Come, come, George, the way one dies here.

THE CHIEF OF POLICE: Indeed? Meaning. . . .

IRMA: The Minister . . . (*She is interrupted by the voice of* CARMEN.)

CARMEN (*in the wings*): Lock Studio 17! Elyane, hurry up! And lower the studio . . . no, no, wait. . . . (*Enter* CARMEN.) Madame, the Queen's Envoy is in the drawing-room. . . .

IRMA: Nonsense! There's no one there. It was I . . . (*She breaks off.*) I'll go and receive him.

> The door opens, left, and ARTHUR *appears, trembling and with his clothes torn.*

ARTHUR: Oh, I'm sorry, I thought you were alone. My respects, sir.

IRMA: Well, what's new? You may speak. Carmen's on our side.

ARTHUR (*panting*): Well, I delivered the stuff, as agreed. The whole city's lit up with fires. The Rebels are in control practically everywhere. I doubt if you can get home, sir. I was able to reach the Royal Palace, and I saw the Grand Chamberlain. He said he'd try to come. I might add that he shook my hand. And then I left. The women are the most excited. They're urging the men to loot and kill. But what was most awful was a girl who was singing. . . .

> A shot is heard. A windowpane is shivered. Also a mirror near the bed. ARTHUR *falls down, hit in the forehead by a bullet coming from outside.* CARMEN *bends over him, then rises to her feet again.* IRMA *goes to the window, then comes back.*

THE CHIEF OF POLICE: In short, I'm stuck here?

CARMEN (*softly*): If the house is to be blown up. . . . Is Saint Theresa's costume in the closet, Mme. Irma?

IRMA (*anxiously*): Yes, at the left. But first have Arthur removed. I'm going to receive the Envoy.

SCENE SIX

*The interior of an old-fashioned café. Mirrors. Bottles on the shelves.
Bar.*

ROGER, *aged 40, model of the proletarian leader, is writing at a small
table, rear, without raising his head.*

ARMAND, *aged 25, is sitting silently on a wall-bench.*

MARK, *who is standing, is holding a map on which he places little
flags according to instructions he receives by telephone.*

In the foreground, CHANTAL *finishes bandaging the arm of a wounded
rebel. She hesitates to insert the pin.*

GEORGETTE, *aged about 30, nervously snatches it from her and pins the
bandage herself.*

GEORGETTE: Your eyes fondle everything you do.

CHANTAL: I've got to look and see where to put the pin.

GEORGETTE: You don't look. You contemplate. You stand back and
observe. (*To* THE WOUNDED MAN.) Go to the back room. The
comrades'll get you out of here. You'll be evacuated in a little
while.

THE WOUNDED MAN: Any good news? Except for the things we're directly involved in, we have no idea what's happening.

GEORGETTE (*putting away the compresses*): We don't get much news
in this place either. But I've heard that almost all the contacts
have been made.

THE WOUNDED MAN (*anxiously*): Is there any hope?

GEORGETTE (*curtly*): No. A man who hopes is already dreaming. Stop
hoping. We'll win.

THE WOUNDED MAN: But what about the Archbishop? And the General?
And the Judge? What's being done about them?

GEORGETTE: No one bothers about them any more. We're fighting
against men. When men start losing, the Great Figures crumble.

315

(*She leads* THE WOUNDED MAN *to the door at the left.*) When you get to the window, hug the wall and walk on all fours. They're shooting from the roofs.

THE WOUNDED MAN *exits.* GEORGETTE *returns to* CHANTAL.

I'm sorry, Chantal. I was a little rough with you just before.

CHANTAL: Forget it. The main thing is that I learn to dress wounds right. (*She smiles.*) To do a good job as a nurse.

ARMAND, *who has been seated, stands up, stretches and looks at himself complacently in a mirror.*

ROGER (*without raising his head*): How long are you going to stand there primping.

ARMAND: I'm arranging my hardware for the ball.

ROGER (*severely*): Not the ball, the fight. . . .

A pause.

Do you admire yourself in your role? You want it to last?

ARMAND (*gaily*): It has its charm. And it's better than being at the shop. (*He laughs as he looks at himself in the mirror; then, spreading his legs, he plants himself in the middle of the stage.*) Like on the enlistment posters for the Marines: the tanks roll between my legs! (*He strikes another pose.*) Taras Bulba! (*He laughs, takes out his revolver and aims at the bottles.*) Big Chief Buffalo! *We* don't have the right to play. The other side would have painted the town red long ago. They'd have smashed the crockery and shivered the mirrors!

ROGER: You itching to do it?

ARMAND: It's a little dismal on our side. All week long we operate machines, and on a red-letter day like this, instead of raising hell, we fuss around with a mechanism that may run away with us.

ROGER: If ever we had the misfortune of taking pleasure in shooting at men and bottles, it would be good-bye to the revolutionary spirit! As for a red-letter day, this is it! The Law Court's been burned to the ground. The churches have been looted. There are

men who are going out to fight in judges' robes and surplices.
It's a regular carnival. That ought to please you.

ARMAND: Our red-letter days are always a mockery of theirs!

ROGER: Later on, we'll organize leisure activities. . . .

ARMAND (*taking a stance like a movie character, he pretends to
machine-gun the entire café*): Bangbangbangbangbang! (*He
laughs and looks at himself in the mirror. Then, by the street-
door enters a wounded man supported by another man who
leaves almost at once.*)

THE MAN (*to* GEORGETTE, *who rushes up*): Been shot in the right thigh.
I don't think it's serious, but better attend to him right away.

ARMAND (*jokingly*): Or finish him off. The wounded get in our way.

ROGER (*to* ARMAND): This is no time for kidding a comrade.

GEORGETTE (*to* THE WOUNDED MAN): He's young. (*To* CHANTAL.) Attend
to him. Here, take the scissors . . . cut it. . . .

> CHANTAL *cuts and tears the man's trousers. Then she takes
> the cotton and alcohol that* GEORGETTE *hands her. She cleans
> the wound.*

SECOND WOUNDED MAN: Take it easy! You're not washing a corpse!
For Christ's sake, take it easy!

CHANTAL (*aggressively*): Does a drop of alcohol make you keel over?

GEORGETTE (*curtly*): Being rough is also a game.

CHANTAL (*hurrying to dress the wound*): The main thing is that the
wounded be attended to.

GEORGETTE: The main thing, as Roger says, is that the rebellion start
off by despising make-believe. (*A pause.*) And complacency.

CHANTAL (*to* ROGER): If I don't feel I have a talent for dressing
wounds. . . .

ROGER: Georgette's right, Chantal. What we . . .

GEORGETTE (*to* THE WOUNDED MAN, *and interrupting* ROGER): Come
over here. (*She takes him to the door by which* THE FIRST
WOUNDED MAN *went out.*) Turn left, and be careful they don't
spot you.

ROGER (*pedantically*): I repeat, Georgette's right. What we're engaged
in is too serious to be undertaken lightly. If we behave like those
on the other side, then we *are* the other side. Instead of changing
the world, all we'll achieve is a reflection of the one we want to
destroy.

GEORGETTE (*same tone*): Everything must be aimed at utility.

ROGER: If we use charm, we're in danger of being taken in by that of the others. It's better to remain silent and motionless than make a remark or gesture that can't be utilized. . . .

GEORGETTE (*in the same tone*): . . . for purposes of the revolution.

ARMAND (*to* ROGER): In two minutes I'm going out for a leak. You mean I really don't have the right to amuse myself by squirting it up along the wall?

ROGER (*shocked*): You mean you usually fool around like that, you, who've been involved in the revolution from the very beginning?

ARMAND (*acting as if he were hurt*): If not that, then what *am* I allowed?

ROGER (*beginning a lecture*): At the basis . . .

LUKE (*interrupting him*): I'm not impressed by your speeches. I still maintain that in certain cases you've got to use the enemy's weapons. That it's indispensable. Enthusiasm for freedom? It's a fine thing, I don't deny it, but it would be even finer if freedom were a pretty girl with a warm voice. After all, what does it matter to you if we storm the barricades by following a female like a pack of males in heat? And what of it if the groans of the dying are groans of love?

ROGER: Men don't revolt in order to go chasing after a female.

LUKE (*stubbornly*): Even if the chase leads them to victory?

ROGER: Then their victory is already sick. Their victory has a dose of clap, to talk like you. . . .

LOUIS *enters. Aged about 40. Gay and good-humored.*

LOUIS: Well, boys, it looks pretty good. All our forces, or almost all, are in contact. The Palace is expected to surrender tonight, or tomorrow morning at the latest. Lots of soldiers and a large part of the police force are already fighting on our side. We don't have everything in hand yet, but we've got reason for more than just hoping. . . .

GEORGETTE: Before, too, we did better than just hope. We were sure of winning.

LOUIS: Luck is with us tonight. Unless those fine gentlemen, those gentlemen who smoke and fart in silk, are planning to pull a fast one on us. (*Noticing* ARMAND.) That worked out all right. I've already heard about it. But you had a pretty close shave!

ARMAND (*laughing*): Are you telling me! I went out to plant the bomb. When I got half-way up the street, some son of a bitch started firing away, but he missed me. I saw the machine gun almost in front of me. The guy was reloading. I just stood and stared at him, cool as a cucumber. He looked as if he were posing, with the light beaming on him. The guy took aim. And then, he toppled over. One of our boys had picked him off. I continued on my way, calm as could be. I planted my bomb, and here I am. I wasn't scared for a second. Didn't even bat an eyelash.

LOUIS: Even so, go take a rest in the back room. We'll be needing you in a little while.

ARMAND: Don't be shy, if you want me. (ARMAND *exits left.*)

ROGER (*as if to himself*): Too much youth, too hot-blooded.

LOUIS: You sound as if you were put out because he wasn't scared.

ROGER: I know him and a thousand like him. He wasn't scared because the danger and the foiling of the danger didn't depend on him. But if ever once in his life he warded off death by his intelligence, you'd see him tremble. He'd realize that he had to accomplish things by intelligence and will-power! He'd be less sure of himself. For the time being, he thinks he's the darling of fate.

LOUIS (*ironically*): You don't dare say "of the gods."

ROGER (*glumly*): I don't mean of the gods. If the heavens are studded with such constellations as that of the Archbishop and the Hero, then we've got to tear heaven down. Not invoke it, nor even ever name it, but strip it, and make it dance naked on the cathedral squares.

LOUIS (*to* MARK): Any news from the Central Committee?

MARK (*still planting flags*): They're electing a president tonight.

LOUIS: Where'll the government be set up?

ROGER: That's a secret.

MARK: At the Royal Palace, if it's taken tonight.

LOUIS: What if things don't work out?

MARK: The fight'll continue, but in shit and darkness. Incognito. Let me get on with my work.

Silence.

ROGER (*to* LOUIS): We were waiting for you. (*He points to* LUKE.) He claims they need someone to spur on the section.

LUKE (*to* LOUIS): It's not that they lack courage. It's not that. But they've got to be keyed up. Just a little.

LOUIS (*to* LUKE): So? Can't you work them up? Can't you give them a pep-talk? You need a bugle?

LUKE (*to* LOUIS): Words aren't enough, and you know it. We came to ask you to lend us Chantal. . . .

ROGER: No. Chantal was useful—I won't deny it—at the beginning of the revolution. She's played her part. Now it's over.

LOUIS: Chantal was taking on too much importance. That's true. On the other hand, if they're really inarticulate. . . . (*To* ROGER.) Did you ask for the bazookas?

ROGER: Again? Bazookas, bazookas! That's the magic word, it's a regular fetish. Bazookas for everyone!

LOUIS: We've got to take advantage of youthful enthusiasm. And youngsters can't fight unless they adorn themselves with war cries. They try to get wounded so as to show their scars. They want bazookas.

ROGER (*bluntly*): No bazookas.

LOUIS (*irritably*): Then according to you we ought to be fighting hand-to-hand?

ROGER: As the word implies, hand-to-hand fighting eliminates distance.

LOUIS: Do you distrust enthusiasm?

ROGER: I distrust nervousness. The rebellion's riding high, and the people are having a carnival. They're shooting for the fun of it.

LUKE: They're right. Damn it, let them have their fling. I've never seen such excitement: one hand on the trigger, the other on the fly. They shoot and screw.

ROGER: Must you use such language! (*With sudden anger.*) What exactly is it you're after? If I yanked Chantal from the brothel, it wasn't to plant her in another—or in the same one—that's a mockery of the old one. Carnival! Carnival! You know well enough we ought to beware of it like the plague, since its logical conclusion is death. You know well enough that a carnival that goes to the limit is a suicide!

LOUIS: Without the people's anger there'd be no revolt. And anger is a carnival.

GEORGETTE: Then we must fight without anger. Reason should be enough.

ROGER: The enemy's losses are high; ours are incalculable. We've got to win at any cost. Those gentlemen on the other side are as happy as can be about our war. Because of it, they'll be able to attain, as they put it, even greater renown. The people mustn't enjoy themselves. And they mustn't play. Starting now, they've got to be in dead earnest.

Enter a WOUNDED MAN.

LOUIS (*to* THE WOUNDED MAN): Is it serious?

THE WOUNDED MAN: No. In the shoulder. But I think the bullet's still there.

CHANTAL (*to* GEORGETTE): Take care of him.

GEORGETTE: Right away. (*To* THE WOUNDED MAN.) Sit down. (*To* CHANTAL.) But what about you?

CHANTAL: I've had enough.

THE WOUNDED MAN: I know how you feel. It's no fun patching up the wounded. All the same, that's a woman's job. . . . My own wife's always busy with that kind of thing: plastering up a kid who gets hurt, mending a broken broomstick. . . .

ROGER (*going up to* CHANTAL): Are you giving up already?

CHANTAL: Forgive me, Roger, but I don't feel I'm cut out for that. I know you despise me. I'm just about ready to drop out. Yet I can't be on the other side either. And I want to sing.

ROGER (*gravely*): I told you, that's over. And you promised.

CHANTAL: I want to sing! To sing the excitement of the brawl, that and nothing else! For the sake of justice, if you like, I agree, but above all for the fighters for justice.

ROGER: You know where that can lead you?

CHANTAL: To the vaudeville stage. Is that what you're thinking?

ROGER (*ardently*): I've placed all my hope in you, Chantal. It was on you that I worked first. I wanted to disenchant you. Singer or whore, it comes to the same thing. You've got to stop charming and serve.

THE WOUNDED MAN (*turning his head in the direction of* CHANTAL): Is that you, Chantal? I didn't recognize you! What the hell are you doing here instead of leading the men forward the way you did yesterday, on the parapet? (*A silence.*) It takes women like you to loosen us up. It's your voice that tears out the cobblestones. It's your voice that stretches the barbed wire. It's your voice. . . .

GEORGETTE (*to* THE WOUNDED MAN): That does it. Keep your arm folded. Now come along. You've got to lie down and rest.

She accompanies him to the door, left. Exit THE WOUNDED MAN.

LUKE (*to* ROGER, *pointing to* CHANTAL): We're asking you to let us
have her for two hours. . . .

ROGER: Chantal belongs . . .

CHANTAL: To nobody!

ROGER: To my section . . . and to me.

LUKE: To the insurrection.

ROGER: If you want a woman to lead men forward, then create one.

LUKE (*seriously*): We tried to. We looked for one. We tried to build
one up: nice voice, nice bosom, with the right kind of free and
easy manner, but . . . her eyes lacked fire, and you know that
without fire . . . we asked the north quarter and the port
quarter to let us have theirs; they weren't free.

CHANTAL: A woman like me? Another one? You really mean another
one? All I have is the face of an inspired owl and my hoarse
voice. I give them or lend them for hatred's sake. All I am is
my face, my voice, and inside me a sweet and deadly kindness.
You mean I have two popular rivals, two other poor devils? Let
them come. I'll walk all over them. I have no rival.

LUKE (*to* LOUIS): She'll have hardly anything to do. As you know,
we're attacking the bridge at dawn. Under our protection, she'll
enter a house overlooking the dock. And she'll sing from the
balcony. . . .

LOUIS: If we lend her to you . . .

LUKE: That's not what we're asking. If we take her, we'll hire her.

CHANTAL (*banteringly*): How much?

ROGER (*to* CHANTAL): You think that's funny?

LOUIS (*to* LUKE): What if we let you have her to sing and spur on
your district and if she got bumped off? We'd lose everything.
She's irreplaceable.

LUKE: It's for her to decide.

LOUIS: She's no longer her own master. She belongs to us. All that
your women are good for is tearing up and carrying cobblestones
or reloading your guns. I know that's useful, but . . .

LUKE: How many women do you want in exchange?

ROGER (*dumfounded*): Is a singer on the barricades as precious as all
that?

LUKE: How many? Ten women for Chantal? (*Silence.*) Twenty?

Silence.

ROGER: Twenty women? Would you be ready to lend us twenty measly women, twenty oxen, twenty head of cattle? So Chantal's something special?

CHANTAL: Chantal? Here's the picture: every morning I go back—because at night I'm ablaze—I go back to a hovel to sleep and knock myself out with red wine. And I, with my raspy voice, my sham anger, my glassy eyes, my painted illumination, my Andalusian hair, I comfort and enchant the rabble. They'll win out, and my victory'll be a queer sort of thing. Maybe I get my talent from the brothel, but I'll never know how to swab a wound.

Suddenly the telephone rings. MARK *answers.*

MARK (*into the telephone*): Hello . . . this is Mark . . . B. 880. . . . Yes . . . yes . . . she's here. . . . (*A long silence.*) Is it serious? . .

A silence. Everyone is still and attentive.

O.K. . . . no, no . . . there's no objection. . . . But . . . is there any possible danger? No? . . . You don't know? . . . In any case, I'll send her. When the time comes, you'll have both sections. . . . (*A silence.*) So long. (*He hangs up.*)

LOUIS: The Central Committee?

MARK: Yes. Everything's working out right. The Palace is surrounded. The enemy has collapsed. It's the end. The bodies of several high dignitaries have been identified. (*A pause.*) Since there's no longer any central authority, we'll have to set up something at once to prevent anarchy. But there's a plot afoot. We've got to work fast.

ROGER: Are they asking you to be a member of the provisional government?

MARK: I've been appointed.

ROGER (*to* MARK): What's to be done?

MARK: Give orders to design posters showing Chantal on the barricades and on the balcony of the Palace. See to it that they're pasted on every wall and billboard. (ROGER *makes a gesture.*) Do as I tell you. According to information, the Grand Chamberlain has gone to The Balcony, which is where the Chief of Police is said to be. They've gone there to work out the usual kind of operation. They know very well that as far as they're concerned the revolt must have only one purpose: to heighten their glory by putting down the insurrection. We're going to cramp their carnival by countering with our own.

ROGER: A carnival?

MARK (*forcefully*): We're going to use Chantal. Her job is to embody the revolution. The job of the mothers and widows is to mourn the dead. The job of the dead is to cry for revenge. The job of our heroes is to die with a smile. . . . The Palace will be occupied this evening. From the balcony of the Palace Chantal will rouse the people, and sing. The time for reasoning is past; now's the time to get steamed up and fight like mad. Chantal embodies the struggle; the people are waiting for her to represent victory.

ROGER: And when we're the victors, what'll we have gained?

MARK: There'll be time enough to think of that. For the moment, there's not a minute to waste. We're racing against the clock. If they succeed in working out their scheme, we're up the creek . . . The royal carriage has managed to get through the lines. It's parked near The Balcony. . . . Was the Queen in it? . . . Does anyone know? (*To* LUKE.) You'll escort Chantal. To get to the Palace you'll have to go along the river. . . . (*He goes back to pinning his flags.*)

LUKE: I know. I'm used to it.

ROGER (*to* CHANTAL, *in a hurt voice*): But it was I who . . . if Chantal . . . (*Humbly, but with resolution.*) I love you, Chantal.

CHANTAL (*to* ROGER): You're the first, the only one, the only one there'll ever be, but let me leave.

ROGER: The minutes without you will be unbearable.

GEORGETTE: Is that why you wanted her to learn to dress wounds?

ROGER: That was why, and also that she be born again.

CHANTAL: We won't be separated. I'll speak to them in an icy voice, and at the same time I'll murmur words of love for you. You'll hear them from here, and I'll listen to those you say to me.

ROGER: They may keep you, Chantal. They're strong—strong as death.

CHANTAL: Don't be afraid, I know their power. Your sweetness and tenderness are stronger. I'll speak to them in a tone of severity. They'll listen to me, and they'll be afraid. All *they* can do is fight, and all *you* can do is talk. That's the role you've learned to play. The brothel has at least been of some use to me, for it has taught me the art of shamming and acting. I've had to play so many roles that I know almost all of them. And I've had so many partners. . . .

ROGER: Be still.

CHANTAL: . . . And such artful ones, such crafty ones, that my skill and guile are incomparable.

GEORGETTE: You'll never forget the brothel. . . .

CHANTAL: Never completely. You and your kind who are pure and just, you resent never having had the experience.

GEORGETTE: Personally, I didn't have a calling for it.

ROGER (*vehemently*): But I dragged you—dragged you!—from the grave! And you're already escaping me and mounting to the sky. . . . Your name's on the lips of people who've never seen or heard you. Before long, they'll think it's for you they're fighting. You're already a kind of saint. Women try to imitate you. . . . (*In a fury.*) I didn't carry you off, I didn't steal you, for you to become a unicorn or two-headed eagle. . . .

GEORGETTE (*contemptuously*): Don't you like unicorns?

CHANTAL (*to* ROGER): I'll come back, and everything will be the same. We love each other. . . .

ROGER: Nothing will be the same, and you know it. You'll be what you've always dreamt of being: an emblem forever escaping from her womanliness.

LOUIS: You're forgetting that it's for the revolution and that she may remain there.

ROGER: That's the only thing that could save her.

MARK (*still planting his flags*): It's time to go.

CHANTAL (*to* ROGER): Shall I kiss you?

ROGER *hugs her; then she leaves, preceded by* LUKE. *A silence.*

GEORGETTE (*to the men*): Excuse me, but I've got medicines to prepare.

GEORGETTE *exits. A silence.*

LOUIS (*to* ROGER): You love her, and she's escaping you. I can understand your anger.

ROGER (*sadly*): She's flying into the other camp!

LOUIS: You're dreaming!

ROGER: Me?

LOUIS: You're dreaming. Dreaming of an impossible revolution that's carried out reasonably and cold-bloodedly. You're fascinated by it, the way those in the other camp are by other games. But you've got to realize that the most reasonable man always manages, when he pulls the trigger, to become a dispenser of justice.

ROGER: In the eyes of whom?

LOUIS: I wonder. (*A pause. Musingly.*) Chantal! But . . . it's Georgette that you ought to love.

ROGER (*surprised*): Georgette?

LOUIS: Because she loves you. . . . But what you love in Chantal is the very thing you're bent on destroying, the thing that made it possible for her to enter the brothel, the thing that's still part of her. . . .

> *Suddenly a terrible explosion. The windowpanes tremble. The three men pull themselves together. They look at each other anxiously.*

Ring up the Central Committee.

> MARK *removes the receiver. He waits a few seconds.*

MARK: Is that you, Robert? This is Mark, B. 880. . . . Did you hear that? . . . Eh? . . . The Palace? . . . Who? . . . The North Section? . . . Good! So long. (*He hangs up.*) Did you get that? (*He smiles.*) The Royal Palace has been blown up.

ROGER: Chantal is saved!

MARK: This time it seems pretty sure that we've got the upper hand. The streets around the cathedral are occupied. So are the bridges. . . . The revolutionary tribunal is in permanent session. . . .

LOUIS: Have there been any executions?

MARK: Quite a number. Execution follows immediately upon condemnation. No standing on ceremony.

ROGER: Chantal's coming back. She'll help Georgette. . . .

LOUIS (*to* MARK): If the Royal Palace has been blown up, the Queen must be under the rubble?

MARK: Let's hope so. But the Grand Chamberlain managed to get to The Balcony. He's still there, and the royal carriage. . . .

ARMAND *enters in a state of wild excitement.*

ARMAND: The Palace has been blown up! You can see it blazing from the windows! The opposition has completely collapsed. Everything's giving way. . . . It's all over. And The Balcony's on fire!

MARK: Is that why you're pale?

ARMAND: Me? Pale?

MARK: I didn't say you're scared. I said you're pale.

ARMAND: I didn't think we'd make it as soon as that. Who's going to take over the controls. And what's to be done with the Queen, and the Archbishop, and the others?

ROGER: First undress them.

ARMAND: What if they don't give in? They've good reason for knowing they're sacred. I personally don't believe in their masquerade, not one bit. But is there any stronger force to replace them?

ROGER: You, and everybody.

LOUIS: The Central Committee's already been set up.

ARMAND: The Central Committee—they're pals. . . .

MARK (*roughly*): Go get your gun. You're coming with me.

ARMAND (*after a very brief hesitation*): O.K. And The Balcony's on fire? No more Balcony, no more whores. . . .

MARK: I was appointed an hour ago. You're to obey me. Get going. (ARMAND *exits. To* ROGER, *in a hurried tone.*) Invent a Chantal who becomes more and more fabulous! She's the only one who'll be able to electrify the people, precisely because she comes from the brothel. Get going. Encourage them. Loudspeakers everywhere. Her voice on all the barricades. Photos. Her face on all the billboards. Have tracts printed, by the thousands, and see that they're distributed. Brightly colored. With a picture of her and a declaration. Invent a historic statement signed Chantal. Write a poem to the glory of wrath, rebellion and war.

ROGER: Yes, a poem hailing freedom, the people and their virtue. . . .

MARK (*weightily*): Hell, no! None of that. That kind of thing would shoot them up into a heaven of abstractions, where they'd hang permanently. If you magnify freedom and the people and virtue, if you make them untouchable, how can you approach them, how can you love them? You've got to leave them in their living reality. Let there be poems and pictures, but they mustn't give pleasure, they've got to sting. And do what I say—Committee orders.

The Funeral Studio mentioned in MME. IRMA's *listing of the studios. The studio is in ruins. The lace and velvet are torn. The artificial wreaths are tattered. An impression of desolation.* IRMA's *dress is in rags. So is the suit of the* CHIEF OF POLICE. ARTHUR's *corpse is lying on a kind of fake tomb of fake black marble. Nearby, a new character: the Court* ENVOY. *Embassy uniform. He is the only one unscathed.* CARMEN *is dressed as at the beginning; she is carrying the Saint Theresa outfit.*

IRMA (*touching the corpse with her foot*): He didn't think he'd be acting his role of corpse this evening in earnest.

THE ENVOY (*smiling*): Our dear Minister of the Interior would have been delighted had not he himself met the same fate. It is unfortunately I who have had to replace him in his mission here, and I have no taste for pleasures of this kind. (*He pinches* CARMEN's *chin.*) We prefer this modest rose! I'm pleased with her. Everything has gone off splendidly, to our great joy. (*Suddenly embarrassed.*) And despite the Fair One's apparent irritation.

CARMEN (*curtly*): I did my job.

IRMA (*to* CARMEN): Be still. (*To* THE ENVOY.) Forgive her, your Excellency, she feels humiliated, because with you she's only a saint. With one of these gentlemen she had higher ranking. But she knows her duty.

THE ENVOY: It's therefore for me to apologize. I know only too well how hard it is to assume the appearance of our abyss. (*He touches* ARTHUR's *corpse with his foot.*) Yes, this body would have sent our dear Minister into raptures.

IRMA: Not at all, your Excellency. It's make-believe that these gentlemen want. The Minister desired a fake corpse. But this one is real. Look at it: it's truer than life. His entire being was speeding towards immobility.

THE ENVOY: He was therefore meant for grandeur.

THE CHIEF OF POLICE: Him? He was a spineless dummy.

THE ENVOY: He was, like us, haunted by a quest of immobility. By what we call the hieratic. And, in passing, allow me to pay tribute to the imagination responsible for there being a funeral parlor in this house. Whose idea was it?

IRMA: The Wisdom of Nations, your Excellency.

THE ENVOY: It does things well. But we were talking about the Queen, to protect whom is my mission.

THE CHIEF OF POLICE: You're going about it in a curious way. The Palace, according to what you say. . . .

THE ENVOY (*smiling*): For the time being, Her Majesty is in safety. But time is pressing. The prelate is said to have been beheaded. The Archbishop's Palace has been ransacked. The Law Court and Military Headquarters have been routed. . . .

THE CHIEF OF POLICE: But what about the Queen?

THE ENVOY (*in a very light tone*): She's embroidering. For a moment she thought of nursing the wounded. But it was pointed out to her that, as the throne was threatened, she had to carry to an extreme the Royal prerogatives.

IRMA: Which are?

THE ENVOY: Absence. Her Majesty has retired to a chamber, in solitude. The disobedience of her people saddens her. She is embroidering a handkerchief. The design of it is as follows: the four corners will be adorned with poppy heads. In the middle of the handkerchief, embroidered in pale blue silk, will be a swan, resting on the water of a lake. That's the only point about which Her Majesty is troubled: will it be the water of a lake, a pond or a pool? Or simply of a tank or a cup? It is a grave problem. We have chosen it because it is insoluble, and the Queen can engross herself in an infinite meditation.

IRMA: Is the Queen amused?

THE ENVOY: Her Majesty is occupying herself in becoming entirely what she must be: the Queen. (*He looks at the corpse.*) She, too, is moving rapidly towards immobility.

IRMA: And she's embroidering?

THE ENVOY: No, Madame, I say the Queen is embroidering a handkerchief, for though it is my duty to describe her, it is also my duty to conceal her.

IRMA: Do you mean she's not embroidering?

THE ENVOY: I mean that the Queen is embroidering and that she is not embroidering. She picks her nose, examines the pickings and lies down again. Then, she dries the dishes.

IRMA: The Queen?

THE ENVOY: She is not nursing the wounded. She is embroidering an invisible handkerchief. . . .

THE CHIEF OF POLICE: By God! What have you done with Her Majesty? I want a straight answer. I'm not amused. . . .

THE ENVOY: She is in a chest. She is sleeping. Wrapped in the folds of Royalty, she is snoring. . . .

THE CHIEF OF POLICE (*threateningly*): Is the Queen dead?

THE ENVOY (*unperturbed*): She is snoring and she is not snoring. Her head, which is tiny, supports, without wavering, a crown of metal and stones.

THE CHIEF OF POLICE (*more and more threateningly*): Enough of that. You said the Palace was in danger. . . . What's to be done? I still have almost the entire police force behind me. Those who are still with me are ready to die for me. . . . They know who I am and what I'll do for them. . . . How far has the rebellion gone? I want a clear answer.

THE ENVOY: You can judge from the state of this house. And from your own. . . . All seems lost.

IRMA: You belong to the Court, your Excellency. Before coming here, I was with the troops. That's where I won my first spurs. I can assure you I've known worse situations. The populace—from which I broke away with a kick of my heels—the populace is howling beneath my windows, which have been multiplied by the bombs: my house stands its ground. My rooms aren't intact, but they've held up. My whores, except for one lunatic, are on the job. If the center of the Palace is a woman like me . . .

THE ENVOY (*imperturbably*): The Queen is standing on one foot in the middle of an empty room, and she . . .

THE CHIEF OF POLICE: That'll do! I've had enough of your riddles. For me, the Queen has to be someone. And the situation has to be concrete. Describe it to me exactly. I've no time to waste.

THE ENVOY: Whom do you want to save?

THE CHIEF OF POLICE: The Queen!

IRMA: My hide!

THE ENVOY (*to* THE CHIEF OF POLICE): If you're eager to save the Queen—and, beyond her, our flag, and all its gold fringe, and its eagle, cords and pole, would you describe them to me?

THE CHIEF OF POLICE: Until now I've served the things you mention, and served them with distinction, and without bothering to know any more about them than what I saw. And I'll continue. What's happening about the rebellion?

THE ENVOY (*resignedly*): The garden gates will, for a moment longer, hold back the crowd. The guards are devoted, like us, with an obscure devotion. They'll die for their sovereign. They'll give their blood. Unhappily there won't be enough of it to drown the rebellion. Sandbags have been piled up in front of the doors. In order to confuse even reason, Her Majesty removes herself from one secret chamber to another, from the servants' hall to the Throne Room, from the latrines to the chicken-coop, the chapel, the guard-room. . . . She makes herself unfindable and thus attains a threatened invisibility. So much for the inside of the Palace. Outside—and from here you cannot be aware of it— the insurrection has attained such proportions that the very nation is in peril.

THE CHIEF OF POLICE: I've been getting reports from my agents. . . .

THE ENVOY (*interrupting him*): I don't doubt their courage or cleverness, but my spies are in the thick of the revolution, and in some cases they're rebels themselves. Now, the populace, which is intoxicated with its first victories, has reached the point of exaltation at which one light-heartedly forsakes actual combat for useless sacrifice. It will be easy to take the leap. The people are not engaging in battle. They're indulging in revelry.

IRMA: When a person's on a spree, he no longer knows what he's doing. While roaring with laughter, one can grab hold of a live wire. . . .

THE ENVOY: Exactly. And you're not the only one who knows it. A revolutionary committee has been set up. You don't quite realize it, but we, who have eyes everywhere, can tell you that the situation is increasingly dangerous for you. It's composed of grim technicians. Dressed in black. . . .

IRMA: As in Studio 28 . . .

THE ENVOY (*interrupting her*): Not at all. That's precisely the difference. Those gentlemen—and this seems a new phenomenon— aren't playing, or rather, don't realize what they're playing. They calculate. Their faces are pale and sad, their gestures sharp and precise, their speech always exact. They don't cheat. They have tremendous power over the people. They want to save them. . . .

IRMA: What if I let loose my army among them—though it *has* suffered from the course of events—and if they were lured into my studios?

THE ENVOY: They've anticipated that. They're taking no risks. Now, for the time being, though they haven't triumphed, they're gaining ground. . . .

THE CHIEF OF POLICE: What about the Generalissimo?

THE ENVOY: Gone mad. He wanders among the crowd, where nobody will harm him, protected by his madness.

THE CHIEF OF POLICE: What about the Attorney General?

THE ENVOY: Died of fright.

THE CHIEF OF POLICE: And the Bishop?

THE ENVOY: His case is more difficult. The Church is secretive. Nothing is known about him. Nothing definite. His decapitated head was said to have been seen on the handlebars of a bicycle. Of course, the rumor was false. We're therefore relying entirely on you. But your orders aren't getting through.

IRMA: We want to win, and not in death.

THE ENVOY: To save whom?

A pause.

Won't you answer? Would it perturb you to see things as they are? To gaze at the world tranquilly and accept responsibility for your gaze, whatever it might see?

THE CHIEF OF POLICE: But, after all, in coming to see me, you did have something definite in mind, didn't you? You had a plan? Let's hear it.

Suddenly a terrific blast. Both men, but not IRMA, fall flat on the floor, then stand up again and dust each other off.

THE ENVOY: That may have been the Royal Palace. Long live the Royal Palace!

THE CHIEF OF POLICE (*aghast*): But the Queen. . . . Then the Queen's under the rubble?

THE ENVOY (*smiling mysteriously*): You need not worry. Her Majesty is in a safe place. And that phoenix, when dead, can rise up from the ashes of a Royal Palace. I can understand your impatience to prove your valor, your devotion . . . but the Queen will wait for you as long as necessary. (*To IRMA.*) I must pay tribute, Madame, to your coolness. And to your courage. They are worthy of the highest respect.... (*Musingly.*) Of the highest....

IRMA: You're forgetting to whom you're speaking. I may run a brothel, but I wasn't born of the marriage of the moon and a crocodile. I've lived among the people. . . . All the same, it was a heavy blow. And the people . . .

THE ENVOY (*severely*): That's behind you. When life departs, the hands cling to a sheet. What significance has that rag when you're about to penetrate into the providential fixity?

IRMA: Sir? Do you mean I'm at my last gasp?

THE ENVOY (*examining her, part by part*): Splendid head! Sturdy thighs! Solid shoulders!

IRMA (*laughing*): So I've been told, and it didn't make me lose my head. In short, I'll make a presentable corpse if the rebels act fast and if they leave me intact. But if the Queen is dead . . .

THE ENVOY (*bowing*): Long live the Queen, Madame.

IRMA (*anxiously*): What? You wouldn't dare . . .

THE ENVOY (*spiritedly*): I've described the situation. The populace, in its joy and fury, is at the brink of ecstasy. It's for us to press it forward. The Queen was less beautiful than you.

IRMA: Her lineage was more ancient . . . she was older. . . . And, after all, maybe she was just as frightened as I.

THE CHIEF OF POLICE: It is in order to approach her, to be worthy of her, that one makes such a mighty effort. But what if one is Herself?

IRMA: And I don't know how to talk. I'm always hemming and hawing.

THE ENVOY: All must unfold in a silence that etiquette allows no one to break.

THE CHIEF OF POLICE: I'm going to have the rubble of the Palace cleared away. If, as you said, the Queen was in a chest, it may be possible to save her.

THE ENVOY (*shrugging his shoulders*): It was made of rosewood! And it was so old, so worn. . . . (*To* IRMA, *running his hand over the back of her neck.*) Yes, it requires solid vertebrae . . . they've got to carry several pounds. . . .

THE CHIEF OF POLICE: . . . and resist the axe, don't they? Irma, don't listen to him!

IRMA (*to* THE ENVOY): But, your Excellency, I'm really very weak, and very frail. Though a while ago I was boasting . . .

THE ENVOY: Around this delicate and precious kernel we'll forge a shell of gold and iron. But you must make up your mind quickly. If it's noticed . . .

IRMA: Allow me just a little more respite. . . .

THE ENVOY: A few seconds, for time is pressing.

THE CHIEF OF POLICE: If only there were some way of knowing what the late sovereign would have thought of it. We can't decide just like that. To appropriate a heritage . . .

THE ENVOY (*scornfully*): You're knuckling under already. Do you tremble if there's no authority above you to decide? But it's for Mme. Irma to declare. . . .

IRMA (*in a highfalutin tone*): In the records of our family, which goes a long way back, there was some question of . . .

THE ENVOY (*severely*): Nonsense, Mme. Irma. In our vaults, genealogists are working day and night. History is submitted to them. I said we hadn't a minute to waste in conquering our people, but beware! Although the populace may worship you, its high-flown pride is capable of sacrificing you. It sees you as red, either crimson or blood-red. If it kills its idols and thrusts them into the sewers, it will sweep us up with them. . . .

THE CHIEF OF POLICE: And you say that without trembling, you who survive all revolutions?

IRMA (*to* THE CHIEF OF POLICE): Let the Grand Chamberlain finish what he has to say. It concerns me. If necessary, I'll take you all under my protection.

THE ENVOY (*to* THE CHIEF OF POLICE): Sir, in the northern part of the country lies a vast plain. Nearby is a mountain. Laborers were already at work when the revolt broke out, but we'll be able to bring them back. In addition to that mountain, and a few others, the country is rich in marble quarries. . . .

THE CHIEF OF POLICE (*marveling*): Marble? And granite? Is there pink granite?

THE ENVOY: And even porphyry, sir. I refer to a project for a tomb. The plan of it is in my possession.

THE CHIEF OF POLICE (*eagerly*): Let me see it.

THE ENVOY: Later. The architect who conceived it was a poet, philosopher and man of science. Imagine a splendid structure. Five or six law-courts piled one on top of the other, a dozen opera houses, twenty large stations, thirty pagodas, a hundred memorial monuments, and you'll have a slight idea of what it will be.

Upon one mountain will be placed another, and on that other still another, and in the middle of the first a tiny diamond sentry-box.

THE CHIEF OF POLICE (*greedily*): Will I be able to stand there—or sit—and keep vigil over my entire death?

THE ENVOY (*banteringly*): Who said anything about designating it for you? But he who gets it will be there—dead—for eternity. The world will center about it. About it will rotate the planets. It will no doubt be the most imposing funeral-pile in the universe. From a secret point of the third mountain will run a road that will lead, after many and many a complication, to a room where mirrors will reflect to infinity—I say to infinity!—the image of the dead man. To infinity—and for eternity—in the depths of a vault ... His image. . . .

THE CHIEF OF POLICE: It's an enormous risk. . . .

THE ENVOY: That is for Mme. Irma to decide.

IRMA (*to* THE ENVOY): Are you quite sure of what you're saying? Do you really know what's going on? What about your spies?

THE ENVOY: They inform us as accurately as the peep-holes that peer into your studios. (*Smiling.*) And I may add that we consult them with the same pleasurable thrill.

IRMA: Too bad I can't peep into the rebellion as I can into Studio 23. . . .

THE ENVOY: You would see faces wrought with anger and hatred and the lust of murder. The populace has ceased to be the submissive animal that tamely licks our feet, or rather our patent-leather pumps. It has become a kind of wild beast that drools blood at the corners of its mouth. . . .

THE CHIEF OF POLICE: Don't you worry. I'll tame it all right! When it comes to action, I'm all there.

IRMA (*to* THE CHIEF OF POLICE): Well, then, you accept?

THE ENVOY: . . . Nothing is ever wholly lost. Our latest information is a few hours old. We know that those gentlemen, who are a tough-minded lot, think they have us. What they want is that each individual be both himself and a shining specimen of himself. More nonsense! They're unaware that our resources are inexhaustible, that we need only choose from the storehouse of mummery. But we must act fast. We're engaged in a race against the clock. It's we or they. Mme. Irma, think speedily.

IRMA (*holding her head in her hands*): I'm hurrying, sir. I'm approach-

ing my destiny as fast as I can. (*To* CARMEN.) Are our Great
Figures there?

CARMEN: The gentlemen tried to return home, Madame, but the
house is surrounded. They all had to come back and take
refuge here.

IRMA: Go see what they're doing. Hurry. . . .

THE ENVOY (*to* CARMEN): What about you, what's to be done w th
you?

CARMEN: I'll stick to my post, sir. (CARMEN *exits.*)

THE ENVOY: One other matter, a more delicate one. I mentioned an
image that for some days now has been mounting in the sky of
the revolution.

IRMA: The revolution has its sky too?

THE ENVOY: Don't envy it. Chantal's image is circulating in the streets.
A stylized image that resembles her and does not resemble her.
She towers above the battles. At first, people were fighting
against illustrious and illusory tyrants, then for freedom. Tomorrow they'll be ready to die for Chantal alone.

IRMA: The ungrateful wretch! She who was in such demand as
Lucrezia Borgia.

THE CHIEF OF POLICE: She won't last. She's like me: she has neither
father nor mother. And if she becomes an image, we'll make use
of it.

Suddenly a bell rings. IRMA *is about to dart forward, but stops.*

IRMA (*to* THE CHIEF OF POLICE): It's Carmen. What's she saying? What
are they doing?

THE CHIEF OF POLICE *lifts one of the earphones.*

THE- CHIEF OF POLICE (*transmitting the message*): While waiting to
go home, they're standing around looking at themselves in the
mirrors.

IRMA: Tell her to smash the mirrors or veil them.

A silence. Then a burst of machine-gun fire.

Good. My mind's made up. I presume I've been summoned from

all eternity and that God will bless me. I'm going to prepare myself by prayer.

THE ENVOY (*gravely*): Do you have the outfits?

IRMA: My closets are as famous as my studios. (*Suddenly worried.*) But everything must be in an awful state! The bombs, the plaster, the dust. Tell Carmen to brush the costumes! (*To* THE CHIEF OF POLICE.) George . . . this is our last minute together! From now on, we'll no longer be us. . . .

THE ENVOY *discreetly moves off and goes to the window.*

THE CHIEF OF POLICE: Are you sure that something of us won't subsist?

IRMA: We'll have to strive to reduce it until it disappears. And when we die, what will seem to die will be only a gilded corpse. In a few minutes the metamorphosis will begin. We'll be strangers to each other, for good and all. Do you consent, George?

THE CHIEF OF POLICE: I've got to. If I didn't, what would become of me?

IRMA *and* THE CHIEF OF POLICE *draw apart from each other.*

IRMA (*to* THE ENVOY): So I'll be real? My robe will be real? My lace, my jewels will be real? The rest of the world will be a copy of what I'll be?

Machine-gun fire.

THE ENVOY (*after a last glance through the shutters*): Yes, Madame, but make haste. As I've told you, the people is awaiting its idol in order to grovel before it. . . . It will be you . . . or the other. Go to your apartments. Embroider an interminable handkerchief. . . . (*To* THE CHIEF OF POLICE.) You, give your last orders to your last men.

IRMA *and* THE CHIEF OF POLICE *exit.* THE ENVOY *remains alone for a few seconds. He goes to a mirror, takes from his pocket a whole collection of decorations and fastens them to his tunic.*

VOICE OF THE BISHOP (*from the wings*): But you yourself, Carmen, you know perfectly well it's sheer madness! It was stupid of me to come back here to hide. . . .

THE BISHOP *enters in civilian clothes, followed by* CARMEN. *On seeing* THE ENVOY *and the unfamiliar studio, he is taken aback. He looks about him.*

THE ENVOY (*to* THE BISHOP, *after bowing to him*): I myself am here— though I've been here longer than you—for a reason not unlike your own. Before Carmen went to get you, she succeeded in convincing me. (*To* CARMEN.) As I have nothing further to do here, I shall return to Her Majesty.

He bows and leaves.

CARMEN: Do you love the Queen?

THE BISHOP: What a question!

CARMEN: I'm not so sure. Last night you managed to get home. It was dangerous in the streets, but you were smart enough to find your way, your house, your wife and your son. Then . . . you fought against us . . . I mean . . .

THE BISHOP: The rebels were blocking the streets. There was shooting from the roofs, from the cellars. . . . Bullets were whizzing high and low. . . . (*Pointing to* THE ENVOY *as he leaves.*) Who's that?

CARMEN: And you preferred to come and take refuge at Irma's place, knowing that they were going to attack the house and that you'd die there. If I understood correctly, you wanted to go up in flames in the midst of what you cherish?

THE BISHOP: I forbid you. . . .

CARMEN: Let's not joke. And above all, let's not put on an act, not even one of delicacy. No one knows better than I the charming drama of which you're the hero. No, no, don't protest. I'm playing in another one myself. . . . But you won't know which. Let's get back to ourselves. Orders have been issued from very high. . . .

THE BISHOP: I'm only a gas-man.

CARMEN: How could you still be a gas-man if nobody recognizes you as the gas-man? Because you know how to do sums? So does a bishop. But you won't be doing that any more. You'll start by knowing nothing. You'll make your appearance—but first, you'll bow to the Queen. . . .

THE BISHOP: Is she here?

CARMEN: You'll bow to your sovereign. The Judge, the General and you will pay homage to her. She'll accept it. Then the Hero will appear. The Queen and he, with the three of you about them, will appear on the Grand Balcony of this house. The acclamation of the crowd will ring out. The Queen will bow. The Hero will bow. Then . . . (*She hesitates.*)

THE BISHOP: Then?

CARMEN: You will go in a carriage to . . . amidst the spellbound or raging crowd, to the cathedral . . . or to the scaffold.

THE BISHOP (*horror-stricken*): What death have you in store for me?

CARMEN: You'll ride in a carriage through a city which has been pacified by your gesture, or you'll be trampled by the horses.

THE BISHOP: But I'll never be able to. . . . I'll be recognized. . . . My acne . . . my mannerisms . . . my voice. . . .

CARMEN: They'll become either your personal, endearing idiosyncrasies—or the permanent stamp of the Bishop.

THE BISHOP: But I won't be alone, will I?

CARMEN: Several of the gentlemen—regular clients, of course—have already complied, and very eagerly.

THE BISHOP: But then, they'll see me, they'll recognize me?

CARMEN: You'll see them, you'll recognize them. You'll see and recognize each other . . . faintly—and withdraw into the most secret chamber of your dignity.

    Enter THE ENVOY.

THE ENVOY (*in a vulgar tone*): Make it snappy. I don't have time to listen to your crap. (*To* CARMEN.) If the gentleman doesn't fill the bill, then get a dummy, but get a move on.

SCENE EIGHT

THE BALCONY

The scene is the balcony itself, which projects beyond the façade of the brothel. The shutters, which face the audience, are closed. Suddenly, all the shutters open by themselves. The edge of the balcony is at the very edge of the footlights. Through the windows can be seen THE BISHOP, THE GENERAL *and* THE JUDGE, *who are getting ready. Finally the French windows are flung wide open. The three men come out on the balcony. First* THE BISHOP, *then* THE GENERAL, *then* THE JUDGE. *They are followed by* THE HERO. *Then comes* THE QUEEN: MME. IRMA, *wearing a diadem on her brow and an ermine cloak. All the characters step forward and take their positions with great timidity. They are silent. They simply show themselves. All are of huge proportions, gigantic—except* THE HERO, *that is,* THE CHIEF OF POLICE—*and are wearing their ceremonial garments, which are torn and dusty. Then, near them, but not on the balcony, appears* THE BEGGAR. *In a gentle voice, he cries out:*

THE BEGGAR: Long live the Queen! (*He goes off timidly, as he came.*)

Finally, a strong wind stirs the curtains: CHANTAL *appears.* THE QUEEN *bows to her. A shot.* CHANTAL *falls.* THE GENERAL *and* THE QUEEN *carry her away dead.*

341

SCENE NINE

IRMA'S *room, which looks as if it had been hit by a hurricane. Rear, a large two-panelled mirror which forms the wall. Right, a door; left, another. Three cameras on tripods. The stage is empty. Enter, in turn, very timidly, right,* THE BISHOP *and, left,* THE JUDGE *and* THE GENERAL. *On seeing each other, they bow deeply. Then,* THE GENERAL *salutes and* THE BISHOP *blesses* THE GENERAL.

THE JUDGE (*with a sigh of relief*): What we've been through!

THE GENERAL: And it's not over! We have to invent an entire life.... That's hard....

THE BISHOP: Hard or not, we've got to go through with it. We can no longer back out. Before entering the carriage . . .

THE GENERAL: The slowness of the carriage!

THE BISHOP: . . . . entering the carriage, it was still possible to chuck the whole business. But now....

THE JUDGE: Do you think we were recognized? I was in the middle, hidden by your profiles. Opposite me, Irma. . . . (*The name astonishes him.*) Irma? The Queen. . . . The Queen hid my face.... Do you think we were?

THE BISHOP: No danger of that. You know whom I saw . . . at the right (*Unable to keep from laughing.*) with his fat, good-natured mug and pink cheeks, though the town was in smith-ereens? (*The other two smile.*) With his pimples and decayed teeth? and who threw himself on my hand . . . I thought to bite me, and I was about to pull away my fingers . . . to kiss my ring? Who? My fruit-and-vegetable man.

THE JUDGE *laughs.*

THE GENERAL (*grimly*): The slowness of the carriage. The carriage wheels on the people's feet and hands! The dust!

THE JUDGE (*uneasily*): I was opposite the Queen. Through the back window, a woman . . .

THE BISHOP (*continuing his account*): I saw her too, at the left-hand door, she was running along and throwing kisses at us!

THE GENERAL (*more and more grimly*): The slowness of the carriage!

We moved forward so slowly amidst the sweaty mob! Their roars were like threats, but they were only cheering. Someone could have hamstrung the horses, fired a shot, could have unhitched the traces and harnessed *us*, attached us to the shaft or the horses, could have drawn and quartered us or turned us into draft-horses. But no. Just flowers tossed from a window, and a people hailing its Queen, who stood upright beneath her golden crown. (*A pause.*) And the horses going at a walking pace . . . and the Envoy standing on the footboard!

A silence.

THE BISHOP: No one could have recognized us. We were in the gold and glitter. They were blinded. It hit them in the eye. . . .

THE JUDGE: It wouldn't have taken much. . . .

THE BISHOP: Exhausted by the fighting, choked by the dust, the people stood waiting for the procession. The procession was all they saw. In any case, we can no longer back out. We've been chosen.

THE GENERAL: By whom?

THE BISHOP: By glory in person.

THE GENERAL: This masquerade?

THE BISHOP: It lies with us for this masquerade to change meaning. First, we must use words that magnify. We must act fast, and with precision. No errors allowed. (*With authority.*) As for me, instead of being merely the symbolic head of the country's church, I've decided to become its actual head. Instead of blessing and blessing and blessing until I've had my fill. I'm going to sign decrees and appoint priests. The clergy is being organized. A basilica is under construction. It's all in there. (*He points to a folder under his arm.*) Full of plans and projects. (*To* THE JUDGE.) What about you?

THE JUDGE (*looking at his wristwatch*): I have an appointment with a number of magistrates. We're drafting bills, we're revising the legal code. (*To* THE GENERAL.) What about you?

THE GENERAL: Oh, me, your ideas drift through my poor head like smoke through a log shanty. The art of war's not something you can master just like that. The general-staffs . . .

THE BISHOP (*interrupting*): Like everything else, the fate of arms can be read in your stars. Read your stars, damn it!

THE GENERAL: That's easy to say. But when the Hero comes back, planted firmly on his rump, as if on a horse . . . For, of course, nothing's happened yet? (

THE BISHOP: Nothing. But let's not crow too soon. Though his image hasn't yet been consecrated by the brothel, it still may. If it does, we're done for. Unless we make a positive effort to seize power.

Suddenly, he breaks off. With a slamming of doors enter, right, three photographers. They are dressed like newspaper reporters. Their voices are loud, their speech brash. Their gestures contrast sharply with the delicate manners of THE THREE FIGURES, *to whom they toss a rather familiar sign of greeting.*

FIRST PHOTOGRAPHER: Evening, gentlemen.

A pause. THE THREE FIGURES *look bewildered.* THE BISHOP *is the first to pull himself together.*

THE BISHOP (*aloof*): Good evening, my friends. We've been expecting you.

SECOND PHOTOGRAPHER (*looking at the lights*): Well, we made it, as you can see.

THE BISHOP (*severely*): Indeed, you have come. Please do your job quickly, and in silence, if possible. You're to take each of our profiles, one smiling, the other rather stern.

FIRST PHOTOGRAPHER: We'll do our job, don't worry. (*To* THE BISHOP.) Get set for prayer, because the world ought to be bombarded with the picture of a pious man.

THE BISHOP (*without moving*): In fervent meditation.

FIRST PHOTOGRAPHER: Right, fervent. Get set.

THE BISHOP (*ill at ease*): But . . . how?

FIRST PHOTOGRAPHER: Don't you know how to compose yourself for prayer? Okay, facing both God and the camera. Hands together. Head up. Eyes down. That's the classical pose. A return to order, a return to classicism.

THE BISHOP (*kneeling*): Like this?

FIRST PHOTOGRAPHER (*looking at him with curiosity*): That's it. . . . (*He looks at the camera.*) No. you're not in the frame. . .

(*Shuffling on his knees,* THE BISHOP *places himself in front of the camera.*) Okay.

SECOND PHOTOGRAPHER (*to* THE JUDGE): Would you mind pulling a longer face? You don't quite look like a judge. A little longer.

THE JUDGE: Horselike? Sullen?

SECOND PHOTOGRAPHER: Horselike and sullen, Mr. Attorney General. And both hands in front, on your brief. What I want is a shot of *the* Judge. A good photographer is one who gives a de*fin*itive image. Perfect.

FIRST PHOTOGRAPHER (*to* THE BISHOP): Turn your head . . . just a little. . . . (*He turns* THE BISHOP's *head.*)

THE BISHOP (*angrily*): You're unscrewing the neck of a prelate!

FIRST PHOTOGRAPHER: I want a three-quarter view of you praying, Monsignor.

SECOND PHOTOGRAPHER (*to* THE JUDGE): Mr. Attorney General, if you possibly can, a little more severity . . . with a pendulous lip. (*Crying out.*) That's it! Perfect! Stay that way! (*He rushes behind his camera, but there is a flash before he gets there.* THE FIRST PHOTOGRAPHER *has just taken his shot.* THE SECOND PHOTOGRAPHER *puts his head under the black hood of his camera.*)

THE GENERAL (*to* THE THIRD PHOTOGRAPHER): The finest pose is Poniatovsky's.

THIRD PHOTOGRAPHER (*striking a pose*): With the sword?

THE GENERAL: No, no. That's Lafayette. No, with the arm extended and the marshal's baton. . . .

THIRD PHOTOGRAPHER: Ah, you mean Wellington?

THE GENERAL: Unfortunately, I don't have a baton. . . .

Meanwhile, THE FIRST PHOTOGRAPHER *has gone back to* THE BISHOP, *who has not moved, and looks him over silently.*

THIRD PHOTOGRAPHER (*to* THE GENERAL): We've got just what we need. Here, now strike the pose. (*Rolls up a sheet of paper in the form of a marshal's baton. He hands it to* THE GENERAL, *who strikes a pose, and then dashes to his camera. A flash:* THE SECOND PHOTOGRAPHER *has just taken his shot.*)

THE BISHOP (*to* THE FIRST PHOTOGRAPHER): I hope the negative comes out well. Now we'll have to flood the world with a picture of me receiving the Eucharist. Unfortunately, we don't have a Host on hand. . . .

FIRST PHOTOGRAPHER: Leave it to us, Monsignor. Newspapermen are a resourceful bunch. (*Calls out.*) Mr. Attorney General!

THE JUDGE *approaches.*

I'm going to try a stunt. Lend me a hand a minute. (*Without further ado, he takes him by the hand and sets him in place.*) But I want only your hand to show . . . there . . . roll up your sleeve a little . . . above Monsignor's tongue. More. Okay. (*Still fumbling in his pocket. To* THE BISHOP.) Stick out your tongue. More. Okay. (*Still fumbling in his pocket. A flash:* THE GENERAL *has just been photographed; he resumes his natural pose.*) Damn it! I don't have a thing! (*He looks about. To* THE GENERAL.) That's perfect. May I? (*Without waiting for an answer, he takes* THE GENERAL'S *monocle from his eye and goes back to the group formed by* THE BISHOP *and* THE JUDGE. *He makes* THE JUDGE *hold the monocle above* THE BISHOP'S *tongue as if it were a Host, and he rushes to his camera. A flash.*)

THE QUEEN (*who has entered with* THE ENVOY, *has been watching these proceedings for some moments*): Curious. Curious method. (*To* THE PHOTOGRAPHERS.) You're presenting the people with a false image? I won't tolerate . . .

THE ENVOY: It's a true image, born of a false spectacle.

FIRST PHOTOGRAPHER (*cynically*): That's common practice, your Majesty. When some rebels were captured, we paid a militiaman to bump off a chap I'd just sent to buy me a pack of cigarettes. The photo shows a rebel shot down while trying to escape.

THE QUEEN: Monstrous!

THE ENVOY: But have things ever happened otherwise? History was lived so that a glorious page might be written, and then read. It's reading that counts. (*To* THE PHOTOGRAPHERS.) Gentlemen, the Queen informs me that she congratulates you. She asks that you return to your posts.

THE THREE PHOTOGRAPHERS *put their heads under the black hoods of their cameras.*

A silence.

THE QUEEN (*looking about her*): Isn't he here?

THE ENVOY (*with irony, but elegantly*): Invisible, in any case. One encounters him occasionally wandering through the corridors, looking very pensive and taciturn. Most of the time, he has appointments with specialists and tailors. He tries on uniforms.

THE QUEEN (*to* THE ENVOY): It's no laughing matter. In his effort to win renown, he has chosen a more difficult path than ours. (*She reads to* THE THREE FIGURES *from a paper she holds in her hand.*) I wished to thank you, gentlemen, for your devotion to my cause, to my people's cause, and for your gallant conduct. Thanks to you and the Chief of Police, the rebellion has been bathed in blood. There is nothing more to fear. . . . (*She returns the paper to* THE ENVOY, *who keeps it in his hand.*) I hope so.

THE BISHOP: Madame, if it has to be done all over again, we're ready. (*To the others.*) Aren't we, gentlemen?

THE QUEEN (*with a wan, sad smile*): I observe in passing that it is you, Monsignor, who are gaining the ascendancy. No, no, don't defend yourself. It's well that it emanates from the highest spirituality. . . . (*A pause.*) Well, gentlemen . . .

THE THREE FIGURES *hesitate to speak.*

THE ENVOY: The Queen would like to know what you're doing, what you plan to do.

THE BISHOP: We've been recovering as many dead bodies as possible. We were planning to embalm them and lodge them in our heaven. Your grandeur requires your having slaughtered the rebels wholesale. We shall keep for ourselves only a few of our fallen martyrs, to whom we shall pay honor that will honor us.

THE QUEEN (*to* THE ENVOY): That will serve my glory, will it not?

THE ENVOY (*smiling*): The massacres, too, are revels wherein the people indulge to their heart's content in the pleasure of hating us. I am speaking, to be sure, of "our" people. They can at last set up a statue to us in their hearts so as to shower it with blows. At least, I hope so.

THE QUEEN: Does that mean that leniency and kindness are of no avail?

THE ENVOY (*smiling*): A St. Vincent de Paul Studio?

THE QUEEN: You're right. It's hard to imagine. (*Evasively.*) Yet, I've seen old men . . .

THE ENVOY: Old men, perhaps. But to experience the thrill of brushing against galley-slaves. However, our hero is still young.

THE QUEEN (*to* THE ENVOY): Isn't anyone going to tell me about the Mausoleum? How far along is the construction?

THE ENVOY: The work's going on, Madame.

THE QUEEN (*testily*): But not fast enough. You, Your Honor, what's being done? I'd ordered fewer death penalties and more sentences to forced labor. I hope the underground galleries are finished? (*To* THE ENVOY.) It's the word galley-slaves that made me think of the galleries of the Mausoleum. Are they finished?

THE JUDGE: Completely. And open to the public on Sundays. Some of the arches are completely adorned with the skeletons of prisoners who died during the digging.

THE QUEEN (*in the direction of* THE BISHOP): Very good. What about the Church? I suppose that anyone who hasn't done at least a week's work on this extraordinary chapel is in a state of mortal sin?

THE BISHOP *bows.*

(*To* THE GENERAL.) As for you, I'm aware of your severity. Your soldiers are watching over the workers, and they thoroughly deserve the fine name of builders. (*Smiling gently, with feigned fatigue.*) For, as you know, gentlemen, I plan to present this tomb to the Hero. You know how downcast he feels, don't you, and how he suffers at not yet having been impersonated?

THE GENERAL (*plucking up courage*): He'll have a hard time attaining glory. The places have been filled for ages. Every niche has its statue. (*Fatuously.*) We, at least . . .

THE JUDGE: That's how it always is when one wants to start from the bottom. And particularly by rejecting or neglecting the traditional. The established order of things, as it were.

THE QUEEN (*suddenly vibrant*): Yet it was he who saved everything. He wants glory. He insists on breaking open the gates of legend, but he has allowed you to carry on with your ceremonies.

THE BISHOP (*arrogantly*): To be frank, Madame, we're no longer concerned with that. As for me, my skirt hampers me, and my hands get caught in the lace. We're going to have to act.

THE QUEEN (*indignantly*): Act? You? You mean to say you're going to strip us of our power?

THE JUDGE: We have to fulfill our functions, don't we?

THE QUEEN: Functions! You're planning to overthrow him, to lower him, to take his place! That's right, isn't it? And you think I'm going to let you? I, too, have my fanatics. If I've decorated and ennobled him, I've done so to heighten his prestige.

THE BISHOP: Somewhere in time—in time or in space!—perhaps there exist high dignitaries invested with absolute dignity and attired with veritable ornaments. . . .

THE QUEEN (*very angrily*): Veritable! And what about those? You mean that those you're wrapped and swathed in—my whole paraphernalia!—which come from my closets, aren't veritable?

THE BISHOP (*pointing to* THE JUDGE's *ermine, the silk of his robe, etc.*): Rabbit, sateen, machine-made lace . . . you think we're going to be satisfied with make-believe to the end of our days?

THE QUEEN (*outraged*): But this morning . . .

She breaks off. Enter THE CHIEF OF POLICE, *quietly, humbly.*

George, beware of them.

THE CHIEF OF POLICE (*trying to smile*): I think that . . . victory . . . we've won the day. May I sit down?

He sits down. Then he looks about, as if questioning everyone.

THE ENVOY (*ironically*): No, nobody's come yet. Nobody has yet felt the need to abolish himself in your fascinating image.

THE CHIEF OF POLICE: That means the projects you submitted to me aren't very effective. (*To* THE QUEEN.) Nothing? Nobody?

THE QUEEN (*very gently*): Nobody. And yet, the blinds have been drawn again. The men ought to be coming in. Besides, the apparatus has been set up; so we'll be informed by a full peal of bells.

THE ENVOY (*to* THE CHIEF OF POLICE): You didn't care for the project I submitted to you this morning. Yet that's the image that haunts you and that ought to haunt others.

THE CHIEF OF POLICE: Ineffectual.

THE ENVOY (*showing a photographic negative*): The executioner's red coat and his axe. I suggested amarinth red and the steel axe.

THE QUEEN (*testily*): Studio 14, known as the Studio of Executions. Already been done.

THE CHIEF OF POLICE (*to* THE ENVOY): You see. These masquerades prove how unimaginative you are. Maybe you're exhausted? As a matter of fact, you look anemic to me. No. I want my image to be both legendary and human. It should, of course, accord with eternal principles, but my face should be recognizable in it.

THE JUDGE (*making himself agreeable*): Yet you're feared. You're dreaded. You're envied. The people's hymns of love are proof of it.

THE CHIEF OF POLICE: I'm afraid that they fear and envy a man, but . . . (*Groping for words.*) . . . but not a wrinkle, for example, or a curl . . . or a cigar . . . or a whip. The latest image that was proposed to me . . . I hardly dare mention it to you.

THE JUDGE: Was it . . . very audacious?

THE CHIEF OF POLICE: Very. Too audacious. I'd never dare tell you what it was. (*Suddenly, he seems to make up his mind.*) Gentlemen, I have sufficient confidence in your judgment and devotion. After all, I want to carry on the fight by boldness of ideas as well. But the fact is—I don't know where to turn first. It was this: I've been advised to appear in the form of a gigantic phallus. A prick of great stature. . . .

THE THREE FIGURES *and* THE QUEEN *are dumfounded.*

THE QUEEN: George! You?

THE CHIEF OF POLICE: What do you expect? If I'm to symbolize the nation, your joint. . . .

THE ENVOY (*to* THE QUEEN): Allow him, Madame. It's the tone of the age.

THE JUDGE: A phallus? Of great stature? You mean—enormous?

THE CHIEF OF POLICE: Of my stature.

THE JUDGE: That'll be very difficult to bring off.

THE ENVOY: Not so very. What with new techniques and our rubber industry, remarkable things can be worked out. No, I'm not worried about that, but rather . . . (*Turning the* THE BISHOP.) . . . what the Church will think of it?

THE BISHOP (*after reflection, shrugging his shoulders*): No definite pronouncement can be made this evening. To be sure, the idea is a bold one. (*To* THE CHIEF OF POLICE.) But if your case is desperate, we shall have to examine the matter. For . . . it would be a formidable figure-head, and if you were to transmit yourself in that guise from generation to generation . . .

THE QUEEN (*alarmed*): No room's been provided for it. No studio is equipped. . . . After all, though my house is reputed for its imaginativeness, it's known for its decency, and for a certain tone as well.

THE CHIEF OF POLICE (*gently*): Would you like to see the model?

THE GENERAL (*briskly*): No, no. Even if one did imagine you with that rigor, your appearance would scare off your most fanatical followers!

THE JUDGE (*to* THE CHIEF OF POLICE): It's wrong of you to be impatient. *We* waited two thousand years to perfect our roles. Keep hoping . . .

THE GENERAL (*interrupting him*): Glory is achieved in combat. You haven't enough illustrious Waterloos to your credit. Keep fighting, or sit down and wait out the regulation two thousand years.

Everyone laughs.

THE QUEEN (*violently*): You don't care a damn about his suffering. And it was I who singled you out! I who fished you out of the rooms of my brothel and hired you for his glory. And you agreed to serve him.

A pause.

THE BISHOP (*firmly*): It is at this point that a question, and a very serious one, arises: are you going to use what we represent, or are we (*He points to the other two* FIGURES.) going to use you to serve what we represent?

THE QUEEN (*flaring up*): Your conditions, you? Puppets who without their rabbit, as you put it, would be nothing, you, a man who was made to dance naked—in other words, skinned!—on the public square of Seville and Toledo! To the click of castenets! Your conditions, Monsignor?

THE BISHOP: That day I *had* to dance. As for the rabbit, it's what it *must* be—the sacred image of ermine—it has the same power.

THE QUEEN: George! Go on, defend yourself. It's God Himself Who has chosen us. . . .

THE ENVOY (*admiringly*): Sublime! Continue. . . .

THE QUEEN (*to* THE CHIEF OF POLICE): Help yourself. Help us. Keep the power. Outdo yourself. . . . Real blood flows in my veins, real sweat in my armpits. I'm all afever, and I want power.

THE CHIEF OF POLICE: I'm weak, I'm inept. . . .

THE QUEEN (*imploring him*): Pull yourself together, I beg of you . . they'll devour us!

THE BISHOP: You can see that his failure is preying on him. Our power . . .

THE CHIEF OF POLICE (*with sudden violence*): I have force, intelligence and passion on my side!

THE BISHOP: With your intelligence and its clear notions, the people can engage in a two-sided discussion—as the weekly magazines would say. They can argue. Our power is obscure and beyond argument.

THE BISHOP (*beside himself*): Exactly. So long as we were in a room in a brothel, we belonged to our own fantasies. But once having exposed them, having named them, having proclaimed them, we're now tied up with human beings, tied to you, and forced to go on with this adventure according to the laws of visibility.

THE CHIEF OF POLICE: You have no power.

THE BISHOP: No one has power. But you want us to have power over the people. In order for us to have power over them, you must first recognize that we have power over you.

THE CHIEF OF POLICE: Never!

THE BISHOP: Very well. Then we shall go back to our rooms and there continue the quest of an absolute dignity. We ought never to have left them. For we were content there, and it was you who came and dragged us away. For ours was a happy state. And absolutely safe. In peace, in comfort, behind shutters, behind padded curtains, protected by a police force that protects brothels, we were able to be a general, judge and bishop to the point of perfection and to the point of rapture! You tore us brutally from that delicious, enviable, untroubled state, but we have since tasted other delights, the bitter delights of action and responsibility. We were judge, general and bishop in order to be bishop, judge and general beneath a perfect, total, solitary and sterile appearance. You wanted us to be these dignitaries this evening in order to conspire in a revolution, or rather in an order, and to round it off, to ground it, as it were. Our public appearance was already a participation in the adventure.

THE GENERAL (*interrupting* THE BISHOP): My breeches! What joy when I pulled on my breeches! I now sleep in my general's breeches, I eat in my breeches, I waltz—*when* I waltz—in my breeches, I live in my general's breeches. I'm a general the way one is a priest.

THE BISHOP: As for my lace, I no longer look forward to it—it's myself.

THE JUDGE: I'm just a dignity represented by a robe.

THE GENERAL (*to* THE BISHOP:) At no moment can I prepare myself—I used to start a month in advance!—prepare myself for pulling on my general's boots and breeches. I'm rigged in them for all eternity. By Jove, I no longer dream.

THE BISHOP (*to* THE CHIEF OF POLICE): You see, he no longer dreams. Our ornamental purity, our luxurious and barren—and sublime—appearance has been eaten away. It's gone forever. Well and good. But the taste of that bitter delight of responsibility of which I've spoken has remained with us, and we find it to our liking. Our rooms are no longer secret. You hurt us by dragging us into the light. But as for dancing? You spoke of dancing? You referred to that notorious afternoon when, stripped—or skinned, whichever word amuses you—stripped of our priestly ornaments, we had to dance naked on the cathedral square. I danced, I admit it, with people laughing at me, but at least I danced. Whereas now, if ever I have an itch for that kind of thing, I'll have to go on the sly to the Balcony, where there probably is a room prepared for prelates who like to be ballerinas a few hours a week. No, no. . . . We're going to live in the light, but with all that that implies. We—magistrate, soldier, prelate—we're now going to act in such a way as to impoverish these ornaments and dignities unceasingly! We're going to render them useful! But in order that they be of use, and of use to you—since it's your order that we've chosen to defend (I mean that it's the only one our dignity could defend)—you must recognize their power and pay homage to them.

THE QUEEN: Careful, George! Watch out for their saliva!

THE CHIEF OF POLICE (*calmly*): I shall be not the hundred-thousandth-reflection-within-a-reflection in a mirror, but the One and Only, into whom a hundred thousand want to merge. If not for me, you'd have all been done for. The expression "beaten hollow" would have had meaning.

THE BISHOP: If you didn't have our age-old glory—which has demonstrated its worth—to back up your success, what would you be? A rebel, faced with the insipid problems of freedom.

THE QUEEN (*to* THE BISHOP, *insinuatingly*): You happen to be wearing that robe this evening simply because you were unable to clear out of the studios in time. You just couldn't tear yourself away from one of your hundred thousand reflections, but the clients are beginning to come back. . . . There's no rush yet, but Carmen has recorded several entries. . . . (*To* THE CHIEF OF POLICE.) Don't let them intimidate you. Before the revolt, there were lots of them. . . . (*To* THE BISHOP.) If you hadn't had the abominable idea of having Chantal assassinated. . . .

THE BISHOP (*frightened*): A stray bullet!

THE QUEEN: Who can say? Whether the bullet was stray or not, Chantal was assassinated on *my* balcony! When she came back here to see me, to visit her boss . . .

THE BISHOP: I had the presence of mind to make her one of our saints.

THE CHIEF OF POLICE: A traditional attitude. A churchman's reflex. But there's no need to congratulate yourself. The image of her on our flag has hardly any power. Or rather . . . I've had reports from all quarters that owing to the possibility that she was playing a double game, Chantal has been condemned by those she was supposed to save.

THE QUEEN: But then the whole business is starting all over again?

THE CHIEF OF POLICE: No doubt about it. Another revolt—that has nothing to do with the one I put down—is beginning to brew. . . .

THE GENERAL: Are we going to have to . . . to get into the carriage again? The slowness of the carriage!

THE CHIEF OF POLICE: And that's why I'm sure of you. At least, as long as I've not been impersonated, because after that I'll just sit back and take it easy. (*Inspired.*) Besides, I'll know by a sudden weakness of my muscles that my image is escaping from me to go and haunt men's minds. When that happens, my visible end will be near. For the time being, and before long, we'll have to act. (*To* THE BISHOP.) Who will assume real responsibilities?

THE BISHOP (*hesitantly*): We can, all the same . . . express, as it were . . . a glimmer of a desire . . . perform an act. . . .

THE QUEEN (*sharply*): Be careful! Don't grant anything!

THE CHIEF OF POLICE: You! (*Shrugs his shoulders.*) Be logical: if you are what you are, judge, general, bishop, it's because you wanted to become that and wanted it known that you had become it.

You therefore did what was necessary to achieve your purpose and to be a focus of attention. Is that right?

THE JUDGE: Pretty much.

THE CHIEF OF POLICE: Very well. That means you've never performed an act for its own sake, but always so that, when linked with other acts, it would make a bishop, a judge, a general. . . .

THE BISHOP: That's both true and false. For each act contained within itself its leaven of novelty.

THE CHIEF OF POLICE (*correcting him*): Forgive me, Monsignor, but this leaven of novelty was immediately nullified by the fact that the act turned in on itself.

THE JUDGE: We acquired greater dignity thereby.

THE CHIEF OF POLICE: No doubt, Your Honor, but this dignity, which has become as inhuman as a crystal, makes you unfit for governing men. No, no, gentlemen, above you, more sublime than you, is the Queen. It's from her, for the time being, that you derive your power and your rights. Above her—that to which she refers —is our standard, on which I've blazoned the image of Chantal Victorious, our saint.

THE BISHOP (*aggressively*): Above Her Majesty, whom we venerate, and above her flag, is God, Who speaks through my voice. As for Chantal, who's painted on the flag . . .

THE CHIEF OF POLICE: Stop talking nonsense!

THE BISHOP: Listen to me . . .

THE CHIEF OF POLICE (*irritably*): And above God?

A silence.

THE BISHOP *moves off, looking extremely troubled until his next speech.*

THE CHIEF OF POLICE: Well, gentlemen, above God are you, without whom God would be nothing. And above you shall be I, without whom . . .

THE JUDGE: What about the people? The photographers?

THE CHIEF OF POLICE: On their knees before the people who are on their knees before God. Therefore . . .

They all burst out laughing.

That's why I want you to serve me. But a while ago you were holding forth quite volubly. I should therefore like to pay homage to your eloquence, your facility of elocution, the limpidity of your timbre. As for me, I'm a mere man of action who gets tangled up in words and ideas when they're not immediately applied. That's why I was wondering whether to send you back to your kennel. I won't do it. In any case, not right away, since you're already there.

THE GENERAL: Sir!

THE CHIEF OF POLICE: Lie down! Lie down, General! You're stuck. And it's not I who forbid you to act, but your dignities themselves.

THE JUDGE: My skirt can be tucked up. . . .

THE CHIEF OF POLICE: Lie down! Since you want to be recognized as a judge, do you want to hold on to your dignity according to my idea of it? And according to the general meaning attached to such a dignity? Very well. Must I therefore grant you increasing recognition along these lines? Yes or no?

No one answers.

Well gentlemen, yes or no?

THE QUEEN (*very blandly*): Excuse him, if he gets carried away. I'm quite aware of what you used to come here for: you, Monsignor, to seek by devious ways a manifest saintliness. No, no, I'm not being ironic. The gold of my chasubles had little to do with it, I'm sure. It wasn't mere gross ambition that brought you behind my closed shutters. Love of God was hidden there. I realize that. You, Mr. Attorney General, you were indeed guided by a concern for justice, since it was the image of a magistrate that you wished to see reflected a thousand times in my mirrors. And you, General, it was bravery and military glory and the heroic deed that haunted you. So let yourselves go, relax, without too many scruples. . . .

THE JUDGE (*timidly*): We can try, carefully of course, to make a slight shift along a different line. . . .

THE GENERAL: Are you mad? If we think, people may start following us in our thinking, and then where'll we stop?

THE CHIEF OF POLICE: Well spoken, General. And now, back to the kennel! Well, gentlemen, if I—and through me, the entire people—recognize your dignity, and increasingly so, and in its strictest sense, well, gentlemen, but . . . you're still in the brothel!

THE QUEEN (*thrilled*): My hero—how well he speaks!

One after the other, the three men heave a deep sigh.

THE CHIEF OF POLICE (*continuing*): That's a relief to you, isn't it? You never really wanted to get out of yourselves and communicate, if only by acts of meanness, with the world. I understand you. (*Amiably.*) You see, I too, when I'm too tired of inventing for people, when I'm too harassed by the burden of power and responsibility, I, too, occasionally have the desire to flee into an image of myself. Unfortunately, my role is still a fighting one. It's still effective in carrying out an action. It's not impersonated. It keeps inciting to further progress. And if I try to crawl into my role, I find no rest in it. My role, unfortunately, is in motion. In short, as you probably know, it's not in the nomenclature of the brothels. . . .

THE QUEEN: In the pink handbook. . . .

THE CHIEF OF POLICE: Yes, in the pink handbook. (*To* THE THREE FIGURES.) Come now, gentlemen, don't you feel sorry for a poor fellow like me? (*He looks at them one after the other.*) Come, come, gentlemen, you're not hardhearted are you? It's for you that these Studios and Illustrious Rites were perfected, by means of exquisite experimentation. They required long labor, infinite patience. You have the good fortune to benefit from them, and you want to go back to the light of day? (*To* THE BISHOP.) You, Monsignor, you're silent. . . .

THE BISHOP: There's still the matter of Chantal. . . . I'm thinking of your glory.

THE CHIEF OF POLICE: Let's forget about that. . . .

THE BISHOP (*very gravely*): On the contrary, I ask that you listen to me. If I had her shot, and then canonized, if I had her image blazoned on our flag, it was for a reason. . . .

THE QUEEN: It's *my* image that ought to be there. . . .

THE ENVOY (*to* THE QUEEN): You're on the postage stamps, on the banknotes, on the seals in the government offices . . . and even that's too much. Your Majesty can be represented only by an abstraction.

THE CHIEF OF POLICE (*to* THE BISHOP): You were saying . . . that for my glory . . .

THE BISHOP (*after a brief hesitation*): The rebels, and perhaps the entire populace as well, must have had high hopes for this rebellion. The fighting—and you realize it more than anyone else —has been murderous. They've been fighting in desperation.

THE QUEEN: The people love their Queen. . . .

THE ENVOY *motions her to be still.*

THE BISHOP: No doubt they do, Madame. But their wrath proves their longing to be rid of us. You, sir, have been seeking the glory accorded by the nomenclature of the brothels. You have crushed the rebellion. You have, as the saying goes, bathed it in blood, but you've done so in a curious way! Without quite knowing whether you have or not, the populace has a right to assume you've triumphed—doubtless because you were the stronger—but also because Chantal's image wanted to return to the brothel that was its starting point. . . .

THE CHIEF OF POLICE: You mean . . . ?

THE BISHOP: That, in a very strange and delightfully equivocal way, your image may merge with Chantal's. The people must be in a state of frightful despair, but they must have a way out, a way that is ghastly, horrendous. Every beaten and humiliated rebel is perhaps haunted by Chantal's image, which is likewise defiled— forgive me, but that's your chance for salvation!—defiled by yours. If my expectations are correct. . . .

THE QUEEN (*to* THE CHIEF OF POLICE): That woman again! Clinging to you even in her death! And I, doomed to be represented formally, merely by four blue bands and three red ones! I don't want to lose you! Or lose myself!

THE ENVOY: Silly jealousy! We've reached the point at which we can no longer be actuated by human feelings. Our function will be to support, establish and justify metaphors.

THE QUEEN: But *I* haven't yet decided to go along with you in this adventure. I love love and I love power and I want to experience them with my body.

THE ENVOY (*sternly*): Then you should have sided with the rebels. Among them one can, if need be, dominate through personal qualities.

THE QUEEN: Will I therefore never be who I am?

THE ENVOY: Never again.

THE QUEEN (*as if frightened*): Never again? Nothing will ever again relate to my person alone? Nothing concerning me will ever again be able to happen to others?

THE ENVOY (*curtly*): Quite.

THE QUEEN: Every event of my life—my blood that trickles if I scratch myself . . .

THE ENVOY: Quite, Madame. Each event will be written with a capital. And now . . .

THE QUEEN: But that's Death?

THE ENVOY: It is indeed. Here's Carmen.

Enter CARMEN *from the door at the left.*

CARMEN: Madame? (*She stands there without moving.*)

THE QUEEN (*crossly*): I gave orders that we were not to be disturbed. And you enter without warning. Come here. What do you want?

CARMEN *goes to her.*

CARMEN: I tried to ring, but the apparatus is out of order. I beg your pardon. I'd like to speak with you.

THE QUEEN: Well, what is it? Speak up!

CARMEN (*hesitantly*): It's . . . I don't know . . .

THE QUEEN (*resignedly*): Well, when at Court do as the Court does. Let's speak in an undertone. (*She conspicuously lends ear to* CARMEN, *who leans forward and murmurs a few words.* THE QUEEN *seems very upset.*)

THE QUEEN: Are you sure?

CARMEN: Quite, Madame.

THE QUEEN *bolts from the room, followed by* CARMEN. THE CHIEF OF POLICE *starts to follow them, but* THE ENVOY *intervenes.*

THE ENVOY: One does not follow Her Majesty.

THE CHIEF OF POLICE: What's going on? Where's she going?

THE ENVOY (*ironically*): To embroider. The Queen is embroidering, and she is not embroidering . . . you know the refrain? The

Queen attains her reality when she withdraws, absents herself, or dies.

THE CHIEF OF POLICE: What's happening outside? (*To* THE JUDGE.) Do you have any news?

THE JUDGE: What you call outside is as mysterious to us as we are to it. His Lordship described it quite well.

THE BISHOP: I shall try to depict the grief of this people which thought it had liberated itself by rebelling. Alas—or rather, thank Heaven! —there will never be a movement powerful enough to destroy our imagery.

THE CHIEF OF POLICE: So you think I have a chance?

THE BISHOP: You're in the best possible position. There's consternation everywhere, in all families, in all institutions. People have trembled so violently that your image is beginning to make them doubt themselves.

THE CHIEF OF POLICE: Am I their only hope?

THE BISHOP: Their only hope lies in utter collapse. Since they've lost everything: a hypothetical but intoxicating freedom, their guides —a criminal lot, I might add—and Chantal who was the very illustration of their efforts, you're all that's left.

THE CHIEF OF POLICE: In short, I'm like a pool in which they behold themselves?

THE GENERAL (*delighted, with a burst of laughter*): And if they lean over too far, they fall in and drown. Before long, you'll be full of drowned bodies! (*No one seems to share his merriment.*) Oh well . . . they're not yet at the brink! (*Embarrassed.*) Let's wait.

A silence.

THE CHIEF OF POLICE: Well, gentlemen, so you really think the people had a wild hope? And that in losing all hope they lose everything? And that in losing everything they'll come and lose themselves in me?

THE BISHOP: That may very well happen. But, believe me, not if we can help it.

THE CHIEF OF POLICE: When I am offered that final consecration. . . .

THE ENVOY (*ironically*): For you, but for you alone, for a second the Earth will stop rotating. . . .

Suddenly the door at the left opens and THE QUEEN *appears, beaming.*

THE QUEEN: George! (*She falls into the arms of* THE CHIEF OF POLICE.)
THE CHIEF OF POLICE (*incredulous*): It's not true. (THE QUEEN *nods yes.*) But where? . . . When?
THE QUEEN (*deeply moved*): There! . . . Now! The studio. . . .
THE CHIEF OF POLICE: You're pulling my leg. I didn't hear anything.

Suddenly a tremendous ringing, a kind of peal of bells.

So it's true? It's for me? (*He pushes* THE QUEEN *away. Solemnly.*) Gentlemen, I belong to the Nomenclature! (*To* THE QUEEN.) But are you really sure?
THE QUEEN: It was I who received him and ushered him into the Mausoleum Studio. The one that's being built in your honor. I left Carmen behind to attend to the preparations and I ran to let you know. I'm trembling like a leaf. . . .
THE BISHOP (*gloomily*) : We're up the creek.
THE CHIEF OF POLICE: The apparatus is working. You can see. . . . (*He goes to the left, followed by* THE QUEEN.)
THE ENVOY: That is not the practice. Matters of that kind are secret.
THE CHIEF OF POLICE (*shrugging his shoulders*): Where's the mechanism? (*To* THE QUEEN.) Let's watch together.

She stands at the left, facing a small porthole. After a brief hesitation, THE JUDGE, GENERAL *and* BISHOP *place themselves at the right, at another porthole symmetrical with the first. Then, the two panels of the double mirror forming the back of the stage silently draw apart, revealing the interior of the Special Studio.* THE ENVOY, *with resignation, joins* THE CHIEF OF POLICE.

Description of the Mausoleum Studio: The stones of the wall, which is circular, are visible. At the rear, a stairway that descends. In the center of this well there seems to be another, in which the steps of a stairway are visible. On the walls, four laurel wreaths, adorned with crape. When the panels separate, ROGER *is at the middle of the stairway, which he is descending.* CARMEN *seems to be guiding him.* ROGER *is dressed like* THE CHIEF OF POLICE, *though, mounted on the same cothurni as* THE THREE FIGURES, *he looks taller. His shoulders have also been broadened. He descends the stairs to the rhythm of a drum.*

CARMEN (*approaching, and handing him a cigar*): It's on the house.

ROGER (*putting the cigar into his mouth*): Thanks.

CARMEN (*taking the cigar from him*): That end's for the light. This one's for the mouth. (*She turns the cigar around.*) Is this your first cigar?

ROGER: Yes. . . . (*A pause.*) I'm not asking for your advice. You're here to serve me. I've paid. . . .

CARMEN: I beg your pardon, sir.

ROGER: The slave?

CARMEN: He's being untied.

ROGER: He knows what it's about?

CARMEN: Completely. You're the first. You're inaugurating this Studio, but, you know, the scenarios are all reducible to a major theme. . . .

ROGER: Which is . . . ?

CARMEN: Death.

ROGER (*touching the walls*): And so this is my tomb?

CARMEN (*correcting him*): Mausoleum.

ROGER: How many slaves are working on it?

CARMEN: The entire people, sir. Half of the population during the day and the other half at night. As you have requested, the whole mountain will be burrowed and tunnelled. The interior will have the complexity of a termite nest or of the Basilica of Lourdes —we don't know yet. No one will be able to see anything from the outside. All they'll know is that the mountain is sacred, but, inside, the tombs are already being enshrined in tombs, the cenotaphs in cenotaphs, the coffins in coffins, the urns . . .

ROGER: What about here, where I am now?

CARMEN (*with a gesture of disdain*): An antechamber. An antechamber called the Valley of the Fallen. (*She mounts the underground stairway.*) In a little while, you'll go farther down.

ROGER: I'm not to hope to see the light of day again?

CARMEN: But . . . do you still want to?

A silence.

ROGER: It's really true that no one's ever been here before me?

CARMEN: In this . . . tomb, or in this . . . Studio?

A silence.

ROGER: Is everything really on right? My outfit? My toupee?

THE CHIEF OF POLICE *turns to* THE QUEEN.

THE CHIEF OF POLICE: He knew I wear a toupee?

THE BISHOP (*snickering, to* THE JUDGE *and* THE GENERAL): He's the only one who doesn't know that everyone knows it.

CARMEN (*to* ROGER): Everything was carefully planned long ago. It's all been worked out. The rest is up to you.

ROGER (*anxiously*): You realize I'm feeling my way too. I've got to imagine what the Hero's like, and he's never shown himself much.

CARMEN: That's why we've taken you to the Mausoleum Studio. It's not possible to make many errors here, nor indulge your imagination.

> *A pause.*

ROGER: Will I be alone?

CARMEN: Everything is padded. The doors are lined. So are the walls.

ROGER (*hesitantly*): What about ... the Mausoleum?

CARMEN (*forcefully*): Built into the rock. The proof is that there's water oozing from the walls. Deathly silent. As for light, the darkness is so thick that your eyes have developed astounding qualities. The cold? Yes, the coldness of death. It's been a gigantic job drilling through the mountain. Men are still groaning in order to hollow out a granite niche for you. Everything proves that you're loved and that you're a conqueror.

ROGER: Groaning? Could . . . could I hear the groaning?

> CARMEN *turns toward a hole dug out at the foot of the wall, from which emerges the head of* THE BEGGAR.

CARMEN: Come here!

> THE BEGGAR *crawls in.*

ROGER (*looking* THE SLAVE *over*): Is that it?

CARMEN: A fine specimen, isn't he? Skinny. With lice and sores. He dreams of dying for you. I'll leave you alone now.

ROGER: With him? No, no. (*A pause.*) Stay. Everything always takes place in the presence of a woman. It's in order for a woman's face to be a witness that, usually . . .

> Suddenly, the sound of a hammer striking an anvil. Then a cock crows.

Is life so near?

CARMEN (*in a normal voice, not acting*): As I've told you, everything's padded, but some sounds always manage to filter through. Does it bother you? Life's starting up again little by little . . . as before. . . .

ROGER (*he seems anxious*): Yes, as before. . . .

CARMEN (*gently*): You were . .

ROGER: Yes. Everything's washed up. . . . And what's saddest of all is people's saying: "the rebellion was wonderful!"

CARMEN: You mustn't think about it any more. And you must stop listening to the sounds from outside. Besides, it's raining. The whole mountain has been swept by a tornado. (*Stage voice.*) You are at home here. (*Pointing to* THE SLAVE.) Make him talk.

ROGER (*playing his role*): For you can talk? And what else can you do?

THE SLAVE (*lying on his belly*): First, bow; then, shrink into myself a little more (*He takes* ROGER'S *foot and places it on his own back.*) like this! . . . and even . . .

ROGER (*impatiently*): Yes . . . and even?

THE SLAVE: Sink into the earth, if it's possible.

ROGER (*drawing on his cigar*): Sink in, really? But there's no mud?

THE QUEEN (*to the others*): He's right. We should have provided mud. In a well-run house. . . . But it's opening day, and he's the first client to use the Studio. . . .

THE SLAVE (*to* ROGER): I feel it all over my body, sir. It's all over me, except in my mouth, which is open so that I can sing your praises and utter the groans that made me famous.

ROGER: Famous? You're famous, you?

THE SLAVE: Famous for my chants, sir, which are hymns to your glory.

ROGER: So your glory accompanies mine? (*To* CARMEN.) Does he mean that my reputation will be kept going by his words? And . . . if he says nothing, I'll cease to exist . . . ?

CARMEN (*curtly*): I'd like very much to satisfy you, but you ask questions that aren't in the scenario.

ROGER (*to* THE SLAVE): But what about you, who sings to you?

THE SLAVE: Nobody. I'm dying.

ROGER: But without me, without my sweat, without my tears and blood, what would you be?

THE SLAVE: Nothing.

ROGER (*to* THE SLAVE): You sing? But what else do you do?

THE SLAVE: We do all we possibly can to be more and more unworthy of you.

ROGER: What, for example?

THE SLAVE: We try hard just to stand and rot. And, believe me, it's not always easy. Life tries to prevail. . . . But we stand our ground. We keep shrinking more and more every . . .

ROGER: Day?

THE SLAVE: Week.

THE CHIEF OF POLICE (*to the others*): That's not much. With a little effort. . . .

THE ENVOY (*to* THE CHIEF OF POLICE): Be still. Let them play out their roles.

ROGER: That's not much. With a little effort. . . .

THE SLAVE (*with exaltation*): With joy, Your Excellency! You're so splendid! So splendid that I wonder whether you're aglow or whether you're all the darkness of all the nights?

ROGER: What does it matter, since I'm no longer to have any reality except in the reality of your phrases.

THE SLAVE (*crawling in the direction of the upper stairway*): You have not mouth nor ears nor eyes, but all of you is a thundering mouth and at the same time a dazzling and watchful eye. . . .

ROGER: *You* see it, but do the others know it? Does the night know it? Does death? Do the stones? What do the stones say?

THE SLAVE (*still dragging on his belly and beginning to crawl up the stairs*): The stones say . . .

ROGER: Well, I'm listening.

THE SLAVE (*he stops crawling, and facing the audience*): The cement that holds us together to form your tomb . . .

THE CHIEF OF POLICE (*facing the audience and joyfully beating his breast*): The stones venerate me!

THE SLAVE (*continuing*): . . . the cement is molded of tears, spit and blood. The workers' eyes and hands that rested upon us have matted us with grief. We are yours, and only yours.

THE SLAVE *starts crawling up the stairs again.*

ROGER (*with rising exaltation*): Everything proclaims me! Everything breathes me and everything worships me! My history was lived so that a glorious page might be written and then read. It's reading that counts. (*He suddenly notices that* THE SLAVE *has disappeared. To* CARMEN.) But . . . where's he going? . . . Where is he? . . .

CARMEN: He's gone off to sing. He's going up into the light of day. He'll tell . . . that he carried your footsteps . . . and that . . .

ROGER (*anxiously*): Yes, and that? What else will he tell?

CARMEN: The truth: that you're dead, or rather that you don't stop dying and that your image, like your name, reverberates to infinity.

ROGER: He knows that my image is everywhere?

CARMEN: Yes, everywhere, inscribed and engraved and imposed by fear.

ROGER: In the palms of stevedores? In the games of children? On the teeth of soldiers? In war?

CARMEN: Everywhere.

THE CHIEF OF POLICE (*to the others*): So I've made it?

THE QUEEN (*fondly*): Are you happy?

THE CHIEF OF POLICE: You've done a good job. That puts the finishing touch to your house.

ROGER (*to* CARMEN): Is it in prisons? In the wrinkles of old people?

CARMEN: It is.

ROGER: In the curves of roads?

CARMEN: You mustn't ask the impossible.

Same sounds as earlier: the cock and the anvil.

It's time to go, sir. The session's over. Turn left, and when you reach the corridor . . .

The sound of the anvil again, a little louder.

You hear? You've got to go home. . . . What are you doing?

ROGER: Life is nearby . . . and far away. Here all the women are beautiful. Their purpose is purely ornamental. . . . One can lose oneself in them. . . .

CARMEN (*curtly*): That's right. In ordinary language, we're called whores. But you've got to leave. . . .

ROGER: And go where? Into life? To carry on, as they say, with my activities. . . .

CARMEN (*a little anxiously*): I don't know what you're doing, and I haven't the right to inquire. But you've got to leave. Your time's up.

> *The sound of the anvil and other sounds indicate an activity: cracking of a whip, humming of a motor, etc.*

ROGER: They give you the rush in this place! Why do you want me to go back where I came from?

CARMEN: You've nothing further to do. . . .

ROGER: There? No. Nothing further. Nor here either. And outside, in what you call life, everything has crashed. No truth was possible. . . . Did you know Chantal?

CARMEN (*suddenly frightened*): Get going! Clear out of here!

THE QUEEN: I won't allow him to create a rumpus in my Studios! Who was it who sent me that individual? Whenever there are disturbances, the riff-raff always crop up. I hope that Carmen . . .

CARMEN (*to* ROGER): Get out! You've no right to ask questions either. You know that brothels are very strictly regulated and that we're protected by the police.

ROGER: No! Since I'm playing the Chief of Police and since you allow me to be here. . . .

CARMEN (*pulling him away*): You're crazy! You wouldn't be the first who thought he'd risen to power. . . . Come along!

ROGER (*disengaging himself*): If the brothel exists and if I've a right to go there, then I've a right to lead the character I've chosen to the very limit of his destiny . . . no, of mine . . . of merging his destiny with mine. . . .

CARMEN: Stop shouting, sir. All the studios are occupied. Come along. . . .

> CARMEN *tries to make him leave. She opens a door, then another, then a third, unable to find the right one.* ROGER *takes out a knife and, with his back to the audience, makes the gesture of castrating himself.*

THE QUEEN: On my rugs! On the new carpet! He's a lunatic!

CARMEN (*crying out*): Doing that here! (*She yells.*) Madame! Mme. Irma! (CARMEN *finally manages to drag* ROGER *out.*)

> THE QUEEN *rushes from the room. All the characters—*THE CHIEF OF POLICE, THE ENVOY, THE JUDGE, THE GENERAL, THE BISHOP—*turn and leave the portholes.* THE CHIEF OF POLICE *moves forward to the middle of the stage.*

THE CHIEF OF POLICE: Well played. He thought he had me. (*He places his hand on his fly, very·visibly feels his balls and, reassured, heaves a sigh.*) Mine are here. So which of us is washed up? He or I? Though my image be castrated in every brothel in the world, I remain intact. Intact, gentlemen. (*A pause.*) That plumber didn't know how to handle his role, that was all. (*He calls out, joyfully:*) Irma! Irma! . . . Where is she? It's not her job to dress wounds.

THE QUEEN (*entering*): George! The vestibule . . . the rugs are covered with blood . . . the vestibule's full of clients. . . . We're wiping up as best we can. . . . Carmen doesn't know where to put them. . . .

THE ENVOY (*bowing to* THE CHIEF OF POLICE): Nice work.

THE CHIEF OF POLICE: An image of me will be perpetuated in secret. Mutilated? (*He shrugs his shoulders.*) Yet a low mass will be said to my glory. Notify the kitchens! Have them send me enough grub for two thousand years.

THE QUEEN: What about me? George, *I'm* alive!

THE CHIEF OF POLICE (*without hearing her*): So . . . I'm. . . . Where? Here, or . . . a thousand times there? (*He points to the tomb.*) Now I can be kind . . . and pious . . . and just. . . . Did you see? Did you see me? There, just before, larger than large, stronger than strong, deader than dead? So I've nothing more to do with you.

THE QUEEN: George! But I still love you!

THE CHIEF OF POLICE (*moving towards the tomb*): I've won the right to go and sit and wait for two thousand years. (*To* THE PHOTOGRAPHERS.) You! Watch me live, and die. For posterity: shoot! (*Three almost simultaneous flashes.*) I've won! (*He walks backwards into the tomb, very slowly.*)

THE QUEEN: But it was I who did everything, who organized everything. . . . Stay. . . . What will. . . .

Suddenly a burst of machine-gun fire.

You hear!

THE CHIEF OF POLICE (*with a burst of laughter*): Think of me!

THE JUDGE *and* THE GENERAL *rush forward to stop him, but the doors start closing as* THE CHIEF OF POLICE *descends the first steps. A second burst of machine-gun fire.*

THE JUDGE (*clinging to the door*): Don't leave us alone!

THE GENERAL (*gloomily*): That carriage again!

THE ENVOY (*to* THE JUDGE): Be careful, you'll get your fingers caught.

The door has definitely closed. The characters remain bewildered for a moment. A third burst of machine-gun fire.

THE QUEEN: Gentlemen, you are free. . . .

THE BISHOP: But . . . in the middle of the night?

THE QUEEN (*interrupting him*): You'll leave by the narrow door that leads into the alley. There's a car waiting for you.

She nods courteously. THE THREE FIGURES *exit right. A fourth burst of machine-gun fire.*

Who is it? . . . Our side? . . . Or rebels? . . . Or? . . .

THE ENVOY: Someone dreaming, Madame. . . .

THE QUEEN *goes to various parts of the room and presses buttons. Each time, a light goes out.*

THE QUEEN (*continuing to extinguish lights*): . . . Irma. . . .
Call me Mme. Irma, and go home. Good night, sir.

THE ENVOY: Good night, Mme. Irma.

THE ENVOY *exits.*

IRMA (*alone, and continuing to extinguish lights*): It took so much light . . . five dollars worth of electricity a day! Thirty-eight studios! Every one of them gilded, and all of them rigged with machinery so as to be able to fit into and combine with each other. . . . And all these performances so that I can remain alone, mistress and assistant mistress of this house and of myself. (*She pushes in a button, then pushes it out again.*) Oh no, that's the tomb. He needs light, for two thousand years! . . . and food for two thousand years. . . . (*She shrugs her shoulders.*) Oh well, everything's in working order, and dishes have been prepared. Glory means descending into the grave with tons of victuals! . . . (*She calls out, facing the wings.*) Carmen? Carmen? . . . Bolt the doors, my dear, and put the furniture-covers on. . . . (*She continues extinguishing.*) In a little while, I'll have to start all over again . . . put all the lights on again . . . dress up. . . . (*A cock crows.*) Dress up . . . ah, the disguises! Distribute roles again . . . assume my own. . . . (*She stops in the middle of the stage, facing the audience.*) . . . Prepare yours . . . judges, generals, bishops, chamberlains, rebels who allow the revolt to congeal, I'm going to prepare my costumes and studios for tomorrow. . . . You must now go home, where everything—you can be quite sure—will be even falser than here. . . . You must go now. You'll leave by the right, through the alley. . . . (*She extinguishes the last light.*) It's morning already.

A burst of machine-gun fire.

THE END

Rhinoceros

by
Eugène Ionesco

Translated by Derek Prouse

RHINOCEROS was first produced in Paris by Jean-Louis Barrault at the Odéon, January 25, 1960, with the following cast:

BERENGER	Jean-Louis Barrault
JEAN	William Sabatier
DAISY	Simone Valère
DUDARD	Gabriel Cattand
THE LOGICIAN	Jean Parédès
THE WAITRESS	Jane Martel
THE HOUSEWIFE	Marie-Hélène Dasté
THE OLD GENTLEMAN	Robert Lombard
MRS. BOEUF	Simone Paris
MR. PAPILLON	Michel Bertay

THE GROCER, THE GROCER'S WIFE, THE CAFE PROPRIETOR, BOTARD, A FIRE-MAN, THE LITTLE OLD MAN, THE LITTLE OLD MAN'S WIFE, AND A LOT OF RHINOCEROS HEADS.

The play is in three acts and four scenes

ACT ONE

The scene is a square in a small provincial town. Up-stage a house composed of a ground floor and one storey. The ground floor is the window of a grocer's shop. The entrance is up two or three steps through a glass-paned door. The word EPICERIE is written in bold letters above the shop window. The two windows on the first floor are the living quarters of the grocer and his wife. The shop is up-stage, but slightly to the left, not far from the wings. In the distance a church steeple is visible above the grocer's house. Between the shop and the left of the stage there is a little street in perspective. To the right, slightly at an angle, is the front of a café. Above the café, one floor with a window; in front, the café terrace; several chairs and tables reach almost to centre stage. A dusty tree stands near the terrace chairs. Blue sky; harsh light; very white walls. The time is almost mid-day on a Sunday in summertime. JEAN *and* BERENGER *will sit at one of the terrace tables.*

The sound of church bells is heard, which stop a few moments before the curtain rises. When the curtain rises, a woman carrying a basket of provisions under one arm and a cat under the other crosses the stage in silence from right to left. As she does so, the GROCER'S WIFE *opens her shop door and watches her pass.*

GROCER'S WIFE: Oh that woman gets on my nerves! (*To her husband who is in the shop.*) Too stuck-up to buy from us nowadays.

The GROCER'S WIFE *leaves; the stage is empty for a few moments.*

JEAN *enters right, at the same time as* BERENGER *enters left.* JEAN *is very fastidiously dressed: brown suit, red tie, stiff collar, brown hat. He has a reddish face. His shoes are yellow and well-polished.* BERENGER *is unshaven and hatless, with unkempt hair and creased clothes; everything about him indicates negligence. He seems weary, half-asleep; from time to time he yawns.*

JEAN (*advancing from right*): Oh, so you managed to get here at last, Berenger!
BERENGER (*advancing from left*): Morning, Jean!

JEAN: Late as usual, of course. (*He looks at his wrist watch.*) Our appointment was for 11:30. And now it's practically mid-day.

BERENGER: I'm sorry. Have you been waiting long?

JEAN: No, I've only just arrived myself, as you saw.

They go and sit at one of the tables on the café terrace.

BERENGER: In that case I don't feel so bad, if you've only just . . .

JEAN: It's different with me. I don't like waiting; I've no time to waste. And as you're never on time, I come late on purpose—at a time when I presume you'll be there.

BERENGER: You're right . . . quite right, but . . .

JEAN: Now don't try to pretend you're ever on time!

BERENGER: No, of course not . . . I wouldn't say that.

JEAN *and* BERENGER *have sat down.*

JEAN: There you are, you see!

BERENGER: What are you drinking?

JEAN: You mean to say you've got a thirst even at this time in the morning?

BERENGER: It's so hot and dry.

JEAN: The more you drink the thirstier you get, popular science tells us that . . .

BERENGER: It would be less dry, and we'd be less thirsty, if they'd invent us some scientific clouds in the sky.

JEAN (*studying* BERENGER *closely*): That wouldn't help you any. You're not thirsty for water, Berenger . . .

BERENGER: I don't understand what you mean.

JEAN: You know perfectly well what I mean. I'm talking about your parched throat. That's a territory that can't get enough!

BERENGER: To compare my throat to a piece of land seems . . .

JEAN (*interrupting him*): You're in a bad way, my friend.

BERENGER: In a bad way? You think so?

JEAN: I'm not blind, you know. You're dropping with fatigue. You've gone without your sleep again, you yawn all the time, you're dead-tired . . .

BERENGER: There is something the matter with my hair . . .

JEAN: You reek of alcohol.

BERENGER: I have got a bit of a hang-over, it's true!

JEAN: It's the same every Sunday morning—not to mention the other days of the week.

BERENGER: Oh no, it's less frequent during the week, because of the office . . .

JEAN: And what's happened to your tie? Lost it during your orgy, I suppose!

BERENGER (*putting his hand to his neck*) : You're right. That's funny! Whatever could I have done with it?

JEAN (*taking a tie out of his coat pocket*) : Here, put this one on.

BERENGER: Oh thank you, that is kind. (*He puts on the tie.*)

JEAN (*while* BERENGER *is unskilfully tying his tie*) : Your hair's all over the place.

BERENGER *runs his fingers through his hair.*

Here, here's a comb! (*He takes a comb from his other pocket.*)

BERENGER (*taking the comb*) : Thank you. (*He vaguely combs his hair.*)

JEAN: You haven't even shaved! Just take a look at yourself!

He takes a mirror from his inside pocket, hands it to BERENGER, *who looks at himself; as he does so, he examines his tongue.*

BERENGER: My tongue's all coated.

JEAN (*taking the mirror and putting it back in his pocket*) : I'm not surprised! (*He takes back the comb as well, which* BERENGER *offers to him, and puts it in his pocket.*) You're heading for cirrhosis, my friend.

BERENGER (*worried*) : Do you think so?

JEAN (*to* BERENGER, *who wants to give him back his tie*) : Keep the tie, I've got plenty more.

BERENGER (*admiringly*) : You always look so immaculate.

JEAN (*continuing his inspection of* BERENGER) : Your clothes are all crumpled, they're a disgrace! Your shirt is downright filthy, and your shoes . . . (BERENGER *tries to hide his feet under the table.*) Your shoes haven't been touched. What a mess you're in! And look at your shoulders . . .

BERENGER: What's the matter with my shoulders?

JEAN: Turn round! Come on, turn round! You've been leaning against some wall. (BERENGER *holds his hand out docilely to*

JEAN.) No, I haven't got a brush with me; it would make my pockets bulge. (*Still docile,* BERENGER *flicks his shoulders to get rid of the white dust;* JEAN *averts his head.*) Heavens! Where did you get all that from?

BERENGER: I don't remember.

JEAN: It's a positive disgrace! I feel ashamed to be your friend.

BERENGER: You're very hard on me . . .

JEAN: I've every reason to be.

BERENGER: Listen, Jean. There are so few distractions in this town—I get so bored. I'm not made for the work I'm doing . . . every day at the office, eight hours a day—and only three weeks' holiday a year! When Saturday night comes round I feel exhausted and so—you know how it is—just to relax . . .

JEAN: My dear man, everybody has to work. I spend eight hours a day in the office the same as everyone else. And I only get three weeks off a year, but even so you don't catch me . . . Will-power, my good man!

BERENGER: But everybody hasn't got as much will-power as you have. I can't get used to it. I just can't get used to life.

JEAN: Everybody has to get used to it. Or do you consider yourself some superior being?

BERENGER: I don't pretend to be . . .

JEAN (*interrupting him*): I'm just as good as you are; I think with all due modesty I may say I'm better. The superior man is the man who fulfils his duty.

BERENGER: What duty?

JEAN: His duty . . . His duty as an employee, for example.

BERENGER: Oh yes, his duty as an employee . . .

JEAN: Where did your debauch take place last night? If you can remember!

BERENGER: We were celebrating Auguste's birthday, our friend Auguste . . .

JEAN: Our friend Auguste? Nobody invited me to our friend Auguste's birthday . . .

At this moment a noise is heard, far off, but swiftly approaching, of a beast panting in its headlong course, and of a long trumpeting.

BERENGER: I couldn't refuse. It wouldn't have been nice . . .

JEAN: Did I go there?

BERENGER: Well, perhaps it was because you weren't invited.

WAITRESS (*coming out of café*): Good morning, gentlemen. Can I get you something to drink?

The noise becomes very loud.

JEAN (*to* BERENGER, *almost shouting to make himself heard above the noise which he has not become conscious of*): True, I was not invited. That honour was denied me. But in any case, I can assure you, that even if I had been invited, I would not have gone, because...

The noise has become intense.

What's going on?

The noise of a powerful, heavy animal, galloping at great speed is heard very close; the sound of panting.

Whatever is it?

WAITRESS: Whatever is it?

BERENGER, *still listless without appearing to hear anything at all, replies tranquilly to* JEAN *about the invitation; his lips move but one doesn't hear what he says;* JEAN *bounds to his feet, knocking his chair over as he does so, looks off left pointing, whilst* BERENGER, *still a little dopey, remains seated.*

JEAN: Oh, a rhinoceros!

The noise made by the animal dies away swiftly and one can already hear the following words. The whole of this scene must be played very fast, each repeating in swift succession: 'Oh, a rhinoceros!'

WAITRESS: Oh, a rhinoceros!

GROCER'S WIFE (*sticks her head out of her shop doorway*): Oh, a rhinoceros! (*To her husband still inside the shop.*) Quick, come and look; it's a rhinoceros!

They are all looking off left after the animal.

JEAN: It's rushing straight ahead, brushing up against the shop windows.
GROCER (*in his shop*): Whereabouts?
WAITRESS (*putting her hands on her hips*): Well!
GROCER'S WIFE (*to her husband who is still in shop*): Come and look!

At this moment the GROCER puts his head out.

GROCER: Oh, a rhinoceros!
LOGICIAN (*entering quickly left*): A rhinoceros going full-tilt on the opposite pavement!

All these speeches from the time when JEAN says 'Oh, a rhinoceros' are practically simultaneous. A woman is heard crying 'Ah!' She appears. She runs to the centre-stage; it is a HOUSEWIFE with a basket on her arm; once arrived centre-stage she drops her basket; the contents scatter all over the stage, a bottle breaks, but she does not drop her cat.

HOUSEWIFE: Ah! Oh!

An elegant OLD GENTLEMAN comes from left stage, after the HOUSEWIFE, rushes into the GROCER'S shop, knocks into the GROCER and his WIFE, whilst the LOGICIAN installs himself against the back wall on the left of the grocery entrance. JEAN and the WAITRESS, standing, and BERENGER, still apathetically seated, together form another group. At the same time, coming from the left, cries of 'Oh' and 'Ah' and the noise of people running have been heard. The dust raised by the animal spreads over the stage.

CAFÉ PROPRIETOR (*sticking his head out of the first-floor window*): What's going on?
OLD GENTLEMAN (*disappearing behind the GROCER and his WIFE*): Excuse me, please!

The OLD GENTLEMAN is elegantly dressed, with white spats, a soft hat and an ivory-handled cane; the LOGICIAN, propped up against the wall has a little grey moustache, an eyeglass, and is wearing a straw hat.

GROCER'S WIFE (*jostled and jostling her husband; to the* OLD GENTLE-MAN) : Watch out with that stick!
GROCER: Look where you're going, can't you!

The head of the OLD GENTLEMAN *is seen behind the* GROCER *and his* WIFE.

WAITRESS (*to the* PROPRIETOR) : A rhinoceros!
PROPRIETOR (*to the* WAITRESS *from his window*) : You're seeing things. (*He sees the rhinoceros.*) Well, I'll be . . . !
HOUSEWIFE: Ah!

The 'Ohs' and 'Ahs' from off-stage form a background accompaniment to her 'Ah.' She has dropped her basket, her provisions and the bottle, but has nevertheless kept tight hold of her cat which she carries under her other arm.

There, they frightened the poor pussy!
PROPRIETOR (*still looking off left, following the distant course of the animal as the noises fade; hooves, trumpetings, etc.*):

BERENGER *sleepily averts his head a little on account of the dust, but says nothing; he simply makes a grimace.*

Well, of all things!
JEAN (*also averting his head a little, but very much awake*) : Well, of all things! (*He sneezes.*)
HOUSEWIFE (*she is centre-stage but turned towards left; her provisions scattered on the ground round her*): Well of all things! (*She sneezes.*)

The OLD GENTLEMAN, GROCER'S WIFE *and* GROCER *up-stage re-opening the glass door of the* GROCER'S *shop that the* OLD GEN-TLEMAN *has closed behind him.*

ALL THREE: Well, of all things!
JEAN: Well, of all things! (*To* BERENGER.) Did you see that?

The noise of the rhinoceros and its trumpeting are now far away; the people are still staring after the animal, all except for BERENGER *who is still apathetically seated.*

ALL (*except* BERENGER) : Well, of all things!

BERENGER (*to* JEAN) : It certainly looked as if it was a rhinoceros. It made plenty of dust. (*He takes out a handkerchief and blows his nose.*)

HOUSEWIFE: Well, of all things! Gave me such a scare.

GROCER (*to the* HOUSEWIFE) : Your basket ... and all your things ...

OLD GENTLEMAN *approaching the lady and bending to pick up her things scattered about the stage. He greets her gallantly, raising his hat.*

PROPRIETOR: Really, these days, you never know ...

WAITRESS: Fancy that!

OLD GENTLEMAN (*to the* HOUSEWIFE) : May I help you pick up your things?

HOUSEWIFE (*to the* OLD GENTLEMAN) : Thank you, how very kind! Do put on your hat. Oh, it gave me such a scare!

LOGICIAN: Fear is an irrational thing. It must yield to reason.

WAITRESS: It's already out of sight.

OLD GENTLEMAN (*to the* HOUSEWIFE *and indicating the* LOGICIAN) : My friend is a logician.

JEAN (*to* BERENGER) : Well, what did you think of that?

WAITRESS: Those animals can certainly travel!

HOUSEWIFE (*to the* LOGICIAN): Very happy to meet you!

GROCER'S WIFE (*to the* GROCER) : That'll teach her to buy her things from somebody else!

JEAN (*to the* PROPRIETOR *and the* WAITRESS): What did you think of that?

HOUSEWIFE: I still didn't let my cat go.

PROPRIETOR (*shrugging his shoulders, at window*) : You don't often see that!

HOUSEWIFE (*to the* LOGICIAN *and the* OLD GENTLEMAN *who is picking up her provisions*) : Would you hold him a moment!

WAITRESS (*to* JEAN) : First time I've seen that!

LOGICIAN (*to the* HOUSEWIFE, *taking the cat in his arms*) : It's not spiteful, is it?

PROPRIETOR (*to* JEAN) : Went past like a comet!

HOUSEWIFE (*to the* LOGICIAN) : He wouldn't hurt a fly. (*To the others.*) What happened to my wine?

GROCER (*to the* HOUSEWIFE) : I've got plenty more.

JEAN (*to* BERENGER) : Well, what did you think of that?

GROCER (*to the* HOUSEWIFE) : And good stuff, too!

PROPRIETOR (*to the* WAITRESS): Don't hang about! Look after these gentlemen! (*He indicates* BERENGER *and* JEAN. *He withdraws.*)

BERENGER (*to* JEAN) : What did I think of what?

GROCER'S WIFE (*to the* GROCER) : Go and get her another bottle!

JEAN (*to* BERENGER) : Of the rhinoceros, of course! What did you think I meant?

GROCER (*to the* HOUSEWIFE) : I've got some first-class wine, in unbreakable bottles! (*He disappears into his shop.*)

LOGICIAN (*stroking the cat in his arms*) : Puss, puss, puss.

WAITRESS (*to* BERENGER *and* JEAN) : What are you drinking?

BERENGER: Two pastis.

WAITRESS: Two pastis—right! (*She walks to the café entrance.*)

HOUSEWIFE (*picking up her things with the help of the* OLD GENTLEMAN) : Very kind of you, I'm sure.

WAITRESS: Two pastis! (*She goes into café.*)

OLD GENTLEMAN (*to the* HOUSEWIFE) : Oh, please don't mention it, it's a pleasure.

> The GROCER'S WIFE *goes into shop.*

LOGICIAN (*to the* OLD GENTLEMAN *and the* HOUSEWIFE *picking up the provisions*) : Replace them in an orderly fashion.

JEAN (*to* BERENGER) : Well, what did you think about it?

BERENGER (*to* JEAN, *not knowing what to say*) : Well ... nothing ... it made a lot of dust ...

GROCER (*coming out of shop with a bottle of wine; to the* HOUSEWIFE) : I've some good leeks as well.

LOGICIAN (*still stroking the cat*): Puss, puss, puss.

GROCER (*to the* HOUSEWIFE) : It's a hundred francs a litre.

HOUSEWIFE (*paying the* GROCER, *then to the* OLD GENTLEMAN *who has managed to put everything back in the basket*) : Oh, you are kind! Such a pleasure to come across the old French courtesy. Not like the young people today!

GROCER (*taking money*) : You should buy from me. You wouldn't even have to cross the street, and you wouldn't run the risk of these accidents. (*He goes back into his shop.*)

JEAN (*who has sat down and is still thinking of the rhinoceros*): But you must admit it's extraordinary.

OLD GENTLEMAN (*taking off his hat, and kissing the* HOUSEWIFE's *hand*): It was a great pleasure to meet you!

HOUSEWIFE (*to the* LOGICIAN): Thank you very much for holding my cat.

> The LOGICIAN *gives the* HOUSEWIFE *back her cat. The* WAITRESS *comes back with drinks.*

WAITRESS: Two pastis!

JEAN (*to* BERENGER): You're incorrigible!

OLD GENTLEMAN (*to the* HOUSEWIFE): May I accompany you part of the way?

BERENGER (*to* JEAN, *and pointing to the* WAITRESS *who goes back into the café*): I asked for mineral water. She's made a mistake.

> JEAN, *scornful and disbelieving, shrugs his shoulders.*

HOUSEWIFE (*to the* OLD GENTLEMAN): My husband's waiting for me, thank you. Perhaps some other time...

OLD GENTLEMAN (*to the* HOUSEWIFE): I sincerely hope so, Madame.

HOUSEWIFE (*to the* OLD GENTLEMAN): So do I! (*She gives him a sweet look as she leaves left.*)

BERENGER: The dust's settled...

> JEAN *shrugs his shoulders again.*

OLD GENTLEMAN (*to the* LOGICIAN, *and looking after the* HOUSEWIFE): Delightful creature!

JEAN (*to* BERENGER): A rhinoceros! I can't get over it!

> The OLD GENTLEMAN *and the* LOGICIAN *move slowly right and off. They chat amiably.*

OLD GENTLEMAN (*to the* LOGICIAN, *after casting a last fond look after the* HOUSEWIFE): Charming, isn't she?

LOGICIAN (*to the* OLD GENTLEMAN): I'm going to explain to you what a syllogism is.

OLD GENTLEMAN: Ah yes, a syllogism.

JEAN (*to* BERENGER): I can't get over it! It's unthinkable!

BERENGER *yawns.*

LOGICIAN: A syllogism consists of a main proposition, a secondary one, and a conclusion.

OLD GENTLEMAN: What conclusion?

The LOGICIAN *and the* OLD GENTLEMAN *go out.*

JEAN: I just can't get over it.

BERENGER: Yes, I can see you can't. Well, it was a rhinoceros—all right, so it was a rhinoceros! It's miles away by now ... miles away ...

JEAN: But you must see it's fantastic! A rhinoceros loose in the town, and you don't bat an eyelid! It shouldn't be allowed!

BERENGER *yawns.*

Put your hand in front of your mouth!

BERENGER: Yais ... yais ... It shouldn't be allowed. It's dangerous. I hadn't realized. But don't worry about it, it won't get us here.

JEAN: We ought to protest to the Town Council! What's the Council there for?

BERENGER (*yawning, then quickly putting his hand to his mouth*): Oh excuse me ... perhaps the rhinoceros escaped from the zoo.

JEAN: You're day-dreaming.

BERENGER: But I'm wide awake.

JEAN: Awake or asleep, it's the same thing.

BERENGER: But there is some difference.

JEAN: That's not the point.

BERENGER: But you just said being awake and being asleep were the same thing ...

JEAN: You didn't understand. There's no difference between dreaming awake and dreaming asleep.

BERENGER: I do dream. Life is a dream.

JEAN: You're certainly dreaming when you say the rhinoceros escaped from the zoo ...

BERENGER: I only said: perhaps.

JEAN: ... because there's been no zoo in our town since the animals were destroyed in the plague ... ages ago ...

BERENGER (*with the same indifference*): Then perhaps it came from a circus.

JEAN: What circus are you talking about?

BERENGER: I don't know ... some travelling circus.

JEAN: You know perfectly well that the Council banned all travelling performers from the district ... There haven't been any since we were children.

BERENGER (*trying unsuccessfully to stop yawning*): In that case, maybe it's been hiding ever since in the surrounding swamps?

JEAN: The surrounding swamps! The surrounding swamps! My poor friend, you live in a thick haze of alcohol.

BERENGER (*naïvely*): That's very true ... it seems to mount from my stomach ...

JEAN: It's clouding your brain! Where do you know of any surrounding swamps? Our district is known as 'little Castille' because the land is so arid.

BERENGER (*surfeited and pretty weary*): How do I know, then? Perhaps it's been hiding under a stone? ... Or maybe it's been nesting on some withered branch?

JEAN: If you think you're being witty, you're very much mistaken! You're just being a bore with ... with your stupid paradoxes. You're incapable of talking seriously!

BERENGER: Today, yes, only today ... because of ... because of ... (*He indicates his head with a vague gesture.*)

JEAN: Today the same as any other day!

BERENGER: Oh, not quite as much.

JEAN: Your witticisms are not very inspired.

BERENGER: I wasn't trying to be ...

JEAN (*interrupting him*): I can't bear people to try and make fun of me!

BERENGER (*hand on his heart*): But my dear Jean, I'd never allow myself to ...

JEAN (*interrupting him*): My dear Berenger, you are allowing yourself ...

BERENGER: Oh no, never. I'd never allow myself to.

JEAN: Yes, you would; you've just done so.

BERENGER: But how could you possibly think ...

JEAN (*interrupting him*): I think what is true!

BERENGER: But I assure you ...

JEAN (*interrupting him*): ... that you were making fun of me!

BERENGER: You really can be obstinate, sometimes.

JEAN: And now you're calling me a mule into the bargain. Even you must see how insulting you're being.

BERENGER: It would never have entered my mind.

JEAN: You have no mind!

BERENGER: All the more reason why it would never enter it.

JEAN: There are certain things which enter the minds of even people without one.

BERENGER: That's impossible.

JEAN: And why, pray, is it impossible?

BERENGER: Because it's impossible.

JEAN: Then kindly explain to me why it's impossible, as you seem to imagine you can explain everything.

BERENGER: I don't imagine anything of the kind.

JEAN: Then why do you act as if you do? And, I repeat, why are you being so insulting to me?

BERENGER: I'm not insulting you. Far from it. You know what tremendous respect I have for you.

JEAN: In that case, why do you contradict me, making out that it's not dangerous to let a rhinoceros go racing about in the middle of the town—particularly on a Sunday morning when the streets are full of children ... and adults, too ...

BERENGER: A lot of them are in church. They don't run any risk ...

JEAN (*interrupting him*): If you will allow me to finish ... and at market time, too.

BERENGER: I never said it wasn't dangerous to let a rhinoceros go racing about the town. I simply said I'd personally never considered the danger. It had never crossed my mind.

JEAN: You never consider anything.

BERENGER: All right, I agree. A rhinoceros roaming about is not a good thing.

JEAN: It shouldn't be allowed.

BERENGER: I agree. It shouldn't be allowed. It's a ridiculous thing all right! But it's no reason for you and me to quarrel. Why go on at me just because some wretched perissodactyle happens to pass by. A stupid quadruped not worth talking about. And ferocious into the bargain. And which has already disappeared, which doesn't exist any longer. We're not going to bother about some animal that doesn't exist. Let's talk about something else, Jean.

please; (*He yawns.*) there are plenty of other subjects for conversation. (*He takes his glass.*) To you!

At this moment the LOGICIAN *and the* OLD GENTLEMAN *come
back on stage from left; they walk over, talking as they go, to
one of the tables on the café terrace, some distance from*
BERENGER *and* JEAN, *behind and to the right of them.*

JEAN: Put that glass back on the table! You're not to drink it.

JEAN *takes a large swallow from his own pastis and puts back
the glass, half-empty, on the table.* BERENGER *continues to hold
his glass, without putting it down, and without daring to drink
from it either.*

BERENGER (*timidly*) : There's no point in leaving it for the proprietor.
(*He makes as if to drink.*)
JEAN: Put it down, I tell you!
BERENGER: Very well.

He is putting the glass back on the table when DAISY *passes.
She is a young blonde typist and she crosses the stage from
right to left. When he sees her,* BERENGER *rises abruptly, and in
doing so makes an awkward movement; the glass falls and
splashes* JEAN'S *trousers.*

Oh, there's Daisy!
JEAN: Look out! How clumsy you are!
BERENGER: That's Daisy...I'm so sorry... (*He hides himself out of
sight of* DAISY.) I don't want her to see me in this state.
JEAN: Your behaviour's unforgivable, absolutely unforgivable! (*He
looks in the direction of* DAISY, *who is just disappearing.*) Why
are you afraid of that young girl?
BERENGER: Oh, be quiet, please be quiet!
JEAN: She doesn't look an unpleasant person!
BERENGER (*coming back to* JEAN, *now that* DAISY *has gone*) : I must
apologize once more for ...
JEAN: You see what comes of drinking, you can no longer control
your movements, you've no strength left in your hands, you're

besotted and fagged out. You're digging your own grave, my friend, you're destroying yourself.

BERENGER: I don't like the taste of alcohol much. And yet if I don't drink, I'm done for; it's as if I'm frightened, and so I drink not to be frightened any longer.

JEAN: Frightened of what?

BERENGER: I don't know exactly. It's a sort of anguish difficult to describe. I feel out of place in life, among people, and so I take to drink. That calms me down and relaxes me so I can forget.

JEAN: You try to escape from yourself!

BERENGER: I'm so tired, I've been tired for years. It's exhausting to drag the weight of my own body about . . .

JEAN: That's alcoholic neurasthenia, drinker's gloom . . .

BERENGER (*continuing*): I'm conscious of my body all the time, as if it were made of lead, or as if I were carrying another man around on my back. I can't seem to get used to myself. I don't even know if I *am* me. Then as soon as I take a drink, the lead slips away and I recognize myself, I become me again.

JEAN: That's just being fanciful. Look at me, Berenger, I weigh more than you do. And yet I feel light, light as a feather! (*He flaps his arms as if about to fly. The* OLD GENTLEMAN *and the* LOGICIAN *have come back and have taken a few steps on stage deep in talk. At this moment they are passing by* JEAN *and* BERENGER. JEAN'S *arm deals the* OLD GENTLEMAN *a sharp knock which precipitates him into the arms of the* LOGICIAN.)

LOGICIAN: An example of a syllogism . . . (*He is knocked.*) Oh!

OLD GENTLEMAN (*to* JEAN): Look out! (*To the* LOGICIAN.) I'm so sorry.

JEAN (*to the* OLD GENTLEMAN) : I'm so sorry.

LOGICIAN (*to the* OLD GENTLEMAN) : No harm done.

OLD GENTLEMAN (*to* JEAN) : No harm done.

The OLD GENTLEMAN *and the* LOGICIAN *go and sit at one of the terrace tables a little to the right and behind* JEAN *and* BERENGER.

BERENGER (*to* JEAN) : You certainly are strong.

JEAN: Yes, I'm strong. I'm strong for several reasons. In the first place I'm strong because I'm naturally strong, and secondly I'm strong because I have moral strength. I'm also strong because I'm not riddled with alcohol. I don't wish to offend you, my dear Berenger, but I feel I must tell you that it's alcohol which weighs so heavy on you.

LOGICIAN (*to the* OLD GENTLEMAN) : Here is an example of a syllogism. The cat has four paws. Isidore and Fricot both have four paws. Therefore Isidore and Fricot are cats.

OLD GENTLEMAN (*to the* LOGICIAN) : My dog has got four paws.

LOGICIAN (*to the* OLD GENTLEMAN) : Then it's a cat.

BERENGER (*to* JEAN) : I've barely got the strength to go on living. Maybe I don't even want to.

OLD GENTLEMAN (*to the* LOGICIAN, *after deep reflection*) : So then logically speaking, my dog must be a cat?

LOGICIAN (*to the* OLD GENTLEMAN) : Logically, yes. But the contrary is also true.

BERENGER (*to* JEAN) : Solitude seems to oppress me. And so does the company of other people.

JEAN (*to* BERENGER) : You contradict yourself. What oppresses you— solitude, or the company of others? You consider yourself a thinker, yet you're devoid of logic.

OLD GENTLEMAN (*to the* LOGICIAN) : Logic is a very beautiful thing.

LOGICIAN (*to the* OLD GENTLEMAN) : As long as it is not abused.

BERENGER (*to* JEAN) : Life is an abnormal business.

JEAN: On the contrary. Nothing could be more natural, and the proof is that people go on living.

BERENGER: There are more dead people than living. And their numbers are increasing. The living are getting rarer.

JEAN: The dead don't exist, there's no getting away from that! ... Ah! Ah...! (*He gives a huge laugh.*) Yet you're oppressed by them, too? How can you be oppressed by something that doesn't exist?

BERENGER: I sometimes wonder if I exist myself.

JEAN: You don't exist, my dear Berenger, because you don't think. Start thinking, then you will.

LOGICIAN (*to the* OLD GENTLEMAN) : Another syllogism. All cats die. Socrates is dead. Therefore Socrates is a cat.

OLD GENTLEMAN: And he's got four paws. That's true. I've got a cat named Socrates.

LOGICIAN: There you are, you see ...

JEAN (*to* BERENGER) : Fundamentally you're just a bluffer. And a liar.

You say that life doesn't interest you. And yet there's somebody who does.

BERENGER: Who?

JEAN: Your little friend from the office who just went past. You're very fond of her!

OLD GENTLEMAN (*to the* LOGICIAN) : So Socrates was a cat, was he?

LOGICIAN: Logic has just revealed the fact to us.

JEAN (*to* BERENGER) : You didn't want her to see you in your present state. (BERENGER *makes a gesture*.) That proves you're not indifferent to everything. But how can you expect Daisy to be attracted to a drunkard?

LOGICIAN (*to the* OLD GENTLEMAN) : Let's get back to our cats.

OLD GENTLEMAN (*to the* LOGICIAN) : I'm all ears.

BERENGER (*to* JEAN) : In any case, I think she's already got her eye on someone.

JEAN: Oh, who?

BERENGER: Dudard. An office colleague, qualified in law, with a big future in the firm—and in Daisy's affections. I can't hope to compete with him.

LOGICIAN (*to the* OLD GENTLEMAN) : The cat Isidore has four paws.

OLD GENTLEMAN: How do you know?

LOGICIAN: It's stated in the hypothesis.

BERENGER (*to* JEAN) : The Chief thinks a lot of him. Whereas I've no future, I've no qualifications. I don't stand a chance.

OLD GENTLEMAN (*to the* LOGICIAN) : Ah! In the hypothesis.

JEAN (*to* BERENGER): So you're giving up, just like that . . . ?

BERENGER: What else can I do?

LOGICIAN (*to the* OLD GENTLEMAN) : Fricot also has four paws. So how many paws have Fricot and Isidore?

OLD GENTLEMAN: Separately or together?

JEAN (*to* BERENGER) : Life is a struggle, it's cowardly not to put up a fight!

LOGICIAN (*to the* OLD GENTLEMAN) : Separately or together, it all depends.

BERENGER (*to* JEAN) : What can I do? I've nothing to put up a fight with.

JEAN: Then find yourself some weapons, my friend.

OLD GENTLEMAN (*to the* LOGICIAN, *after painful reflection*) : Eight, eight paws.

LOGICIAN: Logic involves mental arithmetic, you see.

OLD GENTLEMAN: It certainly has many aspects!

BERENGER (*to* JEAN) : Where can I find the weapons?

LOGICIAN (*to the* OLD GENTLEMAN) : There are no limits to logic.

JEAN: Within yourself. Through your own will.

BERENGER: What weapons?

LOGICIAN (*to the* OLD GENTLEMAN): I'm going to show you . . .

JEAN (*to* BERENGER) : The weapons of patience and culture, the weapons of the mind. (BERENGER *yawns.*) Turn yourself into a keen and brilliant intellect. Get yourself up to the mark!

BERENGER: How do I get myself up to the mark?

LOGICIAN (*to the* OLD GENTLEMAN) : If I take two paws away from these cats—how many does each have left?

OLD GENTLEMAN: That's not so easy.

BERENGER (*to* JEAN) : That's not so easy.

LOGICIAN (*to the* OLD GENTLEMAN) : On the contrary, it's simple.

OLD GENTLEMAN (*to the* LOGICIAN) : It may be simple for you, but not for me.

BERENGER (*to* JEAN) : It may be simple for you, but not for me.

LOGICIAN (*to the* OLD GENTLEMAN) : Come on, exercise your mind. Concentrate!

JEAN (*to* BERENGER) : Come on, exercise your will. Concentrate!

OLD GENTLEMAN (*to the* LOGICIAN) : I don't see how.

BERENGER (*to* JEAN) : I really don't see how.

LOGICIAN (*to the* OLD GENTLEMAN) : You have to be told everything.

JEAN (*to* BERENGER) : You have to be told everything.

LOGICIAN (*to the* OLD GENTLEMAN) : Take a sheet of paper and calculate. If you take six paws from the two cats, how many paws are left to each cat?

OLD GENTLEMAN: Just a moment . . . (*He calculates on a sheet of paper which he takes from his pocket.*)

JEAN: This is what you must do: dress yourself properly, shave every day, put on a clean shirt.

BERENGER: The laundry's so expensive . . .

JEAN: Cut down on your drinking. This is the way to come out: wear a hat, a tie like this, a well-cut suit, shoes well polished. (*As he mentions the various items of clothing he points self-contentedly to his own hat, tie and shoes.*)

OLD GENTLEMAN (*to the* LOGICIAN) : There are several possible solutions.

LOGICIAN (*to the* OLD GENTLEMAN) : Tell me.

BERENGER (*to* JEAN): Then what do I do? Tell me ...

LOGICIAN (*to the* OLD GENTLEMAN) : I'm listening.

BERENGER (*to* JEAN) : I'm listening.

JEAN: You're a timid creature, but not without talent.

BERENGER: I've got talent, me?

JEAN: So use it. Put yourself in the picture. Keep abreast of the cultural and literary events of the times.

OLD GENTLEMAN (*to the* LOGICIAN) : One possibility is: one cat could have four paws and the other two.

BERENGER (*to* JEAN) : I get so little spare time!

LOGICIAN (*to the* OLD GENTLEMAN) : You're not without talent. You just needed to exercise it.

JEAN: Take advantage of what free time you *do* have. Don't just let yourself drift.

OLD GENTLEMAN: I've never had the time. I was an official, you know.

LOGICIAN: One can always find time to learn.

JEAN (*to* BERENGER) : One can always find time.

BERENGER (*to* JEAN) : It's too late now.

OLD GENTLEMAN (*to the* LOGICIAN) : It's a bit late in the day for me.

JEAN (*to* BERENGER) : It's never too late.

LOGICIAN (*to the* OLD GENTLEMAN) : It's never too late.

JEAN (*to* BERENGER) : You work eight hours a day, like me and everybody else, but not on Sundays, nor in the evening, nor for three weeks in the summer. That's quite sufficient, with a little method.

LOGICIAN (*to the* OLD GENTLEMAN) : Well, what about the other solutions? Use a little method, a little method!

The OLD GENTLEMAN *starts to calculate anew.*

JEAN (*to* BERENGER) : Look, instead of drinking and feeling sick, isn't it better to be fresh and eager, even at work? And you can spend your free time constructively.

BERENGER: How do you mean?

JEAN: By visiting museums, reading literary periodicals, going to lectures. That'll solve your troubles, it will develop your mind. In four weeks you'll be a cultured man.

BERENGER: You're right!

OLD GENTLEMAN (*to the* LOGICIAN): There could be one cat with five paws ...

JEAN (*to* BERENGER) : You see, you even think so yourself!

OLD GENTLEMAN (*to the* LOGICIAN) : And one cat with one paw. But would they still be cats, then?

LOGICIAN (*to the* OLD GENTLEMAN) : Why not?

JEAN (*to* BERENGER) : Instead of squandering all your spare money on drink, isn't it better to buy a ticket for an interesting play? Do you know anything about the avant-garde theatre there's so much talk about? Have you seen Ionesco's plays?

BERENGER (*to* JEAN) : Unfortunately, no. I've only heard people talk about them.

OLD GENTLEMAN (*to the* LOGICIAN) : By taking two of the eight paws away from the two cats . . .

JEAN (*to* BERENGER) : There's one playing now. Take advantage of it.

OLD GENTLEMAN (*to the* LOGICIAN) : . . . we could have one cat with six paws . . .

BERENGER: It would be an excellent initiation into the artistic life of our times.

OLD GENTLEMAN (*to the* LOGICIAN) : We could have one cat with no paws at all.

BERENGER: You're right, perfectly right. I'm going to put myself into the picture, like you said.

LOGICIAN (*to the* OLD GENTLEMAN) : In that case, one cat would be specially privileged.

BERENGER (*to* JEAN): I will, I promise you.

JEAN: You promise yourself, that's the main thing.

OLD GENTLEMAN: And one under-privileged cat deprived of all paws.

BERENGER: I make myself a solemn promise, I'll keep my word to myself.

LOGICIAN: That would be unjust, and therefore not logical.

BERENGER: Instead of drinking, I'll develop my mind. I feel better already. My head already feels clearer.

JEAN: You see!

OLD GENTLEMAN (*to the* LOGICIAN) : Not logical?

BERENGER: This afternoon I'll go to the museum. And I'll book two seats for the theatre this evening. Will you come with me?

LOGICIAN (*to the* OLD GENTLEMAN): Because Logic means Justice.

JEAN (*to* BERENGER) : You must persevere. Keep up your good resolutions.

OLD GENTLEMAN (*to the* LOGICIAN): I get it. Justice . . .

BERENGER (*to* JEAN) : I promise you, and I promise myself. Will you come to the museum with me this afternoon?

JEAN (*to* BERENGER) : I have to take a rest this afternoon; it's in my programme for the day.

OLD GENTLEMAN: Justice is one more aspect of Logic.

BERENGER (*to* JEAN) : But you will come with me to the theatre this evening?

JEAN: No, not this evening.

LOGICIAN (*to the* OLD GENTLEMAN) : Your mind is getting clearer!

JEAN (*to* BERENGER) : I sincerely hope you'll keep up your good resolutions. But this evening I have to meet some friends for a drink.

BERENGER: For a drink?

OLD GENTLEMAN (*to the* LOGICIAN) : What's more, a cat with no paws at all . . .

JEAN (*to* BERENGER) : I've promised to go. I always keep my word.

OLD GENTLEMAN (*to the* LOGICIAN): . . . wouldn't be able to run fast enough to catch mice.

BERENGER (*to* JEAN) : Ah, now it's you that's setting me a bad example! You're going out drinking.

LOGICIAN (*to the* OLD GENTLEMAN) : You're already making progress in logic.

A sound of rapid galloping is heard approaching again, trumpeting and the sound of rhinoceros hooves and pantings; this time the sound comes from the opposite direction approaching from backstage to front, in the left wings.

JEAN (*furiously to* BERENGER) : It's not a habit with me, you know. It's not the same as with you. With you . . . you're . . . it's not the same thing at all . . .

BERENGER: Why isn't it the same thing?

JEAN (*shouting over the noise coming from the café*) : I'm no drunkard, not me!

LOGICIAN (*shouting to the* OLD GENTLEMAN) : Even with no paws a cat must catch mice. That's in it's nature.

BERENGER (*shouting very loudly*) : I didn't mean you were a drunkard. But why would it make me one any more than you, in a case like that?

OLD GENTLEMAN (*shouting to the* LOGICIAN) : What's in the cat's nature?

JEAN (*to* BERENGER) : Because there's moderation in all things. I'm a moderate person, not like you!

LOGICIAN (*to the* OLD GENTLEMAN, *cupping his hands to his ears*) : What did you say?

Deafening sounds drown the words of the four characters.

BERENGER (*to* JEAN, *cupping his hands to his ears*) : What about me, what? What did you say?

JEAN (*roaring*): I said that . . .

OLD GENTLEMAN (*roaring*): I said that . . .

JEAN (*suddenly aware of the noises which are now very near*) : Whatever's happening?

LOGICIAN: What is going on?

JEAN (*rises, knocking his chair over as he does so; looks towards left wings where the noises of the passing rhinoceros are coming from*): Oh, a rhinoceros!

LOGICIAN (*rising, knocking over his chair*) : Oh, a rhinoceros!

OLD GENTLEMAN (*doing the same*) : Oh, a rhinoceros!

BERENGER (*still seated, but this time, taking more notice*) : Rhinoceros! In the opposite direction!

WAITRESS (*emerging with a tray and glasses*) : What is it? Oh, a rhinoceros! (*She drops the tray, breaking the glasses.*)

PROPRIETOR (*coming out of the café*): What's going on?

WAITRESS (*to the* PROPRIETOR): A rhinoceros!

LOGICIAN: A rhinoceros, going full-tilt on the opposite pavement!

GROCER (*coming out of his shop*): Oh, a rhinoceros!

JEAN: Oh, a rhinoceros!

GROCER'S WIFE (*sticking her head through the upstairs window of shop*): Oh, a rhinoceros!

PROPRIETOR: It's no reason to break the glasses.

JEAN: It's rushing straight ahead, brushing up against the shop windows.

DAISY (*entering left*): Oh, a rhinoceros!

BERENGER (*noticing* DAISY): Oh, Daisy! [*notices instead of Rhino*]

Noise of people fleeing, the same 'Ohs' and 'Ahs' as before.

WAITRESS: Well, of all things!

PROPRIETOR (*to the* WAITRESS): You'll be charged up for those!

BERENGER *tries to make himself scarce, not to be seen by* DAISY.

The OLD GENTLEMAN, *the* LOGICIAN, *the* GROCER *and his* WIFE
move to centre-stage and say together:

ALL: Well, of all things!
JEAN *and*
BERENGER: Well, of all things!

> *A piteous mewing is heard, then an equally piteous cry of a
> woman.*

ALL: Oh!

> *Almost at the same time, and as the noises are rapidly dying
> away the* HOUSEWIFE *appears without her basket but holding the
> blood-stained corpse of her cat in her arms.*

HOUSEWIFE (*wailing*): It ran over my cat, it ran over my cat!
WAITRESS: It ran over her cat!

> *The* GROCER, *his* WIFE (*at the window*), *the* OLD GENTLEMAN,
> DAISY *and the* LOGICIAN *crowd round the* HOUSEWIFE, *saying*:

ALL: What a tragedy, poor little thing!
OLD GENTLEMAN: Poor little thing!
DAISY *and*
WAITRESS: Poor little thing!
GROCER'S WIFE (*at the window*): ⎫
OLD GENTLEMAN: ⎬ Poor little thing!
LOGICIAN: ⎭
PROPRIETOR (*to the* WAITRESS, *pointing to the broken glasses and the
upturned chairs*): Don't just stand there! Clear up the mess!

> JEAN *and* BERENGER *also rush over to the* HOUSEWIFE *who con-
> tinues to lament, her dead cat in her arms.*

WAITRESS (*moving to the café terrace to pick up the broken glasses and
the chairs, and looking over her shoulder at the* HOUSEWIFE): Oh,
poor little thing!
PROPRIETOR (*pointing, for the* WAITRESS's *benefit, to the debris*): Over
there, over there!

OLD GENTLEMAN (*to the* GROCER): Well, what do you think of that?

BERENGER (*to the* HOUSEWIFE): You mustn't cry like that, it's too heart-breaking!

DAISY (*to* BERENGER): Were you there, Mr. Berenger? Did you see it?

BERENGER (*to* DAISY): Good morning, Miss Daisy, you must excuse me, I haven't had a chance to shave . . .

PROPRIETOR (*supervising the clearing up of the debris, then glancing towards the* HOUSEWIFE): Poor little thing!

WAITRESS (*clearing up the mess, her back to the* HOUSEWIFE): Poor little thing!

> *These remarks must obviously be made very rapidly, almost simultaneously.*

GROCER'S WIFE (*at window*): That's going too far!

JEAN: That's going too far!

HOUSEWIFE (*lamenting, and cradling the dead cat in her arms*): My poor little pussy, my poor little cat.

OLD GENTLEMAN (*to the* HOUSEWIFE): What can you do, dear lady, cats are only mortal.

LOGICIAN: What do you expect, Madame? All cats are mortal! One must accept that.

HOUSEWIFE (*lamenting*): My little cat, my poor little cat.

PROPRIETOR (*to the* WAITRESS *whose apron is full of broken glass*): Throw that in the dustbin! (*He has picked up the chairs.*) You owe me a thousand francs.

WAITRESS (*moving into the café*): All you think of is money!

GROCER'S WIFE (*to the* HOUSEWIFE *from window*): Don't upset yourself!

OLD GENTLEMAN (*to the* HOUSEWIFE): Don't upset yourself, dear lady!

GROCER'S WIFE (*from window*): It's very upsetting a thing like that!

HOUSEWIFE: My little cat, my little cat!

DAISY: Yes, it's very upsetting a thing like that.

OLD GENTLEMAN (*supporting the* HOUSEWIFE, *and guiding her to a table on the terrace followed by the others*): Sit down here, dear lady.

JEAN (*to the* OLD GENTLEMAN): Well, what do you think of that?

GROCER (*to the* LOGICIAN): Well, what do you think of that?

GROCER'S WIFE (*to* DAISY, *from window*): Well, what do you think of that?

PROPRIETOR (*to the* WAITRESS, *who comes back while they are installing the weeping* HOUSEWIFE *at one of the terrace tables, still cradling her dead cat*): A glass of water for the lady.

OLD GENTLEMAN (*to the* HOUSEWIFE): Sit down, dear lady!

JEAN: Poor woman!

GROCER'S WIFE (*from window*): Poor cat!

BERENGER (*to the* WAITRESS): Better give her a brandy.

PROPRIETOR (*to the* WAITRESS): A brandy! (*Pointing to* BERENGER.) This gentleman is paying!

WAITRESS (*going into the café*): One brandy, right away!

HOUSEWIFE (*sobbing*): I don't want any, I don't want any!

GROCER: It went past my shop a little while ago.

JEAN (*to the* GROCER): It wasn't the same one!

GROCER (*to* JEAN): But I could have . . .

GROCER'S WIFE: Yes it was, it was the same one.

DAISY: Did it go past twice, then?

PROPRIETOR: I think it was the same one.

JEAN: No, it was not the same rhinoceros. The one that went by first had two horns on its nose, it was an Asiatic rhinoceros; this only had one, it was an African rhinoceros!

The WAITRESS *appears with a glass of brandy and takes it to the* HOUSEWIFE.

OLD GENTLEMAN: Here's a drop of brandy to pull you together.

HOUSEWIFE (*in tears*): No . . . o . . . o . . .

BERENGER (*suddenly unnerved, to* JEAN): You're talking nonsense . . . How could you possibly tell about the horns? The animal flashed past at such speed, we hardly even saw it . . .

DAISY (*to the* HOUSEWIFE): Go on, it will do you good!

OLD GENTLEMAN (*to* BERENGER): Very true. It did go fast.

PROPRIETOR (*to the* HOUSEWIFE): Just have a taste, it's good.

BERENGER (*to* JEAN): You had no time to count its horns . . .

GROCER'S WIFE (*to the* WAITRESS, *from window*): Make her drink it

BERENGER (*to* JEAN): What's more, it was travelling in a cloud of dust.

DAISY (*to the* HOUSEWIFE): Drink it up.

OLD GENTLEMAN (*to the* HOUSEWIFE): Just a sip, dear little lady . . . be brave . . .

The WAITRESS *forces her to drink it by putting the glass to her lips; the* HOUSEWIFE *feigns refusal, but drinks all the same.*

WAITRESS: There, you see!

GROCER'S WIFE (*from her window*)

and DAISY: There, you see!

JEAN (*to* BERENGER): I don't have to grope my way through a fog. I can calculate quickly, my mind is clear!

OLD GENTLEMAN (*to the* HOUSEWIFE): Better now?

BERENGER (*to* JEAN): But it had its head thrust down.

PROPRIETOR (*to the* HOUSEWIFE): Now wasn't that good?

JEAN (*to* BERENGER): Precisely, one could see all the better.

HOUSEWIFE (*after having drunk*): My little cat!

BERENGER (*irritated*): Utter nonsense!

GROCER'S WIFE (*to the* HOUSEWIFE, *from window*): I've got another cat you can have.

JEAN (*to* BERENGER): What me? You dare to accuse me of talking nonsense?

HOUSEWIFE (*to the* GROCER'S WIFE): I'll never have another! (*She weeps, cradling her cat.*)

BERENGER (*to* JEAN): Yes, absolute, blithering nonsense!

PROPRIETER (*to the* HOUSEWIFE): You have to accept these things!

JEAN (*to* BERENGER): I've never talked nonsense in my life!

OLD GENTLEMAN (*to the* HOUSEWIFE): Try and be philosophic about it!

BERENGER (*to* JEAN): You're just a pretentious show-off— (*Raising his voice.*) a pedant!

PROPRIETOR (*to* JEAN *and* BERENGER): Now, gentlemen!

BERENGER (*to* JEAN, *continuing*): . . . and what's more, a pedant who's not certain of his facts because in the first place it's the Asiatic rhinoceros with only one horn on its nose, and it's the African with two . . .

The other characters leave the HOUSEWIFE *and crowd round* JEAN *and* BERENGER *who argue at the top of their voices.*

JEAN (*to* BERENGER): You're wrong, it's the other way about!

HOUSEWIFE (*left alone*): He was so sweet!

BERENGER: Do you want to bet?

WAITRESS: They want to make a bet!

DAISY (*to* BERENGER): Don't excite yourself, Mr. Berenger.

JEAN (*to* BERENGER): I'm not betting with you. If anybody's got two horns, it's you! You Asiatic Mongol!

WAITRESS: Oh!

GROCER'S WIFE (*from window to her husband*): They're going to have a fight!

GROCER (*to his wife*): Nonsense, it's just a bet!

PROPRIETOR (*to* JEAN *and* BERENGER): We don't want any scenes here!

OLD GENTLEMAN: Now look . . . What kind of rhinoceros has one horn on its nose? (*To the* GROCER.) You're a tradesman, you should know.

GROCER'S WIFE (*to her husband*): Yes, you should know!

BERENGER (*to* JEAN): I've got no horns. And I never will have.

GROCER (*to the* OLD GENTLEMAN): Tradesmen can't be expected to know everything.

JEAN (*to* BERENGER): Oh yes, you have!

BERENGER (*to* JEAN): I'm not Asiatic either. And in any case, Asiatics are people the same as everyone else . . .

WAITRESS: Yes, Asiatics are people the same as we are . . .

OLD GENTLEMAN (*to the* PROPRIETOR): That's true!

PROPRIETOR (*to the* WAITRESS): Nobody's asking for your opinion!

DAISY (*to the* PROPRIETOR): She's right. They're people the same as we are.

The HOUSEWIFE *continues to lament throughout this discussion.*

HOUSEWIFE: He was so gentle, just like one of us.

JEAN (*beside himself*): They're yellow!

The LOGICIAN, *a little to one side between the* HOUSEWIFE *and the group which has formed round* JEAN *and* BERENGER, *follows the controversy attentively, without taking part.*

Good-bye gentlemen! (*To* BERENGER.) You, I will not deign to include!

HOUSEWIFE: He was devoted to us! (*She sobs.*)

DAISY: Now listen a moment, Mr. Berenger, and you, too, Mr. Jean . . .

OLD GENTLEMAN: I once had some friends who were Asiatics! But perhaps they weren't real ones . . .

PROPRIETOR: I've known some real ones.

WAITRESS (*to the* GROCER'S WIFE): I had an Asiatic friend once.

HOUSEWIFE (*still sobbing*): I had him when he was a little kitten.

JEAN (*still quite beside himself*): They're yellow, I tell you, bright yellow!

BERENGER (*to* JEAN): Whatever they are, you're bright red!

GROCER'S WIFE (*from window*)
and WAITRESS: Oh!

PROPRIETOR: This is getting serious!

HOUSEWIFE: He was so clean. He always used his tray.

JEAN (*to* BERENGER): If that's how you feel, it's the last time you'll see me. I'm not wasting my time with a fool like you.

HOUSEWIFE: He always made himself understood.

> JEAN *goes off right, very fast and furious . . . but doubles back before making his final exit.*

OLD GENTLEMAN (*to the* GROCER): There are white Asiatics as well, and black and blue, and even some like us.

JEAN (*to* BERENGER): You drunkard!

> *Everybody looks at him in consternation.*

BERENGER (*to* JEAN): I'm not going to stand for that!

ALL (*looking in* JEAN's *direction*): Oh!

HOUSEWIFE: He could almost talk—in fact he did.

DAISY (*to* BERENGER): You shouldn't have made him angry.

BERENGER (*to* DAISY): It wasn't my fault.

PROPRIETOR (*to the* WAITRESS): Go and get a little coffin for the poor thing . . .

OLD GENTLEMAN (*to* BERENGER): I think you're right. It's the Asiatic rhinoceros with two horns and the African with one . . .

GROCER: But he was saying the opposite.

DAISY (*to* BERENGER): You were both wrong!

OLD GENTLEMAN (*to* BERENGER): Even so, you were right.

WAITRESS (*to the* HOUSEWIFE): Come with me, we're going to put him in a little box.

HOUSEWIFE (*sobbing desperately*): No, never!

GROCER: If you don't mind my saying so, I think Mr. Jean was right.

DAISY (*turning to the* HOUSEWIFE): Now, you must be reasonable!

> DAISY *and the* WAITRESS *lead the* HOUSEWIFE, *with her dead cat, towards the café entrance.*

OLD GENTLEMAN (*to* DAISY *and the* WAITRESS): Would you like me to come with you?

GROCER: The Asiatic rhinoceros has one horn and the African rhinoceros has two. And vice versa.

DAISY (*to the* OLD GENTLEMAN): No, don't you bother.

DAISY *and the* WAITRESS *enter the café leading the inconsolable* HOUSEWIFE.

GROCER'S WIFE (*to the* GROCER, *from window*): Oh you always have to be different from everybody else!

BERENGER (*aside, whilst the others continue to discuss the horns of the rhinoceros*): Daisy was right, I should never have contradicted him.

PROPRIETOR (*to the* GROCER'S WIFE): Your husband's right, the Asiatic rhinoceros has two horns and the African one must have two, and vice versa.

BERENGER (*aside*): He can't stand being contradicted. The slightest disagreement makes him fume.

OLD GENTLEMAN (*to the* PROPRIETOR): You're mistaken, my friend.

PROPRIETOR (*to the* OLD GENTLEMAN): I'm very sorry, I'm sure.

BERENGER (*aside*): His temper's his only fault.

GROCER'S WIFE (*from window, to the* OLD GENTLEMAN, *the* PROPRIETOR *and the* GROCER): Maybe they're both the same.

BERENGER (*aside*): Deep down, he's got a heart of gold; he's done me many a good turn.

PROPRIETOR (*to the* GROCER'S WIFE): If the one has two horns, then the other must have one.

OLD GENTLEMAN: Perhaps it's the other with two and the one with one.

BERENGER (*aside*): I'm sorry I wasn't more accommodating. But why is he so obstinate? I didn't want to exasperate him. (*To the others.*) He's always making fantastic statements! Always trying to dazzle people with his knowledge. He never will admit he's wrong.

OLD GENTLEMAN (*to* BERENGER): Have you any proof?

BERENGER: Proof of what?

OLD GENTLEMAN: Of the statement you made just now which started the unfortunate row with your friend.

GROCER (*to* BERENGER): Yes, have you any proof?

OLD GENTLEMAN (*to* BERENGER): How do you know that one of the two rhinoceroses has one horn and the other two? And which is which?

GROCER'S WIFE: He doesn't know any more than we do.

BERENGER: In the first place we don't know that there were two. I myself believe there was only one.

PROPRIETOR: Well, let's say there were two. Does the single-horned one come from Asia?

OLD GENTLEMAN: No. It's the one from Africa with two, I think.

PROPRIETOR: Which is two-horned?

GROCER: It's not the one from Africa.

GROCER'S WIFE: It's not easy to agree on this.

OLD GENTLEMAN: But the problem must be cleared up.

LOGICIAN (*emerging from his isolation*): Excuse me gentlemen for interrupting. But that is not the question. Allow me to introduce myself . . .

HOUSEWIFE (*coming out of the café in tears*): He's a logician.

PROPRIETOR: Oh! A logician, is he?

OLD GENTLEMAN (*introducing the* LOGICIAN *to* BERENGER): My friend, the Logician.

BERENGER: Very happy to meet you.

LOGICIAN (*continuing*): Professional Logician; my card. (*He shows his card.*)

BERENGER: It's a great honour.

GROCER: A great honour for all of us.

PROPRIETOR: Would you mind telling us then, sir, if the African rhinoceros is single-horned . . .

OLD GENTLEMAN: Or bicorned . . .

GROCER'S WIFE: And is the Asiatic rhinoceros bicorned . . .

GROCER: Or unicorned.

LOGICIAN: Exactly, that is not the question. Let me make myself clear.

GROCER: But it's still what we want to find out.

LOGICIAN: Kindly allow me to speak, gentlemen.

OLD GENTLEMAN: Let him speak!

GROCER'S WIFE (*to the* GROCER, *from window*): Give him a chance to speak.

PROPRIETOR: We're listening, sir.

LOGICIAN (*to* BERENGER): I'm addressing you in particular. And all the others present as well.

GROCER: Us as well . . .

LOGICIAN: You see, you have got away from the problem which instigated the debate. In the first place you were deliberating whether or not the rhinoceros which passed by just now was the same one that passed by earlier, or whether it was another. That is the question to decide.

BERENGER: Yes, but how?

LOGICIAN: Thus: you may have seen on two occasions a single rhinoceros bearing a single horn . . .

GROCER (*repeating the words, as if to understand better*): On two occasions a single rhinoceros . . .

PROPRIETOR (*doing the same*): Bearing a single horn . . .

LOGICIAN: . . . or you may have seen on two occasions a single rhinoceros with two horns.

OLD GENTLEMAN (*repeating the words*): A single rhinoceros with two horns on two occasions . . .

LOGICIAN: Exactly. Or again, you may have seen one rhinoceros with one horn, and then another also with a single horn.

GROCER'S WIFE (*from window*): Ha, ha . . .

LOGICIAN: Or again, an initial rhinoceros with two horns, followed by a second with two horns . . .

PROPRIETOR: That's true.

LOGICIAN: Now, if you had seen . . .

GROCER: If we'd seen . . .

OLD GENTLEMAN: Yes, if we'd seen . . .

LOGICIAN: If on the first occasion you had seen a rhinoceros with two horns . . .

PROPRIETOR: With two horns . . .

LOGICIAN: And on the second occasion, a rhinoceros with one horn . . .

GROCER: With one horn . . .

LOGICIAN: That wouldn't be conclusive either.

OLD GENTLEMAN: Even that wouldn't be conclusive.

PROPRIETOR: Why not?

GROCER'S WIFE: Oh, I don't get it at all.

GROCER: Shoo! Shoo!

The GROCER'S WIFE *shrugs her shoulders and withdraws from her window.*

LOGICIAN: For it is possible that since its first appearance, the rhinoceros may have lost one of its horns, and that the first and second transit were still made by a single beast.

BERENGER: I see, but . . .

OLD GENTLEMAN (*interrupting* BERENGER): Don't interrupt!

LOGICIAN: It may also be that two rhinoceroses both with two horns may each have lost a horn.

OLD GENTLEMAN: That is possible.

PROPRIETOR: Yes, that's possible.

GROCER: Why not?

BERENGER: Yes, but in any case . . .

OLD GENTLEMAN (*to* BERENGER): Don't interrupt.

LOGICIAN: If you could prove that on the first occasion you saw a rhinoceros with one horn, either Asiatic or African . . .

OLD GENTLEMAN: Asiatic or African . . .

LOGICIAN: And on the second occasion a rhinoceros with two horns . . .

GROCER: One with two . . .

LOGICIAN: No matter whether African or Asiatic . . .

OLD GENTLEMAN: African or Asiatic . . .

LOGICIAN: . . . we could then conclude that we were dealing with two different rhinoceroses, for it is hardly likely that a second horn could grow sufficiently in a space of a few minutes to be visible on the nose of a rhinoceros.

OLD GENTLEMAN: It's hardly likely.

LOGICIAN (*enchanted with his discourse*): That would imply one rhinoceros either Asiatic or African . . .

OLD GENTLEMAN: Asiatic or African . . .

LOGICIAN: . . . and one rhinoceros either African or Asiatic.

PROPRIETOR: African or Asiatic.

GROCER: Er . . . yais.

LOGICIAN: For good logic cannot entertain the possibility that the same creature be born in two places at the same time . . .

OLD GENTLEMAN: Or even successively.

LOGICIAN (*to* OLD GENTLEMAN): Which was to be proved.

BERENGER (*to* LOGICIAN): That seems clear enough, but it doesn't answer the question.

LOGICIAN (*to* BERENGER, *with a knowledgeable smile*): Obviously, my dear sir, but now the problem is correctly posed.

OLD GENTLEMAN: It's quite logical. Quite logical.

LOGICIAN (*raising his hat*): Good-bye, gentlemen.

He retires, going out left, followed by the OLD GENTLEMAN.

OLD GENTLEMAN: Good-bye, gentlemen. (*He raises his hat and follows the* LOGICIAN *out.*)

GROCER: Well, it may be logical . . .

At this moment the HOUSEWIFE *comes out of the café in deep mourning, and carrying a box; she is followed by* DAISY *and the* WAITRESS *as if for a funeral. The* cortège *moves towards the right exit.*

. . . it may be logical, but are we going to stand for our cats being run down under our very eyes by one-horned rhinoceroses or two, whether they're Asiatic or African? (*He indicates with a theatrical gesture the* cortège *which is just leaving.*)

PROPRIETOR: He's absolutely right! We're not standing for our cats being run down by rhinoceroses or anything else!

GROCER: We're not going to stand for it!

GROCER'S WIFE (*sticking her head round the shop door, to her husband*): Are you coming in? The customers will be here any minute.

GROCER (*moving to the shop*): No, we're not standing for it.

BERENGER: I should never have quarrelled with Jean! (*To the* PROPRIETOR.) Get me a brandy! A double!

PROPRIETOR: Coming up! (*He goes into the café for the brandy.*)

BERENGER (*alone*): I never should have quarrelled with Jean. I shouldn't have got into such a rage!

The PROPRIETOR *comes out carrying a large glass of brandy.*

I feel too upset to go to the museum. I'll cultivate my mind some other time. (*He takes the glass of brandy and drinks it.*)

Curtain.

ACT TWO

A government office, or the office of a private concern—such as a large firm of law publications. Up-stage centre, a large double door, above which a notice reads: 'Chef du Service.' Up-stage left, near to the Head of the Department's door, stands DAISY'S *little table with a typewriter. By the left wall, between a door which leads to the staircase and* DAISY'S *table, stands another table on which the time sheets are placed, which the employees sign on arrival. The door leading to the staircase is down-stage left. The top steps of the staircase can be seen, the top of a stair-rail and a small landing. In the foreground, a table with two chairs. On the table: printing proofs, an inkwell, pens; this is the table where* BOTARD *and* BERENGER *work;* BERENGER *will sit on the left chair,* BOTARD *on the right. Near to the right wall, another bigger, rectangular table, also covered with papers, proofs, etc.*

Two more chairs stand at each end of this table—more elegant and imposing chairs. This is the table of DUDARD *and* MR. BOEUF. DUDARD *will sit on the chair next to the wall, the other employees facing him. He acts as Deputy-Head. Between the up-stage door and the right wall, there is a window. If the theatre has an orchestra pit it would be preferable to have simply a window frame in front of the stage, facing the auditorium. In the rigt-hand corner, up-stage, a coat-stand, on which grey blouses or old coats are hung. The coat-stand could also be placed down-stage, near to the right wall.*

On the walls are rows of books and dusty documents. On the back wall, left, above the shelves, there are signs: 'Jurisprudence,' 'Codes'; on the right-hand wall which can be slightly on an angle, the signs read: 'Le Journal Officiel,' 'Lois fiscales.' Above the Head of the Department's door a clock registers three minutes past nine.

When the curtain rises, DUDARD *is standing near his chair, his right profile to the auditorium; on the other side of the desk, left profile to the auditorium, is* BOTARD; *between them, also near to the desk, facing*

406

the auditorium, stands the Head of the Department; DAISY *is near to the Chief, a little up-stage of him. She holds some sheets of typing paper. On the table round which the three characters stand, a large open newspaper lies on the printing proofs.*

When the curtain rises the characters remain fixed for a few seconds in position for the first line of dialogue. They make a tableau vivant. *The same effect marks the beginning of the first act.*

The Head of the Department is about forty, very correctly dressed: dark blue suit, a rosette of the Legion of Honour, starched collar, black tie, large brown moustache. He is MR. PAPILLON.

DUDARD, *thirty-five years old; grey suit; he wears black lustrine sleeves to protect his coat. He may wear spectacles. He is a quite tall, young employee with a future. If the Department Head became the Assistant Director he would take his place:* BOTARD *does not like him.* BOTARD: *former schoolteacher; short, he has a proud air, and wears a little white moustache; a brisk sixty year-old: (he knows everything, understands everything, judges everything). He wears a Basque beret, and wears a long grey blouse during working hours; spectacles on a longish nose; a pencil behind his ear; he also wears protective sleeves at work.* DAISY: *young blonde.*

Later, MRS. BOEUF; *a large woman of some forty to fifty years old, tearful, and breathless.*

As the curtain rises, the characters therefore are standing motionless around the table, right; the Chief with index finger pointing to the newspaper; DUDARD, *with his hand extended in* BOTARD's *direction, seems to be saying: 'so you see!'* BOTARD, *hands in the pocket of his blouse, wears an incredulous smile and seems to say: 'You won't take me in.'* DAISY, *with her typing paper in her hand seems, from her look, to be supporting* DUDARD. *After a few brief seconds,* BOTARD *starts the attack.*

BOTARD: It's all a lot of made-up nonsense.
DAISY: But I saw it, I saw the rhinoceros!
DUDARD: It's in the paper, in black and white, you can't deny that.
BOTARD (*with an air of the greatest scorn*): Pfff!

DUDARD: It's all here; it's down here in the dead cats column! Read it for yourself, Chief.

PAPILLON: 'Yesterday, just before lunch time, in the church square of our town, a cat was trampled to death by a pachyderm.'

DAISY: It wasn't exactly in the church square.

PAPILLON: That's all it says. No other details.

BOTARD: Pfff!

DUDARD: Well, that's clear enough.

BOTARD: I never believe journalists. They're all liars. I don't need them to tell me what to think; I believe what I see with my own eyes. Speaking as a former teacher, I like things to be precise, scientifically valid; I've got a methodical mind.

DUDARD: What's a methodical mind got to do with it?

DAISY (*to* BOTARD): I think it's stated very precisely, Mr. Botard.

BOTARD: You call that precise? And what, pray, does it mean by a pachyderm? What does the editor of a dead cats column understand by a pachyderm? He doesn't say. And what does he mean by a cat?

DUDARD: Everybody knows what a cat is.

BOTARD: Does it concern a male cat or a female? What breed was it? And what colour? The colour bar is something I feel strongly about. I hate it.

PAPILLON: What has the colour bar to do with it, Mr. Botard? It's quite beside the point.

BOTARD: Please forgive me, Mr. Papillon. But you can't deny that the colour problem is one of the great stumbling blocks of our time.

DUDARD: I know that, we all know that, but it has nothing to do with . . .

BOTARD: It's not an issue to be dismissed lightly, Mr. Dudard. The course of history has shown that racial prejudice . . .

DUDARD: I tell you it doesn't enter into it.

BOTARD: I'm not so sure.

PAPILLON: The colour bar is not the issue at stake.

BOTARD: One should never miss an occasion to denounce it.

DAISY: But we told you that none of us is in favour of the colour bar. You're obscuring the issue; it's simply a question of a cat being run over by a pachyderm—in this case, a rhinoceros.

BOTARD: I'm a Northerner myself. Southerners have got too much imagination. Perhaps it was merely a flea run over by a mouse. People make mountains out of molehills.

PAPILLON (*to* DUDARD): Let us try and get things clear. Did you yourself, with your own eyes, see a rhinoceros strolling through the streets of the town?

DAISY: It didn't stroll, it ran.

DUDARD: No, I didn't see it personally. But a lot of very reliable people...!

BOTARD (*interrupting him*): It's obvious they were just making it up. You put too much trust in these journalists; they don't care what they invent to sell their wretched newspapers and please the bosses they serve! And you mean to tell me they've taken you in—you, a qualified man of law! Forgive me for laughing! Ha! Ha! Ha!

DAISY: But I saw it, I saw the rhinoceros. I'd take my oath on it.

BOTARD: Get away with you! And I thought you were a sensible girl!

DAISY: Mr. Botard, I can see straight! And I wasn't the only one; there were plenty of other people watching.

BOTARD: Pfff! They were probably watching something else! A few idlers with nothing to do, work-shy loafers!

DUDARD: It happened yesterday, Sunday.

BOTARD: I work on Sundays as well. I've no time for priests who do their utmost to get you to church, just to prevent you from working, and earning your daily bread by the sweat of your brow.

PAPILLON (*indignant*): Oh!

BOTARD: I'm sorry, I didn't mean to offend you. The fact that I despise religion doesn't mean I don't esteem it highly. (*To* DAISY.) In any case, do you know what a rhinoceros looks like?

DAISY: It's a... it's a very big, ugly animal.

BOTARD: And you pride yourself on your precise thinking! The rhinoceros, my dear young lady...

PAPILLON: There's no need to start a lecture on the rhinoceros here. We're not in school.

BOTARD: That's a pity.

During these last speeches BERENGER *is seen climbing the last steps of the staircase; he opens the office door cautiously; as he does so one can read the notice on it: 'Editions de Droit.'*

PAPILLON: Well! It's gone nine, Miss Daisy; put the time sheets away. Too bad about the later-comers.

DAISY *goes to the little table, left, on which the time sheets are placed, at the same moment as* BERENGER *enters.*

BERENGER (*entering, whilst the others continue their discussion, to* DAISY): Good morning, Miss Daisy. I'm not late, am I?

BOTARD (*to* DUDARD *and* PAPILLON): I campaign against ignorance wherever I find it . . . !

DAISY (*to* BERENGER): Hurry up, Mr. Berenger.

BOTARD: . . . in palace or humble hut!

DAISY (*to* BERENGER): Quick! Sign the time sheet!

BERENGER: Oh thank you! Has the Boss arrived?

DAISY (*a finger on her lips*): Shh! Yes, he's here.

BERENGER: Here already? (*He hurries to sign the time sheet.*)

BOTARD (*continuing*): No matter where! Even in printing offices.

PAPILLON (*to* BOTARD): Mr. Botard, I consider . . .

BERENGER (*signing the sheet, to* DAISY): But it's not ten past . . .

PAPILLON (*to* BOTARD): I consider you have gone too far.

DUDARD (*to* PAPILLON): I think so too, sir.

PAPILLON (*to* BOTARD): Are you suggesting that Mr. Dudard, my colleague and yours, a law graduate and a first-class employee, is ignorant?

BOTARD: I wouldn't go so far as to say that, but the teaching you get at the university isn't up to what you get at the ordinary schools.

PAPILLON (*to* DAISY): What about that time sheet?

DAISY (*to* PAPILLON): Here it is, sir. (*She hands it to him.*)

BOTARD (*to* DUDARD): There's no clear thinking at the universities, no encouragement for practical observation.

DUDARD (*to* BOTARD): Oh come now!

BERENGER (*to* PAPILLON): Good morning, Mr. Papillon. (*He has been making his way to the coat-rack behind the Chief's back and around the group formed by the three characters; there he takes down his working overall or his well-worn coat, and hangs up his street coat in its place; he changes his coat by the coat-rack, then makes his way to his desk, from the drawer of which he takes out his black protective sleeves, etc.*) Morning, Mr. Papillon! Sorry I was almost late. Morning, Dudard! Morning, Mr. Botard.

PAPILLON: Well Berenger, did you see the rhinoceros by any chance?

BOTARD (*to* DUDARD): All you get at the universities are effete intellectuals with no practical knowledge of life.

DUDARD (*to* BOTARD): Rubbish!

BERENGER (*continuing to arrange his working equipment with excessive zeal as if to make up for his late arrival; in a natural tone to* PAPILLON): Oh yes, I saw it all right.

BOTARD (*turning round*): Pfff!

DAISY: So you see, I'm not mad after all.

BOTARD (*ironic*): Oh, Mr. Berenger says that out of chivalry—he's a very chivalrous man even if he doesn't look it.

DUDARD: What's chivalrous about saying you've seen a rhinoceros?

BOTARD: A lot—when it's said to bolster up a fantastic statement by Miss Daisy. Everybody is chivalrous to Miss Daisy, it's very understandable.

PAPILLON: Don't twist the facts, Mr. Botard. Mr. Berenger took no part in the argument. He's only just arrived.

BERENGER (*to* DAISY): But you did see it, didn't you? We both did.

BOTARD: Pfff! It's possible that Mr. Berenger thought he saw a rhinoceros. (*He makes a sign behind* BERENGER's *back to indicate he drinks.*) He's got such a vivid imagination! Anything's possible with him!

BERENGER: I wasn't alone when I saw the rhinoceros! Or perhaps there were two rhinoceroses.

BOTARD: He doesn't even know how many he saw.

BERENGER: I was with my friend Jean! And other people were there, too.

BOTARD (*to* BERENGER): I don't think you know what you're talking about.

DAISY: It was a unicorned rhinoceros.

BOTARD: Pff! They're in league, the two of them, to have us on.

DUDARD (*to* DAISY): I rather think it had two horns, from what I've heard!

BOTARD: You'd better make up your minds.

PAPILLON (*looking at the time*): That will do, gentlemen, time's getting on.

BOTARD: Did you see one rhinoceros, Mr. Berenger, or two rhinoceroses?

BERENGER: Well, it's hard to say!

BOTARD: You don't know. Miss Daisy saw one unicorned rhinoceros.

What about your rhinoceros, Mr. Berenger, if indeed there was one, did it have one horn or two?

BERENGER: Exactly, that's the whole problem.

BOTARD: And it's all very dubious.

DAISY: Oh!

BOTARD: I don't mean to be offensive. But I don't believe a word of it. No rhinoceros has ever been seen in this country!

DAISY: There's a first time for everything.

BOTARD: It has never been seen! Except in school-book illustrations. Your rhinoceroses are a flower of some washerwoman's imagination.

BERENGER: The word 'flower' applied to a rhinoceros seems a bit out of place.

DUDARD: Very true.

BOTARD (*continuing*): Your rhinoceros is a myth!

DAISY: A myth?

PAPILLON: Gentlemen I think it is high time we started to work.

BOTARD (*to* DAISY): A myth—like flying saucers.

DUDARD: But nevertheless a cat was trampled to death—that you can't deny.

BERENGER: I was a witness to that.

DUDARD (*pointing to* BERENGER): In front of witnesses.

BOTARD: Yes, and what a witness!

PAPILLON: Gentlemen, gentlemen!

BOTARD (*to* DUDARD): An example of collective psychosis, Mr. Dudard. Just like religion—the opiate of the people!

DAISY: Well I believe flying saucers exist!

BOTARD: Pfff!

PAPILLON (*firmly*): That's quite enough. There's been enough gossip! Rhinoceros or no rhinoceros, saucers or no saucers, work must go on! You're not paid to waste your time arguing about real or imaginary animals.

BOTARD: Imaginary!

DUDARD: Real!

DAISY: Very real!

PAPILLON: Gentlemen, I remind you once again that we are in working hours. I am putting an end to this futile discussion.

BOTARD (*wounded and ironic*): Very well, Mr. Papillon. You are the Chief. Your wishes are our commands.

PAPILLON: Get on, gentlemen. I don't want to be forced to make a

deduction from your salaries! Mr. Dudard, how is your report
on the alcoholic repression law coming along?

DUDARD: I'm just finishing it off, sir.

PAPILLON: Then do so. It's very urgent. Mr. Berenger and Mr. Botard,
have you finished correcting the proofs for the wine trade control
regulations?

BERENGER: Not yet, Mr. Papillon. But they're well on the way.

PAPILLON: Then finish off the corrections together. The printers are
waiting. And Miss Daisy, you bring the letters to my office for
signature. Hurry up and get them typed.

DAISY: Very good, Mr. Papillon.

> DAISY *goes and types at her little desk.* DUDARD *sits at his desk
> and starts to work.* BERENGER *and* BOTARD *sit at their little tables
> in profile to the auditorium.* BOTARD, *his back to the staircase,
> seems in a bad temper.* BERENGER *is passive and limp; he spreads
> the proofs on the table, passes the manuscript to* BOTARD; BOTARD
> *sits down grumbling, whilst* PAPILLON *exits banging the door
> loudly.*

PAPILLON: I shall see you shortly, gentlemen. (*Goes out.*)

BERENGER (*reading and correcting whilst* BOTARD *checks the manu-
script with a pencil*): Laws relating to the control of proprietary
wine produce . . . (*He corrects.*) control with one L . . . (*He corrects.*) proprietary . . . one P, proprietary . . . The controlled
wines of the Bordeaux region, the lower sections of the upper
slopes . . .

BOTARD: I haven't got that! You've skipped a line.

BERENGER: I'll start again. The Wine Control!

DUDARD (*to* BERENGER *and* BOTARD): Please don't read so loud. I can't
concentrate with you shouting at the tops of your voices.

BOTARD (*to* DUDARD, *over* BERENGER'S *head, resuming the recent discussion, whilst* BERENGER *continues the corrections on his own for
a few moments; he moves his lips noiselessly as he reads*): It's all
a hoax.

DUDARD: What's all a hoax?

BOTARD: Your rhinoceros business, of course. You've been making all
this propaganda to get these rumours started!

DUDARD (*interrupting his work*): What propaganda?

BERENGER (*breaking in*): No question of any propaganda.

DAISY (*interrupting her typing*): Do I have to tell you again, I saw it . . . I actually saw it, and others did, too.

DUDARD (*to* BOTARD): You make me laugh! Propaganda! Propaganda for what?

BOTARD (*to* DUDARD): Oh you know more about that than I do. Don't make out you're so innocent.

DUDARD (*getting angry*): At any rate, Mr. Botard, I'm not in the pay of any furtive underground organization.

BOTARD: That's an insult, I'm not standing for that . . . (*Rises.*)

BERENGER (*pleading*): Now, now, Mr. Botard . . .

DAISY (*to* DUDARD, *who has also risen*): Now, now, Mr. Dudard . . .

BOTARD: I tell you it's an insult.

> MR. PAPILLON'S *door suddenly opens.* BOTARD *and* DUDARD *sit down again quickly;* MR. PAPILLON *is holding the time sheet in his hand; there is silence at his appearance.*

PAPILLON: Is Mr. Boeuf not in today?

BERENGER (*looking around*): No, he isn't. He must be absent.

PAPILLON: Just when I needed him. (*To* DAISY.) Did he let anyone know he was ill or couldn't come in?

DAISY: He didn't say anything to me.

PAPILLON (*opening his door wide, and coming in*): If this goes on I shall fire him. It's not the first time he's played me this trick. Up to now I haven't said anything, but it's not going on like this. Has anyone got the key to his desk?

> *At this moment* MRS. BOEUF *enters. She has been seen during the last speech coming up the stairs. She bursts through the door, out of breath, apprehensive.*

BERENGER: Oh here's Mrs. Boeuf.

DAISY: Morning, Mrs. Boeuf.

MRS. BOEUF: Morning, Mr. Papillon. Good morning everyone.

PAPILLON: Well, where's your husband? What's happened to him? Is it too much trouble for him to come any more?

MRS. BOEUF (*breathless*): Please excuse him, my husband I mean . . . he went to visit his family for the week-end. He's got a touch of flu.

PAPILLON: So he's got a touch of flu, has he?

MRS. BOEUF (*handing a paper to* PAPILLON): He says so in the telegram.
He hopes to be back on Wednesday . . . (*Almost fainting.*) Could
I have a glass of water . . . and sit down a moment . . .

BERENGER *takes his own chair centre-stage, on which she flops.*

PAPILLON (*to* DAISY): Give her a glass of water.
DAISY: Yes, straightaway! (*She goes to get her a glass of water, and
gives it to her during the following speeches.*)
DUDARD (*to* PAPILLON): She must have a weak heart.
PAPILLON: It's a great nuisance that Mr. Boeuf can't come. But that's
no reason for you to go to pieces.
MRS. BOEUF (*with difficulty*): It's not . . . it's . . . well I was chased here
all the way from the house by a rhinoceros . . .
BERENGER: How many horns did it have?
BOTARD (*guffawing*): Don't make me laugh!
DUDARD (*indignant*): Give her a chance to speak!
MRS. BOEUF (*making a great effort to be exact, and pointing in the
direction of the staircase*): It's down there, by the entrance. It
seemed to want to come upstairs.

At this moment a noise is heard. The staircase steps are seen to
crumble under an obviously formidable weight. From below an
anguished trumpeting is heard. As the dust clears after the
collapse of the staircase, the staircase landing is seen to be hanging in space.

DAISY: My God!
MRS. BOEUF (*seated, her hand on her heart*): Oh! Ah!

BERENGER *runs to administer to* MRS. BOEUF, *patting her cheeks
and making her drink.*

BERENGER: Keep calm!

Meanwhile PAPILLON, DUDARD *and* BOTARD *rush left, jostling
each other in their efforts to open the door, and stand covered
in dust on the landing; the trumpetings continue to be heard*

DAISY (*to* MRS. BOEUF): Are you feeling better now, Mrs. Boeuf?

PAPILLON (*on the landing*): There it is! Down there! It is one!

BOTARD: I can't see a thing. It's an illusion.

DUDARD: Of course it's one, down there, turning round and round.

DUDARD: It can't get up here. There's no staircase any longer.

BOTARD: It's most strange. What can it mean?

DUDARD (*turning towards* BERENGER): Come and look. Come and have a look at your rhinoceros.

BERENGER: I'm coming.

> BERENGER *rushes to the landing, followed by* DAISY *who abandons* MRS. BOEUF.

PAPILLON (*to* BERENGER): You're the rhinoceros expert—take a good look.

BERENGER: I'm no rhinoceros expert . . .

DAISY: Oh look at the way it's going round and round. It looks as if it was in pain . . . what can it want?

DUDARD: It seems to be looking for someone. (*To* BOTARD.) Can you see it now?

BOTARD (*vexed*): Yes, yes, I can see it.

DAISY (*to* PAPILLON): Perhaps we're all seeing things. You as well . . .

BOTARD: I never see things. Something is definitely down there.

DUDARD (*to* BOTARD). What do you mean, something?

PAPILLON (*to* BERENGER): It's obviously a rhinoceros. That's what you saw before, isn't it? (*To* DAISY.) And you, too?

DAISY: Definitely.

BERENGER: It's got two horns. It's an African rhinoceros, or Asiatic rather. Oh! I don't know whether the African rhinoceros has one horn or two.

PAPILLON: It's demolished the staircase—and a good thing, too! When you think how long I've been asking the management to install stone steps in place of that worm-eaten old staircase.

DUDARD: I sent a report a week ago, Chief.

PAPILLON: It was bound to happen, I knew that. I could see it coming, and I was right.

DAISY (*to* PAPILLON, *ironically*): As always.

BERENGER (*to* DUDARD *and* PAPILLON): Now look, are two horns a characteristic of the Asiatic rhinoceros or the African? And is one horn a characteristic of the African or the Asiatic one. . . ?

DAISY: Poor thing, it keeps on trumpeting and going round and round.

What does it want? Oh, it's looking at us! (*To the rhinoceros.*)
Puss, puss, puss . . .

DUDARD: I shouldn't try to stroke it, it's probably not tame . . .

PAPILLON: In any case, it's out of reach.

The rhinoceros gives a horrible trumpeting.

DAISY: Poor thing!

BERENGER (*to* BOTARD, *still insisting*): You're very well informed, don't
you think that the ones with two horns are . . .

PAPILLON: What are you rambling on about, Berenger? You're still a
bit under the weather, Mr. Botard was right.

BOTARD: How can it be possible in a civilized country. . . ?

DAISY (*to* BOTARD): All right. But does it exist or not?

BOTARD: It's all an infamous plot! (*With a political orator's gesture
he points to* DUDARD, *quelling him with a look.*) It's all your fault!

DUDARD: Why mine, rather than yours?

BOTARD (*furious*): Mine? It's always the little people who get the
blame. If I had my way . . .

PAPILLON: We're in a fine mess with no staircase.

DAISY (*to* BOTARD *and* DUDARD): Calm down, this is no time to quarrel!

PAPILLON: It's all the management's fault.

DAISY: Maybe. But how are we going to get down?

PAPILLON (*joking amorously and caressing* DAISY'S *cheek*): I'll take you
in my arms and we'll float down together.

DAISY (*rejecting* PAPILLON'S *advances*): You keep your horny hands off
my face, you old pachyderm!

PAPILLON: I was only joking!

Meanwhile the rhinoceros has continued its trumpeting. MRS.
BOEUF *has risen and joined the group. For a few moments she
stares fixedly at the rhinoceros turning round and round below;
suddenly she lets out a terribly cry.*

MRS. BOEUF: My God! It can't be true!

BERENGER (*to* MRS. BOEUF): What's the matter?

MRS. BOEUF: It's my husband. Oh Boeuf, my poor Boeuf, what's happened to you?

DAISY (*to* MRS. BOEUF): Are you positive?

MRS. BOEUF: I recognize him, I recognize him!

The rhinoceros replies with a violent but tender trumpeting.

PAPILLON: Well! That's the last straw. This time he's fired for good!

DUDARD: Is he insured?

BOTARD (*aside*): I understand it all now . . .

DAISY: How can you collect insurance in a case like this?

MRS. BOEUF (*fainting into* BERENGER's *arms*): Oh! My God!

BERENGER: Oh!

DAISY: Carry her over here!

> BERENGER, *helped by* DUDARD *and* DAISY, *install* MRS. BOEUF *in a chair.*

DUDARD (*while they are carrying her*): Don't upset yourself, Mrs. Boeuf.

MRS. BOEUF: Ah! Oh!

DAISY: Maybe it can all be put right . . .

PAPILLON (*to* DUDARD): Legally, what can be done?

DUDARD: You need to get a solicitor's advice.

BOTARD (*following the procession, raising his hands to heaven*): It's the sheerest madness! What a society!

> *They crowd round* MRS. BOEUF, *pinching her cheeks; she opens her eyes, emits an 'Ah' and closes them again; they continue to pinch her cheeks as* BOTARD *speaks.*

You can be certain of one thing: I shall report this to my union. I don't desert a colleague in the hour of need. It won't be hushed up.

MRS. BOEUF (*coming to*): My poor darling, I can't leave him like that, my poor darling. (*A trumpeting is heard.*) He's calling me. (*Tenderly.*) He's calling me.

DAISY: Feeling better now, Mrs. Boeuf?

DUDARD: She's picking up a bit.

BOTARD (*to* MRS. BOEUF): You can count on the union's support. Would you like to become a member of the committee?

PAPILLON: Work's going to be delayed again. What about the post, Miss Daisy?

DAISY: I want to know first how we're going to get out of here.

PAPILLON: It is a problem. Through the window.

They all go to the window with the exception of MRS. BOEUF
slumped in her chair and BOTARD *who stays centre-stage.*

BOTARD: I know where it came from.

DAISY (*at window*): It's too high.

BERENGER: Perhaps we ought to call the firemen, and get them to
bring ladders!

PAPILLON: Miss Daisy, go to my office and telephone the Fire Brigade.
(*He makes as if to follow her.*)

> DAISY *goes out up-stage and one hears her voice on the telephone
> say: 'Hello, hello, is that the Fire Brigade?' followed by a vague
> sound of telephone conversation.*

MRS. BOEUF (*rising suddenly*): I can't desert him, I can't desert him
now!

PAPILLON: If you want to divorce him . . . you'd be perfectly justified.

DUDARD: You'd be the injured party.

MRS. BOEUF: No! Poor thing! This is not the moment for that. I won't
abandon my husband in such a state.

BOTARD: You're a good woman.

DUDARD (*to* MRS. BOEUF): But what are you going to do?

> *She runs left towards the landing.*

BERENGER: Watch out!

MRS. BOEUF: I can't leave him, I can't leave him now!

DUDARD: Hold her back!

MRS. BOEUF: I'm taking him home!

PAPILLON: What's she trying to do?

MRS. BOEUF (*preparing to jump; on the edge of the landing*): I'm
coming my darling, I'm coming!

BERENGER: She's going to jump.

BOTARD: It's no more than her duty.

DUDARD: She can't do that.

> *Everyone with the exception of* DAISY, *who is still telephoning,
> is near to* MRS. BOEUF *on the landing; she jumps;* BERENGER
> *who tries to restrain her, is left with her skirt in his hand.*

BERENGER: I couldn't hold her back.

The rhinoceros is heard from below, tenderly trumpeting.

VOICE OF MRS. BOEUF: Here I am, my sweet, I'm here now.
DUDARD: She landed on his back in the saddle.
BOTARD: She's a good rider.
VOICE OF MRS. BOEUF: Home now, dear, let's go home.
DUDARD: They're off at a gallop.

DUDARD, BOTARD, BERENGER, PAPILLON *come back on-stage and go to the window.*

BERENGER: They're moving fast.
DUDARD (*to* PAPILLON): Ever done any riding?
PAPILLON: A bit . . . a long time ago . . . (*Turning to the up-stage door, to* DUDARD.) Is she still on the telephone?
BERENGER (*following the course of the rhinoceros*): They're already a long way off. They're out of sight.
DAISY (*coming on-stage*): I had trouble getting the firemen.
BOTARD (*as if concluding an interior monologue*): A fine state of affairs!
DAISY: . . . I had trouble getting the firemen!
PAPILLON: Are there fires all over the place, then?
BERENGER: I agree with Mr. Botard. Mrs. Boeuf's attitude is very moving; she's a woman of feeling.
PAPILLON: It means one employee less, who has to be replaced.
BERENGER: Do you really think he's no use to us any more?
DAISY: No, there aren't any fires, the firemen have been called out for other rhinoceroses.
BERENGER: For other rhinoceroses?
DAISY: Yes, other rhinoceroses. They've been reported all over the town. This morning there were seven, now there are seventeen.
BOTARD: What did I tell you?
DAISY: As many as thirty-two have been reported. They're not official yet, but they're bound to be cònfirmed soon.
BOTARD (*less certain*): Pff!! They always exaggerate.
PAPILLON: Are they coming to get us out of here?
BERENGER: I'm hungry . . . !
DAISY: Yes, they're coming; the firemen are on the way.

PAPILLON: What about the work?

DUDARD: It looks as if it's out of our hands.

PAPILLON: We'll have to make up the lost time.

DUDARD: Well, Mr. Botard, do you still deny all rhinocerotic evidence?

BOTARD: Our union is against your dismissing Mr. Boeuf without notice.

PAPILLON: It's not up to me; we shall see what conclusions they reach at the enquiry.

BOTARD (*to* DUDARD): No, Mr. Dudard, I do not deny the rhinocerotic evidence. I never have.

DUDARD: That's not true.

DAISY: Oh no, that's not true.

BOTARD: I repeat I have never denied it. I just wanted to find out exactly where it was all leading. Because I know my own mind. I'm not content to simply state that a phenomenon exists I make it my business to understand and explain it. At least I could explain it if . . .

DUDARD: Then explain it to us.

DAISY: Yes, explain it, Mr. Botard.

PAPILLON: Explain it, when your colleagues ask you.

BOTARD: I will explain it . . .

DUDARD: We're all listening.

DAISY: I'm most curious.

BOTARD: I will explain it . . . one day . . .

DUDARD: Why not now?

BOTARD (*menacingly; to* MR. PAPILLON): We'll go into the explanation later, in private. (*To everyone.*) I know the whys and the wherefores of this whole business . . .

DAISY: What whys?

BERENGER: What wherefores?

DUDARD: I'd give a lot to know these whys and wherefores . . .

BOTARD (*continuing; with a terrible air*): And I also know the names of those responsible. The names of the traitors. You can't fool me. I'll let you know the purpose and the meaning of this whole plot! I'll unmask the perpetrators!

BERENGER: But who'd want to . . .

DUDARD (*to* BOTARD): You're evading the question, Mr. Botard.

PAPILLON: Let's have no evasions.

BOTARD: Evading? What, me?

DAISY: Just now you accused us of suffering from hallucinations.

BOTARD: Just now, yes. Now the hallucination has become a provocation.

DUDARD: And how do you consider this change came about?

BOTARD: It's an open secret, gentlemen. Even the man in the street knows about it. Only hypocrites pretend not to understand.

> *The noise and hooting of a fire-engine is heard. The brakes are abruptly applied just under the window.*

DAISY: That's the firemen!

BOTARD: There're going to be some big changes made; they won't get away with it as easily as that.

DUDARD: That doesn't mean anything, Mr. Botard. The rhinoceroses exist, and that's that. That's all there is to it.

DAISY (*at the window, looking down*): Up here, firemen!

> *A bustling is heard below, commotion, engine noises.*

VOICE OF FIREMAN: Put up the ladder!

BOTARD (*to* DUDARD): I hold the key to all these happenings, an infallible system of interpretation.

PAPILLON: I want you all back in the office this afternoon.

> *The firemen's ladder is placed against the window.*

BOTARD: Too bad about the office, Mr. Papillon.

PAPILLON: I don't know what the management will say!

DUDARD: These are exceptional circumstances.

BOTARD (*pointing to the window*): They can't force us to come back this way. We'll have to wait till the staircase is repaired.

DUDARD: If anyone breaks a leg, it'll be the management's responsibility.

PAPILLON: That's true.

> *A fireman's helmet is seen, followed by the* FIREMAN.

BERENGER (*to* DAISY, *pointing to the window*): After you Miss Daisy.

FIREMAN: Come on, Miss.

> *The* FIREMAN *takes* DAISY *in his arms; she steps astride the window and disappears with him.*

DUDARD: Good-bye Miss Daisy. See you soon.

DAISY (*disappearing*): See you soon, good-bye!

PAPILLON (*at window*): Telephone me tomorrow morning, Miss Daisy. You can come and type the letters at my house. (*To* BERENGER.) Mr. Berenger, I draw your attention to the fact that we are not on holiday, and that work will resume as soon as possible. (*To the other two.*) You hear what I say, gentlemen?

DUDARD: Of course, Mr. Papillon.

BOTARD: They'll go on exploiting us till we drop, of course.

FIREMAN (*reappearing at window*): Who's next?

PAPILLON (*to all three of them*): Go on!

DUDARD: After you, Mr. Papillon.

BERENGER: After you, Chief.

BOTARD: You first, of course.

PAPILLON (*to* BERENGER): Bring me Miss Daisy's letters. There, on the table.

BERENGER *goes and gets the letters, brings them to* PAPILLON.

FIREMAN: Come on, hurry up. We've not got all day. We've got other calls to make.

BOTARD: What did I tell you?

PAPILLON, *the letters under his arm, steps astride the window.*

PAPILLON (*to the* FIREMAN): Careful of the documents! (*Turning to the others.*) Good-bye, gentlemen.

DUDARD: Good-bye, Mr. Papillon.

BERENGER: Good-bye, Mr. Papillon.

PAPILLON (*he has disappeared; one hears him say*): Careful of my papers. Dudard! Lock up the offices!

DUDARD (*shouting*): Don't you worry, Mr. Papillon. (*To* BOTARD.) After you, Mr. Botard.

BOTARD: I am about to descend, gentlemen. And I am going to take this matter up immediately with the proper authorities. I'll get to the bottom of this so-called mystery. (*He moves to window.*)

DUDARD (*to* BOTARD): I thought it was all perfectly clear to you!

BOTARD (*astride the window*): Your irony doesn't affect me. What I'm after are the proofs and the documents—yes, proof positive of your treason.

DUDARD: That's absurd . . .

BOTARD: Your insults . . .

DUDARD (*interrupting him*): It's you who are insulting me . . .

BOTARD (*disappearing*): I don't insult. I merely prove.

VOICE OF FIREMAN: Come on there!

DUDARD (*to* BERENGER): What are you doing this afternoon? Shall we meet for a drink?

BERENGER: Sorry, I can't. I'm taking advantage of this afternoon off to go and see my friend Jean. I do want to make it up with him, after all. We got carried away. It was all my fault.

The FIREMAN's *head reappears at the window.*

FIREMAN: Come along there!

BERENGER (*pointing to the window*): After you.

DUDARD: After you.

BERENGER: Oh no, after you.

DUDARD: No, I insist, after you.

BERENGER: No, please, after you, after you.

FIREMAN: Hurry up!

DUDARD: After you, after you.

BERENGER: No, after you, after you.

They climb through the window together. The FIREMAN *helps them down, as the curtain falls.*

ACT TWO

JEAN's *house. The layout is roughly the same as Act Two, Scene One. That is to say, the stage is divided into two. To the right, occupying three-quarters or four-fifths of the stage, according to size, is* JEAN's *bedroom. Up-stage, a chair or an armchair, on which* BERENGER *will sit. Right centre, a door leading to* JEAN's *bathroom. When* JEAN *goes in to wash, the noise of a tap is heard, and that of the shower. To the left of the room, a partition divides the stage in two. Centre-stage, the door leading to the stairs. If a less realistic, more stylized décor is preferred, the door may be placed without a partition. To the left is the staircase; the top steps are visible, leading to* JEAN's *flat, the banister and the landing. At the back, on the landing level, is the door to the neighbour's flat. Lower down, at the back, there is a glass door, over which is written: 'Concierge.'*

When the curtain rises, JEAN *is in bed, lying under the blanket, his back to the audience. One hears him cough.*

After a few moments BERENGER *is seen, climbing the top steps of the staircase. He knocks at the door;* JEAN *does not answer.* BERENGER *knocks again.*

BERENGER: Jean! (*He knocks again.*) Jean!

    The door at the end of the landing opens slightly, and a little old man with a white goatee appears.

OLD MAN: What is it?
BERENGER: I want to see Jean. I am a friend of his.
OLD MAN: I thought it was me you wanted. My name's Jean as well, but it's the other one you want.
VOICE OF OLD MAN'S WIFE (*from within the room*): Is it for us?
OLD MAN (*turning to his wife who is not seen*): No, for the other one.
BERENGER (*knocking*): Jean!

OLD MAN: I didn't see him go out. But I saw him last night. He looked in a bad temper.

BERENGER: Yes, I know why; it was my fault.

OLD MAN: Perhaps he doesn't feel like opening the door to you. Try again.

VOICE OF OLD MAN'S WIFE: Jean, don't stand gossiping, Jean!

BERENGER (*knocking*): Jean!

OLD MAN (*to his wife*): Just a moment. Oh dear, dear . . . (*He close the door and disappears.*)

JEAN (*still lying down, his back to the audience, in a hoarse voice*) What is it?

BERENGER: I've dropped by to see you, Jean.

JEAN: Who is it?

BERENGER: It's me, Berenger. I hope I'm not disturbing you.

JEAN: Oh it's you, is it? Come in!

BERENGER (*trying to open the door*): The door's locked.

JEAN: Just a moment. Oh dear, dear . . . (JEAN *gets up in a pretty bad temper. He is wearing green pyjamas, his hair is tousled.*) Just a moment. (*He unlocks the door.*) Just a moment. (*He goes back to bed, gets under the blanket.*) Come in!

BERENGER (*coming in*): Hello Jean!

JEAN (*in bed*): What time is it? Aren't you at the office?

BERENGER: You're still in bed; you're not at the office, then? Sorry if I'm disturbing you.

JEAN (*still with his back turned*): Funny, I didn't recognize your voice.

BERENGER: I didn't recognize yours either.

JEAN (*still with his back turned*): Sit down!

BERENGER: Aren't you feeling well?

JEAN *replies with a grunt.*

You know, Jean, it was stupid of me to get so upset yesterday over a thing like that.

JEAN: A thing like what?

BERENGER: Yesterday . . .

JEAN: When yesterday? Where yesterday?

BERENGER: Don't you remember? It was about that wretched rhinoceros.

JEAN: What rhinoceros?

BERENGER: The rhinoceros, or rather, the two wretched rhinoceroses we saw.

JEAN: Oh, yes, I remember . . . How do you know they were wretched?

BERENGER: Oh I just said that.

JEAN: Oh. Well let's not talk any more about it.

BERENGER: That's very nice of you.

JEAN: Then that's that.

BERENGER: But I would like to say how sorry I am for being so insistent . . . and so obstinate . . . and getting so angry . . . in fact . . . I acted stupidly.

JEAN: That's not surprising with you.

BERENGER: I'm very sorry.

JEAN: I don't feel very well. (*He coughs.*)

BERENGER: That's probably why you're in bed. (*With a change of tone.*) You know, Jean, as it turned out, we were both right.

JEAN: What about?

BERENGER: About . . . well, you know, the same thing. Sorry to bring it up again, but I'll only mention it briefly. I just wanted you to know that in our different ways we were both right. It's been proved now. There are some rhinoceroses in the town with two horns and some with one.

JEAN: That's what I told you! Well, that's just too bad.

BERENGER: Yes, too bad.

JEAN: Or maybe it's all to the good; it depends.

BERENGER (*continuing*): In the final analysis it doesn't much matter which comes from where. The important thing, as I see it, is the fact that they're there at all, because . . .

JEAN (*turning and sitting on his unmade bed, facing* BERENGER): I don't feel well, I don't feel well at all!

BERENGER: Oh I am sorry! What do you think it is?

JEAN: I don't know exactly, there's something wrong somewhere . .

BERENGER: Do you feel weak?

JEAN: Not at all. On the contrary, I feel full of beans.

BERENGER: I meant just a passing weakness. It happens to everybody.

JEAN: It never happens to me.

BERENGER: Perhaps you're too healthy then. Too much energy can be a bad thing. It unsettles the nervous system.

JEAN: My nervous system is in perfect order. (*His voice has become more and more hoarse.*) I'm sound in mind and limb. I come from a long line of . .

BERENGER: I know you do. Perhaps you've just caught a chill. Have you got a temperature?

JEAN: I don't know. Yes, probably I have a touch of fever. My head aches.

BERENGER: Just a slight migraine. Would you like me to leave you alone?

JEAN: No, stay. You don't worry me.

BERENGER: Your voice is hoarse, too.

JEAN: Hoarse?

BERENGER: A bit hoarse, yes. That's why I didn't recognize it.

JEAN: Why should I be hoarse? My voice hasn't changed; it's yours that's changed!

BERENGER: Mine?

JEAN: Why not?

BERENGER: It's possible. I hadn't noticed.

JEAN: I sometimes wonder if you're capable of noticing anything. (*Putting his hand to his forehead.*) Actually it's my forehead that hurts. I must have given it a knock. (*His voice is even hoarser.*)

BERENGER: When did you do that?

JEAN: I don't know. I don't remember it happening.

BERENGER: But it must have hurt you.

JEAN: I must have done it while I was asleep.

BERENGER: The shock would have wakened you up. You must have just dreamed you knocked yourself.

JEAN: I never dream . . .

BERENGER (*continuing*): Your headache must have come on while you were asleep. You've forgotten you dreamed, or rather you only remember subconsciously.

JEAN: Subconsciously, me? I'm master of my own thoughts, my mind doesn't wander. I think straight, I always think straight.

BERENGER: I know that. I haven't made myself clear.

JEAN: Then make yourself clearer. And you needn't bother to make any of your unpleasant observations to me.

BERENGER: One often has the impression that one has knocked oneself when one has a headache. (*Coming closer to* JEAN.) If you'd really knocked yourself, you'd have a bump. (*Looking at* JEAN.) Oh, you've got one, you do have a bump, in fact.

JEAN: A bump?

BERENGER: Just a tiny one.

JEAN: Where?

BERENGER (*pointing to* JEAN's *forehead*): There, it starts just above your nose.

JEAN: I've no bump. We've never had bumps in my family.

BERENGER: Have you got a mirror?

JEAN: That's the limit! (*Touching his forehead.*) I can feel something. I'm going to have a look, in the bathroom. (*He gets up abruptly and goes to the bathroom.* BERENGER *watches him as he goes. Then, from the bathroom.*) It's true, I have got a bump. (*He comes back; his skin has become greener.*) So you see I did knock myself.

BERENGER: You don't look well, your skin is quite green.

JEAN: You seem to delight in saying disagreeable things to me. Have you taken a look at yourself lately?

BERENGER: Forgive me. I didn't mean to upset you.

JEAN (*very hoarse*): That's hard to believe.

BERENGER: Your breathing's very heavy. Does your throat hurt?

JEAN *goes and sits on his bed again.*

If your throat hurts, perhaps it's a touch of quinsy.

JEAN: Why should I have a touch of quinsy?

BERENGER: It's nothing to be ashamed of—I sometimes get it. Let me feel your pulse. (*He rises and takes* JEAN's *pulse.*)

JEAN (*in an even hoarser voice*): Oh, it'll pass.

BERENGER: Your pulse is normal. You needn't get alarmed.

JEAN: I'm not alarmed in the slightest—why should I be?

BERENGER: You're right. A few days' rest will put you right.

JEAN: I've no time to rest. I must go and buy some food.

BERENGER: There's not much the matter with you, if you're hungry. But even so, you ought to take a few days' rest. It's wise to take care. Has the doctor been to see you?

JEAN: I don't need a doctor.

BERENGER: Oh but you ought to get the doctor.

JEAN: You're not going to get the doctor because I don't want the doctor. I can look after myself.

BERENGER: You shouldn't reject medical advice.

JEAN: Doctors invent illnesses that don't exist.

BERENGER: They do it in good faith—just for the pleasure of looking after people.

JEAN: They invent illnesses, they invent them, I tell you.

BERENGER: Perhaps they do—but after they invent them they cure them.

JEAN: I only have confidence in veterinary surgeons. There!

BERENGER (*who has released* JEAN'S *wrist, now takes it up again*): Your veins look swollen. They're jutting out.

JEAN: It's a sign of virility.

BERENGER: Of course it's a sign of health and strength. But . . . (*He examines* JEAN'S *forearm more closely, until* JEAN *violently withdraws it.*)

JEAN: What do you think you're doing—scrutinizing me as if I were some strange animal?

BERENGER: It's your skin . . .

JEAN: What's my skin got to do with you? I don't go on about your skin, do I?

BERENGER: It's just that . . . it seems to be changing colour all the time. It's going green. (*He tries to take* JEAN'S *hand.*) It's hardening as well.

JEAN (*withdrawing his hand again*): Stop mauling me about! What's the matter with you? You're getting on my nerves.

BERENGER (*to himself*): Perhaps it's more serious than I thought. (*To* JEAN.) We must get the doctor. (*He goes to the telephone.*)

JEAN: Leave that thing alone. (*He darts over to* BERENGER *and pushes him.* BERENGER *staggers.*) You mind your own business.

BERENGER: All right. It was for your own good.

JEAN (*coughing and breathing noisily*): I know better than you what's good for me.

BERENGER: You're breathing very hard.

JEAN: One breathes as best one can. You don't like the way I breathe, and I don't like the way you breathe. Your breathing's too feeble, you can't even hear it; it's as if you were going to drop dead any moment.

BERENGER: I know I'm not as strong as you.

JEAN: I don't keep trying to get you to the doctor, do I? Leave people to do as they please.

BERENGER: Don't get angry with me. You know very well I'm your friend.

JEAN: There's no such thing as friendship. I don't believe in your friendship.

BERENGER: That's a very hurtful thing to say.

JEAN: There's nothing for you to get hurt about.

BERENGER: My dear Jean ...

JEAN: I'm not your dear Jean.

BERENGER: You're certainly in a very misanthropic mood today.

JEAN: Yes, I am misanthropic, very misanthropic indeed. I like being misanthropic.

BERENGER: You're probably still angry with me over our silly quarrel yesterday. I admit it was my fault. That's why I came to say I was sorry ...

JEAN: What quarrel are you talking about?

BERENGER: I told you just now. You know, about the rhinoceros.

JEAN (*not listening to* BERENGER): It's not that I hate people. I'm just indifferent to them—or rather, they disgust me; and they'd better keep out of my way, or I'll run them down.

BERENGER: You know very well that I shall never stand in your way.

JEAN: I've got one aim in life. And I'm making straight for it.

BERENGER: I'm sure you're right. But I feel you're passing through a moral crisis.

> JEAN *has been pacing the room like a wild beast in a cage, from one wall to the other.* BERENGER *watches him, occasionally stepping aside to avoid him.* JEAN'S *voice has become more and more hoarse.*

You mustn't excite yourself, it's bad for you.

JEAN: I felt uncomfortable in my clothes; now my pyjamas irritate me as well. (*He undoes his pyjama jacket and does it up again.*)

BERENGER: But whatever's the matter with your skin?

JEAN: Can't you leave my skin alone? I certainly wouldn't want to change it for yours.

BERENGER: It's gone like leather.

JEAN: That makes it more solid. It's weatherproof.

BERENGER: You're getting greener and greener.

JEAN: You've got colour mania today. You're seeing things, you've been drinking again.

BERENGER: I did yesterday, but not today.

JEAN: It's the result of all your past debauches.

BERENGER: I promised you to turn over a new leaf. I take notice when friends like you give me advice. And I never feel humiliated—on the contrary!

JEAN: I don't care what you feel. Brrr .

BERENGER: What did you say?

JEAN: I didn't say anything. I just went Brrr . . . because I felt like it.

BERENGER (*looking fixedly at* JEAN): Do you know what's happened to Boeuf? He's turned into a rhinoceros.

JEAN: What happened to Boeuf?

BERENGER: He's turned into a rhinoceros.

JEAN (*fanning himself with the flaps of his jacket*): Brrr . . .

BERENGER: Come on now, stop joking.

JEAN: I can puff if I want to, can't I? I've every right . . . I'm in my own house.

BERENGER: I didn't say you couldn't.

JEAN: And I shouldn't if I were you. I feel hot, I feel hot. Brrr . . . Just a moment. I must cool myself down.

BERENGER (*whilst* JEAN *darts to the bathroom*): He must have a fever.

> JEAN *is in the bathroom, one hears him puffing, and also the sound of a running tap.*

JEAN (*off*): Brrr . . .

BERENGER: He's got the shivers. I'm jolly well going to 'phone the doctor. (*He goes to the telephone again then comes back quickly when he hears* JEAN's *voice.*)

JEAN (*off*): So old Boeuf turned into a rhinoceros, did he? Ah, ah, ah . . . ! He was just having you on, he'd disguised himself. (*He pokes his head round the bathroom door. He is very green. The bump over his nose is slightly larger.*) He was just disguised.

BERENGER (*walking about the room, without seeing* JEAN): He looked very serious about it, I assure you.

JEAN: Oh well, that's his business.

BERENGER (*turning to* JEAN *who disappears again into the bathroom*): I'm sure he didn't do it on purpose. He didn't want to change.

JEAN (*off*): How do you know?

BERENGER: Well, everything led one to suppose so.

JEAN: And what if he did do it on purpose? Eh? What if he did it on purpose?

BERENGER: I'd be very surprised. At any rate, Mrs. Boeuf didn't seem to know about it . . .

JEAN (*in a very hoarse voice*): Ah, ah, ah! Fat old Mrs. Boeuf. She's just a fool!

BERENGER: Well fool or no fool . . .

JEAN (*he enters swiftly, takes off his jacket, and throws it on the bed.* BERENGER *discreetly averts his gaze.* JEAN, *whose back and chest are now green, goes back into the bathroom. As he walks in and out.*) Boeuf never let his wife know what he was up to . . .

BERENGER: You're wrong there, Jean—it was a very united family.

JEAN: Very united, was it? Are you sure? Hum, hum, Brr . . .

BERENGER (*moving to the bathroom, where* JEAN *slams the door in his face*): Very united. And the proof is that . . .

JEAN (*from within*): Boeuf led his own private life. He had a secret side to him deep down which he kept to himself.

BERENGER: I shouldn't make you talk, it seems to upset you.

JEAN: On the contrary, it relaxes me.

BERENGER: Even so, let me call the doctor, I beg you.

JEAN: I absolutely forbid it. I can't stand obstinate people.

> JEAN *comes back into the bedroom.* BERENGER *backs away a little scared, for* JEAN *is greener than ever and speaks only with difficulty. His voice is unrecognizable.*)

Well, whether he changes into a rhinoceros on purpose or against his will, he's probably all the better for it.

BERENGER: How can you say a thing like that? Surely you don't think . . .

JEAN: You always see the black side of everything. It obviously gave him great pleasure to turn into a rhinoceros. There's nothing extraordinary in that.

BERENGER: There's nothing extraordinary in it, but I doubt if it gave him much pleasure.

JEAN: And why not, pray?

BERENGER: It's hard to say exactly why; it's just something you feel.

JEAN: I tell you it's not as bad as all that. After all, rhinoceroses are living creatures the same as us; they've got as much right to life as we have!

BERENGER: As long as they don't destroy ours in the process. You must admit the difference in mentality.

JEAN (*pacing up and down the room, and in and out of the bathroom*): Are you under the impression that our way of life is superior?

BERENGER: Well at any rate, we have our own moral standards which I consider incompatible with the standards of these animals.

JEAN: Moral standards! I'm sick of moral standards! We need to go beyond moral standards!

BERENGER: What would you put in their place?

JEAN (*still pacing*): Nature!

BERENGER: Nature?

JEAN: Nature has its own laws. Morality's against Nature.

BERENGER: Are you suggesting we replace our moral laws by the law of the jungle?

JEAN: It would suit me, suit me fine.

BERENGER: You say that. But deep down, no one . . .

JEAN (*interrupting him, pacing up and down*): We've got to build our life on new foundations. We must get back to primeval integrity.

BERENGER: I don't agree with you at all.

JEAN (*breathing noisily*): I can't breathe.

BERENGER: Just think a moment. You must admit that we have a philosophy that animals don't share, and an irreplaceable set of values, which it's taken centuries of human civilization to build up . . .

JEAN (*in the bathroom*): When we've demolished all that, we'll be better off!

BERENGER: I know you don't mean that seriously. You're joking! It's just a poetic fancy.

JEAN: Brrr. (*He almost trumpets.*)

BERENGER: I'd never realized you were a poet.

JEAN (*comes out of the bathroom*): Brrr. (*He trumpets again.*)

BERENGER: That's not what you believe fundamentally—I know you too well. You know as well as I do that mankind . . .

JEAN (*interrupting him*): Don't talk to me about mankind!

BERENGER: I mean the human individual, humanism . . .

JEAN: Humanism is all washed up! You're a ridiculous old sentimentalist. (*He goes into the bathroom.*)

BERENGER: But you must admit that the mind . . .

JEAN (*from the bathroom*): Just clichés! You're talking rubbish!

BERENGER: Rubbish!

JEAN (*from the bathroom in a very hoarse voice, difficult to understand*): Utter rubbish!

BERENGER: I'm amazed to hear you say that, Jean, really! You must be out of your mind. You wouldn't like to be a rhinoceros yourself, now would you?

JEAN: Why not? I'm not a victim of prejudice like you.

BERENGER: Can you speak more clearly? I didn't catch what you said. You swallowed the words.

JEAN (*still in the bathroom*): Then keep your ears open.

BERENGER: What?

JEAN: Keep your ears open. I said what's wrong with being a rhinoceros? I'm all for change.

BERENGER: It's not like you to say a thing like that . . .

> BERENGER *stops short, for* JEAN'S *appearance is truly alarming.* JEAN *has become, in fact, completely green. The bump on his forehead is practically a rhinoceros horn.*

Oh! You really must be out of your mind!

> JEAN *dashes to his bed, throws the covers on the floor, talking in a fast and furious gabble, and making very weird sounds.*

You mustn't get into such a state—calm down! I hardly recognize you any more.

JEAN (*hardly distinguishable*): Hot . . . far too hot! Demolish the lot, clothes itch, they itch! (*He drops his pyjama trousers.*)

BERENGER: What are you doing? You're not yourself! You're generally so modest!

JEAN: The swamps! The swamps!

BERENGER: Look at me! Can't you see me any longer? Can't you hear me?

JEAN: I can hear you perfectly well! I can see you perfectly well! (*He lunges towards* BERENGER, *head down.* BERENGER *gets out of the way.*)

BERENGER: Watch out!

JEAN (*puffing noisily*): Sorry! (*He darts at great speed into the bathroom.*)

BERENGER (*makes as if to escape by the door left, then comes back and goes into the bathroom after* JEAN, *saying*): I really can't leave him like that—after all he is a friend. (*From the bathroom.*) I'm going to get the doctor! It's absolutely necessary, believe me!

JEAN (*from the bathroom*): No!

BERENGER (*from the bathroom*): Calm down, Jean, you're being ridiculous! Oh, your horn's getting longer and longer—you're a rhinoceros!

JEAN (*from the bathroom*): I'll trample you, I'll trample you down!

A lot of noise comes from the bathroom, trumpetings, objects falling, the sound of a shattered mirror; then BERENGER *reappears, very frightened; he closes the bathroom door with difficulty against the resistance that is being made from inside.*

BERENGER (*pushing against the door*): He's a rhinoceros, he's a rhinoceros!

BERENGER *manages to close the door. As he does so, his coat is pierced by a rhinoceros horn. The door shakes under the animal's constant pressure and the din continues in the bathroom; trumpetings are heard, interspersed with indistinct phrases such as: 'I'm furious! The swine!' etc.* BERENGER *rushes to the door right.*

I never would have thought it of him—never!

He opens the staircase door and goes and knocks at the landing door; he bangs repeatedly on it with his fist.

There's a rhinoceros in the building! Get the police!

OLD MAN (*poking his head out*): What's the matter?

BERENGER: Get the police! There's a rhinoceros in the house!

VOICE OF OLD MAN'S WIFE: What are you up to, Jean? Why are you making all that noise?

OLD MAN (*to his wife*): I don't know what he's talking about. He's seen a rhinoceros.

BERENGER: Yes, here in the house. Get the police!

OLD MAN: What do you think you're up to, disturbing people like that. What a way to behave! (*He shuts the door in his face.*)

BERENGER (*rushing to the stairs*): Porter, porter, there's a rhinoceros in the house, get the police! Porter!

The upper part of the porter's lodge is seen to open; the head of a rhinoceros appears.

Another!

> BERENGER *rushes upstairs again. He wants to go back into* JEAN'S
> *room, hesitates, then makes for the door of the* OLD MAN *again.*
> *At this moment the door of the room opens to reveal two*
> *rhinoceros heads.*

Oh, my God!

> BERENGER *goes back into* JEAN'S *room where the bathroom door*
> *is still shaking. He goes to the window which is represented*
> *simply by the frame, facing the audience. He is exhausted,*
> *almost fainting; he murmurs.*

My God! Oh my God!

> *He makes a gigantic effort, and manages to get astride the win-*
> *dow (that is, towards the audience) but gets back again quickly,*
> *for at the same time, crossing the orchestra pit at great speed,*
> *move a large number of rhinoceros heads in line.* BERENGER *gets*
> *back with all speed, looks out of the window for a moment.*

There's a whole herd of them in the street now! An army of rhinoceroses, surging up the avenue . . . ! (*He looks all around.*)
Where can I get out? Where can I get out? If only they'd keep to
the middle of the road! They're all over the pavement as well.
Where can I get out? Where can I get out?

> *Distracted, he goes from door to door and to the window, whilst*
> *the bathroom door continues to shake and* JEAN *continues to*
> *trumpet and hurl incomprehensible insults. This continues for*
> *some moments; whenever* BERENGER *in his disordered attempts*
> *to escape reaches the door of the Old People's flat or the stair-*
> *way, he is greeted by rhinoceros heads which trumpet and*
> *cause him to beat a hasty retreat. He goes to the window for*
> *the last time and looks out.*

A whole herd of them! And they always said the rhinoceros was
a solitary animal! That's not true, that's a conception they'll have

to revise! They've smashed up all the public benches. (*He wrings his hands.*) What's to be done?

He goes once more to the various exits, but the spectacle of the rhinoceros halts him. When he gets back to the bathroom door it seems about to give way. BERENGER *throws himself against the back wall, which yields; the street is visible in the background; he flees, shouting:*

Rhinoceros! Rhinoceros!

Noises. The bathroom door is on the point of yielding.

Curtain.

ACT THREE

The arrangement is roughly the same as in the previous scene.

It is BERENGER's *room, which bears a striking resemblance to that of* JEAN. *Only certain details, one or two extra pieces of furniture, reveal that it is a different room. Staircase to the left, and landing. Door at the end of the landing. There is no porter's lodge. Up-stage is a divan. An armchair, and a little table with a telephone. Perhaps an extra telephone, and a chair. Window up-stage, open. A window frame in the foreground.*

BERENGER *is lying on his divan, his back to the audience.* BERENGER *is lying fully dressed. His head is bandaged. He seems to be having a bad dream, and writhes in his sleep.*

BERENGER: No. (*Pause.*) Watch out for the horns! (*Pause.*)

> *The noise of a considerable number of rhinoceroses is heard passing under the up-stage window.*

No! (*He falls to the floor still fighting with what he has seen in his dream, and wakes up. He puts his hand to his head with an apprehensive air, then moves to the mirror and lifts his bandage, as the noises fade away. He heaves a sigh of relief when he sees he has no bump.*

He hesitates, goes to the divan, lies down, and instantly gets up again. He goes to the table where he takes up a bottle of brandy and a glass, and is about to pour himself a drink. Then after a short internal struggle he replaces the bottle and glass.) Now, now, where's your will-power! (*He wants to go back to his divan, but the rhinoceroses are heard again under the up-stage window. The noises stop; he goes to the little table, hesitates a moment, then with a gesture of 'Oh what's it matter!' he pours himself a glass of brandy which he downs at one go. He puts the bottle and glass back in place. He coughs. His cough seems to worry him; he coughs again and listens hard to the sound. He looks at him-*

439

self again in the mirror, coughing, then opens the window; the panting of the animals becomes louder; he coughs again.) No, it's not the same! (*He calms down, shuts the window, feels his bandaged forehead, goes to his divan, and seems to fall asleep.*)

DUDARD *is seen mounting the top stairs; he gets to the landing and knocks on* BERENGER'S *door.*

BERENGER (*starting up*): What is it?

DUDARD: I've dropped by to see you, Berenger.

BERENGER: Who is it?

DUDARD: It's me.

BERENGER: Who's me?

DUDARD: Me, Dudard.

BERENGER: Ah, it's you, come in!

DUDARD: I hope I'm not disturbing you. (*He tries to open the door.*) The door's locked.

BERENGER: Just a moment. Oh dear, dear! (*He opens the door.* DUDARD *enters.*)

DUDARD: Hello Berenger.

BERENGER: Hello Dudard, what time is it?

DUDARD: So, you're still barricaded in your room! Feeling any better, old man?

BERENGER: Forgive me, I didn't recognize your voice. (*Goes to open the window.*) Yes, yes, I think I'm a bit better.

DUDARD: My voice hasn't changed. I recognized yours easily enough.

BERENGER: I'm sorry, I thought that ... you're right, your voice is quite normal. Mine hasn't changed either, has it?

DUDARD: Why should it have changed?

BERENGER: I'm not a bit ... a bit hoarse, am I?

DUDARD: Not that I notice.

BERENGER: That's good. That's very reassuring.

DUDARD: Why, what's the matter with you?

BERENGER: I don't know—does one ever know? Voices can suddenly change—they do change, alas!

DUDARD: Have you caught cold, as well?

BERENGER: I hope not ... I sincerely hope not. But do sit down, Dudard, take a seat. Sit in the armchair.

DUDARD (*sitting in the armchair*): Are you still feeling a bit off colour? Is your head still bad? (*He points to* BERENGER'S *bandage.*)

BERENGER: Oh yes, I've still got a headache. But there's no bump, I haven't knocked myself...have I? (*He lifts the bandage, shows his forehead to* DUDARD.)

DUDARD: No, there's no bump as far as I can see.

BERENGER: I hope there never will be. Never.

DUDARD: If you don't knock yourself, why should there be?

BERENGER: If you really don't want to knock yourself, you don't.

DUDARD: Obviously. One just has to take care. But what's the matter with you? You're all nervous and agitated. It must be your migraine. You just stay quiet and you'll feel better.

BERENGER: Migraine! Don't talk to me about migraines! Don't talk about them!

DUDARD: It's understandable that you've got a migraine after all that emotion.

BERENGER: I can't seem to get over it!

DUDARD: Then it's not surprising you've got a headache.

BERENGER (*darting to the mirror, lifting the bandage*): Nothing there ...You know, it can all start from something like that.

DUDARD: What can all start?

BERENGER: I'm frightened of becoming someone else.

DUDARD: Calm yourself, now, and sit down. Dashing up and down the room like that can only make you more nervous.

BERENGER: You're right, I must keep calm. (*He goes and sits down.*) I just can't get over it, you know.

DUDARD: About Jean you mean?—I know.

BERENGER: Yes, Jean, of course—and the others, too.

DUDARD: I realize it must have been a shock to you.

BERENGER: Well, that's not surprising, you must admit.

DUDARD: I suppose so, but you mustn't dramatize the situation; it's no reason for you to...

BERENGER: I wonder how you'd have felt. Jean was my best friend. Then to watch him change before my eyes, and the way he got so furious!

DUDARD: I know. You felt let down; I understand. Try and not think about it.

BERENGER: How can I help thinking about it? He was such a warm-hearted person, always so human! Who'd have thought it of him! We'd known each other for...for donkey's years. He was the last person I'd have expected to change like that. I felt more sure of him than of myself! And then to do that to me!

DUDARD: I'm sure he didn't do it specially to annoy you!

BERENGER: It seemed as if he did. If you'd seen the state he was in ... the expression on his face ...

DUDARD: It's just that you happened to be with him at the time. It would have been the same no matter who was there.

BERENGER: But after all our years together he might have controlled himself in front of me.

DUDARD: You think everything revolves round you, you think that everything that happens concerns you personally; you're not the centre of the universe, you know.

BERENGER: Perhaps you're right. I must try to re-adjust myself, but the phenomenon in itself is so disturbing. To tell the truth, it absolutely shatters me. What can be the explanation?

DUDARD: For the moment I haven't found a satisfactory explanation. I observe the facts, and I take them in. They exist, so they must have an explanation. A freak of Nature, perhaps, some bizarre caprice, an extravagant joke, a game—who knows?

BERENGER: Jean was very proud, of course. I'm not ambitious at all. I'm content to be what I am.

DUDARD: Perhaps he felt an urge for some fresh air, the country, the wide-open spaces ... perhaps he felt a need to relax. I'm not saying that's any excuse ...

BERENGER: I understand what you mean, at least I'm trying to. But you know—if someone accused me of being a bad sport, or hopelessly middle class, or completely out of touch with life, I'd still want to stay as I am.

DUDARD: We'll all stay as we are, don't worry. So why get upset over a few cases of rhinoceritis. Perhaps it's just another disease.

BERENGER: Exactly! And I'm frightened of catching it.

DUDARD: Oh stop thinking about it. Really, you attach too much importance to the whole business. Jean's case isn't symptomatic, he's not a typical case—you said yourself he was proud. In my opinion—if you'll excuse me saying this about your friend—he was far too excitable, a bit wild, an eccentric. You mustn't base your judgments on exceptions. It's the average case you must consider.

BERENGER: I'm beginning to see daylight. You see, you couldn't explain this phenomenon to me. And yet you just provided me with a plausible explanation. Yes, of course, he must have been in a critical condition to have got himself into that state. He must have been temporarily unbalanced. And yet he gave his reasons for it, he'd obviously given it a lot of thought, and weighed the pros and cons... And what about Boeuf then, was he mad, too...? and what about all the others...?

DUDARD: There's still the epidemic theory. It's like influenza. It's not the first time there's been an epidemic.

BERENGER: There's never been one like this. And what if it's come from the colonies?

DUDARD: In any case you can be sure that Boeuf and the others didn't do what they did—become what they became—just to annoy you. They wouldn't have gone to all that trouble.

BERENGER: That's true, that makes sense, it's a reassuring thought ...or on the other hand, perhaps that makes it worse? (*Rhinoceroses are heard, galloping under the up-stage window.*) There, you hear that? (*He darts to the window.*)

DUDARD: Oh, why can't you leave them alone!

BERENGER *closes the window again.*

They're not doing you any harm. Really, you're obsessed by them! It's not good for you. You're wearing yourself out. You've had one shock, why look for more? You just concentrate on getting back to normal.

BERENGER: I wonder if I really am immune?

DUDARD: In any case it's not fatal. Certain illnesses are good for you. I'm convinced this is something you can cure if you want to. They'll get over it, you'll see.

BERENGER: But it's bound to have certain after-effects! An organic upheaval like that can't help but leave..

DUDARD: It's only temporary, don't you worry.

BERENGER: Are you absolutely certain?

DUDARD: I think so, yes, I suppose so.

BERENGER: But if one really doesn't want to, really doesn't want to catch this thing, which after all is a nervous disease—then you don't catch it, you simply don't catch it! Do you feel like a brandy? (*He goes to the table where the bottle stands.*)

DUDARD: Not for me, thank you, I never touch it. But don't mind me if you want some—you go ahead, don't worry about me. But watch out it doesn't make your headache worse.

BERENGER: Alcohol is good for epidemics. It immunizes you. It kills influenza microbes, for instance.

DUDARD: Perhaps it doesn't kill all microbes. They don't know about rhinoceritis yet.

BERENGER: Jean never touched alcohol. He just pretended to. Maybe that's why he ... perhaps that explains his attitude. (*He offers a full glass to* DUDARD.) You're sure you won't?

DUDARD: No, no, never before lunch, thank you.

> BERENGER *empties his glass, continues to hold it, together with the bottle, in his hands; he coughs.*

You see, you can't take it. It makes you cough.

BERENGER (*worried*): Yes, it did make me cough. How did I cough?

DUDARD: Like everyone coughs when they drink something a bit strong.

BERENGER (*moving to put the glass and bottle back on the table*): There wasn't anything odd about it, was there? It *was* a real human cough?

DUDARD: What are you getting at? It was an ordinary human cough. What other sort of cough could it have been?

BERENGER: I don't know ... Perhaps an animal's cough ... Do rhinoceroses cough?

DUDARD: Look, Berenger, you're being ridiculous, you invent difficulties for yourself, you ask yourself the weirdest questions ... I remember you said yourself that the best protection against the thing was will-power.

BERENGER: Yes, I did.

DUDARD: Well then, prove you've got some.

BERENGER: I have, I assure you ...

DUDARD: Prove it to yourself—now, don't drink any more brandy. You'll feel more sure of yourself then.

BERENGER: You deliberately misunderstand me. I told you the only reason I take it is because it keeps the worst at bay; I'm doing it quite deliberately. When the epidemic's over, then I shall stop drinking. I'd already decided that before the whole business began. I'm just putting it off for the time being!

DUDARD: You're inventing excuses for yourself.

BERENGER: Do you think I am ... ? In any case, that's got nothing to do with what's happening now.

DUDARD: How do we know?

BERENGER (*alarmed*): Do you really think so? You think that's how the rot sets in? I'm not an alcoholic. (*He goes to the mirror and examines himself.*) Do you think, by any chance ... (*He touches his face, pats his bandaged forehead.*) Nothing's changed· it hasn't done any harm so it must have done good ... or it's harmless at any rate.

DUDARD: I was only joking. I was just teasing you. You see the black side of everything—watch out, or you'll become a neurotic When you've got over your shock completely and you can get out for a breath of fresh air, you'll feel better—you'll see! All these morbid ideas will vanish.

BERENGER: Go out? I suppose I'll have to. I'm dreading the moment. I'll be bound to meet some of them ...

DUDARD: What if you do? You only have to keep out of their way. And there aren't as many as all that.

BERENGER: I see them all over the place. You'll probably say that's being morbid, too.

DUDARD: They don't attack you. If you leave them alone, they just ignore you. You can't say they're spiteful They've even got a certain natural innocence, a sort of frankness. Besides I walked right along the avenue to get to you today. I got here safe and sound, didn't I? No trouble at all.

BERENGER: Just the sight of them upsets me. It's a nervous thing. I don't get angry—no, it doesn't pay to get angry, you never know where it'll lead to, I watch out for that. But it does something to me, here! (*He points to his heart.*) I get a tight feeling inside.

DUDARD: I think you're right to a certain extent to have some reaction. But you go too far. You've no sense of humour, that's your trouble, none at all. You must learn to be more detached, and try and see the funny side of things.

BERENGER: I feel responsible for everything that happens. I feel involved, I just can't be indifferent.

DUDARD: Judge not lest ye be judged. If you start worrying about everything that happens you'd never be able to go on living.

BERENGER: If only it had happened somewhere else, in some other country, and we'd just read about it in the papers, one could discuss it quietly, examine the question from all points of view and come to an objective conclusion. We could organize debates with professors and writers and lawyers, and blue-stockings and artists and people. And the ordinary man in the street, as well—it would be very interesting and instructive. But when you're involved yourself, when you suddenly find yourself up against the brutal facts you can't help feeling directly concerned—the shock is too violent for you to stay cool and detached. I'm frankly surprised, I'm very very surprised. I can't get over it.

DUDARD: Well I'm surprised, too. Or rather I was. Now I'm starting to get used to it.

BERENGER: Your nervous system is better balanced than mine. You're lucky. But don't you agree it's all very unfortunate...

DUDARD (*interrupting him*): I don't say it's a good thing. And don't get the idea that I'm on the rhinoceroses' side...

More sounds of rhinoceroses passing, this time under the downstage window-frame.

BERENGER (*with a start*): There they are, there they are again! Oh, it's no use, I just can't get used to them. Maybe it's wrong of me, but they obsess me so much in spite of myself, I just can't sleep at night. I get insomnia. I doze a bit in the daytime out of sheer exhaustion.

DUDARD: Take some sleeping tablets.

BERENGER: That's not the answer. If I sleep, it's worse. I dream about them, I get nightmares.

DUDARD: That's what comes of taking things too seriously. You get a kick out of torturing yourself—admit it!

BERENGER: I'm no masochist, I assure you.

DUDARD: Then face the facts and get over it. This is the situation and there's nothing you can do about it.

BERENGER: That's fatalism.

DUDARD: It's common sense. When a thing like this happens there's bound to be a reason for it. That's what we must find out.

BERENGER (*getting up*): Well, I don't want to accept the situation.

DUDARD: What else can you do? What are your plans?

BERENGER: I don't know for the moment. I must think it over. I shall write to the papers; I'll draw up manifestos; I shall apply for an audience with the mayor—or his deputy, if the mayor's too busy.

DUDARD: You leave the authorities to act as they think best! I'm not sure if morally you have the right to butt in. In any case, I still think it's not all that serious. I consider it's silly to get worked up because a few people decide to change their skins. They just didn't feel happy in the ones they had. They're free to do as they like.

BERENGER: We must attack the evil at the roots.

DUDARD: The evil! That's just a phrase! Who knows what is evil and what is good? It's just a question of personal preferences. You're worried about your own skin—that's the truth of the matter. But you'll never become a rhinoceros, really you won't . . . you haven't got the vocation!

BERENGER: There you are, you see! If our leaders and fellow citizens all think like you, they'll never take any action.

DUDARD: You wouldn't want to ask for help from abroad, surely? This is an internal affair, it only concerns our country.

BERENGER: I believe in international solidarity . . .

DUDARD: You're a Don Quixote. Oh, I don't mean that nastily, don't be offended! I'm only saying it for your own good, because you really need to calm down.

BERENGER: You're right, I know—forgive me. I get too worked up. But I'll change, I will change. I'm sorry to keep you all this time listening to my ramblings. You must have work to do. Did you get my application for sick leave?

DUDARD: Don't worry about that. It's all in order. In any case, the office hasn't resumed work.

BERENGER: Haven't they repaired the staircase yet? What negligence! That's why everything goes so badly.

DUDARD: They're repairing it now. But it's slow work. It's not easy to find the workmen. They sign on and work for a couple of days, then don't turn up any more. You never see them again. Then you have to look for others.

BERENGER: And they talk about unemployment! At least I hope we're getting a stone staircase.

DUDARD: No, it's wood again, but new wood this time.

BERENGER: Oh! The way these organizations stick to the old routine. They chuck money down the drain but when it's needed for something really useful they pretend they can't afford it. I bet Mr. Papillon's none too pleased. He was dead set on having a stone staircase. What's he say about it?

DUDARD: We haven't got a Chief any more. Mr. Papillon's resigned.

BERENGER: It's not possible!

DUDARD: It's true, I assure you.

BERENGER: Well, I'm amazed . . . Was it on account of the staircase?

DUDARD: I don't think so. Anyway that wasn't the reason he gave.

BERENGER: Why was it then? What got into him?

DUDARD: He's retiring to the country.

BERENGER: Retiring? He's not the age. He might still have become the Director.

DUDARD: He's given it all up! Said he needed a rest.

BERENGER: I bet the management's pretty upset to see him go; they'll have to replace him. All your diplomas should come in useful—you stand a good chance.

DUDARD: I suppose I might as well tell you . . . it's really rather funny—the fact is, he turned into a rhinoceros.

Distant rhinoceros noises.

BERENGER: A rhinoceros!!!! Mr. Papillon a rhinoceros! I can't believe it! I don't think it's funny at all! Why didn't you tell me before?

DUDARD: Well you know you've no sense of humour. I didn't want to tell you . . . I didn't want to tell you because I knew very well you wouldn't see the funny side, and it would upset you. You know how impressionable you are!

BERENGER (*raising his arms to heaven*): Oh that's awful . . . Mr. Papillon! And he had such a good job.

DUDARD: That proves his metamorphosis was sincere.

BERENGER: He couldn't have done it on purpose. I'm certain it must have been involuntary.

DUDARD: How can we tell? It's hard to know the real reasons for people's decisions.

BERENGER: He must have made a mistake. He'd got some hidden complexes. He should have been psychoanalysed.

DUDARD: Even if it's a case of dissociation it's still very revealing. It was his way of sublimating himself. *Papillon*

BERENGER: He let himself be talked into it, I feel sure.

DUDARD: That could happen to anybody!

BERENGER (*alarmed*): To anybody? Oh no, not to you it couldn't—could it? And not to me!

DUDARD: We must hope not.

BERENGER: Because we don't want to . . . that's so, isn't it? Tell me, that *is* so, isn't it?

DUDARD: Yes, yes, of course . . .

BERENGER (*a little calmer*): I still would have thought Mr. Papillon would have had the strength to resist. I thought he had a bit more character! Particularly as I fail to see where his interest lay—what possible material or moral interest ...

DUDARD: It was obviously a disinterested gesture on his part.

BERENGER: Obviously. There were extenuating circumstances ... or were they aggravating? Aggravating, I should think, because if he did it from choice ... You know, I feel sure that Botard must have taken a very poor view of it—what did he think of his Chief's behaviour?

DUDARD: Oh poor old Botard was quite indignant, absolutely outraged. I've rarely seen anyone so incensed.

BERENGER: Well for once I'm on his side. He's a good man after all. A man of sound common sense. And to think I misjudged him.

DUDARD: He misjudged you, too.

BERENGER: That proves how objective I'm being now. Besides, you had a pretty bad opinion of him yourself.

DUDARD: I wouldn't say I had a bad opinion. I admit I didn't often agree with him. I never liked his scepticism, the way he was always so incredulous and suspicious. Even in this instance I didn't approve of him entirely.

BERENGER: This time for the opposite reasons.

DUDARD: No, not exactly—my own reasoning and my judgment are a bit more complex than you seem to think. It was because there was nothing precise or objective about the way Botard argued. I don't approve of the rhinoceroses myself, as you know—not at all, don't go thinking that! But Botard's attitude was too passionate, as usual, and therefore over-simplified. His stand seems to me entirely dictated by hatred of his superiors. That's where he gets his inferiority complex and his resentment. What's more he talks in clichés, and commonplace arguments leave me cold.

BERENGER: Well forgive me, but this time I'm in complete agreement with Botard. He's somebody worthwhile.

DUDARD: I don't deny it, but that doesn't mean anything.

BERENGER: He's a very worthwhile person—and they're not easy to find these days. He's down-to-earth, with four feet planted firmly on the ground—I mean, both feet. I'm in complete agreement with him, and I'm proud of it. I shall congratulate him when I see him. I deplore Mr. Papillon's action; it was his duty not to succumb.

DUDARD: How intolerant you are! Maybe Papillon felt the need for a bit of relaxation after all these years of office life.

BERENGER (*ironically*): And you're too tolerant, far too broadminded!

DUDARD: My dear Berenger, one must always make an effort to understand. And in order to understand a phenomenon and its effects you need to work back to the initial causes, by honest intellectual effort. We must try to do this because, after all, we are thinking beings. I haven't yet succeeded, as I told you, and I don't know if I shall succeed. But in any case one has to start out favourably disposed—or at least, impartial; one has to keep an open mind—that's essential to a scientific mentality. Everything is logical. To understand is to justify.

BERENGER: You'll be siding with the rhinoceroses before long.

DUDARD: No, no, not at all. I wouldn't go that far. I'm simply trying to look the facts unemotionally in the face. I'm trying to be realistic. I also contend that there is no real evil in what occurs naturally. I don't believe in seeing evil in everything. I leave that to the inquisitors.

BERENGER: And you consider all this natural?

DUDARD: What could be more natural than a rhinoceros?

BERENGER: Yes, but for a man to turn into a rhinoceros is abnormal beyond question.

DUDARD: Well, of course, that's a matter of opinion . . .

BERENGER: It is beyond question, absolutely beyond question!

DUDARD: You seem very sure of yourself. Who can say where the normal stops and the abnormal begins? Can you personally define these conceptions of normality and abnormality? Nobody has solved this problem yet, either medically or philosophically. You ought to know that.

BERENGER: The problem may not be resolved philosophically—but in practice it's simple. They may prove there's no such thing as movement . . . and then you start walking . . . (*He starts walking up and down the room.*) . . . and you go on walking, and you say to yourself, like Galileo, 'E pur si muove' . . .

DUDARD: You're getting things all mixed up! Don't confuse the issue. In Galileo's case it was the opposite; theoretic and scientific thought proving itself superior to mass opinion and dogmatism.

BERENGER (*quite lost*): What does all that mean? Mass opinion, dogmatism—they're just words! I may be mixing everything up in my head but you're losing yours. You don't know what's nor-

mal and what isn't any more. I couldn't care less about Galileo
... I don't give a damn about Galileo.

DUDARD: You brought him up in the first place and raised the whole
question, saying that practice always had the last word. Maybe
it does, but only when it proceeds from theory! The history of
thought and science proves that.

BERENGER (*more and more furious*): It doesn't prove anything of the
sort! It's all gibberish, utter lunacy!

DUDARD: There again we need to define exactly what we mean by
lunacy...

BERENGER: Lunacy is lunacy and that's all there is to it! Everybody
knows what lunacy is. And what about the rhinoceroses—are they
practice or are they theory?

DUDARD: Both!

BERENGER: How do you mean—both?

DUDARD: Both the one and the other, or one or the other. It's a de-
batable point!

BERENGER: Well in that case... I refuse to think about it!

DUDARD: You're getting all het up. Our opinions may not exactly coin-
cide but we can still discuss the matter peaceably. These things
should be discussed.

BERENGER (*distracted*): You think I'm getting all het up, do you? I
might be Jean. Oh no, no, I don't want to become like him. I
mustn't be like him. (*He calms down.*) I'm not very well up in
philosophy. I've never studied; you've got all sorts of diplomas.
That's why you're so at ease in discussion, whereas I never know
what to answer—I'm so clumsy. (*Louder rhinoceros noises passing
first under the up-stage window and then the downstage.*) But I
do feel you're in the wrong... I feel it instinctively—no, that's
not what I mean, it's the rhinoceros which has instinct—I feel it
intuitively, yes, that's the word, intuitively.

DUDARD: What do you understand by 'intuitive'?

BERENGER: Intuitively means... well, just like that! I feel it, just
like that. I think your excessive tolerance, and your generous
indulgence... believe me, they're really only weakness... just
blind spots...

DUDARD: You're innocent enough to think that.

BERENGER: You'll always be able to dance rings round me. But, you
know what? I'm going to try and get hold of the Logician...

DUDARD: What logician?

BERENGER: The Logician, the philosopher, a logician, you know you know better than I do what a logician is. A logician I met, who explained to me . . .

DUDARD: What did he explain to you?

BERENGER: He explained that the Asiatic rhinoceroses were African and the African ones Asiatic.

DUDARD: I don't follow you.

BERENGER: No . . . no . . . he proved the contrary—that the African ones were Asiatic and the Asiatic ones . . . I know what I mean. That's not what I wanted to say. But you'll get on very well with him. He's your sort of person, a very good man, a very subtle mind, brilliant.

> *Increasing noises from the rhinoceroses. The words of the two men are drowned by the animals passing under the windows; for a few moments the lips of* DUDARD *and* BERENGER *are seen to move without any words being heard.*

There they go again! Will they never stop! (*He runs to the up-stage window.*) Stop it! Stop it! You devils!

> *The rhinoceroses move away.* BERENGER *shakes his fist after them.*

DUDARD (*seated*): I'd be happy to meet your Logician. If he can enlighten me on these obscure and delicate points, I'd be only too delighted.

BERENGER (*as he runs to the down-stage window*): Yes, I'll bring him along, he'll talk to you. He's a very distinguished person, you'll see. (*To the rhinoceroses, from the window.*) You devils! (*Shakes his fist as before.*)

DUDARD: Let them alone. And be more polite. You shouldn't talk to people like that . . .

BERENGER (*still at the window*): There they go again!

> *A boater pierced by a rhinoceros horn emerges from the orchestra pit under the window and passes swiftly from left to right.*

There's a boater impaled on a rhinoceros horn. Oh, it's the

Logician's hat! It's the Logician's! That's the bloody limit! The Logician's turned into a rhinoceros!

DUDARD: That's no reason to be coarse!

BERENGER: Dear Lord, who can you turn to—who? I ask you! The Logician a rhinoceros!

DUDARD (*going to the window*): Where is he?

BERENGER (*pointing*): There, that one there, you see!

DUDARD: He's the only rhinoceros in a boater! That makes you think. You're sure it's your Logician?

BERENGER: The Logician . . . a rhinoceros!!!

DUDARD: He's still retained a vestige of his old individuality.

BERENGER (*shakes his fist again at the straw-hatted rhinoceros, which has disappeared*): I'll never join up with you! Not me!

DUDARD: If he was a genuine thinker, as you say, he couldn't have got carried away. He must have weighed all the pros and cons before deciding.

BERENGER (*still shouting after the ex-Logician and the other rhinoceroses who have moved away*): I'll never join up with you!

DUDARD (*settling into the armchair*): Yes, that certainly makes you think!

BERENGER *closes the down-stage window; goes to the up-stage window where other rhinoceroses are passing, presumably making a tour of the house. He opens the window and shouts.*

BERENGER: No, I'll never join up with you!

DUDARD (*aside, in his armchair*): They're going round and round the house. They're playing! Just big babies!

DAISY *has been seen mounting the top stairs. She knocks on* BERENGER's *door. She is carrying a basket.*

There's somebody at the door, Berenger!

He takes BERENGER, *who is still at the window, by the sleeve.*

BERENGER (*shouting after the rhinoceroses*): It's a disgrace, masquerading like this, a disgrace!

DUDARD: There's someone knocking, Berenger, can't you hear?

BERENGER: Open, then, if you want to! (*He continues to watch the rhinoceroses whose noise is fading away.*)

DUDARD *goes to open the door.*

DAISY (*coming in*): Morning, Mr. Dudard.

DUDARD: Oh, it's you, Miss Daisy.

DAISY: Is Berenger here, is he any better?

DUDARD: How nice to see you, my dear. Do you often visit Berenger?

DAISY: Where is he?

DUDARD (*pointing*): There.

DAISY: He's all on his own, poor thing. And he's not very well at the moment, somebody has to give him a hand.

DUDARD: You're a good friend, Miss Daisy.

DAISY: That's just what I am, a good friend.

DUDARD: You've got a warm heart.

DAISY: I'm a good friend, that's all.

BERENGER (*turning, leaving the window open*): Oh Miss Daisy! How kind of you to come, how very kind!

DUDARD: It certainly is.

BERENGER: Did you know, Miss Daisy, that the Logician is a rhinoceros?

DAISY: Yes, I did. I caught sight of him in the street as I arrived. He was running very fast for someone his age! Are you feeling any better, Mr. Berenger?

BERENGER: My head's still bad! Still got a headache! Isn't it frightful? What do you think about it?

DAISY: I think you ought to be resting...you should take things quietly for a few more days.

DUDARD (*to* BERENGER *and* DAISY): I hope I'm not disturbing you!

BERENGER (*to* DAISY): I meant about the Logician...

DAISY (*to* DUDARD): Why should you be? (*To* BERENGER.) Oh, about the Logician? I don't think anything at all!

DUDARD (*to* DAISY): I thought I might be in the way!

DAISY (*to* BERENGER): What do you expect me to think? (*To both.*) I've got some news for you: Botard's a rhinoceros!

DUDARD: Well, well!

BERENGER: I don't believe it. He was against it. You must be mistaken. He protested. Dudard has just been telling me. Isn't that so, Dudard?

DUDARD: That is so.

DAISY: I know he was against it. But it didn't stop him turning, twenty-four hours after Mr. Papillon.

DUDARD: Well, he must have changed his mind! Everybody has the right to do that.

BERENGER: Then obviously anything can happen!

DUDARD (*to* BERENGER): He was a very good man according to you just now.

BERENGER (*to* DAISY): I just can't believe you. They must have lied to you.

DAISY: I saw him do it.

BERENGER: Then he must have been lying; he was just pretending.

DAISY: He seemed very sincere; sincerity itself.

BERENGER: Did he give any reasons?

DAISY: What he said was: we must move with the times! Those were his last human words.

DUDARD (*to* DAISY): I was almost certain I'd meet you here, Miss Daisy.

BERENGER: ... Move with the times! What a mentality! (*He makes a wide gesture.*)

DUDARD (*to* DAISY): Impossible to find you anywhere else, since the office closed.

BERENGER (*continuing, aside*): What childishness! (*He repeats the same gesture.*)

DAISY (*to* DUDARD): If you wanted to see me, you only had to telephone.

DUDARD (*to* DAISY): Oh you know me, Miss Daisy, I'm discretion itself.

BERENGER: But now I come to think it over, Botard's behaviour doesn't surprise me. His firmness was only a pose. Which doesn't stop him from being a good man, of course. Good men make good rhinoceroses, unfortunately. It's because they are so good that they get taken in.

DAISY: Do you mind if I put this basket on the table? (*She does so.*)

BERENGER: But he was a good man with a lot of resentment...

DUDARD (*to* DAISY, *and hastening to help her with the basket*): Excuse me, excuse us both, we should have given you a hand before.

BERENGER (*continues*): ... He was riddled with hatred for his superiors, and he'd got an inferiority complex...

DUDARD (*to* BERENGER): Your argument doesn't hold water, because the example he followed was the Chief's, the very instrument of the people who exploited him, as he used to say. No, it seems to me that with him it was a case of community spirit triumphing over his anarchic impulses.

BERENGER: It's the rhinoceroses which are anarchic, because they're in the minority.

DUDARD: They are, it's true—for the moment.

DAISY: They're a pretty big minority, and getting bigger all the time. My cousin's a rhinoceros now, and his wife. Not to mention leading personalities like the Cardinal de Retz...

DUDARD: A prelate!

DAISY: Mazarin.

DUDARD: This is going to spread to other countries, you'll see.

BERENGER: And to think it all started with us!

DAISY: ... and some of the aristocracy. The Duke of St. Simon.

BERENGER (*with uplifted arms*): All our great names!

DAISY: And others, too. Lots of others. Maybe a quarter of the whole town.

BERENGER: We're still in the majority. We must take advantage of that. We must do something before we're inundated.

DUDARD: They're very potent, very.

DAISY: Well for the moment, let's eat. I've brought some food.

BERENGER: You're very kind, Miss Daisy.

DUDARD (*aside*): Very kind indeed.

BERENGER: I don't know how to thank you.

DAISY (*to* DUDARD): Would you care to stay with us?

DUDARD: I don't want to be a nuisance.

DAISY: Whatever do you mean, Mr. Dudard? You know very well we'd love you to stay.

DUDARD: Well, you know, I'd hate to be in the way...

BERENGER: Of course, stay, Dudard. It's always a pleasure to talk to you.

DUDARD: As a matter of fact I'm in a bit of a hurry. I have an appointment.

BERENGER: Just now you said you had nothing to do.

DAISY (*unpacking her basket*): You know, I had a lot of trouble finding food. The shops have been plundered; they just devour everything. And a lot of the shops are closed. It's written up outside: 'Closed on account of transformation.'

BERENGER: They should be all rounded up in a big enclosure, and kept under strict supervision.

DUDARD: That's easier said than done. The animals' protection league would be the first to object.

DAISY: And besides everyone has a close relative or a friend among them, and that would make it even more difficult.

BERENGER: So everybody's mixed up in it!

DUDARD: Everybody's in the same boat!

BERENGER: But how can people be rhinoceroses? It doesn't bear thinking about! (*To* DAISY.) Shall I help you lay the table?

DAISY: No, don't bother. I know where the plates are. (*She goes to a cupboard and takes out the plates.*)

DUDARD (*aside*): She's obviously very familiar with the place. .

DAISY (*to* DUDARD): I'm laying for three—all right? You are staying with us?

BERENGER (*to* DUDARD): Yes, of course you're staying.

DAISY (*to* BERENGER): You get used to it, you know. Nobody seems surprised any more to see herds of rhinoceroses galloping through the streets. They just stand aside, and then carry on as if nothing had happened.

DUDARD: It's the wisest course to take.

BERENGER: Well I can't get used to it.

DUDARD (*reflectively*): I wonder if one oughtn't to give it a try?

DAISY: Well right now, let's have lunch.

BERENGER: I don't see how a legal man like yourself can...

A great noise of rhinoceroses travelling very fast is heard outside. Trumpets and drums are also heard.

What's going on?

They rush to the down-stage window.

What is it?

The sound of a wall crumbling is heard. Dust covers part of the stage, enveloping, if possible, the characters. They are heard speaking through it.

BERENGER: You can't see a thing! What's happening?

DUDARD: You can't see, but you can hear all right.

BERENGER: That's no good!

DAISY: The plates will be all covered in dust.

BERENGER: How unhygienic!

DAISY: Let's hurry up and eat. We won't pay any attention to them.

The dust disperses.

BERENGER (*pointing into the auditorium*): They've demolished the walls of the Fire Station.

DUDARD: That's true, they've demolished them!

DAISY (*who after moving from the window to near the table holding the plate which she is endeavouring to clean, rushes to join the other two*): They're coming out.

BERENGER: All the firemen, a whole regiment of rhinoceroses, led by drums.

DAISY: They're pouring up the streets!

BERENGER: It's gone too far, much too far!

DAISY: More rhinoceroses are streaming out of the courtyard.

BERENGER: And out of the houses . . .

DUDARD: And the windows as well!

DAISY: They're joining up with the others.

A man comes out of the landing door left and dashes downstairs at top speed; then another with a large horn on his nose; then a woman wearing an entire rhinoceros head.

DUDARD: There aren't enough of us left any more.

BERENGER: How many with one horn, and how many with two?

DUDARD: The statisticians are bound to be compiling statistics now. There'll be plenty of erudite controversy you can be sure!

BERENGER: They can only calculate approximately. It's all happening so fast. It leaves them no time. No time to calculate.

DAISY: The best thing is to let the statisticians get on with it. Come and eat, my dear. That'll calm you down. You'll feel better afterwards. (*To* DUDARD.) And you, too.

They move away from the window. DAISY *takes* BERENGER'S *arm; he allows himself to be led docilely.* DUDARD *suddenly halts.*

DUDARD: I don't feel very hungry—or rather, to be frank, I don't like tinned food very much. I feel like eating outside on the grass.

BERENGER: You mustn't do that. Think of the risk!

DUDARD: But really I don't want to put you to the trouble.

BERENGER: But we've already told you ...

DUDARD (*interrupting* BERENGER): I really mean it.

DAISY (*to* DUDARD): Of course if you really don't want to stay, we can't force you ...

DUDARD: I didn't mean to offend you.

BERENGER (*to* DAISY): Don't let him go, he mustn't go.

DAISY: I'd like him to stay ... but people must do as they please.

BERENGER (*to* DUDARD): Man is superior to the rhinoceros.

DUDARD: I didn't say he wasn't. But I'm not with you absolutely either. I don't know; only experience can tell.

BERENGER (*to* DUDARD): You're weakening too, Dudard. It's just a passing phase which you'll regret.

DAISY: If it's just a passing phase then there's no great danger.

DUDARD: I feel certain scruples! I feel it's my duty to stick by my employers and my friends, through thick and thin.

BERENGER: It's not as if you were married to them.

DUDARD: I've renounced marriage. I prefer the great universal family to the little domestic one.

DAISY (*softly*): We shall miss you a lot, Dudard, but we can't do anything about it.

DUDARD: It's my duty to stick by them; I have to do my duty.

BERENGER: No you're wrong, your duty is to ... you don't see where your real duty lies ... your duty is to oppose them, with a firm, clear mind.

DUDARD: I shall keep my mind clear. (*He starts to move round the stage in circles.*) As clear as ever it was. But if you're going to criticize, it's better to do so from the inside. I'm not going to abandon them. I won't abandon them.

DAISY: He's very good-hearted.

BERENGER: He's too good-hearted. (*To* DUDARD, *then dashing to the door.*) You're too good-hearted, you're human. (*To* DAISY.) Don't let him go. He's making a mistake. He's human.

DAISY: What can I do?

> DUDARD *opens the door and runs off; he goes down the stairs at top speed followed by* BERENGER *who shouts after him from the landing.*

BERENGER: Come back, Dudard! We're fond of you, don't go! It's too late! (*He comes back.*) Too late!

DAISY: We couldn't do anything. (*She closes the door behind* BEREN-GER, *who darts to the down-stage window.*)

BERENGER: He's joined up with them. Where is he now?

DAISY (*moving to the window*): With them.

BERENGER: Which one is he?

DAISY: You can't tell. You can't recognize him any more.

BERENGER: They all look alike, all alike. (*To* DAISY.) He *did* hesitate. You should have held him back by force.

DAISY: I didn't dare to.

BERENGER: You should have been firmer with him, you should have insisted; he was in love with you, wasn't he?

DAISY: He never made me any official declaration.

BERENGER: Everybody knew he was. He's done this out of thwarted love. He was a shy man. He wanted to make a big gesture to impress you. Don't you feel like going after him?

DAISY: Not at all. Or I wouldn't be here!

BERENGER (*looking out of the window*): You can see nothing but them in the street. (*He darts to the up-stage window.*) Nothing but them! You were wrong, Daisy. (*He looks through the down-stage window again.*) Not a single human being as far as the eye can see. They're all over the street. Half with one horn and half with two, and that's the only distinction!

> *Powerful noises of moving rhinoceroses are heard, but some-how it is a musical sound. On the up-stage wall stylized heads appear and disappear; they become more and more numerous from now on until the end of the play. Towards the end they stay fixed for longer and longer, until eventually they fill the entire back wall, remaining static. The heads, in spite of their monstrous appearance, seem to become more and more beauti-ful.*

You don't feel let down, do you, Daisy? There's nothing you regret?

DAISY: No, no.

BERENGER: I want so much to be a comfort to you. I love you, Daisy; don't ever leave me.

DAISY: <u>Shut the window</u>, darling. They're making such a noise. And the dust is rising even up to here. Everything will get filthy.

BERENGER: Yes, you're right. (*He closes the down-stage window and* DAISY *closes the up-stage one. They meet centre-stage.*) I'm not afraid of anything as long as we're together. I don't care what happens. You know, Daisy, I thought I'd never be able to fall in love again. (*He takes her hands, strokes her arms.*)

DAISY: Well you see, everything is possible.

BERENGER: I want so much to make you happy. Do you think you can be happy with me.

DAISY: Why not? If you're happy, then I'll be happy, too. <u>You say nothing scares you, but you're really frightened of everything. What can possibly happen to us?</u>

BERENGER (*stammering*): My love, my dear love . . . let me kiss your lips. I never dreamed I could still feel such tremendous emotion!

DAISY: You must be more calm and more sure of yourself, now.

BERENGER: I am; let me kiss you.

DAISY: I'm very tired, dear. Stay quiet and rest yourself. Sit in the armchair.

BERENGER, *led by* DAISY, *sits in the armchair.*

BERENGER: There was no point in Dudard quarrelling with Botard, as things turned out.

DAISY: Don't think about Dudard any more. I'm here with you. We've no right to interfere in other people's lives.

BERENGER: But you're interfering in mine. You know how to be firm with me.

DAISY: That's not the same thing; I never loved Dudard.

BERENGER: I see what you mean. If he'd stayed he'd always have been an obstacle between us. Ah, happiness is such an egotistical thing!

DAISY: You have to fight for happiness, don't you agree?

BERENGER: I adore you, Daisy; I admire you as well.

DAISY: Maybe you won't say that when you get to know me better.

BERENGER: The more I know you the better you seem; and you're so beautiful, so very beautiful. (*More rhinoceroses are heard passing.*) Particularly compared to them . . . (*He points to the window.*) You probably think that's no compliment, but they make you seem more beautiful than ever . . .

DAISY: Have you been good today? You haven't had any brandy?

BERENGER: Oh yes, I've been good.

DAISY: Is that the truth?

BERENGER: Yes, it's the truth I assure you.

DAISY: Can I believe you, I wonder?

BERENGER (*a little flustered*): Oh yes, you must believe me.

DAISY: Well all right then, you can have a little glass. It'll buck you up.

BERENGER *is about to leap up.*

You stay where you are, dear. Where's the bottle?

BERENGER (*pointing to it*): There, on the little table.

DAISY (*going to the table and getting the bottle and glass*): You've hidden it well away.

BERENGER: It's out of the way of temptation.

DAISY (*pours a small glass and gives it to* BERENGER): You've been a good boy. You're making progress.

BERENGER: I'll make a lot more now I'm with you.

DAISY (*handing him the glass*): Here you are. That's your reward.

BERENGER (*downing it at one go*): Thank you. (*He holds up his empty glass to* DAISY).

DAISY: Oh no, dear. That's enough for this morning. (*She takes his glass, puts it back on the table with the bottle.*) I don't want it to make you ill. (*She comes back to him.*) How's your head feel now?

BERENGER: Much better, darling.

DAISY: Then we'll take off the bandage. It doesn't suit you at all.

BERENGER: Oh no, don't touch it.

DAISY: Nonsense, we'll take it off now.

BERENGER: I'm frightened there might be something underneath.

DAISY (*removing the bandage in spite of his protests*): Always frightened, aren't you, always imagining the worst! There's nothing there, you see. Your forehead's as smooth as a baby's.

BERENGER (*feeling his brow*): You're right; you're getting rid of my complexes. (DAISY *kisses him on the brow.*) What should I do without you?

DAISY: I'll never leave you alone again.

BERENGER: I won't have any more fears now I'm with you.

DAISY: I'll keep them all at bay.

BERENGER: We'll read books together. I'll become clever.

DAISY: And when there aren't so many people about we'll go for long walks.

BERENGER: Yes, along the Seine, and in the Luxembourg Gardens...

DAISY: And to the Zoo.

BERENGER: I'll be brave and strong. I'll keep you safe from harm.

DAISY: You won't need to defend me, silly! We don't wish anyone any harm. And no one wishes us any, my dear.

BERENGER: Sometimes one does harm without meaning to, or rather one allows it to go unchecked. I know you didn't like poor old Mr. Papillon very much—but perhaps you shouldn't have spoken to him so harshly that day when Boeuf turned into a rhinoceros. You needn't have told him he had such horny hands.

DAISY: But it was true—he had!

BERENGER: I know he had, my dear. But you could have said so less bluntly and not hurt his feelings so much. It had a big effect on him.

DAISY: Do you think so?

BERENGER: He didn't show it—he was too proud for that—but the remark certainly went home. It must have influenced his decision. Perhaps you might have been the means of saving him.

DAISY: I couldn't possibly foresee what was going to happen to him ... besides he was so ill-mannered.

BERENGER: For my own part, I shall never forgive myself for not being nicer to Jean. I never managed to give him a really solid proof of the friendship I felt for him. I wasn't sufficiently understanding with him.

DAISY: Don't worry about it. You did all you could. Nobody can do the impossible. There's no point in reproaching yourself now. Stop thinking about all those people. Forget about them. You must forget all those bad memories.

BERENGER: But they keep coming back to me. They're very real memories.

DAISY: I never knew you were such a realist—I thought you were more poetic. Where's your imagination? There are many sides to reality. Choose the one that's best for you. Escape into the world of the imagination.

BERENGER: It's easy to say that!

DAISY: Aren't I enough for you?

BERENGER: Oh yes, more than enough!

DAISY: You'll spoil everything if you go on having a bad conscience.

Everybody has their faults, but you and I have got less than a lot of people.

BERENGER: Do you really think so?

DAISY: We're comparatively better than most. We're good, both of us.

BERENGER: That's true, you're good and I'm good. That's true.

DAISY: Well then we have the right to live. We even owe ourselves a duty to be happy in spite of everything. Guilt is a dangerous symptom. It shows a lack of purity.

BERENGER: You're right, it can lead. to that ... (*He points to the window under which the rhinoceroses are passing and to the up-stage wall where another rhinoceros head appears.*) ... a lot of them started like that!

DAISY: We must try and not feel guilty any more.

BERENGER: How right you are, my wonderful love ... You're all my happiness; the light of my life ... We are together, aren't we? No one can separate us. Our love is the only thing that's real. Nobody has the right to stop us from being happy—in fact, nobody could, could they?

The telephone rings.

Who could that be?

DAISY (*fearful*): Don't answer.

BERENGER: Why not?

DAISY: I don't know. I just feel it's better not to.

BERENGER: It might be Mr. Papillon, or Botard, or Jean or Dudard ringing to say they've had second thoughts. You did say it was probably only a passing phase.

DAISY: I don't think so. They wouldn't thave changed their minds so quickly. They've not had time to think it over. They're bound to give it a fair trial.

BERENGER: Perhaps the authorities have decided to take action at last; maybe they're ringing to ask our help in whatever measures they've decided to adopt.

DAISY: I'd be surprised if it was them.

The telephone rings again.

BERENGER: It is the authorities, I tell you, I recognize the ring—a long drawn-out ring, I can't ignore an appeal from them. It can't be anyone else. (*He picks up the receiver.*) Hallo? (*Trumpetings are heard coming from the receiver.*) You hear that? Trumpeting! Listen!

DAISY *puts the telephone to her ear, is shocked by the sound, quickly replaces the receiver.*

DAISY (*frightened*): What's going on?
BERENGER: They're playing jokes now.
DAISY: Jokes in bad taste!
BERENGER: You see! What did I tell you?
DAISY: You didn't tell me anything.
BERENGER: I was expecting that; it was just what I'd predicted.
DAISY: You didn't predict anything. You never do. You can only predict things after they've happened.
BERENGER: Oh yes, I can; I can predict things all right.
DAISY: That's not nice of them—in fact it's very nasty. I don't like being made fun of.
BERENGER: They wouldn't dare make fun of you. It's me they're making fun of.
DAISY: And naturally I come in for it as well because I'm with you. They're taking their revenge. But what have we done to them?

The telephone rings again.

Pull the plug out.
BERENGER: The telephone authorities say you mustn't.
DAISY: Oh you never dare to do anything—and you say you could defend me!
BERENGER (*darting to the radio*): Let's turn on the radio for the news!
DAISY: Yes, we must find out how things stand!

The sound of trumpeting comes from the radio. BERENGER *peremptorily switches it off. But in the distance other trumpetings, like echoes, can be heard.*

Things are getting really serious! I tell you frankly, I don't like it! (*She is trembling.*)
BERENGER (*very agitated*): Keep calm! Keep calm!

DAISY: They've taken over the radio stations!

BERENGER (*agitated and trembling*): Keep calm, keep calm!

DAISY *runs to the up-stage window, then to the down-stage window and looks out;* BERENGER *does the same in the opposite order, then the two come and face each other centre-stage.*

DAISY: It's no joke any longer. They mean business!

BERENGER: There's only them left now; nobody but them. Even the authorities have joined them.

They cross to the windows as before, and meet again centre-stage.

DAISY: Not a soul left anywhere.

BERENGER: We're all alone, we're left all alone.

DAISY: That's what you wanted.

BERENGER: You mean that's what you wanted!

DAISY: It was you!

BERENGER: You!

Noises come from everywhere at once. Rhinoceros heads fill the up-stage wall. From left and right in the house, the noise of rushing feet and the panting breath of the animals. But all these disquieting sounds are nevertheless somehow rhythmical, making a kind of music. The loudest noises of all come from above; a noise of stamping. Plaster falls from the ceiling. The house shakes violently.

DAISY: The earth's trembling! (*She doesn't know where to run.*)

BERENGER: No, that's our neighbours, the Perissodactyles! (*He shakes his fist to left and right and above.*) Stop it! You're preventing us from working! Noise is forbidden in these flats! Noise is forbidden!

DAISY: They'll never listen to you!

However the noise does diminish, merely forming a sort of musical background.

BERENGER (*he, too, is afraid*): Don't be frightened, my dear. We're together—you're happy with me, aren't you? It's enough that I'm with you, isn't it? I'll chase all your fears away.

DAISY: Perhaps it's all our own fault.

BERENGER: Don't think about it any longer. We mustn't start feeling remorse. It's dangerous to start feeling guilty. We must just live our lives, and be happy. We have the right to be happy. They're not spiteful, and we're not doing them any harm. They'll leave us in peace. You just keep calm and rest. Sit in the armchair. (*He leads her to the armchair.*) Just keep calm! (DAISY *sits in the armchair.*) Would you like a drop of brandy to pull you together?

DAISY: I've got a headache.

BERENGER (*taking up his bandage and binding* DAISY's *head*): I love you, my darling. Don't you worry, they'll get over it. It's just a passing phase.

DAISY: They won't get over it. It's for good.

BERENGER: I love you. I love you madly.

DAISY (*taking off the bandage*): Let things just take their course. What can we do about it?

BERENGER: They've all gone mad. The world is sick. They're all sick.

DAISY: We shan't be the ones to cure them.

BERENGER: How can we live in the same house with them?

DAISY (*calming down*): We must be sensible. We must adapt ourselves and try and get on with them.

BERENGER: They can't understand us.

DAISY: They must. There's no other way.

BERENGER: Do you understand them?

DAISY: Not yet. But we must try to understand the way their minds work, and learn their language.

BERENGER: They haven't got a language! Listen...do you call that a language?

DAISY: How do you know? You're no polyglot!

BERENGER: We'll talk about it later. We must have lunch first.

DAISY: I'm not hungry any more. It's all too much. I can't take any more.

BERENGER: But you're the strong one. You're not going to let it get you down. It's precisely for your courage that I admire you so.

DAISY: You said that before.

BERENGER: Do you feel sure of my love?

DAISY: Yes, of course.

BERENGER: I love you so.

DAISY: You keep saying the same thing, my dear.

BERENGER: Listen, Daisy, there *is* something we can do. We'll have children, and our children will have children—it'll take time, but together we can regenerate the human race.

DAISY: Regenerate the human race?

BERENGER: It happened once before.

DAISY: Ages ago. Adam and Eve ... They had a lot of courage.

BERENGER: And we, too, can have courage. We don't need all that much. It happens automatically with time and patience.

DAISY: What's the use?

BERENGER: Of course we can—with a little bit of courage.

DAISY: I don't want to have children—it's a bore.

BERENGER: How can we save the world, if you don't?

DAISY: Why bother to save it?

BERENGER: What a thing to say! Do it for me, Daisy. Let's save the world.

DAISY: After all, perhaps it's we who need saving. Perhaps we're the abnormal ones.

BERENGER: You're not yourself, Daisy, you've got a touch of fever.

DAISY: There aren't any more of our kind about anywhere, are there?

BERENGER: Daisy, you're not to talk like that!

> DAISY *looks all around at the rhinoceros heads on the walls, on the landing door, and now starting to appear along the footlights.*

DAISY: Those are the real people. They look happy. They're content to be what they are. They don't look insane. They look very natural. They were right to do what they did.

BERENGER (*clasping his hands and looking despairingly at* DAISY): We're the ones who are doing right, Daisy, I assure you.

DAISY: That's very presumptuous of you!

BERENGER: You know perfectly well I'm right.

DAISY: There's no such thing as absolute right. It's the world that's right—not you and me.

BERENGER: I *am* right, Daisy. And the proof is that you understand me when I speak to you.

DAISY: What does that prove?

BERENGER: The proof is that I love you as much as it's possible for a man to love a woman.

DAISY: Funny sort of argument!

BERENGER: I don't understand you any longer, Daisy. You don't know what you're saying, darling. Think of our love! Our love ...

DAISY: I feel a bit ashamed of what you call love—this morbid feeling, this male weakness. And female, too. It just doesn't compare with the ardour and the tremendous energy emanating from all these creatures around us.

BERENGER: Energy! You want some energy, do you? I can let you have some energy! (*He slaps her face.*)

DAISY: Oh! I never would have believed it possible ... (*She sinks into the armchair.*)

BERENGER: Oh forgive me, my darling, please forgive me! (*He tries to embrace her, she evades him.*) Forgive me, my darling. I didn't mean it. I don't know what came over me, losing control like that!

DAISY: It's because you've run out of arguments, that's why.

BERENGER: Oh dear! In the space of a few minutes we've gone through twenty-five years of married life.

DAISY: I pity you. I understand you all too well ...

BERENGER (*as* DAISY *weeps*): You're probably right that I've run out of arguments. You think they're stronger than me, stronger than us. Maybe they are.

DAISY: Indeed they are.

BERENGER: Well, in spite of everything, I swear to you I'll never give in, never!

DAISY (*she rises, goes to* BERENGER, *puts her arms round his neck*): My poor darling, I'll help you to resist—to the very end.

BERENGER: Will you be capable of it?

DAISY: I give you my word. You can trust me.

The rhinoceros noises have become melodious.

Listen, they're singing!

BERENGER: They're not singing, they're roaring.

DAISY: They're singing.

BERENGER: They're roaring, I tell you.

DAISY: You're mad, they're singing.

BERENGER: You can't have a very musical ear, then.

DAISY: You don't know the first thing about music, poor dear—and look, they're playing as well, and dancing.

BERENGER: You call that dancing?

DAISY: It's their way of dancing. They're beautiful.

BERENGER: They're disgusting!

DAISY: You're not to say unpleasant thing about them. It upsets me.

BERENGER: I'm sorry. We're not going to quarrel on their account.

DAISY: They're like gods.

BERENGER: You go too far, Daisy; take a good look at them.

DAISY: You mustn't be jealous, my dear.

> *She goes to* BERENGER *again and tries to embrace him. This time it is* BERENGER *who frees himself.*

BERENGER: I can see our opinions are directly opposed. It's better not to discuss the matter.

DAISY: Now you mustn't be nasty.

BERENGER: Then don't you be stupid!

DAISY (*to* BERENGER, *who turns his back on her. He looks at himself closely in the mirror*): It's no longer possible for us to live together.

> *As* BERENGER *continues to examine himself in the mirror she goes quietly to the door, saying:*

He isn't very nice, really, he isn't very nice. (*She goes out, and is seen slowly descending the stairs.*)

BERENGER (*still looking at himself in the mirror*): Men aren't so bad-looking, you know. And I'm not a particularly handsome specimen! Believe me, Daisy! (*He turns round.*) Daisy! Daisy! Where are you, Daisy? You can't do that to me! (*He darts to the door.*) Daisy! (*He gets to the landing and leans over the banister.*) Daisy! Come back! Come back, my dear! You haven't even had your lunch. Daisy, don't leave me alone! Remember your promise! Daisy! Daisy! (*He stops calling, makes a despairing gesture, and comes back into the room.*) Well, it was obvious we weren't getting along together. The home was broken up. It just wasn't working out. But she shouldn't have left like that with no explanation. (*He looks all around.*) She didn't even leave a message. That's no way to behave. Now I'm all on my own. (*He locks the door carefully, but angrily.*) But they won't get me. (*He carefully closes the windows.*) You won't get me! (*He addresses all the rhinoceros heads.*) I'm not joining you; I don't understand you! I'm staying as I am. I'm a human being. A human being. (*He sits in the armchair.*) It's an impossible situation. It's my fault she's gone. I meant everything to her. What'll become of her? That's one more person on my conscience. I can easily picture the worst, because the worst can easily happen. Poor little thing left all alone in this world of monsters! Nobody can help me find her, nobody, because there's nobody left.

Fresh trumpetings, hectic racings, clouds of dust.

I can't bear the sound of them any longer, I'm going to put cotton wool in my ears. (*He does so, and talks to himself in the mirror.*) The only solution is to convince them—but convince them of what? Are the changes reversible, that's the point? Are they reversible? It would be a labour of Hercules, far beyond me. In any case, to convince them you'd have to talk to them. And to talk to them I'd have to learn their language. Or they'd have to learn mine. But what language do I speak? What is my language? Am I talking French? Yes, it must be French. But what is French? I can call it French if I want, and· nobody can say it isn't—I'm the only one who speaks it. What am I saying? Do I understand what I'm saying? Do I? (*He crosses to the middle of the room.*) And what if it's true what Daisy said, and they're the ones in the right? (*He turns back to the mirror.*) A man's not ugly to look at, not ugly at all! (*He examines himself, passing his hand over his face.*) What a funny-looking thing! What do I look like? What? (*He darts to a cupboard, takes out some photographs which he examines.*) Photographs! Who are all these people? Is it Mr. Papillon—or is it Daisy? And is that Botard or Dudard or Jean? Or it is me? (*He rushes to the cupboard again and takes out two or three pictures.*) Now I recognize me: that's me, that's me! (*He hangs the pictures on the back wall, beside the rhinoceros heads.*) That's me, that's me!

When he hangs the pictures one sees that they are of an old man, a huge woman, and another man. The ugliness of these pictures is in contrast to the rhinoceros heads which have become very beautiful, BERENGER *steps back to contemplate the pictures.*

I'm not good-looking, I'm not good-looking. (*He takes down the pictures, throws them furiously to the ground, and goes over to the mirror.*) They're the good-looking ones. I was wrong! Oh, how I wish I was like them! I haven't got any horns, more's the pity! A smooth brow looks so ugly. I need one or two horns to give my sagging face a lift. Perhaps one will grow and I needn't be ashamed any more—then I could go and join them. But it will never grow! (*He looks at the palms of his hands.*) My hands are so limp—oh, why won't they get rough! (*He takes his coat off, undoes his shirt to look at his chest in the mirror.*) My skin is so slack. I can't stand this white, hairy body. Oh I'd love to have a hard skin in that wonderful dull green colour—a skin that looks decent naked without any hair on it, like theirs! (*He listens to the trumpetings.*) Their song is charming—a bit raucous perhaps, but it does have charm! I wish I could do it! (*He tries to imitate them.*) Ahh, Ahh, Brr! No, that's not it! Try again, louder! Ahh, Ahh, Brr! No, that's not it, it's too feeble, it's got no drive behind it. I'm not trumpeting at all; I'm just howling. Ahh, Ahh, Brr. There's a big difference between howling and trumpeting. I've only myself to blame; I should have gone with them while there was still time. Now it's too late! Now I'm a monster, just a monster. Now I'll never become a rhinoceros, never, never! I've gone past changing. I want to, I really do, but I can't, I just can't. I can't stand the sight of me. I'm too ashamed! (*He turns his back on the mirror.*) I'm so ugly! People who try to hang on to their individuality always come to a bad end! (*He suddenly snaps out of it.*) Oh well, too bad! I'll take on the whole of them! I'll put up a fight against the lot of them, the whole lot of them! I'm the last man left, and I'm staying that way until the end. I'm not capitulating!

Curtain.

The Birthday Party

by
Harold Pinter

THE BIRTHDAY PARTY was first presented by Michael Codron and David Hall at the Arts Theatre, Cambridge, April 28, 1958, and subsequently at the Lyric Opera House, Hammersmith; directed by Peter Wood and with the following cast:

PETEY, *a man in his sixties* . . . . Willoughby Gray

MEG, *a woman in her sixties* . . . . Beatrix Lehmann

STANLEY, *a man in his late thirties* . . . . . . Richard Pearson

LULU, *a girl in her twenties* . . . . Wendy Hutchinson

GOLDBERG, *a man in his fifties* . . . . John Slater

MCCANN, *a man of thirty* . . . . John Stratton

Act I, *A morning in summer*

Act II, *Evening of the same day*

Act III, *The next morning*

To Vivien

ACT ONE

The living-room of a house in a seaside town. A door leading to the hall down left. Back door and small window up left. Kitchen hatch, centre back. Kitchen door up right. Table and chairs, centre.

PETEY enters from the door on the left with a paper and sits at the table. He begins to read. MEG's voice comes through the kitchen hatch.

MEG: Is that you, Petey? (*Pause.*) Petey, is that you? (*Pause.*) Petey?
PETEY: What?
MEG: Is that you?
PETEY: Yes, it's me.
MEG: What? (*Her face appears at the hatch.*) Are you back?
PETEY: Yes.
MEG: I've got your cornflakes ready. (*She disappears and reappears.*) Here's your cornflakes.

> *He rises and takes the plate from her, sits at the table, props up the paper and begins to eat. MEG enters by the kitchen door.*

Are they nice?
PETEY: Very nice.
MEG: I thought they'd be nice. (*She sits at the table.*) You got your paper?
PETEY: Yes.
MEG: Is it good?
PETEY: Not bad.
MEG: What does it say?
PETEY: Nothing much.
MEG: You read me out some nice bits yesterday.
PETEY: Yes, well, I haven't finished this one yet.
MEG: Will you tell me when you come to something good?
PETEY: Yes.

Pause.

MEG: Have you been working hard this morning?

PETEY: No. Just stacked a few of the old chairs. Cleaned up a bit.
MEG: Is it nice out?
PETEY: Very nice.

Pause.

MEG: Is Stanley up yet?
PETEY: I don't know. Is he?
MEG: I don't know. I haven't seen him down yet.
PETEY: Well then, he can't be up.
MEG: Haven't you seen him down?
PETEY: I've only just come in.
MEG: He must be still asleep.

> *She looks round the room, stands, goes to the sideboard and takes a pair of socks from a drawer, collects wool and a needle and goes back to the table.*

What time did you go out this morning, Petey?
PETEY: Same time as usual.
MEG: Was it dark?
PETEY: No, it was light.
MEG (*beginning to darn*): But sometimes you go out in the morning and it's dark.
PETEY: That's in the winter.
MEG: Oh, in winter.
PETEY: Yes, it gets light later in winter.
MEG: Oh. (*Pause.*) What are you reading?
PETEY: Someone's just had a baby.
MEG: Oh, they haven't! Who?
PETEY: Some girl.
MEG: Who, Petey, who?
PETEY: I don't think you'd know her.
MEG: What's her name?
PETEY: Lady Mary Splatt.
MEG: I don't know her.
PETEY: No.
MEG: What is it?
PETEY (*studying the paper*): Er—a girl.
MEG: Not a boy?

PETEY: No.

MEG: Oh, what a shame. I'd be sorry. I'd much rather have a little boy.

PETEY: A little girl's all right.

MEG: I'd much rather have a little boy. (*Pause. Vaguely.*) Is it nice out?

PETEY: Yes, it's a nice day.

MEG: Is the sun shining?

PETEY: Yes.

MEG: I wish Stanley would take me for a walk along the front one day. When was I last along the front? Why don't you ask him to take me for a walk one day, Petey?

PETEY: Why don't you ask him yourself?

MEG: No. You ask him. (*Pause.*) He goes through his socks terrible.

PETEY: Why? He's in bed half the week.

MEG: That boy should be up. Why isn't he up? What's the time?

PETEY: About half past ten.

MEG: He should be down. He's late for his breakfast.

PETEY: I've finished my cornflakes.

MEG: Were they nice?

PETEY: Very nice.

MEG: I've got something else for you.

PETEY: Good.

> *She rises, takes his plate and exits into the kitchen. She then appears at the hatch with two pieces of fried bread on a plate.*

MEG: Here you are, Petey.

> *He rises, collects the plate, looks at it, sits at the table.* MEG *re-enters.*

Is it nice?

PETEY: I haven't tasted it yet.

MEG: I bet you don't know what it is.

PETEY: Yes, I do.

MEG: What is it, then?

PETEY: Fried bread.

MEG: That's right.

> *He begins to eat.*

PETEY: No bacon?

MEG: I've run out.

PETEY: Ah.

MEG: I'm going out soon, to do some shopping.

She watches him eat.

PETEY: Very nice.

MEG: I knew it was.

PETEY (*turning to her*): Oh, Meg, two men came up to me on the beach last night.

MEG: Two men?

PETEY: Yes. They wanted to know if we could put them up for a couple of nights.

MEG: Put them up? Here?

PETEY: Yes.

MEG: How many men?

PETEY: Two.

MEG: What did you say?

PETEY: Well, I said I didn't know. So they said they'd come round to find out.

MEG: Are they coming?

PETEY: Well, they said they would.

MEG: Had they heard about us, Petey?

PETEY: They must have done.

MEG: Yes, they must have done. They must have heard this was a very good boarding house. It is. This house is on the list.

PETEY: It is.

MEG: I know it is.

PETEY: They might turn up today. Can you do it?

MEG: Oh, I've got that lovely room they can have.

PETEY: You've got a room ready?

MEG: I've got the room with the armchair all ready for visitors.

PETEY: You're sure?

MEG: Yes, that'll be all right then, if they come today.

PETEY: Good.

She takes the socks etc. back to the sideboard drawer.

MEG: I'm going to wake that boy.

PETEY: There's a new show coming to the Palace.

MEG: On the pier?

PETEY: No. The Palace, in the town.

MEG: Stanley could have been in it, if it was on the pier.

PETEY: This is a straight show.

MEG: What do you mean?

PETEY: No dancing or singing.

MEG: What do they do then?

PETEY: They just talk.

Pause.

MEG: Oh.

PETEY: You like a song, eh, Meg?

MEG: I like listening to the piano. I used to like watching Stanley play the piano. Of course, he didn't sing. (*Looking at the door.*) I'm going to call that boy.

PETEY: Didn't you take him up his cup of tea?

MEG: I always take him up his cup of tea. But that was a long time ago.

PETEY: Did he drink it?

MEG: I made him. I stood there till he did. I tried to get him up then. But he wouldn't, the little monkey. I'm going to call him. (*She goes to the door.*) Stan! Stanny! (*She listens.*) Stan! I'm coming up to fetch you if you don't come down! I'm coming up! I'm going to count three! One! Two! Three! I'm coming to get you! (*She exits and goes upstairs. In a moment, shouts from* STANLEY, *wild laughter from* MEG. PETEY *takes his plate to the hatch. Shouts. Laughter.* PETEY *sits at the table. Silence. She returns.*) He's coming down. (*She is panting and arranges her hair.*) I told him if he didn't hurry up he'd get no breakfast.

PETEY: That did it, eh?

MEG: I'll get his cornflakes.

MEG *exits to the kitchen.* PETEY *reads the paper.* STANLEY *enters. He is unshaven, in his pyjama jacket and wears glasses He sits at the table.*

PETEY: Morning, Stanley.

STANLEY: Morning.

Silence. MEG *enters with the bowl of cornflakes, which she sets on the table.*

MEG: So he's come down at last, has he? He's come down at last for his breakfast. But he doesn't deserve any, does he, Petey? (STANLEY *stares at the cornflakes.*) Did you sleep well?

STANLEY: I didn't sleep at all.

MEG: You didn't sleep at all? Did you hear that, Petey? Too tired to eat your breakfast, I suppose? Now you eat up those cornflakes like a good boy. Go on.

He begins to eat.

STANLEY: What's it like out today?

PETEY: Very nice.

STANLEY: Warm?

PETEY: Well, there's a good breeze blowing.

STANLEY: Cold?

PETEY: No, no, I wouldn't say it was cold.

MEG: What are the cornflakes like, Stan?

STANLEY: Horrible.

MEG: Those flakes? Those lovely flakes? You're a liar, a little liar. They're refreshing. It says so. For people when they get up late.

STANLEY: The milk's off.

MEG: It's not. Petey ate his, didn't you, Petey?

PETEY: That's right.

MEG: There you are then.

STANLEY: All right, I'll go on to the second course.

MEG: He hasn't finished the first course and he wants to go on to the second course!

STANLEY: I feel like something cooked.

MEG: Well, I'm not going to give it to you.

PETEY: Give it to him.

MEG (*sitting at the table, right*): I'm not going to.

Pause.

STANLEY: No breakfast. (*Pause.*) All night long I've been dreaming about this breakfast.

MEG: I thought you said you didn't sleep.

STANLEY: Day-dreaming. All night long. And now she won't give me any. Not even a crust of bread on the table. (*Pause.*) Well, I can see I'll have to go down to one of those smart hotels on the front.

MEG (*rising quickly*): You won't get a better breakfast there than here.

She exits to the kitchen. STANLEY *yawns broadly.* MEG *appears at the hatch with a plate.*

Here you are. You'll like this.

PETEY *rises, collects the plate, brings it to the table, puts it in front of* STANLEY, *and sits.*

STANLEY: What's this?

PETEY: Fried bread.

MEG (*entering*): Well, I bet you don't know what it is.

STANLEY: Oh yes I do.

MEG: What?

STANLEY: Fried bread.

MEG: He knew.

STANLEY: What a wonderful surprise.

MEG: You didn't expect that, did you?

STANLEY: I bloody well didn't.

PETEY (*rising*): Well, I'm off.

MEG: You going back to work?

PETEY: Yes.

MEG: Your tea! You haven't had your tea!

PETEY: That's all right. No time now.

MEG: I've got it made inside.

PETEY: No, never mind. See you later. Ta-ta, Stan.

STANLEY: Ta-ta.

PETEY *exits, left.*

Tch, tch, tch, tch.

MEG (*defensively*): What do you mean?

STANLEY: You're a bad wife.

MEG: I'm not. Who said I am?

STANLEY: Not to make your husband a cup of tea. Terrible.

MEG: He knows I'm not a bad wife.

STANLEY: Giving him sour milk instead.

MEG: It wasn't sour.

STANLEY: Disgraceful.

MEG: You mind your own business, anyway. (STANLEY *eats.*) You won't find many better wives than me, I can tell you. I keep a very nice house and I keep it clean.

STANLEY: Whoo!

MEG: Yes! And this house is very well known, for a very good boarding house for visitors.

STANLEY: Visitors? Do you know how many visitors you've had since I've been here?

MEG: How many?

STANLEY: One.

MEG: Who?

STANLEY: Me! I'm your visitor.

MEG: You're a liar. This house is on the list.

STANLEY: I bet it is.

MEG: I know it is.

He pushes his plate away and picks up the paper.

Was it nice?

STANLEY: What?

MEG: The fried bread.

STANLEY: Succulent.

MEG: You shouldn't say that word.

STANLEY: What word?

MEG: That word you said.

STANLEY: What, succulent—?

MEG: Don't say it!

STANLEY: What's the matter with it?

MEG: You shouldn't say that word to a married woman.

STANLEY: Is that a fact?

MEG: Yes.

STANLEY: Well, I never knew that.

MEG: Well, it's true.

STANLEY: Who told you that?

MEG: Never you mind.

STANLEY: Well, if I can't say it to a married woman who can I say it to?

MEG: You're bad.

STANLEY: What about some tea?

MEG: Do you want some tea? (STANLEY *reads the paper*.) Say please.

STANLEY: Please.

MEG: Say sorry first.

STANLEY: Sorry first.

MEG: No. Just sorry.

STANLEY: Just sorry!

MEG: You deserve the strap.

> *She takes his plate and ruffles his hair as she passes.* STANLEY *exclaims and throws her arm away. She goes into the kitchen. He rubs his eyes under his glasses and picks up the paper. She enters.*

I brought the pot in.

STANLEY (*absently*): I don't know what I'd do without you.

MEG: You don't deserve it though.

STANLEY: Why not?

MEG (*pouring the tea, coyly*): Go on. Calling me that.

STANLEY: How long has that tea been in the pot?

MEG: It's good tea. Good strong tea.

STANLEY: This isn't tea. It's gravy!

MEG: It's not.

STANLEY: Get out of it. You succulent old washing bag.

MEG: I am not! And it isn't your place to tell me if I am!

STANLEY: And it isn't your place to come into a man's bedroom and—wake him up.

MEG: Stanny! Don't you like your cup of tea of a morning—the one I bring you?

STANLEY: I can't drink this muck. Didn't anyone ever tell you to warm the pot, at least?

MEG: My father wouldn't let you insult me the way you do.

STANLEY: Your father? Who was he when he was at home?

MEG: He would report you.

STANLEY (*sleepily*): Now would I insult you, Meg? Would I do a terrible thing like that?

MEG: You did.

STANLEY (*putting his head in his hands*): Oh God, I'm tired.

Silence. MEG *goes to the sideboard, collects a duster, and vaguely dusts the room, watching him. She comes to the table and dusts it.*

Not the bloody table!

Pause.

MEG: Stan?

STANLEY: What?

MEG (*shyly*): Am I really succulent?

STANLEY: Oh, you are. I'd rather have you than a cold in the nose any day.

MEG: You're just saying that.

STANLEY (*violently*): Look, why don't you get this place cleared up! It's a pigsty. And another thing, what about my room? It needs sweeping. It needs papering. I need a new room!

MEG (*sensual, stroking his arm*): Oh, Stan, that's a lovely room. I've had some lovely afternoons in that room.

He recoils from her hand in disgust, stands and exits quickly by the door on the left. She collects his cup and the teapot and takes them to the hatch shelf. The street door slams. STANLEY *returns.*

MEG: Is the sun shining? (*He crosses to the window, takes a cigarette and matches from his pyjama jacket, and lights his cigarette.*) What are you smoking, Stan?

STANLEY: A cigarette.

MEG: Are you going to give me one?

STANLEY: No.

MEG: I like cigarettes. (*He stands at the window, smoking. She crosses behind him and tickles the back of his neck.*) Tickle, tickle.

STANLEY (*pushing her*): Get away from me.

MEG: Are you going out?

STANLEY: Not with you.

MEG: But I'm going shopping in a minute.

STANLEY: Go.

MEG: You'll be lonely, all by yourself.

STANLEY: Will I?

MEG: Without your old Meg. I've got to get things in for the two gentlemen.

A pause. STANLEY *slowly raises his head. He speaks without turning.*

STANLEY: What two gentlemen?

MEG: I'm expecting visitors.

He turns.

STANLEY: What?

MEG: You didn't know that, did you?

STANLEY: What are you talking about?

MEG: Two gentlemen asked Petey if they could come and stay for a couple of nights. I'm expecting them. (*She picks up the duster and begins to wipe the cloth on the table.*)

STANLEY: I don't believe it.

MEG: It's true.

STANLEY (*moving to her*): You're saying it on purpose.

MEG: Petey told me this morning.

STANLEY (*grinding his cigarette*): When was this? When did he see them?

MEG: Last night.

STANLEY: Who are they?

MEG: I don't know.

STANLEY: Didn't he tell you their names?

MEG: No.

STANLEY (*pacing the room*): Here? They wanted to come here?

MEG: Yes, they did. (*She takes the curlers out of her hair.*)

STANLEY: Why?

MEG: This house is on the list.

STANLEY: But who are they? I mean, why. . . . ?

MEG: You'll see when they come.

STANLEY (*decisively*): They won't come.

MEG: Why not?

STANLEY (*quickly*): I tell you they won't come. Why didn't they come last night, if they were coming?

MEG: Perhaps they couldn't find the place in the dark. It's not easy to find in the dark.

STANLEY: They won't come. Someone's taking the Michael. Forget all about it. It's a false alarm A false alarm. (*He sits at the table.*) Where's my tea?

MEG: I took it away. You didn't want it.

STANLEY: What do you mean, you took it away?

MEG: I took it away.

STANLEY: What did you take it away for?

MEG: You didn't want it!

STANLEY: Who said I didn't want it?

MEG: You did!

STANLEY: Who gave you the right to take away my tea?

MEG: You wouldn't drink it.

STANLEY *stares at her.*

STANLEY (*quietly*): Who do you think you're talking to?

MEG (*uncertainly*): What?

STANLEY: Come here.

MEG: What do you mean?

STANLEY: Come over here.

MEG: No.

STANLEY: I want to ask you something. (MEG *fidgets nervously. She does not go to him.*) Come on. (*Pause.*) All right. I can ask it from here just as well. (*Deliberately.*) Tell me, Mrs. Boles, when you address yourself to me, do you ever ask yourself who exactly you are talking to? Eh?

Silence. He groans, his trunk falls forward, his head falls into his hands.

MEG (*in a small voice*): Didn't you enjoy your breakfast, Stan? (*She approaches the table.*) Stan? When are you going to play the piano again? (STANLEY *grunts.*) Like you used to? (STANLEY *grunts.*) I used to like watching you play the piano. When are you going to play it again?

STANLEY: I can't, can I?

MEG: Why not?

STANLEY: I haven't got a piano, have I?

MEG: No, I meant like when you were working. That piano.

STANLEY: Go and do your shopping.

MEG: But you wouldn't have to go away if you got a job, would you? You could play the piano on the pier.

He looks at her, then speaks airily.

STANLEY: I've . . . er . . . I've been offered a job, as a matter of fact.

MEG: What?

STANLEY: Yes. I'm considering a job at the moment.

MEG: You're not.

STANLEY: A good one, too. A night club. In Berlin.

MEG: Berlin?

STANLEY: Berlin. A night club. Playing the piano. A fabulous salary. And all found.

MEG: How long for?

STANLEY: We don't stay in Berlin. Then we go to Athens.

MEG: How long for?

STANLEY: Yes. Then we pay a flying visit to . . . er . . . whatsisname. . . .

MEG: Where?

STANLEY: Constantinople. Zagreb. Vladivostock. It's a round the world tour.

MEG (*sitting at the table*): Have you played the piano in those places before?

STANLEY: Played the piano? I've played the piano all over the world. All over the country. (*Pause.*) I once gave a concert.

MEG: A concert?

STANLEY (*reflectively*): Yes. It was a good one, too. They were all there that night. Every single one of them. It was a great success. Yes. A concert. At Lower Edmonton.

MEG: What did you wear?

STANLEY (*to himself*): I had a unique touch. Absolutely unique. They came up to me. They came up to me and said they were grateful. Champagne we had that night, the lot. (*Pause.*) My father nearly came down to hear me. Well, I dropped him a card anyway. But I don't think he could make it. No, I—I lost the address, that was it. (*Pause.*) Yes. Lower Edmonton. Then after that, you know what they did? They carved me up. Carved me up. It was all arranged, it was all worked out. My next concert. Somewhere else it was. In winter. I went down there to play.

Then, when I got there, the hall was closed, the place was shuttered up, not even a caretaker. They'd locked it up. (*Takes off his glasses and wipes them on his pyjama jacket.*) A fast one. They pulled a fast one. I'd like to know who was responsible for that. (*Bitterly.*) All right, Jack, I can take a tip. They want me to crawl down on my bended knees. Well I can take a tip . . . any day or the week. (*He replaces his glasses, then looks at* MEG.) Look at her. You're just an old piece of rock cake, aren't you? (*He rises and leans across the table to her.*) That's what you are, aren't you?

MEG: Don't you go away again, Stan. You stay here. You'll be better off. You stay with your old Meg. (*He groans and lies across the table.*) Aren't you feeling well this morning, Stan? Did you pay a visit this morning?

He stiffens, then lifts himself slowly, turns to face her and speaks low and meaningfully.

STANLEY: Meg. Do you know what?

MEG: What?

STANLEY: Have you heard the latest?

MEG: No.

STANLEY· I'll bet you have.

MEG· I haven't.

STANLEY: Shall I tell you?

MEG: What latest?

STANLEY: You haven't heard it?

MEG: No.

STANLEY (*advancing*): They're coming today.

MEG: Who?

STANLEY: They're coming in a van.

MEG: Who?

STANLEY: And do you know what they've got in that van?

MEG: What?

STANLEY: They've got a wheelbarrow in that van.

MEG (*breathlessly*): They haven't.

STANLEY: Oh yes they have.

MEG: You're a liar.

STANLEY (*advancing upon her*): A big wheelbarrow. And when tne

van stops they wheel it out, and they wheel it up the garden
path, and then they knock at the front door.

MEG: They don't.

STANLEY: They're looking for someone.

MEG: They're not.

STANLEY: They're looking for someone. A certain person.

MEG (*hoarsely*): No, they're not!

STANLEY: Shall I tell you who they're looking for?

MEG: No!

STANLEY: You don't want me to tell you?

MEG: You're a liar!

> *A sudden knock on the front door.* MEG *edges past* STANLEY
> *and collects her shopping bag. Another knock on the door.*
> MEG *goes out.* STANLEY *sidles to the door and listens.*

VOICE: Hullo Mrs. Boles. It's come.

MEG: Oh, has it come?

VOICE: Yes, it's just come.

MEG: What, is that it?

VOICE: Yes. I thought I'd bring it round.

MEG: Is it nice?

VOICE: Very nice. What shall I do with it?

MEG: Well, I don't ... (*Whispers.*)

VOICE: No, of course not ... (*Whispers.*)

MEG: All right, but ... (*Whispers.*)

VOICE: I won't ... (*Whispers.*) Ta-ta, Mrs. Boles.

> STANLEY *quickly sits at the table. Enter* LULU.

LULU: Oh, hullo.

STANLEY: Ay-ay.

LULU: I just want to leave this in here.

STANLEY: Do. (LULU *crosses to the sideboard and puts a solid, round
parcel upon it.*) That's a bulky object.

LULU: You're not to touch it.

STANLEY: Why would I want to touch it?

LULU: Well, you're not to, anyway.

STANLEY: Sit down a minute.

LULU *walks upstage.*

LULU: Why don't you open the door? It's all stuffy in here.

She opens the back door.

STANLEY (*rising*): What are you talking about? I disinfected the
place this morning.

LULU (*at the door*): Oh, that's better.

STANLEY: Don't you believe me, then?

LULU: What?

STANLEY: Don't you believe I scrubbed the place out with Dettol this
morning?

LULU: You didn't scrub yourself, I suppose?

STANLEY: I was in the sea at half past six.

LULU: Were you?

STANLEY: Sit down.

LULU: A minute.

She sits, takes out a compact and powders her nose.

STANLEY: So you're not going to tell me what's in that parcel?

LULU: Who said I knew?

STANLEY: Don't you?

LULU: I never said so.

STANLEY (*triumphantly*): Well, how can you tell me what's in it if
you don't know what's in it?

LULU: I'm not going to tell you.

STANLEY: I think it's going to rain today, what do you think?

LULU: Why don't you have a shave?

STANLEY: Don't you believe me then, when I tell you I was in the sea
at half past six this morning?

LULU: I'd rather not discuss it.

STANLEY: You think I'm a liar then?

LULU (*offering him the compact*): Do you want to have a look at your
face? (STANLEY *withdraws from the table.*) You could do with a
shave, do you know that? (STANLEY *sits, right, at the table.*) Don't
you ever go out? (*He does not answer.*) I mean, what do you do,
just sit around the house like this all day long? (*Pause.*) Hasn't

Mrs. Boles got enough to do without having you under her feet all day long?

STANLEY: I always stand on the table when she sweeps the floor.

LULU: Why don't you ever go out?

STANLEY: I was out—this morning—before breakfast—

LULU: I've never seen you out, not once.

STANLEY: Well, perhaps you're never out when I'm out.

LULU: I'm always out.

STANLEY: We've just never met, that's all.

LULU: Why don't you have a wash? You look terrible.

STANLEY: A wash wouldn't make any difference.

LULU (*rising*): Come out and get a bit of air. You depress me, looking like that.

STANLEY: Air? Oh, I don't know about that.

LULU: It's lovely out. And I've got a few sandwiches.

STANLEY: What sort of sandwiches?

LULU: Cheese.

STANLEY: I'm a big eater, you know.

LULU: That's all right. I'm not hungry.

STANLEY (*abruptly*): How would you like to go away with me?

LULU: Where.

STANLEY: Nowhere. Still, we could go.

LULU: But where could we go?

STANLEY: Nowhere. There's nowhere to go. So we could just go. It wouldn't matter.

LULU: We might as well stay here.

STANLEY: No. It's no good here.

LULU: Well, where else is there?

STANLEY: Nowhere.

LULU: Well, that's a charming proposal. (*He gets up.*) Are you going to wash?

STANLEY (*going round to her*): Listen. I want to ask you something.

LULU: You've just asked me.

STANLEY: No. Listen. (*Urgently.*) Has Meg had many guests staying in this house, besides me, I mean before me?

LULU: Besides you?

STANLEY (*impatiently*): Was she very busy, in the old days?

LULU: Why should she be?

STANLEY: What do you mean? This used to be a boarding house, didn't it?

LULU: Did it?

STANLEY: Didn't it?

LULU: Did it?

STANLEY: Didn't . . . oh, skip it.

LULU: Why do you want to know?

STANLEY: She's expecting two guests, for the first time since I've been here.

LULU: Oh. Do you have to wear those glasses?

STANLEY: Yes.

LULU: So you're not coming out for a walk?

STANLEY: I can't at the moment.

LULU: You're a bit of a washout, aren't you?

> *She exits, left.* STANLEY *stands. He then goes to the mirror and looks in it. He goes into the kitchen, takes off his glasses and begins to wash his face. A pause. Enter, by the back door,* GOLDBERG *and* MCCANN. MCCANN *carries two suitcases,* GOLDBERG *a briefcase. They halt inside the door, then walk downstage.* STANLEY, *wiping his face, glimpses their backs through the hatch.* GOLDBERG *and* MCCANN *look round the room.* STANLEY *slips on his glasses, sidles through the kitchen door and out of the back door.*

MCCANN: Is this it?

GOLDBERG: This is it.

MCCANN: Are you sure?

GOLDBERG: Sure I'm sure.

> *Pause.*

MCCANN: What now?

GOLDBERG: Don't worry yourself, McCann. Take a seat.

MCCANN: What about you?

GOLDBERG: What about me?

MCCANN: Are you going to take a seat?

GOLDBERG: We'll both take a seat. (MCCANN *puts down the suitcases and sits at the table, left.*) Sit back, McCann. Relax. What's the matter with you? I bring you down for a few days to the seaside. Take a holiday. Do yourself a favour. Learn to relax, McCann, or you'll never get anywhere.

MCCANN: Ah sure, I do try, Nat.

GOLDBERG (*sitting at the table, right*): The secret is breathing. Take my tip. It's a well-known fact. Breathe in, breathe out, take a chance, let yourself go, what can you lose? Look at me. When I was an apprentice yet, McCann, every second Friday of the month my Uncle Barney used to take me to the seaside, regular as clockwork. Brighton, Canvey Island, Rottingdean—Uncle Barney wasn't particular. After lunch on Shabbuss we'd go and sit in a couple of deck chairs—you know, the ones with canopies—we'd have a little paddle, we'd watch the tide coming in, going out, the sun coming down—golden days, believe me, McCann. (*Reminiscent.*) Uncle Barney. Of course, he was an impeccable dresser. One of the old school. He had a house just outside Basingstoke at the time. Respected by the whole community. Culture? Don't talk to me about culture. He was an all-round man, what do you mean? He was a cosmopolitan.

MCCANN: Hey, Nat. . . .

GOLDBERG (*reflectively*): Yes. One of the old school.

MCCANN: Nat. How do we know this is the right house?

GOLDBERG: What?

MCCANN: How do we know this is the right house?

GOLDBERG: What makes you think it's the wrong house?

MCCANN: I didn't see a number on the gate.

GOLDBERG: I wasn't looking for a number.

MCCANN: No?

GOLDBERG (*settling in the armchair*): You know one thing Uncle Barney taught me? Uncle Barney taught me that the word of a gentleman is enough. That's why, when I had to go away on business I never carried any money. One of my sons used to come with me. He used to carry a few coppers. For a paper, perhaps, to see how the M.C.C. was getting on overseas. Otherwise my name was good. Besides, I was a very busy man.

MCCANN: I didn't know you had any sons.

GOLDBERG: But of course. I've been a family man.

MCCANN: How many did you have?

GOLDBERG: I lost my last two—in an accident. But the first, the first grew up to be a fine boy.

MCCANN: What's he doing now?

GOLDBERG: I often wonder that myself. Yes. Emanuel. A quiet fellow. He never said much. Timmy I used to call him.

MCCANN: Emanuel?

GOLDBERG: That's right. Manny.

MCCANN: Manny?

GOLDBERG: Sure. It's short for Emanuel.

MCCANN: I thought you called him Timmy.

GOLDBERG: I did.

MCCANN: What about this, Nat? Isn't it about time someone came in?

GOLDBERG: McCann, what are you so nervous about? Pull yourself together. Everywhere you go these days it's like a funeral.

MCCANN: That's true.

GOLDBERG: True? Of course it's true. It's more than true. It's a fact.

MCCANN: You may be right.

GOLDBERG: What is it, McCann? You don't trust me like you did in the old days?

MCCANN: Sure I trust you, Nat.

GOLDBERG: I'm glad. But why is it that before you do a job you're all over the place, and when you're doing the job you're as cool as a whistle?

MCCANN: I don't know, Nat. I'm just all right once I know what I'm doing. When I know what I'm doing, I'm all right.

GOLDBERG: Well, you do it very well.

MCCANN: Thank you, Nat.

GOLDBERG: As a matter of fact I was talking about you only the other day. I gave you a very good name.

MCCANN: That was kind of you, Nat.

GOLDBERG: And then this job came up out of the blue. Naturally they approached me to take care of it. And you know who I asked for?

MCCANN: Who?

GOLDBERG: You.

MCCANN: That was very good of you, Nat.

GOLDBERG: No, it was nothing. You're a capable man, McCann.

MCCANN: That's a great compliment, Nat, coming from a man in your position.

GOLDBERG: Well, I've got a position, I won't deny it.

MCCANN: You certainly have.

GOLDBERG: I would never deny that I had a position.

MCCANN: And what a position!

GOLDBERG: It's not a thing I would deny.

MCCANN: Yes, it's true, you've done a lot for me. I appreciate it.

GOLDBERG: Say no more.

MCCANN: You've always been a true Christian.

GOLDBERG: In a way.

MCCANN: No, I just thought I'd tell you that I appreciate it.

GOLDBERG: It's unnecessary to recapitulate.

MCCANN: You're right there.

GOLDBERG: Quite unnecessary.

Pause. MCCANN *leans forward.*

MCCANN: Hey Nat, just one thing. . . .

GOLDBERG: What now?

MCCANN: This job—no, listen—this job, is it going to be like anything we've ever done before?

GOLDBERG: Tch, tch, tch.

MCCANN: No, just tell me that. Just that, and I won't ask any more.

GOLDBERG *sighs, stands, goes behind the table, ponders, looks at* MCCANN, *and then speaks in a quiet, fluent, official tone.'*

GOLDBERG: The main issue is a singular issue and quite distinct from your previous work. Certain elements, however, might well approximate in points of procedure to some of your other activities. All is dependent on the attitude of our subject. At all events, McCann, I can assure you that the assignment will be carried out and the mission accomplished with no excessive aggravation to you or myself. Satisfied?

MCCANN: Sure. Thank you, Nat.

MEG *enters, left.*

GOLDBERG: Ah, Mrs. Boles?

MEG: Yes?

GOLDBERG: We spoke to your husband last night. Perhaps he mentioned us? We heard that you kindly let rooms for gentlemen. So I brought my friend along with me. We were after a nice place, you understand. So we came to you. I'm Mr. Goldberg and this is Mr. McCann.

MEG: Very pleased to meet you.

They shake hands.

GOLDBERG: We're pleased to meet you, too.

MEG: That's very nice.

GOLDBERG: You're right. How often do you meet someone it's a pleasure to meet?

MCCANN: Never.

GOLDBERG: But today it's different. How are you keeping, Mrs. Boles?

MEG: Oh, very well, thank you.

GOLDBERG: Yes? Really?

MEG: Oh yes, really.

GOLDBERG: I'm glad. What do you say, McCann? Oh, Mrs. Boles, would you mind if my friend went into your kitchen and had a little gargle?

MEG (*to* MCCANN): Why, have you got a sore throat?

MCCANN: Er—yes.

MEG: Do you want some salt?

MCCANN: Salt?

MEG: Salt's good.

GOLDBERG: Good? It's wonderful. Go on, off you go, McCann.

MCCANN: Where is the kitchen?

MEG: Over there. (MCCANN *goes to the kitchen.*) There's some salt on the shelf.

MCCANN *exits.* GOLDBERG *sits at the table, right.*

GOLDBERG: So you can manage to put us up, eh, Mrs. Boles?

MEG: Well, it would have been easier last week.

GOLDBERG: Last week.

MEG: Or next week.

GOLDBERG: Next week.

MEG: Yes.

GOLDBERG: How many have you got here at the moment?

MEG: Just one at the moment.

GOLDBERG: Just one?

MEG: Yes. Just one. Until you came.

GOLDBERG: And your husband, of course?

MEG: Yes, but he sleeps with me.

GOLDBERG: What does he do, your husband?

MEG: He's a deck-chair attendant.

GOLDBERG: Oh, very nice.
MEG: Yes, he's out in all weathers.

She begins to take her purchases from her bag.

GOLDBERG: Of course. And your guest? Is he a man?
MEG: A man?
GOLDBERG: Or a woman?
MEG: No. A man.
GOLDBERG: Been here long?
MEG: He's been here about a year now.
GOLDBERG: Oh yes. A resident. What's his name?
MEG: Stanley Webber.
GOLDBERG: Oh yes? Does he work here?
MEG: He used to work. He used to be a pianist. In a concert party on the pier.
GOLDBERG: Oh yes? On the pier, eh? Does he play a nice piano?
MEG: Oh, lovely. (*She sits at the table.*) He once gave a concert.
GOLDBERG: Oh? Where?
MEG (*falteringly*): In . . . a big hall. His father gave him champagne. But then they locked the place up and he couldn't get out. The caretaker had gone home. So he had to wait until the morning before he could get out. (*With confidence.*) They were very grateful. (*Pause.*) And then they all wanted to give him a tip. And so he took the tip. And then he got a fast train and he came down here.
GOLDBERG: Really?
MEG: Oh yes. Straight down.

Pause.

MEG: I wish he could have played tonight.
GOLDBERG: Why tonight?
MEG: It's his birthday today.
GOLDBERG: His birthday?
MEG: Yes. Today. But I'm not going to tell him until tonight.
GOLDBERG: Doesn't he know it's his birthday?
MEG: He hasn't mentioned it.
GOLDBERG (*thoughtfully*): Well, well, well. Tell me. Are you going to have a party?

MEG: A party?

GOLDBERG: Weren't you going to have one?

MEG (*her eyes wide*): No

GOLDBERG: Well, of course, you must have one. (*He stands.*) We'll have a party, eh? What do you say?

MEG: Oh yes!

GOLDBERG: Sure. We'll give him a party. Leave it to me.

MEG: Oh, that's wonderful, Mr. Gold—

GOLDBERG: Berg.

MEG: Berg.

GOLDBERG: You like the idea?

MEG: Oh, I'm so glad you came today.

GOLDBERG: If we hadn't come today we'd have come tomorrow Still, I'm glad we came today. Just in time for his birthday.

MEG: I wanted to have a party. But you must have people for a party.

GOLDBERG: And now you've got McCann and me. McCann's the life and soul of any party.

MCCANN *enters from the kitchen.*

MEG: I'll invite Lulu this afternoon. (*To* MCCANN.) We're going to have a party tonight.

MCCANN: What?

GOLDBERG: There's a gentleman living here, McCann, who's got a birthday today, and he's forgotten all about it. So we're going to remind him. We're going to give him a party.

MCCANN: Oh, is that a fact?

MEG: Tonight.

GOLDBERG: Tonight. Did you have a good gargle?

MCCANN: Yes, thanks.

MEG: I'll put on my party dress.

GOLDBERG: And I'll get some bottles.

MEG: Oh, this is going to cheer Stanley up. It will. He's been down in the dumps lately.

GOLDBERG: We'll bring him out of himself.

MEG: I hope I look nice in my dress.

GOLDBERG: Madam, you'll look like a tulip.

MEG: What colour?

GOLDBERG: Er—well, I'll have to see the dress first.

MCCANN: Could I go up to my room?

MEG: Oh, I've put you both together. Do you mind being both together?

GOLDBERG: I don't mind. Do you mind, McCann?

MCCANN: No.

MEG: What time shall we have the party?

GOLDBERG: Nine o'clock.

MCCANN (*at the door*): Is this the way?

MEG (*rising*): I'll show you. If you don't mind coming upstairs.

GOLDBERG: With a tulip? It's a pleasure.

> MEG *and* GOLDBERG *exit laughing, followed by* MCCANN. STANLEY *appears at the window. He enters by the back door. He goes to the door on the left, opens it and listens. Silence. He walks to the table. He stands. He sits, as* MEG *enters. She crosses and hangs her shopping bag on a hook. He lights a match and watches it burn.*

STANLEY: Who is it?

MEG: The two gentlemen.

STANLEY: What two gentlemen?

MEG: The ones that were coming. I just took them to their room. They were thrilled with their room.

STANLEY: They've come?

MEG: They're very nice, Stan.

STANLEY: Why didn't they come last night?

MEG: They said the beds were wonderful.

STANLEY: Who are they?

MEG (*sitting*): They're very nice, Stanley.

STANLEY: I said, who are they?

MEG: I've told you, the two gentlemen.

STANLEY: I didn't think they'd come.

> *He rises and walks to the window.*

MEG: They have. They were here when I came in.

STANLEY: What do they want here?

MEG: They want to stay.

STANLEY: How long for?

MEG: They didn't say.

STANLEY (*turning*): But why here? Why not somewhere else?

MEG: This house is on the list.

STANLEY (*coming down*): What are they called? What are their names?

MEG: Oh, Stanley, I can't remember.

STANLEY: They told you, didn't they? Or didn't they tell you?

MEG: Yes, they. . . .

STANLEY: Then what are they? Come on. Try to remember.

MEG: Why, Stan? Do you know them?

STANLEY: How do I know if I know them until I know their names?

MEG: Well . . . he told me, I remember.

STANLEY: Well?

She thinks.

MEG: Gold—something.

STANLEY: Goldsomething?

MEG: Yes. Gold. . . .

STANLEY: Yes?

MEG: Goldberg.

STANLEY: Goldberg?

MEG: That's right. That was one of them.

STANLEY *slowly sits at the table, left.*

Do you know them?

STANLEY *does not answer.*

Stan, they won't wake you up, I promise. I'll tell them they must be quiet.

STANLEY *sits still.*

They won't be here long, Stan. I'll still bring you up your early morning tea.

STANLEY *sits still.*

You mustn't be sad today. It's your birthday.

A pause.

STANLEY (*dumbly*): Uh?

MEG: It's your birthday, Stan. I was going to keep it a secret until tonight.

STANLEY: No.

MEG: It is. I've brought you a present. (*She goes to the sideboard, picks up the parcel, and places it on the table in front of him.*) Here. Go on. Open it.

STANLEY: What's this?

MEG: It's your present.

STANLEY: This isn't my birthday, Meg.

MEG: Of course it is. Open your present.

(*He stares at the parcel, slowly stands, and opens it. He takes out a boy's drum.*

STANLEY (*flatly*): It's a drum. A boy's drum.

MEG (*tenderly*): It's because you haven't got a piano. (*He stares at her, then turns and walks towards the door, left.*) Aren't you going to give me a kiss? (*He turns sharply, and stops. He walks back towards her slowly. He stops at her chair, looking down upon her. Pause. His shoulders sag, he bends and kisses her on the cheek.*) There are some sticks in there. (STANLEY *looks into the parcel. He takes out two drumsticks. He taps them together. He looks at her.*)

STANLEY: Shall I put it round my neck?

She watches him, uncertainly. He hangs the drum around his neck, taps it gently with the sticks, then marches round the table, beating it regularly. MEG, *pleased, watches him. Still beating it regularly, he begins to go round the table a second time. Halfway round the beat becomes erratic, uncontrolled.* MEG *expresses dismay. He arrives at her chair, banging the drum, his face and the drumbeat now savage and possessed.*

Curtain.

ACT TWO

MCCANN *is sitting at the table tearing a sheet of newspaper into five equal strips. It is evening. After a few moments* STANLEY *enters from the left. He stops upon seeing* MCCANN, *and watches him. He then walks towards the kitchen, stops, and speaks.*

STANLEY: Evening.
MCCANN: Evening.

Chuckles are heard from outside the back door, which is open.

STANLEY: Very warm tonight. (*He turns towards the back door, and back.*) Someone out there?

> MCCANN *tears another length of paper.* STANLEY *goes into the kitchen and pours a glass of water. He drinks it looking through the hatch. He puts the glass down, comes out of the kitchen and walks quickly towards the door, left.* MCCANN *rises and intercepts him.*

MCCANN: I don't think we've met.
STANLEY: No, we haven't.
MCCANN: My name's McCann.
STANLEY: Staying here long?
MCCANN: Not long. What's your name?
STANLEY: Webber.
MCCANN: I'm glad to meet you, sir. (*He offers his hand.* STANLEY *takes it, and* MCCANN *holds the grip.*) Many happy returns of the day. (STANLEY *withdraws his hand. They face each other.*) Were you going out?
STANLEY: Yes.
MCCANN: On your birthday?
STANLEY: Yes. Why not?
MCCANN: But they're holding a party here for you tonight.
STANLEY: Oh really? That's unfortunate.
MCCANN: Ah no. It's very nice.

Voices from outside the back door.

STANLEY: I'm sorry. I'm not in the mood for a party tonight.
MCCANN: Oh, is that so? I'm sorry.
STANLEY: Yes, I'm going out to celebrate quietly, on my own.
MCCANN: That's a shame.

They stand.

STANLEY: Well, if you'd move out of my way—
MCCANN: But everything's laid on. The guests are expected.
STANLEY: Guests? What guests?
MCCANN: Myself for one. I had the honour of an invitation.

MCCANN *begins to whistle "The Mountains of Morne."*

STANLEY (*moving away*): I wouldn't call it an honour, would you? It'll just be another booze-up.

STANLEY *joins* MCCANN *in whistling "The Mountains of Morne." During the next five lines the whistling is continuous, one whistling while the other speaks, and both whistling together.*

MCCANN: But it is an honour.
STANLEY: I'd say you were exaggerating.
MCCANN: Oh no. I'd say it was an honour.
STANLEY: I'd say that was plain stupid.
MCCANN: Oh no.

They stare at each other.

STANLEY: Who are the other guests?
MCCANN: A young lady.
STANLEY: Oh yes? And. . . . ?
MCCANN: My friend.
STANLEY: Your friend?
MCCANN: That's right. It's all laid on.

STANLEY *walks round the table towards the door.* MCCANN *meets him.*

STANLEY: Excuse me.

MCCANN: Where are you going?

STANLEY: I want to go out.

MCCANN: Why don't you stay here?

STANLEY *moves away, to the right of the table.*

STANLEY: So you're down here on holiday?

MCCANN: A short one. (STANLEY *picks up a strip of paper.* MCCANN *moves in.*) Mind that.

STANLEY: What is it?

MCCANN: Mind it. Leave it.

STANLEY: I've got a feeling we've met before.

MCCANN: No we haven't.

STANLEY: Ever been anywhere near Maidenhead?

MCCANN: No.

STANLEY: There's a Fuller's teashop. I used to have my tea there.

MCCANN: I don't know it.

STANLEY: And a Boots Library. I seem to connect you with the High Street.

MCCANN: Yes?

STANLEY: A charming town, don't you think?

MCCANN: I don't know it.

STANLEY: Oh no. A quiet, thriving community. I was born and brought up there. I lived well away from the main road.

MCCANN: Yes?

Pause.

STANLEY: You're here on a short stay?

MCCANN: That's right.

STANLEY: You'll find it very bracing.

MCCANN: Do you find it bracing?

STANLEY: Me? No. But you will. (*He sits at the table.*) I like it here, but I'll be moving soon. Back home. I'll stay there too, this time. No place like home. (*He laughs.*) I wouldn't have left, but business calls. Business called, and I had to leave for a bit. You know how it is.

MCCANN (*sitting at the table, left*): You in business?

STANLEY: No. I think I'll give it up. I've got a small private income,

you see. I think I'll give it up. Don't like being away from home.
I used to live very quietly—played records, that's about all. Everything delivered to the door. Then I started a little private business, in a small way, and it compelled me to come down here
—kept me longer than I expected. You never get used to living in
someone else's house. Don't you agree? I lived so quietly. You
can only appreciate what you've had when things change. That's
what they say, isn't it? Cigarette?

MCCANN: I don't smoke.

STANLEY *lights a cigarette. Voices from the back.*

STANLEY: Who's out there?

MCCANN: My friend and the man of the house.

STANLEY: You know what? To look at me, I bet you wouldn't think
I'd led such a quiet life. The lines on my face, eh? It's the drink.
Been drinking a bit down here. But what I mean is . . . you
know how it is . . . away from your own . . . all wrong, of course
. . . I'll be all right when I get back . . . but what I mean is, the
way some people look at me you'd think I was a different person.
I suppose I have changed, but I'm still the same man that I
always was. I mean, you wouldn't think, to look at me, really . . .
I mean, not really, that I was the sort of bloke to—to cause any
trouble, would you? (MCCANN *looks at him.*) Do you know what
I mean?

MCCANN: No. (*As* STANLEY *picks up a strip of paper.*) Mind that.

STANLEY (*quickly*): Why are you down here?

MCCANN: A short holiday.

STANLEY: This is a ridiculous house to pick on. (*He rises.*)

MCCANN: Why?

STANLEY: Because it's not a boarding house. It never was.

MCCANN: Sure it is.

STANLEY: Why did you choose this house?

MCCANN: You know, sir, you're a bit depressed for a man on his
birthday.

STANLEY (*sharply*): Why do you call me sir?

MCCANN: You don't like it?

STANLEY (*to the table*): Listen. Don't call me sir.

MCCANN: I won't, if you don't like it.

STANLEY (*moving away*): No. Anyway, this isn't my birthday.

MCCANN: No?

STANLEY: No. It's not till next month.

MCCANN: Not according to the lady.

STANLEY: Her? She's crazy. Round the bend.

MCCANN: That's a terrible thing to say.

STANLEY (*to the table*): Haven't you found that out yet? There's a lot you don't know. I think someone's leading you up the garden path.

MCCANN: Who would do that?

STANLEY (*leaning across the table*): That woman is mad!

MCCANN: That's slander.

STANLEY: And you don't know what you're doing.

MCCANN: Your cigarette is near that paper.

Voices from the back.

STANLEY: Where the hell are they? (*Stubbing his cigarette.*) Why don't they come in? What are they doing out there?

MCCANN: You want to steady yourself.

STANLEY *crosses to him and grips his arm.*

STANLEY (*urgently*): Look—

MCCANN: Don't touch me.

STANLEY: Look. Listen a minute.

MCCANN: Let go my arm.

STANLEY: Look. Sit down a minute.

MCCANN (*savagely, hitting his arm*): Don't do that!

STANLEY *backs across the stage, holding his arm.*

STANLEY: Listen. You knew what I was talking about before, didn't you?

MCCANN: I don't know what you're at at all.

STANLEY: It's a mistake! Do you understand?

MCCANN: You're in a bad state, man.

STANLEY (*whispering, advancing*): Has he told you anything? Do you know what you're here for? Tell me. You needn't be frightened of me. Or hasn't he told you?

MCCANN: Told me what?

STANLEY (*hissing*): I've explained to you, damn you, that all those years I lived in Basingstoke I never stepped outside the door.

MCCANN: You know, I'm flabbergasted with you.

STANLEY (*reasonably*): Look. You look an honest man. You're being made a fool of, that's all. You understand? Where do you come from?

MCCANN: Where do you think?

STANLEY: I know Ireland very well. I've many friends there. I love that country and I admire and trust its people. I trust them. They respect the truth and they have a sense of humour. I think their policemen are wonderful. I've been there. I've never seen such sunsets. What about coming out to have a drink with me? There's a pub down the road serves draught Guinness. Very difficult to get in these parts— (*He breaks off.*)

> *The voices draw nearer.* GOLDBERG *and* PETEY *enter from the back door.*

GOLDBERG (*as he enters*): A mother in a million. (*He sees* STANLEY.) Ah.

PETEY: Oh hullo, Stan. You haven't met Stanley, have you, Mr. Goldberg?

GOLDBERG: I haven't had the pleasure.

PETEY: Oh well, this is Mr. Goldberg, this is Mr. Webber.

GOLDBERG: Pleased to meet you.

PETEY: We were just getting a bit of air in the garden.

GOLDBERG: I was telling Mr. Boles about my old mum. What days. (*He sits at the table, right.*) Yes. When I was a youngster, of a Friday, I used to go for a walk down the canal with a girl who lived down my road. A beautiful girl. What a voice that bird had! A nightingale, my word of honour. Good? Pure? She wasn't a Sunday school teacher for nothing. Anyway, I'd leave her with a little kiss on the cheek—I never took liberties—we weren't like the young men these days in those days. We knew the meaning of respect. So I'd give her a peck and I'd bowl back home. Humming away I'd be, past the children's playground. I'd tip my hat to the toddlers, I'd give a helping hand to a couple of stray dogs, everything came natural. I can see it like yesterday. The sun falling behind the dog stadium. Ah! (*He leans back contentedly.*)

MCCANN: Like behind the town hall.

GOLDBERG: What town hall?

MCCANN: In Carrikmacross.

GOLDBERG: There's no comparison. Up the street, into my gate, inside the door, home. "Simey!" my old mum used to shout, "quick before it gets cold." And there on the table what would I see? The nicest piece of gefilte fish you could wish to find on a plate.

MCCANN: I thought your name was Nat.

GOLDBERG: She called me Simey.

PETEY: Yes, we all remember our childhood.

GOLDBERG: Too true. Eh, Mr. Webber, what do you say? Childhood. Hot water bottles. Hot milk. Pancakes. Soap suds. What a life.

Pause.

PETEY (*rising from the table*): Well, I'll have to be off.

GOLDBERG: Off?

PETEY: It's my chess night.

GOLDBERG: You're not staying for the party?

PETEY: No, I'm sorry, Stan. I didn't know about it till just now. And we've got a game on. I'll try and get back early.

GOLDBERG: We'll save some drink for you, all right? Oh, that reminds me. You'd better go and collect the bottles.

MCCANN: Now?

GOLDBERG: Of course, now. Time's getting on. Round the corner, remember? Mention my name.

PETEY: I'm coming your way.

GOLDBERG: Beat him quick and come back, Mr. Boles.

PETEY: Do my best. See you later, Stan.

PETEY *and* MCCANN *go out, left.* STANLEY *moves to the centre.*

GOLDBERG: A warm night.

STANLEY (*turning*): Don't mess me about!

GOLDBERG: I beg your pardon?

STANLEY (*moving downstage*): I'm afraid there's been a mistake. We're booked out. Your room is taken. Mrs. Boles forgot to tell you. You'll have to find somewhere else.

GOLDBERG: Are you the manager here?

STANLEY: That's right.

GOLDBERG: Is it a good game?

STANLEY: I run the house. I'm afraid you and your friend will have to find other accommodation.

GOLDBERG (*rising*): Oh, I forgot, I must congratulate you on your birthday. (*Offering his hand.*) Congratulations.

STANLEY (*ignoring hand*): Perhaps you're deaf.

GOLDBERG: No, what makes you think that? As a matter of fact, every single one of my senses is at its peak. Not bad going, eh? For a man past fifty. But a birthday, I always feel, is a great occasion, taken too much for granted these days. What a thing to celebrate —birth! Like getting up in the morning. Marvellous! Some people don't like the idea of getting up in the morning. I've heard them. Getting up in the morning, they say, what is it? Your skin's crabby, you need a shave, your eyes are full of muck, your mouth is like a boghouse, the palms of your hands are full of sweat, your nose is clogged up, your feet stink, what are you but a corpse waiting to be washed? Whenever I hear that point of view I feel cheerful. Because I know what it is to wake up with the sun shining, to the sound of the lawnmower, all the little birds, the smell of the grass, church bells, tomato juice—

STANLEY: Get out.

Enter MCCANN, *with bottles.*

Get that drink out. These are unlicensed premises.

GOLDBERG: You're in a terrible humour today, Mr. Webber. And on your birthday too, with the good lady getting her strength up to give you a party.

MCCANN *puts the bottles on the sideboard.*

STANLEY: I told you to get those bottles out.

GOLDBERG: Mr. Webber, sit down a minute.

STANLEY: Let me—just make this clear. You don't bother me. To me, you're nothing but a dirty joke. But I have a responsibility towards the people in this house. They've been down here too long. They've lost their sense of smell. I haven't. And nobody's going to take advantage of them while I'm here. (*A little less forceful.*) Anyway, this house isn't your cup of tea. There's nothing here for you, from any angle. So why don't you just go, without any more fuss?

GOLDBERG: Mr. Webber, sit down.

STANLEY: It's no good starting any kind of trouble.

GOLDBERG: Sit down.

STANLEY: Why should I?

GOLDBERG: If you want to know the truth, Webber, you're beginning to get on my breasts.

STANLEY: Really? Well, that's—

GOLDBERG: Sit down.

STANLEY: No.

GOLDBERG *sighs, and sits at the table, right.*

GOLDBERG: McCann.

MCCANN: Nat?

GOLDBERG: Ask him to sit down.

MCCANN: Yes, Nat. (MCCANN *moves to* STANLEY.) Do you mind sitting down?

STANLEY: Yes, I do mind.

MCCANN: Yes now, but—it'd be better if you did.

STANLEY: Why don't you sit down?

MCCANN: No, not me—you.

STANLEY: No thanks.

Pause.

MCCANN: Nat.

GOLDBERG: What?

MCCANN: He won't sit down.

GOLDBERG: Well, ask him.

MCCANN: I've asked him.

GOLDBERG: Ask him again.

MCCANN (*to* STANLEY): Sit down.

STANLEY: Why?

MCCANN: You'd be more comfortable.

STANLEY: So would you.

Pause.

MCCANN: All right. If you will I will.

STANLEY: You first.

MCCANN *slowly sits at the table, left.*

MCCANN: Well?

STANLEY: Right. Now you've both had a rest you can get out!

MCCANN (*rising*): That's a dirty trick! I'll kick the shite out of him!

GOLDBERG (*rising*): No! I have stood up.

MCCANN: Sit down again!

GOLDBERG: Once I'm up I'm up.

STANLEY: Same here.

MCCANN (*moving to* STANLEY): You've made Mr. Goldberg stand up.

STANLEY (*his voice rising*): It'll do him good!

MCCANN: Get in that seat.

GOLDBERG: McCann.

MCCANN: Get down in that seat!

GOLDBERG (*crossing to him*): Webber. (*Quietly.*) SIT DOWN.

> *Silence.* STANLEY *begins to whistle "The Mountains of Morne."*
> *He strolls casually to the chair at the table. They watch him.*
> *He stops whistling. Silence. He sits.*

STANLEY: You'd better be careful.

GOLDBERG: Webber, what were you doing yesterday?

STANLEY: Yesterday?

GOLDBERG: And the day before. What did you do the day before that?

STANLEY: What do you mean?

GOLDBERG: Why are you wasting everybody's time, Webber? Why are you getting in everybody's way?

STANLEY: Me? What are you—

GOLDBERG: I'm telling you, Webber. You're a washout. Why are you getting on everybody's wick? Why are you driving that old lady off her conk?

MCCANN: He likes to do it!

GOLDBERG: Why do you behave so badly, Webber? Why do you force that old man out to play chess?

STANLEY: Me?

GOLDBERG: Why do you treat that young lady like a leper? She's not the leper, Webber!

STANLEY: What the—

GOLDBERG: What did you wear last week, Webber? Where do you keep your suits?

MCCANN: Why did you leave the organization?

GOLDBERG: What would your old mum say, Webber?

MCCANN: Why did you betray us?

GOLDBERG: You hurt me, Webber. You're playing a dirty game.

MCCANN: That's a Black and Tan fact.

GOLDBERG: Who does he think he is?

MCCANN: Who do you think you are?

STANLEY: You're on the wrong horse.

GOLDBERG: When did you come to this place?

STANLEY: Last year.

GOLDBERG: Where did you come from?

STANLEY: Somewhere else.

GOLDBERG: Why did you come here?

STANLEY: My feet hurt!

GOLDBERG: Why did you stay?

STANLEY: I had a headache!

GOLDBERG: Did you take anything for it?

STANLEY: Yes.

GOLDBERG: What?

STANLEY: Fruit salts!

GOLDBERG: Enos or Andrews?

STANLEY: En—An—

GOLDBERG: Did you stir properly? Did they fizz?

STANLEY: Now, now, wait, you—

GOLDBERG: Did they fizz? Did they fizz or didn't they fizz?

MCCANN: He doesn't know!

GOLDBERG: You don't know. What's happened to your memory, Webber? When did you last have a bath?

STANLEY: I have one every—

GOLDBERG: Don't lie.

MCCANN: You betrayed the organization. I know him!

STANLEY: You don't!

GOLDBERG: What can you see without your glasses?

STANLEY: Anything.

GOLDBERG: Take off his glasses.

MCCANN *snatches his glasses and as* STANLEY *rises, reaching for them, takes his chair downstage centre, below the table,* STANLEY *stumbling as he follows.* STANLEY *clutches the chair and stays bent over it.*

Webber, you're a fake.

They stand on each side of the chair.

When did you last wash up a cup?
STANLEY: The Christmas before last.
GOLDBERG: Where?
STANLEY: Lyons Corner House.
GOLDBERG: Which one?
STANLEY: Marble Arch.
GOLDBERG: Where was your wife?
STANLEY: In—
GOLDBERG: Answer.
STANLEY (*turning, crouched*): What wife?
GOLDBERG: What have you done with your wife?
MCCANN: He's killed his wife!
GOLDBERG: Why did you kill your wife?
STANLEY (*sitting, his back to the audience*): What wife?
MCCANN: How did he kill her?
GOLDBERG: How did you kill her?
MCCANN: You throttled her.
GOLDBERG: With arsenic.
MCCANN: There's your man!
GOLDBERG: Where's your old mum?
STANLEY: In the sanatorium.
MCCANN: Yes!
GOLDBERG: Why did you never get married?
MCCANN: She was waiting at the porch.
GOLDBERG: You skedaddled from the wedding.
MCCANN: He left her in the lurch.
GOLDBERG: You left her in the pudding club.
MCCANN: She was waiting at the church.
GOLDBERG: Webber! Why did you change your name?
STANLEY: I forgot the other one.
GOLDBERG: What's your name now?
STANLEY: Joe Soap.
GOLDBERG: You stink of sin.
MCCANN: I can smell it.
GOLDBERG: Do you recognise an external force?
STANLEY: What?

GOLDBERG: Do you recognise an external force?

MCCANN: That's the question!

GOLDBERG: Do you recognise an external force, responsible for you, suffering for you?

STANLEY: It's late.

GOLDBERG: Late! Late enough! When did you last pray?

MCCANN: He's sweating!

GOLDBERG: When did you last pray?

MCCANN: He's sweating!

GOLDBERG: Is the number 846 possible or necessary?

STANLEY: Neither.

GOLDBERG: Wrong! Is the number 846 possible or necessary?

STANLEY: Both.

GOLDBERG: Wrong! It's necessary but not possible.

STANLEY: Both.

GOLDBERG: Wrong! Why do you think the number 846 is necessarily possible?

STANLEY: Must be.

GOLDBERG: Wrong! It's only necessarily necessary! We admit possibility only after we grant necessity. It is possible because necessary but by no means necessary through possibility. The possibility can only be assumed after the proof of necessity.

MCCANN: Right!

GOLDBERG: Right? Of course right! We're right and you're wrong, Webber, all along the line.

MCCANN: All along the line!

GOLDBERG: Where is your lechery leading you?

MCCANN: You'll pay for this.

GOLDBERG: You stuff yourself with dry toast.

MCCANN: You contaminate womankind.

GOLDBERG: Why don't you pay the rent?

MCCANN: Mother defiler!

GOLDBERG: Why do you pick your nose?

MCCANN: I demand justice!

GOLDBERG: What's your trade?

MCCANN: What about Ireland?

GOLDBERG: What's your trade?

STANLEY: I play the piano.

GOLDBERG: How many fingers do you use?

STANLEY: No hands!

GOLDBERG: No society would touch you. Not even a building society

MCCANN: You're a traitor to the cloth.

GOLDBERG: What do you use for pyjamas?

STANLEY: Nothing.

GOLDBERG: You verminate the sheet of your birth.

MCCANN: What about the Albigensenist heresy?

GOLDBERG: Who watered the wicket in Melbourne?

MCCANN: What about the blessed Oliver Plunkett?

GOLDBERG: Speak up Webber. Why did the chicken cross the road?

STANLEY: He wanted to—he wanted to—he wanted to. . . .

MCCANN: He doesn't know!

GOLDBERG: Why did the chicken cross the road?

STANLEY: He wanted to—he wanted to. . . .

GOLDBERG: Why did the chicken cross the road?

STANLEY: He wanted. . . .

MCCANN: He doesn't know. He doesn't know which came first!

GOLDBERG: Which came first?

MCCANN: Chicken? Egg? Which came first?

GOLDBERG and MCCANN: Which came first? Which came first? Which came first?

> STANLEY *screams.*

GOLDBERG: He doesn't know. Do you know your own face?

MCCANN: Wake him up. Stick a needle in his eye.

GOLDBERG: You're a plague, Webber. You're an overthrow.

MCCANN: You're what's left!

GOLDBERG: But we've got the answer to you. We can sterilise you.

MCCANN: What about Drogheda?

GOLDBERG: Your bite is dead. Only your pong is left.

MCCANN: You betrayed our land.

GOLDBERG: You betray our breed.

MCCANN: Who are you, Webber?

GOLDBERG: What makes you think you exist?

MCCANN: You're dead.

GOLDBERG: You're dead. You can't live, you can't think, you can't love. You're dead. You're a plague gone bad. There's no juice in you. You're nothing but an odour!

> *Silence. They stand over him. He is crouched in the chair. He*

looks up slowly and kicks GOLDBERG *in the stomach.* GOLDBERG *falls.* STANLEY *stands.* MCCANN *seizes a chair and lifts it above his head.* STANLEY *seizes a chair and covers his head with it.* MCCANN *and* STANLEY *circle.*

GOLDBERG: Steady, McCann.
STANLEY (*circling*): Uuuuuhhhhh!
MCCANN: Right, Judas.
GOLDBERG (*rising*): Steady, McCann.
MCCANN: Come on!
STANLEY: Uuuuuuuhhhhh!
MCCANN: He's sweating.
GOLDBERG: Easy, McCann.
MCCANN: The bastard sweatpig is sweating.

A loud drumbeat off left, descending the stairs. GOLDBERG *takes the chair from* STANLEY. *They put the chairs down. They stop still. Enter* MEG, *in evening dress, holding sticks and drum.*

MEG: I brought the drum down. I'm dressed for the party.
GOLDBERG: Wonderful.
MEG: You like my dress?
GOLDBERG: Wonderful. Out of this world.
MEG: I know. My father gave it to me. (*Placing drum on table.*) Doesn't it make a beautiful noise?
GOLDBERG: It's a fine piece of work. Maybe Stan'll play us a little tune afterwards.
MEG: Oh yes. Will you, Stan?
STANLEY: Could I have my glasses?
GOLDBERG: Ah yes. (*He holds his hand out to* MCCANN. MCCANN *passes him his glasses.*) Here they are. (*He holds them out for* STANLEY, *who reaches for them.*) Here they are. (STANLEY *takes them.*) Now. What have we got here? Enough to scuttle a liner. We've got four bottles of Scotch and one bottle of Irish.
MEG: Oh, Mr. Goldberg, what should I drink?
GOLDBERG: Glasses, glasses first. Open the Scotch, McCann.
MEG (*at the sideboard*): Here's my very best glasses in here.
MCCANN: I don't drink Scotch.
GOLDBERG: You drink that one.
MEG (*bringing the glasses*): Here they are.

GOLDBERG: Good. Mrs. Boles, I think Stanley should pour the toast, don't you?

MEG: Oh yes. Come on, Stanley. (STANLEY *walks slowly to the table.*) Do you like my dress, Mr. Goldberg?

GOLDBERG: It's out on its own. Turn yourself round a minute. I used to be in the business. Go on, walk up there.

MEG: Oh no.

GOLDBERG: Don't be shy. (*He slaps her bottom.*)

MEG: Oooh!

GOLDBERG: Walk up the boulevard. Let's have a look at you. What carriage. What's your opinion, McCann? Like a Countess, nothing less. Madam, now turn about and promenade to the kitchen. What a deportment!

MCCANN (*to* STANLEY): You can pour my Irish too.

GOLDBERG: You look like a gladiola.

MEG: Stan, what about my dress?

GOLDBERG: One for the lady, one for the lady. Now madam—your glass.

MEG: Thank you.

GOLDBERG: Lift your glasses, ladies and gentlemen. We'll drink a toast.

MEG: Lulu isn't here.

GOLDBERG: It's past the hour. Now—who's going to propose the toast? Mrs. Boles, it can only be you.

MEG: Me?

GOLDBERG: Who else?

MEG: But what do I say?

GOLDBERG: Say what you feel. What you honestly feel. (MEG *looks un-certain.*) It's Stanley's birthday. Your Stanley. Look at him. Look at him and it'll come. Wait a minute, the light's too strong. Let's have proper lighting. McCann, have you got your torch?

MCCANN (*bringing a small torch from his pocket*): Here.

GOLDBERG: Switch out the light and put on your torch. (MCCANN *goes to the door, switches off the light, comes back, shines the torch on* MEG. *Outside the window there is still a faint light.*) Not on the lady, on the gentleman! You must shine it on the birthday boy. (MCCANN *shines the torch in* STANLEY'S *face.*) Now, Mrs. Boles, it's all yours.

Pause.

MEG: I don't know what to say.

GOLDBERG: Look at him. Just look at him.

MEG: Isn't the light in his eyes?

GOLDBERG: No, no. Go on.

MEG: Well—it's very, very nice to be here tonight, in my house, and I want to propose a toast to Stanley, because it's his birthday, and he's lived here for a long while now, and he's my Stanley now. (And I think he's a good boy, although sometimes he's bad. (*An appreciative laugh from* GOLDBERG.) And he's the only Stanley I know, and I know him better than all the world, although he doesn't think so.) ("*Hear—hear*" *from* GOLDBERG.) Well, I could cry because I'm so happy, having him here and not gone away, on his birthday, and there isn't anything I wouldn't do for him, and all you good people here tonight. . . . (*She sobs.*)

GOLDBERG. Beautiful! A beautiful speech. Put the light on, McCann. (MCCANN *goes to the door.* STANLEY *remains still.*) That was a lovely toast. (*The light goes on.* LULU *enters from the door, left.* GOLDBERG *comforts* MEG.) Buck up now. Come on, smile at the birdy. That's better. We've got to drink yet. Ah, look who's here.

MEG: Lulu.

GOLDBERG: How do you do, Lulu? I'm Nat Goldberg. Stanley, a drink for your guest. You just missed the toast, my dear, and what a toast.

LULU: Did I?

GOLDBERG: Stanley, a drink for your guest. Stanley. (STANLEY *hands a glass to* LULU.) Right. Now raise your glasses. Everyone standing up? No, not you, Stanley. You must sit down.

MCCANN: Yes, that's right. He must sit down.

GOLDBERG: You don't mind sitting down a minute? We're going to drink to you.

MEG: Come on!

STANLEY *sits in a chair at the table.*

GOLDBERG: Right. Now Stanley's sat down. (*Taking the stage.*) Well, I want to say first that I've never been so touched to the heart as by the toast we've just heard. How often, in this day and age, do you come across real, true warmth? Once in a lifetime. Until a few minutes ago, ladies and gentlemen, I, like all of you, was asking the same question. What's happened to the love, the

bonhomie, the unashamed expression of affection of the day
before yesterday, that our mums taught us in the nursery?

MCCANN: Gone with the wind.

GOLDBERG: That's what I thought, until today. I believe in a good
laugh, a day's fishing, a bit of gardening. I was very proud of my
old greenhouse, made out of my own spit and faith. That's the
sort of man I am. Not size but quality. A little Austin, tea in
Fullers, a library book from Boots, and I'm satisfied. But just
now, I say just now, the lady of the house said her piece and I
for one am knocked over by the sentiments she expressed. Lucky
is the man who's at the receiving end, that's what I say. (*Pause.*)
How can I put it to you? We all wander on our tod through this
world. It's a lonely pillow to kip on. Right!

LULU (*admiringly*): Right!

GOLDBERG: Agreed. But tonight, Lulu, McCann, we've known a great
fortune. We've heard a lady extend the sum total of her devotion,
in all its pride, plume and peacock, to a member of her own
living race. Stanley, my heartfelt congratulations. I wish you, on
behalf of us all, a happy birthday. I'm sure you've never been a
prouder man than you are today. Mazoltov! And may we only
meet at Simchahs! (LULU *and* MEG *applaud.*) Turn out the light,
McCann, while we drink the toast.

LULU: That was a wonderful speech.

MCCANN *switches out the light, comes back, and shines the torch
in* STANLEY'S *face. The light outside the window is fainter.*

GOLDBERG: Lift your glasses. Stanley—happy birthday.

MCCANN: Happy birthday.

LULU: Happy birthday.

MEG: Many happy returns of the day, Stan.

GOLDBERG: And well over the fast.

They all drink.

MEG (*kissing him*): Oh, Stanny. . . .

GOLDBERG: Lights!

MCCANN: Right! (*He switches on the lights.*)

MEG: Clink my glass, Stan.

LULU: Mr. Goldberg—

GOLDBERG: Call me Nat.

MEG (*to* MCCANN): You clink my glass.

LULU (*to* GOLDBERG): You're empty. Let me fill you up.

GOLDBERG: It's a pleasure.

LULU: You're a marvellous speaker, Nat, you know that? Where did you learn to speak like that?

GOLDBERG: You liked it, eh?

LULU: Oh yes!

GOLDBERG: Well, my first chance to stand up and give a lecture was at the Ethical Hall, Bayswater. A wonderful opportunity. I'll never forget it. They were all there that night. Charlotte Street was empty. Of course, that's a good while ago.

LULU: What did you speak about?

GOLDBERG: The Necessary and the Possible. It went like a bomb. Since then I always speak at weddings.

> STANLEY *is still.* GOLDBERG *sits left of the table.* MEG *joins* MCCANN *downstage, right,* LULU *is downstage, left.* MCCANN *pours more Irish from the bottle, which he carries, into his glass.*

MEG: Let's have some of yours.

MCCANN: In that?

MEG: Yes.

MCCANN: Are you used to mixing them?

MEG: No.

MCCANN: Sit down. Give me your glass.

> MEG *sits on a shoe-box, downstage, right.* LULU, *at the table, pours more drink for* GOLDBERG *and herself, and gives* GOLDBERG *his glass.*

GOLDBERG: Thank you.

MEG (*to* MCCANN): Do you think I should?

GOLDBERG: Lulu, you're a big bouncy girl. Come and sit on my lap.

MCCANN: Why not?

LULU: Do you think I should?

GOLDBERG: Try it.

MEG (*sipping*): Very nice.

LULU: I'll bounce up to the ceiling.

MCCANN: I don't know how you can mix that stuff.

GOLDBERG: Take a chance.

MEG (*to* MCCANN): Sit down on this stool.

LULU *sits on* GOLDBERG's *lap*.

MCCANN: This?

GOLDBERG: Comfortable?

LULU: Yes, thanks.

MCCANN (*sitting*): It's comfortable.

GOLDBERG: You know, there's a lot in your eyes.

LULU: And in yours, too.

GOLDBERG: Do you think so?

LULU (*giggling*): Go on!

MCCANN (*to* MEG): Where'd you get it?

MEG: My father gave it to me.

LULU: I didn't know I was going to meet you here tonight.

MCCANN (*to* MEG): Ever been to Carrikmacross?

MEG (*drinking*): I've been to King's Cross.

LULU: You came right out of the blue, you know that?

GOLDBERG (*as she moves*): Mind how you go. You're cracking a rib.

MEG (*standing*): I want to dance! (LULU *and* GOLDBERG *look into each other's eyes.* MCCANN *drinks.* MEG *crosses to* STANLEY.) Stanley. Dance. (STANLEY *sits still.* MEG *dances round the room alone, then comes back to* MCCANN, *who fills her glass. She sits.*)

LULU (*to* GOLDBERG): Shall I tell you something?

GOLDBERG: What?

LULU: I trust you.

GOLDBERG (*lifting his glass*): Gesundheit.

LULU: Have you got a wife?

GOLDBERG: I had a wife. What a wife. Listen to this. Friday, of an afternoon, I'd take myself for a little constitutional, down over the park. Eh, do me a favour, just sit on the table a minute, will you? (LULU *sits on the table. He stretches and continues.*) A little constitutional. I'd say hullo to the little boys, the little girls—I never made distinctions—and then back I'd go, back to my bungalow with the flat roof. "Simey," my wife used to shout, "quick, before it gets cold!" And there on the table what would I see? The nicest piece of rollmop and pickled cucumber you could wish to find on a plate.

LULU: I thought your name was Nat.

GOLDBERG: She called me Simey.

LULU: I bet you were a good husband.

GOLDBERG: You should have seen her funeral.

LULU: Why?

GOLDBERG (*draws in his breath and wags head*): What a funeral.

MEG (*to* MCCANN): My father was going to take me to Ireland once. But then he went away by himself.

LULU (*to* GOLDBERG): Do you think you knew me when I was a little girl?

GOLDBERG: Were you a nice little girl?

LULU: I was.

MEG: I don't know if he went to Ireland.

GOLDBERG: Maybe I played piggy-back with you.

LULU: Maybe you did.

MEG: He didn't take me.

GOLDBERG: Or pop goes the weasel.

LULU: Is that a game?

GOLDBERG: Sure it's a game!

MCCANN: Why didn't he take you to Ireland?

LULU: You're tickling me!

GOLDBERG: You should worry.

LULU: I've always liked older men. They can soothe you.

They embrace.

MCCANN: I know a place. Roscrea. Mother Nolan's.

MEG: There was a night-light in my room, when I was a little girl.

MCCANN: One time I stayed there all night with the boys. Singing and drinking all night.

MEG: And my Nanny used to sit up with me, and sing songs to me.

MCCANN: And a plate of fry in the morning. Now where am I?

MEG: My little room was pink. I had a pink carpet and pink curtains, and I had musical boxes all over the room. And they played me to sleep. And my father was a very big doctor. That's why I never had any complaints. I was cared for, and I had little sisters and brothers in other rooms, all different colours.

MCCANN: Tullamore, where are you?

MEG (*to* MCCANN): Give us a drop more.

MCCANN (*filling her glass and singing*): Glorio, Glorio, to the bold Fenian men!

MEG: Oh, what a lovely voice.

GOLDBERG: Give us a song, McCann.

LULU: A love song!

MCCANN (*reciting*): The night that poor Paddy was stretched, the boys they all paid him a visit.

GOLDBERG: A love song!

MCCANN (*in a full voice, sings*):

Oh, the Garden of Eden has vanished, they say,
But I know the lie of it still.
Just turn to the left at the foot of Ben Clay
And stop when halfway to Coote Hill.
It's there you will find it, I know sure enough,
And it's whispering over to me:
Come back, Paddy Reilly, to Bally-James-Duff,
Come home, Paddy Reilly, to me!

LULU (*to* GOLDBERG): You're the dead image of the first man I ever loved.

GOLDBERG: It goes without saying.

MEG (*rising*): I want to play a game!

GOLDBERG: A game?

LULU: What game?

MEG: Any game.

LULU (*jumping up*): Yes, let's play a game.

GOLDBERG: What game?

MCCANN: Hide and seek.

LULU: Blind man's buff.

MEG: Yes!

GOLDBERG: You want to play blind man's buff?

LULU and MEG: Yes!

GOLDBERG: All right. Blind man's buff. Come on! Everyone up! (*Rising.*) McCann. Stanley—Stanley!

MEG: Stanley. Up.

GOLDBERG: What's the matter with him?

MEG (*bending over him*): Stanley, we're going to play a game. Oh come on, don't be sulky, Stan.

STANLEY *rises.* MCCANN *rises.*

GOLDBERG: Right! Now—who's going to be blind first?

LULU: Mrs. Boles.

MEG: Not me.

GOLDBERG: Of course you.

MEG: Who, me?

LULU (*taking her scarf from her neck*): Here you are.

MCCANN: How do you play this game?

LULU (*tying her scarf round* MEG's *eyes*): Haven't you ever played blind man's buff? Keep still, Mrs. Boles. You mustn't be touched. But you can't move after she's blind. You must stay where you are after she's blind. And if she touches you then you become blind. Turn round. How many fingers am I holding up?

MEG: I can't see.

LULU: Right.

GOLDBERG: Right! Everyone move about. McCann. Stanley. Now stop. Now still. Off you go!

> STANLEY *is downstage, right,* MEG *moves about the room.* GOLD-BERG *fondles* LULU *at arm's length.* MEG *touches* MCCANN.

MEG: Caught you!

LULU: Take off your scarf.

MEG: What lovely hair!

LULU (*untying the scarf*): There.

MEG: It's you!

GOLDBERG: Put it on, McCann.

LULU (*tying it on* MCCANN): There. Turn round. How many fingers am I holding up?

MCCANN: I don't know.

GOLDBERG: Right! Everyone move about. Right. Stop! Still!

> MCCANN *begins to move.*

MEG: Oh, this is lovely!

GOLDBERG: Quiet! Tch, tch, tch. Now—all move again. Stop! Still!

> MCCANN *moves about.* GOLDBERG *fondles* LULU *at arm's length.* MCCANN *draws near* STANLEY. *He stretches his arm and touches* STANLEY's *glasses.*

MEG: It's Stanley!

GOLDBERG (*to* LULU): Enjoying the game?

MEG: It's your turn, Stan.

MCCANN *takes off the scarf.*

MCCANN (*to* STANLEY): I'll take your glasses.

MCCANN *takes* STANLEY'S *glasses.*

MEG: Give me the scarf.

GOLDBERG (*holding* LULU): Tie his scarf, Mrs. Boles.

MEG: That's what I'm doing.

LULU (*to* GOLDBERG): Kiss me. (*They kiss.*)

MEG (*to* STANLEY): Can you see my nose?

GOLDBERG: He can't. Ready? Right! Everyone move. Stop! And still!

> STANLEY *stands blindfold.* MCCANN *backs slowly across the stage to the left. He breaks* STANLEY'S *glasses, snapping the frames.* MEG *is downstage, left,* LULU *and* GOLDBERG *upstage centre, close together.* STANLEY *begins to move, very slowly, across the stage to the left.* MCCANN *picks up the drum and places it sideways in* STANLEY'S *path.* STANLEY *walks into the drum and falls over with his foot caught in it.*

MEG: Ooh!

GOLDBERG: Sssh!

> STANLEY *rises. He begins to move towards* MEG, *dragging the drum on his foot. He reaches her and stops. His hands move towards her and they reach her throat. He begins to strangle her.* MCCANN *and* GOLDBERG *rush forward and throw him off.*

Blackout

There is now no light at all through the window. The stage is in darkness.

LULU: The lights!

GOLDBERG: What's happened?

LULU: The lights!

MCCANN: Wait a minute.

GOLDBERG: Where is he?

MCCANN: Let go of me!

LULU: Someone's touching me!

GOLDBERG: Who's this?

MEG: It's me!

MCCANN: Where is he?

MEG: Why has the light gone out?

GOLDBERG: Where's your torch? (MCCANN *shines the torch in* GOLD-
BERG's *face.*) Not on me! (MCCANN *shifts the torch. It is knocked
from his hand and falls. It goes out.*)

MCCANN: My torch!

LULU: Oh God!

GOLDBERG: Where's your torch? Pick up your torch!

MCCANN: I can't find it.

LULU: Hold me. Hold me.

GOLDBERG: Get down on your knees. Help him find the torch.

LULU: I can't.

MCCANN: It's gone.

MEG: Why has the light gone out?

GOLDBERG: Everyone quiet! Help him find the torch.

Silence. Grunts from MCCANN *and* GOLDBERG *on their knees
Suddenly there is a sharp, sustained rat-a-tat with a stick on
the side of the drum from the back of the room. Silence. Whim-
pers from* LULU.

GOLDBERG: Over here. McCann!

MCCANN: Here.

GOLDBERG: Come to me, come to me. Easy. Over there.

GOLDBERG *and* MCCANN *move up left of the table.* STANLEY *moves
down right of the table.* LULU *suddenly perceives him moving
towards her, screams and faints.* GOLDBERG *and* MCCANN *turn
and stumble against each other.*

GOLDBERG: What is it?

MCCANN: Who's that?

GOLDBERG: What is it?

In the darkness STANLEY *picks up* LULU *and places her on the table.*

MEG: It's Lulu!

GOLDBERG *and* MCCANN *move downstage, right.*

GOLDBERG: Where is she?
MCCANN: She fell.
GOLDBERG: Where?
MCCANN: About here.
GOLDBERG: Help me pick her up.
MCCANN (*moving downstage, left*): I can't find her.
GOLDBERG: She must be somewhere.
MCCANN: She's not here.
GOLDBERG (*moving downstage, left*): She must be.
MCCANN: She's gone.

MCCANN *finds the torch on the floor, shines it on the table and* STANLEY. LULU *is lying spread-eagled on the table,* STANLEY *bent over her.* STANLEY, *as soon as the torchlight hits him, begins to giggle.* GOLDBERG *and* MCCANN *move towards him. He backs, giggling, the torch on his face. They follow him upstage, left. He backs against the hatch, giggling. The torch draws closer. His giggle rises and grows as he flattens himself against the wall. Their figures converge upon him.*

Curtain.

ACT THREE

The next morning. PETEY *enters, left, with a newspaper and sits at the table. He begins to read.* MEG's *voice comes through the kitchen hatch.*

MEG: Is that you, Stan? (*Pause.*) Stanny?
PETEY: Yes?
MEG: Is that you?
PETEY: It's me.
MEG (*appearing at the hatch*): Oh, it's you. I've run out of cornflakes.
PETEY: Well, what else have you got?
MEG: Nothing.
PETEY: Nothing?
MEG: Just a minute. (*She leaves the hatch and enters by the kitchen door.*) You got your paper?
PETEY: Yes.
MEG: Is it good?
PETEY: Not bad.
MEG: The two gentlemen had the last of the fry this morning.
PETEY: Oh, did they?
MEG: There's some tea in the pot though. (*She pours tea for him.*) I'm going out shopping in a minute. Get you something nice.
PETEY: Good.
MEG: Oh, I must sit down a minute. (*Sits at the table, right.*)
PETEY: How are you then, this morning?
MEG: I've got a splitting headache.
PETEY (*reading*): You slept like a log last night.
MEG: Did I?
PETEY: Why don't you have a walk down to the shops? It's fresh out. It'll clear your head.
MEG: Will it?
PETEY: Bound to.
MEG: I will then. Did I sleep like a log?
PETEY: Dead out.
MEG: I must have been tired. (*She looks about the room and sees the broken drum in the fireplace.*) Oh, look. (*She rises and picks it up.*) The drum's broken. (PETEY *looks up.*) Why is it broken?
PETEY: I don't know.

529

She hits it with her hand.

MEG: It still makes a noise.

PETEY: You can always get another one.

MEG (*sadly*): It was probably broken in the party. I don't remember it being broken though, in the party. (*She puts it down.*) What a shame.

PETEY: You can always get another one, Meg.

MEG: Well, at least he did have it on his birthday, didn't he? Like I wanted him to.

PETEY (*reading*): Yes.

MEG: Have you seen him down yet? (PETEY *does not answer.*) Petey.

PETEY: What?

MEG: Have you seen him down?

PETEY: Who?

MEG: Stanley.

PETEY: No.

MEG: Nor have I. That boy should be up. He's late for his breakfast.

PETEY: There isn't any breakfast.

MEG: Yes, but he doesn't know that. I'm going to call him.

PETEY (*quickly*): No, don't do that, Meg. Let him sleep.

MEG: But you say he stays in bed too much.

PETEY: Let him sleep . . . this morning. Leave him.

MEG: I've been up once, with his cup of tea. But Mr. McCann opened the door. He said they were talking. He said he'd made him one. He must have been up early. I don't know what they were talking about. I was surprised. Because Stanley's usually fast asleep when I wake him. But he wasn't this morning. I heard him talking. (*Pause.*) Do you think they know each other? I think they're old friends. Stanley had a lot of friends. I know he did. (*Pause.*) I didn't give him his tea. He'd already had one. I came down again and went on with my work. Then, after a bit, they came down to breakfast. Stanley must have gone to sleep again.

Pause.

PETEY: When are you going to do your shopping, Meg?

MEG: Yes, I must. (*Collecting the bag.*) I've got a rotten headache. (*She goes to the back door, stops suddenly and turns.*) Did you see what's outside this morning?

PETEY: What?

MEG: That big car.

PETEY: Yes.

MEG: It wasn't there yesterday. Did you . . . did you have a look inside it?

PETEY: I had a peep.

MEG (*coming down tensely, and whispering*): Is there anything in it?

PETEY: In it?

MEG: Yes.

PETEY: What do you mean, in it?

MEG: Inside it.

PETEY: What sort of thing?

MEG: Well . . . I mean . . . is there . . . is there a wheelbarrow in it?

PETEY: A wheelbarrow?

MEG: Yes.

PETEY: I didn't see one.

MEG: You didn't? Are you sure?

PETEY: What would Mr. Goldberg want with a wheelbarrow?

MEG: Mr. Goldberg?

PETEY: It's his car.

MEG (*relieved*): His car? Oh, I didn't know it was his car.

PETEY: Of course it's his car.

MEG: Oh, I feel better.

PETEY: What are you on about?

MEG: Oh, I do feel better.

PETEY: You go and get a bit of air.

MEG: Yes, I will. I will. I'll go and get the shopping. (*She goes towards the back door. A door slams upstairs. She turns.*) It's Stanley! He's coming down—what am I going to do about his breakfast? (*She rushes into the kitchen.*) Petey, what shall I give him? (*She looks through the hatch.*) There's no cornflakes. (*They both gaze at the door. Enter* GOLDBERG. *He halts at the door, as he meets their gaze, then smiles.*)

GOLDBERG: A reception committee!

MEG: Oh, I thought it was Stanley.

GOLDBERG: You find a resemblance?

MEG: Oh no. You look quite different.

GOLDBERG (*coming into the room*): Different build, of course.

MEG (*entering from the kitchen*): I thought he was coming down for his breakfast. He hasn't had his breakfast yet.

GOLDBERG: Your wife makes a very nice cup of tea, Mr. Boles, you know that?

PETEY: Yes, she does sometimes. Sometimes she forgets.

MEG: Is he coming down?

GOLDBERG: Down? Of course he's coming down. On a lovely sunny day like this he shouldn't come down? He'll be up and about in next to no time. (*He sits at the table.*) And what a breakfast he's going to get.

MEG: Mr. Goldberg.

GOLDBERG: Yes?

MEG: I didn't know that was your car outside.

GOLDBERG: You like it?

MEG: Are you going to go for a ride?

GOLDBERG (*to* PETEY): A smart car, eh?

PETEY: Nice shine on it all right.

GOLDBERG: What is old is good, take my tip. There's room there. Room in the front, and room in the back. (*He strokes the teapot.*) The pot's hot. More tea, Mr. Boles?

PETEY: No thanks.

GOLDBERG (*pouring tea*): That car? That car's never let me down.

MEG: Are you going to go for a ride?

GOLDBERG (*ruminatively*): And the boot. A beautiful boot. There's just room . . . for the right amount.

MEG: Well, I'd better be off now. (*She moves to the back door, and turns.*) Petey, when Stanley comes down. . . .

PETEY: Yes?

MEG: Tell him I won't be long.

PETEY: I'll tell him.

MEG (*vaguely*): I won't be long. (*She exits.*)

GOLDBERG (*sipping his tea*): A good woman. A charming woman. My mother was the same. My wife was identical.

PETEY: How is he this morning?

GOLDBERG: Who?

PETEY: Stanley. Is he any better?

GOLDBERG (*a little uncertainly*): Oh . . . a little better, I think, a little better. Of course, I'm not really qualified to say, Mr. Boles. I mean, I haven't got the . . . the qualifications. The best thing would be if someone with the proper . . . mnn . . . qualifications . . . was to have a look at him. Someone with a few letters after his name. It makes all the difference.

PETEY: Yes.

GOLDBERG: Anyway, Dermot's with him at the moment. He's . . . keeping him company.

PETEY: Dermot?

GOLDBERG: Yes.

PETEY: It's a terrible thing.

GOLDBERG (*sighs*): Yes. The birthday celebration was too much for him.

PETEY: What came over him?

GOLDBERG (*sharply*): What came over him? Breakdown, Mr. Boles. Pure and simple. Nervous breakdown.

PETEY: But what brought it on so suddenly?

GOLDBERG (*rising, and moving upstage*): Well, Mr. Boles, it can happen in all sorts of ways. A friend of mine was telling me about it only the other day. We'd both been concerned with another case—not entirely similar, of course, but . . . quite alike, quite alike. (*He pauses.*) Anyway, he was telling me, you see, this friend of mine, that sometimes it happens gradual—day by day it grows and grows and grows . . . day by day. And then other times it happens all at once. Poof! Like that! The nerves break. There's no guarantee how it's going to happen, but with certain people . . . it's a foregone conclusion.

PETEY: Really?

GOLDBERG: Yes. This friend of mine—he was telling me about it—only the other day. (*He stands uneasily for a moment, then brings out a cigarette case and takes a cigarette.*) Have an Abdullah.

PETEY: No, no, I don't take them.

GOLDBERG: Once in a while I treat myself to a cigarette. An Abdullah, perhaps, or a . . . (*He snaps his fingers.*)

PETEY: What a night. (GOLDBERG *lights his cigarette with a lighter.*) Came in the front door and all the lights were out. Put a shilling in the slot, came in here and the party was over.

GOLDBERG (*coming downstage*): You put a shilling in the slot?

PETEY: Yes.

GOLDBERG: And the lights came on.

PETEY: Yes, then I came in here.

GOLDBERG (*with a short laugh*): I could have sworn it was a fuse.

PETEY (*continuing*): There was dead silence. Couldn't hear a thing. So I went upstairs and your friend—Dermot—met me on the landing. And he told me.

GOLDBERG (*sharply*): Who?

PETEY: Your friend—Dermot.

GOLDBERG (*heavily*): Dermot. Yes. (*He sits.*)

PETEY: They get over it sometimes though, don't they? I mean, they can recover from it, can't they?

GOLDBERG: Recover? Yes, sometimes they recover, in one way or another.

PETEY: I mean, he might have recovered by now, mightn't he?

GOLDBERG: It's conceivable. Conceivable.

PETEY *rises and picks up the teapot and cup.*

PETEY: Well, if he's no better by lunchtime I'll go and get hold of a doctor.

GOLDBERG (*briskly*): It's all taken care of, Mr. Boles. Don't worry yourself.

PETEY (*dubiously*): What do you mean? (*A door slams upstairs. They look towards the door. Enter* MCCANN *with two suitcases.*) Oh, it's you. All packed up?

PETEY *takes the teapot and cups into the kitchen.* MCCANN *crosses left and puts down the suitcases. He goes up to the window and looks out.*

GOLDBERG: Well? (MCCANN *does not answer.*) McCann. I asked you well.

MCCANN (*without turning*): Well what?

GOLDBERG: What's what? (MCCANN *does not answer.*) What is what?

MCCANN (*turning to look at* GOLDBERG, *grimly*): I'm not going up there again.

GOLDBERG: Why not?

MCCANN: I'm not going up there again.

GOLDBERG: What's going on now?

MCCANN (*moving down*): He's quiet now. He stopped all that . talking a while ago.

PETEY *appears at the kitchen hatch, unnoticed.*

GOLDBERG: When will he be ready?

MCCANN (*sullenly*): You can go up yourself next time.

GOLDBERG: What's the matter with you?

MCCANN (*quietly*): I gave him. . . .

GOLDBERG: What?

MCCANN: I gave him his glasses.

GOLDBERG: Wasn't he glad to get them back?

MCCANN: The frames are bust.

GOLDBERG: How did that happen?

MCCANN: He tried to fit the eyeholes into his eyes. I left him doing it.

PETEY (*at the kitchen door*): There's some Sellotape somewhere. We can stick them together.

GOLDBERG *and* MCCANN *turn to see him. Pause.*

GOLDBERG: Sellotape? No, no, that's all right, Mr. Boles. It'll keep him quiet for the time being, keep his mind off other things.

PETEY (*moving downstage*): What about a doctor?

GOLDBERG: It's all taken care of.

MCCANN *moves over right to the shoe-box, and takes out a brush and brushes his shoes.*

PETEY (*moves to the table*): I think he needs one.

GOLDBERG: I agree with you. It's all taken care of. We'll give him a bit of time to settle down, and then I'll take him to Monty.

PETEY: You're going to take him to a doctor?

GOLDBERG (*staring at him*): Sure. Monty.

Pause. MCCANN *brushes his shoes.* PETEY *sits, left, at the table.*

So Mrs. Boles has gone out to get us something nice for lunch?

PETEY: That's right.

GOLDBERG: Unfortunately we may be gone by then.

PETEY: Will you?

GOLDBERG: By then we may be gone.

MCCANN (*breaking in*): You know that girl?

GOLDBERG: What girl?

MCCANN: That girl had nightmares in the night.

GOLDBERG: Those weren't nightmares.

MCCANN: No?

GOLDBERG (*irritably*): I said no.

MCCANN: How do you know?

GOLDBERG: I got up. I went to see what was the matter.

MCCANN: I didn't know that.

GOLDBERG (*sharply*): It may be that you didn't know that. Nevertheless, that's what happened.

MCCANN: Well, what was the matter?

GOLDBERG: Nothing. Nothing at all. She was just having a bit of a sing-song.

MCCANN: A sing-song?

GOLDBERG (*to* PETEY): Sure. You know how young girls sing. She was singing.

MCCANN: So what happened then?

GOLDBERG: I joined in. We had a few songs. Yes. We sang a few of the old ballads and then she went to bye-byes.

PETEY *rises.*

PETEY: Well, I think I'll see how my peas are getting on, in the meantime.

GOLDBERG: The meantime?

PETEY: While we're waiting.

GOLDBERG: Waiting for what? (PETEY *walks towards the back door.*) Aren't you going back to the beach?

PETEY: No, not yet. Give me a call when he comes down, will you, Mr. Goldberg?

GOLDBERG (*earnestly*): You'll have a crowded beach today . . . on a day like this. They'll be lying on their backs, swimming out to sea. My life. What about the deck-chairs? Are the deck-chairs ready?

PETEY: I put them all out this morning.

GOLDBERG: But what about the tickets? Who's going to take the tickets?

PETEY: That's all right. That'll be all right, Mr. Goldberg. Don't you worry about that. I'll be back.

He exits. GOLDBERG *rises, goes to the window and looks after him.* MCCANN *crosses to the table, left, sits, picks up the paper and begins to tear it into strips.*

GOLDBERG: Is everything ready?

MCCANN: Sure.

GOLDBERG *walks heavily, brooding, to the table. He sits right of it noticing what* MCCANN *is doing.*

GOLDBERG: Stop doing that!

MCCANN: What?

GOLDBERG: Why do you do that all the time? It's childish, it's pointless. It's without a solitary point.

MCCANN: What's the matter with you today?

GOLDBERG: Questions, questions. Stop asking me so many questions. What do you think I am?

MCCANN *studies him. He then folds the paper, leaving the strips inside.*

MCCANN: Well?

Pause. GOLDBERG *leans back in the chair, his eyes closed.*

MCCANN: Well?

GOLDBERG (*with fatigue*): Well what?

MCCANN: What's what?

GOLDBERG: Yes, what is what. . . .

MCCANN: Do we wait or do we go and get him?

GOLDBERG (*slowly*): You want to go and get him?

MCCANN: I want to get it over.

GOLDBERG: That's understandable.

MCCANN: So do we wait or do we—?

GOLDBERG (*interrupting*): I don't know why, but I feel knocked out. I feel a bit . . . It's uncommon for me.

MCCANN: Is that so?

GOLDBERG: It's unusual.

MCCANN (*rising swiftly and going behind* GOLDBERG'S *chair. Hissing*): Let's finish and go. Let's get it over and go. Get the thing done. Let's finish the bloody thing. Let's get the thing done and go! (*Pause.*) Will I go up? (*Pause.*) Nat!

GOLDBERG *sits humped.* MCCANN *slips to his side.*

Simey!

GOLDBERG (*opening his eyes, regarding* MCCANN): What—did—you—call—me?

MCCANN: Who?

GOLDBERG (*murderously*): Don't call me that! (*He seizes* MCCANN *by the throat.*) NEVER CALL ME THAT!

MCCANN (*writhing*): Nat, Nat, Nat, NAT! I called you Nat. I was asking you, Nat. Honest to God. Just a question, that's all, just a question, do you see, do you follow me?

GOLDBERG (*jerking him away*): What question?

MCCANN: Will I go up?

GOLDBERG (*violently*): Up? I thought you weren't going to go up there again?

MCCANN: What do you mean? Why not?

GOLDBERG: You said so!

MCCANN: I never said that!

GOLDBERG: No?

MCCANN (*from the floor, to the room at large*): Who said that? I never said that! I'll go up now!

He jumps up and rushes to the door, left.

GOLDBERG: Wait!

He stretches his arms to the arms of the chair.

Come here.

MCCANN *approaches him very slowly*

I want your op n on. Have a look in my mouth.

He opens his mouth wide.

Take a good look

MCCANN *looks.*

You know what I mean?

MCCANN *peers.*

You know what? I've never lost a tooth. Not since the day I

was born. Nothing's changed. (*He gets up.*) That's why I've reached my position, McCann. Because I've always been as fit as a fiddle. All my life I've said the same. Play up, play up, and play the game. Honour thy father and thy mother. All along the line. Follow the line, the line, McCann, and you can't go wrong. What do you think, I'm a self-made man? No! I sat where I was told to sit. I kept my eye on the ball. School? Don't talk to me about school. Top in all subjects. And for why? Because I'm telling you, I'm telling you, follow my line? Follow my mental? Learn by heart. Never write down a thing. No. And don't go too near the water. And you'll find—that what I say is true.
Because I believe that the world ... (*Vacant.*). ..
Because I believe that the world ... (*Desperate.*). ...
BECAUSE I BELIEVE THAT THE WORLD ... (*Lost.*). ...

He sits in chair.

Sit down, McCann, sit here where I can look at you.

MCCANN *kneels in front of the table.*

(*Intensely, with growing certainty.*) My father said to me, Benny, Benny, he said, come here. He was dying. I knelt down. By him day and night. Who else was there? Forgive, Benny, he said, and let live. Yes, Dad. Go home to your wife. I will, Dad. Keep an eye open for low-lives, for schnorrers and for layabouts. He didn't mention names. I lost my life in the service of others, he said, I'm not ashamed. Do your duty and keep your observations. Always bid good morning to the neighbours. Never, never forget your family, for they are the rock, the constitution and the core! If you're ever in any difficulties Uncle Barney will see you in the clear. I knelt down. (*He kneels, facing* MCCANN.) I swore on the good book. And I knew the word I had to remember —Respect! Because McCann— (*Gently.*) Seamus—who came before your father? His father. And who came before him? Before him?
(*Vacant—triumphant.*) Who came before your father's father but your father's father's mother! Your great-gran-granny

Silence. He slowly rises.

And that's why I've reached my position, McCann. Because I've always been as fit as a fiddle. My motto. Work hard and play hard. Not a day's illness. (*He emits a high-pitched wheeze-whine. He looks round.*) What was that?

MCCANN: What?

GOLDBERG: I heard something.

MCCANN: What was it?

GOLDBERG: A noise. A funny noise.

MCCANN: That was you.

GOLDBERG: Me?

MCCANN: Sure.

GOLDBERG (*interested*): What, you heard it too?

MCCANN: I did.

GOLDBERG: It was me, eh? (*A slight chuckle.*) Huh. What did I do?

MCCANN: You gave . . . you let out a class of a wheeze, like.

GOLDBERG: Go on! (*He laughs. They both laugh. Then suddenly, quickly, anxiously.*) Where's your spoon? You got your spoon?

MCCANN (*producing it*): Here.

GOLDBERG: Test me. (*He opens his mouth and sticks out his tongue.*) Here. (MCCANN *places the spoon on* GOLDBERG's *tongue.*) Aaaahhh! Aaaaahhhh!

MCCANN: Perfect condition.

GOLDBERG: You really mean that?

MCCANN: My word of honour.

GOLDBERG: So now you can understand why I occupy such a position, eh?

MCCANN: I can, of course.

GOLDBERG *laughs. They both laugh.*

GOLDBERG (*stopping*): All the same, give me a blow. (*Pause.*) Blow in my mouth.

MCCANN *stands, puts his hands on his knees, bends, and blows in* GOLDBERG's *mouth.*

One for the road.

MCCANN *blows again in his mouth.* GOLDBERG *breathes deeply, shakes his head, and bounds from the chair*

Right. We're here. Wait a minute, just a minute. You got everything packed?

MCCANN: I have.

GOLDBERG: The expander?

MCCANN: Yes.

GOLDBERG: Fetch it to me.

MCCANN: Now?

GOLDBERG: At once.

> MCCANN *goes to the suitcase and takes out a chest expander.*
> *He gives it to* GOLDBERG, *who pulls it playfully, masterfully,*
> *bearing down on* MCCANN. *They both chuckle.* GOLDBERG *pulls*
> *it to full stretch. It breaks. He smiles.*

What did I tell you?

> *He throws it at* MCCANN. *Enter* LULU, *left.*

Well, look who's here.

> MCCANN *looks at them, and goes to the door.*

MCCANN (*at the door*): I'll give you five minutes. (*He exits with the*
expander.)

GOLDBERG: Come over here.

LULU: What's going to happen?

GOLDBERG: Come over here.

LULU: No, thank you.

GOLDBERG: What's the matter? You got the needle to Uncle Natey?

LULU: I'm going.

GOLDBERG: Have a game of pontoon first, for old time's sake.

LULU: I've had enough games.

GOLDBERG: A girl like you, at your age, at your time of health, and
you don't take to games?

LULU: You're very smart.

GOLDBERG: Anyway, who says you don't take to them?

LULU: Do you think I'm like all the other girls?

GOLDBERG: Are all the other girls like that, too?

LULU: I don't know about any other girls.

GOLDBERG: Nor me. I've never touched another woman.

LULU (*distressed*): What would my father say, if he knew? And what would Eddie say?

GOLDBERG: Eddie?

LULU: He was my first love, Eddie was. And whatever happened, it was pure. With him! He didn't come into my room at night with a briefcase!

GOLDBERG: Who opened the briefcase, me or you?

LULU: You got around me. It was only because I was so upset by last night.

GOLDBERG: Lulu, schmulu, let bygones be bygones, do me a turn. Kiss and make up.

LULU: I wouldn't touch you.

GOLDBERG: And today I'm leaving.

LULU: You're leaving?

GOLDBERG: Today.

LULU (*with growing anger*): You used me for a night. A passing fancy.

GOLDBERG: Who used who?

LULU: You made use of me by cunning when my defences were down.

GOLDBERG: Who took them down?

LULU: That's what you did. You quenched your ugly thirst. You took advantage of me when I was overwrought. I wouldn't do those things again, not even for a Sultan!

GOLDBERG: One night doesn't make a harem.

LULU: You taught me things a girl shouldn't know before she's been married at least three times!

GOLDBERG: Now you're a jump ahead! What are you complaining about?

Enter MCCANN *quickly.*

LULU: You didn't appreciate me for myself. You took all those liberties only to satisfy your appetite.

GOLDBERG: Now you're giving me indigestion.

LULU: And after all that had happened. An old woman nearly killed and a man gone mad—How can I go back behind that counter now? Oh Nat, why did you do it?

GOLDBERG: You wanted me to do it, Lulula, so I did it.

MCCANN: That's fair enough.

LULU (*turning*): Oh!

MCCANN (*advancing*): You had a long sleep, Miss.

LULU (*backing upstage left*): Me?

MCCANN: Your sort, you spend too much time in bed.

LULU: What do you mean?

MCCANN: Have you got anything to confess?

LULU: What?

MCCANN (*savagely*): Confess!

LULU: Confess what?

MCCANN: Down on your knees and confess!

LULU: What does he mean?

GOLDBERG: Confess. What can you lose?

LULU: What, to him?

GOLDBERG: He's only been unfrocked six months.

MCCANN: Kneel down, woman, and tell me the latest!

LULU (*retreating to the back door*): I've seen everything that's happened. I know what's going on. I've got a pretty shrewd idea.

MCCANN (*advancing*): I've seen you hanging about the Rock of Cashel, profaning the soil with your goings-on. Out of my sight!

LULU: I'm going.

> *She exits.* MCCANN *goes to the door, left, and goes out. He ushers in* STANLEY, *who is dressed in striped trousers, black jacket, and white collar. He carries a bowler hat in one hand and his broken glasses in the other. He is clean-shaven.* MCCANN *follows and closes the door.* GOLDBERG *meets* STANLEY, *seats him in a chair, right, and puts his hat on the table.*

GOLDBERG: How are you, Stan? (*Pause.*) Are you feeling any better? (*Pause.*) What's the matter with your glasses? (GOLDBERG *bends to look.*) They're broken. A pity.

> STANLEY *stares blankly at the floor.*

MCCANN (*at the table*): He looks better, doesn't he?

GOLDBERG: Much better.

MCCANN: A new man.

GOLDBERG: You know what we'll do?

MCCANN: What?

GOLDBERG: We'll buy him another pair.

> *They begin to woo him, gently and with relish. During the*

following sequence STANLEY *shows no reaction. He remains, with no movement, where he sits.*

MCCANN: Out of our own pockets.

GOLDBERG: It goes without saying. Between you and me, Stan, it's about time you had a new pair of glasses.

MCCANN: You can't see straight.

GOLDBERG: It's true. You've been cockeyed for years.

MCCANN: Now you're even more cockeyed.

GOLDBERG: He's right. You've gone from bad to worse.

MCCANN: Worse than worse.

GOLDBERG: You need a long convalescence.

MCCANN: A change of air.

GOLDBERG: Somewhere over the rainbow.

MCCANN: Where angels fear to tread.

GOLDBERG: Exactly.

MCCANN: You're in a rut.

GOLDBERG: You look anaemic

MCCANN: Rheumatic.

GOLDBERG: Myopic.

MCCANN: Epileptic.

GOLDBERG: You're on the verge.

MCCANN: You're a dead duck.

GOLDBERG: But we can save you.

MCCANN: From a worse fate.

GOLDBERG: True.

MCCANN: Undeniable.

GOLDBERG: From now on, 've'll be the hub of your wheel.

MCCANN: We'll renew your season ticket.

GOLDBERG: We'll take tuppence off your morning tea.

MCCANN: We'll give you a discount on all inflammable goods.

GOLDBERG: We'll watch over you.

MCCANN: Advise you.

GOLDBERG: Give you pr ,per care and treatment.

MCCANN: Let you use the club bar.

GOLDBERG: Keep a table reserved.

MCCANN: Help you acknowledge the fast days.

GOLDBERG: Bake you cakes.

MCCANN: Help you kneel on kneeling days.

GOLDBERG: Give you a free pass.

MCCANN: Take you for constitutionals.

GOLDBERG: Give you hot tips.

MCCANN: We'll provide the skipping rope.

GOLDBERG: The vest and pants.

MCCANN: The ointment.

GOLDBERG: The hot poultice.

MCCANN: The fingerstall.

GOLDBERG: The abdomen belt.

MCCANN: The ear plugs.

GOLDBERG: The baby powder.

MCCANN: The back scratcher.

GOLDBERG: The spare tyre.

MCCANN: The stomach pump.

GOLDBERG: The oxygen tent.

MCCANN: The prayer wheel.

GOLDBERG: The plaster of Paris.

MCCANN: The crash helmet.

GOLDBERG: The crutches.

MCCANN: A day and night service.

GOLDBERG: All on the house.

MCCANN: That's it.

GOLDBERG: We'll make a man of you.

MCCANN: And a woman.

GOLDBERG: You'll be re-orientated.

MCCANN: You'll be rich.

GOLDBERG: You'll be adjusted.

MCCANN: You'll be our pride and joy.

GOLDBERG: You'll be a mensch.

MCCANN: You'll be a success.

GOLDBERG: You'll be integrated.

MCCANN: You'll give orders.

GOLDBERG: You'll make decisions.

MCCANN: You'll be a magnate.

GOLDBERG: A statesman.

MCCANN: You'll own yachts.

GOLDBERG: Animals.

MCCANN: Animals.

GOLDBERG *looks at* MCCANN.

GOLDBERG: I said animals. (*He turns back to* STANLEY.) You'll be able to make or break, Stan. By my life. (*Silence.* STANLEY *is still.*) Well? What do you say?

STANLEY'S *head lifts very slowly and turns in* GOLDBERG'S *direction.*

GOLDBERG: What do you think? Eh, boy?

STANLEY *begins to clench and unclench his eyes.*

MCCANN: What's your opinion, sir? Of this prospect, sir?
GOLDBERG: Prospect. Sure. Sure it's a prospect.

STANLEY'S *hands clutching his glasses begin to tremble.*

What's your opinion of such a prospect? Eh, S anley?

STANLEY *concentrates, his mouth opens, he attempts to speak, fails and emits sounds from his throat.*

STANLEY: Uh-gug . . . uh-gug . . . eeehhh-gag . . . (*On the breath.*) Caahh . . . caahh. . . .

They watch him. He draws a long breatn wnicn snuaders down his body. He concentrates.

GOLDBERG: Well, Stanny boy, what do you say, eh?

They watch. He concentrates. His head lowers, his chin draws into his chest, he crouches.

STANLEY: Uh-gughh . . . uh-gughh. . . .
MCCANN: What's your opinion, sir?
STANLEY: Caaahhh . . . caaahhh. . . .
MCCANN: Mr. Webber! What's your opinion?
GOLDBERG: What do you say, Stan? What do you think of the prospect?
MCCANN: What's your opinion of the prospect?

STANLEY'S *body shudders, relaxes, his head drops, he becomes still again, stooped.* PETEY *enters from door, downstage, left.*

GOLDBERG: Still the same old Stan. Come with us. Come on, boy.
MCCANN: Come along with us.
PETEY: Where are you taking him?

They turn. Silence.

GOLDBERG: We're taking him to Monty.
PETEY: He can stay here.
GOLDBERG: Don't be silly.
PETEY: We can look after him here.
GOLDBERG: Why do you want to look after him?
PETEY: He's my guest.
GOLDBERG: He needs special treatment.
PETEY: We'll find someone.
GOLDBERG: No. Monty's the best there is. Bring him, McCann.

They help STANLEY *out of the chair.* GOLDBERG *puts the bowler hat on* STANLEY's *head. They all three move towards the door left.*

PETEY: Leave him alone!

They stop. GOLDBERG *studies him.*

GOLDBERG (*insidiously*): Why don't you come with us, Mr. Boles?
MCCANN: Yes, why don't you come with us?
GOLDBERG: Come with us to Monty. There's plenty of room in the car.

PETEY *makes no move. They pass him and reach the door.* MCCANN *opens the door and picks up the suitcases.*

PETEY (*broken*): Stan, don't let them tell you what to do!

They exit.

Silence. PETEY *stands. The front door slams. Sound of a car starting. Sound of a car going away. Silence.* PETEY *slowly goes to the table. He sits on a chair, left. He picks up the paper and opens it. The strips fall to the floor. He looks down at them.* MEG *comes past the window and enters by the back door.* PETEY *studies the front page of the paper.*

MEG (*coming downstage*): The car's gone.

PETEY: Yes.

MEG: Have they gone?

PETEY: Yes.

MEG: Won't they be in for lunch?

PETEY: No.

MEG: Oh, what a shame. (*She puts her bag on the table.*) It's hot out. (*She hangs her coat on a hook.*) What are you doing?

PETEY: Reading.

MEG: Is it good?

PETEY: All right.

> *She sits by the table.*

MEG: Where's Stan? (*Pause.*) Is Stan down yet, Petey?

PETEY: No ... he's. ...

MEG: Is he still in bed?

PETEY: Yes, he's ... still asleep.

MEG: Still? He'll be late for his breakfast.

PETEY: Let him ... sleep.

> *Pause.*

MEG: Wasn't it a lovely party last night?

PETEY: I wasn't there.

MEG: Weren't you?

PETEY: I came in afterwards.

MEG: Oh. (*Pause.*) It was a lovely party. I haven't laughed so much for years. We had dancing and singing. And games. You should have been there.

PETEY: It was good, eh?

> *Pause.*

MEG: I was the belle of the ball.

PETEY: Were you?

MEG: Oh yes. They all said I was.

PETEY: I bet you were, too.

MEG: Oh, it's true. I was. (*Pause.*) I know I was.

> *Curtain.*